The Art of Being Jewish in Modern Times

JEWISH CULTURE AND CONTEXTS

Published in association with the Center for Advanced Judaic Studies of the University of Pennsylvania

David B. Ruderman, Series Editor

Advisory Board
Richard I. Cohen
Moshe Idel
Alan Mintz
Deborah Dash Moore
Ada Rapoport-Albert
Michael D. Swartz

A complete list of books in the series is available from the publisher.

The Art of Being Jewish in Modern Times

Edited by
BARBARA KIRSHENBLATT-GIMBLETT
and JONATHAN KARP

PENN

University of Pennsylvania Press

Philadelphia

Publication of this volume was assisted by grants from the Martin D. Gruss Endowment Fund of the Center for Advanced Judaic Studies, University of Pennsylvania, and the Posen Foundation.

Published by
University of Pennsylvania Press
Philadelphia, Pennsylvania 19104–4112

Printed in the United States of America on acid-free paper

10 9 8 7 6 5 4 3 2

A Cataloging-in-Publication record is available from the Library of Congress

ISBN-13: 978-0-8122-4002-3
ISBN-10: 0-8122-4002-2

Contents

Illustrations

Preface

This volume originated in the activities of a research group working at the Center for Advanced Judaic Studies of the University of Pennsylvania over the course of the academic year 2000–2001. Professors Ezra Mendelsohn and Richard I. Cohen had formulated the proposal for an extended and interdisciplinary consideration of the place of performing and visual arts in modern Jewish culture, and from its opening seminar until its closing colloquium, the lively and sometimes contentious group of scholars who convened struggled to understand and define the relationship between Jewish civilization and the arts.

Art historians, ethnomusicologists, cultural historians, and literary critics sat around one table, attempting to understand one another's vocabulary, methodologies, and perspectives. Historians soon learned that such seemingly self-evident concepts as "context" could be understood in a radically different way by art historians. Scholars conversant in the languages and literatures of the Jewish experience were obliged to overcome their suspicions that those trained exclusively in the arts would not be able to interpret Jewish culture in new and daring ways. Those accustomed to working in the arts were obliged to engage explicitly with texts and historical data. The task of breaking down disciplinary boundaries and cultural barriers was formidable and often frustrating. The formal and informal meetings between the participants were sometimes discordant and often exhausting. By the end of the year, we had all come to recognize how exhilarating they were.

It was a tremendous challenge to shape these diverse and discrete voices into a single and coherent volume. The task required not only a strong editorial presence but a clear vision of how a collective statement might emerge from so many individual and disparate inquiries. Barbara Kirshenblatt-Gimblett and Jonathan Karp have filled the roles of volume editors with wonderful creativity and diligence. Their intellectual leadership in soliciting essays, in encouraging each participant to place his or her essay in the context of their own more comprehensive vision, in editing and organizing the contributions, and in producing a masterful introduction will be clear to anyone perusing this significant book. Without their persistence and patience this volume would not have emerged. It is a pleasure to thank them, their contributors, and the others present at the seminars.

Together, their work has both stimulated and enhanced serious discourse on the dynamic relationship between the arts and modern Jewish culture.

David B. Ruderman
Joseph Meyerhoff Profesor of Modern Jewish History
Ella Darivoff Director of the Center for Advanced Judaic Studies
University of Pennsylvania

Introduction

Barbara Kirshenblatt-Gimblett and Jonathan Karp

Much remains to be done if the arts are to figure more fully in Jewish studies and the Jewish experience more fully in the arts disciplines.[1] It was with
the aim of bringing these fields together that the Center for Advanced
Judaic Studies at the University of Pennsylvania convened the research seminar "Modern Jewry and the Arts" during the 2000–2001 academic year.
The work of that seminar forms the basis for this volume.[2] The seminar was
conceived by two historians, Richard I. Cohen and Ezra Mendelsohn, who
have been instrumental in bringing contextual art history to Jewish studies
and, with this seminar, the other arts as well. Such interdisciplinary encounters require respect for disciplinary expertise and openness to disciplinary
transformation. During the 1980s, historians recognized that art historians
had developed methods for dealing with "the evocative, many-leveled
properties of art,"[3] while art historians noted that having "come to consider art as a social practice," it was necessary to consider "what we are
about when we do look at and study art in what might broadly be termed a
society way—or, conversely, when we study society in an aesthetic way "[4] In
the decades following these statements, there have emerged the "new, new
art history" and visual culture studies.[5] The study of the performing arts
has been similarly transformed with the emergence of performance studies
and the "new musicology."

In each case, the disciplinary subject (art or theater or music) has been
disentangled from its traditional objects of inquiry (paintings, sculptures,
plays, concert music). Those objects are then situated within a much wider
range of phenomena (not only fine art but anything visual; not only music
proper but also musical practices; not only plays as dramatic literature but
also theatrical productions, indeed, anything performed). In the process,
the disciplinary subject itself shifts from art to visual culture, from music to
music in society, and from theater to performance. With that shift, new
questions arise about the nature of visuality itself (and not only art proper):
in the words of W. J. T. Mitchell, "The complex field of visual reciprocity
is not merely a by-product of social reality but actively constitutive of it."[6]
Similarly, as Susan McClary writes, music makes us who we are—"our feelings, our bodies, our desires, our very subjectivities" (and not just music

proper).[7] The study of performance as embodied action and event (and not only theater proper) is similarly constitutive.[8] Viewed through a new optic, texts, films, buildings, urban form, popular festivity, and other phenomena normally regarded as remote from the study of the visual and performing arts reveal their performative character. Seen in these terms, such phenomena require more than a contextual approach—studying art in a society way and society in an aesthetic way—if we are to illuminate their constitutive capacities, that is, not only what they say and how but also what they do and to what effect. The essays in this volume take up this challenge.

Like cultural studies and other postdisciplinary formations, visual culture studies and performance studies are big-tent fields that organize themselves around a set of problems and range widely for their approaches and objects.[9] Consistent with this generous mandate, there was theoretically no limit to the range of art forms and approaches allowed during our research year. However, the seminar's architects did focus its temporal scope on the modern period of Jewish history, the era during which Jews became citizens of the countries in which they lived, their aesthetic capacities became an issue, and they entered artistic professions in unprecedented numbers.[10] Modern art, with its universalistic ideals but national character (French Impressionism, Russian Constructivism, Italian Futurism, American Abstract Expressionism), held out the impossible promise of world citizenship in a kind of utopia of pure form, while offering Jewish nationalists a medium for styling the Zionist project. These considerations alone would have warranted the year's focus on modern Jewry and the arts. But, as this volume attests, there is more to the relationship between Jews, the arts, and modernity. The art of being Jewish in the modern world—or, alternatively, the art of being modern in the Jewish world—points to the question of whether the "modern Jewish experience" has in some sense been a pointedly artistic one.

What has been the role of artistic expression in Jewish self-definition? How have Jews used the arts in their individual and collective lives? What are the various styles of contemporary Jewishness? If, following Benedict Anderson, "Communities are to be distinguished, not by their falsity/genuineness, but by the style in which they are imagined," this volume explores how the arts—and the debates they engendered—give sound, shape, and dramatic form to such imaginings in all their local and historical specificity. Such considerations require a broader conception of what counts as art and greater attention to the organized contexts in which it is made, whether, as explored in this volume, the American or German or Russian art world, a culture industry such as the American or Israeli popular music business, or the everyday life of a local community in Philadelphia, Tel Aviv, or Birobidzhan. Though several authors do focus on a singular artist—Mark Antokol'skii, Max Liebermann, Ben Shahn, R. B. Kitaj, Ben Katchor, Vera Frenkel, Marcel Ophuls, and Zehava Ben—the book as a whole has the ambitious aim of identifying the aesthetic as a key conceptual category for treating modern Jewish history. This volume, then, is not simply about modern Jewry and the arts but about the art of being Jewish in modern times.

The Jewish Art Question

"The Jewish art question" is the vexing but unavoidable problem of what makes a work of art Jewish. Is it the artist's provenance or his or her conscious or unconscious intention? Is it the themes and language or the iconography and the symbols a given work employs? Or is Jewish art in the eyes of the beholder? In his landmark study of the painter Maurycy Gottlieb, Ezra Mendelsohn defines Jewish art as "work by artists of Jewish descent that not only depicts Jewish life but may also advance a Jewish agenda."[11] While several essays presented here do deal with Jewish art so defined, the volume as a whole neither presumes a definition nor sets out to create one. Instead, by examining how the "Jewish art question" has been formulated in specific situations—by artists, composers, filmmakers, dealers, collectors, audiences, critics, historians, philosophers, and curators—the volume historicizes the question. We start from the premise that the question is constitutive rather than independent of the phenomena to which it points. For this reason, it is important to put the very posing of the "Jewish art question" to the test. When does "Jewish" matter? Under what circumstances, whether historical or conceptual, is the Jewishness of the artist or the work's subject or style or its contexts of creation or reception relevant? When does Jewishness demand explanation? When is it explanatory? What does it account for? Is the dance critic Joseph Lewitan, discussed by the dance historian Marion Kant in this volume, a Jewish artist because he was persecuted as such by the Nazis, despite his own merely occasional and peripheral Jewish associations? Were the Tin Pan Alley songwriters described here by Jonathan Karp Jewish artists simply because Jews were prominent in the music industry, in both numbers and preeminence, prompting accusations, often anti-Semitic, that that entire industry was "Jewish"? Further, what made 1930s Tel Aviv, as described below by Anat Helman, feel Jewish when in fact the city's planners and architects deliberately set out to create a "Hebrew," rather than a Jewish, city? And what needed to be done to music in the Reform synagogue to make it more Jewish, yet still modern, as addressed here by the ethnomusicologist Mark Kligman?

Clearly no single definition of "Jewish art" can suffice. For this reason, we take Jewishness as contingent and contextual rather than definitive and presumptive. This volume approaches the Jewish art question in relational and transactional terms, rather than in normative ones. We seek the appropriate category of analysis and adduce historically specific practices and understandings rather than ontological certainties. This approach is exemplified in Walter Cahn's account of Max Liebermann (1847–1935), who certainly met two of the criteria set out by Mendelsohn in his definition of a Jewish artist—Liebermann was Jewish and he depicted Jewish life, at least some of the time. Cahn, an art historian, could have stopped there, but instead he demonstrates the ellusive nature of the Jewish art/artist question by charting the disagreements among Liebermann's critics and biographers over the relevance of his Jewish descent.[12] Some critics attributed Liebermann's French Impressionist style to his cosmopolitanism, a derogatory code word for Jewish. He was either decried on that account by Germanophiles or praised by those critical of German parochialism. Others said that his "Jewish talent," while it contributed to his clarity and efficiency, produced art that was good but not great. Some believed that Liebermann was a true German artist, his Jewishness notwithstanding (or even because of it). Others felt that he had a special feeling for Amsterdam's Jewish quarter because he was Jewish. As for Liebermann, the challenge was to capture the essence of an iconic subject, Amsterdam's Jewish quarter, without resorting to the typical—whether the typical Jew (a racialized East European Jew in traditional garb) or the typical ghetto image (a scene of traditional Jewish life rendered in ethnographic detail). His solution was to focus on the crowd, rather than on portraits of Jewish types, and, above all, to use style, in particular French Impressionism and the aesthetics of the sketch, to capture the mood of the tightly compressed space and its swarming throng.

As Cahn indicates in his discussion of Liebermann's painting *The Twelve Year-Old Jesus in the Temple*, the ultimate test of artistic achievement in the nineteenth century was the historical rendering of Jesus. How were Jews to be represented in these works of art, given the rejection of classical conventions and commitment to historical realism—and how in particular were Jewish artists to tackle this question? The Russian sculptor Mark Antokol'skii (1843–1902) found in this same dilemma a way to be "strategically" Jewish. In her analysis of his sculpture *Jesus before the Judgment of the People*, the historian Olga Litvak explores how Antokol'skii's "understanding of what it meant to be a nineteenth-century Russian Jew might itself be a product of his development as an artist." Following the creation, reception, and debates surrounding this sculpture, Litvak asks: How did the process of making modern art contribute to making modern the Jews who engaged in it? Her historically specific answer, which takes into account how national modern Russian art was being conceived during the late nineteenth century and the nature of the European art world at the time, uncovers the ways in which Antokol'skii expressed Jewishness through the back door, so to speak. That is, he asserted his Russianness via ambiguously Jewish symbols such as the image of Jesus as he is about to be judged by the people. Who are "the people" and who the judge?

In her essay on the American artist Ben Shahn, the art historian Diana L. Linden addresses a related question, namely, how museum exhibitions, in constituting art historical narratives, determine when and how an artist or work of art is Jewish.[13] She analyzes *Common Man, Mythic Vision: The Paintings of Ben Shahn*, a major exhibition of Shahn's later works at The Jewish Museum in New York in 1998, the centennial of Shahn's birth, which traveled to the Detroit Institute of Arts (DIA) the following year. Shahn enjoys an honored place in standard histories of American art prior to World War II, but not in the story of postwar American modern art, whose defining moment was Abstract Expressionism, not the realistic and allegorical style of Shahn's later work. *Common Man, Mythic Vision* tried to establish Shahn's rightful place in the history of postwar American art by relating Shahn's later work to the Abstract Expressionists on grounds other than style. To make this case at The Jewish Museum, as opposed to the Whitney Museum of American Art or the Museum of Modern Art, is to say something more—namely, that Shahn is an important American artist both because of and despite the fact that he was Jewish, and notwithstanding his refusal to be labeled anything, least of all a Jewish painter. It is not that The Jewish Museum made Shahn a Jewish artist and his work Jewish art. Indeed, this exhibition aimed to do just the opposite, that is, to establish his place in postwar American modern painting. Rather, the *question* of Jewishness comes to the fore because everything shown in The Jewish Museum becomes "Jewish"—contextually. Jewish becomes a consideration, a lens, a frame of reference, a contingency for what is shown. Jewish becomes subjunctive. As a result, in the overdetermined context of The Jewish Museum, where Shahn would tend to be seen as a Jewish artist, the challenge was to demonstrate what made his work part and parcel of postwar American art (as well as to attract a wider audience). In contrast, the Detroit Institute of Arts, where Shahn would be seen as an American artist, took advantage of his Jewishness to differentiate him from the many other American artists they exhibited and to target a Jewish audience.

Diasporism

One might say that Jews have been doubly disallowed their proper places in the grand narratives of art history. They have been defined either as a diaspora, a condition said to be inimical to originality or distinctiveness, let alone the creation of a national style, or as a "nation without art"—that is, until Zionism prompted a self-conscious effort to create it.[14] According to this view, prior to Zionism one might have found paintings by Jewish artists on Jewish subjects, but their distinctively Jewish quality would not have been found in their style, the sina qua non of an art of one's own.

The art critic Harold Rosenberg identifies the problem in his 1966 *Commentary* essay "Is There a Jewish Art?" Rosenberg begins by discounting several different ways Jewish art might be defined: art produced by Jews, art on Jewish subjects, Jewish ceremonial objects, handicrafts and semi-ceremonial folk art, and a future "metaphysical Judaica" based on Jewish philosophy along the lines of Ben Shahn's Hebrew alphabet. As Rosenberg explains, "Style, not subject matter or theme, will determine whether or not paintings should be considered 'Jewish' or placed in some other category." He then states categorically that "there is no Jewish art in the sense of a Jewish style in painting and sculpture. Whether there ever will be such a style is a matter of speculation—a speculation that ought to take into account the progressive fading of national styles in modern art generally."[15] In a word, modern Jewish artists have historically offered what is at best a peculiar variation on a style that was not authentically their own; but, paradoxically, to attempt to create a Jewish style at this late date would be decidedly unmodern. Indeed, it is precisely thanks to their individualism, what Rosenberg calls "the aesthetics of self," that they have played a central role in creating "a genuine American art." This art, he argues, while "not a Jewish art, is a profound Jewish expression," with universal meaning, and it makes the question of whether or not Jewish art does or can exist irrelevant. Rosenberg has, in essence, provided the rationale for giving Shahn his rightful place both in The Jewish Museum and in the history of postwar American modern art. So too has Arthur Danto, in his review of the Modigliani show at The Jewish Museum in 2004, where, referring to this museum's radical art exhibitions in the 1960s, he wrote that "nothing could be more Jewish than supporting advanced art." Today, it has become an "identity art museum," that is, "It cannot rest satisfied with letting the work stand on its artistic merits alone. It must make an effort to explain in what special ways the Jewishness of the artist contributes to the significance of the art."[16] Although Danto misreads The Jewish Museum's present mandate as one that is narrowly confined to Jewish identity questions, his larger point is instructive. The very idea of a Jewish museum devoted, inter alia, to displaying modern art indexes an important aspect of the Jewish art question.

While such arguments have been made with respect to all forms of Jewish artistic expression, the visual arts have been singled out as particularly disadvantaged because of assumptions about the Jewish sensorium and the hierarchy of artistic expression identified with its structure.[17] Thus, the people of the book are alleged to have privileged the ear over the eye and reason over imagination, so that, while they may have a musical tradition of their own, at the very least a liturgical one, they have not created their own visual art. Moreover, it is argued, many factors—among them the second commandment, which prohibits the making of graven images; the marginal status of Jews in the diaspora; their historical exclusion from guilds; their lack of royal or state patronage for cultural projects (the role of court Jews notwithstanding); their successful assimilation into the larger society in the post-emancipation period; the universalistic aspirations of modern art; and the unrepresentability of the greatest trauma in their history— have militated against their creating their own visual art, even if they had been so disposed.[18] That they were not so inclined has been construed by some as a virtue.[19] Fortunately, recent scholarship has taken issue with this argument and, by historicizing it, has made it an object of study in its own right and cleared the way for exciting new perspectives on the Jewish visual imagination.[20]

Given these considerations (and the modern preoccupation with art as an expression of the nation), the Jewish art question has always been a referendum on whether or not a diaspora can produce an art of its own—in any medium. The answer is usually no, for the kinds of reasons that Rosenberg gives, but there have also been dissenting views and even a "diasporist manifesto," the inspiration for the essay in this volume by the art historian Carol Zemel. Zemel focuses on three artists: R. B. Kitaj, an American artist who has painted in England for much of his career—in Sandor Gilman's apposite formulation, Kitaj is paradoxically "the insider outsider, the marginal centrist"; Ben Katchor, a graphic novelist working in the United States; and Vera Frenkel, an installation artist based in Canada.[21] Zemel takes as her point of departure Kitaj's *First Diasporist Manifesto*, which approaches diaspora not only as a historical and existential condition but also as an aesthetic one—and above all, as a condition that is full of creative possibilities. Diasporism ("diasporism" and "diasporist" are Kitaj's coinages) so defined could become "the foundation of a new Jewish aesthetics," as the cultural critic Sidra Ezrahi has written elsewhere with respect to Kitaj and his close friend Philip Roth.[22]

While Jews are not the only diaspora, they are the paradigmatic one, such that the Jewish art question becomes a prime site for exploring what a diasporist aesthetic might be.[23] Diaspora becomes associated with a thoroughly postmodern state of mind arising from the circumstances of rootlessness, nomadism, and dispersal. In Zemel's view, artists working under diasporic conditions are tactical, anti-essentialist, and labile as a result of their multiple affiliations and subjectivities, uncertainties and ambivalences, tensions and pleasures (we have already seen how such a description could be applied to Liebermann and Antokol'skii). In a word, they possess what W. E. B. Du Bois, referring to the African American experience, designated a "double consciousness." Local and translocal, they are connected to a vast imagined community across space and time.[24]

At the center of Zemel's analysis is Kitaj's *The Jewish Rider* (1984–85), one in a long line of images of the Wandering Jew. For Zemel, *The Jewish Rider* is an ambiguous image, one that calls into question "the stereotyped exilic figure of the Wandering Jew—the Jew as doomed and punished, the Jew as perpetually homeless." He is a dandy on a train, "soberly lost in thought despite his brightly colored surroundings"—a rooted cosmopolitan, a serious dreamer, embarked upon a gay yet dimly ominous excursion. But this partially hopeful deployment of what had been a stock Christian and anti-Semitic symbol of the Wandering Jew, condemned to roam ceaselessly as punishment for spurning Christ during his last hours, also calls into question the relatively recent championing of Jewish diaspora existence, seen most dramatically in the idea, espoused by Simon Dubnow at the beginning of the twentieth century, that diaspora nationalism was superior to Zionism precisely because it was not predicated on land and statehood and therefore was a spiritual form of national autonomy, as Richard I. Cohen discusses in this volume.

The flip side of this upbeat view of diaspora is exile, disenfranchisement, and homelessness. As Cohen details in his contribution here, Christian art and literature have long exploited the Wandering Jew image to underscore Jewish taint and otherness, an image all the more fascinating because wandering itself seems to hold clues to the mystery of Jewish survival. In Cohen's analysis, this quintessential icon of the Jewish diaspora becomes a screen onto which are projected historically specific anxieties about diasporic Jews and their relation to Christians—both negative and positive.[25] Because the images not only index moments of tension between Jews and Christians but also figure in them, they are a particularly rich source for exploring the history of Jewish-Christian relations. Here too the aesthetic domain has functioned as a contested sphere, marked by the dialectic of ascription and affirmation, symbolic appropriation and ironic reappropriation.

Usable Pasts, Uncertain Futures

The historical condition of diaspora has, if anything, intensified the desire in the modern period to identify an authentically Jewish aesthetic, to endow it with a deeply Jewish genealogy, to create a Jewish national art form, with or without a state, and to use the arts in the service of utopian ideals. It could be said that a hallmark of Jewish modernity is precisely a self-conscious concern with the Jewish art question, which, as this volume amply demonstrates, is really many questions, and with deliberate efforts to to provide definitive answers.[26] Programmatic, even ideological, in character, these efforts manifest themselves in a variety of forms, many of which are represented in this volume. They include R. B. Kitaj's diasporist manifestos and Franz Rosenzweig's philosophy of Jewish aesthetics, Abraham W. Binder's proposal for a more "Jewish" music for the Reform synagogue, as well as numerous unabashedly propagandistic uses of the arts, among them the Yiddish marching songs for indoctrinating Jewish children with Soviet ideals and the Jewish Palestine Pavilion at the New York World's Fair, which was intended to mobilize support for the Jewish homeland and eventual state.

Aesthetics was an essential element in the program of Jewish self-emancipation in nineteenth-century Europe, which placed great store in the concepts of *Bildung* (cultivation) and *Sittlichkeit* (civility) as essential preparation for citizenship and full participation in the larger society.[27] It was not enough to exhibit the capacity for aesthetic appreciation. It was also important to be able to create art—and even Jewish art. But what should such art look and sound like? What should it be made from? What resources might be found in the Jewish past for the creation of a contemporary if not explicitly modern Jewish art, music, theater, or dance?

Two authors in this volume, Zachary Braiterman and Mark Kligman, explore the role of aesthetics and the arts in reshaping Jewish theology and religious experience. Braiterman, a historian of Jewish thought, offers a highly original portrait of the philosopher Franz Rosenzweig (1886–1929), depicting him as a sort of director seeking to reinvent the Jewish synagogue experience as a form of ritualized theater. Rosenzweig envisioned Judaism—and particularly ritual and cultic space—as "a sensual spirit in aesthetic terms." That spirit was immanent in the dazzling array of forms created during the course of Jewish history. But Rosenzweig, who was raised in an assimilated German Jewish family and schooled in German Idealist philosophy, had not always seen Judaism in these terms. Indeed, according to the well-known story, he was on the verge of converting to Christianity when he had an epiphany during a Yom Kippur service in an Orthodox synagogue in Berlin. Overwhelmed with its beauty, he was prompted to contemplate a form of Jewish religious observance that felt authentic to him as an individual—and which he believed made him no less (and if anything even more) German. He dedicated much of his life to his theological writings—the work for which he is best known is *The Star of Redemption*, which he wrote while fighting in the German army during World War I—and to the Freies Jüdisches Lehrhaus (Free House of Jewish Learning), which he established in Frankfurt-am-Main in 1920. Not a building, but a program, the Lehrhaus was open to everyone, Jews and non-Jews alike, and was distinguished by its progressive pedagogy and attention to the artfulness of religious observance in everyday life. Attuned to the tenor of prayer, movement of the body, taste of wine, and tactile pleasure of the prayer shawl, Rosenzweig emphasized the importance of the sensory, sensual, architectural, and theatrical aspects of Jewish observance, even before ritual spaces and objects took on a particular artistic style, whether organic *Jugendstil*, Orientalist art nouveau, dissonant Expressionism, or the synthetic abstraction of the Bauhaus. He found beauty in the mitzvoth and, as Braiterman so aptly characterizes Rosenzweig's philosophy, he "drew art out of Jewish life." The "ancient treasure chest" of Judaism provided the basis for a distinctly Jewish aesthetics of everyday life, a fully sensuous, spatial, and theatrical experience, in which all the arts were fused.

Rosenzweig's attempt to define an aesthetic Judaism were preceded by efforts in Germany dating from the early nineteenth century to reform Jewish religious life along aesthetically apposite lines. Culminating in Reform Judaism, those efforts accorded the arts, and especially music, a central place in the reshaping of religious experience and thereby in the transformation of Jews themselves. By the twentieth century, however, there were some, like Abraham Wolf Binder (1895–1966), an American composer associated with the Reform Movement, who felt that Protestant-style hymns and liturgy set to Rossini were standing in the way of an authentically Jewish religious experience. Moreover, Binder argued, these compositions were failing to satisfy sophisticated Jews who expected their synagogue music to be as good as what they heard in the concert hall. How Binder addressed these issues is taken up by the ethnomusicologist Mark Kligman. First and foremost, Binder set out to counter what he saw as the "secular atmosphere" created by such music. He encouraged composers to create a modern (and national) Jewish music for the Reform service based on *nusach ha-tefillah,* traditional Jewish modes and melodies, which he celebrated as a wellspring of musically coded moods specific to each liturgical occasion. The composer's task was to "purify and perpetuate" *nusach,* to harmonize it appropriately, and to respect its modal character, melodic emphasis, and free rhythms. Only then would composers succeed in giving proper— which is to say "authentically Jewish"—sonic form to the Reform service and at the same time create a national Jewish art. Binder's declaration in 1944 that "without a distinctive Jewish art we are not a nation; we cannot speak of a complete culture, nor can we call ourselves a civilization," while never a guiding principle of the Reform movement, does reflect his attachment to the East European Jewish sounds of his childhood and the distinctive character of American Reform Judaism in contrast with its European counterpart. Binder's 1944 statement must also be read in the context in which he wrote it, during the Holocaust and just four years before the establishment of the State of Israel.[28] In this light, it is remarkable, but not surprising, that Binder's formula for authenticity proved to be so unabashedly eclectic, combining East European liturgical modes, Hassidic emotionalism, Palestinian Hebraic Orientalism, and European classical rigor.[29]

A more strictly utilitarian approach to how music might be used to transform Jews can be found in the Yiddish marching songs created for children during the 1920s and 1930s as a way inculcating Soviet ideals in the state's youngest Jewish citizens. Envisioned as little soldiers on the front line of social transformation, children literally embodied a utopian Soviet future as they sang and marched to the rhythm of sung ideology. As Anna Shternshis, a Yiddish studies scholar, explains, youth culture was a priority in the Soviet project because young people were a fresh slate on which to write the future; without a pre-Soviet past, there was nothing to unlearn. But, even in this tightly controlled, indeed coercive framework, Jewish children were able to adapt and identify with the propaganda songs as distinctive makers of their Soviet Jewish identity, one that was to become as much Jewish as it was Soviet. Here, it was the Yiddish language—intended as a temporary if necessarily Jewish tool in the dismantling of pre-Soviet Jewish culture and especially its religious institutions—that played the decisive role. Paradoxically, one of the unintended consequences of these efforts to make Jews into proper Soviet citizens was the creation of a new Jewish subculture. These songs, "often the first 'doves' of propaganda to enter Jewish homes" in the Soviet Union at the time, were interpreted and valued differently from what was intended by their creators and fondly remembered many decades after they were learned, for reasons their makers never anticipated.

Not until the Zionist movement and the establishment of the State of Israel was there a concerted effort to create a national Jewish art and style the nation into being by giving it a distinctive look, sound, and feel.[30] Three authors in this volume explore the role of aesthetics in Palestine and the State of Israel. Barbara Kirshenblatt-Gimblett, working at the intersection of performance studies and visual culture studies, analyzes the Jewish Palestine Pavilion at the New York World's Fair in 1939 and 1940.[31] This pavilion was intended to make the Zionist transformation of Palestine self-evident and convince the world that all the elements necessary for Jewish statehood were already in place. Meyer Weisgal, the great Zionist impresario, intended the Jewish Palestine Pavilion to be a model of what a future state might look like and a demonstration of its de facto existence. To that end, he insisted that the award-winning pavilion and its state-of-the-art displays be designed and fabricated in Tel Aviv and shipped to New York and that they celebrate Jewish Palestine's achievements—its cities, agriculture, industries, and trade; its infrastructure and institutions; its culture and arts. Kirshenblatt-Gimblett shows how, through the agency of display, the Jewish Palestine Pavilion played a vital role in envisioning, performing, and projecting a Jewish state within the virtual world of the fair, thereby hastening its arrival in the world itself.

What was the lived reality of that place for the Jews who settled in Palestine during the 1920s and 1930s? In search of how utopian ideals were given tangible and intangible form, the historian Anat Helman reveals how Tel Aviv's city planners, in their efforts to create the first "Hebrew" city, were at least partly undone by their own creation. No amount of planning could make a city that appeared from the dunes in a flash feel like it had been there forever. Tel Aviv was not "naturally Hebrew." The deliberateness of the Zionist social transformation was at odds with the goal of making that transformation seem self-evident so that it might be experienced as normal—as given, not fabricated. Tel Aviv started out as a garden suburb to the north of the ancient city of Jaffa and in short order it became a bustling cosmopolitan metropolis and rival to "Jewish" Jerusalem. Self-consciously intended as a Hebrew rather than a Jewish city—with Jewish evaluated negatively as diasporic, conservative, and religious—Tel Aviv, according to Helman, could not ultimately escape the appeal of traditional Jewish urbanity, even as it managed to reconfigure it on its streets and in its neighborhoods.

Jews, most of them emigrants from Eastern Europe, made up Tel Aviv's entire population and their sheer density was remarkable and remarked upon by inhabitants and visitors alike. To better understand why the first "Hebrew" city was experienced as Jewish, though pointedly not in the sense of religion or tradition, "high" culture or folklore, language or learning, Helman explores the aesthetics of everyday life. The official "Hebrew" program may have been promulgated from above through formal ideology, "high" culture, and the secularization of religious customs, but the city's Jewish character, its distinctive style and atmosphere, was fashioned from below by those who lived there and made the city their own through their everyday practices, festivities, and popular culture.[32]

More than half a century later, with the State of Israel firmly, if not securely established, dissenting voices were making themselves heard through a popular music that "vocalizes the space" between Ashkenazi and Mizrahi Jews, Israelis and Palestinians, Jews and Arabs. What does that space sound like? The folklorist Amy Horowitz traces the history of that sound from the roots music that Middle Eastern Jewish immigrants brought to Israel to the creation of a new synthesis, Musika Mizrahit (Mediterranean Israeli music). Musika Mizrahit emerged in the 1970s in immigrant neighborhoods, where it was performed live on social and ceremonial occasions. Circulating through the informal economy of cassette tapes sold at bus stations, this music was soon picked up by the popular music industry and has been traveling across disputed territories. Horowitz focuses on one of the most poignant cases explored in this volume, that of the Israeli singer Zehava Ben. Despite the second-class status of Israel's Middle Eastern Jewish citizens (and their music), Ben, who was born in Israel of Andalusian Moroccan parents, not only rose to success but also turned her Middle Eastern pedigree and musical competence to advantage as a peace advocate. Horowitz focuses on the turning point in Ben's career, in 1994, when she decided to perform the repertoire of Umm Kulthum, the Maria Callas of the Arab world, and did so both at Palestinian gatherings and at memorials for Yitzhak Rabin. Despite the surrounding tragedy, the moment seemed ripe with possibility, not just for musical and cultural integration but for social and political reconciliation as well. Attuned to the fine calibrations of the Israeli soundscape, listeners heard not only the sounds but also their sources. Above all, they heard what coming together across divides sounds like. For a brief moment, between the signing of the Oslo Peace Accords and the assassination of Israeli Prime Minister Yitzhak Rabin, the fateful shadow that inevitably separates hopeful dreams from harsh realities lifted.

Art Worlds

To study the arts contextually is also to study art worlds and culture industries. Howard S. Becker defines an art world as "the network of people whose cooperative activity, organized via their joint knowledge of conventional means of doing things, produces the kind of art works that the art world is noted for."[33] While the art world concept seems self-evident and even tautological (by Becker's own admission), "many of its implications are not. . . . The dominant tradition takes the artist and the art work, rather than the network of cooperation, as central to the analysis of art as a social phenomenon."[34] In this light, what better topic for exploring the complex dynamic of art worlds than the history of Jewish participation in the arts? In the modern era seemingly disproportionate numbers of Jews gravitated to the culture industries, often not as artists per se but as agents, mediators, arbiters, publicists, impresarios, dealers, entrepreneurs, managers, and collectors. Yet much work remains to be done to develop the connections between modernity, Jewish art, and Jewish artistic mediation. This volume offers a number of examples, including the theater and movie house entrepreneurs discussed in Judith Thissen's essay on film and vaudeville on New York's Lower East Side, the street corner entrepreneurs peddling the homemade pop music cassettes that Amy Horowitz discusses, and the self-proclaimed Jewish purveyors—composers, musicians, critics, and salesman—of "Negro Jazz" discussed by Jonathan Karp.

The historian Charles Dellheim takes up a key variation on this theme in his examination of the slow-to-emerge but currently salient issue of the Nazi theft of Jewish "art treasures." Before World War II, as he notes, European Jews were prominent as artists, collectors, dealers, curators, and art historians. The legacy of this aesthetic and commercial phenomenon, which Dellheim links to the Jews' assertion of their cultural credentials for membership in modern European society, was significantly occluded by the systematic Nazi confiscation campaign as well as by the victors' postwar obfuscation of the original Jewish sources of much of the stolen art. In recent years many of these confiscated works have been adduced as material witnesses to the Shoah and have become sites of Jewish memory in their own right. But Dellheim suggests that despite the overdue attention to this aspect of the Holocaust, the historical reality that made Jews important to the arts in the first place still remains largely forgotten. Jews, after all, were prominent actors both in the multifarious "art worlds" of Europe, à la Becker, and in the singular European art world in its traditional, elitist sense. Jews' contribution to the integration of these two spheres constitutes a history that ought to be recovered.

This volume manages to rediscover an important but forgotten figure in the art world of modern dance, Joseph Lewitan. Like the subject of Dellheim's essay, Lewitan too was a victim of Nazi racist aesthetics.[35] Moving from the Soviet Union to Berlin in 1920, he established a landmark journal, *Der Tanz: Monatsschrift für Tanzkultur*, seven years later. Given the ephemeral nature of dance performance, dance critics are often on the front lines of dance history, for they are the ones who see and write about performances close to the time of the event, and theirs may well be the only record that remains. As much as any single figure, Lewitan charted a decisive phase in late Weimar German dance, the fractious debates between the anti-modernists and the modernists, and the increasing identification of German modern dance with the *Völkisch* aesthetics embraced by National Socialism. As the dance historian Marion Kant notes, this was an ideological war waged on the human body and how it moved. Lewitan tried, without success, to protect dance from the very politics whose victim he eventually became. Whatever sociological factors led to the disproportionate Jewish participation in mediating roles, Jewishness—by anti-Semitic ascription as much as by self-identification—also functioned to exclude him and many others. With the Nazi advent to power, Lewitan was forced to abandon his journal, flee the country, and forgo the art world he helped to create. While he did not create dance, Lewitan played a vital role in the organized context in which dance was made.

However important it may be to study art worlds such as those signified by Lewitan and others, sociologists of art (and for that matter historians and anthropologists) have sometimes been faulted for studying everything but "the work of art itself" (*l'oeuvre elle-même*).[36] Even art historians have been faulted for neglecting the work itself. In a recent diatribe against the new art history—and the even newer "new, new art history"[37]—Roger Kimball asks if the interest in art has become "ulterior, not aesthetic." Are scholars "enlisting art as an illustration of some extraneous, non-artistic, non-aesthetic narrative"? Is art's fate "relegation to the status of a prop in a drama not its own"?[38] And the same question could be put to any other art form, as indeed it has, in almost identical words. Rose Rosengard Subotnik notes that "critics sometimes complain that authors of studies based on this assumption of social intimacy [the "intimate relationship between music and society"] are not really interested in music but rather in philosophy or anthropology or some other 'extrinsic' discipline." She challenges them to question their cherished assumption of autonomy, not only of music but also of musicology, which positivist musicologists "tend to see as an extension of the autonomous domain of music itself." Musicologists, in her view, need to subject these ideas to the same scrutiny as they do the music itself.[39] The new art historians would say the same for art and art history.[40]

Yet the response to sociology's quandary, to Kimball's complaint, and to critics of contextual musicology need not be defensive, whether by absolving sociology of the necessity to do what it is not "good at" or by rebuilding the barricades around the disciplines of art history and musicology. Rather, Becker asks, what might it mean to treat empirically "the principle of the fundamental indeterminacy of the art work," a daunting task that requires "enormously detailed knowledge of the work and of the organized context in which it was made."[41] A singular strength of this volume is precisely its integration of a close analysis of the work of art with careful attention to the circumstances of its production, dissemination, reception, and efficacy—whether a single piece of wedding music, in the case of Hankus Netsky's musical self-portrait of Philadelphia's Jewish community, or a single film, in the case of Susan Rubin Suleiman's analysis of Marcel Ophuls's fascinating documentary about Klaus Barbie.

With a penetrating focus, Netsky traces the history of the Philadelphia Russian Sher medley from the late nineteenth century to the present on the basis of an extraordinary collection of early manuscripts and recordings. An ethnomusicologist by training, as well as a musician from a long line of Philadelphia klezmorim (traditional East European Jewish instrumentalists), Netsky offers a close musicological reading of a classic East European wedding dance that shows how its shifting role was expressed through its changing form, as it moved with those who danced—and later forgot how to dance—to its rhythms. This one piece of music becomes a sensitive barometer of the relationship of American Jews to their European past and American future. Muting what was once the signature sound of Philadelphia's Jewish community, upwardly mobile Jews who had moved to the suburbs partied to new rhythms. By the 1960s, the Philadelphia Russian Sher medley was rarely heard, except as a nostalgic reminder of an immigrant and European past. Yet, by the 1970s, a new generation had rediscovered the music, and the sher—and this particular version of it—became a cornerstone in the revival of what has come to be known as klezmer music.[42] By exploring the interplay of the music business, the musical taste of Philadelphia Jews, and the ways they chose to party, Netsky's richly textured sonic history of one piece of music reveals the social nature of musical creativity and the historically specific circumstances that shaped Philadelphia's Jewish soundscape over the course of its history.

In her elegant and precise analysis of *Hotel Terminus: The Life and Times of Klaus Barbie*, Susan Suleiman, a literary scholar, explores the moral consequences of making the film—and the making of the film—at least partly its own subject. In this film, released in 1988 the auteur Marcus Ophuls takes up the refusal of the French to "remember" what happened under Klaus Barbie, the infamous "butcher of Lyon" who was responsible for the arrest, torture, deportation, and deaths of Jews as well as members of the French Resistance during the German Occupation of France. In his treatment of Barbie's 1983 capture and trial, which took four years to prepare, Ophuls employs every technique in the documentarian's arsenal to avoid making a film that in any way resembles an exposé, an indictment, a tribute, or a monument. Instead, his unsettling concentration his own persona in an ostensibly nonautobiographical documentary is clearly designed to expose the performative character of even a supposedly factual, truth-telling historical film. This strategy succeeds in unsettling the moral certainty that viewers likely bring to the film, by placing them in an uncomfortable if not untenable position that requires a struggle to arrive at judgment. The conclusions are no longer pat, the moral no longer self-affirming and comforting. Ophuls demands that one situate oneself "affectively, as a subject—an ethical subject as well as the subject of aesthetic perception—in relation to the film's rendering of 'other people's memories.'" Ophuls was worried that this film, both in the making and in its reception, would be just a "Jewish film," that the Holocaust would be a parochial matter rather than a more universal human concern. Paradoxically, the film pursues its universality precisely through its relentless, jolting subjectivity, achieved not least of all by the intrusive on-screen presence of the filmmaker, who confronts his subjects, enrages them, makes asides, and addresses the viewer directly. For Suleiman, it is precisely "in these moments of visually highlighted subjectivity that Ophuls points the viewer to the central moral issues raised by his work." The total effect of applying such extreme distancing techniques to the topic of the Holocaust is among the most radical of Jewish artistic statements possible today.

Stratification of the Cultural Field

The remapping of disciplinary subjects and the formation of new ones have called into question the cultural hierarchies that compartmentalize and stratify the arts and the study of them. Specialized disciplines devoted to the high and largely European end of artistic achievement (fine art, classical music, concert dance, literary drama) left the low end of the cultural spectrum to ethnomusicology, anthropology, and folklore. This arrangement has had profound implications for how the Jewish arts and Jewish participation in the arts broadly conceived are constituted as subjects of study—they are more likely to be treated as ethnic and taken up by ethnomusicologists, folklorists, and anthropologists than art and music historians. Intervening in this arrangement, this volume ranges across a stratified cultural field. The goal is not simply to remedy a history of exclusions by being more inclusive of the so-called low end of the artistic spectrum. Rather, these essays focus on the historical formation of the cultural hierarchies themselves; they seek to understand, in the words of the cultural studies theorist Stuart Hall, "the relations of power which are constantly punctuating and dividing the domain of culture into its preferred and its residual categories."[43]

As the theater historian Nina Warnke chronicles in this volume, Yiddish theater became a battleground for the hearts and minds of the Jewish immigrant masses on New York's Lower East Side during the first decades of the twentieth century. Believing in the power of art to effect social transformation, critics of *shund* or trash, as Yiddish melodrama and vaudeville were dubbed, waged their war in the pages of the Yiddish press in an effort to refine the taste and comportment of immigrant audiences addicted to

spectacular melodrama and vulgar vaudeville. Convinced that good theater, which meant realist literary dramas, would enlighten and uplift the
Jewish masses, Russian Jewish radical intellectuals strived mightily to "elevate" what was performed on the stage.

Why did they fail? What intervened to frustrate the noble plans of the
simultaneously socialist egalitarian and culturally elitist critics? Both Warnke
and Judith Thissen, who explores a similar dynamic in the contemporaneous emergence of nickelodeon films, suggest that the Jewish masses found
a ready ally in the struggle against their erstwhile benefactors in the emerging
mass entertainment industries generated by American consumer capitalism. The result of this alliance, however, was neither the respectful tutelage
to high culture demanded by the ideologues nor the robotic submission to
commodified entertainment desired by the film industry, but rather a
hybrid form of popular American Yiddish culture.

It is by focusing on the programming and exhibition practices associated
with movies (and not just the movies themselves) that Thissen, a film historian, is able to show how movies and vaudeville changed places in the cultural hierarchy. During the first decade of the twentieth century, social
reformers objected to the unsanitary, unsavory, and unsafe conditions of
Lower East Side movie venues, while some critics thought the movies themselves were actually preferable to vaudeville and hoped that movies would
drive out the lowest forms of live entertainment. Worst of all, in their view,
was the promiscuous mixing of movies and live vaudeville in the same program, because the low quality of live performances—tickets were so cheap,
the exhibitors could not afford better—debased the movie experience.
The result was trashy vaudeville and sing-alongs, which encouraged rowdy
sociability. To elevate moviegoing as a social practice, critics insisted that
movie programs be devoted exclusively to movies and that moviegoers
focus on the screen, not on what was going on around them in the theater.
In this way, what had been a boisterous social experience would become a
quiet individual one and moviegoing as a practice would be a more effective agent of Americanization. The tide turned in 1909, when the Grand
Theater ceased to be a Yiddish theater and became a movie venue and movies came to be seen as posing a serious threat to live Yiddish performance
of any kind. Some of the critics who had railed against Yiddish vaudeville
as Americanization of the wrong kind started supporting it "as an authentic
expression of *yidishkayt*." As a result, Yiddish vaudeville shot up the cultural
escalator from lowbrow to middlebrow, while movies, increasingly associated with vice, slid to the bottom, though not everyone who objected to
movies thought Yiddish vaudeville was the antidote. Jewish working-class
taste prevailed: Yiddish vaudeville experienced a revival and mixed programs won out. Moreover, because most of the movies were mainstream,
not Jewish, fare, the interspersing of Yiddish vaudeville between reels made
the experience more "Jewish" and conditioned the movie experience

itself, as well as any Americanizing effects that movies—and above all, moviegoing—might have on Jewish immigrant audiences.[44]

Stratification of the cultural field is not only a source (as well as an outcome) of conflict, but also a resource for the creation of new expressive forms, as Jonathan Karp demonstrates in his account of how early twentieth-century American Jewish composers and songwriters worked with—and not only within—artistic hierarchies.[45] They ragged the classics and classicized the rags, whether to parodic or serious ends, in the hope that a synthesis of American popular music with European art music might form the basis of a national American music. Noting that Tin Pan Alley was a "Jewish" business, at the very least demographically, Karp explores the parallel efforts of Jewish and black musicians to synthesize popular and classical music, as well as differences in their status within a racialized music industry. Karp, a historian by training, calls attention to a peculiar but hardly unique case of cultural substitution and ethnic impersonation. Arising from the contemporary perception that Jews by nature, as well as (diasporic) historical experience, are the cultural mediators par excellence, Jews were thought to be ideally placed to "straddle multiple worlds: black and white, American and European, high and low" in the manner that cultural critics of the era deemed necessary to the creation of a distinctively American form of music. Karp's "maestros" and "minstrels" are thus self-conscious musical mediators between the marginalized and the mainstream who attempted to create a distinctively American music by classicizing what had come to be identified as the singular expression of American musical genius, namely, African American vernacular music. They thus exemplify the problem of cultural stratification wherein the art of the Jews is viewed as either constructive or corrosive, but never constitutive.

These then are the broad contours of *The Art of Being Jewish in Modern Times*. First, by historicizing the Jewish art question, the essays in this volume pose the question in different ways and, above all, keep it alive and unpredictable as a question that can shed light on the relationship between Jews, the arts, and modernity. Second, by attending not only to the work itself but also to the organized context in which it was made, the contributors to this volume illuminate how the social and the aesthetic are mutually constitutive. Third, the range of approaches and sites of analysis highlight the ways in which disciplinary and cultural hierarchies are formed and make their formation an object of analysis in its own right. As noted above, the essays in this volume thus entertain the hypothesis that the "modern Jewish experience" has in some sense been a pointedly artistic one.

To capture these concerns and others that cross-cut the essays, we have organized the volume thematically, rather than chronologically, geographically, or by genre. The first section, "Culture, Commerce, and Class," focuses on art worlds, the art business, and stratifications of class and culture within the Yiddish immigrant world of the Lower East Side (Warnke

and Thissen) and Tin Pan Alley (Karp). The second section, "Siting the
Jewish Tomorrow," explores the role of embodied and concrete practices
in making utopian ideals tangible, whether Soviet Yiddish marching songs
for children (Shternshis) or the Zionist ideals materialized in the Jewish
Palestine Pavilion at the New York World's Fair (Kirshenblatt-Gimblett)
and performed in "the first Hebrew city," Tel Aviv (Helman) and in the
music of Zehava Ben (Horowitz). The third section, "Lost in Place," takes
up the question of Diaspora, both negative (Cohen's analysis of the Wandering Jew) and positive (Zemel's discussion of a diasporist aesthetic). The
fourth section, "Portraits of the Artist as Jew," explores the Jewish art question in Germany (Cahn on Liebermann), Russia (Litvak on Antokol'skii),
and the United States (Linden on Shahn). The fifth section, "In Search of
a Usable Aesthetic," discusses efforts to formulate a Jewish aesthetics (Braiterman on Rosenzweig) and give it sonic form, whether from the top down
(Kligman on Binder) or the bottom up (Netsky on Jewish wedding music).
The volume concludes with the sixth section, "Hotel Terminus," which
explores the relationship between aesthetics and ethics in extremis, from
the Nazification of dance in Germany (Kant on Lewitan) and preoccupation with the recovery and restitution of Nazi loot (Dellheim) to the possibility of a poetics of memory after the Holocaust (Suleiman on Ophuls).
Together, the essays explore how Jewish aesthetic culture (a set of historically specific practices that includes but is broader than the arts proper)
gives tangible, palpable, and affective form—a sound, a look, a feel, a poetics—to understandings and values and to what effect.

It is our hope that these contributions will enliven a conversation across
fields that will make the arts and innovative ways of studying them a more
prominent concern within Jewish studies, while encouraging other disciplines to discover what might be learned from the Jewish experience.

I.
Culture, Commerce, and Class

America's new mass culture industries divided an early twentieth-century New York Jewish community by class and culture. Essays by Nina Warnke, Judith Thissen, and Jonathan Karp illustrate how the struggle between elitist programs for cultural elevation and new and old forms of popular entertainment resulted in a peculiarly American, or American Jewish, hybrid.

Nina Warnke's "Theater as Educational Institution: Jewish Immigrant Intellectuals and Yiddish Theater Reform," explores the efforts by Jewish radical intellectuals to "elevate" the cultural standards of the immigrant masses through the replacement of *shund* (the term meaning "trash" applied to much popular Yiddish entertainment) by literary dramas about "real life problems." The critic and playwright Jacob Gordin, a pivotal figure in the clash between realistic art theater and such *shund* manifestations as popular melodramas, musicals, and vaudeville, strived tirelessly, although ultimately unsuccessfully, to replace stage spectacle with edifying drama. Nevertheless, as Warnke shows, the commercial and populist character of the American setting combined with the sheer stubbornness of Jewish working-class sensibilities to help make *shund* resistant to the high-minded efforts of Gordin and the radical elite.

If in his heyday Gordin saw *shund* as the most serious threat to a didactic theater for the Yiddish masses, New York's Jewish immigrant intelligentsia soon faced a new danger in the form of nickelodeon motion picture houses. As Judith Thissen recounts in "Film and Vaudeville on New York's Lower East Side," reformers like the Yiddish *Daily Forward* editor Abraham Cahan had initially hoped that film entertainment would help wean Jewish audiences from their addiction to unsavory Yiddish vaudeville entertainment. The reformers changed their tune, however, when it became apparent that film was displacing not only vaudeville but Yiddish legitimate theater as well (a trend that became unmistakable when in 1909 Jacob Adler's famed Grand Theater was sold to movie moguls Adolph Zukor and Marcus Loew). Now, operating on the presumption that even Yiddish vaudeville was preferable to vulgar American film shorts, popular forms of live Yiddish entertainment became the objects of the Jewish culture critics' belated solicitude. Yet as in the case described by Warnke, the Jewish working class once again insisted on having its own way. Not wishing to choose between stark alternatives, Jewish nickelodeon audiences interspersed movies with live Yiddish entertainment to create a new synthesis. Thissen's account reveals the complex interaction of modern mass entertainment with a specific ethnic subculture, as socialist paternalism, evolving mass media, and folk consumerism struggled for the soul of New York's Lower East Side.

Jonathan Karp shifts the site of highbrow-lowbrow conflict from the struggle over Yiddish theater to the contest to forge a distinctively American music. "Of Maestros and Minstrels: American Jewish Composers between Black Vernacular and European Art Music" traces the process through which Old World stereotypes depicting Jews as economic and cultural middlemen became applied to the "non-Jewish Jews" who dominated the American popular music business of Tin Pan Alley in the years between 1910 and 1930. He shows how Jewish songwriters like Irving Berlin and the Gershwin brothers self-consciously exploited the presumption of their intrinsic Jewish talent for mediation by proclaiming themselves uniquely qualified to translate and elevate the purportedly instinctive but unrefined musical genius of the African American *Volk*. Karp complicates the picture further by identifying an internecine Jewish competition between Tin Pan Alley tunesmiths, on the one hand, and highbrow modernist composers like Aaron Copland, Mark Blitzstein, and Louis Gruenberg, on the other. Both groups, the "minstrels" and the "maestros" respectively, though starting from different rungs of the cultural hierarchy, found that the imputed attributes of their Jewish origins both facilitated and hindered their efforts to refashion black vernacular song into *the* distinctive American musical sound.

Theater as Educational Institution: Jewish Immigrant Intellectuals and Yiddish Theater Reform

Nina Warnke

The Russian Jewish radical intellectuals who arrived in the United States during the 1880s and 1890s were instrumental in creating a leftist mass press, a strong Jewish labor movement, and an immigrant Yiddish literature. They also devoted much time and energy to turning the existing commercial Yiddish theater into an educational institution and a place that would be artistically on a par with contemporary European art theaters. As has been well documented, these intellectuals considered education a key concept in their program to elevate the immigrants, and their press became the primary agent for its dissemination. Their efforts to reform the stage through the writing of theater criticism and realist plays have been largely overlooked until now but need to be seen as an integral part of the radicals' efforts to lead and shape the immigrant community.[1]

Having grown up in Russia during the 1860s and 1870s, and having been exposed to Russian culture in their youth, these men were deeply influenced by the intellectual climate of Russian populism and positivism.[2] Populism stipulated the intellectuals' moral obligation to lead the *narod* (people) in their struggle to liberate themselves from oppression and to assimilate into the intellectuals' cultural and political orbit. And as the positivist critics and writers Nikolai Chernyshevskii, Nikolai Dobroliubov, and Dmitrii Pisarev stipulated, literature and art were, above all, tools for education and fostering social change. Jewish immigrant intellectuals would transpose these principles to fit American and, in particular, Jewish immigrant working-class conditions. Thus, besides local, national, and international news, as well as information on activities in the Jewish labor movement, the popular press offered articles on science, literature, art, history, medicine, civics, and philosophy. Considering literature, primarily realist literature, an important means for the moral education of the workers, they introduced readers to novels by writers like Zola or Tolstoy and offered them Yiddish stories, sketches, and poems reflecting the lives of the immigrants written by local radical writers. An integral part of their notion of realism—besides the so-called truthful depiction of life and nature—was social criticism and a lesson or moral that would propel the readers or audience to question their own assumptions as well as society's social and moral norms, both Jewish and American. Realist fiction or drama had to tackle issues of contemporary society brought to life by characters with credible psychological development.

Coverage of Yiddish theater in the radical press began in the late 1880s. With the production of Jacob Gordin's first plays in the early 1890s, the press made an impassioned, even if limited, bid to teach audiences and actors to give up their predilection for melodrama with its predictable victory of virtue over evil and declamatory acting style and to appreciate instead realist plays and an acting style that emulated natural speech and behavior. By the early years of the twentieth century, theater criticism turned into a highly politicized and factional campaign against the popular theater, or so-called *shund* (literally, trash) theater—a campaign in which aesthetic discussions were closely linked to the political position and aspirations of an individual paper and its bid for higher circulation. Around the time of Gordin's death in 1909, when formulaic melodramas reigned supreme on the Lower East Side, intellectuals had to face the limitations of their reform efforts. The intelligentsia's considerable success when directly addressing the workers' problems is without question; their influence on the theater, however, was another matter. They had not created this institution, and many actors and audience members disagreed with them on how it was to be defined. While their success in creating and supporting a strong labor movement is undisputed, their impact on the theater remained limited.

Yiddish Theater: The Early Years

The Yiddish theater these Russified intellectuals encountered in New York and tried to reform was a commercial institution with no intellectual pretensions that served the poor and minimally educated immigrants. As a modern, secular institution, Yiddish theater has its roots in two earlier performance traditions: the centuries-old folk genre of Purim plays, which dramatized the story of Esther and other biblical stories during the holiday season, and the secular Maskilic (Enlightenment) tradition, starting in the mid-nineteenth century, of performing songs and comical skits in wine cellars and similar locales. In the mid-1870s, Abraham Goldfaden—beloved folk poet and fledgling dramatist—was the first to succeed in forming a lasting professional Yiddish theater for the masses. Generally acknowledged as the father of Yiddish theater, he soon moved from Maskilic slapstick comedies like *Di tsvey Kuni-Leml* (The Two Kuni-Leml) to crowd-pleasing romantic historical operas and melodramas such as *Shulamis*, laying the foundations for what was essentially a musical theater. His success spurred the creation of wandering troupes and the interest of writers of varying abilities who followed his lead. Since the demand for repertoire was enormous, playwrights usually resorted to quickly adapting European—particularly German and French—melodramas, comedies, and farces, and setting them in a Jewish context. Similarly, the music for these "operas" or "operettas" was taken from a wide variety of sources, from traditional *nigunim* (melodies) and various folksong traditions to nineteenth-century opera. In the 1880s and 1890s, the declining Purim-play tradition continued in a modified form within a secular context as historical operas about Esther. Other biblical stories were also popular on the Yiddish stage. For decades to come, many plays were constructed around an essential element of the Purim story's drama: the conflict with and ultimate Jewish victory over evil anti-Semites.

The flourishing of Yiddish theater all over the Pale of Settlement was suddenly curtailed when, in 1883, the Russian ministry for internal affairs banned performances in Yiddish. While some actors continued to tour the Pale by posing as German troupes, others dispersed, and soon several companies established themselves in New York. Headed by the playwrights Moyshe Hurwitz and Josef Lateiner, they offered primarily historical operas and melodramas that dramatized Jewish themes, either mythological or contemporary. Although the theaters could boast some very talented actors, most had little education and no formal acting training. After all, many had run away from home or from the masters to whom they were apprenticed to join wandering troupes in search of adventure and in the hope of avoiding the predictable life of poverty and exploitation.

The Yiddish theaters in New York were unruly and noisy places. The mostly working-class audience enjoyed plays that emphasized spectacle and music over text, slapstick and risqué jokes over emotional subtlety, visual attractions over logical plot development, entertainment over education. This audience delighted in stories about Jewish heroism and in the spectacular and sensational: the bright and lavish costumes, the big orchestras and choruses, the titillation of men in tights and women in raised skirts, and such special stage effects as live animals or thunder and lightning on stage. The spectators participated actively by hissing at the villains or demanding that the actor repeat a particularly beautiful tune or dance. Like most folk and working-class theater, the Yiddish stage in New York was a performance-centered theater; author and text were secondary to both the actors' performance and the spectators' consciousness. Playing to the audience, the actors often improvised and thus had a direct rapport with their viewers.

Early Voices for Theatrical Reform

When the radical Russian intellectuals encountered the Yiddish theater on the Lower East Side in the 1880s, most of them turned away in disgust. Privately, they looked at it with contempt; publicly, they ignored it. Lacking, as they asserted, artistic value and social merit, the Yiddish stage provided nothing for their cause. Getsl Zelikovitsh, the editor of the pro-labor weekly *Folksadvokat* (People's Advocate) from 1888 to 1889, was the only one to take up the cause to improve the stage. However, besides acerbic reviews of historical operas and attacks on actors for their unprofessional behavior, he also criticized the other papers for their complacency and lack of serious critique. The Yiddish theater, he argued, was only "a very useful institution under the good control and sharp criticism of the Yiddish press." He was especially adamant about the radical papers' duty to enlighten the uneducated and poor workers to make them understand what they "could and should demand from the stage," instead of letting them waste their hard-earned dollars on "nonsense."[3] Thus Zelikovitsh was probably the first to articulate the basic paradigm that was to guide immigrant critics during the following decades: as a commercial institution, the theater exploited the uneducated and, therefore, "helpless" audience. It was the intelligentsia's responsibility, first, to pressure the theater to change its fare and thereby its role in society; and, second, to empower the audience to resist its exploitation by educating it to demand proper art.

Around the same time, Israel Barsky, an avid labor organizer who had been instrumental in launching a tailors' union in 1888, proposed a detailed plan to turn the theater into a "useful" institution for the movement. Unlike his colleagues, Barsky had been involved in Yiddish theater. In 1882 he participated in the first Yiddish performance in New York and subsequently wrote several plays.[4] In a series of articles, published in the *Nyu yorker yidishe folks-tsaytung* (New York Jewish People's Paper) in 1889, he proposed to found a people's theater. "Would we not gain much for the labor movement," he asked, "if we had a true people's theater and our brothers could hear true folksongs and couplets, real folk dramas and comedies and in between also a good popular speaker? Wouldn't such a theater be able to serve the propaganda of the labor movement and at the same time move the labor organizations forward with mighty strides?" In order to create such a people's theater, he suggested founding a "Dramatisher untershtitsungs fareyn" (Dramatic Benevolent Society), to which each member would contribute a monthly fee and have to sell a dollar's worth of tickets per performance. The revenue was to support unemployed members and the families of deceased members.[5] But there seems to have been little support for his ideas at the time and nothing came of his plans. At a meeting of the United Hebrew Trades, for example, where the creation of a people's theater was discussed, a member protested that valuable time was being wasted when it was more important to address the workers' dismal wages.[6]

Most intellectuals thought similarly. The creation of a strong labor movement and radical press seemed more urgent and promising than reforming the theater, an institution to which they had no direct access and which they could not control. Typical of this attitude is Abraham Cahan's statement in 1890 in the recently founded *Arbayter tsaytung* (Workman's Paper). When asked by a reader why the paper did not print theater reviews, he responded, "we cannot devote ourselves to theatre reviews because most Jewish readers, regrettably do not understand what theatre criticism is. Also, it would not help to improve the theatre. Most of the plays on stage do not deserve serious reviews."[7] Ten years later, the *Forverts* (Jewish Daily Forward) critic Moyshe Katz described this period in the following manner: "The situation of the Yiddish stage was like the Jewish story of Genesis: And the earth was without form and void. (*Un es iz geven toyu-vovoyu*) . . . Goldfaden's childish, comical caricatures were exchanged for historical plays by German pseudo-artists which Yiddish 'authors,' who cannot write in a literary style, crippled into Purim-plays."[8]

Jacob Gordin's First Plays

As Katz implied, "creation," or rather "reform," was imminent: in 1891 the noted Russian Jewish journalist Jacob Gordin, whose epithet would soon be "the reformer of the Yiddish stage," arrived in New York, where he joined the staff of the socialist *Arbayter tsaytung*. Since he had some knowledge of theater—in his youth, he was presumably briefly a traveling actor in a Russian troupe and, during the 1880s, he wrote theater reviews for several Russian newspapers—Gordin decided to write for the Yiddish stage in order to supplement his meager income as a Yiddish journalist.

Like the proponents of Russia's people's theater movement, who organized troupes to bring literary plays to the peasants, Gordin placed particular hope in the potential of the stage to serve as a tool to enlighten, educate, and civilize the broad masses of the population. Gordin was deeply influenced by the Russian playwright Aleksandr Ostrovskii, whose ideas inspired much of the people's theater movement. Like Ostrovskii, whose works Gordin intimately knew and emulated, Gordin called the theater a *folks shule* (primary school, literally "people's school"), accessible to those who had no opportunity to study elsewhere.[9] There, Gordin insists, "one should come to learn about the life of society, family, and individual, there one should acquaint oneself with the significance of social phenomena and explanations of life's problems. Theater is created so that the masses educate their feelings, harmonize their concepts, and socialize their ideas about justice and injustice . . . In theater, people from different classes receive one and the same suggestions and become united through one and the same ideals. Theater can only fulfill this task if it describes the truth of life, the truth of nature."[10] Echoing the Russian intelligentsia's desire to create a cultural consensus between themselves and the masses through realist literature and theater, Gordin and his fellow journalists imbued the Yiddish stage with the same enormous task of uniting the different classes and thus bridging the cultural and intellectual gap between the common people and the radical intellectuals.[11] But unlike the organizers of the people's theater movement, who determined their own repertoire and created their own (often amateur) troupes, the Jewish intellectuals in New York attempted to reform an already vibrant commercial theater with its particular well-entrenched conventions.

The new "cultural consensus" that was to be achieved through realism was only possible by turning an actor-centered theater, with its general disregard for author and text, into an author-centered stage. During the rehearsal period of his first drama, *Sibiriya* (Siberia), in 1891, Gordin insisted on the sanctity of the text, breaking the actors' prerogative of ad-libbing and changing texts to suit their needs. In order to create a more realistic representation on stage, he demanded that they speak regular Yiddish instead of the stilted Germanized Yiddish that mirrored the Romantic stage convention of unnatural speech and heightened language. He also insisted on a more natural and nuanced acting style, instead of the booming declamatory style then in vogue in both the American melodrama houses and the Yiddish theater. Furthermore, he refused to allow songs and particularly couplets—songs performed outside the context of the play and in direct interaction with the audience—thus enforcing the idea of a "fourth wall."

The performance of *Sibiriya* was celebrated by Gordin's cohort at the *Arbayter tsaytung* as the first literary and realist drama on the Yiddish stage. Cahan, realizing that with Gordin's presence the intellectuals might begin to exert some influence over the theater, was moved to write his first theater review. He prophesized triumphantly that "the play and the way it was performed will revolutionize the Yiddish stage."[12] Although *Sibiriya* succeeded in bringing the small circle of the intelligentsia into a Yiddish playhouse for the first time, the general audience, expecting a very different show, rejected it. The realism of Gordin's play lacked the theatricality, the rich visual impressions, and the happy ending they demanded. In the 1890s, for the majority of the audience, the theater's appeal lay precisely in forgoing verisimilitude and the stark realism of problem plays in favor of fantasy and spectacle. Those who did see *Sibiriya* expected more action and were bored with the play's first act and, at points, misunderstood the author's intentions. For example, they laughed when they saw the servant (played by the comedian Sigmund Mogulesco) express his pain with some comic mannerisms, as he announced in tears that his master's daughter had killed herself. What to Cahan was an extraordinarily moving moment, the audience interpreted as funny because, as Cahan claimed, "they have a rule that when Mogulesco makes a grimace one has to laugh."[13]

Like *Sibiriya,* Gordin's *Der pogrom in rusland* (The Pogrom in Russia), which was produced in early 1892, was written in calculated opposition to melodrama's one-dimensional character types. After it flopped, Gordin tried to explain the play's meaning and value to the readers of the *Arbayter tsaytung.* The drama, which takes place during the wave of pogroms in 1881 following the assassination of Czar Alexander II, dramatizes the tragic fate of the Halperin family. Well-to-do store owners, the Halperins have two daughters: Manitshke, who is in love with the Ukrainian Pavlusha, and Eda, who reads Russian novels and prepares to enter a Russian gymnasium. Their integrationist hopes are shattered when a pogrom breaks out. The family home and store are destroyed, but Pavlusha is at least able to rescue Manitshke and her parents. Eda, however, is raped by a pogromist, which leaves her emotionally disturbed. When Pavlusha asks Manitshke to marry him, she refuses, declaring she can no longer marry someone who belongs to the people who attacked her family. Devastated, Pavlusha kills the woman he loves.

In both of these early plays, Gordin made a conscious decision to break with the convention of positive Jewish heroes versus non-Jewish villains. Instead he emphasized that positive and negative character traits are not divided along ethnic lines but are part of human nature: "I don't say in order to please the audience that all Russians are murderers and all Jews are angels." On the contrary, he depicted a Jew who "benefited from the pogrom and who also has a human heart" and, in Pavlusha, he created a Gentile whose sincerity and nobleness were well proven before his murder in despair.[14] While from our perspective Gordin's representation of the characters' internal duality of good and bad impulses also seems simplistic, overwrought, and contrived, it has to be understood within the context of his goals at the time: to challenge an audience that was used to clear moral divisions in melodrama and to make them question their own assumptions.

Theater Criticism in the Early 1890s

Gordin, Cahan, and Louis Miller, another contributor to the *Arbayter tsaytung,* quickly realized that in order for the theater to fulfill its function to develop the audience and teach it new ideas, they had to prepare performers and theatergoers for drastically altered conventions. Thus began their decades-long campaign in the radical press to educate actors and audiences alike on how to differentiate between "art" and "cheap entertainment" and to instill in them a sense of "proper" taste. The critics attacked the theater's Romantic and musical tradition, its disregard for historical accuracy, its use of Germanized Yiddish, its emphasis on spectacle, its gratuitous display of sexuality, its rapid succession of emotional climaxes, and its insistence on a happy ending. And they condemned many of the historical operas and melodramas, which, because of their ritualized celebration of the collective victory of the Jews over anti-Semites, smacked of unacceptable parochialism and chauvinism.

The critics did not mince words when they scolded directors for choosing historical operas or actors for performing in an exaggerated manner. Cahan's description of the actors' typical performance may serve as a representative example of the tone of much theater criticism during the following two decades. While praising the actors for their acting in *Sibiriya*, he reminded them how preposterous their usual acting seemed to him. Pointing specifically to the influence of the neighboring American entertainment world, Cahan asked why "a brilliant talent like Mogulesco . . . cannot do without dirty wisecracks that seem to be made for the Bowery liquor saloons. Why should [Jacob P.] Adler, [David] Kessler, [and] Mrs. [Keni] Liptzin not be able to make people cry in the so-called *lebnsbilder* [literally, scenes of life] without putting all their energy into twisting their bodies and throwing themselves like angry lions on words appropriate for *Julius Caesar*, with grimaces taken from a second-rate Bowery theater?"[15]

For intellectuals, the development of Yiddish theater became an important yardstick for the progress of a modern, secular Jewish culture. Intent on accelerating this process, they goaded their readers to participate in a cultural "catching-up" by pressuring them to embrace "higher" standards of art. Thus, informing much of the criticism at the time was the preoccupation with the "progress," or rather with the perceived "stagnation" or "decline," of the stage and an endless attempt to identify the "culprit." This paradigm, of course, did not allow intellectuals to acknowledge that social classes differed in their cultural needs. Performance traditions to which the audiences were accustomed were turned into negative symbols. During the 1890s, as intellectuals attempted to demarcate the line between "primitive" entertainment and the more developed state of Yiddish theater, they regularly called actors "Purim players," or "Kuni Leml" (after the foolish, inept, and crippled character from Goldfaden's early comedy), and referred to historical operas or melodramas as "Purim plays" or "balagan" (Russian fairground entertainment). After 1900, new terms of derision gained popularity with the critics: *shund* became the catchall word for all "unworthy" productions, and actors were accused of playing like Yiddish "vaudeville or music hall performers," in reference to the latest form of entertainment despised by the critics. In typical exaggeration, Gordin taught his readers proper aesthetic criteria: "Only a drama that describes life, portrays real, natural, true human beings with all their character traits, faults and virtues, happiness and suffering, good habits and bad strivings is a dignified play."[16]

Gordin felt that practical steps were needed to further his reform efforts as a playwright, and indeed he was able to win over several intellectuals to the cause. In late 1896 or early 1897, he cofounded the Fraye yidishe folks-bine (Free Yiddish People's Stage). The new organization attracted several writers—most of them regular contributors to the radical press—who would, for years to come, dedicate much of their time, thought, and energy to Yiddish theater. Among them was the sketch writer and literary critic Bernard Gorin, who was to become one of the most astute theater critics and who would publish the first book-length history of Yiddish theater in 1918; Leon Kobrin, at the time an aspiring playwright who presented his first play at the Folksbine; and Joel Entin, who, like Gorin, was soon to con-tribute regular theater reviews to the *Forverts* and other papers and who would be the leading force behind the Progressive Dramatic Club, an ama-teur club devoted to producing literary plays.[17] The other members included the lexicographer Alexander Harkavy, the Marxist scholar Louis Budianov (Boudin), Abraham Kaspe, and Sergei Ingerman, all well-known journalists of the radical press who also occasionally wrote on theater. According to its "platform," which was written by Gordin, the Fraye yidishe folksbine was to educate the audience and help create a new repertory. The organization planned to publish "impartial" reviews in its journal by the same name; sponsor lectures on theater history, dramatic art, and the role of theater in society; organize concerts with explanatory lectures on music; encourage writers to write plays by offering prizes; publish translations and original Yiddish dramas with critical introductions; and select dramas and have them staged by professional actors.[18] However, little came of it, since the organization only lasted for about nine months. It dissolved due to internal frictions.[19]

The following year Gordin enjoyed an unprecedented popular and criti-cal success with *Di yidishe honigin lir, oder Mirele Efros* (The Jewish Queen Lear, or Mirele Efros), which harbingered what all chroniclers of Gordin's career consider his heyday. The papers eagerly published reviews praising the author and, for the most part, the actors for their achievements. The *Abend blatt*'s critic Benjamin Feigenbaum called the play "the 'queen' of all Yiddish dramas" and considered it "the duty of everyone who is serious about the cultural development of the Jewish masses to push this play as much as possible."[20] Moyshe Katz, writing for the *Forverts*, used the opportu-nity to remind his fellow intellectuals that *Mirele Efros* was still such a rare phenomenon on the Yiddish stage because intellectuals like themselves "very rarely attempted to accomplish anything in this educational field" of Yiddish theater.[21]

In response to the success, star actors such as Adler, Liptzin, Kessler, and Bertha Kalich started clamoring for roles in Gordin's plays and began to pay considerably more for his scripts. With the theaters' sudden increased openness to plays by an intellectual, others began to follow in Gordin's footsteps. For his journalist colleagues the prospect of having their plays produced meant not only artistic gratification but also—and just as importantly—much needed additional income. After all, the radical press in those years could rarely afford to pay its contributors adequately for their articles and stories. As Sholem Perlmutter relates, Katz like Gordin before him began writing plays in 1899 because he could not make ends meet despite being a journalist for the *Forverts* and a popular lecturer.[22] B. Gorin saw his first play staged in 1898 and the following year both Miller, then a chief contributor to the *Forverts*, and Kobrin made their stage debuts. In 1900, Zalmen Libin's first play was produced. Unlike most of their journalist colleagues, however, only the latter two were able to create considerable careers as playwrights. The increased number of writers whose dramas were produced on the Yiddish stage was a clear sign that the almost complete control that the company dramatists Hurwitz and Lateiner had enjoyed for over a decade was diminishing. But the growing representation of radical writers on the Yiddish stage was also an indication of the strengthening of the radical movement—a fact that the religiously Orthodox and more politically conservative forces noticed with much consternation.

Realism, Politics, and Newspaper Wars

Around the time of Gordin's first successes on the Yiddish stage, the radical and Orthodox press entered an increasingly bitter rivalry. At bottom, this conflict was motivated by the political antagonism between the radical intelligentsia, on the one hand, and the religiously Orthodox and politically conservative forces on the Lower East Side, on the other, and their competitive struggles to influence the political, social, and moral development of the immigrant community. While this competition had been going on for years, it escalated in the late 1890s and subsequent years with the expansion of radical politics and culture into a mass phenomenon. A significant manifestation of the radicals' increasing sphere of influence was the rapid growth of their press. In 1891, when Gordin arrived, the two small-circulation radical weeklies, the socialist *Arbayter tsaytung* and the short-lived anarchist *Fraye arbayter shtime* (Free Voice of Labor), were no competition to Kasriel Sarasohn's well-established and popular daily *Tageblatt* (Daily Paper). The 1890s, however, witnessed the founding of two socialist dailies, the *Abend blatt* (Evening Paper) in 1894, the *Forverts* in 1897, and, in 1899, the resumption of publication of the weekly *Fraye arbayter shtime*. The radicals' infringement upon Sarasohn's market share was countered in 1899 by Jacob Saphirstein with his daily *Abend post* (Evening Post). Two years later, he launched the much more successful *Morgen zhurnal* (Morning Journal), which, like the *Abend post*, was co-owned by Sarasohn and essentially targeted the same readership as the *Tageblatt*. Despite Sarasohn's efforts, by 1904, after seven years of aggressive competition, the *Forverts* announced that its circulation surpassed that of the *Tageblatt*, thereby breaking the latter's nineteen-year dominance in the newspaper market.[23]

In this competitive struggle, the Yiddish theater became one of the major battlegrounds. Theater productions, after all, raised questions about not only art but also politics and morality. Moreover, it was the most popular form of entertainment on the Lower East Side, and both sides were well aware of its influence in shaping the immigrants' tastes, ideas, and opinions. While in 1891 the community of 135,000 residents could only support two theaters with a total seating capacity of 1,900, ten years later three large theaters with a total daily capacity of nine thousand seats sold tickets to over two and a half million spectators during one season. These figures are dramatic proof of the immense popularity of the theater for the approximately 300,000 residents on the Lower East Side. The growing number of daily and weekly publications is, of course, also testimony that reading papers on a regular basis had become common practice for many immigrants. The exponential growth of the press beginning in the late 1890s increased the possibility for timely reviews, for a wide-ranging critical response to productions, and for ensuing controversies. As one of the acknowledged intellectual leaders of the radical community, Gordin became the key figure for the two warring sides.

His highly controversial dramas that were to follow *Mirele Efros*, such as *Di shkhite* (The Slaughter, 1899), *Di yidishe Safo* (The Jewish Sappho, 1900), *Kreytser sonata* (Kreutzer Sonata, 1902), *Di yesoyme* (The Orphan, 1903), and *Tares hamishpokhe* (Purity of Family Life, 1904), turned Gordin into a culture hero for many radical intellectuals and workers. Most welcomed his growing popularity as a sign that the theater was becoming a forum for their artistic and political ideas. Against all expectation, some of these problem plays, modeled on Ibsen, Ostrovskii, and Hauptmann, even became box office hits. Taking his social criticism a step further than in *Sibiriya* or *Mirele Efros*, Gordin focused in these controversial domestic dramas on the woman's suffering within the patriarchal structure of the Jewish family. He attacked what he saw as the double standards regarding the sexual conduct of men and women and the hypocrisy with which the Jewish bourgeoisie, the immigrant parvenus, and the Orthodox establishment defended the "sanctity of the family." Considered commodities, several of these heroines are married off to inappropriate spouses to relieve the family's financial burden; they are treated like servants by husbands and in-laws and are often sexual prey. While the husbands visit prostitutes or have extramarital affairs with impunity, they condemn and punish the women who, in their search for love, respect, and companiate marriage, have had premarital relationships resulting in pregnancy or extramarital relationships with men whom they consider their soul mates. The plays end with the despondent women either killing their oppressor husbands or themselves, or making a conscious sacrifice for their children and resigning themselves to a loveless marriage.

The socialist press touted Gordin's successes as a clear indication of their increasing political influence, of the theater's progress, and thus of the community's intellectual maturation. Gordin's more popular plays increased the visibility of radical culture beyond newspapers, cafes, and strike meetings and brought it into the community's mainstream. As the radicals celebrated with great fanfare Gordin's tenth anniversary as a dramatist in 1901 and declared the victory of literary art—conveniently ignoring that the great hit of the season was not a literary drama but a historical opera—the politically conservative, Orthodox papers reacted with alarm.

With what was at the time a provocative presentation and discussion of love, sexuality, infidelity, and marriage, Gordin fueled the general anxiety over changing sexual conduct and the stresses on family life that accompanied urbanization and immigration. For many (including the radical intellectuals), the new heterosexual contacts and dating practices among young immigrants were disconcerting, particularly within the sexually charged atmosphere of the dance halls and music halls.[24] However, while the gratuitous display of sexuality in historical operas remained disturbing to the Orthodox press, it seemed relatively harmless compared to an ideologically based attack on traditional family values and on the existing social order in general. Morally outraged by his attack on the family and his supposed advocacy of free love, they branded Gordin and the radicals as subversives whose aims and message were both un-Jewish and anti-American. As a result, they blamed Gordin's plays and, by extension, all radicals for the rise in suicides, the general breakdown of the family, and other social pathologies arising from the immigrant experience. The mudslinging between the two sides contributed to the plays' successes, particularly as the socialist papers, above all the *Forverts*, effectively used their performances as public rallies to further their cause. During the controversy over *Di yesoyme*, for example, the *Forverts* encouraged its readers to show their support by attending these performances/rallies and asked labor organizations to send in statements defending Gordin against the Orthodox press, creating a sense of widespread public support and unity among the readers of the radical press.

The polemics for and against Gordin, over representations on stage and their moral effects, have to be read within the context of ideological politics, newspaper circulation wars, and the arbitration of morality. In the process, Gordin was turned into a powerful symbol that his admirers and critics alike used for their purposes in their battles. The radicals' enthusiasm for the alleged progress of the Yiddish stage, however, could not hide increasing internal dissent, and Gordin's place in the limelight and the headlines did not last much beyond 1905. By that time, due to long-standing animosities between him and *Forverts* editor Cahan, he had lost the all-important backing of the paper. Their rivalry, ostensibly over artistic matters but fueled by personal dislike, dated back to the mid-1890s. It was interrupted during Cahan's five-year absence from the Yiddish press, which coincided with Gordin's rise to stardom. Upon his return to the *Forverts* in 1902, Cahan allowed Miller to continue championing Gordin and to lead the fight over *Di yesoyme*. But in 1904, with the circulation war won, Cahan resumed his public criticism of Gordin's plays, which contributed to Miller leaving the *Forverts* and founding *Di varhayt* in 1905.

The "Decline" of the Yiddish Theater

While the hostilities between Cahan and Gordin certainly affected Gordin's career, various economic factors and cultural developments had a decisive impact on Yiddish theater in general. The sudden rise of the music halls and nickelodeons, which began in 1905, proved to be devastating competition. Yiddish music halls quickly captured the imagination of large numbers of pleasure-seeking immigrants. With admission prices between ten cents and twenty-five cents, they appealed to both the poor and the young segments of the population. Their much lower overhead costs (as compared to the theaters) gave them a competitive advantage over the large playhouses. By 1906, there were about twelve Yiddish music halls on the Lower East Side and two in Brooklyn.[25] But the same year also saw the beginning of the nickelodeon boom, which at five to ten cents even undercut the music hall admission rates (earlier movie theaters were called nickelodeons because the price of admission was as low as a nickel). The popularity of moving pictures was so great that at the end of 1907 most music halls featured them as their main entertainment.

The theaters were hard pressed to compete. In 1904, when attendance at Yiddish theaters still seemed to be increasing, a fourth playhouse, the Grand Theater, had opened, the first theater built for a Yiddish company. That year three million spectators were estimated to have attended 1,500 performances. Yet despite the dramatic increase in the immigrant population in the wake of the Kishinev pogrom of 1903 and the failed Russian revolution of 1905—635,000 Jews entered the United States between 1904 and 1908—the four theaters could not be maintained. The economic depression that began in the fall of 1907 and lasted through much of 1908 put 25 percent of the Jewish immigrant workforce on the street. Those immigrants who could still afford to go out preferred to visit the movies. Indeed, not only the theaters lost significant numbers of patrons. As Judith Thissen demonstrates in this volume, by the summer of 1908, the nickelodeons had also pushed the Yiddish music halls almost entirely out of the market.

Starting in 1906, intellectuals began discussing the reasons behind the theaters' "decline." One of the first voices in this new era of pessimism was

Jacob Gordin's. He was convinced that Yiddish theater had no future in the United States because most immigrants, whether intellectual or uneducated, embraced what he considered American materialist attitudes. They showed no interest in Yiddish culture but wanted to break out of the geographical, psychological, and cultural confines of the immigrant sphere and enter the more lucrative American milieu, whether as writers, actors, or audience members.[26] A true Russian *narodnik* (populist) until the end of his days, Gordin felt abandoned with respect to his project to educate the "masses" and create cultural consensus: he accused the intellectuals of having lost their idealism and their sense of obligation to the people, the actors of lacking any interest in art, and a good part of his potential audience—"the younger, semi-educated but thoroughly conceited generations"—of preferring "American sports and vulgar amusements."[27] Writing in January 1906, Gordin was still optimistic that the situation for Jews in Russia would quickly improve—the liberalization of laws that had restricted Yiddish theater performances and a Jewish press seemed evidence of an expanding cultural life. Softening his cosmopolitan stance and identifying with the idealism and cultural program of the Bund, Gordin had great hopes that the organization would be instrumental in elevating the stage. A political and cultural stabilization in Russia, he believed, would result in a further deterioration of the situation of Yiddish theater in the United States since it would lead to a decrease in immigration and rob it of its most important source of spectators.[28]

For B. Gorin, the theater's decline was not a natural phenomenon since it contravened the law of progress. The audience, he explained, resembled a child: the older it got, the more developed its taste and mind became.[29] Thus the reversal to *shund* could best be explained by the new wave of immigrants who, he alleged, had no prior experience with theater due to the czarist government's ban of Yiddish theater in 1883. Gorin held the new arrivals' lack of literary taste responsible for the sudden rise of the music halls and the theaters' change in repertoire, which tried to accommodate the new audience. However, since the theaters' business did not improve despite the increase in potential spectators, Gorin declared—in line with his idea of the earlier immigrants' mental development—that the lowering of standards drove away the previous audience, which was already used to better fare.[30]

Between the fall of 1905 and the spring of 1908, Yiddish theater managers were hard pressed to keep their houses profitable. With no play in this period—neither historical opera, melodrama, drama, nor a play from the European repertoire—becoming a box office hit, most critics came to agree with Gorin in putting the blame primarily on the new immigrants' low taste and their predilection for music hall entertainment and moving pictures. At the same time, they also held the Hebrew Actors Union's admission policy responsible, which effectively barred young actors from joining their ranks and which caused heated discussions in the Yiddish press. While actors, well aware that New York's Jewish immigrant community could only support a limited number of troupes, tried to protect their turf, their critics accused them of violating union rules and undermining the theater's potential artistic development. The focus of the criticism, however, began to shift to actor-managers when the theaters were able to score several hits with melodramas, which the critics considered *shund*.

The instant popularity and overwhelming success of Lateiner's *Dos yidishe harts* (The Jewish Heart) in the fall of 1908 took the theaters and the critics by complete surprise. Yet, in the first weeks of the play's run, few critics were seriously alarmed by the success of a *shund*-play. Cahan, the anti-*shund* campaigner par excellence, even had some good words to say about the play, considering the comic scenes very funny and superbly acted by Mogulesco, as well as others.[31] But the concern rose when *Dos yidishe harts* remained on the bill for the entire season and was joined by Thomashefsky's adaptation of Josef Ter's *Di yidishe neshome* (The Jewish Soul) and when, during the following season, both Thomashefsky's *Dos pintele yid* (The Quintessence of Jewishness) and Isidor Zolotarevsky's *Di vayse shklafin* (The White Slave) were added to the list of *shund*-hits. Critics became so focused on the popularity of these plays that the successes of so-called better theater in 1909—the lengthy run of David Pinski's literary play *Yankl der shmid* (Yankl the Blacksmith) and the celebrated guest performances of the famous Polish Yiddish actress Esther Rokhl Kaminska—hardly registered in their evaluation of the Yiddish theater's state.[32]

With respect to story line, characterization, and message, the *shund*-hits represented everything Gordin and the critics had tried to fight and supplant with socially critical dramas. *Dos yidishe harts*, *Di yidishe neshome*, and *Dos pintele yid* celebrate both the heroes' steadfast clinging to their Jewishness in the face of rampant anti-Semitism, and America and/or Palestine as the new havens for Jews, thus affirming the immigrants' own choice. At the end of *Dos yidishe harts*, the hero announces at his wedding that he and his wife will emigrate to America, and in the wedding scene that concludes *Di yidishe neshome*, the couple opens a present from American cousins: an American flag! In *Dos pintele yid*, two skimpily clad American Jewish girls, on tour in Eastern Europe with an American circus, teach their newfound friends "Three Cheers for Yankee Doodle." The play ends with a Star of David being lowered from the ceiling and the words "Dos pintele yid" illuminated with electric lights. All three plays feature a middle-aged maternal woman with a mysterious past. With the lures of assimilation couched in sexual terms, these women, who reveal their Jewish identity toward the end of the play, were seduced (through love or sexual attraction) to marry a Gentile aristocrat and to convert. For leaving her Jewish husband and child, the mother in *Dos yidishe harts* is punished when her Jewish son kills her anti-Semitic Christian son in self-defense. She then takes the blame,

Figure 1.1. Lola, "Teater kunst tsu der akeyde." The Dorot Jewish Division, The New York Public Library, Astor, Lenox and Tilden Foundations. The cartoon "Teater kunst tsu der akeyde" (The Attempt to Sacrifice Theater Art) by Lola (pseudonym of the painter Leon Israel, 1887–1955) was published on September 2, 1910, in the Yiddish satirical magazine *Der groyser kundes*. It is a trenchant critique of the Yiddish theater managers who after having supported literary plays for years had recently produced a series of very popular sentimental melodramas. To critics invested in creating a literary theater, this amounted to an unforgivable betrayal of the ideal of "art." The image shows "theater art" about to be executed on the sacrificial altar of the dollar. Like Abraham who was prepared to follow God's command and sacrifice Isaac, Jacob P. Adler is willing to behead theater art for the god Mammon: "Colleagues, I am ready for the slaughter . . ." Only a year earlier, Adler had, in the minds of many Yiddish critics, "killed" theater art by selling the lease of his Grand Theater to the moving picture exhibitors Zukor and Loew. The other actors favor less drastic measures. A squeamish Kessler, who for years tried to compete with Adler for the critics' recognition as the preeminent actor of serious drama, suggests, "Oy, oy, oy, I can't watch this, at least give her some chloroform first." Thomashefsky, whose commitment to literary plays was more tenuous, cries out in a self-aggrandizing tone and in typical Germanized stage language: "No, don't you dare. I will take her as a boarder into my Temple of Art where she will quickly expire by herself." Liptzin appears to Adler as God's angel did to Abraham in order to save the life of the condemned. Yet all she offers is to arrange a marriage with an inappropriate spouse, thus sacrificing her as well: "No, no, don't touch her. I have a good match for her with Itsikl Zolotarevsky." In the minds of the critics, Liptzin was the latest traitor. She had just produced *Di vayse shklafin* by Zolotarevsky, the "king" of melodrama.

repents, and dies. The Countess in *Di yidishe neshome* is ultimately redeemed because she was the heroine's protector.

The plays make use of old favorite stock characters, which Gordin had opposed from the beginning of his career: the villainous, or at least, heartless, Gentiles. The true heroes are the members of the young generation who do not give in to the lures of assimilation and stand by their Jewishness (which is presented in terms of an ethnic or national pride rather than overtly religious affiliation) even in the face of virulent and physically violent anti-Semitism. The mixture of heartwrenching conflicts between repenting "fallen" women and their children, beautiful wedding scenes, racy songs, fanciful costumes, and the celebration of Jewish national pride and of America brought together many aspects that appealed to the audience on a variety of levels. They certainly responded to a shifting political climate on the Lower East Side in the wake of the pogroms in Russia and the failed revolution in 1905. The cosmopolitanism that Gordin had promoted in the 1890s and into the new century had given way to various forms of national identities among both the general population and, to a certain degree, the radical intellectuals.

Most critics held the actor-managers responsible for this "return" to what they considered an earlier stage of Yiddish theater. They accused Kessler, Thomashefsky, and Liptzin of having betrayed their responsibilities as theater artists. After the actors professed for years that they wanted to raise the level of the theater, the critics believed that their true desire reemerged. Ignoring the theaters' financial difficulties over the preceding years, many critics declared that greed made the actor-managers give in to audience demands. Their mercantile attitude toward the theater seemed to indicate that they had lost their respect for art and for the critics' opinion of them. To the critics' great consternation, the actors supposedly felt no shame, but rather they denigrated literary plays and exhibited an "arrogant love for everything that is vulgar, wild, and repulsively stupid as long as it brings in money."[33]

The success of these *shund* plays came at a time when the intellectual community was mourning Gordin's premature death in June 1909. In a series of cartoons, the newly founded satirical magazine *Der groyser kundes* (The Big Stick) vividly captured the intellectuals' frustration with the actor-managers' embrace of *shund* plays and their sense of hopelessness about the theater's future. Moreover, it linked the "victory" of *shund*, as critics tended to phrase it, directly to Gordin's death. Without his intellectual and moral presence, the magazine intimated, *shund* was free to reign again. In a cartoon published shortly after Gordin's passing, *shund* personified as a jester reads a note announcing the sad news. With a malicious grin on his face, the jester leaps into the air. The caption reads: "The one who is happy about Jacob Gordin's death."[34]

The radical movement and socialist press would never again have a dra-

Figure 1.2. S. Raskin, ["Yankev Gordin iz toyt"], *Der groyser kundes,* June 18, 1909. The Dorot Jewish Division, The New York Public Library, Astor, Lenox and Tilden Foundations.

matist of Gordin's stature around whom many intellectuals would rally and who would be directly involved with the theater. Without such a figure and without the intense controversies that Gordin's work had sparked, the scene lost much of its momentum. While the critics kept working at raising the level of the theater, some of their previous utopian zeal had eroded. Many slowly began to understand that the factors that contributed to the functioning and development of theater were more complex than they had previously admitted.

The populist ideal of community uplift through theater was illusory, since education alone could not override the complex social, cultural, and economic circumstances that shaped both the theater and the community. While the critics tended to locate the reasons for the relative lack of success of realist plays in deficiencies in the community's intellectual "progress," those reasons were really to be found in the commercial nature of the houses, in the internal organization of the theaters (including the unionization of the entire theater profession), and in the theaters' sizes—with seating capacities ranging from two thousand to thirty-five hundred people, most were indeed mass theaters too large for successful runs of challenging literary plays. Trying to impose a European literary model on immigrants in the processes of Americanization could only fail. After all, this literature and the concept of theater as an educational institution were alien to both the immigrants and their surrounding culture. The intellectuals' concept of empowering them through a critical representation of themselves, their values, and America did reach a sizable minority but could not succeed in radically transforming the masses' psyche.

Chapter 2
Film and Vaudeville on New York's Lower East Side

Judith Thissen

In December 1909, Nathan Fleissig, the manager of a nickel-and-dime theater on New York's Lower East Side, announced triumphantly that the movies had been defeated and that his theater would be devoted again to "first class Yiddish variety."[1] By presenting the shift in programming practice in terms of a cultural war between Yiddish vaudeville and moving pictures, Fleissig shrewdly linked the reopening of his establishment with the "Grand Theater Affair." In September 1909, the Grand—a large legitimate playhouse especially built for Yiddish performances—had fallen into the hands of the movie exhibitors Marcus Loew and Adolph Zukor and was turned into a moving picture theater. The takeover scandalized public opinion and triggered highly emotional responses in the Yiddish press. In particular, it seemed to be a slap in the face of the community's cultural elite, because for several years the Grand Theater had been the home of literary drama. Many immigrant intellectuals, with Abraham Cahan at the forefront, found it difficult to put up with the idea that moving pictures were to replace Jacob P. Adler starring in Jacob Gordin's *Jewish King Lear*. But in the battle for Adler's Grand Theater, pressure from the *Jewish Daily Forward* and the United Hebrew Trades to retain the playhouse for Yiddish performances had been no match for the power of money. Adler eagerly accepted the generous offer that the future Hollywood moguls made him.

By using the rhetoric of power struggle, Fleissig (consciously or not) also tied the revival of Yiddish vaudeville to the demand for Jewish working-class solidarity. The linkage proved timely. The economic recovery following the depression of 1907–8 had revitalized the Jewish labor movement, leading to a series of strikes in the Hebrew trades. In the last week of November 1909, twenty thousand shirtwaist makers had left their work to walk the picket lines. Most shirtwaist shops in New York were still closed when Fleissig's theater reopened its doors as a Yiddish music hall. In what follows I will explore the revival of Yiddish vaudeville around 1910 in the context of the broad-based intensification of Jewish working class consciousness in these years and a growing resistance on the part of the Jewish working-class to top-down forgings of cultural identity. As I will demonstrate, the forces favoring immigrant "Americanization," those who advanced the cause of cultural refinement, and those who sought to promote a synthesis of immigrant and Americanized environments waged a complex struggle over the future of Jewish entertainment on the Lower East Side.

The Jewish Labor Movement

Turn-of-the-century America went through a deep cultural and social crisis. Industrialization, urbanization, and the mass arrival of immigrants from Southern and Eastern Europe were rapidly transforming the American way of life. Native-born Anglo-Saxon Americans became increasingly confused and angered by the displacement they experienced as demographic changes threatened their economic situation, challenged their political leadership, and subverted their cultural authority. Some of them mounted virulent attacks upon recent immigrants whom they held responsible for the imminent collapse of traditional American values. "Unless we Americanize the immigrants, they will foreignize our cities, and in doing so foreignize our civilization," the religious leader and reformer Josiah Strong wrote in *The Challenge of the City* (1907).[2] The foreign born, who formed the bulk of the nation's workforce, were perceived not only as utterly "alien" but as politically radical as well. The Haymarket, Homestead, and Pullman strikes symbolized their power to destabilize the country. Indeed, social unrest constituted a major aspect of the immense changes taking place in America around 1900. Economic upheaval—booms interspersed with stock market panics and severe depressions—provided the context for violent labor disputes and a breeding ground for left-wing radicalism. Trade unions challenged the injustices of capitalism and sought to redress working-class grievances, supported by socialist and anarchist radicals who preached class struggle and revolution.

In the public mind, New York's East Side "ghetto" was intimately linked with radicalism, not least of all because the best-known anarchists—Emma Goldman and Alexander Berkman—were Russian Jews. However, active participation in trade unions was a relatively late phenomenon among Jewish workers. Since the 1880s, considerable numbers of Jewish immigrants had participated in strikes and other collective political actions (such as economic boycotts, for example), but few had truly committed themselves to the cause of organized labor.[3] In 1909, ten years after its creation, the United Hebrew Trades had only five thousand members and most of its forty union locals were held together by a handful of militant workers. Yet this situation was about to change with amazing rapidity. Starting with the return of economic prosperity in the spring of 1909, America witnessed increased industrial unrest and a significant upsurge of socialism nationwide. Radicalism intensified among Jewish workers too. Tens of thousands went on strike for higher wages, shorter hours, and improved working conditions. The first mass walkout was that of the shirtwaist makers in November 1909, which involved almost fifteen thousand young Jewish women. After their strike was settled, in February 1910, they passed on the torch of Jewish labor activism to their male colleagues in the needle trades. On July 7, 1910, seventy thousand cloak makers declared a general strike—the largest in the history of New York City. Over the next few years, the United Hebrew Trades consolidated its power. On the eve of World War I, it encompassed more than one hundred unions with approximately two hundred and fifty thousand members (compared to five thousand in 1909).[4] The renewed labor movement had forged a more explicit place for Eastern European Jews in the American public sphere and helped the Jewish working class to formulate a positive sense of collective identity vis-à-vis the mainstream.

That is one side of the matter. But there is more to it. As Daniel Soyer recently pointed out, the militancy of the Jewish working class coexisted with a strong aspiration of its members to rise out of that class and move into the middle class of shopkeepers, manufacturers, and professionals.[5] Many first-generation immigrants espoused two conflicting ideologies. On the one hand, they embraced working-class militancy, socialist ideals, and collective action. On the other hand, they harbored middle-class impulses toward individual advancement and ambitious entrepreneurship. According to Soyer, this ideological uncertainty "stemmed from their ambivalent attitudes about class and their ambiguous experiences of it." Many Eastern European Jews, he explains, "perceived themselves to be of essentially middle-class backgrounds." Their resentment at downward social mobility—before and after migration—led them to oppose "a class system that seemed to them arbitrary and unfair" and, at the same time, aroused the "desire to restore their (or their families') entrepreneurial independence."[6] The higher wages and better working conditions won by strikes and trade-unionism more generally allowed a considerable number of Jewish workers to leave their wage-earning jobs and become independent businessmen. This was yet another way in which participation in the labor movement pulled Jewish workers deeper into the dynamics of American society.

The mobilization of the Jewish proletariat—as Jews and as workers—and its impact on American Jewish life have been well documented by social historians. What has been largely overlooked, however, is that this mobilization was played out not only on the work floor but also in the realm of leisure. In particular, the new film medium—a national mass medium in the making—was an important arena for the articulation of cultural identities. The rise of the discourse of Americanization within the U.S. film industry led to sharp debates between the Jewish immigrant community and the American host society, as well as within the Jewish immigrant community itself over cinema's nature and function. Like the revitalization of the labor movement, these debates formed a key aspect of a complex, multilayered process of cultural and social renewal, whereby the immigrant community of Eastern European Jews accommodated to "America" and, at the same time, forged a distinctive ethnic identity.

Cinema and the Cultural Crisis

Around 1900, the concentration of workers and immigrants in America's largest cities spurred the emergence of new forms of commercial entertainment. The most popular activity of all was the movies. Largely due to their cheapness—five cents—the nickelodeons provided the lower classes with a regular basis for leisure. By 1908, attendance at moving picture shows in New York City was estimated at three to four hundred thousand people per day.[7] The majority of these moviegoers were foreign-born or first-generation Americans. In the Jewish part of the Lower East Side, there were more than thirty movie theaters, without counting those on the Bowery and East Fourteenth Street.[8]

The "moving picture craze" or "nickel madness" both fascinated and unnerved many New Yorkers of the older stock. Most people saw little difference between a mob of strikers and the unruly patrons of cheap amusements.[9] As the movies turned into a permanent feature of everyday life, the nation's cultural elites grew obsessed with the effects of moviegoing on the allegedly "underdeveloped" minds of uneducated working people, especially immigrants and their children. The concerns about the effects of moviegoing upon the lower classes were closely linked to the intense debates over whether or not the massive arrival of immigrants from Eastern and Southern Europe posed a threat to the American way of life.[10]Most troubling was that the nickelodeons relied heavily on foreign films. By mid-1905, the French company Pathé Frères had become the leading supplier of moving pictures for the American market.[11] Although American producers such as Edison, Vitagraph, and Biograph remained significant players on the domestic film market, the immigrants, who in cities like New York formed the bulk of the nickelodeon audiences, preferred above all the knockabout comedies, blood-and-thunder melodramas, and crime films made by Pathé. This worried social reformers and others who believed that the cinema could encourage the Americanization process of the newcomers, provided of course that they watched pictures that offered appropriate role models. To make sure that the foreign born would learn American values and virtues from clean, wholesome "American" movies, progressive reformers began to collaborate with the leading American film producers. As the film historian Richard Abel has demonstrated, the desire of these companies for economic expansion and control of the American moviegoing market neatly converged with the demands for social control of the new film medium.[12]

The American film industry employed a broad range of strategies to make cinema "respectable" according to the terms defined by the dominant WASP culture. One of the industry's first attempts to uplift the moving pictures was the creation of the National Board of Censorship in 1909. The board was an instrument of self-censorship set up in close collaboration with the People's Institute, a strong advocate of progressive civic reform. Its members reviewed the majority of films, both domestic and foreign, before they were released to the rental exchanges. Significantly, Abel found that "Pathé films were either rejected or returned for alteration much more frequently than were the films of American producers." Thus, the board curtailed what they viewed as an undesirable, immoral, "foreign" influence and, at the same time, helped American manufacturers to curb Pathé's economic power.[13]

But censorship alone was not enough. It exerted little influence on the actual conditions that prevailed inside the nickelodeons. Poor sanitation, insufficient ventilation, obstructed exits, inadequate seating, dim lighting, and lack of chaperonage were all seen as posing physical and moral threats to the well-being of the audience. While reformers and legislators lobbied for stringent safety regulations and better building codes for moving picture theaters, much of the advice given to exhibitors in trade journals underscored the importance of improving storefront theaters or moving into more upscale venues. For the same reason, the Board of Censorship and other reform institutions pressured local exhibitors with site inspections, which targeted in particular nickelodeons located in immigrant neighborhoods. Between September 1909 and February 1910, for instance, inspectors of the People's Institute visited about twenty movie theaters on the Lower East Side, reporting on sanitary conditions, fire exits, audiences, and quality of the show (film and vaudeville). The conditions in the larger theaters on the Bowery were generally found to be satisfactory. The general conclusion about the storefronts in the heart of the Jewish quarter, however, was that "a better class of moving picture shows must be encouraged, then these small proprietors will either have to correct their methods of handling trade or get out of business."[14] That the problem was not so easily remedied is apparent from the fact that two years later, in December 1912, the East Side Neighborhood Association (in collaboration with the New York Motion Pictures Exhibitors' Association) called a conference of East Side nickelodeon managers asking them to cooperate "for better, cleaner and more wholesome picture places, and to report all nuisances to the association."[15]

Special points of concern for those inside and outside the industry were the songs and vaudeville acts that nickelodeon managers interspersed between the films. It should be emphasized that these live "extras" defined the experience of moviegoing as much as the moving pictures themselves. In particular, reformers criticized the mixing of vaudeville and film in five-cent theaters because these outlets could only afford to offer live entertainment of "the poorest grade." "Peculiarly vicious is the Yiddish vaudeville given in many lower East Side picture shows," a social worker complained in 1909.[16] The anti-vaudeville discourse was taken up by the film trade press. Vaudeville—more precisely "cheap" vaudeville—dragged the movies down rather than lifting them up, according to the editor of *Moving Picture World.* "Is it not a disgusting shame for those of us who love the picture for its own sake here in New York City [that] when we go to leading moving picture houses [we] have to endure the stupidity, the inanities, the crudities, sometimes indecencies and the obscenities of cheap low vaudeville?"[17] Trade papers repeatedly urged exhibitors to reduce nonfilmic activities, such as vaudeville acts, songs, and amateur nights. Though rarely expressly thematized, the anti-vaudeville discourse in the trade press was clearly directed against manifestations of working-class culture and ethnicity. The variety format, as Miriam Hansen argues, offered structural conditions around which "working-class and ethnic cultures could crystallize, and responses to social pressures, individual displacement, and alienation could be articulated in a communal setting."[18] To transform the movies into a vehicle for mainstream values, nonfilmic activities that aimed at building audiences on the basis of a shared ethnic and working-class identity had to be eliminated. The "real" social, cultural, and physical space of the movie theater had to become subordinated to the fictional world on the screen so that the film text, rather than the exhibition context, could become the prime site of meaning.

Apparently, the problem with vaudeville acts and sing alongs was not only their content but also the fact that these activities encouraged modes of behavior that stimulated an active sociability between members of the audience. The rowdy behavior of the nickelodeon audiences was considered un-American. Moreover, critics feared that this participatory mode of audience response would lead to more overt political action. As Hansen points out, filmmakers increasingly sought to enhance the viewer's absorption in the imaginary flow on the screen in order to impose a discipline of silence on movie audiences and make the viewing experience an individual experience rather than a collective one.[19] This shift from collective to individual viewing experience marked one of the major differences between early cinema and Hollywood cinema.

While the anxiety of the native-born Americans over changing social, economic, and cultural conditions led to an embourgeoisement of American cinema in the years after 1910 (and eventually to the classical Hollywood style), film exhibition practices remained an arena of considerable conflict throughout the silent cinema period. A closer look at the moviegoing experiences of Jewish immigrants challenges the dominant notion of a fast and consensual process of gentrification and standardization.[20] Nickel-and-dime theaters on Manhattan's Lower East Side and in Brooklyn neither played out the embourgeoisement scenario nor fostered the simple assimilation of their patrons into the mainstream of American entertainment. Significantly, Yiddish vaudeville experienced a revival in Jewish neighborhood movie theaters at the very moment that the American film industry and progressive reformers sought to make cinema "truly" American, in part through banning nonfilmic activities (especially vaudeville) from five-and-ten cent moving picture shows. Does this indicate that Jewish film exhibitors and their audiences sought to counteract the increased demand for conformity to American norms? Was the revival of Yiddish vaudeville around 1909–10 a sign of grassroots resistance to the "Americanization of American cinema"?[21] Before I can begin to answer this question, I must explain how vaudeville and film figured in the Jewish immigrant experience.

American Novelties

The first Yiddish music halls and concert salons appeared on the Lower East Side during the winter of 1901. Nina Warnke found that these new amusement venues met with fierce resistance from the community's cultural elites and guardians of immigrant morality.[22] Both conservative and socialist newspapers condemned the Yiddish music halls as the wrong kind of Americanization. They sharply criticized the bawdy songs, vulgar jokes, and suggestive dances of the vaudeville stage. What was happening in the music halls was "a crime against decency," in the words of Abraham Cahan.[23] According to Warnke, Yiddish music halls "presented exactly those aspects that socialist intellectuals were fighting so hard to reduce in the [legitimate Yiddish] theaters. [. . .] Horrified at realizing their obvious lack of power of immigrant entertainment, the critics constructed the music halls as the new 'low-other,' relegating it to a position even lower than the *shund* [trash] plays in the theaters."[24]

Under the editorship of Cahan, the *Forward* endlessly railed against the vaudeville "*shmuts.*" Time and again, the paper warned "respectable" workers to stay away from the Yiddish music halls. It goes without saying that its anti-vaudeville campaign reflected Cahan's own moralistic bias rather than his readers' responses to this new possibility for leisure. Not unexpectedly, many Jewish workers and their families frequented the music halls on a regular basis, turning a deaf ear to the warnings in the press. By 1906, Yiddish vaudeville had become a prime attraction and big business (by ethnic entertainment standards, at least). The Lower East Side counted a dozen Yiddish vaudeville theaters. Some of them, including Fleissig's Grand Street Music Hall, could seat up to a thousand patrons and offered elaborate shows with at least one playlet or three-act sketch, supplemented by songs, jokes, dances, single turns, and moving pictures.[25]

During the 1905–6 season, the first nickelodeons appeared on East Fourteenth Street and the Bowery, the two main arteries of night life in downtown Manhattan. The following year, five-cent *muving piktshur pletser* were also opening up east of the Bowery, in the heart of the Jewish quarter. One of the first film exhibitors to venture into tenement district was Adolph Zukor, who with his business partners operated a large and elegant seventy-five-thousand-dollar penny arcade and moving picture theater on East Fourteenth Street near Union Square. The success of their Automatic Vaudeville subsidiary at 265 Grand Street (next to Jacob P. Adler's Grand Theater) was emulated by other Jewish immigrant entrepreneurs. Moving picture shows continued to multiply during the recession of 1907–8. The economic downturn fueled the demand for inexpensive entertainment and fed the expansion of five-cent theaters specializing in moving pictures. Yiddish music hall managers, who suddenly saw a falling off of business because many immigrants could no longer afford to pay a dime or a quarter for admission, became increasingly interested in film exhibition. They lowered their ticket prices and switched to moving pictures as their main attraction. Others with no prior experience in the field also tried their luck in the booming nickelodeon business. By mid-1908, Jewish working-class neighborhoods of Manhattan and Brooklyn had the highest density of motion picture shows in New York City.[26]

Initially, the proliferating nickelodeons caused few complaints in the Yiddish press. In May 1908, the socialist *Forward*, by now the leading Yiddish-language newspaper, described the nickel theater as "a novelty which just like the music halls comes from uptown, from the Christians," but this seemed not a matter of concern.[27] On the whole, Cahan's staff showed slight interest in the latest pastime activity of their readers. They occasionally published a human interest story about the nickelodeon boom, but with little of the moralizing commentary that accompanied discussions of Yiddish vaudeville. In fact the *Forward* discussed the popularity of moving pictures with immigrant audiences primarily in relation to the decline of Yiddish vaudeville entertainment.[28] Did Cahan prefer the cinema to Yiddish vaudeville? Perhaps. In the early days of the motion picture craze, he certainly observed with satisfaction the nickelodeons pushing the music halls out of the market. Significantly, the impact of movies on Jewish workers was not an issue at all, despite the fact that *Forward* articles devoted to the East Side picture shows frequently underscored how spellbound audiences were by the events on the screen. This initial indifference was in marked contrast with how other segments of contemporary American society reacted to the popularity of the cinema with working-class immigrants. The progressive reformers, for instance, embraced "Americanizing" movies in their efforts to acculturate immigrant Jews and their children. The

American Federation of Labor, for its part, realized that socialist pictures could help the labor movement and urged workers to boycott theaters that showed anti-labor films. Yet Jewish socialists like Cahan apparently failed to see cinema's potential as an agency for edification, acculturation, and class struggle.[29]

At the other end of the political spectrum, the leading conservative Yiddish newspapers—the *Tageblatt* and *Morgen zhurnal*—satisfied the public's interest in the nickelodeon boom with up-to-date information about the film trade. The *Tageblatt* covered extensively what was happening in the new motion picture business, informing readers about such topics as the formation of the Motion Picture Patent Company, the introduction of a new system for colored pictures, and the first experiments with television.[30] What accounts for this perspective is the targeted readership of the conservative press: predominantly (lower) middle-class immigrants, who were politically moderate and emotionally bound to the Jewish way of life.[31] The *Tageblatt* and the *Morgen zhurnal* played on the traditionalism of these immigrants as far as religion and politics were concerned, but they also served their upwardly mobile aspirations by publishing the latest business news. Inclined to defend the interests of small Jewish businessmen, they consistently rallied to the side of the film exhibitors. After a fatal nickelodeon accident on Rivington Street, for instance, both papers insisted on more stringent rules for picture shows, at the same time defending the proprietors of the theater, who were charged with homicide. According to the *Tageblatt*, "hot-heads" in the audience were responsible for the deadly accident.[32] As a matter of fact, even their socialist competitor did not accuse the proprietors of the Rivington Street nickelodeon outright. In a strongly worded editorial, centering on the physical threats storefront shows posed to moviegoers, Cahan stated:

The masses that are squeezed together in the tenements do not know where to go during the cold evenings. In the gloomy buildings where they sleep and have their sacred homes, there is no space to live. They are forced to go outside. They cannot afford real amusement, so they pass their time for five cents in a moving picture show. This business is booming thanks to the sorrowful life of the masses. These places are crammed like the rooms where they live. Who cares when this human merchandise is crushed? One more person squeezed inside, one more nickel earned.

With the usual socialist rhetoric, Cahan concluded that the capitalist system was to be held responsible for the accident, rather than the individual film exhibitor who was living off the poverty of the workers.[33]

As these examples illustrate, a broad range of descriptions of East Side nickelodeons, their owners, and audiences circulated in the Yiddish press. However, in sharp contrast to the initial reception of Yiddish music hall entertainment in the Yiddish press, or to the depiction of the nickelodeon boom in the mainstream English-language press, the Yiddish dailies did not initially define the cinema as a contested site of Americanization. Regardless of their orientation, almost no Yiddish newspaper touched on the subject of the moral influence movies had on immigrants—that is, until late 1909, when attitudes began to change.

The Grand Theater Affair

The attitude toward the new film medium changed after the takeover of Adler's Grand Theater by Zukor and Loew in September 1909. Throughout the following decade, the Yiddish press expressed deep concern with the power and propriety of the cinema. At stake in the debate over film was the question of who ultimately would define the nature of the Jewish experience in America and direct the Jewish immigrant "masses" toward Americanization. Would it be the East Side's self-acclaimed leadership of newspaper editors, writers, and labor organizers, or would it be the American film industry and its agents? The "Grand Theater Affair" pointed toward the answer.

In September 1909, after weeks of negotiation, Loew and Zukor secured the lease of the two-thousand-seat Grand Theater. The occasion held special significance because, under the management of the Yiddish theater star Jacob P. Adler, the playhouse had become the home of Yiddish literary drama. Although the leading Yiddish newspapers were sharply divided with regard to Adler's motives in selling his lease of the Grand, there existed a virtual consensus on the question of who was to blame for the fact that the playhouse was lost for Yiddish performances. As the Grand drama unfolded, Loew and Zukor were exposed as the true villains. At the same time, the editors of the Yiddish dailies did not wish to antagonize their readers by blaming upwardly mobile Jews for destroying the community's cultural heritage. Hence they carefully avoided revealing the Jewish identity of the Grand's new lessees. At first, commentators insisted that the Grand Theater had fallen into the hands of "*American* theater managers" (italics mine). Eventually, the Yiddish newspapers got so caught up in their efforts to hide the truth that they stripped Zukor and Loew of their Jewishness. For instance, a few days before the reopening of the Grand Theater, the leftist *Warheit* described the people behind the moving picture company that had secured the lease of the playhouse as "*goyim*" (Gentiles) and "Yankees."[34] Thereafter, the paper repeatedly used the term *goyim* in association with the new proprietors of the Grand, although its editor, Louis Miller, clearly knew better, for he himself had played a crucial role in the negotiations between Adler and Zukor. Miller's involvement in the deal was perhaps the very reason why the *Warheit* tried so hard to conceal the fact that both Zukor and his business partner Marcus Loew were Jews. Still, *Forward* readers too were made to believe that "*goyim*" had gained control over the "glorious *kunst tempel* of the East Side."[35] Even the *Tageblatt,* which at first hushed up much of the commotion around the Grand Theater, eventually joined in with its competitors.[36] Evidently, the Yiddish newspapers editors were so horrified to realize that their authority over the immigrant community had been challenged by two "*proste jidn*" (people without learning, taste, or spiritual virtues) that they decided to repress this social and cultural upheaval by redrawing the boundaries of the Jewish ethnic group. They outlawed Loew and Zukor by defining them as "*goyim*" rather than "*alrightniks,*" the sneering Yinglish term that the East Side's intelligentsia normally used for the allegedly uneducated Jews who had done economically well in America.

Di Muving Piktshur Frage

During the decade after 1910, the Yiddish press repeatedly addressed what the *Tageblatt* defined in 1911 as "*di muving piktshur frage*" (the moving picture issue).[37] By far the most remarkable response was that of the *Jewish Daily Forward.* For almost two decades, Jewish socialists like Cahan had promoted Yiddish legitimate drama (especially realist plays) as an instrument of enlightenment and a weapon against "American" influences that threatened to corrupt the uneducated "masses." But now, with legitimate Yiddish theater clearly ill-equipped to do battle with the cinema, they turned to Yiddish vaudeville to keep Jewish immigrants on the "right" road to Americanization.

At first sight, it was an obvious choice. The legitimate Yiddish stage was experiencing a deep economic and artistic crisis. Yiddish vaudeville, on the other hand, was thriving. At the beginning of the 1909–10 season, most former Yiddish music halls on Manhattan's East Side and in Brooklyn, which had turned to moving pictures as their entertainment staple during the depression of 1907–8, were switching back to full-fledged variety shows. In their footsteps, film exhibitors with no previous experience in the Yiddish variety business began to incorporate elaborate Yiddish vaudeville acts into their programs so as to satisfy the increased demand for ethnic entertainment. Until then, nonfilmic activities had played a minor role on the bills of local movie theaters. The time needed to change reels was usually filled with an (illustrated) song, a joke, or a dance, at most a simple sketch. By December 1909, however, moving picture shows were being recognized as important outlets for Yiddish vaudeville entertainment, ranging from single turns to three-act sketches with scenery and props. Over the next few months, most nickel-and-dime theaters in Jewish neighborhoods switched to "vaud-pic" shows.

Still, the *Forward*'s endorsement of the grassroots revival of Yiddish vaudeville came as quite a surprise, given its long-standing hostility to this form of entertainment. Cahan himself had been the driving force behind several campaigns against the Yiddish music halls. Yet Cahan's desire to maintain his leadership position—in the cultural sphere as much as in the domain of immigrant politics—proved even stronger than his aversion to Yiddish vaudeville. In an attempt to protect the status quo, Cahan and his staff had decided to incorporate—or rather "assimilate"—Yiddish vaudeville into the mainstream of Jewish culture. In December 1909, the *Forward* made a remarkable U-turn: from condemning Yiddish vaudeville as the wrong kind of Americanization to promoting it as an authentic expression of *yidishkayt.*

The reinvention of Yiddish vaudeville—now with the Jewish socialist elite's seal of approval—entailed a new emphasis on the "Jewishness" of Yiddish vaudeville and an obfuscation of its American roots. The Yiddish music halls were structurally promoted to a middlebrow position within the cultural hierarchy.[38] The cinema, for its part, was relegated to the bottom end of the scale, the position previously occupied by Yiddish vaudeville. In the process, prostitution, white slavery, and loose sexual behavior—vices of urban America that had been associated with the early Yiddish music hall business—became more and more linked with the moving picture houses on the East Side. Most *Forward* articles and editorials that condemned the cinema focused on the practice of moviegoing rather than on specific films. Put differently, it was primarily a discussion about the corrupting influence of the movie theater as a social space—the movies themselves did not seem to matter. From late 1909 onward, the *Forward* repeatedly wrote about the moral dangers that the nickelodeons held for young people, especially young women. Speculations about the connection between movie houses and the white slave trade gained momentum on May 13, 1910, when the paper's headline screamed: "Don't let your children go alone into the moving picture houses: Mothers beg the *Forward* to save their children from ruin and shame."[39] In addition to highly sensational front page stories that associated moviegoing with the sex trade, short back page news items with titles such as "Break into a home because of moving pictures" and "Movies turn children into gangsters" depicted local movie houses as schools of crime where murder, shoplifting, robbery, and hold-ups were illustrated.[40] Admittedly, such articles highlighting the moral dangers of moviegoing were commonplace in the English-language newspapers too. Yet, in the mainstream press, cinema's critics often used these stories to illustrate the need for regulation and censorship. Many argued that if immoral movies could turn children into criminals, moral subjects might just as well turn them into good citizens. This type of reform discourse was absent in the comments of the *Forward,* whose denunciation of the cinema now seemed unqualified.

Cahan's competitors shared his concern about the corrupting influence of the moving pictures, but they were less convinced that Yiddish vaudeville was the right answer to the *muving piktshur frage.* Hence they merely outlined the potential dangers of cinemagoing to their readers. The editor of the Orthodox *Tageblatt*, for instance, warned parents time and again that the establishment of the National Board of Censorship offered no guarantee that all movies were suitable for *Jewish* children.[41] Like the *Forward*, the conservative Yiddish newspapers primarily addressed the issue in abstract terms, rarely focusing on specific movies. However, the *Tageblatt* did speak out against such ghetto films as *The Jew's Christmas* (Rex, 1913), in which the daughter of a rabbi marries a Gentile. According to *Moving Picture World*, "a large delegation of rabbis witnessed the projection of the picture. They were pleased with the story, with its treatment and with the fidelity with which the producers had followed Jewish ceremonies and customs, but were inclined to look with disfavor on the title."[42] The *Tageblatt* was less enchanted with this holiday release. Particularly offensive for Orthodox Jews was the scene in which the rabbi sells his copy of the Torah to buy a Christmas tree for the poor little girl, who turns out to be his granddaughter, and the "happy ending" with the family reunited around the same Christmas tree.[43]

A remarkably blunt example of the strategy to discourage moviegoing was "Abie's Moving Pictures," a series of cartoons published in the leftist *Warheit*, which depicted the misadventures of little Abie and Izzy after their return from the picture show. Cartoons depicted the boys imitating much of what they saw at the movies, kidnapping a baby, dressing up in their parents' best clothes to go out, and hanging the neighbor's cat. Each and every cartoon concluded with a punitive ending, usually their mother beating the hell out of them.[44] Thus, Yiddish newspaper editors of both left and right came to decry the dangerous influence of the cinema. An "American" entertainment form that had at first attracted admiration (or at least little controversy) among these self-acclaimed leaders of the Jewish immigrant community was by the beginning of the second decade of the century essentially proscribed by them.

The new hostile discourse on the cinema was more than a rescue action on the part of the Yiddish press to protect Jewish culture against the onslaught of Americanization. As we have seen, it followed a deep crisis in the immigrant community itself. In the aftermath of the takeover of the Grand Theater by Loew and Zukor, the immigrant elite of newspaper editors and labor organizers realized that they were losing their grip on community matters. Loew and Zukor had challenged their vested cultural authority and leadership positions. In response to this subversion of the traditional distribution of power between the "educated" and the "uneducated," the editors of the Yiddish press redefined the community's relationship to the newly emerged national mass medium of the movies. Thus, they sought to reestablish their authority over the Jewish "masses."

The anti-cinema discourse in the Yiddish press is but one side of the matter. Its logic should not be confused with the logic that commanded the

Figure 2.1. *Der kidneper* (The Kidnapper), "Eybi's muving piktshurs," *Die wahrheit*, October 30, 1912.

actual entertainment practices and preferences of East Side audiences. As Roger Chartier points out, "there is a radical difference between the lettered, logocentric, and hermeneutic rationality that organizes the production of discourses and the rationality informing all other regimes of practices."[45] Like the leaders of the immigrant community, the Jewish "masses" displayed a strong commitment to the core values of their culture. But in this case, the impetus did not arise from a sustained striving for continued hegemony but from the contemporaneous revitalization of the Jewish labor movement and the increased Jewish ethnic and working-class assertiveness that went with it. The growing prominence of Yiddish vaudeville on the bills of moving picture theaters should thus be explained as a grassroots resistance on the part of working-class Jews to outside interference in their leisure-time activities, especially to mainstream efforts to Americanize the cinema. Programmed in between moving pictures, Yiddish vaudeville shaped the reception of the films that were shown, thus reducing the impact of the growing Americanizing tendency of the silver screen. Moreover, Yiddish vaudeville reinforced feelings of belonging to an ethnic community with shared values and pleasures based on a communal language and history. In sum, what the revitalization of the Jewish labor movement marked at the level of the factory, the revival of Yiddish vaudeville signified in the domain of leisure: a reassertion of Jewish ethnic attachments and loyalties.

What is remarkable in this light is that, unlike Cahan and other socialist leaders, working-class Jewish immigrant audiences embraced Yiddish vaudeville anew without rejecting the film medium. They liked the entertainment of the "American" movies enough not to want to do away with them as an act of cultural correctness. While sympathetic and responsive to the message of ethnic solidarity, both in the workplace and in their leisure time, the Jewish masses did not oppose acculturation into the American mainstream. Rather, they sought to exert some measure of control over their own process of Americanization. At their local movie theaters, they resisted the top-down pressures from mainstream society by embracing Yiddish vaudeville anew. As well, they resisted the top-down pressures from their own cultural elites—by continuing to enjoy the movies. What emerged from this dynamic dialogue was a heterogeneous entertainment product that remained flexible enough to serve multiple, often contradictory purposes: providing the basis for ethnic solidarity among audience members and, at the same time, inviting them to participate in the American dream of the movies.

Chapter 3

Of Maestros and Minstrels: American Jewish Composers between Black Vernacular and European Art Music

Jonathan Karp

This essay describes a contest, informal but nonetheless real, to create the definitively American musical masterpiece. The contest took place during the second and third decades of the twentieth century, a period in which American Jews had begun to play an important role in American musical life. Though the exact nature of the prize would become clear only late in the game, from the start the participants recognized that victory would bring both material success and critical acclaim. The unspoken rules were likewise straightforward: devise the ideal musical synthesis that weds America's indigenous folk spirit to the formal rigors of the European art music tradition.[1]

Of course, such an aim could not be disentangled from the era's racial conceptions. Since the late nineteenth century and particularly under the influence of the Czech composer Anton Dvořák (as discussed below), a growing number of musicians and critics had acclaimed African American music as the nation's most authentic and vivid sound. Such praise of black music—partly rooted in a romanticizing of black culture—often went hand in hand with a prejudice whose effect was to deny African American musicians themselves an equal chance for success. The operative assumption was that blacks lacked a key qualification for victory: the capacity to handle classical and not merely vernacular musical approaches. In light of this imputed disability, the winning contestant, though not black, must be able to venture into—and emerge intact from—the world of black musical culture. He (a male gender was likewise assumed) must refine the "primitive" genius of black folk music into a work of enduring classical value. He must straddle multiple worlds: black and white, American and European, high and low.

As in any competition, self-assurance could provide a psychic edge. The vaunted capacity of Jews to function as mediators between different segments of non-Jewish society (a stereotype, as discussed below, deriving from their European heritage as a "middleman minority")—between different classes and estates, religious groups, ethnicities, and castes—helped give composers of Jewish background a leg up. In fact, the propagation of an image of Jews as a uniquely integrative force took place on so many levels that at times the contest misleadingly appeared to be confined to the world of Jewish music makers alone. For our present purposes that world can be broken down into two basic camps: the first, referred to here as the "minstrels," were the songwriters of Tin Pan Alley, the popular music business headquartered in downtown Manhattan; the second, the "maestros," comprised the art music composers of uptown. Yet despite their contrasting addresses, the members of both groups had originated from some of the same neighborhoods, most recently the Lower East Side, or sections of Brooklyn and the Bronx. And even earlier they (or their immediate forebears) had flourished together in the towns and cities of Eastern Europe, where our account of their battle begins.

Minstrels

The image of Jews as preeminent musical and cultural mediators was rooted in both sociological realities and pervasive stereotypes. Indeed, the Jews' "disproportionality" in certain industries and occupations constitutes a key fact of their historical experience. Not merely an alien religious group in premodern Europe, Jews have constituted a legal, social, and economic category as well. Existing outside the regular feudal and estate categories, but not isolated from them, their very presence in Christendom was partly a consequence of the roles they typically played as economic mediators between different sectors of the non-Jewish society.[2] This middleman functionality persisted into the nineteenth century, despite the fact that Jews came under intense pressure to divest themselves of their occupational "peculiarities."[3] By the late nineteenth century, impressionistic associations in the press between Jews and specific professions provided ballast to charges that the Jews refused to assimilate, and for anti-Semitic accusations that they sought a sinister domination over society.[4] Many of the occupations that drew disproportionate numbers of middle-class Jews—in addition to commerce, law, and medicine—involved activities of cultural mediation, such as education and journalism, as well as brokerage as agents, dealers, impresarios, critics, and interpreters of the arts, including music, a pattern that continued among the two and a half million Jews who emigrated from Eastern Europe to the United States between 1880 and 1924. It was largely from this pool of immigrants and their children that the Jewish songwriters of Tin Pan Alley derived. In short, the Jewish "disproportionality" in various spheres of American life mirrored, under new

and sharply different circumstances, the Jewish occupational distinctiveness of Central and Eastern Europe.[5]

Certainly this was true of the music industry in New York City. By 1920
the Jewish population of New York as a fraction of the city's general population had leveled off to about one-fourth.[6] This was roughly the percentage
of Jews then employed as songwriters in Tin Pan Alley sheet music publishing firms. When one considers that New York was then the capital of the
American popular music industry, a magnet to which composers and musicians gravitated from all regions, the statistic takes on added significance.
If one takes quality into account along with quantity, the Jewish role in Tin
Pan Alley truly astonishes. Edward Pessen, after examining the member
ship records of ASCAP (the American Society of Composers, Authors and
Publishers), concluded that Jews wrote the music to around 50 percent of
the three hundred "great" and three hundred "good" songs of the 1920s
and 1930s (determined both by their commercial success and by acribed
aesthetic merit) and to a whopping 75 percent of the lyrics.[7] It must also
be emphasized that between 1890 and 1920, about 70 percent of the largest
and most important of the sheet music publishing houses—the capitalistic
infrastructure of Tin Pan Alley—were Jewish owned, initially by Jews of Central European background.[8] This last fact may be said to tip the balance in
favor of speaking of Tin Pan Alley as sociologically a "Jewish" business,
since Jews constituted at least a plurality of its occupants.

While in most respects a business like any other, the fact that Tin Pan
Alley involved music rather than, for instance, muslin, ensured that the
character of its cultural fabric would extend, however remotely, into the
realm of the aesthetic. Or, as the Tin Pan Alley historian Isaac Goldberg
put it, "what lives on song, however sordid, must catch the spirit of song."[9]
The related propensity of songwriters to feel themselves commercial func-
tionaries who at the same time transcended mere business was noted early
on by the songwriter/publisher Edward Marks. "Songwriters are a meretri-
cious race," observed Marx, "they write according to the market, yet have
the sneaking feeling that they are a little above the laity to whom they pan-
der." One might go further and speculate that the Jewish songwriters' mercantile filiations, not just with the immediate publishing side of the
business but with an older, often stigmatized ethnic commercial identity,
contributed to the desire on the part of some to produce a higher kind of
art free of such taints. Participating in the contest to elevate American
musical vernacular would provide a means of winning artistic esteem. It
would make separate currencies of what had originally been two sides of
the same coin. It would make it possible to exploit the presumption of a
Jewish talent for cultural mediation while escaping from the taint of Jewish
commercial origins.[10]

As noted, those origins were essentially bourgeois. For this reason, the
image of the ghetto-toughened immigrant youth clawing his way to music

business glory through a mixture of talent and grit seems too simplistic. The class backgrounds of the Tin Pan Alley composers were by no means universally humble. About 60 percent of Pessen's sampling attended college, while half had enrolled in some form of professional school, figures, as Pessen notes, that place these men well outside the contemporary norm.[11] Pessen's statistics apply to the generation of composers who came of age in the 1920s, men such as Richard Rodgers, Lorenz Hart, Oscar Hammerstein II, and Cole Porter, all of whom came from wealthy backgrounds. But even in earlier decades, songwriters such as Louis A. Hirsch, Joseph Meyer, Al Dubin, and Louis Alter came from homes that could have afforded them access to more conventional careers had they not found the lure of writing and selling popular music irresistible.[12] In fact, many Tin Pan Alley songwriters, Jewish and non-Jewish, did start elsewhere: Meyer had been a businessman; Sigmund Romberg an engineer; Dorothy Fields an art teacher; Edgar "Yip" Harburg owned an appliance business; Arthur Schwartz was a lawyer and Jack Yellen and Frank Loesser newspaper reporters before writing songs full time.[13] George Gershwin was born into a modest household (his family moved twenty-eight times before he was twelve), and he himself dropped out of New York's High School for Commerce.[14] But two of his lyricists, Irving Caesar and George's brother Ira, attended City College.[15] Otto Harbach graduated from Columbia University, Harry Woods from Harvard, Jimmy Van Heusen attended Syracuse University, Kay Swift attended Julliard, and Buddy De Sylva the University of Southern California.[16] Though indubitably a song factory, Tin Pan Alley was hardly a proletarian operation.

This points to Tin Pan Alley's unique character as a leveling institution, or at least a meritocratic one. Here men possessing the widest divergence of musical facility and education vied for the prize of creating a hit. Self-trained musicians like Harry Ruby, even musical illiterates like Irving Berlin, cohabited and at times collaborated with harmonic sophisticates and quasi-aristocrats like Kern, Porter, Vernon Duke, and Egbert Van Alstyne. This cacophony of class intensified calls for the creation of a new pecking order, one defined not just by commercial success (always a sine qua non) but by artistic merit too. Elevating the popular song by dressing it up in classical garb would help separate the wheat from the chaff and produce music for the ages. As early as 1910 Berlin had voiced his frustration that, despite commercial success, "we are not producing any living songs." As he informed an interviewer for the *New York World*, "These things I am writing are only for the brief career of the vaudeville stage. They will be a hit for a week or two. They will then be forgotten and new ones will take their place. But I cannot think of a song in years that has come to stay." [17] In the following years, other Tin Pan Alley composers, notably Kern and Gershwin, echoed Berlin's complaint.

Yet theirs was no straightforward case of artistic social climbing. Part of what makes the contest so intriguing is that the desired synthesis could be approached either from above or below. The method of aesthetic transcendence thus involved as much lowering as lifting up. What was to be pulled down was the very "Europeanness" of the art music tradition. The most common approach was through symphonic or operatic parody, by then a hoary tradition in vaudeville and blackface minstrelsy, institutions in which many Tin Pan Alley songwriters had served apprenticeships. The nineteenth-century minstrel show specialized in such effects, based in turn upon the actual practice in antebellum America of punctuating productions of grand Italian operas with deliberate buffoonery and ridiculous musical comic asides.[18]

Tin Pan Alley composers and vaudevillians in the early years of the twentieth century resurrected these practices. In this, as Charles Hamm has shown, there was no more avid practitioner than the young Irving Berlin. In 1909, for example, Berlin penned a put-on of Mendelssohn's "Spring Song" entitled "That Mesmerizing Mendelssohn Tune." The parody depended upon the comic rendering of the song by a blackface duet in which the ill-educated female partner repeatedly mistakes "Mendelssohn" for "meddlesome," a piece of comic confusion that, once dispelled, proceeds to a cheerful reiteration of the chorus: "that's the only music that was ever meant for me/ that tantalizin', hypnotizin', mesmerizin', Mendelssohn tune."[19] Similarly, Berlin's "That Opera Rag" of 1910 and "Ragtime Opera Sextet" from 1912 parodied Bizet's *Carmen* and Donizetti's *Lucia di Lammermoor*, respectively, and depended on the presumably incongruous image of "op'ra darkeys" recreating the classics.[20] In his 1914 *Watch Your Step*, Berlin featured his "Ragtime Opera Medley," a number that promised to "modernize" or rather "hurdy gurdy Mr Verdi":

Aida,
There's not a melody sweeter.
But you'll be sweeter when we begin turning you into a rag.
Aida,
We're gonna chop up your meter.[21]

Ragging the classics involved knocking them down to size by performing them in a Negro minstrel or blackface mode (an act of class ridicule as much as racial denigration), as well as revving up their rhythmic quality by accelerating and syncopating their tempos. It was an approach that would recur throughout the later history of American popular music: "jazzing" the classics in the 1920s, "swinging" them in the 1930s and 1940s, and "rocking" them in the 1950s.[22] As the rock 'n' roll pioneer Chuck Berry famously demanded, "Roll over Beethoven and tell Tchaikovsky the news!"[23]

That reference is not merely ornamental. As noted, incorporating snippets of opera was a staple of African American minstrel performance in the late nineteenth century. The most successful of these, built around the Negro diva Matilda Sisseretta Jones (the "Black Patti"), wedged arias from famous operas between the typical minstrel fare. Supplementing the leveling designs of the vaudevillians, the procedure also intended, according to the American music scholar Thomas L. Riis, to issue "a challenge to the stereotypes of the minstrel show and the coon song."[24] One of the graduates of Jones's organization, Bob Cole, began incorporating comic parodies of opera and symphony into the musical reviews he cowrote with J. Rosamund Johnson in the decade or so before his death in 1911. And until his own untimely death in 1919, the black bandleader James Reece Europe continued to rag Bach and Brahms to the great delight of white and black audiences alike.[25] As with Jews, blacks on Tin Pan Alley ran the gamut from musical illiterates to classically trained composers such as Will Marion Cook, W. C. Handy, the aforementioned J. Rosamund Johnson, and later William Grant Still. These black songwriters/composers, a number of them college educated, were attempting to do roughly the same thing as some of their Jewish counterparts: elevate popular song (or black vernacular forms like blues and spirituals) by combining it with elements of the European concert music tradition (both in parodic and "serious" ways).

Like Cook, Cole, and others, Berlin was after more than mere comic effect in his opera parodies. In his case opera parodies were designed as preparation for a more ambitious project, one he began to plan sometime between 1910 and 1914. In the August 1913 edition of *Green Book Magazine*, Rennold Wolf reported that Berlin intended 'to write an opera in rag-time, if you please." The songwriter confessed: "my readers will perhaps smile when I tell them that I am writing an opera in ragtime; the whole libretto as well as the music. The idea is so new and ambitious that it may be a great big failure, and certainly such a thing has never been tried before."[26] In asserting the project's unprecedented character, Berlin was certainly incorrect and possibly disingenuous. By the time he made his remarks, the black composer Scott Joplin had already written two ragtime operas, the now lost *A Guest of Honor* (1903?) and *Treemonisha* (1911). Berlin may even have heard parts of the latter when his and Joplin's publishers shared offices in the same New York building during the years 1909–10. Joplin apparently believed Berlin had lifted the melody for "Alexander's Ragtime Band" from *Treemonisha*'s "A Real Slow Rag," an accusation Berlin vigorously dismissed.[27] It would not be the last time that black composers believed white, and often in particular Jewish, composers had usurped their claims to priority as well as its rewards.

White and black composers were simultaneously pursuing new syntheses of popular (African American) and classical (European) music in a host of musical styles and genres, including ragtime operas and attempts to introduce "jazz" style into Broadway stage musicals.[28] With regard to Jews, there is evidence that training in the synthesizing of popular and art music styles had already begun in the "Old World" context, such eclecticism perhaps reflecting what the musicologist Mark Slobin has called the "Jewish penchant for filling every available niche in the musical ecology."[29] If so, the penchant was hardly unique to Jews; it could just as easily be applied to black band leaders of the late nineteenth century and the early jazz age. In the years leading up to 1920, the blues-based, polyphonic, and improvisatory jazz music then germinating in cities like New Orleans, Memphis, and Chicago contained its own synthetic qualities that rendered it a type of Euro-American, classical-vernacular hybrid. Indeed, the contemporaneous evolution of jazz included a not dissimilar effort by some of its African American and white practitioners to devise their own distinctive Euro-American art music hybrid (of which Duke Ellington would become the most notable exemplar). The notion that early jazz possessed merely the fortuitous or instinctive genius of the brothel and speakeasy is a distortion. From its early days, many jazz musicians white and black viewed themselves as artists and their music as in some regard akin to the European classical tradition.[30]

That is not, however, how others saw it at the time. Indeed, the degree of technical musicological difference between European music, on the one hand, and ragtime or jazz, on the other, was widely exaggerated. For those who sought to disparage black music, the difference was exaggerated in order to condemn and demonize it as barbaric; for those who wished to praise it, the difference was exaggerated so as to render African American music the vital antithesis, and perhaps the cherished antidote, to the "repressive" culture of Europe and white America. What is striking is that in the years just before 1920, when both black and white Tin Pan Alley composers engaged in similar fusion experiments, only Jewish songwriters appeared to get the credit—or the blame. Part of the reason lies in the fact that Jewish songwriters, as participants in a Jewish "ethnic" business whose bread and butter lay in its appeal to the American mainstream, possessed their own paradoxical self-interest in both promoting and suppressing the black origins of the popular music they were fashioning. As Berlin told readers of the *American Magazine* in 1920, "our popular song writers and composers are not negroes," but mostly "of Russian birth or ancestry." Such "Russians," he noted, enjoyed a special talent for integrating disparate musical elements, as can be seen in their compositions, which combine "the influences of Southern plantation songs, of European music from almost countless countries and of the syncopation that is found in the music of innumerable nationalities—found even in the music of the old master composers."[31] Berlin's remarks prompt a question: if, as some historians have insisted, Jews sought to obscure the key musicological role of blacks and thereby advance their own credentials as America's preeminent "entertaining people," then why did Berlin feel the need to hide behind the "Russian" circumlocution? It is true, as noted earlier, that the Jews of

Tin Pan Alley were mostly of East European or "Russian" descent, just as Berlin was correct to insist upon the eclectic influences behind Tin Pan Alley song. Yet both descriptions manage to avoid any direct mention not just of blacks but of Jews, the other key group in the popular music industry of the time. Did Berlin seriously expect readers to believe that the "Alexander" of his "Ragtime Band" was Borodin or Glazunov?

Berlin's evasion may reflect the ambiguous nature or the Jewish middleman stereotype, whose historical usage had been both flattering and pejorative. On the one hand, traditional Jewish apologetics had included the Jews' supposed capacity for economic and cultural mediation as a component in its repertoire of self-advertisements: "Wherever the Jews have lived," as a classic work of Jewish apologetics put it, "there traffic and business have flourished."[32] At the same time, the middleman image also functioned, as noted above, as a key weapon in the arsenal of European anti-Semitism. Since the Jew adds nothing substantive of his own to the product, he is at best extraneous and at worst parasitical to the creative process. Given Berlin's awareness of the near interchangeability of the business and creative sides of Tin Pan Alley publishing, both of which currently involved Jewish mediation of black vernacular style, he was understandably coy about revealing the full recipe of Tin Pan Alley success. And since, according to his family history, he himself had been a refugee from a pogrom, he may have perceived that the Russian anti-Semitic view of the Jews as exploiters of the peasantry, the oppressed but ultimately redemptive folk, could be readily transferred to the American scene, with the African American now playing the role of the tortured Russian peasant, the *muzhik.*

Curiously, such a connection had earlier been asserted by no less a Russian than Fyodor Dostoevsky, and while Berlin was not likely to have known the source, the underlying concept would have been familiar to him. For Dostoevsky, writing in the 1870s, it was the parasitic déclassé Jews who, in the wake of Lincoln's emancipation, had descended upon the South in order to manipulate and dominate the recently emancipated slaves. If the Jews so readily exploit the Russian peasants, Dostoevsky wondered, what would stop them from preying upon the gullible and childlike blacks? Since "the Negroes have now been liberated from the slave owners, . . . the Jews, of whom there are so many in the world," Dostoevsky predicted, "will jump at this new little victim."[33] As Dostoevsky's remarks suggest, what I have labeled the image of the Jewish maestro/minstrel, whether understood positively in the form of Jews' creative mediation of black folk art, or negatively as the exploitation and purveying of Negro culture, had a long and complex prehistory. It will be worthwhile to summarize the views of a number of authors who, like Dostoevsky, helped develop the ideological premises behind the Jewish minstrel/maestro phenomenon.

Dostoevsky insinuated that the Jews lie in wait to steal something from the helpless blacks. But what? In subsequent decades, after they had been eliminated as a potent electoral force, one commodity blacks still retained was their musical culture. This was the Negroes' uniquely valuable possession that another Slavic commentator, Anton Dvořák, came to champion. Shortly before he completed his "New World Symphony" in May 1893, Dvořák informed the American press that that "the future music of this country must be founded upon what are called negro melodies."[34] In the United States for less than a year, Dvořák had already performed a concert at the Columbia Exposition in Chicago and may even have heard ragtime played there. And although he quickly retreated from his categorical emphasis on the distinctive Americanness of Negro music (ironically, in the face of accusations that he was foisting his European prejudices upon America), the seed he had planted took root.[35] Composers like Henry F. Gilbert and Arthur Farwell devoted much of their careers to mining Negro melodies in an effort to produce the quintessentially American symphony, or opera, or ballet, while other such as Charles Ives and Edward Burlingame Hill at the very least dabbled in Negro music.

While Dvořák's remarks expressed a conception of the Negro as culturally authentic and peasant-like in the vein of contemporary Slavic romanticism, he made no mention of Jews as interpreters of the Negro's music. That claim—and its implicit linkage with Dostoevsky's portrayal of the Jews as exploiters of the black *Volk*—would require several intermediary steps. As has been noted by many commentators, it was the Anglo-Jewish playwright Israel Zangwill who provided a key motif that influenced aesthetic perceptions of the Jewish composer and made possible his eventual link to the Negro folk source. Without rehearsing the plot of his famous 1908 play *The Melting Pot,* suffice it to say that David Quixano, the play's Russian Jewish protagonist, aspires to create a symphonic masterpiece that will seamlessly fuse the disparate elements of American musical life, including (though not centrally) its Negro components, into a representative and democratic whole.[36] What is important here is that Zangwill identified the Jew as chief smelter of the cultural melting pot, the ultimate American artistic and musical middleman.

Though Dostoevsky, Dvořák, and Zangwill supplied its foundation, the figure of the Jewish minstrel/maestro became fully formed only during the years surrounding World War I. Central to this effort was the activity of a small but influential group of New York literary and cultural critics associated with the magazine *The Seven Arts.* These writers believed that the crisis afflicting American culture centered on a rift that rendered its two poles of "highbrow and lowbrow" entirely separate and mutually isolated domains, thereby inhibiting the nation's healthy artistic development. In a 1915 essay titled "Highbrow and Lowbrow" the group's leader, the literary critic Van Wyck Brooks (who coedited the magazine), located the cause of this divide in the paradoxical circumstance of America's colonial origins: its dependency upon Old World aesthetic ideals that abstracted from their original European framework, had left the nation's practical day to day life bereft of a living connection to a higher spiritual purpose. What must therefore be defined, by the perspicacious agency of the critic, is a "middle plane between vaporous idealism and self-interested practicality"—that is, a happy synthesis between the spiritual and material domains that nevertheless eschews any merely middlebrow compromise. The long-postponed integration of high and low, in Brooks's view, would mark America's true maturation, what he called its "Coming of Age."[37]

The circle of critics surrounding Brooks (men like Waldo Frank, Paul Rosenfeld, and Hiram Motherwell, or more indirectly, Carl Van Vechten and Gilbert Seldes) sought ways to apply his prescription. These younger writers adapted Brooks and Zangwill to contemporary urbanized America with its new mass entertainment industries, including Tin Pan Alley. In the July 1917 edition of *The Seven Arts*, Motherwell proclaimed ragtime to be America's "one true music," noting that its distinctive "jerk and rattle" rendered it "the perfect expression of the American city." To demonstrate ragtime's high artistic merit, he proposed that a concert be held at the Aeolian Hall in New York City mixing Negro spirituals and ragtime standards, the latter of which, as can be seen from his suggested program, happened to consist entirely of works produced by Tin Pan Alley Jews (Berlin's "Everybody's Doing It" and "I Love a Piano," Kern's "On the Beach at Wai-ki-ki," and Odessa-born L. Wolfe Gilbert's "Waiting for the Robert E. Lee").[38] Similarly, Carl Van Vechten, in a *Vanity Fair* article from April of the same year (entitled "The Great American Composer") glossed Dvořák by insisting that the popular song of the city rather than the Negro spirituals of the plantation would best supply the raw material for a distinctly American symphonic art. All that awaited was the emergence of a young musical genius to shape this material into "new forms." Van Vechten did not say if he had a David Quixano in mind. But in supplying specific examples of great ragtime songs, he likewise referred mostly to Jewish Tin Pan Alley composers (and exclusively white ones): "Lewis F. Muir, Irving Berlin, and Louis A. Hirsch," he wrote, "[are] the true grandfathers of the Great American Composer of the year 2001."[39]

Perhaps the most original response to Brooks's call came from Gilbert Seldes, a younger contemporary of Van Vechten. The title of his influential book, *The Seven Lively Arts*, underscores its author's sense of continuity as well as distance from the short-lived *Seven Arts*. Seldes took issue with what he saw as the residual elitism of Brooks's circle, one he found especially pronounced in the writings of the magazine's coeditor Waldo Frank and the music critic Paul Rosenfeld, both highly cultured German Jews who were contemptuous of ragtime and jazz. Seldes, who grew up in a secular, largely Russian Jewish anarchist colony in Alliance, New Jersey, believed that the synthesis these men sought existed too much on the high plane of a cerebral modernism.[40] Instead, Seldes aimed to define a more populist approach. He argued that the "lively arts" (including vaudeville, comics, slapstick, and ragtime) offer both a complement and a corrective to the lofty art that strives for high ideals alone. "[The] one is more intense and more noble, yes. But we are under no compulsion always to be intense and noble." While championing Eliot and Pound in the pages of *The Dial*, Seldes treated the "lively arts" as America's real forte. Whereas socialists like Brooks, Frank, and Rosenfeld held mass culture's commercialism in contempt, Seldes regarded the nation's capitalist orientation as a spur to its creativity: intense competition to produce mere entertainment had rendered "the technical mastery displayed in the minor arts . . . far more complete than that of the major arts."[41] And whereas Rosenfeld and Frank despised ragtime and jazz, Seldes championed these forms, especially once they had been refined through the smelting capacity of Jewish cultural brokers. Fully acknowledging that the "lively art" of ragtime had originated entirely with Negroes, Seldes nevertheless felt sure it could achieve apotheosis only when the Negro's "uncorrupted sensibility" had been "worked over . . . by [Jewish] creative intelligence." Irving Berlin and Al Jolson, he insisted, offered the clearest proof.[42]

Van Vechten and Seldes were the principal (though not exclusive) literary concocters of the Jewish minstrel/maestro ideal and the most active agents in fomenting the contest to discover "the great American composer." They knew many of the Jewish songwriters personally and, through their writings in magazines like *The Dial* and *Vanity Fair*, sought to mold the public's conception of them. At the same time, their championing of Jewish maestro/minstrelsy would not have succeeded without the full engagement of the songwriters themselves. Here it is worth noting that by the time Seldes, Van Vechten, and the others had begun actively to promote the contest, the composer who had helped launch it, Irving Berlin, had quietly abandoned the field. While he had earlier broached the idea of a ragtime opera, by 1918 or 1919 his interest had waned—at least momentarily. With regard to the contest, the pistol had been fired but no one had started to run.

In fact, the first to step forward was not a composer at all but the then-novice lyricist Ira Gershwin, who, in his initial collaboration with George, seemed interested in wresting from his brother a joint declaration of aims. The Gershwins' 1918 "The Real American Folk Song Is a Rag" updated Dvořák and lent him a brash American sparkle that, despite the song's playful tone, underscored its nationalist design. "Too much like an essay" was Ira's own later assessment. Indeed, the song has the quality of a manifesto. It opens "allegretto" with the affirmation that though "each nation" possesses its own "creative vein" and "native strain" of folk refrain, it is the American that carries the "stronger appeal," possessing what all the others lack (but feel): "a certain snap . . . that makes you tap," and "the invitation to agitate" and "leave the rest to Fate." All of which owes to its one unmatched virtue, its "syncopated sort of meter," which, compared to "a classic strain," is "sweeter."[43]

Gershwin's effort to follow up on this theme appeared two years later in the form of a "party song" cowritten with brother George. Though never published, the song was "sung by the writers at the slightest provocation," according to Ira's recollections. It concerns four "temperamental Oriental gentlemen" ("Mischa, Jascha, Toscha, Sascha"), who at age three take up the fiddle. Their "notes were sour" until a "Professor Auer" (a reference to the great Hungarian Jewish violin teacher Leopold Auer) "set out to show us, one and all / how we could pack them in, in Carnegie Hall." Though born "in darkest Russia," the virtuosi are happily now relatives of "Uncle Sammy." And though for a living they "play the high-brow stuff," they also "like" (read prefer) their "syncopations":

Our magic bow
Plays Liszt and Schumann;
But then you know
We're only human
And like to shake a leg to jazz
(Don't think we've not the feelings everyone has).

Should anyone miss the Shylockian allusion in the last line, the song contains a more direct Shakespearean reference to the prosaic (or Hebraic) origins of the virtuosi:

Shakespeare says, "What's in a name?"
With him we disagree.
Names like Sammy, Max or Moe
Never bring the heavy dough
Like Mischa, Jascha, Toscha, Sascha—
Fiddle-lee, diddle-lee, dee.

The fact that these "Russian" gentlemen (echoing Berlin) find ragtime and jazz irresistible exposes the virtuosi's true nature and origins. Despite the fancy Russian names and cultivated exoticism, the "High-brow Hebrow" will invariably "play the low-brow in his privacy," reveling to syncopated sounds, but "when concert halls are packed / watch us stiffen up and act / Like Mischa, Jascha, Toscha, Sascha—fiddle-lee, diddle-lee, dee."[44]

As with Berlin's opera parodies, humor supplied a decoy with which to lull the high-minded enemy into complacency and inspire the troops for a conquest of American musical culture. Armed with "the real American folk song," that is, black music, the Jewish minstrels were now prepared to storm America's temples of culture.

Maestros

In an article from the January–February 1933 issue of *Modern Music* entitled "Popular Music—An Invasion: 1923–1933," the composer Marc Blitzstein summed up the crisis that he believed currently afflicted the world of serious music. When, on the one hand, a popular composer like George Gershwin writes "what is, to a stadium full of people, concert music," while on the other, a "serious composer" such as Vladimir Dukelsky occasionally takes on the name of Vernon Duke for his Broadway songwriting career, then it is clear that popular has invaded and threatens to overturn the established musical order. Far from cheering this insurrection, however, Blitzstein bemoaned the "loss of 'constant' values" as well as the "artistic inferiority-complex" the invasion had wrought. The blame, he emphasized, lay not with overweening Tin Pan Alley musicians alone who would not respect their betters. Rather, the fact that Gershwin could foist his "lamentably mediocre, false and sloppy music" onto a gullible concert audience was more a symptom than a cause.[45]

In Blitzstein's view, the true sources of the crisis were both social and aesthetic: in the latter category, Stravinsky's *Rite of Spring* from May 1913, though in itself artistically valid, had unfortunately spawned a sycophantic "school of neo-primitives . . . in full flight from 'culture,' high-mindedness, and civilized music." In the meantime, the war, or rather its conclusion, having induced a mood of "abandon and excitement," added the hedonistic sweetener to the primitivist spice to create a veritable "wave of infantilism." Such childishness was marked, first, by the "noise-esthetic" of the machine, a bogus attempt to simulate the rat-tat-tat of modern wartime, as well as the vicious drone of the postwar assembly line, and second, by "a new dependence upon folk-elements [far] outdoing anything existing before along that line." Dvořák's romanticizing of the folk had given way to Bartók's obsessive academicism. Everywhere the naive and the vulgar had become objects of worship, bringing forth "a new deification—of the savage, the child, the peasant, the artless music-maker."[46] And chief among the new idols, in America and to a lesser extent Europe too, was the cult of jazz: "What was more natural than that some of the most astute of us should alight upon jazz? Here was something new, ours, unused, full of vitality (it turned out to be nothing more than a charming exuberance)— and the great American symphony had yet to be written!"[47] Blitzstein followed this diagnosis of past mistakes with specific critiques of the jazz-inflected works of his (slightly older) contemporaries Ernst Krenek, Louis Gruenberg, Kurt Weill, and Aaron Copland. Though Copland's 1926 "Piano Concerto" remains "the best work I know in the genre," in the final analysis, wrote Blitzstein, it too fails, since it cannot truly reconcile irreconcilables such as good jazz, on the one hand, and "a certain level of intellectual content," on the other. Since Copland's integrity does not allow him to omit the cerebral, his concerto comes out sounding schizo-phrenic. As for the lesser figures, serious music composers who cheapen themselves in an effort to "write down" to the level of popular music, their "reaching down has its counterpart in a reaching up" on the part of the Tin Pan Alley renegades. The only solution, according to Blitzstein, is an amicable divorce. Let serious and popular music prevail, each in its distinct domain, for Tin Pan Alley and jazz do possess a vitality of their own, one derived, Blitzstein adds, from its "predominantly Yiddish material, with strains of the negro and the Celt."[48]

Blitzstein's lumping together of Tin Pan Alley with jazz—and his deriva-tion of the vitality of both from the ethnic strains of the Irish, the Jewish, and the Negro—conformed to commonplace notions regarding "popular music" in the 1920s. Relatively few commentators knew then what later ret-rospectively came to be defined as the era's "real jazz"; until the latter part of the decade most were unfamiliar with the music of Louis Armstrong, Joe "King" Oliver, Jelly Roll Morton, and Sidney Bechet, as well as such with such white jazz musicians as Jack Teagarden, Frank Teschemacher, and Bix Beiderbecke (though all of these had recorded from the early 1920s). In part, this reflected a geographical lag in the 1920s, when jazz as we under-stand it today remained largely a music of New Orleans and Chicago musi-cians. Up through the mid-1920s, even the black bands from Washington D.C. and New York City that would later achieve renown, such as those of Duke Ellington and Fletcher Henderson, still played half in the older rag-time styles associated with Will Marion Cook and James Reece Europe.[49]

At the same time, by the early 1920s, a form of popular music retrospec-tively labeled "symphonic jazz" had taken root in New York and other cities. It was defined by heavily arranged large-band renditions of Tin Pan Alley songs, incorporating some ragtime and jazz rhythms as well as associ-ated gimmicks and effects. Symphonic jazz made signal contributions to jazz music's overall development in terms of instrumentation, personnel, and repertoire, but because it placed relatively little emphasis on improvi-sation, its identification as jazz remains problematic.[50] Swing musicians of the 1930s, even many who had once played symphonic jazz, often went to great lengths retroactively to dissociate themselves from it.[51] But in the 1920s, the linkage between symphonic jazz and songwriters like Gershwin and Berlin echoed those composers' earlier identification with ragtime. Similarly, the fact that many critics could not properly differentiate jazz (of any variety) from ragtime also replicated an older problem, the widespread ignorance of the "classic" ragtime of Scott Joplin and Joseph Lamb and awareness of only the "popular" ragtime of Tin Pan Alley. Hence, to iden-tify "jazz" with East European Jews ("Yiddish"), Negroes, and Irish—albeit a misconception by current standards—was simply to view it as part and parcel of the ethnic history of Tin Pan Alley and minstrelsy, in which the Irish, Negroes, and Jews had played central roles.

Authors who stressed a black-Jewish connection in forging jazz were legion in the 1920s. In a 1929 survey of "Our American Music," John Tasker Howard noted that, while jazz originated with the Negroes, "it has come to Broadway and Tin Pan Alley and in a very real sense it has become a Jewish interpretation of the Negro."[52] Though no friend of jazz, Waldo Frank, writing in the mid-1920s, averred that "the races at once most flexible and most maladjusted—the negro and the Jew—give the best jazz masters."[53] Gilbert Seldes concluded in a 1926 *Vanity Fair* article "at this moment a significant part of American music, is composed almost entirely by the descendents of African Negroes and the descendents of Russian Jews."[54] As late as 1934 the English composer and critic Constant Lambert held that "most jazz is written and performed by cosmopolitan Jews," while only slightly earlier Isaac Goldberg had insisted that though the origins of jazz "go back to the African jungle," it has been transformed, polished, and promoted "at the hands of such Jews as Irving Berlin, George Gershwin and Jerome Kern and—in the symphonic realm—Gershwin, [Louis] Gruenberg and Aaron Copland."[55] If Jews didn't actually start jazz, so the argument went, they had certainly helped to finish it.

Blitzstein too subscribed to the belief that popular song and jazz were basically synonymous and essentially represented a combination of black and Jewish elements. He assumed that the synthesis of modernist art music composition with (symphonic) jazz rhythms and coloration was a largely Jewish accomplishment as well: according to his biographer, he "couldn't help observing that the route through which jazz was beginning to filter up to classical music came through Jews—Copland, Gershwin, Irving Berlin and Richard Rodgers. Even the most famous of the white coon shouters [Blitzstein noted] had been Jews."[56] More surprising, given his harsh condemnations of efforts to synthesize popular and art music in 1933, is that earlier in his career Blitzstein himself had not been averse to deploying jazz in the service of art music. In 1927 he created jazz settings for poems by Walt Whitman. He followed these "Songs for a Coon Shouter" with a 1928 ballet, *Jig Saw,* whose five-part sequence included vaudeville and minstrel sections with titles like "Buck and Wing" and "Cotton-Pickers' Shuffle." The composer defended his mingling of Whitman and jazz against hostile criticisms (accusing him of concocting an "incongruous and debasing" combination) by insisting that it was "perfectly natural to couple two media whose implications are alike universal and whose methods are alike primitive [since] both jazz and Whitman contain a proud and all-pervasive sexuality."[57]

Despite his own nominally Jewish status, Blitzstein must have recognized that his own use of jazz and minstrel motifs put him into a category with other modernist composers of Jewish descent who in the 1920s had become identified with the use of black music.[58] Of course, plenty of composers lacking any Jewish connection were doing precisely the same thing, among them John Alden Carpenter, Ernst Krenek, George Antheil, and Emerson Whithorne. But so powerful was the assumed linkage of Jews and jazz that comic misattributions sometimes occurred: Antheil and Paul Whiteman, for instance, were mistaken by some writers for Jews.[59] Thus in an era when racial generalizations were pervasive even (or especially) within scholarly and artistic circles, contemporaries were not likely to divorce Blitzstein's aesthetic choices from his Jewish origins.

The question is, did Blitzstein's own awareness of the presumed link between Jews and jazz—or perhaps his fear that by deploying jazz he would call attention to his Jewish origins—have anything to do with his renunciation of jazz in 1933? To answer, we need to view Blitzstein's 1933 pronouncements in relation to a larger pattern. A number of young modernist composers of the 1920s, European and American both, had followed a period of mid-1920s experimentation in symphonic jazz with loud public renunciations of it as a possible vehicle for serious art. Virgil Thomson may have been the first to bail out, partly because when it came to jazz he had never been fully in. Writing in the June 1925 edition of *Vanity Fair*, Thomson labeled the current "worship" of jazz "just another form of highbrowism," that is, a fad or cliquish cult, and four months later predicted, "by the end of the season high-brow jazz will probably be as dead as mahjong."[60] Darius Milhaud, who on his 1922 visit to the United States had filled American reporters "with consternation" by enthusiastically endorsing jazz (and a year later, in the ballet *La Création du monde*, composed perhaps the most admired of early symphonic jazz works), unsettled them again when, upon revisiting America in 1926, he declared himself "no longer interested" in it.[61] Ernst Krenek, composer of the sensational "jazz opera" *Johnny spielt auf* (staged at the Metropolitan Opera House in 1929, with Lawrence Tibbett in the title role wearing blackface), indicated by the early 1930s that he thought jazz old hat, even reactionary, a throwback to the system of conventional Romantic tonality now rendered obsolete by Schoenberg's dodecaphonic approach.[62] Aaron Copland, after producing two symphonic jazz pieces in close succession, the 1925 *Music for the Theater* and the 1926 Concerto for Piano and Orchestra, determined by 1928 that he "had done all [he] could with the idiom considering its limited emotional scope."[63] And Louis Gruenberg, throughout the 1920s the most avid experimenter in concertized jazz, let it be known in 1930 that he was through with the "jazz phase" of his career.[64]

Yet in light of these pronouncements it is curious that, with the exception of Krenek, *none of these composers actually did give up jazz*. Thomson employed its rhythms, tonalities, and coloration with no less, and perhaps more, frequency after than before 1925. Milhaud made use of the sonorities and percussive elements he had absorbed in his intensive studies of 1920s jazz records in a host of later compositions, his *Le Bal martiniquais* (1944), *Carnival a la Nouvelle-Orleans* (1947), and Concerto for Clarinet and

Orchestra, which he dedicated to Benny Goodman (1941), among others. As for Copland, his biographer Howard Pollack insists that "jazz remained central to his musical style and imagination" long after the 1920s.[65] Similarly, the jazz phase Louis Gruenberg had declared over in 1930 never actually ended: his magnum opus of three years later, the opera *The Emperor Jones*, incorporated not just jazz but many types of African American music that Gruenberg had struggled for years to master. Gruenberg's 1944 violin concerto, commissioned by Jascha Heifetz, made a similarly extensive use of spirituals, blues, and "jazz born rhythms."[66] Finally, there is the case of Blitzstein himself. Despite his denunciations of four years earlier, his 1937 proletarian opera *The Cradle Will Rock* combined clever, agitprop lyrics with Tin Pan Alley–style song structures, which the composer expertly worked over in a manner designed to make them yield dissonance and complexity in the finest *Entfremdung* manner.

It thus appears that these composers' break with jazz in the late 1920s and early 1930s was more rhetorical than actual. How then to explain the need for a public renunciation of jazz, while continuing in practice to employ it? Surely these composers sought to dampen the unrealistic, even messianic, expectation their earlier pronouncements had fed, namely, that their experimentation with jazz would bring forth some transformational new synthesis of cultures, epochs, classes, and styles. But there were other reasons as well. For the European composers like Milhaud and Krenek, most oppressive of all may have been the sense that the use of jazz in art music was now identified, as Blitzstein indicated, with a primitivist movement that seemed increasingly worn out, especially with Stravinsky's own turn by the 1920s to "neo-classicism." The American composers, in contrast, likely felt oppressed by the enormous pressure placed upon them to devise a national musical style from a Negro vernacular mode that, despite their attraction to it, still seemed alien. For the Jews in particular (the maestros), the presumption that, as Isaac Goldberg put it, the artist of Jewish race and culture "responds naturally to the deeper implications of jazz" eventually had to come face to face with the reality of each artist's sense of his own aesthetic autonomy.[67]

Anti-Semitism, too, constituted a part of the backdrop. Snide remarks were voiced regarding the jazz proclivities of Jewish composers. Edward Burlingame Hill, who on several occasions had tried his own hand at composing symphonic jazz, expressed the opinion that Copland's *Music for the Theater* amounted to "the usual clever Hebraic assimilation of the worst elements of polytonalité."[68] Similar statements were uttered, not just privately but in print, both by the "ultra" modernist Henry Cowell and the conservative Columbia music professor Daniel Gregory Mason.[69] Even among Jews, distinctions emerged on the grounds of acceptable jazz aesthetics. Paul Rosenfeld lambasted Gershwin's crass Yiddish "showmanship," whose "charming bits" are invariably spoilt by "faults of grammar in every line," while offering qualified praise to Copland, whose jazz reveals "the artist's relation to life"; for, although unfortunately reliant upon the "second-rate . . . ragtime" material that is his patrimony, Copland nevertheless manages to deploy it "in a first-rate fashion."[70] Whether or not such comments played a role in making Jewish composers self-conscious and embarrassed about their jazz efforts is a matter of speculation. What can be said definitively is that by the end of the 1920s these modernist composers decided individually, and in a sense collectively, that jazz had disappointed their expectations, had proven itself to be, as Copland characterized it, too "limited" technically and emotionally to supply an alternative to the European classical tradition. In the eyes of most of them, jazz did not perhaps need to be entirely discarded, but it did deserve to be demoted from its formerly preeminent status.

This brings us back to the question of what precisely Copland, Blitzstein, and the others meant when they referred to jazz during the 1920s. For Copland and Thomson, jazz was reducible to its peculiar polyrhythms. As Thomson put it, "there is almost no implication in [jazz] of any intrinsic musical quality beyond [an] elementary muscle jerking" induced by the technique of "sounding two rhythms at once in order to provoke a muscular response."[71] In this regard, and here Copland agreed, jazz was not so much a musical content as a method. Just about any piece of music could thus be rhythmically "jazzed."[72] This brings to mind the old vaudeville ploy of "ragging the classics," mastered by Berlin and Bob Cole but almost universally condemned in the music literature of the 1920s. Viewed in this way, jazz seemed almost merely an effect or musical form that depended on gimmicks to achieve a part of its sound. For Milhaud too, jazz was in essence a form of rhythm, a unique method of polyphony that achieved its flavor through a counterpoint of melodic line "against the [steady] beat of the drum, the two criss-crossing . . . in a breathless pattern of broken and twisted rhythms."[73]

But once shorn of these core rhythmic qualities—that is, once its technical lessons had been absorbed—what would remain of jazz? One early critic thought of jazz as ragtime song with "jazz orchestration superimposed upon it" in the manner of popular bandleaders like Paul Whiteman or Vincent Lopez.[74] In the 1920s, the connection between jazz and ragtime had been a vexing one not just for critics but for musicians and composers as well. In a 1927 article in *Modern Music*, Copland provided a lengthy musical analysis aimed at discerning the key distinction between the two. Because, as noted above, he believed that rhythm was the key to jazz, Copland implied that what remained after the polyrhythmic technique had been extracted was merely a ragtime song, such as (in the example he used) Irving Berlin's "Everybody's Doing It Now." Copland's thinking was fairly typical in this regard: jazz was a continuation of ragtime by other rhythmic means. These means, when applied to classical forms, both he and Thomson insisted, would be of the greatest importance for the future of American concert music, for they would help—indeed, had already helped—to revitalize its "rhythmic sense."[75] But as for ragtime itself, it remained merely a method of syncopating a popular song—with the method deriving characteristically from Negroes and the songs characteristically from Jews. Since ragtime syncopation as a device had now been superseded by jazz polyrhythm, only the actual Tin Pan Alley song remained intact. And since Copland and other composers had now assimilated jazz rhythms as one of the many devices at their disposal, what use could they possibly have for these structurally simple and emotionally limited songs?

It thus appears that the maestros had finally come face to face with their minstrel counterparts, glimpsed their mirror images, and recoiled. They had engaged with jazz, explored its contours, wrestled with its supposed import as the "real American folk song," and flirted with the notion of employing it to compose what Blitzstein and others referred to as the "Great American Symphony." But once the rhythmic element had been extracted, they were left with the simple form of the popular song, something for which they felt only limited respect, if not actual contempt. As Copland quipped, "You can only hear a popular song so many times before you want to hear another popular song."[76] Here too a surprising degree of symmetry existed between the two groups, for in their own assessment of the artistic value of songs, minstrels like Irving Berlin and George Gershwin entirely concurred. "Unfortunately, most songs die at an early age," Gershwin told an interviewer, "and are soon completely forgotten by the selfsame public that once sang them with such gusto." Gershwin confessed that he wished to insert blues music into classical structures in order to make it endure. In this regard he epitomized the program laid out shortly before 1920 by Van Vechten and others: in order to eternalize the Negro's music a "great composer" would need to set it into a "larger and more serious form."[77] The point was not, as Paul Whiteman thought, "to make a lady out of jazz" but rather to make of her a goddess, a work of the highest art.

It would be tempting but facile to explain the minstrels' and maestros' mutual rejection of the "Yiddish" element (the Tin Pan Alley song) in terms of Jewish self-hate. In the contest to devise the American musical masterpiece, social and aesthetic snobbery as much as ethnic or religious self-renunciation were equally at play. To put it otherwise: what both maestros and minstrels feared was not their identification, qua Jews, as gifted musical interpreters, or even middlemen, but rather any labeling of them as the mere *producers* of songs. In their minds, the object was not to make folk or pop music but rather to refashion it into something higher. The raw material of American music belonged to somebody else, to the American peasantry or, more accurately, the American Negro caste. But it was their job—as maestros, minstrels, and Jews—to make it suitable for Carnegie Hall.

Such a goal indeed seemed in reach when in 1925 Otto Kahn, the chairman of the Metropolitan Opera Company (whose son, Roger Wolfe Kahn ran a successful jazz band), publicly appealed to Kern, Berlin, and Gershwin each to try his hand at writing a grand "jazz opera." [78] With Kahn's pronouncement and the contest and prize—a Met debut—finally out in the open, the minstrels proceeded to pick up the pace. In 1927 Kern and Oscar Hammerstein produced a new type of Broadway musical, *Showboat*, characterized by a serious theme, cohesive storyline, and operetta-like score. In fact, *Showboat* constituted an exquisite elegy for the entire bygone era of popular song, a nostalgic tribute to the folk sources that had made Tin Pan Alley possible, written at a moment when the old music publishing business—in the face of Hollywood encroachment—appeared moribund. At roughly the same time, Irving Berlin also revived and revised his earlier plan of creating "the great American opera." Prompted in 1924 by the diva Mary Garden, he proclaimed his intent to write a jazz opera set in the "South during the Civil War." Unfortunately, like Berlin's earlier plan, this proposal too went nowhere.[79] Thus despite *Showboat*'s innovations and Berlin's aspirations, it was George Gershwin who among the Jewish composers proved most determined and successful in the refashioning of Tin Pan Alley song. The culmination of his extended efforts, the 1935 *Porgy and Bess*, followed by a year the death of Kahn, thereby precluding any chance for a premiere at the Met. Even so, Gershwin came closest to realizing the dream: the great American folk song raised to the level of the great American symphony or opera, created by the man in the middle, he "of Russian birth and ancestry," as Berlin had put it, with his special gift for elevation.

Unfortunately for Gershwin, the maestros refused to acknowledge his triumph. Instead, they rewrote the contest rules by now proclaiming themselves the only legitimate players. As Copland put it, after the experimentation of the 1920s, "our search for musical ancestors had been abandoned or forgotten, partly, I suppose, because we became convinced that there were none—that we had none."[80] Their orphaned state rendered impossible the former notion that black music be considered the essential basis for a quintessentially American art. On the contrary, a serious American music would have to be created from scratch, employing disparate folk or "popular" elements (including but not primarily jazz) because none had advanced so high on its own as to enjoy a singular status. But clearly even this formula proved merely provisional. In wake of the Great Depression a new paradigm emerged, rooted in a broad cultural shift toward left-wing populism. By the early 1930s maestros like Copland, Blitzstein, and others had discovered in the aesthetic principles of the Popular Front their preferred mechanism for negotiating the parlous relations of middleman to mass.[81] The Popular Front's modulated Marxism both renewed and broadened the maestros' access to the folk, with the "common man" of Copland's fanfare now heralding mostly white farmers and workers while (consequently but perhaps inadvertently) tending to drown out the voices of the old Negro chorus.

Finally, there were the jazz musicians themselves—black, white, Jewish, and Gentile. They too bore a burden in their relation to classical music and Tin Pan Alley song. For one thing, hardly anyone in either of the other categories seemed to grasp what they were actually about, what jazz music actually was. Copland, Thomson, Blitzstein, Kern, Gershwin, and such admiring critics as Seldes and Van Vechten—none of them truly recognized the centrality of improvisation to jazz, its role as a form of spontaneous composition.[82] Perhaps the nature of their own crafts, ones in which quality invention must always pursue its immortality on the written page, made it difficult for them fully to appreciate this performance art. More important, none appeared to see that jazz musicians did not view themselves as primitives in need of agents to elevate their music along European aesthetic lines. In this light, one might say it was the jazz musician himself who best epitomized the minstrel/maestro's mediating role. It was he who took the melodic and harmonic "raw material" of the popular song and transformed it into new art through the act of improvisational interpretation. And by a curious irony, in doing so he helped preserve for the Jews of Tin Pan Alley their dignity as American musical originators, or—dare we say it?—as the creators of real American folk songs too.

II.
Siting the Jewish Tomorrow

Scenes of ideological persuasion reshaped the Jewish future by establishing rhetorical and visual "facts on the ground." Essays by Anna Shternshis, Barbara Kirshenblatt-Gimblett, Anat Helman, and Amy Horowitz all examine the role of aestheticized ideology in the twentieth-century Jewish experience. How have art, popular and folk music, architecture, and exhibition practices been employed by Jews (or on their behalf) to advance specific political agendas? Modern Jews no less than governments and political parties, it seems, have richly exploited the aesthetic domain to advance their various models of the ideal tomorrow.

In "May Day, Tractors, and Piglets: Yiddish Songs for Little Communists," Anna Shternshis offers an oral history of Soviet Jewish propaganda songs instituted by the Bolshevik regime from the 1920s to the 1940s. Here the Soviet formula of "socialist in content and nationalist in form" meant instilling in Jewish children a secular collectivist sensibility that would be reflected in new Soviet celebratory rituals. The goal was to reinforce the legitimacy of the communist state through a cultural indoctrination that would be at once ethnically particularistic and nationally transcendent. Through interviews with approximately two hundred former students of Yiddish schools, almost half of whom were able to recall music and lyrics from their childhood with remarkable accuracy, Shternshis demonstrates how the skillfully wrought songs utilized Yiddish-Russian homonyms and double entendres to subvert traditional religious culture and inculcate an ethos favoring secularization, modernization, and collectivization. At the same time, however, as Shternshis suggests, the reliance upon Yiddish as a vehicle of Russification ironically reinforced the sense of a distinctive Jewish identity within Soviet life.

While Bolshevik planners aimed their new rituals at the hearts and minds of Yiddish-speaking children, American Zionist visionaries promoted a future statehood in Palestine, nowhere more grandly than in the subjunctive space of the world exposition. In "Performing the State: The Jewish Palestine Pavilion at the New York World's Fair, 1939–40," Barbara Kirshenblatt-Gimblett argues that the architects of the Jewish Palestine

Pavilion, chief among them the Zionist impresario Meyer Weisgal, created, through the "agency of display," an adumbration of an "inevitable" Jewish state. They did so at a time, moreover, when Zionist political fortunes, not to mention world Jewry's existential circumstances, had come under severe threat. The Jewish Palestine Pavilion was in essence a performance, a veritable enactment of statehood through the three-stage process of "envisioning," "visualizing," and "projecting." Kirshenblatt-Gimblett situates this process within the larger framework of the visual culture of the New York World's Fair, which opened on the eve of World War II and reopened for a second season during the war itself. At this fair, Communist, fascist, and New Deal regimes employed the techniques of Madison Avenue to merchandise their respective utopias. The difference was that while the former were states seeking to make propaganda, the Jewish Palestine Pavilion was propaganda seeking to make a state.

The disparity in Zionist history between its prosaic ideological fantasies and more colorful (and certainly messier) human realities emerges sharply in Anat Helman's exploration of the cultural character of Tel Aviv. In her provocatively titled essay, "Was There Anything Particularly Jewish about 'The First Hebrew City'?," Helman argues that Tel Aviv has occupied a unique place in Zionist mythology. Although in modern times Jews have been stereotypically urbanites, Zionists depicted Tel Aviv as the first city since ancient times actually to be built by and for Jews. Yet such assertions begged the question of precisely *how* Tel Aviv should be "Jewishly" experienced. Helman describes the various alternatives posed by Tel Aviv's planners, artists, and residents. She shows that from the time of its creation the city found itself perpetually juxtaposed with the sacral Jewish center of Jerusalem. Embracing the contrast, Tel Aviv sought to forge its counter identity as a "Hebrew" (meaning secular and national) as opposed to "Jewish" (religious and diasporic) metropolis. Despite these efforts, Helman demonstrates that Diaspora Jewishness (in terms, for instance, of taste, speech, and worship) continuously penetrated the city's borders to subvert the official ideology. If Russian Jews in the 1930s were made to sing the Soviet Yiddish future and American Jews persuaded to visualize statehood in Palestine, then the citizens of Tel Aviv were, by necessity, forced to live out the contending narratives of the ideal Jewish tomorrow, a fate which Helman delineates in terms of the city's architecture, languages, artistic "schools," ethnic subcultures, religious orientations, and polemical Zionist debates.

In "Re-Routing Roots: Zahava Ben's Journey between Shuk and Suk," Amy Horowitz revisits Tel Aviv in the 1990s when the conflicts had become as much ethnic as ideological. This was in part because the regnant Ashkenazi population's general disdain for the legacy of Mizrahi Jews (of Middle Eastern descent) ensured that any resurgence of the latter's Arabic-influenced culture could only germinate outside the country's establishment institutions. Horowitz describes how the pent-up anger and aspirations of Mizrahi Jews found an outlet in the makeshift marketplace of Tel Aviv's central bus station, where the sale of homemade cassette tapes of musicians like Zohar Argov (and later Zehava Ben) skyrocketed in the late 1970s and early 1980s. But such signs of growing economic and aesthetic self-affirmation composed merely the first stage of an evolving "folk process" that eventually led to a new fusion of Mizrahi and European popular music, one which even appeared to foster a partial reconciliation between Mizrahi Jews and the Ashkenazic European descendents of the state's founding elite. This, according to Horowitz, opened up the further and still more daring possibility that music might also promote a rapprochement with the Arab populations inside and outside Israel. The story of Zehava Ben, the central figure in Horowitz's account, suggests that this version of the idealized Jewish future was not so much a sighted as a sounded one, with pop music striving to perform political reconciliation proactively, as it were, on the wings of song. During the late 1980s and early 1990s, Ben experimented with performances of the Arabic repertoire of the legendary Egyptian singer Umm Kulthum, a process that culminated in an enormously successful 1995 CD tribute to her hero. But did such musical excursions across enemy lines and into disputed territories really help to redefine political attitudes? Like the other essays in this section, Horowitz's discussion concludes with a sobering meditation on limitations and disappointments that seem to ensue when art and utopian ideology fuse.

Chapter 4

May Day, Tractors, and Piglets: Yiddish Songs for Little Communists

Anna Shternshis

Grigorii B., an eighty-two-year-old retired businessman, takes his daily stroll to his neighborhood coffee shop in midtown Manhattan. Grigorii was born in the Ukrainian *shtetl* Orynin in 1918. On one beautiful April afternoon, I join Grigorii to learn details of his remarkable life story. After he lost his parents in 1927, he moved to Leningrad to live in a Jewish orphanage. During World War II, Grigorii was wounded several times, yet remained in service through 1945. In 1973, he and his family moved to the United States and settled in New York. I ask him whether he has any pleasant memories from before the war. "Oh, yes," he says. "I loved singing, especially Yiddish songs." He immediately begins to sing quietly, but clearly:

Gekoyft hot mame Shimelen	Mother bought Shimele
A shterndl a roytn,	A little red star,
Hot Shimele es ongeton	Shimele put it on
Un hot zikh shtark gefreyt.	And was delighted
Zogt di mame Shimelen:	Mother says to Shimele:
Kum Shimele aher!	Come here, Shimele!
Bavayz nor mit di fiselekh,	Show me with your feet,
Vi geyt a pioner.[1]	How a pioneer walks.

This song, written by L. Rosenblum, appeared in the January 1926 issue of the Yiddish children's literary magazine *Pioner*.[2] Strikingly, Grigorii sings it identically to the published text. He says that he remembers the song because he performed it at a local theater workshop at the Jewish orphanage in 1929. Grigorii explains that the song reflected "the spirit of that era." When I ask him about other Yiddish songs he liked during his childhood, he replies, "The Yiddish songs that I learned at the orphanage are especially dear to my heart. All of us [children] in the orphanage did not have many joys in life. We did not have loving parents, home-cooked meals, and any affection. But these patriotic Yiddish songs made us feel that we had a motherland and that someone loved us. I understand now that these were propagandistic songs, but when I was a little boy, I absolutely loved them."[3] Grigorii is very critical of the Soviet regime, its postwar policies toward Jews, and the Communist ideology. Yet he still sings Yiddish Communist songs from his childhood when he meets old friends. He acknowledges that these songs had a significant influence on the formation of his literary and cultural tastes. He also says that he knows many apolitical Yiddish songs that were popular in that era. So why did Grigorii, who generally disagrees with Soviet propaganda messages, choose to sing a Communist Yiddish song as his favorite example of prewar Yiddish culture?

Grigorii's attitude to Communist Yiddish songs illustrates one of the major successes of early Soviet propaganda in creating a new Jewish culture and identity. As Anne Gorsuch, a historian of Soviet youth, has argued:

Making the new youth culture was one of the most important projects of the Soviet government in the 1920s, as it prepared the path for the future development of Soviet citizens. The successful transformation of young people was essential to the Bolshevik project. The young generation was seen as the part of society which could grow up free from the corruption of pre-revolutionary Russia. The youth were the guarantor of future social and political hegemony, insofar as they were able or willing to replicate the ideology and culture of the Bolshevik Party. As the new model of Soviet men and women, Soviet youth had to be made communist in every aspect of their daily lives—worlds, leisure, gender relations, and family life.[4]

Young people from ages nine to twenty-four constituted about a third of all Soviet Jews in 1926, and a quarter in 1939, which represented 893,607 and 755,000 people respectively.[5] Like all other groups living within the Russian empire, young Jews faced tremendous changes and challenges after the Russian Revolution of 1917. They were subjected to intensive propaganda directed to them both as Jews and as young people. The process of assimilation, urbanization, Russification, and acculturation, which affected the majority of Jews in the country, was especially focused on youngsters. In the 1920s and 1930s, young people were the first to leave the smaller towns within the Pale of Settlement for larger urban centers in Russia.[6] Yet they usually did so after finishing seven years of secondary school, therefore spending the earliest years of their lives in a Yiddish-speaking environment.[7]

In 1918, the *Evsektsii* (the Jewish sections of the Communist Party) began to take steps against the traditional Jewish educational system—*khadorim* (Jewish religious primary schools) and *yeshives* (Jewish religious secondary schools)—as well as against the Jewish religion itself. In 1922–23, committees for the "Liquidation of the *khadorim*" were organized in towns and hamlets where Jews resided. As an alternative to traditional Jewish institutions of education, a great number of Soviet Jewish schools were established in the mid-1920s. These schools were designed for children whose mother tongue was Yiddish. Jewish parents often preferred that their children attend Russian schools because they felt that doing so gave the children more opportunities for the future, but government officials insisted that Yiddish-speaking children study at Soviet-run Yiddish-language schools, since many ideologues believed that children would learn Soviet values better if they were taught in their mother tongue. Despite the fact that a significant number of Jewish parents opposed sending their children to Soviet Yiddish schools, these institutions rapidly expanded from 366 in 1923–24, to 775 in 1926–27, and then to 1,100 in 1929–30.[8] As a result, hundreds of thousands of Soviet Jewish children received their primary education in Yiddish.[9]

Schools were seen by the Soviet government not only as educational institutions but also as an important mechanism that could be used to disseminate propaganda. Their goal was first to "convert" children to a belief in Soviet doctrine and then to use them to gradually educate their parents. Soviet movies, short stories, and theatrical performances from this era were filled with images of "progressive" children who explained new values to their parents and grandparents.[10] The incorporation of songs into curricular as well as extracurricular activities served both purposes. Songs were also a great learning tool, and Soviet Yiddish schools actively integrated them into their curricula. Children learned singing during language and literature classes, and especially during obligatory extracurricular activities.[11] Public performances of these propagandistic songs at meetings, concerts, and theatrical performances helped to "educate" adults as well. In the 1920s and 1930s, more than fifty collections of Yiddish folksongs appeared in the Soviet Union, as well as approximately one hundred pieces of sheet music, approximately half of which were designed specifically for younger audiences.[12] State publishing houses issued at least one or two collections of "suitable" Yiddish children's songs per year from 1921 to 1937.[13] Approved children's songs also appeared in children's magazines and teachers' journals, as well as newspapers.

In this essay, I analyze how the texts and melodies of children's propaganda songs introduced ideological messages to Yiddish-speaking children. Without a consideration of the popular reception of these songs, the analysis would not be complete. To determine which of the officially promoted songs reached their audiences and which remained largely unknown, I interviewed about two hundred former students of Soviet Yiddish schools about the songs they learned in school in the 1920s and 1930s.[14] Most of them were born in the territory of the former Pale of Settlement, the territory within the borders of czarist Russia wherein the residence of Jews was legally authorized. The Pale of Settlement included parts of modern Ukraine, Byelorussia, and parts of Russia. Many of the interview participants had moved to bigger cities after graduation. About half of them both remembered the existence of Soviet Yiddish children's songs and could sing or recite some of them. These are the people whose responses form the basis for this essay. That so many of these Yiddish-speaking respondents (ninety-eight out of one hundred and ninety-five) remembered songs that they had last heard seventy years prior to the interview indicates their impact and significance.

The beauty of the oral history method is that it allows individual stories to be heard and analyzed in a larger historical context. Yet, because the primary goal of this study was to examine the popular reception of Soviet policies, I only use the "least original" testimonies. For example, the appearance of a testimony in this essay means that I heard a similar idea or statement from at least ten respondents, and in some cases from more than fifty.[15] I noticed no significant variations between memories of Yiddish songs among respondents who lived in Moscow and those who immigrated to the United States or Germany. In all cases, those memories were surprisingly fresh. Correlating what they remembered with what has been published reveals a fascinating picture of the reception of official Yiddish culture among people who were children in the late 1920s and early 1930s.

Collectivism and Soviet Holidays

In the early 1920s, compilers of Yiddish children's songs for teachers acknowledged the utilitarian function of music. An anonymous editor of one of the first collections of Yiddish children's songs for kindergarten students, which was produced by a state-sponsored publishing house, asserted, "Songs had to teach the children about the nature that surrounded them, and needed to combine play with work."[16]

M. Limone, an editor of the collection *Thirty Songs for Children*, further asserted, "Songs will make [the] ideological upbringing of children easier and more effective."[17] Indeed, even when songs in these collections were devoted to such seemingly neutral subjects as nature, animals, and games, they still promoted values of significant importance to Soviet ideology, such as collectivism, technical progress, and atheism. The ideas of collectivism were important in all genres of Soviet official mass publications from the 1920s. According to Vladimir Papernyi, a new "horizontal culture" appeared in the Soviet Union soon after the revolution, the main feature of which was a shift of focus from the individual to the masses.[18] Almost all the children's songs published in Yiddish between 1919 and 1921 featured "we" as the main actor (as opposed to a possible "I" as a particular hero). In these songs, "we" were happy to be participants of the revolution, "we" benefited from the policies of the new government, "we" were prepared to build socialism. In the 1930s, this tendency was replaced by a "vertical" culture, which featured individual achievements and aspirations.

A popular way to introduce collectivism in the 1920s was through marching songs. Marching was an important children's activity, and marching songs, which were easy to learn, could contain political information and slogans. The lyrics of these new Yiddish pieces were simple and easy to remember, and the melodies were suitable for marching. One example of such Yiddish march is an anonymous song from *Zamlbukh fun kinder lider* (Collection of Children Songs), published in 1921:

Lomir ale in eynem marshirn,	Let us all march together,
Far di hentlekh zikh nemen getray.	Take each other by the hand.
Lomir ale in eynem zikh rirn,	Let us all move together,
Mit di fislekh geyen fray.[19]	And walk freely with our feet.

In this song, which encourages children to demonstrate their unity by marching together, rhythmic movement conveys an ideological message. Soviets often used marches in conjunction with Communist activities, although many such marches were also common before the revolution, albeit with other meanings.

Poems by non-Soviet writers were also used. The Lithuanian Yiddish poet Itsik Katsenelson (1885–1942) authored one of the most frequently published ones:

Khotsh mir zaynen	Though we are
Yung un kleyn,	Young and small,
Vi di heldn	We have to walk
Darf men geyn![20]	Like heroes!

This song was popular in other countries as well, but only Soviet Jewish children were required to sing such Yiddish marching songs in school, in classes and extracurricular activities.

Singing Yiddish songs while parading around town with red flags was one of the most vivid memories among participants in such events. Ian D. (born in 1919 in Berdichev) explains:

When we saw young people marching in the streets, we immediately wanted to join them. I remember once I saw such a band. It was a small band, and they played musical instruments. For us children it was a big deal at that time, so we all followed them. They were lined up in columns. They were wearing beautiful clothes, some green and blue shirts and white shorts. At that time, the *komyugistn* [Young Communist League members] used to wear uniforms. And we sang together with them, because the words of these songs were so easy to remember.[21]

Ian, who was able to recite several different children's marches, reveals that children enjoyed marching songs not only because they featured easy to memorize lyrics and melodies but also because they were associated with festive and unusual activities, such as public demonstrations, usually conducted during Soviet holidays. Children's performances, which provided not only education but also ideologically appropriate entertainment, played a central role in the creation of new Soviet celebratory rituals designed to legitimate the state. Moreover, children's marching songs were the first element of Soviet mass culture to be deployed in the creation of new Soviet holidays.

The new Soviet calendar was synchronized with the seasons such that spring, for example, was associated with May Day, an official Soviet holiday:

Eyns un tsvey, dray un fir	One and two, three and four,
Es tsegeyt der letster shney	The last snow is melting
Geyt di freylekhe armey . . .	The cheerful army marches . . .
Felder, kinder, zun un may	Fields, children, sun and May
Gasn, fonen, may un mir	Streets, flags, May and we,
Gasn, fonen, may un mir	Streets, flags, May and peace
Eyns, tsvey, dray, fir	One, two, three, four
May un mir	May and peace
Zingen mir.[22]	We sing.

Itsik Fefer (1900–52), the author of this poem, connects signs of spring's awakening, such as melting snow and newly green fields, with new political symbols, such as "cheerful" steps of the army, flags, and children singing revolutionary marches. The song also incorporates the Soviet slogan of the 1920s, "May and peace," but pointedly uses the Russian words *may i mir,* not *sholem,* the Yiddish word for "peace." However, because *mir* also means "we" in Yiddish, the last line can be read in two ways: either as "May and peace" or as "May and we." Fefer incorporates this wordplay into the song to create an impression of organic connection between Soviet slogans and Yiddish, one of several strategies for creating specifically Jewish rituals for Soviet holidays.

Artistic methods were not the only ways to make sure new songs reached their intended audience. Soviet educational institutions incorporated them into rituals of daily life. Children studied Yiddish May Day songs in school and performed them during locally organized parades on that holiday. Such street celebrations are among the most vivid recollections of the 1920s and 1930s. Tsirl B. (born in 1920 in Shepetovka, Ukraine) recalls: "During May Day, all Jewish residents of our *shtetl* went to the market, where a Yiddish meeting was organized. There were speeches and music . . . But in fact, everyone knew that they went to the meeting place because children were performing. We rehearsed for many hours in school before the event, and finally during the meeting, we marched and sang. Some songs were in Russian, others in Yiddish. Our parents and neighbors were delighted."[23] Hearing Jewish children sing Yiddish songs on Soviet holidays clearly made a striking impression on older Jewish audiences. Some testimonies suggest that parents who opposed the Soviet regime and its ideology attended the events during which their children performed Soviet songs.[24] As for the children, they associated singing on festive public celebrations with vacations from school and the approval of adoring parents and teachers.

Almost all those who remember these songs tend to agree that their content was less important than their rhythms, memorable melodies, and, of course, performers. Yet the song lyrics conveyed vital messages. Using catchy marching rhymes, children's songs often described Soviet holiday rituals in detail, explained their meaning, and glorified demonstrations, flags, automobiles, and the festive mood associated with Soviet holidays, as can be seen in the following song by R. Boyarskaya:

Freylekh, lustik	Merry, happy
Ale, ale—fray	Everyone is free
S'geyt der yontev—	The holiday is coming
Ershter may!	May Day!
. . . . .	. . . .
Flien avto,	Cars fly
Ful mit kind	Full of children
Keplekh, hentlekh,	Heads, hands
Shvimt un shvimt![25]	Swim, swim!

This song described not how May Day was celebrated in reality but rather how it was supposed to be celebrated, a typical feature of socialist realism, a style that began to dominate Soviet literary culture in the 1930s.[26] Actual celebrations of Soviet holidays were usually not as colorful or crowded as depicted in this song, since many Jews still lived in smaller towns where cars were not that common. Still, songs depicting an idealized celebration made their way into real celebrations of the holiday as a way adding to the festive atmosphere.

Indeed, these songs may have served as effective tools for indoctrinating the young. Many oral histories suggest that a substantial number of participants in such festivities agreed with Soviet policies and the ideological content of these celebrations. Semyon S. (born in 1918 in Kuty, Ukraine) attests:

In 1927, our *shtetl* celebrated the tenth anniversary of the October revolution. It was a beautiful fall day. The sun shined, as it shines now. In the center of the *shtetl*, near the former mansion of the governor, there was a park. A soapbox was built in the square, and a column of people marched through town. It was a Jewish column. A gym teacher was the leader of the parade. I remember his Yiddish accent when he said [in Russian] "At, dva, at, dva" (one, two, one two). This is a typically Jewish expression. The head of the column was Roza, the daughter of the rabbi. She had a red tie on. She also carried a flag and was singing a song. It was a Komsomol [Young Communist League] song.

I do not remember why I was not in the column. I was standing near one Jew, who was a former Talmud teacher. He was soon surrounded by older people. The column yelled Soviet slogans, sang songs, but he did not pay attention to this. The teacher said, "Listen to me, boys. This will not last long . . ." And people agreed with him.[27]

This testimony provides a colorful picture of the celebration of May Day in Kuty. The respondent's description of a schoolteacher, a rabbi's daughter, and old men speaking about the implications of the Soviet regime vividly portrays popular attitudes toward the new holiday: the younger generation seemed to enjoy themselves more than did their elders, who were cautious and more skeptical.

Semyon refers to "at, dva" as a "specifically Jewish" expression, but there is nothing "Jewish" about it, except, perhaps, the Yiddish accent of the man who pronounced it. This is one of several indications that, although Soviet propaganda attempted to promote the "internationalist" essence of holidays, Semyon and others experienced the celebration of May Day as a Jewish event, conducted in Yiddish with only Jewish participants. Mariya K. (born in 1918 in Ukraine) recalls that Jews celebrated May Day and the anniversary of the October revolution separately from non-Jews: "I remember we were standing in straight columns, and then began singing . . . It was something about May Day. It was in Yiddish . . . We marched around the marketplace, and everyone was waving to us. Jews celebrated May Day in Yiddish, and Ukrainians had their own demonstration in Ukrainian."[28]

Paradoxically, Yiddish songs designed to explain socialist ideas to Yiddish-speaking Jews and to promote universal holidays and universal collectivism served indirectly to establish collective Jewish rituals for celebrating Soviet holidays.

Many respondents even spoke about how Soviet Yiddish songs were incorporated into celebrations of traditional Jewish holidays. Matvey G. (born in 1922 in Zhmerinka, Ukraine) recalls:

My parents celebrated all Jewish holidays. For Rosh Hashanah, all my aunts and uncles and their children gathered at my parents' house. It was a very small house, we sat on wooden benches, and the children had their own table. Then, my mother would say: "Motya, sing for the guests!" I would get up, stand on a bench (I was only five or six years old), and sing a song we learned in school. I still remember it:

S'z geshtorbn undzer Lenin	Our Lenin died
Un er ligt in mavzoley	He lies in a mausoleum
Un mit shvartse royte fonen	And with black and red flags
Geyen kinder eynts un tsvey![29]	Children march, one and two.

Everyone clapped, and I got an apple. My grandfather was sitting next to me, and said, "You are a good boy." And my grandmother gave me another piece of *lekekh* [honey cake].[30]

Matvey and many other respondents (fifty-seven out of ninety-eight) assert that during festive meals of Passover and Rosh Hashanah, children were asked to sing songs that they learned in school for the guests, which usually consisted of extended family. Thus, paradoxically, the inclusion of children's Yiddish songs in Jewish religious celebrations is especially notable because many of these songs were designed to combat religion both directly and indirectly and because Yiddish children's songs, more than any other genre of Soviet Yiddish culture, promoted the idea that human achievements, not divine will, was the driving force of progress.

Images of Technology in Yiddish Children's Songs

Many songs were devoted to the description of various professions (factory and railway workers, peasants, gardeners, drivers, tailors, and shoemakers) and to the role of technology in revolutionizing labor. The literary critic Vladimir Papernyi notes the importance of the idea of technological progress in the construction of socialist culture and its cult of the machine, which was similar to a religious cult.[31] Cars, airplanes, electricity, and the radio symbolized the accomplishments of the Soviet state and evoked feelings of a wonderful socialist future, full of new revolutionary light and energy. Descriptions of technical progress that appear in Yiddish songs are consistent with these ideas, as can be seen in a song that exalts radio:

Iber yam	Over sea
Iber feld	Over field
Iber dorf	Over village
Un shtot	And city
Geyt dos vort	Goes a word
Geyt der klang	Goes a sound
Geyt gezang	Goes a song
Radio, radio, radio![32]	Radio, radio, radio!

Glorifying technical progress was also in keeping with the romanticization of labor, as can be seen in the following song, which has a cheerful melody:

Mashinen hudyen, binen	Machines buzz, hum,
S'tsitern di vent,	The walls shake,
Kh'shtey do bay mashinen	I stand here near the machines
Mit tseglite hent.	With lowered hands.
Vern do geshafn	Here are created
Toyzenter por shikh.	Thousands of pairs of shoes.
Redlekh un pasn	Wheels and stripes
Loyfn azoy gikh.	Run so fast.
Hudyen der baginen	The dawn buzzes
Hudiet der hudok	The hooter buzzes
Shtiler zayt mashinen	Calm down, machines
Rut a bisl op.[33]	Rest a little bit.

This song focuses on the incorporation of technology into the industrial process. The protagonist "stands with lowered hands" because machines do all the work for him, consistent with the government's emphasis on modernizing working conditions. Faina M. (born in 1919 in Arynin,

Ukraine) recalled that this song was used in a children's production in her Yiddish school: "Children were dressed up in working clothes; they had wheels and hammers in their hands. They ran around the stage and pretended to be the machines which made shoes. I was one of those children ... And one boy, I remember his name until now, Misha Groys, was singing, something like 'Shtiler zayt mashinen, rut a bisl op!' [Machines, calm down, get some rest!]. And we would stop. It was such a success, this performance!"[34] Incorporating such songs into a theatrical performance enhanced their popularity.

One of the chief goals of children's songs was to create enthusiasm for labor, and Yiddish ones were no exception. The above song, which portrayed new equipment as essential to improving working conditions, made the profession of shoemaker more modern and industrial and therefore more attractive to potential workers. Factories were highly romanticized by comparing industrial noises with music, for example. Lullabies even suggested that this "music" would help to rock children to sleep:

Rut zhe, shloft zhe	Rest, please, sleep please
Shloft biz tog	Sleep until morning
Biz s'nemt huden	Until the [factory] whistle
Der hudok	Starts buzzing
Hu-hu-hu-hu.	Hu-hu-hu-hu.
In fabrik shoyn	In the factory already
Fun baginen	Since dawn
Chak-chak, chak-chak.	Chak-chak, chak-chak.
Di mashinen	The machines [clack]
Tik-tak, tik-tak.	Tik-tak, tik-tak.
Hamers klapn	Hammers are knocking
Pikh-pekh, pikh-pekh.[35]	Pikh-pekh, pikh-pekh.

Note that while songwriters were instructed not to personify animals by making them speak or think (since "[t]his would mislead the child in understanding the laws of nature"), they were encouraged to animate machines and tools. Like humans, machines could speak an intelligible language.[36] They could communicate with people. They could feel and express themselves—they sniffed and sang.

Songs about industrial equipment glorified not only factory labor but also agriculture. Because of the massive ideological campaign that promoted the resettlement of Jews to collective farms in the mid-1920s, many children's songs promoted agricultural work. Once again, the use of technical equipment was presented as a Soviet achievement:

Aker un aker, traktor	Plough and plough, tractor
Aker un aker tif	Plough and plough deep
Dos, vos eyner kon nit,	What one cannot do alone
Kon a kolektiv	A collective can.

Vos a ferdl kon nit,	What a horse cannot,
Dos a traktor kon—	The tractor can—
Fun a hektar kerner	From a hectare of rye
Nerer vi a ton.	More than a ton.

Aker un aker, traktor	Plough and plough, tractor,
Aker un aker tif	Plough and plough deep
Aker tif di felder	Plough deep the fields
Fun dem kolektiv.[37]	Of the collective.

This song combines ideas of collectivism with the promotion of tractors as a symbol of technological progress. Catchy slogans such as "What one [person] cannot do alone, a collective can" were taken from the official rhetoric of the time. The last verse asserts that combining the strengths of equipment with the collective effort will produce the most effective results in agricultural enterprises. In this way, such songs incorporated easy-to-learn slogans, a clear ideological message, catchy lyrics, and rhythmic melody, all of which made such songs more likely to be remembered.

Images of high-tech tools in descriptions of agriculture not only demonstrated the progressiveness of Soviet technology but also emphasized connections between farming and industry and the workers in each sector through such symbols as the hammer and sickle, which became the official Soviet emblem:

Ikh mit dir getrayer bruder	You and me, my loyal brother
Ikh bam hamer, du—bam serp	Me with the hammer, you with the sickle
Ikh vel shmidn dir an aker	I will forge you a plough
Du vest akern dem feld.[38]	You will plough the field.

Songs combining a description of agricultural labor with details of the daily routine of a Soviet farmer promoted labor, encouraged the Soviet lifestyle, and supported youth movements such as Young Pioneers and the Communist Youth League:

Mitvokh nokhn buker	Wednesday after the combine
Donershtik nokhn plug	Thursday after the plough
Fraytik nokhn brone	Friday after the harrow
Shabes in komyug.[39]	Saturday in the Komsomol [club].

The hero of this song is the ideal Soviet youngster, as seen by the Soviet ideologues: one who dedicates his or her work to the Communist regime, takes advantage of all the benefits provided by the Soviet government, such as latest technical equipment, and socializes in government-sponsored places such as *komyug* (Communist Youth club).

While technological progress was relevant to all ethnic groups of the Soviet Union, Yiddish children's songs helped to universalize this idea by making the young singers feel themselves to be part of a larger Soviet culture. Still, the songs that portrayed and addressed the perfect Soviet Jew were slightly different from songs addressed to their non-Jewish Russian counterparts.

Jewish Notions in Soviet Yiddish Songs for Children

The ways in which Yiddish children's songs differ from Soviet songs in other languages made them especially relevant to young Jewish listeners. The song "Mitvokh nokhn buker," which described a working week on a collective farm and emphasized that it combined work and pleasure, also mentions *shabes* (Sabbath, the Jewish day of rest), which here is associated with Soviet-sponsored recreation, such as entertainment in a Komsomol club. This mention of *shabes* was part of a wider anti-religious propaganda effort to promote the substitution of religious holidays with Soviet equivalents.

Consistent with the Soviet policy of discouraging religious observance, Jews were encouraged to raise pigs, and Yiddish children's songs about Soviet farming are rife with images of these animals. In these songs, children groom pigs, play with them, and take care of them, much more than is the case with any other animals, including cows, dogs, cats, and birds, which are more popular in Russian-language children's songs. One of the most popular "Yiddish pig songs" was "Anna Vanna," which describes the excitement of children observing pigs and piglets. The song became widely known as a children's declamatory poem and later as a song. It was written by Leyb Kvitko (1890–1952), one of the most famous Soviet Yiddish poets, and was later translated into Russian by Sergey Mihalkov, a famous Russian poet and author of both Soviet and Russian national anthems.

"Anna Vanna," which became a favorite poem for many generations of Soviet children, started out as a semi-propagandistic effort to "promote" swine breeding among Jewish children. It takes the form of a dialogue between a brigade leader working with pigs and children who come to watch the process:

Ana Vana brigadir	Anna Vanna, brigade leader,
Efn uf fun shtal di tir.	Open the sty door.
Vayz di naye sheyne	Show the beautiful new
Khazerlekh di kleyne.[40]	Little piglets.

Later in this song, pioneers ask whether the pigs are pink or pale, hairy or bald, clean or dirty. While the descriptions of pigs are elaborated and the cuteness of piglets emphasized, the song treats the interest of children as a casual "part of the landscape" rather than explain directly that growing pigs was a radical departure from Jewish tradition. Because authors of propagandistic songs for adults aimed to destroy existing beliefs and traditions, they had to name what they repudiated. In contrast, the creators of children's songs started from the assumption that children were a tabula rasa and would grow up free of any knowledge of Jewish laws and practices. It was therefore neither necessary nor advisable to mention Jewish tradition, even in negative terms. Thus, songs promoting swine breeding would not call attention to the Jewish taboo against eating pork and the associated aversion to pigs.

Many respondents remembered songs about pigs fondly and did not associate them with anti-religious propaganda. Some sixty-five out ninety-eight respondents remembered the existence of such songs: forty-seven of the sixty-five spoke about these songs without a leading question; and twenty-three were able to sing the above song in a version rather close to the published original. Yet when I asked whether they saw these songs as anti-religious propaganda, all respondents disagreed. The response of Mikhail B. (born in Kiev, Ukraine, in 1921) was typical: "Songs about pigs had nothing to do with propaganda. These were songs for children, and everyone liked them, Jews and non-Jews. Yiddish songs were the same as Russian ones, and they taught children about animals."[41] From this and other similar testimonies, it is easy to conclude that even when the creators of propaganda songs for Yiddish-speaking children included notions considered relevant specifically to a Jewish audience, rapidly acculturating Jewish children, who were departing from a traditional Jewish way of life, often did not recognize them as propagandistic.

At the same time, children did recognize specifically Jewish references in the songs, particularly the promotion of resettlement to Birobidzhan, a province in the far east of Russia that was endorsed by the Soviet government in 1928 and officially established in 1934 as a Jewish autonomous region. David Hofshteyn (1899–1952), a famous Yiddish poet, wrote a song that was entirely devoted to teaching children how to pronounce the difficult word "Birobidzhan":

Biro, biro iz nokh gring,   Biro is still easy to say,
Etvos shverer iz Bidzhan.   A little more difficult to say is Bidzhan.
Itster, kinder, git a kling—   Now, children, let us pronounce together—
Birobidzhan, birobidzhan![42]   Birobidzhan, Birobidzhan!

Numerous testimonies (thirty-two out of ninety-eight) reveal that listeners of that era also thought of such songs as specifically Jewish.

Yet popular interpretations often differed from official ones. Sometimes the messages of Soviet Yiddish songs were reinterpreted to contradict the propaganda's intent (without any alteration of the words or melody). Efim G. (born in 1918 in Parichi, Byelorussia) explained that many people in his hometown did not take propaganda songs seriously and in fact laughed at them. He remembered how one popular song about resettlement was interpreted sarcastically:

During a performance in our amateur theater, actors, who were often children, performed songs about the new way of life. I remember once I was singing a song about Birobidzhan:

S'fort a yidene in mark	A Jewess goes to market,
Mit a groysn kheyshek.	With lots of courage.
Fort a yidene in Birobidzhan	A Jewess goes to Birobidzhan
Hodeven a loshek!	To raise a calf!
Op-lya, op-lya, hodeven a loshek!	Op-lya, op-lya, to raise a calf!

I was singing the song, and other children were acting during this performance. One girl played the *yidene* [a pejorative for a Jewish woman]). She was wearing a big dress with some pillows underneath. She was showing how she loved to go to the market, and how she did not want to go to Birobidzhan. However, she was encouraged by her young energetic sons (played by two boys) to move there. While singing the "Op-lya" refrain, we would take this quite full-bodied girl and flip her up. It looked extremely funny, the audience was laughing.[43]

Yidene is a term that usually refers to a talkative, petty, sentimental woman. Here the term suggests that she is stereotypical of the old order, and the intention of the song is to demonstrate that even such a "backward" person should be eager to go Birobidzhan and build a new life there. Efim's recollection about this satirical play reveals that those who settled in Birobidzhan were seen not as heroes but as foolish eccentrics. Yet, the only Jewish theme in children's Soviet Yiddish songs recognized as such by my respondents was Birobidzhan. They did not interpret the promotion of pig breeding and anti-religious propaganda as specifically Jewish concerns, although their propagandistic messages often had far-reaching, long-term consequences, to cite the overwhelming majority of post-Soviet Jews whom I interviewed, who ate pork regularly and saw no religious problem in so doing. Moreover, for my respondents, the observance of other Jewish religious traditions did not constitute a part of Jewish culture or identity.

Children's songs were one of the most important genres of Soviet propaganda music directed at Jews during the interwar period. Children were a vital part of the Soviet propaganda machine, and songs carrying ideological messages were obligatory in school and were performed in children's amateur theatrical performances. Children's songs therefore had a captive audience, in contrast to other songs, which had to attract listeners. For this and other reasons, Yiddish songs for children were the only genre of Soviet Yiddish official culture that truly reached the masses (children in this case) in the 1920s. After receiving state-approved ideological messages in school, children were expected to deliver them to their parents.[44]

While the majority of people whom I interviewed (176 of 195) emphasized that they never directly protested when their parents celebrated traditional Jewish holidays or went to synagogue, many (61 people) asserted that they performed songs and poems they learned in school during family celebrations of Rosh Hashanah and Passover.[45] These children's Yiddish songs served as a link between traditional Jewish family upbringing and state-imposed ideology. A song in Yiddish performed by an eleven-year-old child could bridge the gap between a traditional Jewish lifestyle and Soviet propaganda. Even though some parents might not have taken the content of the children's songs seriously, they listened simply because their children performed them, even though there is some evidence that some parents soundly disapproved of the ideological messages in these songs.[46] Others did not particularly enjoy their children performing Communist pieces at home but did not say anything, so that the children did not repeat their words in school or other official settings. Still, simple children's marching songs were often the first "doves" of propaganda to enter Jewish homes in the late 1920s and 1930s. By the late 1930s, many of these amateur children's songs were also promoted as Yiddish folk songs sympathetic to the regime. For example, the song "Mitvokh nokhn buker" appeared in Dobrushin and Yuditskii's 1940 collection as just such a folk song.[47]

When rapidly growing and assimilating children moved to a Russian-speaking environment, they stopped speaking Yiddish on daily basis. Yet most of them retained some recollection of the Soviet Yiddish culture of their childhood. The songs they had learned in school and during after-school activities remained ingrained in their memory, sometimes as the only thing they remembered of their youth.

Chapter 5

Performing the State:
The Jewish Palestine Pavilion at the New York
World's Fair, 1939/40

Barbara Kirshenblatt-Gimblett

World's fairs became a prime site for transforming the Holy Land into the Jewish homeland. For most of the history of world's fairs, Jews were defined as a religious group and were included in parliaments, halls, temples, and exhibitions of religion. This was by no means the only context in which Jews might be found at world's fairs, but it was a particularly hospitable one because it let them perform an ideal of citizenship predicated on religious liberty.[1] Even when the basis for their inclusion was religion, Jews defined themselves in broader cultural and historical terms. With the rise of Jewish national aspirations, Zionists seized the opportunity afforded by world's fairs to promote a Jewish homeland in Palestine. If, in earlier fairs, the contest for Palestine was a struggle between Christians and Jews for the Holy Land, the competition for Palestine in later fairs was between Jews and Arabs for national sovereignty. By the 1930s Zionists were taking charge of the "official" Jewish presence at world's fairs in the form of Zionist pageants and Palestine exhibits, the most ambitious of which was the Jewish Palestine Pavilion at the New York World's Fair in 1939/40.

I will argue that the Jewish Palestine Pavilion attempted to perform the state into being by staging de facto statehood in the gap between the world of the fair and the world itself, a gap that widened with the approach of World War II. By *world of the fair*, I mean, first, an envisioned totality and, second, the idea of bringing the entire world into one space. By *performing the state into being*, I mean that the Pavilion itself was a "performance" within the theater of the Fair. By suggesting that the world of the fair—and the Jewish Palestine Pavilion—were also performative, I point to the conviction on the part of their organizers that such displays would help to bring about that which they postulated.[2]

Those who organized the New York World's Fair (and those responsible for the Jewish Palestine Pavilion) expressed precisely this distinction—

Figure 5.1. "Palestine Exhibits Building," New York World's Fair, 1939/40.
Postcard published by Frank E. Cooper, 258 Broadway, New York. "This pavilion,
built about a patio reminiscent of the age-old Mediterranean tradition, houses an
exhibit of the concrete achievements of the Jewish people in the rebuilding of their
National Home. El-Hanani is the architect."

between performance and performative—in their own terms. Listen to
Grover Whalen, president of the Fair Corporation (until the end of the
1939 season), characterize the Fair in his autobiography some years later:
"This then was the Fair—primarily a great theater. Not only the prosce-
nium behind which a thousand entertainments might pass to delight the
spectator, but also an amphitheater—vast enough, deep enough, distinguished enough to show the average man how the powers of the universe
might be alerted to sustain and comfort him."[3] The Fair was thus both a
setting for performances, as in theater or architecture, and a performance
in its own right. But Whalen goes further. Note the sequence of terms in
the passage that he quotes from a brochure that promised that the Fair
would *present* "a clear, unified, and comprehensive picture of . . . ," *depict*
the past, *show* "how the present has evolved out of the past," and *project*
"the average man into the World of Tomorrow."[4] This series leads to the
following summation: "By setting forth what has been beside what is, the
Fair of 1939 will predict, may even dictate, the shape of things to come."[5]
The sequence of terms—present, depict, show, project, predict, dictate—
shifts the ground from the *exhibition as performance* (as show) to the *performativity of exhibition* (as action).

This sequence—from showing to projecting to predicting to dictating—is at the heart of what might be called the agency of display. The official guide to the New York World's Fair is positively rhapsodic on this point:

The true poets of the twentieth century are the designers, the architects, and the engineers who glimpse some inner vision, create some beautiful figment of the imagination and then translate it into valid actuality for the world to enjoy. Such is the poetic process; the poet translates his inspiration into terms that convey vivid sensation to his fellow men. But instead of some compelling pattern of words you have a great articulation that is far more tangible and immediate; exhibits that embody imaginative ideas, buildings, murals, sculptures and landscapes . . . The designer's dream on paper and charts is only a tentative gesture toward reality, for the engineer and the works are the indispensable middlemen who translate a dream into a fact.[6]

Note the sequence: *imagination* to *actuality; inspiration* to *sensation; words* and *ideas* to the *tangible, immediate,* and *embodied; dream* to *reality* and *fact.*

The theme, "World of Tomorrow," referred to a world planned by architects, engineers, and designers—that is, a centrally planned though decentralized world. The generally unstated affinities between the total, the totalizing, and the totalitarian—and the emphasis on "big picture" statements, whether in the form of iconic architecture, photomurals, panoramas, dioramas, or scale models—were everywhere to be found at the Fair, from Democracity and Futurama to the Soviet and Italian pavilions. Democracity was a garden city, with its urban business core (Centerton), surrounded by green countryside, and satellite towns, both residential (Pleasantvilles) and industrial (Millvilles). Democracity, the creation of the prominent industrial designer Henry Dreyfuss, was a "symbol of a perfectly integrated, futuristic metropolis pulsing with life and rhythm and music."[7] Futurama, the featured exhibit of General Motors, showed the world in 1960: seen as if from an airplane, Futurama promoted the automobile by demonstrating what the world would look like when it was properly prepared through "super-highways, speed lanes, and multi-decked bridges."[8]

The Jewish Palestine Pavilion was in keeping with the idea that envisioning, planning, and rehearsal not only made visions of the future immediate within the world of the Fair but could also make them actual in the world itself. First, however, the organizers of the Pavilion had to contend with the reality that Jewish Palestine was not a state and that the Jewish Palestine Pavilion was privately, not state, sponsored.

A Nation among Nations

It is no accident that world's fairs, for all their rhetoric about peace, have often taken place in the context of war, when national claims are at their most contested.[9] Planned in the mid-1930s, during the Great Depression and rise of fascism in Europe, the Fair could barely keep up with changes on the geopolitical map. Even before it opened, the Fair was billed as a peace table of the world "around which the sixty nations will sit down and work out their problems," or so it was hoped.[10] The Fair put itself forward as evidence of the American policy of neutrality, though the organizers were defiant in their opposition to Hitler and refused to invite Germany to participate in the 1939 fair; the Soviet pavilion was demolished before the 1940 fair opened.

However closely the world of the fair was aligned with the world outside the fair when foreign participants first signed up, the gap between them only widened as war approached. No wonder those wanting to make national claims would take the world of the fair as seriously as they took the world itself. They used the world of the fair—a utopian space in any case—to perform a world order as they thought it should be, not as it was or was becoming.

If, as Roland Robertson claims, "the idea of nationalism (or particularism) develops *only* in tandem with internationalism," then the agency of a world's fair lies precisely in how it configures and performs internationalism, understood as a "system, in which each state officially recognizes the internal sovereignty of its neighbours."[11] If, as Michael Billig argues, "The nation is always a nation in a world of nations," then it is the task of a world's fair to create a virtual world of nations such that copresence in the world of the fair, a highly charged space of diplomacy and propaganda, becomes in itself an indication of mutual recognition.[12] For nations aspiring to statehood or trying to regain their sovereignty, the recognition of other states within the world of the fair would be a moral victory. The Jewish Palestine Pavilion was neither the first nor the last to use a world's fair to this end.

Meyer Weisgal, the Zionist impresario who spearheaded the creation of the Jewish Palestine Pavilion, fully appreciated that to treat the Jewish Palestine Pavilion as if it were government sponsored was tantamount to treating Jewish Palestine itself as if it were a state. It is in this sense that the world of the fair was by its very nature a subjunctive space in which the "as if" of the world of the fair would become a reality in the world itself. Weisgal won on most points but not on the most critical one: location within the international landscape of the world of the fair.

Territory was no less important in the world of the fair than it was in the world at large. Try as he might, Weisgal failed to secure a place for the Jewish Palestine Pavilion in the Government Zone, where spaces around the Lagoon of Nations and in the Hall of Nations were reserved for states and state-sponsored exhibits.[13] Insisting that Jewish Palestine was not a state, the Fair organizers allocated the Jewish Palestine Pavilion a plot of land in the Community Interests zone, right next to the Temple of Religion and in the company of the American Radiator Corp., Christian Science, Contemporary Art, Electrified Farm, Gas Exhibits, Inc., House of Jewels, Medicine and

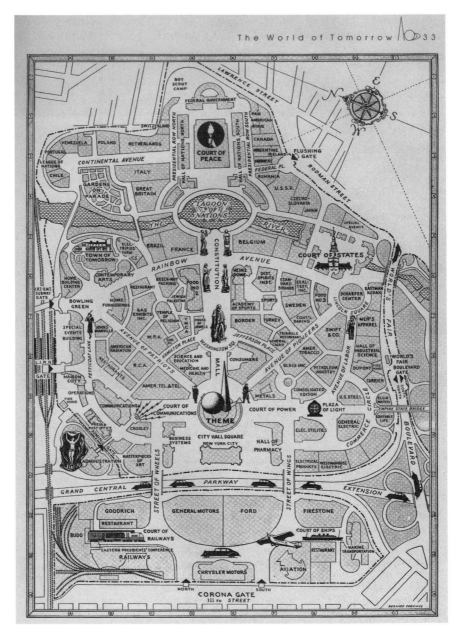

Figure 5.2. Map of the New York World's Fair, 1939. From "The Fair's Huge Exhibit Area," *New York Times*, April 30, 1939, sec. 8: special World's Fair section, p. 127. Map drawn by Bernard Corvinus.

Public Health, Town of Tomorrow, WPA (Works Progress Administration), and YMCA (Young Men's Christian Association), among others.

Having lost the zone war, Weisgal shifted the battle to symbols and ceremonies of national recognition; he used every protocol the Fair could afford to ensure that Jewish Palestine would appear along with other nations in the line of flags, Parade of Nations, *Book of Nations*, and calendar of national days and weeks. Central to the internationalism of world's fairs is the "imagined universal code of nationhood," a modular system of pavilions, flags, anthems, insignia, and uniforms that both make nations recognizable as such and distinguish them from each other.[14] This idea was captured by David Ben-Gurion, who became Israel's prime minister in 1949: "Two basic aspirations underlie all our work in this country: to be like all nations, and to be different from all nations."[15] Speaking in the universal code of nationhood, the Jewish Palestine Pavilion enacted these aspirations within the world of the fair.

Nations without a State

For all its celebration of private enterprise, educational mission, and non-profit claims, the New York World's Fair was both an unabashedly commercial affair and a highly charged diplomatic arena. In contrast with European world's fairs, which were state supported, American ones had to raise their own finances; the only government support they received was generally for city, state, and federal buildings and for public works and improvement. Moreover, although the Fair Corporation was a non-profit educational organization that defined itself as a "civic undertaking," the government of the United States was the official convener of this international gathering; only governments with whom the United States had diplomatic relations could be invited to the Fair, and it was President Roosevelt himself who issued the formal invitation after the Congress of the United States, on June 15, 1936, authorized him to do so.[16] Three traveling commissioners, working with the State Department and through diplomatic representatives, went abroad to meet personally with representatives of invited governments in the hope of getting as many governments as possible to sign on. The final tally of foreign participants was "sixty foreign governments and international bodies."[17]

Consistent with the regulations of the Bureau International des Expositions, the Fair Corporation had to allocate 10,000 square feet of space, without charge, to each participating government and did so in the Hall of Nations. Governments could also lease land and build their own pavilions, with no restriction on how much they spent.[18] France and Great Britain focused their national pavilions on themselves, while presenting their overseas possessions, protectorates, dependencies, and colonies in the less prestigious Hall of Nations. The Republic of Lebanon appeared in the Hall of

Nations as a government that had been organized in 1920 and was a mandate of France at the time of the Fair. Had it so desired, which it clearly did not, Great Britain could have done the same for its mandate, Palestine. There were, in addition, several international bodies, most prominent among them the League of Nations.

Initially, the Fair's organizers invited Palestine to participate under the aegis of Great Britain, which could have either included Palestine along with its other empire displays or approved a Mandate-sponsored display, as it did at the Wembley Empire Exhibition in 1924/25. At Wembley, where "government stalls" showed the accomplishments of the Palestine government under the British Mandate, Jews were responsible for the "Zionist stalls," where they displayed their efforts to build a Jewish homeland, while Britain took responsibility for exhibiting the Arabs.[19] Though recognizing that Palestine under the Mandate was not technically part of the British Empire and that Jewish exhibits left much to be desired, *The Jewish Chronicle* saw in the Jewish presence at Wembley indications of a rapprochement of British and Jewish interests:

The inclusion within the Exhibition of a Palestine Pavilion is . . . a token that, albeit embryonically, the Jewish nation has become part of the British Empire . . . It were well for Great Britain to understand, and for the British Empire to appreciate, the immense moral gain they have acquired . . . in thus enfolding the Jewish nation within their bosom. With a proper understanding of the true position on both sides, there is room ample and to spare for the development to the fullest degree of Jewish National aspirations consistent with the very best interests of the British Empire . . . Thus the great Exhibition, which has drawn together representation from every corner of the Empire upon which the sun never sets, by the inclusion within it of the Palestine exhibit makes manifest to all the new relation that now subsists between the British Empire and the Jewish people.[20]

Between Wembley in 1924 and the New York World's Fair in 1939, the British relationship to the Mandate changed.

Conflicts between Arabs and Jews prompted the British to restrict Jewish land purchases and Jewish immigration and to modify its policy on Jewish statehood, as can be seen from negative responses to the Peel Commission's call in 1936–37 to partition Palestine into a Jewish state and an Arab state and the 1939 McDonald White Paper, which proposed a single binational state. By 1937, when the invitation to participate in the New York World's Fair was issued, Britain showed no interest in including Palestine in its British Empire exhibits at the New York World's Fair. America's ambassador in London presented the invitation for Palestine's participation to the appropriate British authorities but was informed by a representative of the American Economic Commission for Aid to Palestine that although "Palestine's authorities were exceedingly anxious to have an exhibit," they were short on funds.[21] A comment by Sir William McLean, an expert on the empire who was trying to encourage American investment in Britain's colonies, better captures the mood: "Palestine is a costly hobby says noted Briton in Seattle . . . an expensive hobby of the British Government which costs $5,000,000 a year and 'returns nothing but trouble.'" While noting that "these were purely his personal views, Sir William said that England took over Palestine under a League mandate because nobody else wanted it."[22]

When planning its exhibits for the New York World's Fair, Great Britain gave emotional and psychological factors, which were understood as essential to political gains, precedence over commercial considerations, which had been primary at Wembley. Nervous about the hostility of the American public to British imperialism and the likelihood that Hitler would demand that Britain turn its colonies over to Germany, Britain turned for advice on what Americans would find appealing or offensive to Sol Bloom.[23] A Jewish impresario who had been organizing exhibitions for world's fairs since the 1880s and a Democratic congressman since 1923, Bloom was a member of the Board of Directors of the New York World's Fair Corporation and a savvy showman.[24] The upshot was a British Colonial Empire exhibition that would focus on "the humanitarian and social services aspect of our Colonial Empire" in order to stress the "morality of the Empire."[25] The last thing that Great Britain needed was a Palestine exhibit.

Once the British refusal was official, the way was cleared for Jews to go forward with a Palestine exhibit that was not government sponsored, which did not stop the Jewish organizers from presenting their pavilion as if it were an official presence. Not long after the agreement with the Fair Corporation was signed on April 14, 1938, the American consul general in Jerusalem alerted the Department of State in Washington that "the strongly nationalistic 'Arab Women's Committee'" had sent a letter to the high commissioner "protesting against the use of the term 'Palestine' to describe the pavilion in question, i.e. 'one purely Jewish in character.' Such a use, it said, 'would be a gross abuse of the word 'Palestine,' a violation of the international status of the country and calculated to excite the feelings of the Arabs.'"[26] The Fair Corporation insisted that the name be changed; in response, the organizers contemplated such names as "Land of Israel" or "Jewish National Home in Palestine" before settling on "Jewish Palestine Pavilion," although the building continued to be known informally as the Palestine Pavilion to continued protests.

However reluctant the United States might have been to enter another world war, the Fair Corporation did not hesitate to pressure nations already at war to participate in the 1939 fair and to keep their pavilions open for a second season. Grover Whalen traveled throughout Europe in the months between the closing of the 1939 fair in October and the opening of the 1940 fair in March to appeal directly to heads of state, including Mussolini. Never anticipating a war, the Fair Corporation itself and many of the exhibitors had originally hoped the fair would run for five seasons and needed at least a second season to break even let alone make a profit. Many, though not all the national exhibitors, returned.

Whereas the Soviet Union had been the first foreign government to sign on for the 1939 fair, on November 11, 1939—about two weeks before it invaded Finland and almost a month before it was expelled from the League of Nations—it decided not to return for a second season.[27] The gaping space left by the demolished Soviet Pavilion, the largest national pavilion at the Fair and the most popular, was filled by the hastily created American Common, which featured "the richness of the cultures which the various nationalities have brought into the American picture . . . Probably in no other country do the magic words—peace and freedom—mean as much as they do in America today for here you find the greatest variety of peoples living in peace . . . A Gallery of Honor fences in the area. It lists the names of American citizens of every national origin who have made great contributions to our democracy."[28] Jews participated in the American Common and appeared in the Gallery of Honor, where they were listed under the countries where they had been born or spent their formative years, not as Jews. The American Common was the perfect expression of the inverse internationalism of an immigrant society.[29] Jews were also part of the failed effort to create a Freedom Pavilion—an inversion of the Nazi Degenerate Art Exhibit—that would feature the work of writers and artists who were exiled or self-exiled from Germany. No other form of Jewish presence, however, was as prominent or as national and international in its reach as the Jewish Palestine Pavilion.

The possibility that an alliance with the United States might help end American isolationism was a critical factor in the decision of several nations to stay in the Fair for a second season. Participation in the Fair was an "overture to an alliance" at a time when such alliances were most needed: Britain, for example, wanted the United States to join forces with it in the emerging war.[30] That nations at war were prepared to put resources into maintaining their pavilions is a measure of how much was at stake not only in the world but also in the world of the fair. Several national pavilions, including those of Czechoslovakia, Denmark, Finland, and Poland (Arthur Szyk's miniatures depicting the role of Poles in American history were featured in the Polish pavilion), incorporated displays relating to the war. The presence of these pavilions was an indication, according to Grover Whalen, that "the World's Fair of 1940 now becomes international with a far more cogent meaning than when it was first planned."[31]

However, the autonomous world of the fair had become harder to sustain. To insulate the Fair from the war, no war news was to be radio broadcast on its grounds and the bar of McGinnis's fairground restaurant banned any "war talk," though a bomb did go off at the fair on July 4, 1940.[32] While military displays were commonplace at world's fairs, the presence of American soldiers in uniform at the New York World's Fair was a reminder that the world was at war.

At the same time, the principle for determining what counted as an official national pavilion had also become harder to apply. The Jewish Palestine Pavilion was no longer such an anomaly.[33] The war had compromised the sovereignty of other nations who had pavilions, for example, Czechoslovakia and Poland, and they too had to seek support from private and commercial interests, rather than from governments. That alone did not level the playing field, of course, but it did make it harder to maintain the principle of government backing as the basis for national recognition, a factor that eased the way for the Jewish Palestine Pavilion to prevail in its demands: the Pavilion was included in the lineup of flags along the bridge to the foreign buildings, *Book of Nations*, and other such contexts even during the first season, though not without considerable wrangling.

Moreover, despite all the efforts to insulate the Fair from the war, the war made it more acceptable for national pavilions to address their national interests more explicitly. Countries that had been invaded could maintain the appearance of sovereignty within the world of the fair and, by keeping their pavilions open, could also protest the abrogation of their borders and appeal for support. Fair policy had emphatically stressed that there was to be no propagandizing or evangelizing, a policy that became more difficult to enforce when war directly affected participating nations. "Truth and Propaganda," Weisgal's contribution to the Jewish Palestine Pavilion souvenir booklet, was a preemptive strike: acknowledging American antipathy to propaganda, Weisgal defined propaganda as "a message of truth" and boldly stated that "In this sense the Jewish Palestine Pavilion at the New York World's Fair is propaganda."[34]

A Jewish World of Tomorrow

By the time of the New York World's Fair, Jews could bring considerable exhibition experience to world's fairs. Palestine exhibits intended to spur trade and investment, as well as Jewish resettlement in Palestine, had been appearing as early as the 1890s in Germany, England, France, and Palestine itself. Such exhibits, which accompanied the early Zionist Congresses, were soon incorporated into world's fairs or even became world's fairs in their own right. Not surprisingly, the strongest impetus to exhibit Palestine at world's fairs came from Jews advocating the creation of a national Jewish home, support of the fledgling Yishuv (the Jewish settlement in Palestine), and eventually the establishment of a Jewish state.

The real laboratory for developing concepts and techniques for "exhibiting Palestine" came with the creation of Mischar v'Taasia (Commerce and Trade) in Tel Aviv in 1926. This organization dedicated itself to diversifying the economy of the Yishuv, encouraging industry and trade, and supporting urban development. It transferred the power of sophisticated marketing, advertising, and promotion techniques from the economic realm to the political one in order to sell the idea of a Jewish homeland in Palestine. Recognizing the importance of economic viability to statehood, Mischar v'Taasia set out to make Palestine the hub of communication and trade in the region. It organized trade fairs in Tel Aviv and, by the 1930s, had created a permanent exhibition ground for the Levant Fair (as this fair was now called) on the outskirts of Tel Aviv. The Levant Fairs of the 1930s attracted international participation and became miniature world's fairs in their own right. Mischar v'Taasia also took its exhibits and fairs on the road; it made its most spectacular showings at two Paris world's fairs—the Palestine Pavilion at the 1931 Paris International Colonial Exposition and the Pavillon d'Israël en Palestine at the 1937 Exposition internationale des arts et techniques—and, above all, at the New York World's Fair in 1939/40. The Levant Fair even exhibited itself, in the form of a glass model, inside the Jewish Palestine Pavilion at the New York World's Fair.

In the United States, Weisgal was the one who understood best how to use world's fairs to promote the Zionist cause. He had made his world's fair debut with a highly successful Zionist pageant, *The Romance of a People*, which was performed on Jewish Day at the 1933 Century of Progress Exposition in Chicago.[35] Weisgal believed that the way to revivify the Zionist movement in the United States in the 1930s was not through speeches (an exhausted genre) and not through a building (too static) but through an awe-inspiring spectacle. In his 1971 memoir, he described the situation he faced at the time of the Century of Progress Exposition: "The Zionist field in Chicago was strewn with dry bones and a thousand speeches were not going to revive them. The leadership was confined to two or three men, and they were powerless against the inertia of the community. I realized at once that in these circumstances pedestrian Zionist propaganda and routine education, however well intentioned, would produce no effect. There had to be, first, a reawakening, and I turned to the performing arts—music, drama, spectacle."[36] Sponsored by the Jewish Agency for Palestine, which represented Jewish interests to the Mandate authorities, the pageant would tell the 3,000-year history of the Jews using the machinery and properties of the Chicago Opera House, which had recently produced *Aida*. According to Weisgal, "The highlight of the evening was to be: *no speeches!* The spectacle would deliver its own message. This was an unheard of proposal: a great Zionist affair at which the local Zionist orators would keep their mouths shut."[37]

Weisgal had three goals in creating the pageant: to further the Zionist cause by gathering support and raising funds; to amplify the voice of protest against Hitler and raise money to help Jews leave Germany; and, at the same time and through these efforts, to stage a strong show of American Jewish solidarity by involving tens of thousands of people. These goals had not changed when he was invited to lead the effort to create a Jewish Palestine Pavilion at the New York World's Fair three years later, but the strategy for how to achieve them had. The idea of a building, which he had rejected for the Chicago fair, emerged here not as an inert edifice but as a way to materialize the state quite literally, using the material metonyms of plants, stone, and wood brought from Palestine itself. A pavilion would make it possible to enact statehood using every protocol for doing so that the Fair could provide, despite the resistance of the Fair to treat Jewish Palestine as if it were sponsored by a state. Each rebuff produced a social drama that Weisgal quickly turned into a media event that became part of his campaign to gain public recognition of the de facto statehood of Jewish Palestine.

Weisgal later answered the question of why he supported a building rather than a pageant in the chapter of his memoir appropriately entitled "A Jewish State in Flushing Meadows," where he characterized the Jewish Palestine Pavilion as "showmanship of another kind."[38] The major bone of contention was its location on the Flushing Meadows fairgrounds. More than twenty years after the establishment of the State of Israel, he would represent his prescience as follows: "One section had been set aside for the national pavilions, and that is where I wanted us to be. There was of course no Jewish State as yet, but I believed in its impending arrival on the scene of history, and I wanted the idea of Jewish sovereignty to be anticipated there, in Flushing Meadows."[39]

Weisgal realized that to unify American Jewish support it was necessary to stress the upbuilding of a Jewish homeland and downplay statehood. Most American Jews could agree on the former, particularly as the refugee issue became more acute, while the latter was a point of sharp disagreement. However, as the Fair moved into its 1940 season, the world was at war, and the Jewish Palestine Pavilion, including the events it sponsored, encountered less resistance to the message of statehood. Weisgal claimed in retrospect that he had understood this all along. What the record does show is that the strict principle of recognizing only government-sponsored buildings as officially national ones could no longer be upheld, even nominally, which worked to the advantage of the Jewish Palestine Pavilion.

Not only would this be the first Jewish Palestine Pavilion at a world's fair in the United States but also this fair would be located in New York City, home of the largest Jewish community in the United States. Not since 1853 had there been a world's fair in New York City. By the mid-1930s, when the city was selected for the 1939/40 fair, Jews in New York had become an increasingly confident and successful immigrant community. Jewish businessmen and politicians were on the various boards and committees of the Fair. They formed a veritable Who's Who of national and international figures. Several were also active in Jewish communal affairs.[40] Several were men of such enormous wealth—Percy S. Strauss and Felix M. Warburg, to mention but two—that any one of them could probably have underwritten the cost of the Jewish Palestine Pavilion, much as Baron de Rothschild had done for the Palestine Pavilion at the 1931 International Colonial Exposition in Paris.

The Jewish Palestine Pavilion was not the only proposal for Jewish participation in the New York World's Fair. Most of the other proposals were referred to the Temple of Religion because the Fair Corporation had decided that there would be no separate denominational displays.[41] The most serious contender was the proposal made by the Synagogue Council of America, "The Jewish Exhibits at the World's Fair, Jews of All Nations, Their Contribution to the Making of America," which dealt with "Jews as American Pioneers," "Colonial Patriots and Soldiers," "Lands of Origin," "Philanthropy," "Great Jews of the Present," and "Synagogue—The History of its Development," including a re-creation on the fairgrounds of the Touro Synagogue (Newport, Rhode Island), the oldest synagogue in the United States.[42] Projects like the Jewish Palestine Pavilion, which looked to the future, were more in keeping with the Fair's futuristic theme, "Building the World of Tomorrow," and were received more sympathetically than ones that celebrated the past. Not everyone agreed with such strict adherence to the futuristic theme. Dr. S. Margoshes, editor of *The Day*, wrote to the Fair organizers that if there were going to be a "Temple of Religious Liberty," why not a "Building of Jewish Achievement." He would later sign on to the Jewish Palestine Pavilion, which in its own way became an exhibition of Jewish achievement, though not what he had in mind.

The ostensible occasion for the New York World's Fair was the 150th anniversary of the inauguration in New York City of George Washington, but, as the 1939 *Guide* hastened to add, "the future, pregnant with high destiny, seemed even more meaningful than the past with all its fateful achievements."[43] According to the Fair philosophy, the visitor would discover what he "could attain for his community and himself by intelligent coordinated effort and will be made to realize the interdependence of every contributing form of life and work."[44] The Fair would present "a new and clearer view of today in preparation for tomorrow."[45] This could have been the byline for the Jewish Palestine Pavilion, which adopted the Fair's futuristic rhetoric and used it for its own purposes. That said, immigrants were a prominent feature of the Fair, not only in the national pavilions representing their homelands but also on the American Common and in the Temple of Religion.

Whereas the Jewish Palestine Pavilion was specific and concrete in articulating its message, the Temple of Religion was an exercise in strategic vagueness: it was to be a temple to religion without referring to any religion in particular. The challenge was to give architectural form to an abstract concept and create an open space both for individual groups to create their own programs and for groups to come together in an interfaith spirit.

The Temple of Religion invited broad participation, as long as the programs were appropriate to the theme and there was no proselytizing or religious services. In contrast, the organizers of the Jewish Palestine Pavilion exercised tight control over what would be shown and done there. The Temple of Religion was more flexible, and many American Jewish groups found the Temple of Religion a hospitable setting for their own programs.

In many ways, the proximity of the Jewish Palestine Pavilion and the Temple of Religion was fortuitous. Jewish groups took advantage of their closeness to create programs that started in the Temple of Religion and moved to the Palestine Pavilion, as can be seen from the program for B'nai B'rith Day on September 8, 1940. At 6:45 pm, members of the organization gathered at the Temple of Religion for a program that began with Wagner's Fantasia and the "Star Spangled Banner." An address entitled "Religion and the Bill of Rights" was followed by Handel's Largo, "God Bless America," and a benediction. Officiating were Dr. Harry D. Gideonse, president of Brooklyn College, and Reverend John W. Houck, pastor of Pilgrim Congregational Church, Bronx. The program continued, without a break, as the group processed to the Jewish Palestine Pavilion for ceremonies there: "Mr. Monsky will place a wreath at the Eternal Light in commemoration of those who made the supreme sacrifice that Palestine might continue to be a living symbol of Hope."[46] (The Eternal Light had been lit in a formal ceremony at the Western Wall in Jerusalem and kept alight all the way to the New York World's Fair.) There was a response by Weisgal in his capacity as director-general of the Jewish Palestine Pavilion, followed by the Academy Choir singing "Hatikvah" and "America the Beautiful."

"Something Authentically Palestinian"

The design of the Jewish Palestine Pavilion and its contents was in accord with Weisgal's desire for "something authentically Palestinian" to show that "in 1938 Jewish Palestine was a reality; its towns, villages, schools, hospitals and cultural institutions had risen in a land that until our coming had been derelict and waste . . . I wanted a miniature Palestine in Flushing Meadows."[47] Insisting, with no trace of irony, that the Pavilion should steer clear of politics, Weisgal applied himself to the "construction of the Jewish State under the shadow of the Trylon and Perisphere, or, as the Jews were fond of calling it, the Lulav and Esrog."[48]

Everything about the Jewish Palestine Pavilion had to be Palestinian down to the last stone, the designer included. The name of Norman Bel Geddes, the brilliant American stage and industrial designer responsible for Futurama, was brought to the design commission. Weisgal and his team rejected him on the grounds that he was not working in Palestine. They chose instead Arieh El-Hanani (Arieh Sapoznikov), who had immigrated to Palestine from Ukraine in 1922, where he had studied at the Kiev School of Art and Architecture.[49] What might the Jewish Palestine Pavilion have looked like had Bel Geddes received the commission? Surely, nothing like the Bauhaus-inspired International Style building created by Arieh El-Hanani of the Levant Fair Studios in Tel Aviv. El-Hanani's Jewish Palestine Pavilion at the New York World's Fair tied for third prize with Oscar Niemeyer's Brazilian pavilion.

As might be expected, the Jewish Palestine Pavilion thematized Zionist ideology in its programmatic architecture, including "a tower symbolic of those that guard the water supply and lives of Jewish colonists in Palestine."[50] Everything about the Pavilion was intended to transport the visitor into "the atmosphere of Eretz Israel." The cedars of Lebanon in the garden recalled the Temple of Solomon. The eucalyptus used for the main doors to the Pavilion called to mind their role in drying the malarial swamps. Palestinian marble lined the walls of the Memorial Hall, which was dedicated to those who had given up their lives in the building of a Jewish national home.[51]

Each major theme was developed in its own hall as follows:

Memorial Entrance
Section I: Achievements of Jewish Colonization
Hall of Transformation
Hall of Agriculture and Settlement
Hall of Town Planning/Cities
Hall of Industry
Hall of Culture and Education
Hall of Labor and New Social Forms
Hall of Health
Section II: The Holy Land of Yesterday and Tomorrow
Temple of Solomon
Diorama Hall—Famous Palestinian Scenes
Section III: Gallery of Palestinian Arts and Crafts

While a detailed analysis of the installation itself is beyond the scope of this essay, suffice it to say that the archival material reveals exhibition concepts guiding the design and exposes significant differences between the approach of El-Hanani, whose work until then had been in Palestine and Europe, and that of his American collaborator Lee Simonson, a distinguished theater designer associated with the New Stagecraft. El-Hanani's approach was documentary and architectural, whereas Simonson approached installation as a form of theater, with special attention to lighting and special effects.[52] El-Hanani brought his experience with commercial design from Mischar v'Taasia, while Simonson's strength was his grasp of the expressive potential of theater.

PLANNING...DESIGNING...AND BUILDING THE EXHIBIT

Figure 5.3. "Planning, Designing, and Building the Exhibit." Photomontage from *Palestine Book*, ed. Meyer W. Weisgal, art editor, Robert Perlman (New York: Pavilion Publications, Inc. for the American Committee for Jewish Palestine Participation at the New York's World's Fair, [1939]). Collection of Robert Rothstein.

In a period when the lines between advertising, propaganda, publicity, public relations, and public information were blurred, Weisgal exploited the arts of persuasion to the fullest.[53] The Jewish Palestine Pavilion, by dint of the massive organizational effort required to mobilize American Jewry to support it, was part of a process of transformation that David H. Shapiro describes in his study of American Zionism. He delineates the conversion of American Zionism from "an apolitical, philanthropical entity into a powerful, well-organized political influence group that had adopted many of the methods inherent in the American democratic process and had learned to manipulate the diverse forces at play on the American scene."[54] Making no mention of phenomena like the Jewish Palestine Pavilion, Shapiro asserts, "The Zionist movement totally lacked organizational tools; it had no department of information and propaganda, no public relations section, no regular means of feeding news to the press or radio."[55]

However, by searching for the strategic approach that only an established organization could sustain, he overlooks the kind of tactical approach that someone like Weisgal would seize as opportunities arose.[56] Indeed, the Jewish Palestine Pavilion is a prime example of tactics, from beginning to end. Once the Pavilion was up and running, Weisgal made every effort to convert tactics into strategy. That is, he pressured the Fair Corporation to recognize the Pavilion as a national entity on a par with the other national pavilions so that he would not have to proceed tactically, opportunity by opportunity, to fight for this recognition. Even with limited resources, the Jewish Palestine Pavilion organized a systematic public persuasion campaign that involved information services, public relations, publicity, and propaganda on behalf of the Zionist cause.[57]

The tactic, in Palestine and at the Fair, was to make facts on the ground (or grounds). The Jewish Palestine Pavilion played a vital role in projecting statehood as fact. As I have argued here, this was done not only through displays of Jewish Palestine as if it were already a functioning state, a fait accompli awaiting ratification, but also by using the world's fair itself as a stage for performing statehood—that is, as a series of occasions for international recognition. For the Jewish Palestine Pavilion to convey de facto statehood, it had first to envision, then visualize, and finally project the "fact." As discussed above, a pavilion was better suited for the purpose than the kind of pageant Weisgal had produced for the 1933 Century of Progress Exposition in Chicago. A pavilion was more strategic than a pageant because it occupied a nationally defined territory on the fair grounds from which it could project its messages in a sustained and systematic way for the entire duration of the Fair.

This raises a final question: why, until recently, did the Palestinian Arabs not create their own national exhibits at world's fairs?[58] The vital importance of projection is captured by Edward Said in his analysis of what he characterizes as Palestinian powerlessness to claim Jerusalem:

It is a sign of Palestinian powerlessness and, it must be said, collective incompetence that to this day the story of Jerusalem's loss both in 1948 and 1967 has not been told by them, but—insofar as it has been told at all—partially reconstructed either by Israelis sympathetic and unsympathetic or by foreigners. In other words, not only has there been no Palestinian narrative of 1948 and after that can at least challenge the dominant Israeli narrative, there has also been no collective Palestinian projection for Jerusalem since its all-too-definitive loss in 1948 and again in 1967. The effect of this quite extraordinary historical and political neglect has been to deprive us of Jerusalem well *before* the fact.[59]

The Jewish Palestine Pavilion was precisely about projecting statehood before the de jure fact. Said attributes considerable agency to such projections. Referring to Israel's projection of Jerusalem as "an 'eternally' unified, principally Jewish city under exclusive Israeli sovereignty," Said cautions, "Only by doing so first in projections could it then proceed to the changes on the ground during the last eight or nine years [prior to 1995], that is, to undertake the massive architectural, demographic, and political metamorphosis that would then correspond to the images and projections."[60] Would that it were that simple.

There is, however, cause for cautious optimism, given recent efforts to offer "a tangible vision of the benefits of peace." The Arc, a proposal developed under the auspices of the Rand Corporation, is intended as "an urban and infrastructural solution that would embody the iconic power that would dramatize the emergence of a new independent state."[61] The issue is not whether The Arc is the ultimate solution but rather the efficacy of envisioning statehood in concrete as well as symbolically resonant terms. Much is to be learned in this regard from the Jewish Palestine Pavilion.

Chapter 6

Was There Anything Particularly Jewish about "The First Hebrew City"?

Anat Helman

A Zionist promotion pamphlet from 1936 describes Tel Aviv as "the youngest and boldest of all Hebrew cities in Palestine, a wonder city that sprang out, almost instantly, from the sand dunes . . . A symbol and demonstration of the people of Israel's political recovery and of the Jewish creative force, revived in its ancient homeland."[1] Tel Aviv, founded in 1909 as a Jewish "garden suburb" of the predominantly Arab city of Jaffa, grew rapidly and soon became the demographic and economic center of Jewish Palestine. Zionists proudly nicknamed it "the First Hebrew City." Note the significant use of the term "Hebrew," rather than "Jewish." These terms overlap and are often used synonymously, yet in Zionist imagination and rhetoric "Jewish" stood for diasporic inferiority, while "Hebrew" indicated a brave new return to nationalism. Jerusalem, the biblical capital, remained the sanctified and uncontested Jewish center. Clad in its mountains and holy stones, Jerusalem was often depicted as static and conservative in modern Hebrew literature and art. Coastal Tel Aviv, in contrast, stood for openness and dynamism. When the national poet Hayyim Nahman Bialik lectured in 1933 on the importance of the Hebrew University—opened in Jerusalem in 1925—he asserted that Jerusalem held a kind of monopoly over all serious learning (the "Torah"), leaving to Tel Aviv only lighter matters and entertainment.[2]

A sort of rivalry emerged between the Jewish center and the Hebrew one. Before his visit to Tel Aviv, many "decent people" had warned the Yiddish writer Shalom Asch about the new city's shortcomings. Most ardent were the "Jerusalem lovers," who "mention Tel-Aviv with a sigh, their faces twisted in shame, as if they were mentioning some blemish in the family."[3] Unlike Asch, whose positive impressions of Tel Aviv refuted all warnings, the French Zionist writer Edmond Fleg was seized by a strong un-poetic and unprosaic mood when traveling from moonlit Jerusalem to sunlit Tel-Aviv. "But I was even more horrified by the disdain which the citizens of this metropolis, still in its infancy, affect towards its venerable ancestor," he wrote in the early 1930s. Even his host, the painter Reuven Rubin, spoke of Jerusalem as "a museum" he wouldn't wish to live in.[4]

As far as its public image was concerned, Tel Aviv was a *Hebrew* city. But was there anything particularly Jewish about Tel Aviv's culture? My use of the term "Jewish" here does not refer solely to formal religion or tradition. Neither does it allude exclusively to Jewish "high" culture, to conscious and intentional elements such as linguistic creativity, or to learning in Jewish fields and specialized branches of folklore.[5] "Jewishness" can also include cultural traits and everyday lifestyles and behaviors that were associated, by many Zionists at least, with Jewish life in the diaspora. In what follows, I will focus on the city's general atmosphere and the impressions it left on residents and visitors, in an effort to determine whether, how, and why Tel Aviv was *experienced* as "Jewish."[6]

Nationalism, Hebrew Culture, and Religion

The religious Zionist parties viewed the Jewish settlement in Palestine as the worldly beginning of the future messianic deliverance. Holding on to Jewish religion and traditions, religious Zionists insisted that Zionism was merely a political movement, not an alternative culture. For them, settling in the Land of Israel did not mean abandoning Jewish religion but, on the contrary, fulfilling it in its ideal original setting. The second group in Zionist leadership, the majority, was composed mainly of Eastern European secular intelligentsia. Following the ideas of Ahad Ha-am (Asher Hirsch Ginsberg, 1856–1927), they expected and demanded that Zionism develop its own new national culture, as a *substitute* for religious Judaism. The third group, that composed of Western European liberals, tried to avoid the "cultural question" altogether. They wanted to concentrate solely on the practical and political facets of Zionism, and they set aside all issues of Jewish/Hebrew identity for the future. But in vain: the "cultural polemic" over the role of religion and tradition in Jewish nationalism broke out in the late 1890s and its issues echoed in many future debates.[7] As Zionists were settling Palestine, the relations between nationalism and religion remained vague and unresolved. Even socialist Zionists, some of whom were among the most anti-clerical, vacillated between antagonism to religion, romantic secularization of old Jewish customs and symbols, and homesickness for their old way of life in the diaspora.

The Zionist slogan "negation of the diaspora" meant more than objecting to conditions in the diaspora: it presented the very existence of Jews in the diaspora as immoral, insufferable, and degenerating.[8] Some took a radical position, negating all Jews who chose to remain outside Palestine and the entirety of Jewish heritage created in the diaspora. Others expressed a more ambivalent form of negation aimed selectively at rabbinic Judaism. There was also a religious Zionist concept of negation of the diaspora, which viewed the Jews' exile as a condition that distorted their religion. Finally, there was the approach of Ahad Ha-am, who played a key role in the cultural/spiritual Zionist movement. While he saw the persistence of the diaspora itself as a sad yet inevitable reality, he did not believe in a total split from the past and viewed the new national culture that Zionism would create as a continuation of Jewish creativity and heritage that had endured for centuries, including its diasporic phase.[9] All versions of diaspora negation nurtured a wish to create in Palestine a new kind of Jew. In contrast with the stereotypical diaspora Jew, an image strongly influenced by anti-Semitic notions, "the New Jew" was to be productive, deeply rooted in his land, brave, strong, healthful, uncomplicated, and handsome.[10] While "diaspora" (*golah*) could be used as a neutral term indicating the dispersal of the Jewish people, Zionists applied the word "diasporism" (*galut*) to specifically indicate the downright negative nature of Jewish life outside the Land of Israel.[11]

Tel Aviv was populated and governed mainly by Eastern European, secular, lower-middle-class Jews, who usually belonged to the "civil circles," namely, political Zionists who affiliated neither with the socialists on the left, nor the Revisionists on the right.[12] The general atmosphere toward cultural issues was moderate. Even though they did not practice religion, many of these Jews were sympathetic to Jewish tradition and, despite their lack of observance, anti-religious expressions among them were rare. However, choosing to call their city "Hebrew" suggests that Tel Aviv's founders, leaders, and residents were trying to stress that the city—its urban form and lifestyle—was revolutionary and new. At the same time, the designation "Hebrew city" connected Tel Aviv to the land and its past, while dissociating the city and its lifestyle from the immediate diaspora past. In its formal ideology and "high" cultural activity, Tel Aviv's intended Hebrewness was indeed more apparent than its Jewishness. But as we will see, quite a few traces of Jewishness could be detected in Tel Aviv's everyday culture and popular lifestyles, due to the vitality of immigrant communities and the failure of ideology to fully penetrate all spheres of everyday life.[13]

Since Zionism was a new national movement, cultural products played an important role in defining the community, enforcing Hebrew, and consolidating national identity, nowhere as clearly as in Tel Aviv, which had quickly acquired the attributes of an urban cultural center during the 1920s and 1930s: a concentration of artists from different fields, cultural conventions, and artistic standards, "gatekeepers" such as critics and editors, cultural institutions and the architecture to house them, and an influential public of culture consumers.[14] Art created and produced in Tel Aviv, including literature, theater, dance, music, and the visual arts, while consumed mainly in the city itself, was also exported to other towns and settlements in Jewish Palestine.

Most cultural activities in Jewish Palestine were based on an ideological consensus: the aspiration to create a new Hebrew Land-of-Israel culture.[15] Like other national high cultures, Zionist culture strove to transmit and enhance national values. Hebrew writers between the two world wars—most of them living and working in Tel Aviv—considered themselves witnesses to the Zionist drama. They described the Jewish settlement process and echoed reigning national values, thus helping to shape Jewish Palestine's self-identity. Local poetry celebrated the life of the hardworking pioneer, and prose described the struggles of the collective.[16]

By the early 1920s, Tel Aviv had become a center for visual artists and a counterweight to Jerusalem's "Bezalel" school, whose early Zionist aesthetic integrated traditional and religious elements into a national idiom. The younger generation of Bezalel students rebelled against their teachers' utopian idealism and what they viewed as a conservative "rootless Diasporism" (hence Rubin's regard of Jerusalem as "a museum"). The young artists moved to Tel Aviv and replaced iconic prophets and Zionist symbols with concrete though stylized and idealized local landscapes. By depicting the Land, the artists likened themselves to active pioneers, and by concentrating on the territorial and the earthly, they protested against diasporic "displaced spirituality."[17]

The mere intention to *create* localism has something artificial about it, because it makes self-conscious that which we assume to be taken for granted—namely, nativity. Nativity (unlike the wider and more culturally and politically flexible definition of "nationalism") refers to a natural, direct, unconscious, and unintentional connection to one's birthplace. The deliberate effort by European immigrants to create a Hebrew native culture in the Land of Israel was therefore something of a paradox,[18] a dilemma that was not lost on some of the artists themselves. The painter Manahem Shemi, for one, did not approve of such forced and artificial efforts. In 1928, he insisted that art should be judged solely on the basis of artistic standards. Without plastic excellence, it was useless to insist upon local themes such as a donkey, a camel, an olive tree, or an Arab garment. An original local art, he wrote, would and should develop naturally and would only emerge when local painters simply concentrated on pure artistic expression.[19] In the 1930s, many artists returned to Tel Aviv from training in Paris, replacing the primitive style of the 1920s with Expressionism. Some of them forsook local themes and colors, a move lamented in 1935 by a critic who believed that the artists were abandoning their true national vocation.[20] As a cultural center, Tel Aviv did nurture some "purist" artistic trends; yet even when focusing on aesthetic standards and not on ideological propaganda, they were still received in the wider context of a comprehensive national goal.[21]

Artists in all fields viewed themselves as holding a pivotal vocation in the Zionist enterprise: since the old Jewish identity was discarded, they recruited themselves to the urgent mission of forming a new Hebrew one

instead. Most professional dancers, for instance, didn't restrict themselves
to modern European ballet but also choreographed dances depicting supposedly oriental and biblical motives, or stylized movements of agricultural
pioneers at work.[22]

Although the national elite that dominated most cultural activity in Tel
Aviv promoted Hebrewness as opposed to Jewishness, Land-of-Israel as
opposed to diasporic values, and secularism as opposed to religion, shades
of the Jewish, the diasporic, and the religious entered through the back
door, for instance in the form of Hasidic and cantoral music, which
remained very popular in Tel Aviv. The head cantor, Shelomo Ravitz, a
local star, was always a main attraction and in great demand. Secular Sabbath gatherings organized by Bialik (*Oneg Shabbat*) included public singing
of Hasidic songs, before and even after newly written Hebrew "folk songs"
were taught and sung. When people played their gramophones—loudly
and sometimes as late as two or three in the morning—well-known cantorial *nigunim* (melodies) resounded in Tel Aviv's streets. "In any household
owning a record player," mentioned a journalist when discussing Tel Aviv's
enthusiasm for this kind of music, "you'll find at least ten records of the
Hebrew world's famous cantors."[23] Note the appropriation: by defining the
famous cantors as belonging to the *Hebrew* world, not the *Jewish* one, the
journalist legitimized their popularity in the first Hebrew city.

During the 1920s and 1930s, Tel Aviv was described in contradictory
terms: on the one hand, angry accusations of Tel Aviv being irreligious and
debauched, and on the other, apologetic counterarguments about Tel
Aviv's supposedly deep respect for tradition. Tel Aviv acquired a reputation
for being extremely nonreligious, and even secular observers feared that a
total lack of tradition might lead to complete immorality and anarchy,
while others claimed that Tel Aviv was developing its very own tradition,
that the city was maintaining Jewish customs while giving them new life.[24]

Religious leaders and citizens, as well as some visitors, complained that
Tel Aviv's secular majority violated specific religious commandments and
generally disregarded traditional morals. The Tel Aviv municipality
responded to such accusations by stressing the city's support of religious
customs and institutions although the mayor, Meir Dizengoff, treated Jewish tradition not as an obligatory set of rules to be followed but rather as a
selective national asset. Religious factions were furious about the weekly
Sabbath violation, while the municipality emphasized Tel Aviv's special Sabbath atmosphere, "stemming from a religious—or, mostly—from a
national sensibility."[25] Secular Jews tried to put new national meanings into
traditional Jewish holidays, such as Purim, and celebrated them in new civil
forms (for example, a grand Purim parade), presenting them as a vital
regeneration of old rituals that had lost their relevance.[26]

From a religious viewpoint there was something pathetic and even grotesque about Tel Aviv's secular attempts at combining religious customs

with contemporary and local elements. A national-religious weekly, published in Jerusalem, highlighted an example of this in 1925. A cinema house in Tel Aviv decided to conduct penitential prayers (*Selihot*) in its main hall. Some were glad: hundreds of youngsters, who ignored the synagogue all year long, still felt the need to pray publicly during the high holidays. Others were offended: why pray inside a hall, which is usually used for doubtful secular activities and Sabbath desecration? However, a "prologue" put an end to all arguments when an early *Selihot* prayer was arranged on Saturday evening. Since entry was free of charge, about four thousand people filled a hall with a capacity for only one thousand. Some men entered bareheaded and accompanied by young women. The cantor demanded that all heads be covered and that men and women be separated. When ignored, the cantor left the hall and the prayer was cut short. "This is how Tel-Aviv ran to Selihot"—gloated the Jerusalem reporter— "and this is how it returned empty handed."[27]

One of Tel Aviv's most important symbols was the Great Synagogue on Allenby Street. The synagogue was often photographed to promote Tel Aviv's positive image. Important urban events, both religious and secular, took place in the building or around it. The municipality restricted the kinds and shapes of shops to be allowed in the synagogue's proximity, wishing to maintain its whole surroundings in as dignified and as representative a manner as possible. Then again, it took eight years from the beginning of construction until the building was completed. Throughout the 1920s, the domeless synagogue's sides had to be covered with fabric as temporary shelter for prayers. Due to financial difficulties and engineering problems, the Great Synagogue, an icon of Tel Aviv's traditionalism, remained for almost a decade in a state appropriately described as "not yet a synagogue, nor great."[28] Nevertheless, the Great Synagogue and its history reflect both a genuine wish to pay religion and tradition their due respect, and the equally genuine priority of the city's governors and residents to focus on the construction of secular buildings, many of which were completed during the years when the synagogue on Allenby Street remained half-built.

Tel Aviv's Jewishness

In its wider sense, "Jewishness" includes a range of lifestyles, behaviors, and mentalities associated with Jews.[29] In Tel Aviv, which was populated mainly by Eastern European Jews, these were mostly linked to the Eastern European diaspora, where such lifestyles had developed over centuries.[30] Zionist settlers in Palestine were supposed to leave diasporic lifestyles behind and turn over a new leaf in the old-new homeland. Alas, Zionist critics often described Tel Aviv's inhabitants as people who had betrayed the pioneering ideal of agriculturally working the land by retaining and importing "typical" urban diasporic livelihoods. Tel Aviv's urban economy enabled easier

Figure 6.1. The Great Synagogue on Allenby Street in Tel Aviv, 1934. Photo: Kluger Zoltan. Item no. 003773, picture code D23–103, National Photo Collection, Government's Press Office, State of Israel.

absorption of lower-middle-class Jews, who did not necessarily have to forsake their former occupations. This varied economy—although drawing ideological criticism—became one of the city's main attractions for immigrants and a crucial factor in its spectacular growth.[31]

Since the dominant Zionist ideology strove to unify all Jewish immigrants, the mere fact that immigrants had introduced cultural diversity to Palestine was enough to earn them the pejorative label of "Jewish-diasporic." Cultural diversity was presented as "Babel" and as a threat to the Zionist aim of consolidating a monolithic national culture. This threat was acutely felt in a heterogeneous city like Tel Aviv, an immigrant society of numerous subcultures. Hebrew, for instance, was Tel Aviv's formal and dominant language, and yet its streets, buses, shops, and seashore were filled with the sounds of various foreign tongues. Enforcing an exclusive use of Hebrew was much easier in small homogenous settlements than it was in a rapidly growing immigrant city.[32]

It sometimes appeared as if every imported trait from foreign lands was regarded negatively as "Jewish-diasporic," even cultural habits that had no Jewish origins whatsoever and were in no way unique to Jews. For instance, many streets in Tel Aviv looked a lot like typical streets in Polish cities and towns, with their clustered, untidy small shops and shouting peddlers. This similarity was presented as a sign of diasporism, although it could have been regarded simply as an import of *Polish* culture and lifestyles. In any case, Eastern Europe was not a favored model, as Tel Aviv's leaders, most of them Eastern Europeans themselves, strove to create a city according to modern Western ideals. In spite of a preference for Western influences over Eastern ones, even habits imported from the West, such as the Vienna-style coffeehouse culture of the 1930s, were sometimes frowned upon: if it did not stem from the Land of Israel, it was dichotomously dubbed and disparaged as "diasporic."[33]

The obvious continuity of recent foreign (Jewish and non-Jewish) life-styles in Tel Aviv was often viewed as an un-Zionist fault. When people felt dissatisfied with Tel Aviv's appearance or its administration, they scornfully likened it to a typical *shtetl*. The Hebrew writer Y. D. Berkovitch, Sholem Aleichem's son-in-law and translator, became furious at the time it took the municipality to number the houses on his Tel Aviv street. In an angry letter, he exclaimed, "In the world press we ring all bells, in honor of the first Hebrew city's grandness and government. Only those who live in the city . . . know the painful and well kept secret, that even in the smallest matters Tel-Aviv often does not excel over that other famous Jewish town, its predecessor in our literature—over Kasrilevke [the fictional Jewish town of many of Sholem Aleichem's stories]."[34]

Similarly, in 1926 one journalist attended a charity ball conducted by Gemilut Hasadim, a women's charity organization. Quite appalled, he reported about the "diasporic" figures that had gathered there: "When I left the place I felt as if the same Jewish shtetl, which writers and poets have already kissed goodbye, has been rolled with all its characters and types, into the Land of Israel. All year long they are dispersed and nobody knows of their existence, until one ball of 'Gemilut hasadim' brings them all together into one hostel."[35] In this vampire-like description, improper signs of the diaspora are regarded as a rare disturbance of an otherwise undiasporic city, as a hidden and lurking threat to Tel Aviv's aspired-to Hebrewness. Since the writer has already buried the diaspora as a thing of the past, he treats its reappearance in Tel Aviv as an eerie encounter with the living dead.

In contrast, a visitor who described mid-1920s Tel Aviv to the readers of the American Yiddish daily *Der Tag* found its striking and familiar Jewish-ness positively appealing:

The Fourth Aliyah with its white castles in Tel-Aviv, its shops and kiosks, growing in number just like in any other city where the people of Israel are many—this phenomenon is not less Jewish (perhaps even more so) and not less historically important than the Moshavoth and Kevutzoth [agricultural and collective settlements]. This is a continuation, bridging European Jewry and the Land of Israel. And believe me: I felt myself closer and more "involved" about the Tel-Aviv Jew, with his knitted brow, livelihood problems and need for charity, who is too troubled to remember to speak Hebrew, than about all these new and revolutionary idealists who returned to the Land. I share a common language with the sighing Jew who sells soda: the Jewish sorrow, the Jewish sigh . . . The city bears a Hebrew character; not Hebrew-Hebrew like the Moshavoth, but a Hebrew character, which is so very Jewish. Finally, there's a lifestyle closer to the historic Jewish one, a continuation, not a rift.[36]

If "Hebrew" was supposed to replace the old "Jewish," then "Hebrew-Hebrew" stood for a radical negation of the diaspora and a total break from the past. The writer, who disliked such revolutionary forms of Zionism as manifested in collective agricultural settlements, found Tel Aviv's urban culture less estranged: new and Hebrew, certainly, yet also maintaining obvious traces of a familiar Jewishness.

Tel Aviv's totally Jewish population astonished Jewish and non-Jewish visitors alike. It was noticeably the first modern city built and populated exclusively by Jews, a result of a simple demographic fact: 98.8 percent of the city's population was Jewish or, as it was put in Zionist propaganda, Tel Aviv was "the only 100 percent Jewish city in the world."[37] Shalom Asch wrote that "when you walk in the street, there are Jews in front of you and behind you. Wherever you turn, only Jewish eyes."[38] He witnessed a courtroom session in Tel Aviv, delighted to see a Jewish judge, talking simple Yiddish to a Jewish thief, who hadn't spent enough time in Palestine to master Hebrew. The defense lawyer was Jewish, and so were the prosecutor and the policeman who guarded the defendant. The witnesses were Jewish, as were the owners of the stolen rings, the shop from where they were stolen, and even the broken lock.[39]

Tel Aviv's urban society maintained a degree of traditional Jewish heterogeneity, but its demographics turned one of the main characteristics of diaspora urban experience on its head: from a *minority* culture within a hostile majority culture, Jews in Tel Aviv were in the distinct *majority*.[40] Though Jews were often the numerical majority in many towns in the Pale of Settlement, they were structurally a minority, in terms of their position as a religious group, their inferior legal status, and social barriers to their full participation in the host society. In Tel Aviv, Jews reigned and non-Jews were a rarity. In the early 1920s, a Tel Aviv manual laborer sent his brother in Europe a photograph of himself, as a construction worker in Tel Aviv, together with other laborers and a camel. On the back of the photo he mingled complaints with pride, mentioning hardships "in the only city devoid of any aliens [*nokhrim*]."[41] For a change, a few Gentiles—not the many Jews—stood out as the alien element in the city.[42]

The fact that Tel Aviv was founded by Jews also made a crucial difference. When the city celebrated its twenty-fifth anniversary in 1934, a local journalist noted that until Jews built Tel Aviv, seventy generations of them had merely settled in great foreign cities. During the anniversary celebrations, the formal representative of diaspora communities, a writer from Poland, said in his congratulatory public speech that in the diaspora Jews might become the majority in existing towns, "while here we conquer the sands and establish [new] communities."[43]

Long-term visitors and permanent residents rapidly adjusted to this new demographic phenomenon. They started to take for granted Tel Aviv's all-Jewish reality and the unique cultural atmosphere associated with it. They experienced a new feeling of confidence and freedom. Surrounded only by Jews, "[y]ou can do everything and say everything you wish."[44] Asch stated that mid-1930s Tel Aviv is not a city but rather a sanatorium. "Were I a doctor," he wrote, "I'd prescribe three years in Tel-Aviv for every sick Jew who complains about his nerves, because the 100 percent Jewish city is the best relaxation from all gentile plights." In Tel Aviv he met adults who had never heard the "yid" curse nor felt the abuse of a Gentile's blow. Some of Tel Aviv's Jews never even saw a Gentile's face, with the exception of the harmless cinema. "You can therefore imagine how healthful the Jews of Tel-Aviv are, almost as healthful as the Gentiles," he concluded.[45]

When the novelist Ludwig Lewisohn visited Tel Aviv in 1925, he heard people singing and dancing in the streets at night. "Their freedom and naturalness" touched his heart. He had never before heard Jews singing like that in a summer evening, not even in New York's "Jewish" quarters. He said to himself that perhaps they would have liked to do so, but they dared not from fear that an anti-Semite would hear them and call them "loud and vulgar Jews." Tel Aviv's importance for all the Jews in the world, wrote the increasingly Zionist Lewisohn, lies in its Jews' ability to sound their voices with no fear.[46] Even a non-Zionist like the socialist Abraham (Abe) Cahan, the editor of *Der Forverts*, mentioned the atmosphere of Jewish freedom sensed in Tel Aviv. During his 1925 visit he experienced this city as even more Jewish than East Broadway on New York's Lower East Side, and when, instead of the stereotypical Irish policeman, he met a Jewish policeman from Minsk, he almost felt like converting to Zionism himself.[47]

Tel Aviv's distinctive festive culture impressed the writer Ben-Yishai, one of Tel Aviv's main spokesmen, who compared his memories of Christmas Eve in the diaspora to the atmosphere in Tel Aviv: "Bells did not ring, snow did not fall. The windows were not covered with frost, from which the eye of 'that Man' [Jesus Christ] was peeping at us during the night, awaking our deep childhood fears." There was no traditional breaking of Jews' windows, no mysterious dread of living among the Gentiles. Instead, Christmas Eve in Tel Aviv was a warm night after a whole day of sunshine. Doors and windows were wide open. The rabbi was reading his lesson in the Great Synagogue on Allenby Street. No one even remembered it was Christmas Eve. People might feel the fear of Christmas Eve in Jerusalem or Nazareth, but not in Tel Aviv. Perhaps two British soldiers drank a bit too much and could be heard in the main street, "but the sound isn't echoed. It is lost in the darkness."[48]

The Polish Zionist leader Yizhak Greenbaum would have agreed. After visiting Tel Aviv in 1933, Greenbaum wrote that in Eastern Europe Jews always feel insecure, dreading an insult or a blow, but, he continued, "In Tel-Aviv the Jews walk erect and strong: this is their city, their flesh and blood, their labor and toil. All feel equal citizens, Jews who build and develop the land." He wondered why Tel Aviv seemed more attractive than Haifa and Jerusalem and concluded that the latter are mixed cities, where the Jew is confronted by opposing forces, while "in Tel-Aviv the Jew feels at home, free inside his creation."[49] This feeling of freedom, though rooted in the Jews' majority status, was also enhanced by politics. Tel Aviv was governed by an all-Jewish elected municipality, which prompted the religious Zionist leader Meir Berlin to claim that Tel Aviv was more attractive than Jerusalem and Haifa to Jews in Palestine and the world, thanks to Jewish self-rule in this almost 100 percent Jewish city.[50]

Marsha Gitlin, a South African Zionist writer who visited Tel Aviv in 1933, also puzzled over the city's Jewishness: "It is difficult to say for what I was looking, but I think it was for something which to myself I called 'specifically Jewish,' something distinct and individual, infinitely better than what was commonly known as 'Jewish' outside Palestine." Her first impression was extremely disappointing. "Where was that Jewish spirit of which so much had been heard? The only specifically Jewish thing in Tel-Aviv apparent to me was an accumulation of Jewish people from all over the world, and a consequent accumulation of Jewish faults and deficiencies." After seven weeks, however, her impressions changed radically:

I soon realized one thing—that Tel-Aviv may not be "specifically Jewish" but it is permeated with Jewishness.
     And when I say Tel-Aviv is Jewish, I do not necessarily mean to emphasize that everybody—policemen, roadmenders, bus drivers etc.—are Jews. I took it for granted that all that would be so in a hundred per cent Jewish town. Tel-Aviv's Jewishness is a far more subtle thing than this—it is something that insinuates itself into one and gives one a sensation of complete freedom. One is utterly at home. There is no effort whatsoever to be a Jew—one is that automatically . . . One could go on giving countless instances of this feeling of at-homeness, of being among one's own, that envelopes one at Tel-Aviv more than in any other town of Palestine.[51]

Gitlin's enthusiastic portrayal of Tel Aviv can't be explained away as the naive response of a tourist. Though perhaps less exhilarated and more likely to feel homesick than temporary visitors, 40 percent of all Jewish immigrants to Palestine during the mandate era eventually chose to settle in Tel Aviv, an indication of the city's enduring appeal.[52] Tel Aviv was not the only all-Jewish town in Palestine but its lingering "diasporic" traits might have rendered it less alienating and more like home—more familiar and cozy—particularly for Eastern European Jewish immigrants.

Yet feeling confidently at home had its side effects as well. Suddenly freed from their fear of the Gentiles, Tel Aviv Jews were accused of embracing an excessively free, almost anarchic lifestyle.[53] In the mid-1930s, the aging Mayor Dizengoff disapproved of the undisciplined and impolite younger generation of Palestine-born Jews, but he noticed that even older immigrants, educated in Europe, suddenly felt free to neglect their former manners and civilities, which they had kept so meticulously as long as they lived among Gentiles.[54]

As a minority turned into a majority, Tel Aviv Jews were put to a new test. The Hebrew writer Eliezer Steinman wrote about his chance meeting with a young Arab boy. The boy was leading his donkey in a Tel Aviv street at sunrise and, when noticing Steinman, he started and rushed by. The boy's fear was so familiar to Steinman, who remembered such horror as a child among Gentile brats in the diaspora. First, he viewed the incident happily, as a testimony of this city's strength and his ownership of the land. But then the Jew inside him abruptly called him to order: why is it that he, yesterday's victim, can only exist as either the persecuted or the persecutor?[55]

Tel Aviv's residents always strove to achieve "normality," and being Jewish in Tel Aviv was indeed the norm.[56] Practical issues caused tensions and conflicts between religious and nonreligious Jews, yet essential questions about Jewish identity were generally not addressed, not because these questions did not arise in Tel Aviv but rather because its residents simply took Jewishness for granted. The political, religious, and cultural question of "who is a Jew?"—heatedly discussed in Israel a few decades later—was not posed in Tel Aviv during the 1920s and 1930s. If one wasn't an Arab from Jaffa, or a British policeman or soldier, or a Gentile tourist, then one was presumed to be Jewish. Despite the dichotomy of Land of Israel versus the diaspora, a wider concept of a Jewish collectivity enveloped both Palestine's Jews *and* Jews in the rest of the world.[57] If Palestine's Jews had totally dissociated themselves from their diaspora kin, the "negation of the diaspora" would have become redundant. Instead, a comprehensive concept of a "Jewish People" lingered on, even among practicing Zionists, which made the diaspora option an ongoing issue of debate.

Tel Aviv's nonchalant Jewishness was different both from the formal Zionist ideology, with its clean break from the past, and from diaspora experience, with its constant need to negotiate and clarify Jewish identity. Thus, paradoxically, while the Zionist immigrants who built "The First Hebrew City" could not take their Hebrewness and their "nativity" for granted and therefore had to define it in a highly self-conscious way, they could casually assume their *Jewish* identity, which required no justification in their all-Jewish city.

Chapter 7

Re-Routing Roots: Zehava Ben's Journey between *Shuk* and *Suk*

Amy Horowitz

In 1990, Zehava Ben made her commercial cassette debut in the outdoor marketplace (*shuk*) at Tel Aviv's Central Bus Station. In market booths far from the sophisticated Dizengoff Center, the chic northside cafes, and the rejuvenated beach promenades, Zehava Ben's cassettes occupied retail space next to vegetables, poultry, and household supplies, and her Arabic and Turkish mellismatic vocals competed for air time with the guttural shouts of market vendors and the drone of idling buses. Although confined to the Tel Aviv's urban underbelly, Zehava Ben's "ornate and Oriental noise"[1] disturbed European Israelis throughout Israel, her Eastern overtones momentarily challenging Tel Aviv's image as a center of Western culture.

Yet, for working-class Mizrahim (Israeli Jews with roots in Islamic countries), who raced to buy her new cassette at the Central Bus Station, Zehava Ben's voice was not an unwilling audio caress, and the Central Bus Station *shuk* was not reducible to an exoticized carnival of smell and noise. This was where they caught buses to and from work and paused on the run to pick up affordable necessities, odds and ends, and music. This was where Zehava Ben's voice blared from loudspeakers, her cassettes selling by the tens of thousands, well before radio editors, journalists, and record company executives even knew her name. In a small country like Israel, where gold records are often based on sales of twenty thousand CDs, unconfirmed but nevertheless astounding estimates that her cassette sold eighty thousand copies signaled a landmark event for disenfranchised Mizrahi musicians.[2]

Zehava Ben grew up in the impoverished Shkhuna Dalet neighborhood on the outskirts of Be'er Sheva. In neighborhoods such as these, emerging from the 1950s transit camps for Middle Eastern immigrants (like her Moroccan-born parents, Simon and Aliza Benista), Arab music, such as the songs of the legendary Muslim Egyptian singer Umm Kulthum (1907–75), coexisted peacefully with Hebrew liturgical traditions chanted in Middle Eastern vocal styles.[3] Ben was born in 1968, five years before the Yom Kippur War, and her childhood years coincided with significant political, ethnic, technological, and musical revolutions out of which a new, neighborhood music—Mediterranean Israeli music—emerged and became commercially viable. By the late 1970s, the growing frustration of poor, disenfranchised Mizrahim expressed itself in a pan-ethnic movement that challenged economic, social, and cultural discrimination.

As a teenager, Zehava Ben encountered the neighborhood Yemenite singer Zohar Argov, whose rendition of songs such as Avihu Medina's composition "Perakh B'Gani" (Flower in My Garden) created a hybrid soundscape that utilized the newly invented cassette recorder and four-way duplicating machine to become a competitive alternative music industry.[4] By the 1980s, during her teenage years, Zehava, like other young singers, studied Zohar's Middle Eastern vocal style on pirated cassettes. She played them over and over again in the cramped apartment that she shared with nine brothers and sisters, as well as her Arabic-speaking parents. Youngsters like Zehava imitated and improvised on Zohar Argov's captivating sound at local weddings, bar mitzvahs, and holiday parties. They bought cheap cassettes of his music, as well as of the music of Daklon, Avner Gedassi, and other singers, at the outdoor marketplaces in their towns and cities. These bus station marketplaces provided them with readily accessible Mizrahi music that enjoyed only tiny air pockets of broadcast time on radio stations largely controlled by Israeli Jews of European descent.

Zehava Ben's first major success came with the sound track to *Tipat Mazal* (A Drop of Luck), a feature-length film based on the story of her father's descent from Andalusian Moroccan musician to discouraged Moroccan Israeli janitor. The sound track, which captured the airwaves in Tel Aviv's Central Bus Station *shuk* in 1990, was followed by her mainstream vocal breakthrough, "Ketourna Masala" (1991), an East-West duet with the musical group Etnix, which won first place in the 1992 Israeli hit parade.[5] A turning point in Zehava's career came in 1994, when she decided to master the repertoire of Umm Kulthum, the most famous singer in the twentieth-century Arab world. This repertoire allowed Zehava to serve as a musical ambassador for the hopeful, yet in hindsight fragile, mid-1990s peace process, during which Zehava sang at Palestinian gatherings in Nablus and Jericho, as well as at the memorials for Yitzhak Rabin, the assassinated Israeli prime minister.

Accidental Ethnography in Tel Aviv's Central Bus Station Marketplace: Bus Routes, Immigration Waves, and Music Markets

It was only after several bus trips that I understood the Tel Aviv Central Bus Station *shuk* as more than a photogenic transit point, the place from which I would depart for cities throughout Israel, where I would interview performers, radio editors, cassette company owners, distributors, and consumers. One day, while searching for the Bar Ilan University bus, I stopped to ask for directions at a cassette booth pumping out a pulsating Mediterranean beat.

At the entrance to the booth, a young Georgian merchant shouted through a bullhorn above the equally distorted tones of an amplified cassette. It was difficult to distinguish the advertisement—one free leather belt for each purchase of three cassettes—from the elevated bass end feedback of the cassette itself. I noticed that every consumer gravitated toward one particular cassette, from whose pale yellow cover a lean man stared out with hungry eyes. When the booth attendant noticed my interest, he pointed to the overhead speaker and tried to shout above the Yemenite mellisma (several notes sung to a single syllable), which had wrapped itself around Greek *bouzouki* and Western beats, following the opening flamenco *muwwal* (improvised rhythmic introduction).[6]

I purchased the tape and only then remembered to ask for directions to the Bar Ilan bus. Exiting the booth with me, the young Georgian merchant pointed ahead: "There, you see that big red building over there, the one under construction? Head that way and take your second right."

Turning to go, I asked him: "What is that big red building?"

"Oh that! That's the 'new' Central Bus Station! It's been under construction for forty years," he laughed.

Heading toward the building, I shouted back over my shoulder: "Excuse me! And who's this singer?"

"Zohar Argov," he shouted back.

Later that evening I puzzled over why, in all my discussions about alternative Israeli music, none of the people I had interviewed ever mentioned Zohar Argov. When I shared the story of my cassette purchase with colleagues in North Tel Aviv, they issued a stream of unexpected ethnic buzzwords. The designation "cheap" referred not only to the price of this music but also its aesthetic. The names of the music—*Musikat HaTahanah HaMerkazit* (Central Bus Station Music) or *Musikat HaKasetot* (Cassette Music)—clearly placed this music outside the mainstream. I had unknowingly touched a deep cultural nerve.

Taking Note: Scholarly Attention to Mediterranean Israeli Music

The cassette debut of Mediterranean Israeli music in the marketplace in 1974 was followed by a handful of articles in the daily Hebrew-language newspapers in the late 1970s through the mid-1980s. Newspapers covered the music as either local gossip or a sidebar to the emerging Mizrahi ethnic revolution. In the early 1980s some scholars took note. Among the first were the ethnomusicologist Amnon Shiloah in collaboration with the sociologist Erik Cohen, who published two landmark articles on the musical, social, and political dimensions of Israeli popular music.[7] Shiloah and

Cohen identified five chronological stages in the development of this music from the 1950s through the 1980s: Israelization, Orientalization, ethnicization, popularization, and academization. Building on their work, the anthropologist Jeff Halper and the ethnomusicologists Edwin Seroussi and Pamela Kidron observe that *Musika Mizrahit* (one of several designations for Mediterranean Israeli music) remains marginal, not only because of its unaccepted sound but also because it is associated with "low culture," as evidenced in its compositional aesthetics (musical clichés and imitations rather than originality), the locations of performances (gas stations, wedding halls in industrial areas, and working-class neighborhood events), and by the nature of the audience itself.[8] Motti Regev elaborates Shiloh's and Cohen's notion of Israelization as Israeliness in his study of Israeli rock 'n' roll, following Pierre Bourdieu's notion of "the production of meaning."[9] In his consideration of how marginal popular music struggles for elite recognition, Regev suggests that *Musikat HaKasetot* was considered a poor imitation of rock artistry rather than an Israeli cultural phenomenon specific to a time and place.[10] These scholars attempt to understand Mediterranean Israeli music as a context-sensitive Israeli local expression and to lay the ground for exploring the circulation and recontextualization of sounds separated from their originating contexts. Seroussi and Regev's recently published work, *Popular Music and National Culture in Israel*, covers *Shirey Eretz Yisrael* (The Song of the Land of Israel), Israeli rock, and *Musika Mizrahit*, noting that *Musika Mizrahit* is the most studied genre of the three, in part, they claim, due to "public activism," that is, to the recruitment by Mizrahi singers and producers of "scholars interested in their art."[11] They call for a critique of both the genre and the attention that this music has received, while questioning whether such a "mishmash" of diverse styles can be said to form a genre at all.[12] In the close reading offered here of one singer, Zehava Ben, which is based on ethnographic research, I will address these issues.

Track 1: Umm Kulthum Comes to Shkhuna Dalet

The story of Mediterranean Israeli music and the career of Zehava Ben that follows is organized as a series of sound tracks—Umm Kulthum's *Enta Omri*, Zohar Argov's "Perakh B'Gani," Zehava Ben's "Tipat Mazal," Zehava Ben and Etnix's "Ketourna Masala," and Zehava Ben's "Enta Omri"— that make audible the political and historical currents shaping Zehava Ben's development as an Israeli singer.

When Zehava Ben was growing up, the music that her North African parents loved was marginalized by Israelis of European descent and even by some young Mizrahi Jews. Yehudit Ravitz, one of Israel's leading popular music singer/songwriters, shared a story about coming to terms with her rejection of her Egyptian mother's culture in the mid-1980s, before Mediterranean Israeli and Arab music had become fashionable in Ashkenazi

Figures 7.1 and 7.2. Left: Umm Kulthum's CD, *Enta Omri*. Right: In early 1995, Zehava Ben released a CD on her own label, entitled *Zehava Ben Sings Arabic*. The silver and gold cover portrays Ben inscribed within the profile of the renowned Egyptian singer Umm Kulthum. Soon after Prime Minister Rabin's assassination, Ben released a CD of Umm Kulthum repertoire on the Helicon label.

communities: "As a child I begged my mother to hide her Arab music in the back room where none of my friends would make ugly comments about Umm Kulthum's whiny voice. My mother loved this music which reminded her of her childhood in Egypt. I was much more drawn to my father's Israeli folk music; he was from Poland and knew all the early songs, even those that had been composed in Europe. When I grew up and realized how cruel I had been to my mother, I begged for her forgiveness."[13] Simon Benista, Zehava Ben's father, was a neighborhood oud player in Morocco and had hoped to build his career in Israel but discovered instead that North African and Middle Eastern music was often raw material for European compositions. The music of Yemenite Jews was especially valued because it was thought to be closer to ancient Jewish music and therefore more "authentically" Jewish than the music of other Jewish groups.[14] As a result, from at least the end of the nineteenth century, Ashkenazi composers and performers used elements derived from Yemenite Jewish music to create the national Israeli musical canon, *Shirey Eretz Yisrael*. The "Middle Eastern" sound of Jewish Palestinian (and later Israeli) music owes much to Yemenite Jewish music.[15]

In contrast, Middle Eastern and North African music—whether classical or folk, urban or rural, live, recorded, or broadcast—was most often heard in Middle Eastern and North African Jewish neighborhoods and festivals. Beloved Middle Eastern singers such as the Muslim Egyptian Umm Kulthum or the Egyptian Coptic Farid el Atrash (or Jewish singers who performed such repertoire) might be heard on Israel's Arab-language radio shows. For continuous Arab music, Middle Eastern and North African Jewish listeners had only to turn the radio dial slightly to tune into stations in Jordan, Lebanon, or Syria.

However, the ethnic and musical rejection that the Benistas encountered also laid the groundwork for the emergence of a Mizrahi coalition, expressed musically and in other ways, that would coalesce in the twenty-year period during which their daughter Zehava was growing up. This coalition arose not only from cultural and social affinities but also in response to the shortcomings of an immigration program that treated North African and Middle Eastern Jews unfairly. Israeli ethnomusicologist Amnon Shiloah, who is of Syrian descent, and Cohen characterize the cultural insensitivity to North African and Middle Eastern music as "Israeliza tion," by which he means the absorption of selected North African and Middle Eastern musical motifs into a European musical aesthetic. However, many Middle Eastern and North African Jews did not recognize themselves in this music. Nor was the practice of incorporating fragments of their musical styles—understood as more closely connected to an ancient collective past than European Jewish music—a substitute for an appreciation of their music in its own right. While the North African popular music that neighborhood artists such as Simon Benista had performed in Morocco was rejected by the European-dominated Israeli music industry, it was far from becoming a memory of a lost past in Mizrahi neighborhoods, where such music merged with other styles to create a new musical genre.

The relationship between Mizrahi and European musical styles has long been asymmetrical—that is, while European Israelis showed little interest in Mizrahi music in its own right, they valued elements of the music considered ancient and authentically Jewish. Ironically, the music of neither Simon Benista nor Umm Kulthum qualified. Neither of them were "folk" performers from an ancient, rural past. Simon Benista performed classical and popular Arab music in Morocco. Umm Kulthum combined classical Arab vocal styles with elements from classical European music traditions. Both musicians were part of a modern musical dialogue between East and West. By relegating contemporary Mizrahi music to the category of heritage music (for display and appropriation rather than ongoing development and performance), European Israelis failed to appreciate this music its own right, tokenized and trivialized it, and were initially blind to the emergence of a vital new Mizrahi hybrid musical genre.

The marginalization of musicians like Zehava Ben's father, the relegating of elements of Middle Eastern and North African music to "heritage," and attempts to incorporate those elements into European-derived musical compositions occurred in large measure during the 1950s and 1960s, as European Israeli cultural and artistic preferences were institutionalized in the form of chamber choirs, concert halls, and classical music festivals like the Abu Ghosh festival (1957). No comparable institutions for the advancement of Middle Eastern or North African music or culture were founded during the period. Instead, recordings of Umm Kulthum and other Middle Eastern and North African musicians continued to flourish in crowded, poor Mizrahi neighborhoods like Shkhuna Dalet, where older generations of working-class people spoke primarily Arabic. Although the Academy of the Hebrew Language was established as the supreme authority on Hebrew in 1953, the year of the major Moroccan *aliyah* (immigration), Middle Eastern and North African mothers like Zehava Ben's, whose lives were overwhelmed with concerns of daily survival, had little time to attend the *ulpan* (intensive Hebrew language instruction) programs.

In Shkhuna Dalet of the 1970s, Umm Kulthum's music was not confined to backrooms, as it was in Yehudit Ravitz's Ashkenazi neighborhood, but rather it was integrated into the emerging Mediterranean Israeli music genre of the neighborhoods and into the everyday lives of children. Zehava Ben came into the world as Yemenite bands like Lahaqat Tsliley HaKerem were composing multiethnic soundtracks for Kurdish, Moroccan, or Iraqi Jewish weddings. They combined Arab music with the Eastern European sounds of *Shirey Eretz Yisrael*, to which they added Greek and rock 'n' roll sounds. Some musicians took the frets off their guitars in order to bend the notes. What youngsters like Zehava Ben appreciated most was that the singers retained Eastern vocal elaborations rarely heard on Israeli radio.

The journey from Yehudit Ravitz's embarrassment when her mother played Umm Kulthum to Zehava Ben's reclamation of Umm Kulthum's repertoire as her own is a retrospective story that brings into relief a history of exclusions, appropriations, and relocalizations. It is a lesson in the significance of style as a cultural map that displays the complexities of time (never a unidirectional series of influences) and space (disrupting rather than asserting the correspondence between cultures and territories).

"Perakh B'Gani" (The Flower in My Garden): Zohar Argov Comes to Shkhuna Dalet

> We needed a champ. If there hadn't been a Zohar, we would have had to invent one.[16]
>
> —Chaim Moshe and Asher Reuveni

For young Mizrahi Israeli singers like Zehava Ben, Zohar Argov was the champion whose cassette breakthrough in the *shuk* and appearances on radio and even television in the 1980s opened up the possibility of success beyond local neighborhood events. Zohar provided a model for young singers like Zehava by defying the limits of his own impoverished neighborhood music scene in Rishon L'Tzion. In 1981, sales of his first cassette, *Elinor,* exceeded the expectations of its producers, the Reuveni Brothers, a small company in Tel Aviv's Shkhunat HaTikvah neighborhood.[17] The commercial success of this cassette forced the Reuveni Brothers to expand their marketing and distribution beyond Tel Aviv's Central Bus Station marketplaces to Be'er Sheva and other cities. Zohar Argov, like Zehava Ben a decade later, would credit Tel Aviv's Central Bus Station *shuk* for his first commercial visibility: "With a cassette I reached the Central Bus Station and Shuk HaKarmel [Carmel Market]. That's my radio. Who doesn't come to buy vegetables in the market? And that's where I am played from morning to night. That's my clientele. Only after I became famous and sold tens of thousands of cassettes and records, the television came to check . . . what's the noise? Who's terrorizing around here? So they took my picture and they took my mother's picture also."[18] Zehava Ben's cassette *Tipat Mazal* would set even greater sales records here a decade later. In addition to its commercial success, Zohar's "Perakh B'Gani" won first place at the 1981 Festival of Eastern Song, which led to a limited number of radio and television appearances.

With Zohar Argov's commercial success in the early 1980s, Mizrahi musicians could command more airtime. By 1981, the Israeli army's official station, Galey Zahal, and Israel Radio's popular music channel, Reshet Gimel, each added a two-hour weekly Mizrahi segment. While these were significant advances, Zohar claimed ghettoization: "Over 55% of Israel is my audience, but to hear me on the radio they have to wait until 2:00 p.m. on Wednesday in the Mizrahi corner. We live in 1981 and those programs were old ten years ago. We are fed up!!! Why are we being locked in a—I didn't say ghetto, that's your word. I only said it hurts. Scatter us on all the hours or don't play us at all."[19] Fellow Mizrahi musicians, Ashkenazi journalists, and scholars canonized Zohar Argov after his death in 1987. The Yemenite guitarist Moshe Ben Moshe noted that "Argov presented music like it's written in the Bible, with the same cantillations [the Hebrew text of the Bible is marked to indicate how it is to be chanted]. When it is done with the right emphasis it makes the listener understand. And this is what came to Zohar spontaneously."[20]

As a child singer in Be'er Sheva, Zehava Ben studied Zohar Argov's performance style on cassettes and occasionally on television and radio and in live performance. She was drawn to the measured intensity of his voice and incorporated Zohar's sonic juxtaposition of Jewish text with Arab vocal styles into her own emerging style; he became, by default, her music teacher in the absence of a formal institutional structure through which she might become proficient in Middle Eastern and North African musical systems. Young singers like Zehava Ben studied the way Zohar Argov's music (composed and arranged by another Yemenite musician, Avihu Medina) selectively incorporated Spanish, Greek, and Western instrumentation and arrangements in order to embellish a Middle Eastern vocal line, which remained the most resilient element of the music. In his compositions and arrangements for Zohar Argov, such as "Perakh B'Gani" (composed and arranged by Avihu Medina and Nanci Brandeis), Medina adapted specific components of Arab vocal style, such as a shortened version of the traditional *muwwal*, an introduction highlighting melismatic nasal vocalization. In Bakhtinian terms, the prolonged *muwwal* can itself be considered an "uncrowning" of the authorial voice of Israeli popular culture.[21]

In "Perakh B'gani," which he recorded and performed in concerts throughout Israel in the 1980s, Zohar Argov demonstrated the remixed musical styles that emerged during Zehava Ben's youth. During this period, Argov often performed the song at Shoni Gavriel's Club Ariana. Located in Jaffa, this club was one of the leading Mizrahi venues in the 1970s and 1980s, and Zohar Argov, who was the leading Mizrahi Israeli singer of the 1980s, considered the club his home base. To make a living, Zohar and other Mizrahi performers would appear at clubs, weddings, and other neighborhood events, sometimes performing at three different events in one night. Even so, few could survive on music alone, a function of not only their exclusion from mainstream European-centered Israeli music channels, but also of the small and limited music market of the country.

In one performance of "Perakh B'Gani" at Club Ariana in the summer of 1984, the opening bars of the synthesizer's horn section seem to prepare the ear for a Spanish bullfight. Brassy tones crest, then cool down, then pause expectantly. But the matador does not enter the ring. Instead, Zohar Argov, a slender Yemenite man in a tight-fitting Western suit, appears at stage left. He walks to the microphone and fills the air with a single clear, piercing tone. The sound shoots out from a deep well somewhere between his heart and his head. It streams through every inch of his throat and nose, lips and cheeks, like unexpected rain winding down the interior crevices of a desert canyon. It is neither a cry nor a roar, but evokes both. Overtones reverberate, as he bends the note into a melismatic arch that conjures up Muslim and Jewish prayer.

Zohar Argov's abbreviated *muwwal* answers the linear horn opening with carefully placed vocal spirals and twists of Eastern melisma (*silsulim*). The *muwwal* is an improvisation on a syllable such as "ah" or on word such as "Yalel," with which a singer opens a vocal performance. The opening *muwwal* focuses the singer and the audience and sets a meditative mood. Zohar's timbres soar like a bird in mid-air. His vocal lines retrace the melody outlined by the horns, creating an interior path that bends the pitches and liberates the myriad microtones that live between the whole and half-tones of Western scales. The *muwwal* lasts forty seconds, giving way to Western drumbeats, which underline the rhythmic drive of the song. In this well-known song, which the composer Avihu Medina classifies as "one of my Spanish works," the *muwwal* marks the cultural nerve center. Between Spanish Mediterranean horns and Western beat, Zohar Argov's *muwwal* assures the listener that the voice, with its Middle Eastern attitude and aesthetic, is the signature line. Zohar's voice subverts expectation. He over-takes but does not obliterate the Spanish orchestra with Hebrew lyrics, which reclaim and celebrate the language's guttural sounds. He renders improvisational *silsulim* where Western notation calls for rest bars.

It is not only the intensity of his voice and its unlikely coalition with the musical accompaniment that shocks younger singers like Zehava Ben into emotional attentiveness; it is the man himself. He has piercing black eyes and a hungry face (which, he had confessed in an interview with Michael Ohad, was deemed "too ugly for airtime" by an apologetic television pro-ducer)—hungry for approval.[22] His movements are understated, yet the audience feels the volcanic center from which the sound flows. The audi-ence, a mixture of teen- and middle-aged adults, most of them from Moroc-can, Yemenite, Iraqi, Iranian, Georgian, and other Mizrahi communities, is on its feet, clapping, singing, and dancing, with arms raised above their heads, swaying to the music. Some audience members climb onto the low stage in the smoke-filled club. Zohar offers them the microphone to sing a few bars. Others throw dollars and flowers and undulate toward the beloved singer.

Argov's mercurial rise in Mizrahi communities was cut short just as he began to penetrate mainstream Israeli channels. His suicide in prison in 1987 silenced a powerful Mizrahi voice. Within the next few years, Zehava Ben and other young singers had refashioned Zohar Argov's performances of "Perakh B'Gani." Zehava performed his signature song as a memorial at an anti-drug concert in 1993. Zehava bowed her head for a brief second and then, as Zohar had a decade earlier, captured the audience's emo-tional attention with her opening note. But now, almost ten years later, this song had become popular throughout Israel, symbolizing a growing aware-ness if not acceptance of Middle Eastern and North African hybrid music forms.

Unlike Zohar's hungry and piercing *muwwal*, Zehava's opening improvi-sation at the outdoor concert across from the HaMashbir building in down-town Jerusalem, on June 11, 1993, engulfed the listener in a sonic moment that unfolded slowly like the garden flower, the song's central metaphor. Zehava Ben stood before a breathless crowd, eyes closed, barely moving, except for her left arm, which she gently raised in beat with the soaring note that echoed off the surrounding buildings. Zehava Ben's *muwwal* charted an emotional territory through which the ensuing song lyric could be contextualized. Resounding in Zehava Ben's improvisation were the economic and ethnic struggles of Mizrahim like Zohar Argov, as well as a call for determination and optimism. Sadness and hope were woven into the carefully executed quartertones, as if to catch and comfort the listener, between the notes, weary from his or her daily struggle. As the drumbeats signaled the beginning of the song's first verse, the audience cheered, danced, hugged each other, and began singing in full voice. Here in a cen-tral Jerusalem park, as the Palestinian Intifada still raged and the nascent

Palestinian-Israeli peace process had not yet been reduced to a CNN sound bite, European, Middle Eastern, and North African Israelis, along with a handful of Palestinians from Ramallah and Bethlehem, rose to their feet and danced together to Zehava Ben's new version of the song that had brought Zohar Argov and Mizrahi music into the mainstream Israeli canon of popular music and across the borders to Jordan, Lebanon, Syria, and Palestine.

Zehava Ben's Crying Songs: "Tipat Mazal" (A Drop of Luck) and Two Drops of Turkish Turkish

Like Zohar Argov's performances of "Perakh B'Gani" in the 1980s, Zehava Ben's interpretation in the summer of 1993 also straddled Mediterranean and Middle Eastern aesthetics. She framed and centered the song's Spanish and Greek arrangement with her precise Arab *muwwal* and convincing vocal quartertones, maintaining a delicate position between the Arab East and the more acceptable (more European) Greek and Mediterranean domains, both aesthetically and politically.

Yet, as the journalist Rino Tsror observed, Mizrahi singers such as Zehava Ben were beginning to record more "risky" (read: Middle Eastern) styles, abandoning the earlier Greek and Mediterranean songs for what he refers to as "Turkish Turkish." In the following statement, he sums up European Israeli discomfort with the unabashed combination of musical styles embraced by Mizrahi composers and condemns the Arabizing (North African "curl" refers to Zehava Ben's melismatic vocal elaboration) of the literary Hebrew song lyrics composed by European Israeli superstars such as Nomi Shemer, one of the best-known Israeli singer/songwriters, who wrote, among other things, the song "Yerushalayim Shel Zahav" (Jerusalem of Gold):[23]

No one came up with a less insulting definition [of Mediterranean Israeli music] than the combination of Greek tone with the spice of an oud, of the North African curl with Nomi Shemer's Hebrew.[24] So it's all over. There is no continuation of the Mediterranean experiment, not a real one, anyway—there are no buyers. The separation from the Hebrew is final, period. The market only buys heavy Arabic, or Turkish Turkish. They want Arab stuff, not Greek Hebrew. . . .

The public's request climaxes in Zehava Ben and Ofer Levi. These are the two making business boil. She is from the Be'er Sheva borough, and he is from the Kiryat Ata borough [both are poor industrial neighborhoods]. Eli Luzon is from the Netanya quarter. There's a difference between a black guy from one borough and a black guy from another, especially in the level of openness, the tolerance for white. The Be'er Sheva quarter is tougher and less open than Netanya borough—and Zehava came from Shkhuna Dalet (a notoriously poor neighborhood in Be'er Sheva). Take the history or the twenty-one years of her life there and you'll understand what Shkhuna Dalet is, and why they don't speak White Hebrew there.[25]

The Moroccan Israeli songwriter Danny Shoshan, who wrote "Tipat Mazal" by overlaying his original Hebrew lyrics on a Turkish folk tune, explained the appeal of the new "Turkish Turkish" trend for Mizrahim. For Shoshan, Greek music was safely European, while Turkish folk music's unequivocally Middle Easternness resonated with Mizrahi reclamations of their cultural roots. Shoshan also noted that Greek tunes required royalty payments, whereas Turkish tunes did not, because there was no intellectual property agreement between Turkey and Israel. As a result, he was able to take "Tipat Mazal"'s Turkish tune from the "public domain."

The radio editor Yoel Rekem contends, however, that it was not the Turkish Turkishness of Shoshan's new composition for Zehava Ben that kept it from being broadcasted on Israeli radio but rather the poor quality of the production itself: "During the cassette era, feelings of deprivation intensified. Singers and impresarios cried out, 'You don't play us on Kol Yisrael.' The greatest revolution was not cultural but technological. Once the producers of the Central Bus Station singers understood that they would not be played on Kol Yisrael because of the bad quality, they started investing in better productions and searching for singers who had a chance of becoming popular and not recording just anyone who sang. In that sense, the radio policy was productive, since it initiated a kind of quality control."[26] The poor technical quality of the *Tipat Mazal* cassette resulted partly from Shoshan's overuse of new computer-based music compositional technologies, sequencing and quantizing, as well as his lack of fluency in Turkish music. Shoshan, like other computer music technicians, expanded his possibilities through the use of a MIDI (musical instrument digital interface) technology. In so doing he could capture (synthesize or sample) and utilize the sounds of traditional Middle Eastern and North African as well as European instruments.

Like the cassette technology of the 1970s, these new technologies provided accessible music compositional tools for anyone who could learn to operate a MIDI, computer, and module.[27] Although these techniques save time and allow for the incorporation of musical instruments that usually require very specialized training in creating precise rhythmic patterns and removing rhythmic inaccuracies, there is also a "canned" quality lacking in the improvisational textures and feelings that bring music alive.

Despite the poor technical quality of the recording, Zehava Ben's rendition of this Turkish tune demonstrated her competence in Eastern singing, including the performance of quartertones. She made no attempt to sound European in her vocal style, and the only sign that the song was Israeli, albeit of Turkish origin, was the Hebrew lyrics. After the sales of that cassette exceeded Zohar Argov's earlier figures, a remastered version of the *Tipat Mazal* (1992) cassette eventually caught the attention of European Israeli radio editors, who finally broadcast it on Israeli radio.[28] Increasing recognition for the singer and the song followed the release of a feature-length film, also called *Tipat Mazal* (1992), starring Zehava Ben.[29] The film fictionalizes her father's difficult transition from stardom in North Africa to artistic rejection and subsequent economic ruin in Israel, followed by his death. During the production of this film, Zehava Ben traveled to Morocco to research her father's roots. With the film Zehava not only reclaimed her North African music but also the tragic story of her father's life.

Zehava Ben's Mainstream Duet with the Etnix: "Ketourna Masala"

In the early 1990s, the influence of Mizrahi singers could be felt in Israel's shifting mainstream popular music soundscape. "Legitimate" pop stars such as Yehuda Poliker began to mark the prevailing rock aesthetic with their own ethnic musical signatures. Poliker, the son of Greek Holocaust survivors, fought with his record producers until they agreed to release an album featuring Greek songs. The Tunisian-Israeli pop singer Etti Ankry, who had previously performed primarily Western rock, added a few Arabic songs (for example, Safy Boutella's "Eshebo") to her repertoire and displayed her skill at traditional drumming during live performances. These singers distinguished their "acceptable" incorporation of Middle Eastern motifs from cassette music associated with the Tel Aviv Central Bus Station. In 1992 a popular rock band called Etnix (Ethnics) invited Zehava Ben to perform one song with them for their new recording, *Ketourna Masala*. In her guest appearance on this mainstream recording, Zehava shares the vocal lead with Zev Nehama, the band's Bulgarian lead singer.

While Etnix incorporates some Eastern motifs within their rock sound, their music is basically Western pop/rock. The band's duet with Zehava Ben in the song "Ketourna Masala" shifts more to the East than most of their repertoire. The main meeting of Eastern and Western styles occurs in the refrain, which takes the form of call and response between Zev Nehama and Zehava Ben. Nehama sings the verses in a standard rock vocal style, though he inserts some slow and simple trills reminiscent of his Bulgarian heritage, while Zehava Ben sings the refrain in an Arabic vocal style, demonstrating her mastery of quarter tones and Eastern aesthetics. Although the instrumental arrangements are almost entirely Western, an Eastern feeling is achieved through a rhythmic shift between the refrain (4/4 time) and the verses (6/4 time). This rhythmic shift punctuates the distinction between Zev Nehama's Western vocals on the verses and Zehava Ben's Eastern style on the refrain. A syncopated rendering of the Hebrew word for love, *ahava*, in Zehava Ben's vocal refrain lead momentarily interrupts Zev Nehama's Western style on the verses. The sequencer provides an Eastern feeling by emulating the sounds of the *santur*, a hammered dulcimer, and other "indigenous" instruments. Although the *santur* track is sequenced, it is not quantized, as are the Western instruments. This gives the listener the feeling that the *santur* track remains rhythmically free.

"Ketourna Masala," the song from which the album takes its title, is based on the common Middle Eastern folkloric theme of searching for an appropriate gift for one's beloved. Written jointly by Zev Nehama and the synthesizer player Tamir Kalisky, and featuring Zehava Ben's compelling vocal line, the song was extremely popular in the early 1990s and won first place in the 1992 Israeli Mitza'ad HaPizmonim (Israeli Hit Parade). Two seemingly oppositional directions meet in collaborations such as this, where Mizrahi musicians perform mainstream duets with well-known European Israeli performers, while re-Arabizing the music. The Mizrahi vocalists maintain and even embellish their Middle Eastern vocal elaboration as a counterpart to the European vocal styles of their singing partners. Do these collaborations represent a true reciprocity? Do they make up for previous lack of appreciation of Mizrahi music on the part of European Israelis, who were otherwise willing to incorporate elements of this music into their own compositions? Although Zehava Ben's Eastern vocal refrain reverberates only faintly within the Western rock frame of "Ketourna Masala," her collaboration with Etnix—in bringing together the two styles without blending them—searches for a different kind of meeting ground.

"You are my life" Umm Kulthum: Zehava Ben Sings "Enta Omri"

Zehava Ben's rise to fame roughly corresponds with the period from the early 1990s Israeli Palestinian peace process to the assassination of Yitzhak Rabin in 1995. It was in the course of this period that the homespun soundtrack of Mediterranean Israeli music began shifting its position in the national landscape. In 1995, Zehava Ben, who was dubbed "queen of crying songs" for such numbers as "Tipat Mazal," issued a CD of Umm Kulthum's repertoire, entitled *Zehava Ben Shara Aravit* (Zehava Ben Sings Arabic).[30] Zehava Ben's highly successful covers of Umm Kulthum's repertoire brought Arab music out into the mainstream for Mizrahim, who had kept their unwavering appreciation of this iconic Egyptian singer quietly confined to neighborhood events. In the context of seemingly forward-moving peace negotiations with Palestinians and Arab countries, Ashkenazi audiences who had rejected both Mizrahi attempts to emulate *Shirey Eretz Yisrael* as too Arab-sounding, and the emerging pan-ethnic genre of Mediterranean Israeli music as too hybrid and confusing, embraced Zehava Ben's performances of an unquestionably "authentic" Arab music, a music that they could now claim as their own. World music, a marketing concept and emergent genre that took hold in the late 1980s, had resituated Arab music as legitimate for Ashkenazi music consumers, who might own a copy of an Umm Kulthum recording without personally appreciating the music itself. In a way, the world music boom prepared the European Israeli ear for Zehava Ben's reclamation of Umm Kulthum.

Why did Zehava Ben decide to perform Umm Kulthum's repertoire? Was the Egyptian repertoire recognized as more generically "pure" than hybrid Mizrahi popular music? While Zehava Ben's manager, the savvy Ely Banai,[31] no doubt saw the commercial potential of producing an Israeli cover of a renowned Egyptian singer, her performance was more than a successful marketing ploy. She presented her cover of Umm Kulthum and other Arab singers as homage to revered masters. The cover image for *Zehava Ben Shara Aravit*, which features primarily Umm Kulthum as well as several other Arab selections, merges a drawing of Zehava Ben's face with that of Umm Kulthum and includes photographs of her pilgrimage to Umm Kulthum's grave in Egypt. The director Erez Laufer also filmed Zehava Ben's pilgrimage to Umm Kulthum's grave, in a scene following an announcement of restricted travel to Egypt, in the feature documentary *Solitary Star.*[32] In these ways, she defined herself as a daughter of the tradition rather than an outsider. Consistent with that tradition, she learned and emulated the style of her forebear. Although this move was contested by some, her boldness and the quality of her performance of decidedly Arab music were generally appreciated.

Several months later, in the fall of 1995, in the aftermath of Prime Minister Rabin's assassination, Zehava Ben released a sequel, *Zehava Ben Shara Aravit: Enta Omri*, on the mainstream Helicon label.[33] Umm Kulthum's "Enta Omri" was well known in the classical Arab music repertoire. Written by Mohammed Abdul Wahab, a composer who intentionally mixed European and Arab forms, "Enta Omri" sounded like "pure" Arab music, even when rendered by a Moroccan Israeli who reduced the fifty-seven-minute classic to a five-minute cover. In the time between her first two Arabic CDs, Zehava Ben had been studying classical Arabic music, language, and performance, had developed competency in the repertoire of Umm Kulthum, and employed the Haifa Arab Orchestra to accompany her. As many Israelis and Palestinians grieved together over Rabin's death and the unresolved prospects for peace, Zehava Ben's CDs, her appearances in Nablus and Jericho, and her presence at ceremonies marking the (cold) peace with Egypt acquired new meaning.

With these Arab CDs and live performances of Arab songs, Zehava Ben defied single-voiced categorizations and claimed conflictual identities and multiple indigeneities. Her encounter with Umm Kulthum's life story and artistry was personal and emotional. Umm Kulthum's flexible religious identity and poor rural background resonated with Zehava Ben's own traditional religious upbringing, impoverished childhood, and cultural marginality. Umm Kulthum taught Zehava Ben more than proper classical Arab music. Umm Kulthum opened Zehava Ben to her own Arab Jewish heritage. Moreover, Umm Kulthum was an important role model as a woman. That this bold revoicing of Arab Jewish heritage should emanate from a woman is particularly important in the context of the Israel-Palestine conflict.[34] Women's coalitions such as Women in Black have played an important role in creating personal, grassroots institutional connections as a parallel track supporting male-dominated official diplomatic channels. As Zehava Ben herself said, "I am braver than a man and so I went to perform in Arab communities. I was always treated with great gentleness and kindness."[35]

While Zehava Ben's music reaches across hostile national boundaries, audio penetration of enemy territory does not create peace, even if it creates aesthetic common ground. At the time of this writing, in 2007, Zehava Ben's travel to Palestinian communities is not possible. Still, her cassettes continue to be sold on the streets, even by Muslim vendors in Jerusalem, and she continues to perform Umm Kulthoum's repertoire for Israelis, claiming, "I will always sing in Arabic. I pray that my music, my singing can bring real peace. I wish it were so. I wish my music would create some sort of connection. That is the most important thing right now."[36]

On November 12, 2003, the *Jerusalem Post* announced that al-Jazeera, the Arab TV network, planned to feature Zehava Ben in a celebration of the centennial of the birth of Umm Kulthum.[37] Community artists the world over are selectively acclaimed as token representatives of their groups while simultaneously experiencing social and economic marginalization. Zehava Ben has responded to this condition by challenging the opposition between authentic and hybrid, traditional and contemporary, marginal and mainstream. Her performances defy such compartmentalized identities. Her music charts soundscapes that challenge geopolitical maps of disputed territories, where affiliations and loyalties have heightened significance and life and death consequences.

III.
Lost in Place

Territorially specific sitings of the Jewish tomorrow, whether in Palestine or the Soviet Union, stand in contrast with diaspora, a condition of displacement and ubiquity whose enduring emblem is the "Wandering Jew." In this section, essays by Richard I. Cohen and Carol Zemel offer contrasting artistic perspectives on this figure and on Jewish diaspora generally. Cohen focuses on the figure of the Wandering Jew in Christian Europe from the late Middle Ages to the end of the nineteenth century, while Zemel explores the possible meanings and definitions of a "diasporist" aesthetic, informed by postmodern and post-Zionist cultural theory.

While literary treatments of the Wandering Jew have been amply studied, the visual images of this symbol have not received comparable attention. Righting the imbalance, Richard I. Cohen offers a pioneering analysis of the figure's iconographic history. According to legend, the Wandering Jew (often named Ahasuerus in European legends) was condemned to roam the globe until the Second Coming for his cruel spurning of a suffering Christ. As Cohen notes, despite the persistence of traditional theological antipathy, the figure of Ahasuerus proved remarkably supple, often reflecting social concerns that transcended the "Jewish Question" itself. Early modern Europeans wondered at the wanderings of the Jews, sensing in their perpetual displacement a potent metaphor for contemporary political and spiritual turbulence. Similarly, in Restoration France, interest in the Wandering Jew paralleled the hopes pinned on the figure of Napoleon: exiled and humiliated, but soon to return to rehabilitate a defeated France. In the fin de siècle period, Ahasuerus even came to epitomize a universal human condition, personifying heroic perseverance and paradoxical freedom in the face of harsh existential necessity. Cohen notes that in the early twentieth century the overtly anti-Semitic function of the Wandering Jew (as a marker of Jewish execrable otherness) did return, but in contrast with the late medieval theological formulae, it now bore the ineradicable stigma of racial rather than religious ostracism. Finally, and perhaps in response to this radicalization, Jews themselves took up and refashioned the image, whether to transvalue the diaspora in positive terms or to make the case for Zionism.

If wandering and the accompanying disease of anti-Semitism constituted the very pathologies that Zionism hoped to cure, Carol Zemel's treatment of "diasporism," a term coined by the artist R. B. Kitaj, exposes a current-day Jewish aesthetic and ideological movement that locates the authentic wellsprings of Jewish cultural creativity in the millennial condition of mobility and adaptation. In her essay, Zemel depicts the dual aim of diasporism as a simultaneous effort to "interrogate national cultural limits and to embrace or transmit its fluidities." It is in these terms that she reads the visual imagery and formal devices of such diverse figures as the painter R. B. Kitaj, the graphic novelist Ben Katchor, and the multimedia installation artist Vera Frenkel. All three, Zemel argues, have self-consciously embraced displacement, transience, and a perspectivism arising from shifting locales. These qualities—or so the distilled consciousness of these three figures suggests—are emblematic of the modern artist generally and symptomatic of the Jew in particular. Instead of viewing diaspora in religious and mythical terms as exile and punishment, they interpret it as an existential condition of mixed blessing, one that is characterized by a rich and complex "double relationship" to reality and by "multiple subjectivities."

Chapter 8

The "Wandering Jew" from Medieval Legend to Modern Metaphor

Richard I. Cohen

Wanderers—real and fictional—have engaged the imagination in different cultures and times. For the settled and the sedentary, they arouse a sense of fear and attraction, offering a glimpse of another world and of other civilizations, appearing in moments of crisis and tension, at junctures of a dramatic nature when new currents of thought or social transformations are emerging. Legendary figures ranging from the Ancient Mariner and Wild Huntsman to Pindola and Al-Sameri, to name but a few, have been condemned to wander, either interminably or for a defined time.[1] References to the Wandering Jew, however, far exceed those relating to the other wanderers, and he—seldom she—has remained a constant cultural trope in our time as well.

The legend has attracted the interest of collectors, researchers, and observers for over a hundred and fifty years. A scholar of English Jewry, Frank Felsenstein, argued that the Wandering Jew has had a "chameleon-like ability to take a form that reflects a given age."[2] In contrast, Galit Hasan-Rokem, who has studied many folkloric variations on the theme, claimed that the attraction of the figure lies in his paradox: "His simultaneous presentation as local and itinerant, almost autochtonous as a nature spirit and as exotic as a complete stranger . . . signal the paradoxical identity of European Jews in their own eyes and in the eyes of their Christian neighbours as at the same time completely local and familiar and on the other as deeply alien." The image has thus reinforced for the Europeans their identity as the opposite of the wanderer, that is, "as belonging to a specific locality as well as to their self-image rooted in stability."[3] Finally, the Wandering Jew has had the power to represent issues in society that are not intrinsically related to Jews or the Jewish historical evolution. He seems to mirror certain social and cultural issues of a universal nature.[4]

This essay explores how the visual image of the Wandering Jew reflects the historical tension between Jews and non-Jews in different periods, how it represents various internal traditions relating to the legend, and how the imagined figure transmitted aspects of the historical experience of Jews in the modern period. To what extent did images of "real Jews" inform the depiction of the imaginary figure, and how did the representation of the Wandering Jew enable mythic notions of the Jew to surface and persist? What can the changing iconography of the Wandering Jews tell us about the history of the relationship of Jews and non-Jews? Although my concern here is with how non-Jewish artists have treated the legend, I conclude the essay with a brief discussion of some artists of Jewish origin who have also taken up the visual image of Ahasuerus.

Although the visual image of the Wandering Jew has undergone constant evolution, it has received little scholarly attention. The nineteenth-century critic and writer Champfleury (Jules-François Felix Husson), who served on a censorship commission for popular art during the Second Republic in France, was fascinated by the popular imagery of le Juif errant and made a list of some extant prints. His study was sketchy and marred by his dislike of images that strayed from what he considered popular art.[5] Though Champfleury included several illustrations in his work, they failed to suggest the scope of the phenomenon.[6] Since Champfleury, specific depictions of the Wandering Jew have been studied, and images from the classic prints (e.g., from Gustave Doré's series of 1856 or from one of the flourishing publishing houses in Épinal, the home of French popular culture in the nineteenth century) have illustrated the occasional article or book, but the visual phenomenon had not been examined in its wider context until an exhibition in Paris in 2001 on the Wandering Jew opened up the area extensively.[7] This essay builds on that work.

At the center of the legend is the encounter between Christ and a Jew in Jerusalem, while Christ was carrying his cross to Calvary. On the road Christ paused for a moment to rest on the Jew's doorstep but was driven away by the cry "Walk faster!" Christ replied, "I go, but you will walk until I come again." Two themes emerge from this brief but hostile meeting: first, Christ's promise that he will return at some indefinite period of time, before which the victim will know no rest; second, the indignity with which the Jew treated Christ. Two other stories contributed additional themes to the Wandering Jew legend. In the story of Malchus (Gospel of St. John), the offender is punished and suffers for his insulting behavior. In contrast, the legend of St. John (Gospel of Matthew) emphasizes waiting and doing the will of Christ.[8]

Though some see the precursor to the legend already in the story of Cain and Abel, it was not until the thirteenth century that the various threads of the story emerged into a full-blown legend. But nothing compared with its later reception, following the publication in 1602 of the anonymous chapbook *Kurtze Beschreibung und Erzehlung von einem Juden mit Namen Ahasverus*. An immediate success, twenty different editions of the pamphlet appeared within a single year in Germany, reaching a wide and diverse audience. Probably authored by a German Lutheran, the slim volume, with a vignette portraying the Wandering Jew in crude outline, bearded and wearing head-gear in the form of a turban, brought the legend into the internal battle between Catholicism and Protestantism by associating the Wandering Jew with the Antichrist. As narrated in this influential version, the Wandering Jew was born in Jerusalem with the name of Ahasuerus and worked as a shoemaker. He had been present at the crucifixion of Christ, but, con-demned to wander, he traveled through many lands. In his travels he repeatedly appears as a man of grave demeanor and few words. He is upstanding, avoids oaths and blasphemy, and is charitably inclined. Inter-estingly enough, though his past is checkered, nothing damning is said about him and his actions, and he carries himself with the temperament of a missionary. Constantly questioned by scholars of all countries, Ahasuerus responds in the language in which he is addressed. In the *Kurtze Beschrei-bung* Ahasuerus is a man of about fifty years of age. The pamphlet provides a good description of his physical appearance: he is shabbily dressed and barefoot, tall, lean, and gaunt, with long, wild hair and a ragged counte-nance, features that arouse interest. Ahasuerus appears both bearded and beardless and may or may not have a head covering.

The growing interest in the legend in the seventeenth century came at a time when European society and Jews in Europe were undergoing signifi-cant changes. This period saw a fascination with worlds beyond Europe, but also the emergence of internal strife from the Reformation and Counter-Reformation and ensuing confrontations between Catholics and Protestant/Lutheran denominations. The turbulent atmosphere gave birth to a dramatic rise in magic, witch hunts, cults of different kinds, char-latans, astrologers, and the like. Folklorists and others have shown that such unsettling and contradictory developments lend themselves to the dis-semination of legends like *le Juif errant*.[9]

Jews in Central and Western Europe during this period were particularly vulnerable to such representations. Following the major expulsions of Jews from Christian Europe in the late Middle Ages, a reversal in the attitude of European powers to the Jews began to unfold in the last quarter of the sixteenth century. Jonathan Israel has meticulously documented how Jews returned to Germanic lands, resettled in England, consolidated themselves in France, and flourished in Holland.[10] Although the Khmelnytskyi rebel-lion and massacres in Poland (1648–49) cast a dark shadow over these new currents, the renewed presence of Jews in Western and Central Europe could not be denied. Without attempting to offer these developments in European and Jewish society as the sole or overriding factor in the receptiv-ity of the legend, we may assume that the reappearance of the Jew rekin-dled classic associations that had been crystallized in the medieval legend.

The Popularization of the Legend

England, where discussions on the return of the Jews (expelled in 1290) became widespread among various Christian groups in the first half of the seventeenth century, produced an early and popular rendition of the Wandering Jew. In a chapbook entitled *The Wandering-Jew, Telling Fortunes to English-Men* (1640), Egremont, an English gentleman—who, like many Englishmen of the century, took to travel—reached Venice, whereupon he encountered a Jew. Considered by many as his double, Egremont agreed to disguise himself as a Venetian Jew. On his return to London he was sought out by various marginal characters who wanted to have their fortunes told. The ruse enables the author to imply that the Wandering Jew possesses certain important secrets that cause others to seek him out. A woodcut on the cover shows him standing in front of a townhouse, wearing a long cloak with a badge and a flat beret. His arrival arouses interest. Taller than the other figures and barefoot, Egremont or the Wandering Jew is clearly an "other" who the locals believe has some truth to reveal.

The Wandering Jew makes his next visual appearance in England in *The Wandering Jew, or The Shoe-maker of Jerusalem* (c. 1720), a slim volume authored by four ministers associated with millenarianism. Millenarian movements had been active in the struggle for readmission of the Jews to England and continued to figure prominently in English thought even after Jews returned in the period of Oliver Cromwell. This volume discusses the origins of the legend and insists on the authenticity of the Wandering Jew. Once convinced of his existence, the authors had a painter draw his picture, "in which he looked neither Old or Young, but just as he did seventeen hundred and sixty seven years ago when he began his journey. The King of France, hearing this, wrote for his picture."[11] The work ends in characteristically millenarian style, prophesying the return of all the Jews to Jerusalem, the rebuilding and flourishing of the city, and eventually their conversion: "they, and all others, shall become Christians, and that Wars shall cease, and the whole World live in Unity one with another."[12] The Wandering Jew will thus cease to wander when he and his kind return to Jerusalem and convert to Christianity.

At about the same time as the appearance of this chapbook, *The Wandring Jew's Chronicle* was published in London, a broadside that contained a monologue in verse by the Wandering Jew about the history of English rulers from William the Conqueror to George I. It included illustrations of all the English rulers up to Queen Anne and its text was to be sung "to the Tune of, The Wandring Jew's Chronicle." Meant to be for "meer Recreation / To put off Vexation," the broadside did not characterize or provide images of the Wandering Jew. Rather, the Wandering Jew becomes the eternal chronicler who documents the events of the past hundred years of the English crown as one who was "present" throughout.[13] (The Jew's absence from England from 1290 to the seventeenth century carried no weight for the creator of the broadside, nor was he disturbed by the implication that it is the Wandering Jew who is granted this unique function.)

Though a keeper of secrets, a forerunner of a Jewish return to Jerusalem and Christianity, and a chronicler of the English past, the Wandering Jew, relatively prominent in literary accounts, was not adopted as a model for visualizing Jews. Even during the 1753 controversy over the naturalization of the Jews (the "Jew Bill"), when a range of visual depictions was produced, mainly to stress Jewish "otherness" and raise objections to their naturalization, the visual depictions drew overwhelmingly on "Jewish physiognomy" rather than on the image of the Wandering Jew.[14] The Wandering Jew became associated with the growing number of Ashkenazic pedlars and hucksters who entered London in the eighteenth century. One text in the naturalization controversy did, however, speak of "a certain Person commonly and emphatically stiled *the wandering Jew*, who, though already upwards of 1700 Years old, is however sure of living several hundred years longer . . . Now if this strange old Vagrant should chance to be tired of his present pedling way of Life . . . what alas! May be apprehended from a man in his extraordinary circumstances."[15]

The phenomenon of the Jew penetrating a sedentary society, bringing new occupations and habits to English society, created an association between the Wandering Jew and the Jewish itinerant pedlar, which is apparent in *Moses Gorden or the Wandering Jew in the Dress he now wears in Newgate* (1788). (See Figure 8.1.) A Protestant of Scottish birth, Gordon is known for having incited the Gordon riots in 1780 (against Roman Catholics, wealthy aristocracy, and the Bank of England) and was prosecuted for publishing libel against Queen Marie Antoinette. He reappeared in public in the late 1780s as a recent convert to Judaism (probably between 1786 and 1787) who had observed Orthodox practice while in prison.[16] Preferring to be considered *leader of the Jews* (the traditional title accorded Christ) rather than a humble *disciple* of *Jesus*, Gordon appeared with straggling reddish brown hair and an unkempt beard. His behavior and conversion occasioned many ballads, pamphlets, and caricatures. In some, he is depicted in all his outlandish eccentricity as a spoof of the popular perception of what constitutes a Jew. In the print *Moses Gorden or the Wandering Jew*, which was published apparently a month after Gordon's arrest in Birmingham, he appears bearded, with long hair and black hat, against the background of several buildings.[17] Dressed as an Ashkenazic Jew, he holds a bag under one arm and rabbit skins in his other hand.

Why was the association made between Gordon and the Wandering Jew? As can be seen from the etching, the occupation of a pedlar (rabbit skins and bag) is conflated with the legend of the Wandering Jew. The anonymous artist turned Gordon (and the Jew) into the perpetual alien, a theme that was becoming common among English caricaturists (for example, in

MOSES GORDEN or the WANDERING JEW.
In the Dress he now wears in Newgate.
Pub. Jan 5 1788 by A. Davis Birming[...]

Figure 8.1. *Moses Gorden [Gordon] or the Wandering Jew in the Dress he now wears in Newgate*, Birmingham, 1788. Aquatint, green pencil, aquarelle. AR 1513 (136), Jewish Museum, London.

caricatures by Thomas Rowlandson). Gordon becomes identified with the itinerant pedlar, already an icon of his fellow Jews, who are understood to lack a sedentary nature and the capacity to assimilate. In this way, he becomes a fulfillment of the biblical prophecy (Acts 19:13) that he will find no rest no matter where he turns. Gordon's case notwithstanding, images of the Wandering Jew in England were rare, possibly, as Felsenstein has implied, because the extensive engagement of caricaturists with the Jew as the itinerant pedlar found in a real-life figure all the iconography it needed for visualizing wandering as a mark of Jewish otherness.

It was in France, from the late eighteenth century, that the Wandering Jew became a larger than life image and veritable public figure. The image was often accompanied by a *complainte*, a lyric lament that originated in France in the early seventeenth century and circulated in six versions. Its more prominent themes touched on the nature of the Wandering Jew and his physical appearance. It describes the Wandering Jew as an individual with five sous in his pocket (corresponding to the five injuries inflicted on Christ) who always wore unkempt shoes and clothes. On his travels he would encounter respectable individuals who, struck by his appearance (particularly his extraordinary long beard), engage him in conversation and try to coax him to join them for a drink, but he refuses, claiming that he is committed to travel. He relates to them accounts of his past, his birth in Jerusalem, and his long journeys, occasioned by Christ's response to his rejection of him. Though the *complainte* grants his longevity greater attention than his wandering, its most widely circulated version, attached to a visual image, celebrates the alleged visit of the Wandering Jew to Brussels on April 22, 1774, at six in the evening, an event said to have been recorded around 1800. (See Figure 8.2.) Sold for small sums by merchants and pedlars as broadsheets and in chapbooks, which often added a touch of the supernatural to the text, the *complainte* was sung and read aloud in France and later translated into other languages, including Flemish, Danish, and Dutch.[18]

The visual image surged forward from the Restoration period (following Napoleon's demise) in a remarkable way, feeding into the growing popular desire not only for religious imagery but also for a certain stability in an age of tremendous change and flux. One example will suffice. One of the leading publishers was the Pellerin publishing company whose founder, Jean-Claude Pellerin, was a deist involved with Freemasonry. His background and beliefs did not prevent him from becoming a major publisher and disseminator of religious icons. Pellerin obviously knew his clientele and their religious practices associated with devotional art. Though his catalogue listings from 1814 contained much religious literature and art, he added to his list, in the two years following the Restoration, sixty images of saints alongside many portraits of the Bourbon family and prints of Napoleon. From 1822 the Wandering Jew appeared in his catalogue and became a staple, together with other popular images—Napoleon's above all. The

Figure 8.2. *Véritable Portrait du Juif-Errant . . . remarquables*, Paris, 1804. Engraving, colored. Mouers PC 140-3, Musée Carnavalet, Paris. © Photothèque des Musées de la Ville de Paris. Photo: Marie-Laure Berthier.

wide variety of images of Napoleon embodied secular and religious perspectives, since he was seen as the harbinger of an impending democratic
revolution and as a savior who would redeem his people from social and
economic injustice. Napoleon was also thought to have supernatural powers. Pellerin employed Pierre-Germain Vadet and François Georgin, two
artists who were to a large extent responsible for creating this integrated
image of Napoleon. It unleashed populist aspirations for the renewal of
French glory and egalitarian justice.[19]

Georgin was also the artist behind one of the most successful and popular representations of the Wandering Jew. (See Figure 8.3.) Created in
1826, Georgin's image depicted the Wandering Jew walking sturdily and
determinedly on shore, near water, with a ship in the distance. Georgin
veered away from the more common Épinal images. They commonly told
the story of the Wandering Jew in stages by showing him in the center of
the print, while in the background three scenes appeared: the shoemaker
rejecting Christ, Christ on his way to Calvary, and the Wandering Jew being
met by several individuals on his entrance to a city. Georgin, on the other
hand, placed him in the center of the lithograph, dressed in a bonnet and
wearing a turban, with no allusions to the originary legend.

Notwithstanding his long beard and hair, his physical appearance
arouses no negative associations. The *complainte* is printed beneath the figure, unassumingly. The print's attraction can be attested by its repeated
reproduction and retouching by others until the early twentieth century.[20]
Evidently, Georgin succeeded in capitalizing on the pagan and para-
Christian practices in regional France to turn the immortality of the Wandering Jew into a desired talisman, similar to the way he found the key to
making Napoleon's image so widely attractive.

Épinal imagery of the Wandering Jew flourished throughout the nineteenth century, bolstered by a wide variety of visual images, first and foremost a series of twelve engravings by Gustave Doré. Attractively published
under the imprimatur of Michel Lévy *frères* of Paris (1856), the work had
immediate success. An English version appeared in 1859 and another
French one in 1862 with many versions subsequently reprinted. Based on
the very popular, melodramatic poem by Pierre-Jean de Béranger (1831),
with additional verses by Pierre Dupont in cooperation with Doré, the
series joined the artist's fascination with the occult and fantastic with his
unique ability as an illustrator. Using the *complainte*, Béranger presented
Ahasuerus roaming through tempests as a result of his iniquity to a suffering fellow man, even more than as a result of his action against God. His
song was put to music several times. Charles Gounod's composition
became the most popular version.

Doré shows his knowledge of the earlier images and various versions of
the legend in his highly imaginative graphic creation. (See Figure 8.4.) He
does not see le *Juif errant* in the romantic sense of the heroic figure but

Figure 8.3. François Georgin (1801–63), *Le Juif-Errant*, 1826–30. Épinal, Pellerin publisher. Printed paper, colored by hand. MAHJ 95.41.1, Musée d'art et d'histoire du Judaïsme, Paris. Photo: Mario Goldman. © Musée d'art et d'histoire du Judaïsme.

Figure 8.4. Gustave Doré (1832–83), *On thro' the storm he speeds . . . The Legend of the Wandering Jew*, 10:1856. Wood engraving on wove paper. Published by Michel Lévy frères. Musée d'art et d'histoire du Judaïsme, Paris. Photo: Christophe Fouin. © Musée d'art et d'histoire du Judaïsme.

rather very much within the traditional contours of the legend. His own romantic style, prevalent in his illustrations to Milton's *Paradise Lost*, Coleridge's *Ancient Mariner*, and Dante's *Divine Comedy*, is clearly present, previewing what would follow in his monumental illustrative Bible. What did Doré try to preserve with respect to the legend and how did he attempt to depict the Wandering Jew? Above all, he tried to dramatize the life of the Wandering Jew, from his condemnation to wander until his judgment day, emphasizing his remorse over his earlier behavior to Christ. Doré has the Wandering Jew face the cross and Christ in a variety of ways, implying that his original rejection of Christ remains with him forever. The ever-present cross and the crucified hover over him, appearing in phantasmagoric reflections in the sky, mountains, and water, and serve as constant reminders of why he must wander. His wandering is even construed as a mirror image to Christ's ascent to Calvary. The Wandering Jew is given clear attributes: a purse (with his five sous), a large walking stick, a huge beard, and meager clothing (hat and shoes).

Doré incorporated themes that were addressed both in the *complainte* and in Épinal material, including the Wandering Jew's capacity to draw people's intense interest, their desire to see him, hear stories of his travels, and attempt to cajole him to drink with them at a tavern. However, Doré places his main emphasis on the Wandering Jew's lonely trek. Doré depicts the stamina of the Wandering Jew to walk through hills, water, and land, to survive storms and wreckages ("while helpless vessels sink before his eyes"), overcome death, both by natural and unnatural causes ("Trees intertwined with snakes") and reach his judgment day. In the climax to his wandering, he is finally seen sitting amid an array of skeleton bones, animals, demons attending to the purgatory fire, guards, and others, as he hears the sounds of trumpets announcing the end of his wandering as the Day of Judgment/Redemption has come.

Each of Doré's twelve images was reproduced in various media, and their impact upon the development of visual interest in the *Juif errant* in the following decades was extensive.[21] This was not to Champfleury's liking. He chastised Doré's work for being too bombastic and for being interested only in "the setting; he sacrifices Ahasuerus for the old Belgian homes, for the storms, whirlwinds, forests of fir trees, and crocodiles." Champfleury concluded that "[Doré] does not possess the secret of the figure of the Wandering Jew."[22] Champfleury's desire to preserve the simple "popular images" revealed his misunderstanding of the magnetic power of the legend and the ways in which popular imagery could be imported into other forms of art.

This was certainly the case for Champfleury's close friend Gustave Courbet. In *The Meeting* (1854), Courbet documents a meeting with Alfred Bruyas, his patron, together with the latter's servant and dog. However, it seems that this realistic interpretation of the painting overlooks its connection to popular imagery and in particular to an Épinal image of the Wandering Jew.[23] Linda Nochlin has convincingly argued that *The Meeting* was simply a gloss on the meeting that often took place in Épinal imagery between two bourgeois gentlemen and the Wandering Jew. Courbet was likely aware of Champfleury's interest in the Wandering Jew and probably saw certain images of this figure in Champfleury's possession. Courbet admired folk-lore and felt that popular imagery held a certain charm and insight into the nature of people. In the 1850s, he relied on such images for key paint-ings. In *The Meeting*, there is a resonance between the encounter of the Wandering Jew with strangers on the road and the encounter of the artist with his patron. In the painting, the artist is a wanderer with a mission (like Ahasuerus in the French novelist Eugene Sue's famous 1844–45 account, *Le Juif errant*), who meets his patron on the road and speaks his mind. As Nochlin remarks: "The work must be regarded not only as a portrait of the artist as a Wandering Jew, but as a portrait of Courbet as a free man."[24] She also notes how the proud stance and gesture of the Wandering Jew/Cour-bet asserts his claim to the important role the artist must play in society. Thus, the Wandering Jew became a marker of attachment to popular cul-ture and to freedom of expression. Yet, several years later, Manet incorpo-rated the figure, only partially visible on the right side of the canvas, in *The Old Musician* (1862). Standing among a group of "outsiders"—Pierrot, the absinthe drinker, and the gypsy fiddler—the Wandering Jew would appear to represent the artist as a marginalized figure, not fully part of society.

These transformations of the popular image in France were to become more pronounced in the latter half of the century, when artists from vari-ous European countries privileged one or another theme in the Wander-ing Jew saga. All of them would draw from the variety of popular imagery in circulation.

Ahasuerus and the Fin de Siècle

Interest in the theme of Ahasuerus was extremely prevalent in the second half of the nineteenth century in a variety of languages and literary media. His mortality and, at times, his wish to bring an end to his eternal state were in keeping with romantic themes such as the end of days, destruction, suffering, and mortal ruin. The sense of an impending fin de siècle fed a fascination with Ahasuerus, whether as the main protagonist or a minor character in a variety of settings, from classical to modern. Pre-Raphaelites, Symbolists, and academic realists identified aspects of the Ahasuerus leg-end with religious, classical, and mythic images. These works were so remote from contemporary Jewish society that a commentator in an Anglo-Jewish orthodox newspaper described *The Wandering Jew* by Evelyn Picker-ing (later Evelyn De Morgan, 1855–1919), an epigone of Pre-Raphaelites, as a "beautiful and altogether admirable picture."[25]

For De Morgan and others, engagement with the Wandering Jew reflected wider concerns. The forever restless Wandering Jew stands in her painting solemnly and mournfully, as he looks over a dead young girl lying on a couch, her arms folded tranquilly on her breast. Above her, a view of an ancient city is seen at a distance. Wearing a floor-length cape that covers his head, his hands clasped in anguish, the white-bearded Wandering Jew, personifying immortality, would appear to contrast sharply with the mortality of the young girl. De Morgan was deeply involved during this period with Spiritualism, a movement that viewed death as only a stage in the spiritual continuation of life.[26] Thus, the Wandering Jew's presence at the bedside of the dead woman could be viewed as an actualization of the transition from the lower physical stage of existence to the spiritual one. In this context the Wandering Jew emerges as the embodiment of the spiritual level. De Morgan, like other Pre-Raphaelites and Spiritualists, treated many mythological and allegorical figures and scenes (e.g., *Medea* [1889], *Flora* [1894]), and, earlier in her career, also religious and biblical themes (e.g., *By the Waters of Babylon* [1883]).[27] *The Wandering Jew* fits neatly into her inclinations and thematic interests. Traces of William Blake's inspiration attest to their common spiritual quests. In *Hela Contemplating Tiriel Dead in a Vineyard* (c. 1789), Blake, the English artist and mystic, reverses the relationship of the Wandering Jew and the dead girl: the young Hela stands over the elderly Tiriel, who lies prostrate, as does the young woman in De Morgan's work.[28]

As it was for other artists of her age, De Morgan's concern with this theme was fleeting. But in the space of a few years, many artists across Europe turned to Ahasuerus as a signifier of the end of days. Relying upon Doré's treatment, in which the Wandering Jew is seen gazing on Calvary as he walks on, artists like the Viennese-born Anton Hlávaček (1842–1926) and the Parisian-born Gustave Moreau (1826–98) created works that captured the encounter between the figures of Ahasuerus and Christ. Moreau was especially taken by the fate of the Wandering Jew, whose predicament invoked for him associations with Cain, doomed to wander the earth for killing his brother Abel. Various preparatory studies for a large oil painting—together with his own interpretive texts—emphasized the terror sensed by *le Juif errant* as he saw the "sublime appearance" of Christ on the cross. In the painting, Christ's unorthodox gesture on the cross, beckoning the Wandering Jew with outstretched arms and gentle gaze, overwhelms him with emotion. It is as if Christ pardons the Wandering Jew for his iniquity and he, in turn, "finally worships his God."[29] Moreau's engagement with this theme, especially in the latter days of his life, seems to echo De Morgan's spiritualist search, though with a more clearly Christian orientation.

The correlation between the legend and the sense of the end of days generated interest among Symbolists in different countries. Ferdinand

Figure 8.5. Ferdinand Hodler (1853–1918), *Ahasver*, 1886. Oil on canvas. Museum Oskar Reinhart am Stadtgarten, Winterthur, Switzerland.

Hodler (1853–1918), a Swiss artist who combined a realistic style with ideal-istic elements, came into close contact with a group of Symbolist poets and artists in Geneva in the 1880s. One in particular, the poet Louis Duchosal, befriended Hodler, and his poetry found expression in the latter's paint-ings. In *Poèmes en Prose* (1886), dedicated to Hodler, Duchosal included "Sosie," a poem in which an elderly man dealt with the disillusionment of old age, his inability to remember his youth, and the compulsion to con-tinue walking to his end, notwithstanding great pain. "I walk, I must walk, wandering Jew of fatality . . . How long this route is, and how weary I am." Duchosal's poem, and his own physical disabilities, encouraged Hodler to take up the legend, which continued to occupy him long after his early works. Hodler's *Ahasuerus* (1886) focused on the individual's interminable restlessness and fate, and his studies of the figure show how he derived the head of *Ahasuerus* from realistic portrayals of solitary old men. (See Figure 8.5.) Ahasuerus becomes, in Hodler's work, a study on the determination of man to persevere in the face of adversity, expressing a clear, universalist message.[30]

The works highlighted here, and others whose whereabouts are un-known today, indicate how certain themes in the work of Doré and the German Romantic artist Caspar David Friedrich (1774–1840) became sig-nificant at the turn of the century. Some continued to interpret the origi-nal legend by confronting the Wandering Jew with the image of Christ on the cross, but others granted Ahasuerus a more universal message. Consis-tent with the contemporary literary meanings accorded him, these images focused on his personification of immortality as well as his association with the impending end of time, emanating qualities of either (or both) resil-ience or decadence. Driven by their engagement with allegorical and myth-ological material, the artists transformed the Wandering Jew into a European metaphor of the fin de siècle, minimizing the engagement with the conflict between Judaism and Christianity. Nonetheless, the theme of religious tension continued to be pursued in other contexts.

The Wandering Jew as an Anti-Semitic Motif

Though the traditional image and legend of the Wandering Jew are part of the historic Jewish-Christian polemic, many of the images discussed above are not part of a particularly anti-Jewish or anti-Semitic agenda. Certainly, an argument could be made for placing the entire body of material into that realm, yet in attempting to sift expressions of a more malignant nature from the entire corpus of benign material, I follow the orientation of schol-ars of the legend itself. The works discussed below have been singled out either by virtue of the artist's outright enunciation of an anti-Jewish posi-tion or by an unambiguous signifier in the work that utilizes the legend to further an anti-Jewish/anti-Semitic orientation.

The appearance of the Wandering Jew in Wilhelm von Kaulbach's immense painting *The Destruction of Jerusalem by Titus* (585 x 705 cm, 1846), commissioned by Ludwig I of Bavaria, was unprecedented.[31] (See Figure 8.6.) Never before was the legendary figure integrated into such a major work of art, and never before was the visual image granted such a profound anti-Jewish connection as in this work. Kaulbach (1804–74), a well-known historical painter and director of the Munich Academy (1849–74), had also been commissioned by Ludwig I to create a series of frescoes for the outside walls of the Neue Pinakothek in Munich, inaugurated in 1853. Thus *The Destruction* was clearly part of the staging of the new museum. The painting, for which the artist wrote a detailed explanation, focuses on the destruction of Jerusalem, prophesied by Isaiah, Jeremiah, Ezekiel, and Daniel, who appear above the smoke in the upper part of the painting. Kaulbach dramatically depicts the destruction and burning of the city by the Romans and portrays the victorious Romans gallantly entering the city on the upper right-hand corner of the painting. In response to their entry and the burning city, the high priest, at the center of the canvas, stabs himself while gazing in the direction of Titus and his followers. At the lower left, the Wandering Jew is seen escaping the burning city with his frightened coreligionists, pursued by three male demons. Kaulbach thus transformed the original legend to imply that the Wandering Jew began his wandering only after the city was destroyed by the Romans. Moreover, Kaulbach saw the fleeing Wandering Jew as the antithesis to the Christian family, positioned at the lower right of the painting, which embodied the Nazarenes' ideal of beauty. The Wandering Jew has none of the more common features of anti-Jewish/anti-Semitic iconography, but his harried look and ragged appearance are in sharp contrast to the image of stability and peacefulness that exudes from his counterpart, the family. Avraham Ronen has observed that "the contrasting images of the defeated Jew and the triumphant Christian family follow the traditional representations in art of the opposing images of the defeated *Synagoga* and the Triumphant *Ecclesia*."[32] Indeed, Kaulbach himself commented that the meaning of this historical painting was "a judgment which God intended and carried out."[33] Kaulbach's historical-religious painting was a powerful work with a significant statement: Jews and Judaism had been defeated and replaced by Christianity. For Kaulbach the implication was clear—the Wandering Jew was a personification of the Jew throughout history.

Granted pride of place in the Neue Pinakothek from the day the museum opened, the painting was widely known and coveted. A replica was prepared by Kaulbach for a fresco for the New Museum in Berlin (1853), and engravings were made of both the original in Munich (by Eduard Eichens) and of the Berlin fresco (by H. Merz). Special engravings, lithographs, and other media focusing solely on the expulsion of the Wandering Jew also appeared, while others centered the expulsion but added new motifs that highlighted the condemnation of the Jew.[34] Created in Germany and

Figure 8.6. Wilhelm von Kaulbach (1804–74), *The Destruction of Jerusalem by Titus*, Munich, 1841–46. Oil on canvas. INV.-NR. WAF Y03, München, Neue Pinakothek.

France, these visual depictions gave resonance to the phenomenon of the Wandering Jew as a rejected figure and carried a strong message.

Yet it seems that Kaulbach's influence on later artists and caricaturists was minimal, even on those who turned the Wandering Jew into a staple of anti-Jewish imagery. Others turned to the legend for their own local and specific anti-Semitic purposes and refashioned the image accordingly. Several examples from different countries will suffice to illuminate these transformations.

In 1852 a colored caricature of the Wandering Jew was published in Paris on the front page of *Journal pour rire*, a journal devoted to humor, satire, and criticism. Accompanied by a *complainte,* it appeared several years after the publication of Eugène Sue's novel and preceded Doré's series by four years. Collaboratively produced by Gustave Doré and Pierre-Jean-Louis Dumont (the engraver), the striking image visualized the legend with outright anti-Semitic attributes. (See Figure 8.7.) Its pungent character explains why it was chosen to be on the cover of Eduard Fuchs's classic work *Die Juden in der Karikatur* (1921).[35] Apparently the first artist to place a cross on the figure's forehead, representing both the crucifixion and the mark of Cain, Doré portrayed the Wandering Jew with an extremely hooked nose, deformed mouth, wild hair and beard, and thin, bony legs. A halo in the form of devils' horns looms in the background. The Wandering Jew walks determinedly through a barren area, carrying no possessions, assisted by his large walking staff. Doré's use of different shades of red, both for the mark and for the hair, add to the Wandering Jew's haunting character. The color red may have aroused in itself further negative associations.[36] Certainly Doré was inspired by Sue's work, then at the height of its success, and possibly also by Matthew Gregory Lewis's novel, *The Monk* (1796). Lewis created the association with Cain's mark and, like Sue, represented the Wandering Jew in positive terms. Why the twenty-year-old artist rejected these positive images of the Wandering Jew and resorted to an anti-Jewish representation is unclear, but it may have had some connection to the satirical nature of the journal.[37] In contrast, Doré's subsequent series, discussed above, though rife with references to the original legend and traditional interpretations of the Wandering Jew, muted, in my estimation, an anti-Semitic import.

Despite its potential, the Wandering Jew did not become a central element in French anti-Semitic iconography. Though the figure was embedded in French popular culture and easily available for those who wanted to slant its meaning, few in fact did so. Even amid the tremendous outpouring of visual imagery during the Dreyfus Affair, the Wandering Jew was seldom utilized to advocate an anti-Dreyfusard position. Its association with Christian tradition and with the notion of homelessness could have provided grist for the mill for those who desired to showcase these perspectives in the Dreyfusard/anti-Dreyfusard divide that pitted Christian and monarchical groups against liberal and republican ones. Anti-Dreyfusard visual imagery was neither short of Christian themes nor of "otherness," but they were by no means the dominant mode, and associations with the Wandering Jew were scarce. Prior to the Affair, the image of the Wandering Jew was picked up by *Le Pèlerin*, an organ of the Catholic right. On April 3, 1892, it discussed the phenomenon of "Jewish migration for wealth," mixing together the legend (the commonly used French name of the Wandering Jew—Isaac Laquedem—creates the allusion) with contemporary Jewish migration. Appended to the text was a visual triptych, where, from right to left, a long procession of Jews is seen climbing a hill, carrying their packs and their children. The artist depicts them as fleeing Russia, which is personified by an officer with a whip. The center of the triptych recreates the encounter between Christ and the Wandering Jew. It places Christ, with a heavy cross in the background, as if in the clouds. In the foreground, slightly removed from the procession, the Wandering Jew, shabbily dressed and heavily weighed down by packages (money?), struggles on. He is oblivious to all, especially to Christ, determined to continue his wandering, or, as in the

Figure 8.7. Gustave Doré (1832–83), *Le Juif Errant*, in *Le journal pour rire*, June 5, 1852. Engraving by Pierre Jean-Louis Dumont. Accompanied by a *complainte* composed by Joseph Prud'homme. Bibliothèque Nationale de France, Paris, Tf 484a.

spirit of the article, his pursuit of money. His form creates a haunting shadow. Other Jews, more caricatured in their appearance, have reached the hill and join others in their descent to the ocean and departure for the United States, symbolized by the figure of Uncle Sam, waiting to receive them. The *Pèlerin* image obviously appealed to its Catholic readership, who knew both the legend and the contemporary litany on Jews and money, but the image was rarely seen in later issues of the journal or in depictions of the Dreyfus Affair.[38]

The restlessness and nomadism that became identified with the Wandering Jew and central to anti-Semitic iconography was given a psychopathological twist by the psychiatric school of Jean-Martin Charcot at Salpêtrière. Charcot identified a Jewish "nervousness" and new sickness, a form of "traveling insanity," akin to a "somnambulism provoked by hypnosis." Charcot presented one such figure, who suffered from pains in his leg, extreme exhaustion, and excessive frugality, to his audience in 1889 "as a true descendant of Ahasuerus or Cartophilus," a person "driven by an irresistible need to change his surroundings, to travel, without being able to settle down anywhere."[39] Charcot's lead was pursued by his student Henry Meige, who in his dissertation of 1893 set out to study the neuropathology of *le Juif errant*. Meige pursued the historical origins of the legend and added several images that he regarded as valuable from a medical standpoint.[40] (See Figure 8.8.) Meige argued that their neuropsychological studies proved the existence of a "Jewish pathology" that expressed itself in the form of a nervous, insatiable need to travel. Second, the Jew's image and gaze were consistent with such a condition. Third, and central to our concerns, Meige analyzed a series of illustrations of the Wandering Jew, including some Épinal images, and claimed repeatedly that they showed that "the artist rendered reliably and naively the expression of his model." To do so, he claimed, the artist obviously must have observed the model. Indeed, Meige compared the clinical patients at Salpêtrière with the images, several of which he drew himself. His comparison produced the remarkable conclusion "that the Wandering Jew of the legend and the Wandering Jew of the clinics are but one and the same type: a neurotic traveller, interminable wanderer, who appears one day and disappears the next, followed shortly by another who resembles him in every manner: a Jew who wanders, around the world, lamenting and gasping."[41] Meige had thus moved the eternal wandering of the Jew from the theological to the medical realm, adding another link to the growing contemporary literature on anti-Semitism and disease.[42] Folk legend had proposed a supernatural explanation for what (in the eyes of this literature) was actually a medical condition. In this way Charcot and Meige furthered their design to undermine clerical and historical explanations of the eternal Jew.

Few images pursued directly the connections created by Charcot and Meige between contemporary Jews and the Wandering Jew, but at least one

Figure 8.8. Albert Londe (1858–1917), *M. Gottlieb, a Neurotic Jewish Wanderer*, in Henri Meige, *Le Juif errant à La Salpêtrière, étude sur certains névropathes voyageurs* (Paris: L. Battaille and Co., 1983). Photograph. Library of the Alliance Israélite Universelle, Paris.

would appear to derive from their perspective. During the intensive anti-Semitic campaign against Léon Blum in France in the 1930s, when he was often vilified for being a Wandering Jew, a caricature appeared portraying Blum as "la juive errante."[43] The defamatory iconography gave visual expression to the anti-Semitic arguments leveled against him. First and foremost, Blum was feminized. Blum's controversial book on marriage (1907) aroused great antagonism among Catholic and right-wing circles, who in the 1930s renewed their campaign against him and his critique of traditional marital practice. He was perceived as a weak and unassertive prime minister, his political image merging with his cultural one. Second, he was attacked for lacking deep roots in French soil, implying that he could have settled just as easily in "New York, Cairo or Vilna." Indeed, the "subtle Talmudist" (in the words of Xavier Vallat) appears in the caricature wearing a long cloak or dress, holding a staff in one hand and a sack over his/her back as s/he walks on to an undetermined goal. This rare visual image of a female Wandering Jew fit neatly into the battle waged against Blum and gave credence to the claim that Jewish rootlessness, symbolized by the Wandering Jew, was a permanent Jewish trait.[44]

Figure 8.9. *Der ewige Jude*, Germany, 1937. Exhibition poster. Lithograph. Kunstbibliothek, Staatliche Museen zu Berlin, Berlin. Photo: Bildarchiv Preussischer Kulturbesitz/ Art Resource, NY.

In contrast with the extensive French engagement with the theme of *le Juif errant* during the modern period, German artists turned to the *ewige Jude* less often, and it was not a dominant aspect of anti-Semitic iconography. Yet, in November 1937, the National Socialist Party staged an extensive exhibition in Munich, entitled *Der ewige Jude*, organized by Dr. Hans Diebow, a Nazi official, and opened in the presence of Julius Streicher and Josef Goebbels, who both addressed the gathering.[45] This was the largest anti-Semitic exhibition prior to the war and contained several hundred documents and anti-Semitic images. The exhibition implied that, at least for the National Socialists, *ewige Jude* clearly meant the "eternal Jew," a more encompassing concept than *le Juif errant*. In fact, few images treated the theme of the Wandering Jew, and the vicious exhibition poster reveled in an ugly, more stereotypical anti-Semitic caricature.[46] (See Figure 8.9.) It featured a heavyset orthodox Jew with a black scraggly beard and an unpleasant grimace, wearing a black coat, holding several coins in one hand, and in the other, a stick or whip. Under his right arm he holds a map with a hammer and sickle engraved on it. The anti-Semitic depiction was meant to identify the Jew as the progenitor of capitalism and of communism, a common theme in the Nazi ideological battle against Jews, while his uncomely appearance intensified his "otherness." Yet, some association with the classic legend was maintained in the exhibition brochure that carried on its cover a poem, "Ahasvers Fröhlich Wanderlied," written ostensibly by a German Jew. On August 2, 1938, the exhibition opened in Vienna, and Viennese school children were required to view it.[47]

From what has been described thus far, it would appear that the folk legend did not become a major element in the arsenal of anti-Jewish visual imagery. Certainly, powerful negative associations were created, as in the case of Kaulbach's *Destruction* and Doré's caricature, but they did not constitute the major form of representation of the Wandering Jew in either Germany or France.[48] Possibly, the religious dimension embedded in the legend appeared to be too insurmountable for artistic expression, especially in societies that were growing more estranged from religion and its visual language.

Jewish Reinterpretations of the Wandering Jew

No treatment of the visual characterization of the Wandering Jew would be complete without reference to the ways artists of Jewish origin refashioned its meaning and converted the figure into an expression of their particular predicaments and perspectives. In a period of widespread Jewish migration, occasioned both by persecution and economic need, the affinity with this legendary figure loomed large and was evoked by diverse artists.[49]

Alfred Nossig provided a Zionist interpretation. Born in Lemberg, Galicia (now Lviv in the Ukraine), in 1864, Nossig struggled with issues of identity. Attracted in his teens to Polish nationalism, he advocated in the early 1880s the full integration of Jews into Polish society and identified New Poland with Old Israel. But by the mid-1880s Nossig had became one of the leading spokespersons for the Jewish national cause in Galicia. A sculptor as well as a secular thinker, Nossig was influenced by the pulsating atmosphere in Lemberg. Caught in the ideological crossfire of contemporary Jewish politics, Nossig then shifted intellectually to a religious-nationalist position, seeing the key collective survival in Jewish Orthodoxy. After studying sculpture in Vienna, he sought to express these sentiments through depictions of the Wandering Jew.

Nossig's version offers a clear confrontation with the traditional interpretations. (See Figure 8.10.) His *Wandering Jew* (whereabouts unknown), first exhibited in 1899, holds a large staff (larger than the figure itself) and wears an unkempt and unwieldy beard. Wearing a large cape over his head, Nossig's virile figure stands proudly erect. His countenance displays intensity and firmness. But what has given this Wandering Jew his strength is not the sign of Cain (as in Doré's anti-Semitic lithograph) but the Torah scroll he holds close to his heart. The Star of David is its sole decoration. Strong, muscular arms hold the staff and scroll, unlike the thin, bony legs often associated with the Wandering Jew in some European interpretations.

Presenting the Wandering Jew in this vein, Nossig attested to the Jew's capacity to withstand hatred and opposition, when shielded by the Hebrew Bible. Nossig's Wandering Jew stood as a visionary, holding tightly to the Torah as the symbol of Jewish perseverance. Nossig transvalued the negative connotations associated with the Wandering Jew by attributing the secret of his endurance to Mosaic determination rather than Christian condemnation.[50] This was a depiction of Jewish piety that owed as much to modern nationalist visions of political redemption as to the Jewish religious tradition.[51]

But it was not only the nationalist turn in Jewish life that brought artists of Jewish extraction to turn to the legend of the Wandering Jew. An important 1906 exhibition of Jewish art and antiquities at Whitechapel Art Gallery in the East End of London featured a wide array of paintings by artists of Jewish origin, including works by Lizzie Hands, a minor English artist from the West End of London. A photograph of her *Outcast among the Nations* (whereabouts unknown) shows how Hands incorporated the Wandering Jew legend into contemporary times. The Wandering Jew appears old and tired, leaning both on his walking stick and on a young female (?) companion, herself barefoot. As they leave a village several figures (non-Jews?) look on, while the young companion turns partially in their direction. It would appear that the small hill in the background is studded with crosses. The painting's title seems to imply that the Wandering Jew has again been cast out from society and can find no refuge or home. The crosses in the background may intimate that Christian attitudes are the

A. Nossig.   Kunstverlag „Phönix“, Berlin

Der ewige Jude.

Figure 8.10. Alfred Nossig (1864–1943), *Der ewige Jude*. Postcard of the sculpture, assumed lost. Collection Gérard Silvain, Paris.

source of his exile; they recall in some fashion Épinal imagery, although with different associations.[52] What inspired Hands to turn to this theme is still unclear, but it is likely that the presence of thousands of Eastern European Jews in London's East End at the turn of the century, many of them destitute and shabby, drew her attention and empathy.

In contrast to Hands's perspective as a sympathetic if detached observer, Marc Chagall (1887–1985), more than any other twentieth-century artist, turned the Wandering Jew into a reflection of his own state of mind and self-perception.[53] According to Ziva Amishai-Maisels, Chagall "sporadically returned to this figure whenever he himself was on the move," especially after Hitler came to power and the artist sought refuge.[54] From his early teens onward, Chagall inserted the Wandering Jew into a variety of paintings, providing him with the common attributes—most prominently a sack and at times a walking stick—and associated him with the notions of exile and Jewish destiny. Often he appears as one of the characters in the wide cast of figures Chagall grafted into certain paintings (for instance, *La guerre*, 1943), but at other times he is seen alone. Though Chagall claimed that "the man in the air in my paintings . . . is me . . . *I have no place of my own . . . I have to live someplace*," it is clear that one cannot connect all the figures walking over homes as Wandering Jews.[55] Issues of homelessness, flight, exile, and wandering are so pronounced in his work—even when he treats sedentary figures (as in *The Jew in Bright Red* [1914–15])—that a certain blurring of the quintessential Wandering Jew often occurs. His Wandering Jew almost always appears as an Orthodox Jew in traditional dress, and in some cases he is endangered by a fire burning around him (e.g., *The White Crucifixion* [1938]). This then is not voluntary wandering but an exile imposed on the Jew by callous pogroms and persecution, an experience that Chagall knew all too well from his own experience, as well as his family's.

Despite his remoteness from Chagall's own stormy upbringing, the Cleveland-born R. B. Kitaj (alias Ronald Brooks, born in 1932) produced equally striking images of the Wandering Jew. After close to forty years of creative work in London, where he became a leading representative of "The School of London," he returned in 1997 to the United States, where he presently resides in Los Angeles. Jewish themes have become more important to Kitaj and he has articulated thoughts on "homelessness, existential as well as artistic," on the nature of "Jewish art," and on the Holocaust.[56] Two works in particular are relevant here. In both *The Jew, Etc.* (1976–79) and *The Jewish Rider* (1984–85), a solitary Jew sits in a railway carriage that for Kitaj serves as a symbol of homelessness, solitude, and constant movement.[57] Unlike the perennial Wandering Jew, the passenger on a train usually knows his ultimate destination. In *The Jewish Rider* the destination is clear. Kitaj himself acknowledged on several occasions an association between *The Polish Rider* (attributed to Rembrandt) and *The Jewish*

Rider, which relates directly to the Holocaust and the modern Jewish predicament.[58] The train—a modern and public means of transport—replaced
the horse, which is often identified with more aristocratic and refined
forms of movement. Kitaj has created a triptych with the central frame concentrating on a modern-looking figure sitting in an awkward position, a
horse's head and rump appearing to his right and left side (the reference
to *The Polish Rider*). Dressed in white shoes and a shirt with an open collar,
the Jewish rider has put his book—his sole possession—on the window sill,
as he lapses into deep contemplation. Apparently a portrait of Kitaj's
friend, the philosopher Richard Wollheim, the rider is meant to represent
the modern intellectual Jew and the Jewish crisis of displacement.[59] He is
the Wandering Jew. To his left, from the window of the train, a chimney
emitting smoke can be seen amid a dark and hilly landscape. As Vivianne
Barsky has perceptively noted, the smoke creates an arch in the direction
of a cross at the edge of the hill, "like an accusing figure," and links the
gas chambers with Christian persecution. The cross on the ridge recalls its
position in many works of art (such as Caspar David Friedrich's *Das Kreuz
im Gebirge Tetschener Altar,* 1808) as well as those dealing with the Wandering
Jew. To the right of the rider, at the end of a narrow corridor of the train,
a conductor/Nazi officer stands in a dandy-like position, as his right arm
holds high a baton forming "a visual echo of the smoke issuing from the
chimney."[60] Thus this rider has a destination. Kitaj has eloquently recre-
ated the fate of many Jews in World War II: the Wandering Jew has been
deported by the officer to his final end—to the crematorium. In presenting
this as a sequence, or, in the formulation of Julián Ríos, as "cinematic-emo-
tion picture(s)," Kitaj avoided turning this painting into a lurid scene of
the Holocaust.[61] He opted for a more symbolic and subdued portrayal
where individual figures and images assume a metaphorical function.

Kitaj avoided associating his Wandering Jews with traditional ones, driving home the point that many of the victims of Christian-influenced anti-
Semitism were secular, intellectual Jews. He presented the conductor/offi-
cer in an atypical and unrepresentative position to demythologize the Nazi
oppressors. Last, Kitaj created a link between Auschwitz and the Church
that, while uncharacteristic of most historical interpretations of the Holocaust, is not out of character for an artist who, in several works, intimated
Christianity's link to anti-Semitism. Thus, in an ironic manner, *The Jewish
Rider* brings us back to an interpretation that places the cross as a cause of
the Wandering Jew's suffering, as well as a direct threat.

The range of visual material treating the Wandering Jew (only some of
which has been explored here) illuminates the repeated invocation of the
legend during the last two hundred years. Caricaturists, artists, artisans,
sculptors, and craftspeople of different political and cultural backgrounds
were intrigued by the legend and incorporated the image in myriad ways
into their creations. The Wandering Jew's presence was ubiquitous. A true

folk figure, he could be found on popular broadsheets, labels for Bitter-mouth, an Àpéritif Tonique, or for El Judio Errante, a name brand of Havana cigars, as an ex libris, a small statuette, a board game with the fig-ures from Sue's famous novel, or on ceramic plates and other items. He could clearly appeal to different audiences, more or less familiar with the legend, and provoke humor, sarcasm, anger, affection, and wonder. Yet, he could also be found in paintings and sculptures that developed the symbol-ism associated with the legend into areas that mirrored the problematic of Jewish life and modern society. As such, the Wandering Jew was an anvil upon which political, theological, social, and personal ideas and idylls could be designed and refashioned. The medieval myth had indeed become a modern metaphor for Jews and non-Jews alike.

Chapter 9

Diasporic Values in Contemporary Art: Kitaj, Katchor, Frenkel

Carol Zemel

The Diasporist feels uneasy, alert to his new freedom, groundless, even foreign until or unless he feels very much at home[.]

—R. B. Kitaj [1]

Exile is always the beginning of narrative—and Diaspora is the place where people talk.

—Sidra DeKoven Ezrahi [2]

I begin with a challenge posed in the epigraphs cited above concerning life in Jewish diaspora, and the nature of artistic production in that environment. For the painter R. B. Kitaj, writing in his aphoristic manifesto of 1989 and coining in it the notion of "Diasporism" in modern art, the situation is fundamentally ambivalent. It encompasses both the exhilaration and anxiety of being unfettered, free of convention and proscriptive ties, as well as uneasiness in that "groundless" state. But, Kitaj suggests, this discomfort passes for the diasporist with recognition that this state can also be "home." Writing a decade later, the literary scholar Sidra Ezrahi also evokes the modern diaspora's creative possibilities. In *Booking Passage*, she argues that if exile begins a tale, a history to be told and handed on, diaspora—a long enduring exile—augments and elaborates that story. Less a site of alienation, though some tensions of difference always remain, diaspora is an important site of a modern Jewish aesthetic, in Ezrahi's terms an "imaginative theatre," the place or condition where "people talk."[3]

Although they revise (with some resistance) traditional Jewish concepts 1znof *galut* (Hebrew: diaspora), these notions of diaspora and its cultural energies offer, I believe, a new and useful framework for considering modern Jewish art. Diaspora implies multiple affiliations and multiple communities and so corresponds more accurately to the situation of many modern peoples, not only Jews. At its core, diaspora culture constitutes a double relationship: an outward relation between its minority voice or vision and that of the majority or "host," and an inner relation among dispersed communities of its own. Seen in these terms, diasporic art complicates and challenges conventional categories of art history premised on identifiable national cultures produced in homogenous nation-states. The challenge need not be militant, for diaspora need not be a condition of the oppressed. Neither separatist nor liberationist, diaspora communities may flourish in multicultural states, where their culture is always negotiated, coextensive and intertwined with mainstream forms and institutions, varying with historical moment and circumstance. In this sense, the notion of diaspora culture avoids the pitfalls of essentialism, for if we dispute the idea of an unchanging national essence, then we must also maintain diaspora's historically labile features and specificities.

To explore these issues and to suggest some of the distinguishing features of diasporic art, I consider work by R. B. Kitaj (born in Cleveland), Ben Katchor (born in New York), and Vera Frenkel (born in Bratislava, in the former Czechoslovakia): three Jewish artists who work mainly in the United States and Canada and exhibit their art in mainstream international art venues. Kitaj's *The Jewish Rider* (1984–85) is one of many pictures by the artist dealing with diaspora, displacement, and foreignness. Katchor's comic strip book, *The Jew of New York: A Historical Romance* (1999) tells an illustrated tale of immigration, intercultural relationships, and searching for home.[4] Frenkel's installation . . . *from the Transit Bar* (1992) provides an environment for travelers/visitors forming a temporary community and telling their tales of home. All three works deal with journeying, with travel and fantasized adventure, but also—and especially when seen through a Jewish lens—with upheaval and uncertainty. The works' similarities and differences illuminate the ways in which diasporic culture functions, the ways in which diasporic pleasures are coupled with tension and ambivalence, and the ways in which they assert the multiple subjectivities that are the hallmark of diaspora's "double consciousness."[5]

As diasporic societies are increasingly a focus of globalization and immigrant studies, attention to the Jewish diaspora—perhaps the oldest model of this social form—acquires new relevance and urgency. Indeed, the character of "diaspora" is one of the more vexed issues in modern Jewish studies. As an enforced expulsion, diaspora may warrant a redemptive promise of return; this is implied in the Hebrew term *galut.* But along with expulsions and displacements, voluntary dispersal has also been the condition of Jews since ancient times. Indeed, as many scholars point out—Yitzhak Baer, A. B. Yehoshua, and Arnold Eisen among them—since at least the second century CE, Jews have been scattered as a minority community through many lands.[6] But if the spiritual yearning for Jerusalem is bound by Jewish collective memory, the pain of *galut* has been tempered by duration; no one would dispute the fact that Jews have flourished in diaspora at least as much as they have suffered, with lengthy periods of cultural distinction, to mention only Sephardic Spain and Maghreb, Ashkenazic Eastern Europe, and contemporary North America.

I emphasize duration and the sense of being "at-home-in-diaspora" in order to underscore diaspora's productive character. Indeed, in contrast to the condition of exile, where uprootedness or never-at-home-ness is a conscious and often stimulating fact of daily life, for the diasporist, home is where one lives, happily and unhappily, for long periods and several generations, simultaneously in one's own community and in other peoples' territories. Always a double geography, without a single center or fixed borders, diaspora is best charted as a palimpsest, with multiple centers and capitals and overlapping or porous border zones. One layer of the map corresponds to the nation-state and its citizenry, the other layer marks the experiential space of diasporic community.

In contrast to the stereotyped exilic figure of the Wandering Jew—the Jew as doomed and punished, the Jew as perpetually homeless—most Jews remain where they were born; even those who undertake some migration, whether forced or voluntary, do not make this a habit. Not a nomadic people, they settle in a place that they willfully experience as home. Thus, while debates continue about the possibility of an authentic Jewish life outside Israel, the evidence indicates that Jews flourish as Jews in many diaspora geographies. Rather than assimilate and lose their identities, they inhabit instead a culture of diversity and simultaneity, diasporically Jewish and national citizens at once.[7]

Seeing this condition in positive rather than punitive terms, Simon Dubnow argued for "diaspora nationalism" as a feature of modern Jewish identity. Writing in the first decades of the twentieth century, a period of burgeoning nationalisms in Eastern Europe, Dubnow called for maintenance of Jewish cultural autonomy within Gentile nation-states. The Jews were a "spiritual nation"—he deemed this the loftiest national form—and the tenacity of this spiritual identity assured their survival over the centuries. Without forgoing the notion of a spiritual center in Israel, Dubnow was unwilling to accept the Zionist position of relinquishing the positive possibility of a Jewish diaspora (though it might be a less complete Jewish experience). "If the Diaspora cannot live a full national life without the center in Palestine," he argued, "then the latter cannot possibly exist without a national Diaspora."[8] To counter both the provincial isolation of the "ghetto" and the modern dangers of assimilation, Dubnow called for "national autonomy." Encompassing all Jews in his vision of the future, no matter what their language or geographic location, Dubnow argued that modern Jews must move beyond the diaspora's religious separatism to forge a distinctive and cosmopolitan Jewish national culture, varying according to circumstance, even as they function as citizens of a Gentile state. "In the Diaspora," he wrote in 1909, "we must strive, within the realm of the possible, to demand and to attain national-cultural autonomy for the majority of the nation . . . the powerful vital instinct will tell the people what style to use for building the wall of national autonomy which will replace the former religious 'fence to fence,' and will not at the same time shut out the flow of world culture."[9] Dubnow's diasporic perspective was from inside the Jewish community looking out, but the reciprocities in his vision were multiple: between diaspora and Israel, between diaspora and national majority or host.

A similar doubling may characterize the production of modern Jewish art. Not merely a local phenomenon, modern Jewish art is not an insider's art. It is instead a flexible cultural weave, combining Jewish elements with the cultural features of the national context or international matrix. What determines its diasporic success is the breadth of its address and audience, its ability to engage a wide range of viewers and to deliver a cultural statement in multiple geographies. Unlike the effort of contemporary Israeli art to distinguish itself among national cultures, diaspora art has very a different project: to push at or interrogate national cultural limits and to embrace or transmit its fluidities.

The resources of diaspora, then, are especially rich. In her discussion of Philip Roth's diasporist novel *Operation Shylock*, Sidra Ezrahi describes diaspora as a site of cultural fiction and imaginative play, a "masked ball" of performativity, which, precisely because of its unrealized fantasy of return, encourages qualities of dream and possibility often repressed in the ideological confines of modern Israel. Ezrahi's study concerns the implications for cultural production in post-1948 Israel, the modern and necessarily imperfect state that exists but cannot actualize diaspora's utopian promise and myth. Outside Israel, Ezrahi observes, for artists like Roth and for Kitaj, "Diasporism has taken on a new cultural agenda . . . [as] the foundation of a new Jewish aesthetics."[10]

With these issues in mind, let me return to my examples. Kitaj's *The Jewish Rider* (Figure 9.1) pictures a middle-aged gentleman on a passenger train, soberly lost in thought despite his brightly colored surroundings. Ever eager to attach his work to mainstream art history, Kitaj derives his passenger from the equestrian knight of *The Polish Rider*, a seventeenth-century painting formerly attributed to Rembrandt in the Frick Collection in New York. The Jewish dandy in the train—the model was the Jewish British art historian Michael Podro—retains the proud posture of the Polish hero on horseback, though his mount is squashed beneath him, and its protruding greenish head and white tail turn him into a strange hybrid.[11] But unlike the misty hills surrounding Rembrandt's steed, Kitaj's train moves through an ominous landscape, where a smoking chimney, visible through the window, sends its smoke up to the cross on a hill. Kitaj breaks the figure, train setting, and window view into wildly colored, loosely brushed segments, and in this excited sea of color, the balding head and

Figure 9.1. R. B. Kitaj, *The Jewish Rider*, 1984–85. Oil on canvas. © R. B. Kitaj. Courtesy, Marlborough Gallery, New York.

face is a somber spot of dullish gray, downshifting the demeanor of the Jewish man from the dashing confidence of the Polish knight. To underscore his confinement, a steep and narrow blood-red corridor at the right edge of the image tunnels back to the stick figure conductor—a uniformed authority—arms also akimbo, waving a weapon-like baton. We observe this scene as if standing to one side, pausing in the passage between compartment and corridor. But there is no refuge beside this passenger. The vivid zone of fragments also threatens to slide apart. Its painted restlessness loosens the figure's form, our attention lodges in the blood-red trousers, and it requires effort to see the whole coherently. In this charged and dislocating combination of color, space, and mood, the Polish-Jewish Rider—unlike the self-assured equestrian figure—travels to some unknown destiny.

A resident of London for nearly four decades, in 1989 the American-born Kitaj published the *First Diasporist Manifesto*, whose text, illustrated with his drawings, proclaims displacement as a central condition of modernity and modern art. "Diasporist painting, which I just made up," Kitaj writes, "is enacted under peculiar historical and personal freedoms, stresses, dislocation, rupture and momentum. The Diasporist lives and paints in two or more societies at once."[12] Kitaj sees diasporism as a characteristic of modern artists generally. "In my time," he states a few pages later, "half the painters of the great schools of Paris, New York and London were not born in their host countries."[13] One might note that Kitaj's multiple diasporic identities begin with his childhood. Raised in the Midwest, in Cleveland, the adopted son of a Viennese Jewish immigrant father whose name he took, Kitaj lived the expatriate artist's life, first in Vienna and then London. There is, he wrote, a real advantage to this condition for the artist. "As a painter, I've come to detect something like moral power or destiny, living in more than one society, wrapped about in art, in its histories and antitheses."[14] But however broad its cultural base and mainstream success, and however eager the artist is to see it as a modern condition, Kitaj's diasporism is clearly Jewish: "Diasporic painting is unfolding commentary on its life-source, the contemplation of a transience, a *Midrash* . . . in paint . . . these circumstantial allusions form themselves into secular *Responsa* or reactions to one's transient restlessness, un-at-homeness, groundlessness."[15] Feeling his difference as an American Jew in Britain, Kitaj's diasporist identity is prompted both by his need to address a catastrophic Jewish history and his desire to bind his work to some larger community.[16] Diaspora provides this larger "theater . . . where human artistic instinct comes into play."[17] Thus, while there is much that is celebrative in Kitaj's work, the diasporic imagery in pictures like *Germania (The Tunnel)* (1985), *Cecil Court, London, WC2 (The Refugees)* (1984–85), or *The Jewish School (Drawing a Golem)* (1980) is fraught with expressions of disquiet, dislocation, disruption, and fear.

Some scholars put a positive spin on Kitaj's diasporism. Andrew Benjamin sees the Wandering Jew/Jewish Rider not in terms of a punitive Jewish homelessness but, more existentially—or theologically, like the Jewish God—as a people unfixed, always in the process of becoming.[18] Janet Wolff argues that the layered allusions and unresolved meanings in Kitaj's work—problematic features for many of his critics—are effective pictorial homologies to the condition of diaspora itself.[19] But these approaches to the diasporist pictures, or to diasporism generally, are still bound to the distressing condition of nomadism or exile. Despite invocations in his text and pictures of Jewish diasporists like Walter Benjamin, Franz Kafka, Philip

Roth, and the moral-critical edge that Kitaj believes is diaspora's claim, it is the plight—not the purpose—of the Wandering Jew/Jewish Rider, the smoking chimneys of concentrations camps, the anxieties and uncertainties of *galut* emigration that he depicts, not the positive potential of diaspora's imaginative theater.

Produced as unique objects and displayed in galleries and museums, Kitaj's pictures reach a broader community through art books and photo reproductions. Ben Katchor's work, however, appears first as newspapers cartoon strips, a medium that fosters what Benedict Anderson has termed "imagined community," and so effectively conjoins segments of diaspora's far-flung geography.[20] Nationally syndicated, the work is a regular feature of the weekly English edition of the Jewish *Forward*, a "natural" site given the paper's history and its new diasporist purpose. Once the most widely read Yiddish daily in North America, with the declared mission of Americanizing its readers, the paper now draws on an acculturated but self-consciously Jewish American readership, for whom it reports and reinforces the continuing vitality of Jewish life in the diaspora—in English. Katchor, who teaches at New York's School of Visual Arts, and whose Guggenheim and MacArthur fellowships certify his place in the American mainstream art world, also publishes his strips in book form. These include *The Beauty Supply District* (2000); *Julius Knipl, Real Estate Photographer* (1996); and *Cheap Novelties: The Pleasures of Urban Decay* (1991). The titles are high art parodies: they play on beauty and its commercial supply; on the photography of property, not landmarks; on the joys of vulgar novelties, not artistic innovation or delight. Katchor uses irony and humor to create a critical aesthetic layering; he sets the viewer/reader in a framework not unlike a diasporist's double consciousness. This is certainly true of *The Jew of New York: A Historical Romance* (1998), which is designed to resemble a nineteenth-century history, with special end papers, introductory pages, book flaps and bookmarks. As a highly stylized volume, it moves from its cheap journalistic origins into the realm of the art book and a more sophisticated commerce.

Katchor's strips habitually depict the adventures of Jewish men engaged in small-time commercial enterprise in the urban world. *The Jew of New York* combines notions of Jewish immigration and diaspora with the mythic framework of America as a promised land. But the storytelling is decidedly kaleidoscopic, as Katchor plays fast and loose with any easy-to-follow sequence or narrative. A dizzying cast of male characters appear and reappear, and despite their distinctive Jewish monikers—Enoch Letushim, Yosl Feynbrot, Nathan Kishon, Isaac Azarael—they are not easy to tell apart. Angular and stiff in contour, the figures are rather like manikins, and they enact their drama through puppet-like gesture and pose. This produces a primitive quality appropriate to a comic strip mode, and, as a repudiation of high art figure styles, it invokes popular print traditions and broadsides. But the drawing is also an expressive strategy, for the physiognomic awk-

Figure 9.2. Page 35, from *The Jew of New York* by Ben Katchor, copyright © 1998 by Ben Katchor. Used by permission of Pantheon Books, a division of Random House, Inc.

wardness of the characters brings them close to caricature in the spirit of parody, thereby reinforcing critical distance in the viewer.

This approach also governs the graphic design of the page. *The Jew of New York* stays close to its newspaper format, with regular frames and only occasional interruptions of important symbolic forms, settings, and chapter breaks (Figure 9.2). From frame to frame, however, close-ups, panoramas, and perspectives leap about like cinematic jump-cuts or montage, disrupting the ease of narrative sequence and refusing to draw a single point of view. For a graphic novel, moreover, the text is remarkably wordy and visually dense (Figure 9.3.). Characters deliver lengthy speeches and large blocks of text tell the story in a sophisticated literary style that belies the figures' woodenness. But it is this very "mismatch"—the puppet-like fig-

Figure 9.3. Page 23, from *The Jew of New York* by Ben Katchor, copyright © 1998 by Ben Katchor. Used by permission of Pantheon Books, a division of Random House, Inc.

ures, the perspectival jumpiness, the witty text—that produces our own omniscient or specially informed presence and the story's sardonic tone.

The historical tale is well researched: Katchor's knowledge of United States and Jewish history is evident in this drama, which pairs myths of the bustling entrepreneurial energy of early nineteenth-century New York with Jewish immigration and the search for a promised land. The American Jewish historian Jonathan Sarna has described the desire for linked mythologies as almost a Jewish American propensity. "Among America's ethnic and religious groups," Sarna writes, "only one, the Jews, has linked itself to so many of the nation's founding myths," a habit that says less about real history than it does "about American Jews, their loyalties, and their insecurities."[21] *The Jew of New York* derives its narrative from a project of Mordecai

Manuel Noah, a playwright, newspaper editor, and politician whom the *Jewish Encyclopedia* (1901–6) described as the "most influential Jew in the United States in the early nineteenth-century."[22] Noah sought to establish a Jewish homeland called Ararat on Grand Island in the Niagara River, just north of Buffalo. (Now a suburb, the area is currently the subject of land claim disputes between Tuscarora Iroquois and suburban homeowners.) In Katchor's tale, Jews and Indians are paired as dispossessed partners. Reviving nineteenth-century accounts of Native Americans as the Ten Lost Tribes (a mythic population who have been repeatedly "discovered" in unexplored geographies), the combination offers some telling couplings or binary stereotypes:

1. Jews are seen as a sophisticated people detached from nature, unlanded and unnatural, while Indians are seen as simple primitives embedded in nature, the "natural man."
2. Jews are seen as traditionally entrepreneurial and mercantile, while Indians are seen as living entirely in a subsistence or natural economy.[23]
3. Jews, often ghettoized in Europe, are thought to be in perpetual search for their home and promised land, while Native people, their land wrested from them by European colonizers, live ghettoized on reserves.

Katchor intertwines diasporic Jews and ghettoized Indians, not only through the Lost Tribes myth and Grand Island project, but also through his characters' adventures: Nathan Kishon, the disgraced *shoykhet* (Yiddish: ritual slaughterer), lives au naturel as a trapper, marketing muskrat skins, taming nature by carbonating Lake Erie to ease the *grepsing* (Yiddish: burping) of New York digestive tracts, shuttling between city and nearby frontier. If it is hard to keep track of plot details, with this crowded cast and their restless to-ings and fro-ings, what emerges is the always moving population and the shifting identities that these Jews acquire.

On one narrative level, however, the play's the thing in Katchor's diasporic theater. The story opens with plans for a dramatic staging of Manuel Noah's project as "The Jew of New York." Characters are self-consciously costumed in diving suits, togas, business suits, and buckskins to fit the mythic terms of their mission. One of the commercial ploys in the story (along with the muskrat skin trade and the sale of kabbalistically themed printed handkerchiefs) is more costume illusion: the manufacture of a flesh-colored body stocking to disguise the nakedness of the play's star and only woman in the story, the aging diva Ms. Patella. Katchor's tales describe the seedy or marginal worlds of men. Women, if they do appear, are merely incidental objects of desire. More important than Ms. Patella is the body stocking's commercial potential, and significantly, it widens the

Figure 9.4. Title page from *The Jew of New York* by Ben Katchor, copyright © 1998 by Ben Katchor. Used by permission of Pantheon Books, a division of Random House, Inc.

masquerade, as identities are made, enacted, and circumstantial. As the floating top hat at the top of the book's title page suggests, New York's Jew is an airborne figure, a *luftmentsh* (Yiddish: one who lives on air or fanciful daydreams) (Figure 9.4). Borne by the wind, his bourgeois identity hovers over his diasporic home.

If Katchor's restless characters are forever seeking their place in an America of promise and opportunity, the diaspora of Vera Frenkel's installation . . . *from the Transit Bar* evokes a less determinate geography. Born in Czechoslovakia, Frenkel emigrated as a teenager with her family from England to Canada, where the national rhetoric proclaims not a promised land but a protected colony, not a melting pot but rather a diverse social

Figure 9.5. Vera Frenkel, . . . *from the Transit Bar,"* 6-channel videodisk installation and functional piano bar. Partial view. Museum Fredericianum, Documenta IX, Kassel, 1992. Photo: Dirk Bleicker.

mosaic. For the *Transit Bar,* Frenkel collects a diverse group of participants to stand for the world's dislocated and diasporic populations. As an installation first constructed for *Documenta IX* at Kassel, Germany in 1992, . . . *from the Transit Bar* has since been installed in galleries and museums in Toronto, Ottawa, Tokyo, Stockholm, and Warsaw. Its high art settings and audiences notwithstanding, the work has considerable public appeal. The gallery space is transformed into a railway bar (Figure 9.5); café tables and racked newspapers are available; drinks can be ordered from a handsome barman, or, on occasion, from the artist playing bartender. Wall cutouts reveal glimpses of auxiliary spaces: stacks of old-fashioned suitcases and topcoats clutter a left-luggage room; another space opens onto a palm-treed paradise. The vaguely art deco décor and the melodies coming from the player piano suggest the 1930s, but in a more contemporary vein, TV monitors scattered about play a forty-minute loop of interviews. The fifteen respondents sit, as we do, at a train bar or in a railway club car. They are a diverse company of eight men and seven women, young adults to middle-aged, but old enough to have some past and to tell us, as fellow travelers, about their journeys, displacements, and homes. Sound—as Jean Gagnon has noted in calling the bar a space of orality and address, a space to say—is crucial here: the romantic tunes coming from the piano (always some sort of "You must remember this . . .") are punctuated by the background noise of passing trains.[24] And the videotape, in Polish and Yiddish (the languages of the artist's grandparents), is subtitled in French, English, and German (Figure 9.6).

. . . *from the Transit Bar* can also be visited through another work, Frenkel's *Body Missing* project, which began as a separate installation in Linz, Austria, and which is now located on the Internet at *The Body Missing Project*, http://www.yorku.ca/BodyMissing. In this global setting, clearly a space of representation as well as communication, the bar appears in fragments, with glimpses of the mise-en-scène, the personnel, the interviewees, and other visitors. Access here, of course, is as easy as an electronic click, but always partial, as the text warns, depending on where you sit and what's around you. One page of the website, *The Site Map*, is a cartographic drawing of great elegance, but like many diasporic journeys, it charts somewhat baffling terrain. Indeed, hunting through the frames of the website reminds us that the journey, like the writing of history, always offers a situational view.

Still, everyone is an equal traveler in the *Transit Bar*. Mass culture codes of leisure and romance, familiar to most Western audiences, entice us into a space of nostalgia and fantasy. To enter the bar is to begin a journey of encounter and discovery, to enjoy the bar's voyeuristic disclosures, its transient society, its sense of possibility. Even the title, with its opening ellipsis and prepositional *from*, suggests a prior or already ongoing existence, lack of fixity, an open site, and message relay. Indeed, if bars are ideal spaces in which to speak, to pour out one's story to an ever-listening barman or companion, this bar's design, décor, music, and pictures urge us to remember and imagine. Citing Paul Ricoeur's notion of "a prenarrative quality," Jean Gagnon notes Frenkel's tendency to work at this liminal level, where the desire for story effectively draws us into the game.[25] Thus, the bar creates a place for us—it even allows for solitude and loneliness—as one spins one's own narrative fantasy, weaving together filaments from the environment, personal history, cultural recollection, and the bar's community history.

This is not to overlook the tension and foreboding stirred by the setting and the travelers' tales. Nor is the *Bar* a safe harbor, or more than temporary shelter. Irit Rogoff and others astutely discuss the *Transit Bar's* capacity to evoke traumatic memory and a tragic past—the glimpses of stacked luggage, the sound of shuttling trains evoking Nazi prisoner transports, forced expulsions, and running for refuge to a fantasized natural Paradise, glimpsed in the palms.[26] This may be the predicament of Jews for much of our history, but by now it is also a widespread refugee experience. So are the allusions in the video texts, whose words sound the ethnic expressiveness of M/other tongue translated into the authoritative, cosmopolitan

Figure 9.6. Vera Frenkel, . . . *from the Transit Bar,* 6-channel videodisk installation and functional piano bar. Detail: Narrator Ian Robertson on monitor above immigrant community newspapers. Museum Fridericianum, Documenta IX, Kassel, 1992. Photo: Vera Frenkel.

script of Euro-American power. But what makes . . . *from theTransit Bar* particularly effective is the mix of its experiences. If there is painful history here, there is also promise and well-being. Which part is illusory? Which is real? The erotic space of the bar, the use of nostalgia to draw us in, and only then, amid that pleasure, to awaken uneasy associations of home, travel, and flight: all this enables multiple participants, multiple subject positions, and reconsideration of one's own geography along a broad emotional continuum. From Holocaust refugees to more recent emigrants and travelers, the visitors in or . . . *from the Transit Bar* are another diaspora pondering their relation to home.

With these three examples let me briefly suggest some main contours of diasporic art. The necessary qualities seem to me to be a positing of multiple subjectivities and an appeal to both widespread and multiple audiences. If, as Benedict Anderson describes it, modern print culture was essential for the development of national consciousness, then easy access for a dispersed community is similarly crucial to diaspora's cultural forms. To be sure, these artists' first-line audiences are limited—visitors to museums and galleries. Still, in an age of mechanical and digital reproduction, this work reaches beyond an "actual" audience into a "virtual" diasporic space.

Among these three artists, moreover, there are features that reinforce diaspora's variant possibilities. Despite their differences, all three artists set the Jewish diaspora as their landmark or cornerstone, and all three allude to diaspora's darker side. Indeed for Kitaj—generationally closer to the shadow of the Holocaust—the diasporic condition is fundamentally uneasy. He may proclaim the "Diasporism" of modernity in general, but his diasporist pictures allude only to Jews and represent only the dispossessed and their anguish. What there is of home and comfort in his paintings does not bear a diasporic stamp. Instead, images like *The Jewish Rider* or *Cecil Court, London, WC2* articulate Jewish diasporism as that of the post-Holocaust immigrant and anxious guest. Stylistically, the pictures participate in an international vanguard, but their content offers little sign of diaspora's pleasures or imaginative environment.

Katchor's *Jew of New York* clearly centers on Jewish experience, and in their comic representation, the adventures of his characters evoke both anxiety and irony. Similarly, Frenkel's fellow travelers are surrounded by nostalgia and discomforting allusions to the Holocaust. The ambivalence of diaspora, its pleasures along with its tensions, is striking in both artists' works. Key features affirm diaspora's labile character, its play with several viewpoints, its meandering and mutable borders rather than existence within fixed cultural frames, and its aesthetic pact with the viewer as included participant or knowing and critical spectator.

All three artists convey the experience of modernity's migrations and resettlements, with their combination of upheaval and idealism. Katchor's

Jewish American saga and Frenkel's transient barroom are probing frameworks for diasporic identities, old and new. Characters change, assert, and re-imagine themselves as they encounter new hosts and new ways to be-at-home. Both works complicate and extend their putative subject matter, and in doing so, they call attention to the exhilarating, uncertain, and always negotiated status of home and community. If for Kitaj, the uneasy and displaced immigrant views are separate from his often joyous, non-Jewish, or "assimilated," work, for Katchor and Frenkel, the ambivalence, the pleasure, as well as the problems of diaspora are evident and compelling. Despite their explicitly Jewish references, these works propose new affinities as well as displacements. Such positions allow for diaspora's simultaneity, for the pleasures of diasporic imagination as well as the tensions embedded in the more exilic *galut*. This is a different notion of diaspora, one that supersedes the singular identities of the modern nation-state. Relinquishing the choice between separatism or assimilation, this diasporic culture signals a new kind of home as a negotiated, dynamic, and changing space between.

IV.
Portraits of the Artist as Jew

When is "Jewish" pertinent to the evaluation of an artist and his or her work? This question remains central to analyses of *modern* Jewish art in particular, since the ambiguity of Jewish identity, though hardly absent from earlier eras, is a hallmark of the modern age. In this section, essays by Diana L. Linden, Walter Cahn, and Olga Litvak treat the "Jewish art question" from substantively disparate but methodologically complementary perspectives. All three resituate the question by examining it in light of specific institutional and biographical contexts where the Jewish ascription is at bottom not a reflection of essences and absolutes but a self-conscious strategy on the part of artists, patrons, and critics to advance specific artistic and nonartistic ends.

Diana L. Linden's "Modern? American? Jew? Museums and Exhibitions of Ben Shahn's Late Paintings" proceeds from the premise that art historical narratives are constructed—by collectors, curators, critics, and art historians—and performed in exhibitions. In the case at hand, Shahn has been excluded from the story of American postwar modern art because critics deemed the personal realism of the work he did in the 1940s and 1950s incompatible with abstract expressionism, presumably the defining moment of postwar American modern art. Yet by demonstrating commonalities other than style between Shahn's later work and abstract expressionism, The Jewish Museum in New York's 1998 exhibition of Shahn's late work, *Common Man, Mythic Vision*, set out to revise the art historical narrative by defining a place within it for Shahn. The results were ironic. Since it was The Jewish Museum that made the case for Shahn's *general* relevance, the exhibition inadvertently left the impression that Shahn's own Jewishness was key to his artistic achievement, despite the artists's own protestations to the contrary throughout his lifetime. This confusion was only aggravated when the Shahn exhibition traveled to the Detroit Institute of Arts (DIA). There overt references to his leftist political affiliations were minimized and the artist's thematic focus on oppression and use of Hebrew and Yiddish inscriptions accentuated—all to suggest a Jewishness defined by both a universalist humanism and ethnic pride, rather than the specific tradition of secular Jewish working-class politics that Shahn had embraced. Linden's sophisticated analysis provokes us to consider how institutional identity, the merchandising exigencies of the museum industry, as well as the ideological agendas of art critics can often promote a claim for aesthetic relevance by carving out convenient ethnic "niches."

The relevance of Jewishness to the work of the painter Max Liebermann, who flourished some fifty years earlier in Germany, was also the subject of heated debate. In "Max Liebermann and the Amsterdam Jewish Quarter," Walter Cahn uses the series of *Judengasse* scenes painted by Liebermann between 1905 and 1909 to address the nature of the relationship between the painter, of acculturated and middle-class German Jewish background, and the nearly three-hundred-year-old Amsterdam ghetto, a "place of authentic Jewish life" captured by Liebermann immediately prior to its dissolution. He tackles this problem in three ways: first, by analyzing the ghetto scene genre itself; second, by examining the painter's iconographic, formal, and stylistic choices; and third, by tracing the reception history of Liebermann's *Judengasse* paintings. Cahn's multifaceted analysis, focusing like Liebermann's paintings on the Jewish street, reveals the complexity of this seemingly straightforward Jewish locale. The pictoral representation of the "ghetto," *Judengasse,* or Jewish quarter (or, in the case of Eastern Europe, the *shtetl*) is a veritable Rorschach test of a given artist's attitude toward Judaism and modernity. Modern Jews have alternatively seen the crowded Jewish quarter as an impediment to their integration or a wellspring of authentic Jewish culture threatened by the corrosive forces of emancipation and modernity. With the transformation and disappearance of these neighborhoods, such ambivalence would often turn to melancholy. Liebermann evoked all of these conflicting sentiments by capturing the mood of the swarming throng in the tightly compressed space of the *Judengasse,* suggesting his own simultaneous status as insider and outsider, participant and observer.

In 1885 Max Liebermann outraged anti-Semitic critics with his deliberately "Semitic" rendering of *The Twelve-Year-Old Jesus in the Temple.* Given the centrality of the image of Christ in the history of Western art, modern Jewish artists who have treated this subject have faced enormous challenges and inevitable controversies. Indeed, their very portrayal of Christ by Jewish artists begs the question of whether his depiction by a Jew should inevitably be understood as an act of aesthetic reappropriation. In her "Rome and Jerusalem: The Figure of Jesus in the Creation of Mark Antokol'skii," Olga Litvak turns this notion on its head. She demonstrates how the sculptor deliberately manipulated the presumption of contemporary critics that his Jewish origins provided the key to a proper understanding his work. According to Litvak, by coyly playing off of such an assumption, Antokol'skii pursued a serious aim: fashioning an oeuvre and a reputation that that would enable him to elide the deadly binary slashes of Jew/Christian, Occident/Orient, East/West, and Rome/Jerusalem. In her conclusion, Litvak suggests that it is precisely in this effort to devise an aesthetically driven "cultural promiscuity" that Antokol'skii reveals himself as a modern Jew.

Chapter 10

Modern? American? Jew?
Museums and Exhibitions of Ben Shahn's Late Paintings

Diana L. Linden

The year 1998 marked the centennial of the birth of artist Ben Shahn (1898–1969). Coupled with the approach of the millennium, which many museums celebrated by surveying the cultural production of the twentieth century, the centennial offered a perfect opportunity to mount a major exhibition of Shahn's work (the last comprehensive exhibition had taken place at The Jewish Museum in New York in 1976).[1] The moment was also propitious because a renewed interest in narrative and figurative art and in the social history of art encouraged scholarly and popular appreciation of Ben Shahn, whose reputation within the history of American art had been eclipsed for many decades by the attention given to the abstract expressionists. The Jewish Museum responded in 1998 with *Common Man, Mythic Vision: The Paintings of Ben Shahn*, organized by the museum's curator Susan Chevlowe, with the abstract expressionism scholar Stephen Polcari. The exhibition traveled to the Allentown Art Museum in Pennsylvania and closed at the Detroit Institute of Arts (DIA) in 1999.

Smaller Shahn exhibitions then in the planning stage (although not scheduled to open during the centennial year) were to focus on selected aspects of Shahn's oeuvre: the Fogg Museum was to present his little-known New York photographs of the 1930s in relationship to his paintings, and the Jersey City Museum intended to exhibit his career-launching series, *The Passion of Sacco and Vanzetti* (1931–32).[2] Knowing this, Chevlowe chose to focus on the later years of Shahn's career and on his lesser-known easel paintings of the post–World War II era. In so doing, Chevlowe challenged viewers to expand their understanding of both the artist and his place in twentieth-century American art.[3]

In the textbook version of art history, the 1940s and 1950s are known for the triumph of abstract expressionism, from which Shahn is normally excluded. Similarly, most art museums today do not display works by Shahn alongside those of abstract expressionists like Jackson Pollock and Mark

Rothko, and many scholars do not acknowledge that Shahn worked concurrently with them.[4] This "triumph of American painting," to use Irving Sandler's term, implies that in the postwar period, realists like Shahn either gave up the brush or became irrelevant, as reflected in most museum exhibitions.[5] But in her foreword to the exhibition catalogue, the director of The Jewish Museum, Joan Rosenbaum, highlighted the heretofore forgotten commonalities between Shahn and the abstract painters of the 1940s and 1950s, proposing that the artist's mythic and allegorical paintings of the post–World War II era shared with other American artists a response to the traumas of the period, including the Holocaust, nuclear age, and Cold War. Like them, Shahn struggled to find an artistic vocabulary to express, rather than merely document, such experiences.[6] Nevertheless, Shahn has been presented increasingly in the context of "Jewish art and artists."

Exhibitions of Shahn's work have been instrumental in defining his position within the history of twentieth-century American art, whether at its center during his early career or at its margins during his later years. Whereas at The Jewish Museum, *Common Man, Mythic Vision* attempted to reinscribe Shahn within the history of postwar American art, the Detroit Institute of Arts marketed Shahn as a Jewish artist, an identification that Shahn himself refused. This essay explores how this exhibition, in two different museums, shaped expectations of Shahn's work. I draw upon my experience as an essayist for the exhibition catalogue; participant in one of two scholars' forums at The Jewish Museum during the planning stage; trainer of docents at the DIA; and speaker during the show's run there. While intimately familiar with the exhibition, I had no control over its content. Indeed, mine was the only catalogue essay to deal with works that predate the postwar easel paintings at the heart of the exhibition.[7]

Ben Shahn and New York's Museums

No single museum lays sole claim to launching and supporting Shahn's long career. Nor is there just one repository for the work of this prodigious and multitalented artist. Shahn was a photographer for the Farm Security Administration/Resettlement Administration; a muralist under the auspices of federal art projects (and one of the few New Deal muralists to work in true fresco, which he learned while serving as an apprentice to the famed Mexican muralist Diego Rivera); a mosaicist for the William E. Grady Vocational High School in Manhattan (1957), Syracuse University (1967), and for various synagogues; an illustrator for such magazines as *Harpers, Fortune,* and *The Nation*; a designer of political posters and graphics for such organizations as the Office of War Information (1942–44) and the Congress of Industrial Organization/Political Action Committee (1944–46); as well as the painter of numerous temperas, most often working on board or paper applied to board (these tempera paintings were the focus of *Common Man, Mythic Vision*).[8] Despite this eclecticism and mobility, Shahn's life and work remained anchored in New York City. He lived in New York from the time of his arrival in America at age eight (he was born in 1898 in Kovno, then part of the Russian empire, today in Lithuania) until the late 1930s, when he moved to the utopian workers' community of the Jersey Homesteads, New Jersey.[9] For this reason, New York—central to the Jewish immigrant experience, the site of the most formative period of the artist's life, a center for labor and radical politics during Shahn's lifetime, and today, the heart of the American art world—appeared to be the most appropriate city to host the artist's centennial exhibition.

Given this setting, it is instructive to note that it was The Jewish Museum, one of several New York museums capable of organizing a centennial exhibition on Shahn, that took the lead. All museums have specific curatorial and programmatic missions. In Shahn's case, his work could have fit the broad mandates of such encyclopedic museums as the Metropolitan Museum of Art and the Brooklyn Museum of Art or the more focused missions of the Whitney Museum of American Art, the Museum of Modern Art, and The Jewish Museum. Each museum would have told a different story about the artist and his paintings. Shahn would have been seen in the context of twentieth-century American painting (the Whitney), or European and American modernism (MoMA), or Jewish culture, art, and history (The Jewish Museum). It was The Jewish Museum that ventured a Shahn retrospective and focused it on the phase of his work that was critical for assessing his relation to postwar American painting.

Ben Shahn as an American Artist

Why not the Whitney? In the early 1930s, on the basis of Shahn's breakthrough series, *The Passion of Sacco and Vanzetti* (1931–32), the Whitney Museum of American Art became a champion of the young artist and selected Shahn's paintings for display in its very first biennale.[10] Adam D. Weinberg, a curator at the Whitney in 1998, later praised both the series and the Whitney's paintings as "among the greatest achievements of twentieth-century art."[11] Given its mission, a commitment "to collecting, preserving, interpreting, and exhibiting American art . . . to serve a wide variety of audiences and to celebrate the complexity, heterogeneity, and diversity of American art and culture," and its strong Shahn holdings—the Whitney was the second largest institutional lender to *Common Man, Mythic Vision* at The Jewish Museum—why does the Whitney emphasize its pre-1940 Shahns over such (later) paintings in its collection as *Cherubs and Children*, and *Everyman*, both lent to the 1998 Shahn exhibition, along with *Reconstruction* (1945) and *Conversations* (1954)?[12] Because the New York School continues to dominate postwar American modernism.

Thus, while Whitney curator Barbara Haskell included Shahn's photographs, paintings, and graphics in her 1999 exhibition, *The American Century: Art and Culture, 1900–1950*, the curator Lisa Phillips neither displayed nor mentioned Shahn in the companion exhibition and volume, *The American Century: Art and Culture, 1950–2000*, even though the artist was active and popular until his death in 1969.[13] The Whitney has chosen to display works by realist painters only from their initial years of productivity, creating a chronology of twentieth-century American art that is subdivided into discrete styles, each confined to a specific time period, moving from realism to abstraction. As a result, Shahn, as well as Isaac and Raphael Soyer, Reginald Marsh, and Isabel Bishop, become realists from the 1930s, rather than artists who remained productive for decades to come. It was precisely this periodization of Shahn and American art that Susan Chevlowe and The Jewish Museum sought to counter.

Even the exhibition titles (The Jewish Museum's *Common Man* and the Whitney Museum's *American Century*, the latter phrase coined by the newspaper and magazine publisher Henry Luce), wittingly or unwittingly, evoked the climate of the postwar era and the ways that artists were identified politically, a factor in how critics assessed their postwar work. Shahn had strongly supported the presidential candidacy of Henry Wallace, who declared the twentieth century to be the "Century of the Common Man" and who had sought to expand New Deal policies globally, whereas Luce's "American Century" encapsulates what Frances K. Pohl has called the publisher's "benevolent imperialism." Echoes of this contrast can be heard in Serge Guilbaut's classic argument that the promotion of abstract expressionism was part of the expansionist policies and rhetoric of the Cold War.[14] Whether the argument is correct or not, images of the "Common Man" produced by such realists as Shahn, Max Weber, and Jack Levine, which were relegated decades ago to the historical dustbin, and have yet—even long after the Cold War—to be retrieved.

Ben Shahn as a Modern Artist

In terms of both quality and quantity, the Museum of Modern Art's vast holdings of Shahn's work—over 138 paintings, photographs, temperas, illustrated books, prints, works on paper, sketches, and studies, as well as important correspondence between the artist and several MoMA curators—are even more impressive than those of the Whitney. MoMA had started exhibiting Shahn's work in 1932 as part of Lincoln Kirstein's *Murals by American Painters and Photographers* and continued to collect and exhibit Shahn's work into the early 1960s. In 1947, as abstract expressionism gained both institutional and critical approval, MoMA organized Shahn's first career retrospective. At that time, the curator James Thrall Soby wrote that Shahn's commitment to non-abstraction was evidence of the artist's importance and his against-the-grain Americanness. (Of differing opinion was Clement Greenberg, who upon viewing the 1947 retrospective asserted that Shahn's art "is not important, is essentially beside the point as far as ambitious present-day painting is concerned.")[15] In 1954, MoMA curators selected Shahn and Willem de Kooning to represent the nation at the Venice Biennale's American Pavillion.[16] MoMA, with its extensive Shahn holdings, was the single largest institutional lender to *Common Man, Mythic Vision* at The Jewish Museum.

Since the 1970s, MoMA has rarely displayed works by Shahn, with one important recent exception. In 2000, MoMA presented numerous smaller exhibitions that were focused thematically during a two-part examination of its collection of twentieth-century art. One such exhibition, *The Rhetoric of Persuasion*, included Shahn's painting *Welders* (1943), which was displayed alongside works by Diego Rivera, Jose Clemente Orozco, and Jacob Lawrence. In 1944, the artist had turned this painting into a poster for the Congress of Industrial Organizations/Political Action Committee and retitled it *Welders, or For Full Employment after the War*.[17] In a curious irony, the presentation of Shahn's pro-labor painting coincided with MoMA's staff walking out on strike at the moment when MoMA's own labor policies were under public scrutiny. Shahn, Lawrence, and the great Mexican artists had made it onto interior gallery walls normally reserved for the mainstream.

In light of this complex legacy, a MoMA exhibition of Shahn in 1998 could have occasioned an exploration of the changing relationship between museum and artist, the factors shaping how his work looked and its reception, when and why MoMA's enthusiasm for Shahn diminished, and how other artists with similar stylistic, thematic, or philosophical characteristics fared. But by refusing to acknowledge the relevance of realists and social/political artists to postwar American art, the Whitney and MoMA advanced a vision of modernism that emphasized formalist innovation over political expression. Nor is Shahn the only artist of his generation to be excluded from MoMA's vision of pure modernism. Many women artists and artists of color were also left out.[18]

In the canonical MoMA narrative, rooted in European modernism, one style progresses into the other, in the direction of greater formal abstraction, such that, as Carol Duncan has observed, "earlier American artists like Stuart Davis and [Edward] Hopper, who cannot be so easily fitted in, are hung in corners or alcoves out of the way of the 'mainstream': likewise the Mexican artists Rivera and Orozco, who have often ended up out in the hall."[19] Moreover, to the extent that MoMA identified "artistic invention with moral achievement . . . the more artists freed themselves from representing recognizable objects in space, the more exemplary they became as moral beings and the more pious and spiritually meaningful their artistic efforts."[20] The abstract expressionists reigned supreme in this regard, in contrast with Shahn, whose moral stance was expressed in a figurative art of social viewpoint and humanistic concern. Yet again, in 1998, MoMA and the Whitney mounted major exhibitions celebrating abstract expressionist artists: Jackson Pollock at MoMA and Mark Rothko at the Whitney.[21]

Ben Shahn as Jewish Artist

When asked in 1966 at a synagogue community forum if he was a Jewish artist, Shahn denounced the label, saying, "I am a human artist. I don't like categorization in groups. I wouldn't be interested in an exhibit of Jewish painters."[22] In his 1957 book, *The Shape of Content*, Shahn wrote, "I believe that if it were left to artists to choose their own labels most would chose none. For most artists have expended a great deal of energy in scrambling out of classes and categories and pigeon-holes, aspiring toward some state of perfect freedom which unfortunately neither human limitations nor the law allows—not to mention the critics."[23] While *Common Man, Mythic Vision* was intended to restore to Shahn his rightful place in the history of postwar American art, the venue, The Jewish Museum, ensured that he would be received as a Jewish artist, Shahn's views and the curators' intentions notwithstanding.

In the catalogue foreword, the museum's director, Joan Rosenbaum, notes that, just like the abstract expressionists Jackson Pollock, Barnett Newman, and Willem de Kooning, Shahn, in the postwar era, explored the "universal themes of war, destruction and renewal, the fate of humanity in the face of catastrophic upheaval."[24] In this way, the museum asked its visitors to view Shahn as equal to or at least in dialogue with the more celebrated abstractionists. It is true that Shahn's postwar work shifted away from his earlier social realism into what he termed "personal realism," and later, "symbolic realism," that is, the use of symbol and allegory to interpret rather than document and a focus more on individual experience and identity than on the collective. Accordingly, The Jewish Museum featured Shahn's lesser-known temperas of the 1940s and 1950s, which showed his deft use of the medium, his balance of broad expanses of paint with minute detail, his matte application of paint, varied strokes, and quirky characteristic sense of outline and calligraphic line.[25]

What The Jewish Museum ultimately presented in *Common Man, Mythic Vision* was a revisionist narrative of postwar American art. The exhibition opposed MoMA's mainstream narrative of modernism by inserting Shahn's work—not all of it, but only works that conformed to high-modernist criteria—into that narrative. As a result, visitors to *Common Man, Mythic Vision* saw only Shahn's easel paintings, with the exception of a limited number of magazine illustrations and ephemera that were also on view. Thus, the painting *Cat's Cradle* (c. 1959) appeared without the related poster *Stop H-Bomb Tests* (c. 1960s).[26] The decision not to include Shahn's graphics and posters, which The Jewish Museum had previously included as part of its comprehensive 1976 retrospective, created the visual impression that

Shahn had left organized partisan politics and the graphic arts behind. In fact, nothing could have been further from the truth, as Stephen Polcari himself indicated in his exhibition catalogue essay. Even with the artist's stylistic switch to personal realism and allegorical and symbolic work, "Shahn continued to make partisan political art"; he created posters for the Office of War Information (OWI), the CIO-Political Action Committee (CIO-PAC), for Roosevelt's and Wallace's campaigns.[27] The omission had the curious effect of distorting the nature of Shahn's postwar output in order to focus attention on his paintings and rewrite the history of postwar American art.

But situating Shahn in a Jewish context also shaped (or misshaped) the interpretation of his work as the expression of a Jewish artist. A case in point is Shahn's *Spring*, which The Jewish Museum selected for the cover of the exhibition catalogue, the promotional poster, and the invitation to the opening. Shahn based this painting on a newspaper clipping of two young lovers lying intertwined on a city park lawn and enjoying a spring day, the woman coyly wearing her companion's fedora on her head.[28] As discussed by the art historian Laura Katzman, Shahn often used images from newspaper and documentary photos as source materials, altering and adapting them in his painted interpretations.[29] In *Spring*, the two lovers fill the foreground yet appear emotionally disconnected from each other, despite their physical closeness. At left, the man's face and hand are darkened and partially obscured by the thistle plant, held upright in the young woman's hand, which separates the pair. Frances K. Pohl, one of the catalogue authors, suggests that the painting is a fitting metaphor for the spring of 1947, when "talk of another world war clouded the future and the search for communists sowed suspicion and distrust among the survivors of a more optimistic New Deal era."[30] But as the promotional image for The Jewish Museum's exhibition, *Spring* suggests two young *Jewish* lovers in a New York City park, as it does subsequently on the cover of the Yiddish novelist Isaac Bashevis Singer's *Meshugah*. The novel tells the story of a love triangle, informed by experiences of surviving the Holocaust, in New York City at the close of World War II. Thus, *Spring* becomes Jewish by context, and Shahn becomes a Jewish artist by attribution, not by personal identification or iconography.

Common Man Travels to Detroit

When *Common Man, Mythic Vision* left its Jewish institutional context and traveled to non-Jewish museums, it should have been easier to establish Shahn as a major figure in the history of postwar American art, one of the goals of the original exhibition. But this was not to be the case. The exhibition first went to Allentown, Pennsylvania, from March 28 to June 27, 1999, before arriving at its final destination, the Detroit Institute of Arts (DIA), where it ran from July 25 to October 31, 1999. Unfortunately, MoMA withdrew its paintings from the Detroit venue, which reduced the number of works in the exhibition to forty-one from the original fifty-five and created gaps in the original logic and design of the exhibition. As a result, Rebecca Hart, assistant curator of modern and contemporary art at the DIA, reconfigured the exhibition around several new themes, including Social Realism to Personal Realism; Religious Sources and Traditions; War and Conflict; The Human Condition; and Saga of the Lucky Dragon. An expanded display of Shahn's graphics and career ephemera was arranged in several vitrines. In addition, a small show of works lent by local Detroit collectors, many from the 1930s, was presented concurrently.[31]

With the new configuration, the Detroit curators and promotional staff now decided to make Shahn's connection with Jewish culture more explicit and to target a Jewish audience: the DIA reached out to synagogues and advertised in the Jewish press. Thus, the DIA did not use Shahn's *Spring* as its main promotional image—*Spring* did appear on the cover of the exhibition catalogue and would have tied in with the exhibition's marketing—but rather *Soapbox* (1936), which was doubly removed, by period and style, from the original exhibition's emphasis on Shahn's postwar symbolic work. A gouache from The Jewish Museum's collection, *Soapbox* portrays a labor rally in which one man brandishes a sign in Yiddish that reads "Nature gave everybody an appetite, but our bosses have stolen the bowl from us." *Soapbox* is based on a 1916 photograph of the labor organizer Paul Thompson, a reproduction of which was included in the exhibition. Shahn transformed the central figure into a composite portrait that resembled John L. Lewis in the Jersey Homesteads mural and substituted the Yiddish verse for a quotation, in English, from Lewis's 1937 CIO address. The second promotional image was *Hebrew Books, Holy Day Bookstore* (1953), a genre scene from Detroit's own collection. To underscore the Jewishness of Shahn's *Hebrew Books, Holy Day Bookstore*, the DIA displayed a photo of Levine's bookstore in 1920s Chicago in a vitrine near the painting, though this was not a photograph taken by Ben Shahn or even the actual Levinson's storefront portrayed by Shahn in his easel painting.

Rather than veil his Jewish identity, as Ziva Amishai-Maisels posits, Shahn fused ethnic identity—understood here as *yidishkayt*, the culture, values, and politics of Eastern European Jews—with an inclusive working-class politics that involved cross-union, Popular Front coalition building during the 1930s.[32] However, once these paintings—and *Soapbox,* in particular— became promotional images for *Common Man,* they no longer signified this fusion. Few visitors to the DIA would have been able to read the sign in *Soapbox,* but many would have recognized the writing as "Jewish." For them, *Soapbox* would become a generic sign for "Jewish." While Shahn's commitment to secular Jewish culture and leftist politics would have continued to resonate during the 1940s and 1950s, the period treated by *Com-*

mon Man, Mythic Vision, would today's museum audiences recognize these themes? Or would they only identify Shahn as a Jewish artist through paintings bearing explicit signs of Jewishness, narrowly conceived—ritual objects, holy books, Hebrew script? While a "Jewish" context is by no means irrelevant to Shahn's paintings, it is only one of several contexts for viewing his work.

The Audience for Shahn's Paintings

Since the early 1930s, critics have characterized Shahn's audience as different from the art crowd because their primary interest was in the social and political content of his work rather than its artistic form and style. They commended Shahn for speaking directly to "the people."[33] No less a figure than Diego Rivera declared that Shahn's paintings were "technically within the school of modernistic painting, but they possess the necessary qualities, accessibility, and power to make them important to the proletariat."[34] Shahn's 1947 MoMA retrospective prompted one reviewer to quip that Shahn's audience "is the common folk, who are interested in the next meal and not a whit in aesthetics."[35] At The Jewish Museum's 1976 Shahn retrospective, Hilton Kramer opened his review as follows:

Almost more interesting than the Ben Shahn retrospective is the public that comes to see it. Some were young, to be sure, but most of them were not. They were not only older but looked less prosperous and less sophisticated, less used to being in a museum, than one commonly observes at the Whitney or at the Museum of Modern Art. Such impressions are always subjective, of course. Mine on this occasion, were of a people, mainly New Yorkers and mainly Jewish, close to retirement age or beyond it, who were probably members of a labor union during much of their lives.[36]

What were the demographics of visitors to the DIA exhibition and what did they learn?

A survey directed by Jennifer Czajkowski of the DIA's Education Department and carried out by undergraduate students enrolled in a seminar I taught on Shahn at the University of Michigan showed that most of the approximately 100 visitors surveyed were museum members and identified their political views as liberal. Many said that they were unfamiliar with Shahn's late work (41 percent), and that their main reason for coming to the DIA on that day was just to look at art (46 percent) or as a social activity (39 percent), whereas only 24 percent came specifically to see the Shahn exhibition. The majority listed their race/ethnicity as European (63 percent), with incomes in excess of US$50,000 (63 percent). Many knew that Shahn was a Jew, attributed his concern with social justice to that fact, and thought the work was about "the Jewish experience." Thirty-two percent of visitors said they had no religion, 27 percent identified as Catholic, 20 percent were Protestant, and just 15 percent self-identified as Jews, although some of those stating no religious affiliation may be nonreligious Jews. In conversation, visitors who attended public lectures and gallery talks said that their expectations and perceptions of Shahn's paintings were shaped by the knowledge that he was a Jew. Visitors frequently ascribed Shahn's liberal political beliefs and his anger at social injustice to his Jewishness, as formed in his early childhood. While some critics and art historians cite Shahn's childhood yeshiva education as the source of his political vision, claiming that Shahn's Orthodox religious training fostered his *liberal* political beliefs, the sociologist Arthur Liebman has suggested a direct link between religious education and *conservative* politics.[37] In neither case do they look to the turbulent era in which Shahn was formed. Visitors also inquired about Shahn's feelings toward Israel, even though there is little visual evidence that Shahn strongly identified with the Jewish state. He did once illustrate an advertisement for Israel that appeared in *Time* magazine in 1951, but he never visited the country and never mentioned Israel in his writings, articles, and lectures.[38]

How did Shahn deal with the Holocaust, an important marker of what it means to be Jewish today? In the post–World War II period, Shahn created a series of paintings entitled *Europa*. Drawing on newspaper photos of Spanish refugees, OWI photographs, and other sources, the artist's work mourned the devastation wrought by war in Italy.[39] As Shahn recalled in the late 1950s:

During the war I worked in the Office of War Information. We were supplied with a constant stream of material, photographic and documentation of the decimation within enemy territory. There were the secret confidential horrible facts of the cartloads of dead; Greece, India, Poland. There were the blurred pictures of bombed-out places, so many of which I knew well and cherished. There were the churches destroyed, the villages, the monasteries—Monte Cassino and Ravenna. At that time, I painted only one theme, "Europa," you might call it. Particularly I painted Italy as I lamented it, or feared that it might have become.[40]

Shahn's *Europa* paintings, *Italian Landscape* (1943–44), *Italian Landscape II: Europa* (1944), *The Red Stairway* (1944), and *Liberation* (1945), were prominently featured in *Common Man, Mythic Vision*.

Yet the DIA's audience sought from Shahn a bolder, more explicit statement on the war, and more specifically on the Holocaust. They wanted him to be as graphic as a documentary news photo, perhaps, and wished that he had located his narratives in Poland, rather than Italy. As the historian Peter Novick writes, now that so many American Jews no longer define themselves in terms of religion, what they have in common is "the knowledge that but for their parents' or (more often) grandparents' or great-grandparents' immigration, they would have shared the fate of European Jewry . . . The Holocaust, as virtually the only common denominator of

American Jewish identity in the late twentieth-century, has filled a need for a consensual symbol."[41] Visitors came to Shahn looking for Zionism and the Holocaust, not the labor unions, *yidishkayt*, and "mythic vision" that spoke to their grandparents and great-grandparents.

The Jewish Museum's exhibition *Common Man, Mythic Vision* brought much-needed attention to the later years of Ben Shahn's career as a painter, while questioning the conception of American modernism put forward by the Museum of Modern Art, among others. *Common Man, Mythic Vision* argued for a pluralistic conception of postwar American art. A more expansive vision of modernism, one that includes the distinct contributions of racially and ethnically diverse artists to postwar art, is emerging. This is, however, a mixed blessing for Ben Shahn. When Shahn is presented as a Jewish artist, audiences and critics search for, and sometimes find, specific themes in his work that they can identify as Jewish. But to see Shahn solely as a Jewish artist—rather than as an American or New York or twentieth-century artist or as a figurative or politically engaged artist—is to narrow the frame of reference and lose sight of the many contexts in which his work was produced and received.

Chapter 11

Max Liebermann and the Amsterdam Jewish Quarter

Walter Cahn

Between the years 1905 and 1909, Max Liebermann devoted his energies to a series of paintings and a production of numerous etchings that have the Amsterdam Jewish Quarter as their theme. He was then fifty-eight years old, and at the height of his powers: president of the Berliner Sezession, member of the Prussian Academy of Fine Arts, bearer of the title of Honorary Professor. The city as subject, and the life of contemporaneous Jewry within an urban setting, were new themes to him. Born in 1847 into a wealthy, assimilated family that had established itself in Berlin two generations earlier, he received his first art lessons in the studio of a fashionable though mediocre painter of horses in the Prussian capital. His initial successes were bleak and darkly lit scenes of workshops with earnest and absorbed laborers, which reflect the impact upon him of realist works by the Hungarian artist Mihaly Munkacsy and, somewhat later, of the sober agrarian romanticism of the French painter J.-F. Millet, which he discovered during his formative two years in Paris from 1873 to 1875. He was, however, especially drawn to Holland and active there, after an initial voyage in 1872, for extended periods of time from 1876 onward. He formed there what was to be a lifelong admiration for the Dutch landscape and the particular quality of the light from which it gained much of its poetry, and he came to closely identify himself with the Dutch masters of the seventeenth century, notably Rembrandt and Frans Hals, whose accomplishments he considered to be the summit of art.[1]

The Jews of Amsterdam, initially Sephardic refugees from Spain and Portugal, were settled since the seventeenth century in a warren of streets, alleys, and canals situated along the southeastern rim of the expanding city. Because of Amsterdam's mercantile activities and relative religious tolerance, the area was early on noted for its colorful mixture of peoples and the exotic character of its religious observances. While other Jewish communities like those of Venice and Frankfurt lived almost entirely hidden behind ghetto walls, the Jews of Amsterdam were "visible" to an unprecedented degree. Initially, the curiosity of travelers was solicited primarily by the Portuguese and German synagogues, which were generally admired for their beauty. The picturesque costumes worn by the congregants attracted much attention, but the cultic ceremonial was judged to be strange if not altogether bizarre, unfolding as it appeared to do in an unintelligible cacophony.[2] The English traveler-antiquarian John Evelyn, who visited Amsterdam in 1641, arrived on a Saturday and went straight to the Sephardic synagogue, for the "Ceremonys, Lamps, Laws, & Scholes [of the Jews]," he tells us, "afforded matter for my Contemplation: The Women were secluded from the Men, in Gallerys above, shut with lattices: having their heads mabbl'd with linnen, after a fantastical shape: The Men wearing a large Calico mantle yellow Coloured over their Hatts: all the while Waving their bodys, whilst at their Devotions, & that the Rabby brought out the Law . . . written on Velum & rolled on two staves to which hung divers little Bells."[3]

At this time and especially in the aftermath of the Thirty Years War (1618–48), the composition of the Jewish community in Amsterdam was being altered by new arrivals of Ashkenazim from Germany and points further east. When Liebermann discovered it, the neighborhood had become notorious for its crowded conditions and the appalling poverty of its residents. It was the most densely settled part of the city, with roughly 1,400 dwellings for a population of nearly 8,000 persons, according to a survey made in 1903.[4] The optic of observers also shifted from an interest in antiquities and the ceremonial to the physical setting and the wretched appearance of the inhabitants. Edmondo de Amicis, the much-traveled and hugely prolific author of *Holland* (1874), a book of observations and opinions about that country and its people, describes the Jewish Quarter in a tone indebted to Zola's naturalism that is at once fascinated and horrified. It is "one of the marvels of Amsterdam," he begins, with evident sarcasm:

a labyrinth of narrow streets, foul and dark, with very old houses on either side, which seemed as though they would crumble to pieces if one kicked the walls. From cords strung from window to window, from the window-sills, from the nails driven in the doors, dangled and fluttered tattered shirts, patched petticoats, greasy clothes, dirty sheets and ragged trousers, flapping against the damp walls. In front of the doors, on the broken steps, in the midst of tottering railings, old goods were exposed for sale. Broken furniture, fragments of weapons, objects of devotion, shreds of uniforms, parts of machinery, splinters of toys, iron tools, broken china, fringes, rags, things that have no name in any language; everything that has been ruined or destroyed by rust, worms, fire, disorder, dissipation, disease, poverty, death; all those things that servants sweep away, rag-merchants throw away, beggars trample underfoot, and animals neglect; all that encumbers, smells, disgusts, contaminates—all this is to be found there in heaps and layers destined for a mysterious commerce, for unforeseen combinations, and for incredible transformations. In the midst of this cemetery of things, this Babylon of uncleanliness, swarms of a sickly, wretched, filthy race, beside which the Gypsies of Albaycin in Granada are clean and sweet.[5]

This mixture of fascination and revulsion exercised an attraction also on painters and photographers, whose views of the Jewish Quarter provide a certain context for Liebermann's own efforts. The small panel by the Viennese painter Tina Blau, who visited Amsterdam in the mid-1870s, endows the street with an autumnal glow in a nostalgic evocation of urban life in the Dutch Golden Age.[6] Among local painters, G. J. Staller's street scene of circa 1900 presents, by contrast, a resolutely modern view of the subject, while Willem Witsen's wintry aquatint of 1906 adopts for his treatment the very different, crepuscular manner of Whistler.[7] The production of views on postcards documents the involvement of photography in this process of aesthetization at a more popular level (Figure 11.1).[8]

The Jews of Amsterdam were chiefly active in the diamond trade and various kinds of petty commerce, among which ragpickers and vendors of fruit, vegetables, and fish (generally recorded as peddlers) were most heavily represented. The municipal authorities who compiled these and other data were, to an increasing degree in the later nineteenth century, concerned to improve the appearance and sanitary conditions of the district, and after much delay usual in these circumstances, they finally carried out in the years preceding World War I the drastic cleanup and rebuilding that effectively destroyed its character.[9] Taking note of this situation, Liebermann, in a letter from Holland dated October 1912, advised his dealer Cassirer in Berlin: "So, cover your demand [for my work] as soon as you can. *Judenstrassen* altogether are no longer to be discovered, and new paintings impossible, as the Jewish Quarter as such has ceased to exist."[10] But the perception of misery, squalor, and social anachronism that made this outcome an inevitable or even welcome development in progressive eyes had as a counterpart the discovery, in Amsterdam and elsewhere, of the Ghetto as a place of authentic Jewish life and feeling, or of picturesque customs and decencies made all the more poignant by their seemingly inexorable disappearance.

It was perhaps Liebermann's identification with Rembrandt that first drew him to the Jewish Quarter. For, as is well known, the house into which the painter had moved in 1631 was located on the major thoroughfare of this district, the Jodenbreestraat, and had become in the later nineteenth century something like a place of pilgrimage, while Rembrandt himself enjoyed a position of special favor among educated German Jews. "To be with Rembrandt in Amsterdam!," Liebermann later wrote in a review of a book devoted to the exploration of that theme, "With him in whom the dramatic genius of Shakespeare, the poetic lyricism of Goethe, the childlike soul of Mozart and the melancholy depth of Beethoven are united."[11] He considered Amsterdam to be the most beautiful city in the world. It was in 1876, during his first extended stay in Holland, that he seems first to have visited the Jewish Quarter. But although this journey to the Low Lands had a decisive impact on the development of his art, the excursion to the

Figure 11.1. Jodenhouttuinen, Amsterdam. From a postcard, early twentieth century. Kunstanstalt Herz, Amsterdam.

Jewish Quarter, undertaken in the company of a fellow painter, August Allebé, does not seem to have inspired him in a major way and is reflected in his surviving oeuvre in a fairly unemphatic manner.[12] A sketch-like pencil drawing, made at a site that has been tentatively identified as lying along Jodenhouttuinen, a thoroughfare bordering a canal to the north and parallel to the Jodenbreestaat, shows a group of typically gabled houses bordering a dock on which small and summarily indicated figures busy themselves.[13] Greater interest attaches to the view of the interior of the Portuguese synagogue, a painting that evokes Jewish life in seventeenth-century Amsterdam in a more literal way, and the famous images of the synagogue by Bernard Picart and Romeyn de Hooghe in particular (Figure 11.2).[14] Executed in an almost monochrome palette of earthen colors and dashing brushwork, the painting is also Liebermann's first work to concern itself explicitly with a Jewish subject, if only through the index of topography.

The composition draws the eye obliquely into a space that is at once crowded with incident, yet largely empty, supplying the eye with cut-off parts of the *bimah*, rows of benches, and an ornamental chandelier. The three men clad in black and engaged in prayer, whose presence in the distance seems almost accidental, tend more to convey a sense of the remoteness of the painter/observer from the event depicted than to alert anyone to its significance. One is led to ponder what attitudes or convictions might be embodied in the artist's arresting pictorial conception. A reminiscence of a later visit by Liebermann to the synagogue in the company of his friend and biographer Erich Hancke, which is said to have taken place in 1911,

Figure 11.2. Max Liebermann, *Interior of the Portuguese Synagogue, Amsterdam*, 1876. After F. Stuttmann, *Max Liebermann*. Private collection, Zurich.

betrays a similar mixture of curiosity and detachment, of nostalgia and estrangement. If Hancke's report is to be trusted, the painter had wanted to show him the famous synagogue where Spinoza had been excommunicated. Smoking cigars, the two men stood in the darkness of the courtyard outside, peering at the light within visible through the windows, and Liebermann remarked that in former days he would never have been seen smoking in public on the eve of the Sabbath, nor been without his silk top hat, which, like other respectable German Jews of some social standing, he always wore out of respect for the holy day. In this vaguely melancholic mood, the men approached the entrance but went no further, observing the cantor wearing his *talit*, with his back turned to them.[15]

Liebermann told Hancke that he began at this time to make studies for his painting *The Twelve-Year-Old Jesus in the Temple*, which he exhibited in Munich three years later. It is the work, as is well known, that brought against him the furious hostility of the national and conservative political establishment in Bavaria, incensed by what was perceived to be a scurrilous treatment of a noble Christian subject at the hands of a Jew.[16] The blond, long-haired Christ child demonstrating his precocious wisdom to the rabbis assembled around him is not what anyone but the most rabid anti-Semite would call provocative, though it has recently been shown that the present appearance of the young Jesus is the result of a modification by the painter of an originally much less idealized and stereotypically Jewish-looking portrayal, which is documented by an old photograph. What prompted the irreverent though hardly contentious Liebermann to choose this theme is not wholly clear. He might have wanted to demonstrate his skill in the vaunted genre of history painting, which, in academic circles of his time, still stood at the pinnacle of artistic achievement. This required the ability to depict in persuasive fashion edifying stories and events of the past, animated by heroic protagonists, for which the Bible was regarded as a major source. The ardent nineteenth-century concern for historical verisimilitude complicated the task, since these biblical personages could no longer be represented in conventional classical garb and in Arcadian settings, as had been done by artists since the seventeenth century. But who were the Jews, and how could they be depicted at once accurately and in a manner that would adequately convey to a modern audience—Christian audience, by and large—the religious significance of the event in which they were the actors?

Holman Hunt's picture of Jesus in the Temple, painted between the years 1854 and 1860, puts the subject in a richly detailed setting of an Oriental coloration, which he made on the basis of personal observation in the Holy Land.[17] The impulse for Liebermann's painting likely came from another quarter, the treatment of the theme by Adolph Menzel in a lithograph of 1851.[18] Menzel, a Berlin artist of an older generation who was highly regarded by Liebermann, rejected this archeological approach and sought to portray the scene instead in some indeterminate yet present time. For this purpose, he gave to the rabbis of the Temple the swarthy complexions, hooked noses, and demonstrative gestures thought to typify the Jewry of Eastern Europe, thus rejecting what one of his biographers calls "the merely superficial recording of external appearance through the trappings of Oriental costumes" and attempting instead to reach "a more authentic historical truth through an immersion into the racial particularities (*Rasseneigentümlichkeiten*) of the Jewish people."[19]

This procedure is criticized by Liebermann in a letter written some thirty years after the execution of his painting on the grounds that Jews seemed to him to be too "*charakteristisch*," that is, to possess too marked a physical character, thus tending to lend themselves too much to caricature.[20] Thus, although committed, like Menzel, to a portrayal of biblical Jews in the guise of modern ethnic types, Liebermann sharply toned down the outlandish theatrical deportment attributed to them by the older painter, as well as what one might call their ethnic otherness. This is consistent with the objective and emotionally understated cast of his art, though it can hardly be understood without some reference to the issue of German Jewish identity, continually circumscribed as it was by the challenge of Eastern European Orthodoxy on the one hand and assimilation on the other. But the outrage provoked by the picture, and perhaps as well an unavowed sense that he had reached an impasse, led him, in the ensuing years, to avoid overtly religious themes almost entirely.[21] He was to devote himself now primarily to scenes of laboring men and women, Dutch farms and market scenes, and after the painter's discovery of French Impressionism in the early 1890s, depictions of recreation out of doors and fashionable pastimes.

Liebermann made it a habit to visit the Amsterdam Jewish Quarter during his trips to Holland, which took place on a nearly annual basis until the outbreak of World War I. The theme of the *Judengasse* emerged in his work with the oil sketch, now in Hanover, painted after his move from Munich to Berlin, and marriage, in December 1884 (Figure 11.3).[22] It is a head-on, severely foreshortened view of a narrow street closed off at one end, into which we peer from a larger thoroughfare in the foreground that is revealed by the section of a building façade along the left side of the composition. The dominant tonality of the work is a mixture of murky browns and grays, and like the artist's earlier depiction of the interior of the Portuguese synagogue, it is, save for a few sketchy hints of human presence—a woman with an apron and white headgear in the middle ground, several small and unsubstantial figures in the distance, and a dark, profiled silhouette approaching the doorway on the lower left—largely devoid of incident, an expression of mood and milieu rather than the record of a specifiable action. Matthias Eberle has noted the connection of the painting with views of streets in Venice made by Liebermann six years earlier and has drawn attention to the seventeenth-century antecedents in the genre of streetscape. It is uncertain, however, whether the painter originally intended a Jewish association to be attached to the work. A notation on the back gives it merely the title *Holländische Strasse*, and it probably acquired its present title only when it entered public ownership in 1909. At that time, Lieber-

Figure 11.3. Max Liebermann, *Judengasse in Amsterdam*, 1884. Niedersächsiche Landesmuseum Hannover.

mann's *Judengassen* had become a staple and highly successful item in his production.

When, in August 1905, Liebermann set out on his now habitual journey to Holland that would inaugurate the series of *Judengassen*, he had achieved nearly unrivalled preeminence in the German-speaking art world. On the death of his father in 1894, he became the occupant of the palatial residence on the Pariser Platz, abutting the Brandenburg Gate on its northern side, a badge not only of wealth but of the most solid respectability. In 1900 appeared Hans Rosenhagen's first book-length biography of the artist, to be followed by the monographs of Karl Scheffler (1906), Wilhelm Burr (1910), and Gustav Pauli's volume in the *Klassiker der Kunst* series, an unusual tribute that placed Liebermann in the enviable company of the great masters of the past. The collection of essays edited by Martin Buber under the title *Juedische Kuenstler* (1903) accorded him a place in a constellation of modern painters in whom the promise of a Jewish cultural renewal seemed to be realized.[23] Overt anti-Semitic hostility toward Liebermann receded, though conservative or xenophobic critics now found fault with his championship of French Impressionism. Thus, in the early months of 1905, the painter was on the receiving end of a diatribe by Henry Thode, a professor of art history in Heidelberg and an ardent Germanophile of Wagnerian sensibilities, over the alleged dangers that his "cosmopolitan" outlook posed for the health of native art.[24]

Liebermann's production of *Judengassen* began in 1905 with the painting acquired soon after its execution by the Wallraf-Richartz Museum in Cologne, indeed a fact of some note since it was apparently his first work to enter a major public collection (Figure 11.4).[25] The number of *Judengassen*, all of them executed in the next four years, is not known with certainty, though Eberle's recently published oeuvre catalogue lists eighteen pictures (several of them variant versions), of which eight are now lost or unaccounted for. They range from the fully finished performance to the remarkable and almost free improvisation. The painter was in the habit of sometimes making more than one version of a picture, or working up a salient motif from a composition into an independent work. But Liebermann's concentration on the theme over a period of five years and the number of pictures that he devoted to it represent an exception in his practice. Beyond the paintings, a substantial number of drawings pertain to the theme, though these have never been comprehensively inventoried or coordinated with the related paintings.[26] Finally, Liebermann in these years developed proficiency as a printmaker, and studies he made for his *Judengassen* achieved a wide diffusion through the medium of etchings.[27]

The series of *Judengassen* form three distinct groups whose character and sequence in time helps us to plot the stages of the artist's development of his theme and working methods. Characteristic of the first group, the painting in Cologne and its offshoots shows a street corner seen at fairly close range, with a bustle of men and women, some of them engaged in conversation, others huddling over pushcarts, the largest of which, near the middle, is piled high with green vegetables. The site, now profoundly transformed, has been identified with the help of an old photograph as the corner of Uilenburgersteeg and Jodenbreestraat, where a popular café named *De Twee Zwaantjes* (The Two Swans) and a bakery, visible at the left, once stood.[28] The painter must have stationed himself more or less at the

Figure 11.4. Max Liebermann, *Judengasse in Amsterdam*, 1905. Rheinisches
Bildarchiv, Köln.

same spot where the photograph was taken, probably a first-floor window
of a house on the opposite side of the larger Jodenbreestraat. A comparison of the two views shows that he flattened the angle formed by the meeting of the two streets and closed off the perspectival recession into the
distance on the right side, bringing the eye closer to the scene. The architectural setting, composed of dark painted wall surfaces punctuated by
doors and rows of windows framed in white, retains the prominence that
Liebermann had given it in the Hanover painting of 1884, but life now
makes its presence felt in these stark surroundings and a certain gritty
energy inhabits even the loose brushwork and the thick dabs of paint that
cake the surface.

   During the next four years, Liebermann regularly spent part of the summer in Amsterdam's Jewish Quarter, making numerous drawings from
which the paintings were derived (Figure 11.5). Already in connection with
his painting *The Twelve-Year-Old Jesus in the Temple*, he had remarked on the
difficulty of persuading religious Jews to pose as models, and this seems to
have been one of the reasons that led him to rent space well above ground
in a private house, where he could work without attracting attention.[29] He

Figure 11.5. Max Liebermann, *Judengasse in Amsterdam*, 1907. After E. Hancke, *Max Liebermann*. Chalk drawing. Private collection, Bad Neuenahr.

thus also obtained plunging views onto the street below, lined on both sides with pushcarts stationed under awnings and filled, as always on Friday afternoon before the Sabbath and on Sundays, with crowds of shoppers. The drawings that record this view, among his finest, now convey more fully the impression of a street rather than a scattering of people among fragments of buildings. In this, the second phase of his works on the Amsterdam Jewish Quarter, the artist focused his attention more insistently on the meandering flow of anonymous ghetto dwellers around the peddlers' carts, which may be registered with an eye for a characteristic detail, or as a dense, more undifferentiated mass.

Liebermann, as already noted, had become since the mid-1890s an active proponent of French Impressionism as well as a collector of Impressionist pictures, and it is likely that this new conception of the *Judengasse* in his work owes much to city views by such painters as Monet and Pissarro. This is made clear by a juxtaposition of Pissarro's *Boulevard Montmartre on a Winter Morning* of 1897 (Metropolitan Museum of Art)—one of a number of compositions of this kind by the artist—with its plunging view onto one of Baron Haussmann's wide new thoroughfares in Paris, and Liebermann's painting, formerly preserved at Magdeburg and dated 1907, with its subject observed from a similar angle (Figures 11.6 and 11.7).[30] But the comparison also brings out significant differences. While Pissarro's strollers move about unconstrained in airy and spacious surroundings, Liebermann's crowds have little room for maneuver, confined as they are within darkly colored walls that stretch into the distance and offer no prospect of release.

A third and final phase of Liebermann's involvement with the Amsterdam Jewish Quarter is represented by a series of drawings and paintings executed in the years 1908 and 1909. This version of the subject is now better known by the sketchy rendering of the left side of the composition in the Städel-Museum at Frankfurt (Figure 11.8) than through the more complete and finished version, long thought to be lost, that has recently resurfaced. It is a very large work by Liebermann's standards, measuring about four to six feet, and dated 1909 (Figure 11.9).[31] To the eye captivated by the dashing brushstrokes and flickering colors of the artist's earlier labors concerned with this theme, it is a disconcerting performance, prosaic and almost plodding, which the painter realized in his Berlin studio on the basis of drawings made in situ. The setting is again the junction of two streets, though the observer's point of view is much closer to ground level, and the angle of vision is such that any sight of the sky is entirely eliminated, recession into the distance being curtailed all around by blank walls punctuated by opaque windows. Near the center, in the middle ground, a young girl observes a pushcart filled with vegetables over which three older women and a man hover. Behind them, a woman at the top of a flight of stairs disappears into an open doorway. In the foreground at the right is a fish cart attended by a woman engaged with several customers.

Figure 11.6. Camille Pissarro (1830–1903), *The Boulevard Montmartre on a Winter Morning*, 1897. Oil on canvas. 60. 174, Metropolitan Museum of Art, gift of Katrin S. Vietor, in loving memory of Ernest G. Vietor, 1960.

Behind this group, there is another vegetable cart, barely visible in the surrounding crowd of shoppers. On the left side of the composition, the space in the rear where the two streets meet is densely packed with people on their errands.

Liebermann's success with his smaller, rapidly executed, and heavily impastoed canvasses, betokening the increasing prestige of the aesthetics of the sketch, makes the motive that led him to carry out this painstaking exercise difficult to comprehend. Having apparently decided to bring the series of *Judengassen* to an end, he may have deemed it appropriate to do so with a final, grandiose gesture. The more precise delineation of all the elements of the composition to which the painter committed himself, however, is of more than stylistic or procedural interest, since it affected what could be called the evidence of its Jewish content. Whereas he and the observer of his earlier versions of the subject could rely on the suggestive intimations of his bold brushwork, the last, monumental treatment committed the painter to greater specificity (Figure 11.9). Perhaps because the setting was no longer materially present before him but had to be recon-

Figure 11.7. Max Liebermann, *Judengasse in Amsterdam*, 1907. After G. Pauli, *Max Liebermann*. Formerly Magdeburg, Kaiser-Friedrich-Museum.

structed from drawings, interest is to a greater degree focused on figurative action, while details which gave hints of the character of the setting in the earlier version—the café at the corner, the fluttering sheets hanging out of windows, hints of rubbish piled here and there—are eliminated altogether. The men and women depicted in the painting seem to be people of modest means, but they are by no means miserably poor. The men's heads are uni-

Figure 11.8. Max Liebermann, *Judengasse in Amsterdam*, 1909. Courtesy Städtische Galerie im Städelschen Kunstinstitut, Frankfurt am Main. Photo: © Ursula Edelmann.

formly covered by hats, caps, or skullcaps. A few have short beards but do not exhibit in their clothes or deportment a pronounced or particularized "Jewish" ethnicity. The title of the painting, once more, contributes a good deal to our perception of the meaning.

What of the artist's intentions and the opinions of those, more or less close to him, who sought to explicate them to a broad public? The critics saw themselves confronted with the task of coming to grips not only with a subject unavoidably invested with a religious and social dimension but also

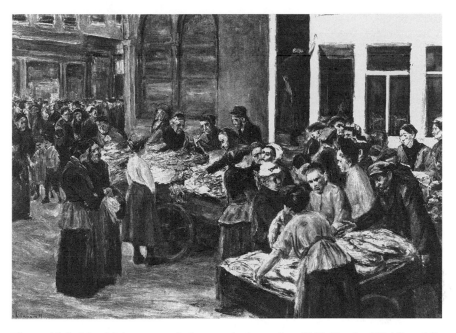

Figure 11.9. Max Liebermann, *Judengasse in Amsterdam,* 1909. Kaufhof Holding AG, Köln.

of assessing what the painter's Jewish identity may have contributed to the work. The first edition of Hans Rosenhagen's biography preceded the execution of the *Judengassen,* and though it mentions the scandal aroused by *The Twelve-Year-Old Jesus in the Temple,* it omits any notice of the fact that the painter was a Jew.[32] No doubt this was sufficiently well known, but Rosenhagen and like-minded critics probably also believed it to be either irrelevant or damaging to the painter's cause in the public eye. Karl Scheffler's monograph, whose third edition appeared after the completion of the *Judengassen* in 1912 cites the series once in passing and features two illustrations, the large painting of 1909 and one of the artist's spirited drawings of the subject, both disguised with more innocuous captions, the first called *Markt in Amsterdam,* the second *Holländische Strasse.* But unlike Rosenhagen, Scheffler's book faces the painter's Jewishness head on. Although Germany and Berlin in particular counted for much more, he argues, Liebermann's religion could not be ignored, as it entailed both advantages and disabilities for him. His chief merit was to have opened German art to the fructifying influence of French Impressionism, which Scheffler considered vastly superior to contemporaneous German art, because, as a Jew, he had an outlook more worldly and cosmopolitan than that dominant in the Gentile, parochially Germanophile culture. On the other hand, the qualities ascribed by Scheffler to Jewish talent—clarity, efficiency, adaptability—led to respectable, middling results, without great heights or depth, for which a demonically genial sensibility was required. Liebermann's accomplishments were therefore fated to remain, like those of Moses Mendelssohn, Heine, Börne, Mendelssohn-Bartholdy, and Meyerbeer, thoroughly admirable, though unable to rise beyond a certain level.[33] Gustav Pauli's much shorter study reproduces four of the *Judengassen* and gives them their "correct" titles. The concluding peroration emphatically assures the reader that Liebermann is a thoroughly German artist and, if his Judaism must intrude at all on one's appreciation of his work, it does so in a manner that ingeniously renders his German qualities even more authentic: "That he is a Jew and feels himself to be proud to be the son of an old and pure race does not much count for us, since his pictures talk to us in our mother tongue and have drawn their best inspiration from the ancestral German soil of the Netherlands."[34]

Judaism is the elusive but indispensable ingredient of Liebermann's art also for Erich Hancke, whose massive and apparently "authorized" biography of 1914 supplies the most extended and reliable information concerning the creation of the *Judengassen*. In the introduction, Hancke positions the artist as the reformer of German painting, who managed through his sheer talent to perpetuate its finer qualities, without yielding to its ingrained constraints and narrowness. There have been many guesses as to the source of this talent, Hancke reports, "his racial origin having been especially favored as an explanation."[35] But it is sufficient, he goes on to say, that the talent exists, that Germany again possesses a painting worthy of the name. With the greater perspective of distance in time, Hancke regarded the *Judengassen* of the years 1905 to 1908 as Liebermann's supreme achievement, the subject that engaged the painter's sensibility more deeply than any other. One could not say what was the basis of this special empathy, since it lay beneath the surface of consciousness. But it could not be found, Hancke believed, in the realm of purely painterly procedures and was rather bound up with reflection on the past, "with thoughts about the history of this place and the race that inhabited it, with the tragedy of an ancient people."[36]

Liebermann's *Judengassen* have been called *Gruppenbilder*, and it is indeed the case that while the streetscape of gabled and darkly painted houses situates the action in space and time, the painter's primary focus of interest was the crowd, though this is perhaps more evident in his graphic renderings than in the paintings.[37] We have already noted that he chose to make his views on days of greatest activity and elected more or less elevated points of view from which he could more easily survey the hustle and bustle below as a comprehensive whole. It is not the case, however, that his recorded reaction to this scene is particularly marked by insight or sympathy. Hancke, who in 1912 accompanied the artist on a visit to the site of his earlier triumphs, recalled that he and Liebermann entered a dirty store

and climbed a rickety and nearly upright flight of stairs onto a narrow landing and into a room with a window facing the street, where Liebermann
could work unnoticed: "One saw lying below a swarm of carts full of apples
and vegetables, fish, coconuts and all imaginable and unimaginable wares,
a true cornucopia of delicacies emerging from the filth, surrounded by a
buzzing crowd of men," he continues, adding further observations in the
same unsparing vein.[38] Hancke's terse and unromantic Berlin sensibility
may be at work here, but surely also in play is a process whereby description
helps to establish some distance between the observer and his subject. Liebermann's innate Jewishness, as intuited by his biographers, harbored a
large measure of ambivalence and complexity.

Liebermann's investment in his theme, pictorial and verbal, invites one
to consider its relation to the nineteenth-century discovery of the crowd
and the various interpretations that it fostered. Gustave Le Bon's grimly
energetic *Psychologie des foules* (1895) is still a necessary point of reference
for modern discussions of this topic, though the propensity to violence and
pathological impulses that he ascribes to crowds—colored as these opinions were by reactionary political resentments—is hardly applicable to
scenes of street life painted by Liebermann or his Impressionist forerun-
ners. If, nevertheless, something useful for my purposes can still be salvaged from the author's doctrine, it is Le Bon's perception that the
behavior of crowds, unlike that of individuals, reveals the workings of
unconscious habits and thus discloses to us deep-seated patterns of conduct that are common to a group. Groups, according to Le Bon, are at
once irrational and profoundly conservative.[39] There is no reason to believe
that Liebermann or Hancke were familiar with these ideas on a firsthand
basis. But the descriptive vocabulary that the latter applies to the denizens
of the Jewish Quarter uncannily echoes Le Bon's characterization of the
crowd's instability or volatility. We hear of the *Judengasse*'s busy shoppers as
Menschenknäule and *surrenden Menschenschwarm*, constructions that fasten
on them the image of a coiling or swarming throng, which is described in
terms of *wimmeln* (teeming, swarming) and *schwirr[en]* (whirring), and as
people who *sich rottendenden*—who congregate like a mob. Even the specter
of the crowd's criminal instincts makes an appearance in Hancke's report,
which states that having heard that the painter commanded high prices for
his *Judengassen*, a group of men assembled in his room in order to pressure
him for higher payments than he previously made to them in order to
enlist their cooperation. As Liebermann himself wrote in frustration to
Hermann Struck: "I have again attempted to work in the Jewish Quarter,
and I have already had to put up with some resistance to my studies, but
our dear co-religionists are setting a record in this business. They are not
even to be satisfied with money."[40]

Liebermann's *Judengassen* were undoubtedly intended to convey a sense
of authenticity, though they are not an ethnographic record. Indeed, Han-

cke praises the painter for having been able to rise above the difficult conditions and disagreeable challenge that the reality of life in the Jewish Quarter presented to him and produce his "masterpieces of space, light and mood." The erasure of the subject's asperities, which has led one writer to observe that the beholder of Liebermann's pictures "hardly learns from them anything about the inhabitants of the Jewish Quarter or of their mode of living," was consistent with the painter's progressive assumptions about art and those of his growing circle of admirers, for whom the achievement of the formal and poetical effects noted by Hancke took precedence over descriptive precision.[41] No doubt commitment to these values also helped to spare viewers any semblance of ambivalence that this mode of living might have aroused in them.

The attitudes of emancipated Jews and of Gentiles in Liebermann's time toward the life of the ghetto were contradictory. For some, it was the repository of a once vital tradition threatened with extinction by modern forgetfulness and apostasy. The eponymous hero of George Eliot's novel *Daniel Deronda* (1876) rediscovers his real identity as a result of a process that culminates in the revelatory experience of a visit to the Frankfurt Ghetto. He had been there long before, but "what his eyes chiefly dwelt now were the human types there; and his thought, busily connecting them with the past phases of their race, stirred that fibre of historic sympathy which had helped to determine in him certain traits worth mentioning for those who are interested in his future." His feelings were stirred:

the forms of the Juden-gasse [*sic*], rousing the sense of union with what is remote, set him musing on two elements of our historic life which that sense raises into the same region of poetry—the faint beginnings of faiths and institutions, and their obscure lingering decay; the dust and weathered remnants with which they are apt to be covered, only enhancing for the awakened perception the impressiveness either of a sublimely penetrating life, as in the twin green leaves that will become the sheltering tree, or of a pathetic inheritance in which all the grandeur and the glory have become a sorrowing memory.[42]

Liberal opinion, by contrast, found in the ghetto only the fossilized survival of Judaism in the Dark Ages. In Heine's *Rabbi of Bacherach*, the Frankfurt Ghetto is described in the following terms: "The part of the Jewish Quarter which remained standing after the great fire, and which is called the Alte Gasse, those high, blackened houses where a damp and whimpering population scurries about, is a frightful monument of the Middle Ages."[43] Goethe, whose writings Liebermann knew well and liked to quote, similarly found the place distressing: "The narrowness, the filth, the swarming crowd, the accents of an unhappy speech, all together made an unhappy impression, when one merely passed by the gate and looked in." But the writer immediately adds that this people remained, in spite of everything, the Chosen of God, whose loyalty to their ancient customs deserved respect.[44] Zionist authors, though sometimes inclined to celebrate the beauty of the communal life in former times, not surprisingly regarded the contemporary ghetto as a symptom of the evils that had befallen Jewry living in the diaspora.

Where Liebermann might have stood on this issue can only be conjectured. While he was fascinated by the Amsterdam Jewish Quarter, he is not known to have taken an interest in Berlin's so-called Scheunenviertel district much closer to home, where poor Jews of the city and recent arrivals from Eastern Europe resided in equally crowded conditions, and which in the years 1904–5 was itself the object of a "sanitizing" campaign that eventually led to its destruction.[45] Perhaps he might have been attracted by Martin Buber's ideas on this subject, which were published in the same first decade of the century. Buber, in several passages, praises the ghetto as a preserver of Jewish values and a bulwark against emancipation, which he saw as a forerunner of assimilation. But elsewhere he deprecates the narrowness of ghetto culture, its enslavement of Jewry into "an unproductive money economy and the hollow-eyed homelessness which destroys all will to unity." A distinctive aspect of his views, however, is his emphasis on the aesthetic impoverishment suffered by the ghetto dweller. Beyond the damage inflicted by the teaching of a misunderstood and constricted religious tradition, "blossoming flowers and growing plants beyond the ghetto were unknown to our forebears and detested like the wonders of the human body."[46]

Nietzschean after Buber's fashion, Dickensian after that of Israel Zangwill's *Children of the Ghetto* (1892), or traditionalist in its various shadings, the fin de siècle discourse on the *shtetl* articulated some of the larger tensions in Jewish self-understanding exposed to the relentless pressures of modernization. Liebermann's own sense of identity adds a complicating dimension to the picture. He felt himself to be a Jew and never sought to deny that fact. But he was equally certain that this had no bearing on his art, which, following his idealizing convictions, he described in terms of formal processes and values that were universal in their application.[47] In the light of his own experience and that of German Jewry in the twentieth century, it is not surprising that his admirable stance has failed to be wholly persuasive.

Chapter 12

Rome and Jerusalem: The Figure of Jesus in the Creation of Mark Antokol'skii

Olga Litvak

Throughout his prolific career, the Russian sculptor Mark Matveevich Antokol'skii (1841–1902) subjected his Jewishness to polemical negotiation in the name of Russian art. The persona of Russia's first modern Jewish artist emerged against the background of nineteenth-century populist discourse that privileged homegrown genius at the expense of Western European cosmopolitanism. A milestone in Antokol'skii's career and singularly important for understanding the contemporary cultural politics that informed the poetics of his work, *Jesus before the Judgment of the People (Ecce homo)* bears the visual traces of the construction of Jewishness as a Russian cultural style.

The title of Antokol'skii's work calls attention to its connection with an established Christian iconographic tradition that the sculpture visually subverts. The phrase *Ecce homo*—"Here is the man!"—invokes a scene from the Passion according to the gospel of John, in which Pilate displays the wounded body of Jesus to the people of Jerusalem before dispatching him to be crucified:

Pilate then had Jesus taken away and scourged; and after this, the soldiers twisted some thorns into a crown and put it on his head and dressed him in a purple robe. They kept coming up to him and saying, "Hail, king of the Jews!" and slapping him in the face. Pilate came outside again and said to them, "Look, I am going to bring him out to you to let you see that I find no case against him." Jesus then came out wearing the crown of thorns and the purple robe. Pilate said, "Here is the man [*Ecce homo*]." When they saw him, the chief priests and the guards shouted, "Crucify him! Crucify him!" Pilate said, "Take him yourselves and crucify him; I find no case against him." The Jews replied, "We have a Law, and according to that Law he ought to be put to death because he has claimed to be Son of God." When Pilate heard them say this, his fears increased. (Jn 19:1–8)

The passage, which appears in none of the synoptic gospels, highlights the primary thematic concern of John's narrative, to present the significance of Jesus' descent from heaven as accessible exclusively to the Johannine community.[1] The movement of the drama depends on the tension, captured in this scene, between the collective unregenerate blindness of "the Jews," the paradigmatic community of unbelievers, and the perfected vision of "whoever comes from God" (Jn 8:47). Jesus, the physical marks of his abased and tortured humanity objectified by Pilate's act of public revelation, remains silent and "imperturbable" to the struggle taking place below the balcony and ultimately in the consciousness of John's implied reader. The confrontation between Pilate and the Jews, staged for the benefit of the "children of God" concentrates the irony implicit in John's attitude to the humanity of Jesus; "the Jews," the agents of Christ's suffering, effectively become the bearers of the truth of his divine nature. The mockery of Jesus, the signs of the scourge, the purple robe, the crown of thorns actually reveal that he is the Christ. Unknowingly, his tormentors proclaim his true identity: "He really is the king of the Jews as the Romans sarcastically call him; he really is the Son of God as the Jews accuse him of claiming and [as] Pilate dimly senses."[2] In fact, Pilate's "dimmed," equivocal perception of the truth before his eyes serves as a foil for the position of John's audience, uneasily poised between the apparent evidence of Jesus' earthly humiliation and death and faith in the invisible, the eternal, the real life of the Christ. "You believe because you have seen me," says Jesus to the apostle Thomas who witnesses the resurrection and touches the wounds of crucifixion for himself, but "blessed are those who have not seen and yet believe" (Jn 20:29).

John locates the narrative tension in the Passion story at the point of crisis occasioned by the "response" to Jesus' presence in the world.[3] John's Jesus manifests all the physical signs of suffering humanity but himself remains impassive and virtually without affect; the drama lies precisely in the events of the Passion unfolding according to a divinely ordained script that Jesus himself carefully follows (Jn 19:23–30). The *Ecce homo* scene—the moment of divine *anagnorisis*—concentrates the theatrical effect of the Johannine Passion, central to the poetics of Christian devotion exemplified in the complementary relationship between liturgy and iconography. In fact, *Ecce homo* entered into the canon of late medieval "devotional pictures" (Ger. *Andachtsbilder*) during the same era that the Passion according to John emerged as the key text in the expanded Good Friday service, meant to commemorate Christ's suffering and death.[4] The enduring connection of this scene with the institutionalization of affective piety shaped the canonic representation of *Ecce homo* in Christian art.

Between the beginning of the fifteenth century and the end of the seventeenth, Western European artists produced scores of paintings of *Ecce homo*, all remarkably consistent in their allegiance to the devotional tradition of the Late Middle Ages. Subject to strict canons of representation, *Ecce homo* provided the context for the image of Christ as Man of Sorrows displaying his wounds explicitly as objects of meditation; depicted mostly as a half-length figure, the latter actually appeared as a close-up of the former.[5] The relationship between the iconic Man of Sorrows, "condensing" the suffering of Jesus into an allegory of the Passion, and the source of the image in the *Ecce homo* episode rendered all visual references to the gospel text fraught with devotional significance.[6] Graphic and scenically elaborate exhibitions of Jesus' humanity—the focus of *Ecce homo*—implicitly made "visual accuracy its standard of truth."[7] Such claims contributed to the development of affective Christian imagery in the masterworks of Renaissance and Baroque art. At the same time, the spiritual importance of Christian vision found expression in a constellation of theologically pregnant motifs that endowed the faithful description of the *Ecce homo* scene with the weight of an icon. In this case, God really *was* in the details. But as *Ecce homo* moved from panel and altarpiece to canvas, artists began to explore the potentialities of representing it not merely as an allegory of the Passion tout court but as a historic confrontation between Jesus, the Roman governor, and the people of Jerusalem. The iconic image of Jesus as Man of Sorrows emerged most clearly in the references to the mystery of Jesus' kingship, the signs of his utter humiliation on earth that alluded to his eternal sovereignty in heaven: the crown of thorns; the purple robe; the hands, bound at the wrists, often holding a reed; and the marks of the scourge. All of these details accessorized the suffering persona of Jesus as the Christ; they alone constituted and confirmed the theological truth of *Ecce homo* even in paintings that strove to situate the person of Jesus within his own contemporary moment and milieu.

The depiction of the crowd, often taking up so much of the foreground as to overshadow Jesus entirely, mirrored the difficult position of the viewer, caught between being made aware of the presentness of the truths of Christian belief and being overwhelmed by the spectacular exotic pastness of first-century Jerusalem. Echoing the gospel text itself, the problem of perception often became the implicit subject of the visual representation of *Ecce homo*. Similarly driven by the drama of looking, Antokol'skii's *Ecce homo* actively subverted the spiritual claims of Christian iconography, transforming the pious intimacy of devotion into an act of secular connoisseurship. In fact, Ankol'skii's Jesus challenged the Christian claim that the realism of iconography inhered in repetition, that is to say, in the recapitulation of the originary moment of divine revelation of Jesus' "true image" (Lat. *vera icon*), faithfully transmitted to the viewer.[8] On the contrary, Antokol'skii's brand of realism called attention to the artist's ability to produce elaborately illusionistic effects of truthfulness. Highlighting his originality and the viewer's willingness to be constantly surprised and deceived, Antokol'skii transformed the open gaze of the worshipper into the secular stare of an audience, defined precisely by its remove from the artist.

Antokol'skii's *Ecce homo* (Figure 12.1) deliberately showcases its polemical association with the Christian devotional ideal. Imposing, austere, and isolated from his scenic background, Antokol'skii's Jesus invokes the iconic Man of Sorrows. However, absent the allusions to the Passion—the accessories of suffering linking image to text—the sculpture does not structure its relationship to the viewer in any normative way and precludes immediate emotional identification. The self-conscious divorce of *Ecce homo* from its conventional symbolic markers presented the possibility that a life-size statue of Jesus could be detached from its Christian context and displayed somewhere other than in a church or chapel.

The secular repertoire of contemporary European sculpture was limited to political subjects, genre scenes, and Graeco-Roman models, all inspired by the neoclassical revival, which had its roots in the Enlightenment.[9] Devotional statuary remained confined to public and private sites of worship, including, increasingly, graveside memorials.[10] Antokol'skii's *Ecce homo* did not fit any of these established categories. Whereas no previous version of *Ecce homo* actually required a title, so conservative and accessible were the established canons of representation, Antokol'skii's version, stripped as it was of all secure iconographic indices, rendered its subject indeterminate—compromising *what* it means, as well as complicating the question of *how* it means.[11]

It is important to stress that Antokol'skii did not simply erase the crown of thorns, the bound wrists holding a reed, the purple robe, and the wounds of the scourge; rather, he referenced the signs of the Passion through deliberate revision, creating a kind of countericonography. In fact, he drew the eye precisely to the points that made the work of subversion most evident; to say that he depicted a human or a Jewish or even a historical Jesus does not capture in full the aesthetic and ideological provocation of his *Ecce homo*.[12] For instance, scholars looking for the "origins" of "Jewish national art" in Antokol'skii's "Jewish Jesus" focus on the skullcap.[13] But there was nothing inherently iconoclastic or "Jewish" in marking Jesus' Jewishness in this way.[14] I. E. Repin (1844–1930), Antokol'skii's friend, former roommate, and fellow member of the St. Petersburg Academy of Arts, had depicted a skullcapped Jesus as healer and miracle worker more than a decade earlier and won first place and a gold medal for this work upon his graduation.[15] Repin's *Raising of Jairus' Daughter* (1871, Russian Museum, St. Petersburg) illustrates a scene from the gospel of Mark (5:35–43), the subject of an assignment in Repin's historical painting class. Executed in Russian realist style, this work treated what had been a religious topic as a historical one and gave it a contemporary relevance by linking the characterization of Jesus as a Jewish physician to nineteenth-century Russian social life.

The treatment of the skullcap marks a critical difference between Antokol'skii's Jewish Jesus and that of Repin. Repin's depiction of Jesus' Jewish milieu is scrupulously faithful to its gospel source: Jairus, according to Mark, is the president of a synagogue and Jesus is a Jewish preacher and

39
ХРИСТОС ПЕРЕД СУДОМ НАРОДА. 1876
Статуя. Мрамор. ГТГ

Figure 12.1. Mark Antokol'skii, *Jesus before the Judgment of the People (Ecce homo)*.
Bronze, 1878. Property of the Collection of the State Tretiakov Gallery, Moscow.
Photo: E. V. Kuznetsova, *M. M. Antokol'skii, zhizn' i tvorchestvo* (Moscow: Iskusstvo,
1989), pl. 39.

miracle worker ministering to the communities of Galilee. The skullcap of Antokol'skii's Jesus, which lacks explicit literary precedent in the gospel of John, marks the absence of the crown of thorns, an ironic double for Christ's halo and anticipation of the Passion. In this case, the Passion attests to the reality of the ministry, not the other way around. Antokol'skii's sculpture, by contrast to Repin's painting, which relies on the historical truth of Christian scripture, dispenses with scriptural authority as such, and, by extension, with the Christian ideal of truth in representation. The presence of the Jewish skullcap does not *mean*, however, that Antokol'skii's Jesus is a Jew; rather, the skullcap throws the meaningfulness of the difference between Christian and Jew—scripturally constituted and visually transparent—into question.

The Jewish countericonography of Antokol'skii's *Ecce homo* asserts itself even more insistently in his depiction of Jesus' garments. As in the case of the skullcap, scholars have noted Jesus' "Jewish" dress: the "long shirt tied around the waist and covered with a broad striped cloak, called an *abbas*" worn, allegedly, by "Biblical prophets and apostles."[16] Another reading goes so far as to suggest that the overgarment's "delicately chiseled broad stripes suggest those of a prayer shawl."[17] Actually, Antokol'skii left the texture of the overgarment grainy and coarse in contrast to the neck and the planes of the face, which he assiduously polished.[18] The contrast is particularly evident in the earlier marble version of the sculpture (1876, Tretiakov Gallery, Moscow) and in its bronze copy (1878, Russian Museum, St. Petersburg), poured from the original plaster cast (1874, Museum of the Academy of Arts, St. Petersburg). Jesus wears this roughly textured robe almost like a shield. It forms a carapace around his body, the outline of which remains completely obscure. The clasp at the neck resembles a hinge, another suggestion of armor-like enclosure. Virtually every line of drapery goes straight down to heighten the effect of rigid verticality; there is not a billow or a curve in sight, defying an effect that characteristically both reveals and conceals the contours of the human shape it covers. Here, the drapery—which does not drape—displaces the body by its sheer and massive, almost geometric, presence.

This effect works polemically against the canonic focus in the *Ecce homo* scene on Jesus' nude or semi-nude body, his robe slipping off one or both shoulders. Nudity, a key feature of the image of the Man of Sorrows, heightens the spectacle of vulnerability embodied in the suffering Jesus and, more importantly, alludes to the corpse of the dead Christ. The nude torso likewise offers itself as a white canvas for the graphic display of the bloody wounds of flagellation, not only absent but counterindicated in Antokol'skii's *Ecce homo* by the protective bulk of Jesus' coat. The stony mantle not only obscures the body—conventionally the site of his physical suffering— but makes him appear resistant to it in a way that forecloses the experience of the Passion. In fact, the visual rhetoric of concealment counters the promise of revelation, implicit in the exposure of Jesus' naked torment. Even the eyes do not provide a point of entry into the mystery of *Ecce homo*. Heavy-lidded and hooded, they preclude identification.

Antokol'skii breaks the predominantly vertical line of the sculpture at its widest point, just above the waist. Two narrow bands throw Jesus' broad chest into bold relief and bind his arms to the sides. The split emphasizes the torso, again linking Antokol'skii's *Ecce homo* to the close-up image of Christ as Man of Sorrows, which is similarly focused on the upper body. At the same time, the bands reference polemically the convention of depicting Jesus with his wrists tied together and usually held in front of the body. Linking all these various depictions of the bound wrists is the devotional interest in the mystery of the Passion, inscribed into the iconography of *Ecce homo*. As in the case of the skullcap, Antokol'skii foregrounds the idea of confinement but changes its implications entirely. In his *Ecce homo*, Jesus' upper arms are fully encased by the sleeves of the robe and form an extension of his clothing. Cut off at the elbows by the bands, the bare forearms seem to be detached from the mass of the body altogether. In this way, unlike the binding of the hands at the wrists, which indicates submission, the binding of Antokol'skii's Jesus serves to free the limbs from their captivity in the clothes. Entirely insufficient to their ostensible function, the bands actually underscore Jesus' bulk. Integral to the clothing Jesus wears and positioned precisely in the same place where a belt would be—from the side, they actually look like a belt—the bands do not so much constrain as contain the body.[19]

In light of the liturgical significance of the belt in Jewish tradition and its role in separating the upper body from its lower half, the bands can be read as suppressing the spectacle of the Incarnation. The Talmud assigns particular semiotic value to the belt.[20] This derives from the dual conception of prayer, particularly the all-important Eighteen Benedictions, otherwise known as the 'Amidah. It is at once a form of service akin to the sacrificial cult and a dialogue with God. In the first instance, the requirement to wear a belt alludes to one of the four garments worn by the priests in the Temple: a fringed tunic, breeches, a headdress, and a sash.[21] In the second instance, the respect due the divine majesty of the King of Kings calls for a rigid separation between the upper and the lower body, specifically between the "genitals" (Heb. *'ervah*) and the "mouth and heart."[22] In this context, rabbinic sources rely on the martial metaphor of "girding the loins" with armor and sword (Heb. *hogar et motnav be'oz*) in order to link the readiness for prayer to the preparation for war.[23]

The idea of prayer as ritualized behavior similar to Temple sacrifice and the conception of prayer as a dialogic, even combative exchange potentially conflict with one another. Yet both express the premise that the approach to God demands the recognition of His ultimate transcendence as signified by the required separation of the holy from the profane. The relationship between the human and the Divine is one of proximity at best because the distinction between God's incorporeal essence and man's physical presence is absolute. The belt inscribes the notion of transcendence onto the body of the worshipper and heightens a sense of awareness of God's essential separateness. Among the customary observances of nineteenth-century Eastern European Jews, wearing a special double-woven silk *gartl* (the Yiddish word for "belt")—in addition to the belt holding up one's trousers—during prayer had become associated with Hasidism. As a ritual garment, the *gartl* was specifically designated to shield the devotee from the involuntary invasion of "alien [i.e., sexual] thoughts," that is, from the insistent intrusion of his own body.[24]

The narrow double bands around the waist of Antokol'skii's Jesus can be read here as playing a similar semiotic role. The bands are critical to the overall effect of transcendence—distance—reified in the excess of clothing, a direct contrast with the immanent nakedness of Jesus' exposed body, which is so central to the canonic depiction of *Ecce homo*. Jesus' robe, here encasing his entire physical form, recalls the Jewish practice of wrapping the body during prayer as a way of heightening the sense of the unbridgeable divide between the human and the divine. At the same time, the sense of verticality, manifest in the rigid downward creases of the robe, brings to mind the presence of a curtain (Heb. *parokhet*), a critical feature of Temple and synagogue décor, which cordons off the Holy of Holies or the Ark from the congregation of worshippers.[25] The radical disappearance of Jesus' body into his Jewish garb—the skullcap, the tunic, and the sash—references the liturgical displacement of the priest's person by the "elaborate" recollection of his garb in the Yom Kippur service.[26] In the absence of the High Priest himself, the vestments retain the power to atone for the sins of Israel.[27] In this case, the clothes quite literally constitute the man. Like Antokol'skii's Jesus, the High Priest of Jewish ritual memory is an elaborately bedecked cipher, ultimately hidden in plain view.

Antokol'skii drew on this rich stock of Jewish associations with the instrumentality of priestly vestments not because he was interested in making Jesus look like a Jewish High Priest. He wanted access to a set of complicating images that would negate the notion of iconography inherent in the ideal of representing perfect likeness. Locating the Christian ideal of art in the miracle of the Incarnation—a triumph of imagination over reason —Antokol'skii invoked the visual rhetoric of *Ecce homo* to question the possibility of vision as revelation. His attempt to create a Jewish countericonography drew explicitly on the rabbinic insistence on divine transcendence and implicitly on the biblical prohibition against making three-dimensional, that is to say, life-like representations of God: "You shall not make for yourself a sculptured image, any likeness of what is in the heavens above or on the earth below or in the waters below the earth. You shall not bow to these or serve them" (Deut. 5:8–9). This taboo, paradoxically, did not inhibit the creation of art but contributed to the exposure of art as artifice. Antokol'skii's Jesus was, therefore, not so much about being Jewish as about *seeing* Jewish, a strategy that ultimately enabled the secularization of the image and hinted at the possibility that the truth in art was not revealed but manufactured.

This possibility is, I think, already implicit in *Ecce homo* itself, particularly in the rendering of Jesus' feet. Encased in a filigree of straps, the feet, like the bands across the torso, break into the vertical line of the sculpture. Both the forearms and the feet detach themselves from the overall geometry of the body; the feet, however, are richly detailed in a way that seems at odds with the severity of the rest of the figure. In fact, this is just the kind of ornamental detail that distinguished Antokol'skii's realism. Both contemporaries and later critics commented on the way that excessive attention to "jewel-like relief work on the lower parts" of historical portraits, such as the throne in *Ivan the Terrible* (1870–75, Tretiakov Gallery, Moscow), as well as the buttons on the breeches and the spurs on the boots in *Peter the Great* (1872, Tretiakov Gallery, Moscow), distracted from the "integrity of visual expression."[28]

In most iconic images related to the Passion, Jesus is unshod, his lower body fully exposed as an integral part of the corporeal hierarchy that links his humanity with his divinity, signified by the head.[29] His bare feet at once anticipate the wounds of the Crucifixion and allude to the imminent triumph of the Resurrection. Before his death, Jesus exhorts the disciples to "proclaim the kingdom of Heaven" without "haversack for the journey, or spare tunic or footwear" (Mt. 10: 7–10) and, again, "Start off now but, look, I am sending you like lambs among wolves. Take no purse with you, no haversack, no sandals" (Lk. 10:4). Given this evangelical emphasis on the performance of humility—a pregnant sign of the approaching "kingdom of Heaven"—the explicit focus on Jesus' sandals in Antokol'skii's *Ecce homo*, rather than on his naked limbs, is, precisely, unseemly. Making the feet appear from beneath the tunic as if from nowhere, disconnected from the theological economy of the body in which every aspect of representation links up with the promise of salvation, effectively turns Jesus' person into a decorative object, the sum of its beautiful parts.

The humanization of Antokol'skii's Jesus does not portend the communion of revelation here, as the title suggests, but its opposite. Typified by a reflexive gesture, the ostensible realism of the sculpture constitutes an act of aesthetic withdrawal, analogous in its effect to the countericonography of the Passion. Antokol'skii placed the figure on a pedestal that consists of two steps. Jesus balances on the lower step, his left foot jutting out slightly. The figure appears to descend from a height to enter the same space as the viewer. The illusion of intimacy is, however, completely unsettling. The teetering foot implies suspended movement, as if Antokol'skii imagines Jesus walking away from his fate and removing himself from the scenario of the Passion. Poised in defiance of Christian history and the teleology of *Ecce homo,* the beautiful feet of Antokol'skii's Jesus signify a shift toward a radically different frame of reference for the depiction of *Ecce homo.* Two other sculptures, *Socrates* (1875, Russian Museum, St. Petersburg) and *Spinoza* (1886–87, Russian Museum, St. Petersburg) exhibit a similar formal strategy.

Both *Socrates* (Figure 12.2) and *Spinoza* (Figure 12.3) thematize acts of willful defiance by contrasting images of pose with a striking detail that seems to fall outside the space inhabited by the figures. In both cases, the objects—Socrates' empty chalice lying on its side at the back of his chair to the right and Spinoza's open book, just touching the hem of his coat also at the right—suggest arrested movement, in contrast with the principal subjects, who are frozen in a state of self-contained, inaccessible stillness. Socrates slouches, his head down and his eyes closed, already dead; Spinoza sits in his chair, his hands folded neatly across his chest in anticipation of being placed in a coffin. In the case of *Ecce homo,* the artificially animated foot is the most realistic effect in a sculpture otherwise devoted to the hieratic articulation of stasis. In its emphasis on décor at the expense of decorum, the foot, like the cup and the book, intercepts the relationship between the sculpture and the viewer to bring the work of art into view as a made *thing.*

Antokol'skii's suggestive formal grouping of Jesus, Socrates, and Spinoza points to Ernest Renan, whose phenomenally popular *Life of Jesus* (1863) was the source for the sculptor's subversive misreading of the iconography of *Ecce homo.* Antokol'skii was inspired not by Renan's descriptions of Jesus but by the bold transformation of the Christian ideal of revelation into the modern act of reading, exemplified in the invocation of the gospel as an imaginative text. Renan compares the three figures as follows: "Opposition always glorifies a country. The greatest men of a nation are often those whom it puts to death. Socrates was the glory of Athens which proved unable to live with him. Spinoza was the greatest of modern Jews and the synagogue excluded him with disgrace. Jesus was the glory of the people of Israel and they crucified him."[30] Renan positions Jesus between the Greek philosopher and his modern Jewish counterpart, who rejected Torah from Sinai; in this context, Jesus is a secular hero whose life unfolded not within the redemptive teleology of the gospel but within the scope of the conflict between religion and reason.

Renan severed the modern "quest of the historical Jesus" from Christian hermeneutics of the New Testament. His immediate scholarly predecessors had recovered from the gospel a Jesus dwarfed by the providential significance of his death for the coming of the Christian community.[31] The Jesus of the Tübingen school of biblical criticism, exemplified in the magisterial two-volume *Life of Jesus, Critically Examined* (1835–36) of David Friedrich Strauss, virtually faded into the background of the gospel text, the realiza-

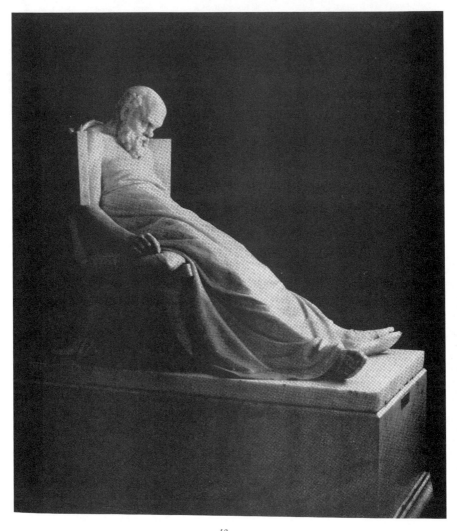

46
СМЕРТЬ СОКРАТА
Статуя. Мрамоп

Figure 12.2. Mark Antokol'skii, *Death of Socrates*. Russian Museum, St. Petersburg. Photo: E. V. Kuznetsova, *M. M. Antokol'skii, zhizn'i tvorchestvo* (Moscow: Iskusstvo, 1989), pl. 46. © 2006, State Russian Museum, St. Petersburg.

tion, according to Strauss, of the ideal of divine immanence signified in the words of the early Christians. At the heart of the revelation lay the death of Jesus, and his merger with Christian memory, at which point he ceased to be a historical person at all.

Renan explicitly rejected the "petty certainty" of German biblical criticism in order to return Jesus to the site of his heroic confrontation. He saw

Figure 12.3. Mark Antokol'skii, *Spinoza*. Russian Museum, St. Petersburg. Photo: E. V. Kuznetsova, *M. M. Antokol'skii, zhizn'i trorchestvo* (Moscow: Iskusstvo, 1989), pl. 50. cW 2006, State Russian Museum, St. Petersburg.

in the pietism of the Tübingen school a form of bibliolatry, hardly secular in its pedantic focus on the material details of Scripture, which, Renan said, were "impossible to verify." Renan's own style, rooted as much in the scientific rejection of the "unverifiable" as in the nineteenth-century romance with the past best exemplified in the historical fiction of Sir Walter Scott, relied instead on the "truth of color."[32] Enlivened by Renan's personal encounter with the landscape of Palestine, the evidence of literary design signified the necessary remove of the author from his reader.[33] Like the clothes of Antokol'skii's over-dressed Jesus, the exotic artfulness of Renan's distinction between the ancient "East" and the modern "West" instantiated a sense of imaginative distance from the "unverifiable" events of the gospel. Relegating the sustaining Christian belief in the significance of the Passion to the overwrought "enthusiasm" of a "few devoted women,"[34] Renan produced a life of Jesus unillumined by the "good news" of his death. The book read and sold like a French novel. First published in 1863, it had been reprinted fourteen times by 1875. Such secular signs of success did not go unremarked; the author's learned colleagues complained that Renan, in his quest for the "truth of color," had "painted [Christ] over with a brush which has been dipped in the melancholy blue of modern poetry, in the rose of the eighteenth-century idyll, and in the grey of a moral philosophy derived from La Rochefoucauld."[35]

Renan had, in fact, transformed the inscrutable Messiah of the gospel of John into a Greek among Jews, a lover of the good life ill-placed among his own God-fearing but barbarous people. Renan's protagonist exemplified the Hellenic principles of "profane life" and beauty overcoming the patriarchal "oriental" religion.[36] In pastoral Galilee, Renan's Jesus becomes a child of nature, "a young villager who sees the world through the prism of his own naïveté."[37] Among the vulgar crowd in Jerusalem, he appears as an artist, "with an exquisite feeling for nature, which furnished him with expressive images" for his parables. His teachings display "a wonderful keenness, like what we call wit [Fr. *l'esprit*], which put his aphorisms in sharp relief; at other times, his vivacity consisted in the felicitous invocation of popular proverbs."[38] Jesus displays great disdain for the "social susceptibilities of the time" and openly prefers "people of questionable lives" to "orthodox leaders," who have no taste and no appreciation for beauty.[39] At the same time, he is a man of "infinite charm," who makes numerous social "conquests."[40] In life, Renan's Jesus does not "shrink from pleasure," but in death he maintains a "calm and dignified attitude," which makes an impression, even on the Roman procurator.[41] Thus, Jesus presents a series of contradictory appearances, "susceptible to indefinite interpretations."[42]

Renan had, in this radical claim, presented the possibility of reading the gospel as literature. He destabilized the commanding authority of scripture by locating its aesthetic power in textual "magic," composed of metaphoric effects, "literalized" into Christian dogma.[43] In the succeeding six volumes of the *History of Christianity*, Renan traversed the "interpretive" distance that lay between Jesus and Christ. Antokol'skii traveled the same road, rendering in *Ecce homo* the aesthetic detachment of "symbol" from "theology."[44] The insistence on the aggressive impenetrability of art and the attendant secularization of Christian vision became increasingly evident in the sculptor's work after *Ecce homo*, most strikingly in the devotional representations of blind women (*Christian Martyr*, 1887, Tretiakov Gallery, Moscow; *Blind Girl for K. K. Groot Memorial*, 1898, Russian Academy of Arts, St. Petersburg, *Memorial for the Daughter of I. A. Tereshchenko*, 1888, Kiev Museum of Russian Art, Kiev; *The Angel, Memorial for T. N. Yusupova*, 1895, Estate-Museum at Arkhangel'skoe). The alienation of vision from revelation brought into sharp focus Antokol'skii's realism as a mode of artistic practice, based not on the representational ideal of the *vera icon* but on the objective—secular—otherness of art. What realism meant within the context of Antokol'skii's career as a nineteenth-century Russian artist is another matter, however. Indeed, the contemporary reception of Antokol'-skii's controversial Jesus indexed the tension between the increasing cultural autonomy of art in Russia and the explicitly ideological investment in realism as the social ethos of Russian art. *Ecce homo* thus entered critical discourse in its refractory "capacity as hermeneutic," marking the "limits of representation."[45]

Realism formed the credo of the first Russian movement of organized resistance to the institutional monopoly of the state on artistic production. The commitment of the Wanderers (Rus. *peredvizhniki*) to the critical exposure of the social evils that plagued contemporary Russian life went hand in hand with the desire to emancipate the artist from the tutelage of the Academy and from the authority of official patronage.[46] In reality, things were far more complicated; the Wanderers grew into a movement within the halls of the Academy itself. Both their careers and the exhibition of their work became possible in the wake of the state-sponsored efforts at the general unserfment (Rus. *raskreposhchenie*) of Russian society that began with the abolition of serfdom in 1861, followed by the creation of an independent judiciary, the relaxation of censorship restrictions, the introduction of universal conscription, the establishment of more effective institutions of urban and rural self-government, and a host of other measures associated with the creation of civil society. The compass of Great Reforms effectively diminished the significance of estate privileges and restrictions and contributed in no small measure to the creation of modern Russian culture, the tenor of which reflected the ambivalence of opposition to the state.[47] Its purveyors, ideologically unmoored from the establishment, found themselves caught between the heady sense of freedom and the need to establish their credentials within the new and very contentious Russian public sphere. In the case of the Wanderers, the investment in realism signified the turn to the nation as the repository of Russian authenticity, the source of the Wanderers' own claims about the contemporary social significance of their work. According to their own lights, the Wanderers spoke directly to and from the people (Rus. *narod*).

In the work of the Wanderers, the image of Jesus served the heroic apotheosis of Russian radicalism. During the period between the disastrous "pilgrimage to the people" in 1873 and the wave of arrests that followed the political assassination of Alexander II in 1881, Repin in particular began to associate various stages of the Passion with the martyrdom of the Russian "moral community," the embattled self-sacrificing rebellious children of educated society (see, for example, the four major thematically linked canvases, all at the Tretiakov Gallery, Moscow: *Refusing Confession before Execution* , 1879–85; The Arrest of the Propagandist, 1880–91; *Secret Meeting,* 1883; and *They Did Not Expect Him,* 1883–84).[48] Russian realists of the second half of the nineteenth century were, in fact, less interested in the "historical Jesus" then in mining the allegorical potential of scripture to provide a pictorial language for the representation of contemporary scenes.[49] This approach to the gospel as the "mythological subtext" of current events actually presented problems for the realistic—historically contextualized—representation of Jesus and turned self-described realists like N. N. Ge (1831–94) and I. N. Kramskoi (1837–87) into "secret romantics,"[50] seeking to free their depiction of gospel scenes from the "objectification of scenery."[51] More generally, the tendency toward historical symbolism, paradoxically embraced in the name of the commitment to authenticity, bespoke the urgency of the conflict between the contemporary function of realism as a painterly style and the Wanderers' embrace of realism as ideologically normative. The emphasis on the "expression" of truth, here inhibited the insistence on the self-conscious production of verisimilitude. Antokol'skii's secular inclinations toward the latter in the creation of *Ecce homo* placed him in direct confrontation with I. N. Kramskoi, the chief exponent among the Wanderers of the spiritual relevance of "expression."[52] The exchange between the two artists over the meaning of *Ecce homo* brought out the importance that Antokol'skii attached to the polemical deployment of Jewishness in the defense of the radical unserfment of Russian art, enabled by the experience of emancipation from the confessional discipline of Jewish Vilna, the Lithuanian Jerusalem.

The story of Antokol'skii's career as a Russian artist and a self-made Russian Jew manifests the uneasy relationship between the politics of emancipation and the moral claims of Russian populism.[53] Antokol'skii arrived in St. Petersburg in 1862, at the age of twenty, among the hundreds of young and ambitious Jewish provincials who streamed into Russian institutions of higher learning during the era of the Great Reforms in search of a life beyond the geographic and cultural confines of the Pale of Jewish Settlement. He was the first Jewish student to enroll in the St. Petersburg Academy of Arts, initially as an auditor. In 1863, he met Repin; the two became roommates and lifelong friends. In 1865, after winning two major academic prizes for the genre pieces, *Jewish Tailor* (Russian Museum, St. Petersburg), and *The Miser* (Russian Museum, St. Petersburg) he was awarded a regular stipend. Beginning in 1866, he and Repin joined the unofficial St. Petersburg Artists' Cooperative (Rus. *artel'*) that also included Kramskoi. The group formed the seedbed for the Wanderers, with whom Antokol'skii continued to maintain ties even though he did not exhibit with them regularly. In 1867, he showed his work at the Paris Exposition universelle. In 1868, he began work on a relief called *The Attack of the Inquisition on the Jews of Spain during a Secret Celebration of the Passover,* the second and still incomplete version of which won another academic prize.[54] This work also brought him to the attention of St. Petersburg society, particularly V. V. Stasov (1824–1906), art critic and chief spokesman of Russian populism in art and music.[55] Stasov became Antokol'skii's most enthusiastic supporter, intellectual patron, and correspondent.[56]

In 1870, the sculptor attained the rank of "honorary citizen," which made him an official resident of St. Petersburg; from 1862 until 1870, he was still technically under the jurisdiction of Vilna's Jewish community. Between 1870 and 1871, Antokol'skii completed the initial version of *Ivan the Terrible,* which earned him full membership in the Academy; Alexander II bought the sculpture for four thousand rubles. In the fall of 1871, Antokol'skii left Russia for Rome as a *pensionnaire* of the Academy.[57] While in Rome, he met the railroad magnate S. I. Mamontov (1841–1918) and his wife, E. G. Mamontova, both enthusiastic art patrons. Antokol'skii, joined the Mamontovs' intimate circle, which also included the art critic A. V. Prakhov (1846–1916) and the painter V. D. Polenov (1844–1927).[58] The group formed the nucleus of the larger society of artists that eventually congregated at Mamontov's estate of Abramtsevo, Russia's first artists' colony and museum dedicated expressly to modern Russian art.[59]

In 1872, Antokol'skii completed the first version of *Peter the Great,* exhibited at the All-Russian Polytechnic Exhibition in Moscow. In the same year, he showed plaster versions of *Ivan the Terrible* at the first Wanderers' Exhibition in Moscow and at the International Exhibition in London. In October–November of the same year, Antokol'skii traveled to Russia for the first official exhibition of his works at the Academy in St. Petersburg. Early in 1873, he began *Ecce homo* and *Spinoza;* in April, Mamontov commissioned the former in marble for nine thousand rubles and brought it back to Abramtsevo, which housed the sculpture until its relocation to the Tretiakov Gallery in the twentieth century. In 1877, Antokol'skii moved permanently to Paris; his studio became the meeting place for Russian artists traveling abroad. He received an impressive number of private commissions for portraits and funerary sculptures; throughout the next twenty-five years, until his death in 1902, Antokol'skii never stopped working, returning as well to historical and literary subjects. And he never went back to Russia for an extended stay.

The success of *Ecce homo* marked a turning point in his career. The marble version, along with the bronze of *Peter the Great*, was exhibited at the Paris Exposition universelle of 1878, won the prestigious *medaille d'honneur*, and earned Antokol'skii the ribbon of the French Legion of Honor. Formally emancipated from the Academy, he was now a citizen of Europe. The transformation depended, however, on the careful cultivation of his Russian ties through the continuous flow of correspondence. Antokol'skii's letters to Russia—primarily to Stasov but also to Repin, Kramskoi, the Mamontovs, and all his colleagues and friends on the Russian art scene— became the stage upon which the sculptor enacted the drama of homesickness. The thousand-page-volume of correspondence published by Stasov shortly after Antokol'skii's death is the most important source for reconstructing the sculptor's Russian Jewish persona, which was as deliberately crafted as any of his other works.[60]

During the first decade of the Great Reforms, the government of Alexander II passed a series of measures permitting categories of Jewish individuals who had distinguished themselves professionally, economically, or in military service to the empire to leave the confines of the Pale of Settlement and to enroll in the social estates commensurate with their civil status. This emergence of Jewishness from the boundaries of the Pale of Settlement created unprecedented opportunities for the development of competing visions of Jewish experience. Part of contemporary Russian discourse, secular Jewish culture now pressed its claims on Jewish self-consciousness primarily in moral and aesthetic—rather than religious and social—terms. Before the political turn toward Zionism at the turn of the century, it was very hard to tell where Russian populism ended and Jewish populism began. Stasov, for instance, saw in Antokol'skii's Jewish origins the source of his expressly Russian genius, such that Antokol'skii's position as a Russian artist depended both on his emancipation from the Lithuanian Jerusalem and on his imaginary return to his Jewish roots. By the time he entered into conversation with Kramskoi about the meaning of his *Ecce homo*, the sculptor was primed to marshal Jewishness as the means of translating the vocabulary of secular art into a Russian idiom.

Kramskoi's reservations regarding *Ecce homo* grew out of aesthetic, religious, and professional concerns.[61] The enduring suspicion of Russian Orthodoxy toward freestanding sculptures of Jesus dovetailed with the spiritual proclivities and social commitments of the Wanderers. While the Latin West embraced three-dimensional images of Jesus as part of the same devotional tradition that gave pride of place to the graphic depiction of Jesus' suffering, the Russian Orthodox East, which focused on icon painting, did not.[62] In the aftermath of the Schism (1650–66), Old Believers— the sectarians who rejected official Russia in the name of authentic Russian faith—deplored the "life-like" representations of Jesus as a demonic foreign import. Where Western European artists and audiences located compelling symbolic values, their Russian counterparts saw only illusionistic effects, elaborate fictions that obscured the gospel truth (Rus. *istina*). The archpriest Avvakum, hero-martyr of Old Belief, seethed in his *Table-talk* (1669–75) against the "imitators" (Rus. *izugrafy*) who painted the Savior "his face all puffy, his lips scarlet, his hair curly, his arms and his thighs stout, his fingers inflated . . . all of him fattened up like a German [i.e., foreigner] only a sword missing at the hip." Such "fat" images, he said, were all done "after the flesh" and could not convey Jesus' "subtle [Rus. *tonkostny*, lit. "thin"] feelings." In the pointed contrast between fat and thin Avvakum referenced the distinction between the Western European embrace of perspective and the flat—thin—picture plane of the icon. Particularly provoking, though, were Jesus' feet; they looked too solid, like "little stools."[63]

The persistent association of life-size sculptures of Christian saints and of Jesus with "idolatry" underlay the 1722 decree, enacted by Peter I—the same czar who persecuted Old Believers and also introduced neoclassical sculpture to Russia—forbidding their installation not only in churches but also in private homes.[64] In the eighteenth century, probably under the impact of the spread of Western European norms, life-size figures of the *Scourged Christ*, carved and wood and colored, began to feature in provincial northern churches.[65] But by the beginning of the nineteenth century, only mystically inclined eccentrics, like the freemason I. V. Lopukhin (1756–1816), who had a private garden dedicated to the "spiritual knights" of his own "inner church," placed devotional statuary in their gardens.[66] At the Academy, Antokol'skii's predecessors confined themselves to allegorical figures of the "virtues" and to the Graeco-Roman pantheon.[67] And while Russian painters studying in Rome copied the Old Masters as a matter of course, no Russian sculptor had ever attempted to imitate the religious work of Michelangelo and Bernini, even as an exercise.[68] The nineteenth-century search for the "historical Jesus," however, put new pressure on Russian artists seeking to resolve the tension between native traditions and Western European visual culture, urgently relevant to the work of Kramskoi.

Throughout his career, Kramskoi maintained a commitment to the politics of realism that brought the Wanderers together; in other words, he believed in the political significance of representing the reality—mostly grim—of contemporary Russian life as fully and as faithfully to its dark colors as possible. So far so good; however, when it came to matters of "expression," Kramskoi strove to avoid illusionistic effects. In his letters, he returned over and over again to the conflict between the "dramas of the human heart" and "dramas of form." This conflict plagued his work with endless "difficulties of execution" and made the background of his canvases, particularly the portraits, look ill-defined and unfinished.[69] The problem became especially acute with regard to the representation of Jesus. When Kramskoi began work on his *Christ in the Desert* (1872, Tretiakov Gallery, Moscow) in the fall of 1871, he wrote of his recent trip to Crimea as having inspired the authentic "oriental" setting of the painting.[70] He repeatedly asked for photographs of Chufut-Kale, a tenth-century fortress near the old town of Bakhchisarai; the landscape, remarkably close in appearance to the eastern Mediterranean, served as the background for *Christ in the Desert*.[71] But throughout the time that he worked on *Christ in the Desert* and for years afterward, Kramskoi could not come to terms with the realistic "exposure" of Jesus that such details implied. He talked about "veiling" the painting altogether and referred to "smearing the paint over the face," as if he were engaged in the dirty work of covering up a preexisting, ideal vision.[72] In 1878, responding to the writer V. M. Garshin (1855–88), who inquired about the meaning that Kramskoi attached to his own painting, by then considered a masterpiece, the painter went on to describe the psychological "crisis" that holds the central figure in its grip. But as to the identity of this figure, Kramskoi demurred: "This is not Christ. That is, I have no idea who it is. It is an expression of my personal thoughts."[73] It proved easier to disavow the painting as an image of Jesus than to come to terms with the necessity of depicting the Savior's "sandal straps."[74]

The pregnant reference to Jesus' "sandal straps" evoked the meaning that Christ's feet held as an ambivalent symbol of his humanity, referenced in Avvakum's diatribe two hundred years earlier and then polemically by Antokol'skii. More in the spirit of the former than of the latter, Kramskoi made a nasty comment about Titian's Jesus (*The Tribute Money,* 1518, Gemäldgalerie Alte Meister, Dresden): "Really, these Italians were the most naïve crowd. He went and painted an Italian diplomat, delicate, sly, a shrewd dry egoist—there are many such people around—and put next to him a type from among the people, himself a crafty sort, stuck a dinar in his hand, did an outstanding job conveying the body, touching it up with the most extraordinary precision, and said: 'This is Christ!' And, imagine, everyone believed. But, then again, this isn't so surprising. They believe still."[75]

Kramskoi was deeply invested, even obsessed, with *Ecce homo.* Just as he was completing *Christ in the Desert*, he talked about being "relentlessly" pursued by the "mocking laughter" (Rus. *khokhot*) of the "crowd" watching the "spectacle" of the suffering Christ before Pilate.[76] The vision would express itself on a monumental canvas called *Mocking Christ "Hail, King of the Jews!"* (1877–82, Russian Museum, St. Petersburg). Working on it for close to ten years, Kramskoi intended it to be the definitive Russian Christ, both contemporary and fully historical, a response, on the proper scale, to A. A. Ivanov's *Christ's Appearance to the People* (1837–57, Tretiakov Gallery, Moscow), as well as a visual commentary on the condition of the Russian intelligentsia caught between government persecution and popular ignorance and disdain. He never finished it.

The earliest reference to *Mocking Christ* in Kramskoi's correspondence appears in a letter dated December 1, 1872; the earliest reference to *Ecce homo* appears in Antokol'skii's letter to Stasov, dated May 8, 1872.[77] In his letter to Stasov, Antokol'skii pointedly stressed that his own *Jesus before the Judgment of the People* would be "entirely original." In the spring of 1876, Kramskoi was in Rome, "looking at Romans," in preparation for *Mocking Laughter*, which he began the following year.[78] It is impossible to ascertain whether Antokol'skii turned to *Ecce homo* independently of Kramskoi; there is evidence, however, that Kramskoi could not dismiss the sculptor's choice of subject as mere coincidence. When Tretiakov asked the painter, who had visited Antokol'skii's studio in Rome, for his opinion of the marble *Ecce homo*, which was nearly complete, Kramskoi averred: his verdict would of necessity be "partial and unjust."[79] In the exchange with Antokol'skii himself, ideological and aesthetic differences were sharpened by the painter's sense of personal pique.

At the end of August in 1874, Kramskoi first saw the sculpture in a photo of the recently completed plaster cast that Antokol'skii sent to Stasov.[80] He wrote Antokol'skii a letter, which has not survived, but we do have Antokol'skii's response, dated September 6, 1874, and Kramskoi's subsequent letter to Repin, dated September 28, 1874, in which he rehearsed his original remarks to the sculptor.[81] What exactly had Kramskoi said? In his response, Antokol'skii bristled particularly at the charge that the "feet were no good at all." He quoted Kramskoi as saying: "Say what you like, but the influence of Italy is not entirely healthy." Kramskoi had apparently remarked that the "steps" (Rus. *sledki*) of Jesus looked too much like those of the Roman *Germanicus*, on exhibit not, as it happened, "in Italy" but at the Louvre, "in Paris." But Antokol'skii shot back, "I can assure you that I have always hated *Germanicus* for its soulless monumentality [Rus. *statuarnost*] and I can tell you (and even prove if necessary) that the steps of *Christ* were done from a live model." As to Kramskoi's alleged remark that the face of Jesus was altogether too "traditional," Antokol'skii agreed, adding that he wished for the figure to have expressly "eastern-Jewish features," to avoid the justifiable claim that this was not Jesus but "God knows who."

At this time, Kramskoi wrote to Repin that Antokol'skii had entirely misjudged the severity of his criticism; he liked the sculpture very much and, for the most part, agreed with Repin that Antokol'skii's Jesus embodied the "most faithful representation of the way in which Jesus is imagined in our own nineteenth century." He had taken minor exception to the feet ("decidedly stone-like, reminiscent of *Germanicus*") and the nose ("too low . . . although that's natural for it belongs to a Jew [Rus. *iudei*, lit. Judean]"). Kramskoi used the biblical term to highlight the sarcastic tone of the remark that immediately followed: "I would agree with him entirely if I had proof that a nose of such a cut could belong to a person of the highest moral stature." This attack on Jesus' Jewish physiognomy may have been a thinly veiled thrust against Antokol'skii for "stealing" *Ecce homo* from the painter.

The problem of the feet revealed precisely the stakes attendant on the difference between the ways in which Kramskoi and Antokol'skii tackled the problem of Jesus in Russian art and, more generally, on the values that each artist attached to the meaning of realism. It hardly mattered to Kramskoi whether Antokol'skii had used a "live model" to make Jesus' *sledki*; what mattered was that the feet, prominent and entwined with those very conspicuous "sandal straps," signified that the sculpture was a secular work of "imitation." The suggestion of Western European precedent—like Avvakum, Kramskoi invoked the "German" in *Germanicus* to mean "foreign"— had nothing to do with whether the feet actually resembled those of the Roman sculpture (they don't).[82] It is not even clear whether or not Kramskoi saw *Germanicus* and was in a position to make the call. Antokol'skii chided him for his ignorance of the fact that *Germanicus* was exhibited in Paris, not in Rome. Rather, Kramskoi's point called attention to the workmanship involved in making Jesus' feet appear real.

We are left with the "Jewish" face and Antokol'skii's remark that it was the only way to identify the sculpture as a figure of Jesus. In the conspicuous absence of conventional Christian iconography, Jesus' Jewish look made him recognizable by turning an anonymous "God knows who" into a compelling historical subject. Jesus' Jewishness paradoxically made the sculpture accessible to a Christian audience. But, in this case, the sculpture failed to testify to the artist's Christian humility, his recourse to revelation. Antokol'skii was not a Christian and his *Ecce homo* explicitly celebrated the powers of human invention over the authority of scripture and Christian tradition. Ultimately, contemporaries who gazed in wonder at Antokol'skii's work could not be sure whether they were venerating Jesus or admiring *Jesus*. As admiration of *Jesus* slipped into the veneration of Mark Antokol'skii, the image of the modern artist displaced the icon.

The confrontation with Kramskoi underscores the importance of Antokol'skii's social connections in the creation of his artistic persona. To say that his Jewishness was similarly contingent is to argue not only that modern Jews created art but that art created modern Jews. In this instance, Stasov—the patron who appropriated Antokol'skii's Jewishness in the name of Russian art—forced the presence of Vilna to the surface. In the summer of 1873, just as the work on *Ecce homo* neared completion, Antokol'skii and the art critic Prakhov met Stasov in Vienna to attend the Wiener Weltausstellung (Vienna World's Fair). In the course of this encounter, the unfinished *Ecce homo* figured as the subject of an argument that nearly destroyed the close relationship between the critic and the sculptor. Stasov indignantly reported to his sister that the influence of Italy and the Roman friendship with Prakhov—Prakhov, we recall, was a member of Mamontov's circle in Rome—eroded the originality of Antokol'skii's art. Stasov lamented that Antokol'skii was becoming too much of a Westerner, exhibiting an unhealthy predilection for antiquity and for "flabby" idealism. He said that he now despaired of Antokol'skii's developing potential as a realist, infected by "filthy [lit. "pagan"] Rome" and "all of the baseness of Italy." In the same letter, Stasov assailed Prakhov as an "omnivorous and well-tempered liberal" and blamed him for corrupting not only Antokol'-skii but Repin too.[83] In a letter that Stasov sent to Antokol'skii, upon the latter's return to Rome, the critic now urged the sculptor to make a choice between himself and Prakhov, a choice, he claimed, that Repin had already made. Although this crucial letter has not survived, traces of it remain in Antokol'skii's response, dated September 30, 1873.[84] The sculptor refers to Stasov's insistence that he abandon "cursed Italy" and return to Russia. Stasov apparently urged Antokol'skii to take up subjects that would imbue his art with the integrity and wholesomeness of his authentic Russian talent. Antokol'skii's true vocation, Stasov had said, lay not in the derivative depiction of "old-time" Christian myths but in the representation of contemporary Jewish subjects of the sort that had informed the sculptor's early genre scenes.

To be sure, Stasov's radical criticism of Prakhov centered on the opposition between "art for art's sake," which he considered alien and Western, and the ostensible social embeddedness of the realist ethos.[85] One might argue, however, that what really angered Stasov was the competing presence of Prakhov in Vienna, and presumably in the life of his own protégé. Antokol'skii also derived his own sense of Russianness from his connections with the Russian artistic community. This can be seen in *Ecce homo*: the way that Jesus is bound around his middle is a subtle, but unmistakeably native, allusion to a sketch of Repin's *Volga Barge Haulers* (1870–73, Russian Museum, St. Petersburg; Figure 12.4), a nationalist masterpiece.

The distinction between Western European art and Russian art upon which Stasov so stridently insisted was, in fact, largely invented. Antokol'-skii's so-called Roman Jesus represented a native thrust against the regnant Russian Jesus as envisioned by Ivanov and perhaps Kramskoi. Ivanov had also arrived at his subject in Rome, under the influence of the contemporary European quest for the historical Jesus. Antokol'skii's *Jesus* entered into the pantheon of Russian national art—Mamontov's collection in Abramtsevo—through the transnational art market. Antokol'skii and Mamontov met and became friends in Rome, as Russian Europeans. They both wanted to draw Russian artists closer to the artistic and commercial development of Western Europe. Thus, the conflict between Europe and Russia that Stasov projected onto *Jesus before the Judgment of the People* sharpened differences that were, in reality, elusive. In his response to Stasov's call that he return to Russia, Antokol'skii staged an imaginary journey to a

Figure 12.4. I. E. Repin, studies on the Volga for the *Volga Barge-Haulers*. © National Gallery in Prague, 2005. Photo: Elizabeth Kridl Valkenies, *Ilya Repin and the World of Russian Art*, New York, 1990, pl. 2.8.

place that, conveniently, could be reached only through the power of recall: the Vilna of his childhood.

In December of 1873, Antokol'skii wrote to Stasov to announce his intention to leave Rome "forever."[86] He was planning to return to Russia, he said, and to remain there "as long as possible," in order to begin work on a relief that he described as "the most fundamental and serious" work of his life, "the dramatization of an historical fact." The subject would be an episode culled from memories of his Vilna childhood: the military conscription of Jewish minors, which he claimed to have witnessed firsthand in 1851. What followed was a vivid account of an imaginary scene that has become a staple in the literary depiction of the particular horrors of Russian Jewish life—Jewish children ripped from their mothers' breasts and delivered into the arms of the autocracy by the cruel *khappers*, agents of a venal communal leadership. Such stories of suffering and persecution began to shape Russian Jewish expression precisely when Russian Jewish experience began to reflect the realities of emancipation. Here is Antokol'-skii's description of one Jewish mother's grief, with its stark aesthetic claim on Russian Jewish memory:

I shall never forget the image of one lone woman, running without rest and almost unconscious onto a field, where she was meant to take her leave from her son. She was about thirty-five or so. Her face was thin and weary, her eyes red and sunken, her lips half-open and almost black. She was covered with an old, faded kerchief, under her arm she carried a small bundle, and in her hands she held a pair of old, worn-out shoes, none of which got in the way of her running. She ran with quick, small steps and with her whole body leaning forward. At times, with a great deal of effort, she drank in air as if she was having difficulty breathing. At times, she glanced down at her fingers which seemed as if they were frozen and shook . . . It seemed to me that she would collapse as soon as she reached her destination.[87]

In fact, Antokol'skii had no plans to exchange his rented European studio for the "rheumatic" northern climate of his homeland or to dismiss from his mind his current project in favor of this new one.[88] The plans for the conscription relief remained on paper; he made no preliminary sketches, and he never again returned to this or any other Russian Jewish subject. Even his experimental and much-admired early relief on an explicitly Jewish theme, *The Assault of the Inquisition on the Jews* (1868), remained unfinished. Yet, in the conscription letter, Antokol'skii patently reveled in the aesthetic potentialities of his own personal past.

The conscription letter served to restore the sculptor in the critic's good graces by reestablishing the link between art and life that Stasov considered the most important measure of Antokol'skii's native genius, in spite of the fact that Antokol'skii actively detested Vilna, and St. Petersburg only marginally less so. Indeed, Antokol'skii's so-called eyewitness account revealed the traces not just of what he was inclined to remember of his past in the Jerusalem of Lithuania—which was not much—but also of what he saw around him in Rome, particularly the art of Christian Western Europe. The scenes of Jewish maternal suffering that ostensibly appeared before his eyes were filtered through explicitly Christian iconography, obviously connected to the work he was doing on *Ecce homo*. The artist, as it were, retraced the steps of Calvary, now strewn with the signs of historical indifference, the details rendered significant by their link with the original

Christian "drama." This path became the symbolic structure of Antokol'-skii's Jewish reminiscences: "We began our journey home and again returned to that same spot, when just a few moment ago the drama had played itself out. And there was nothing there anymore! The sun still shone and warmed us. Here is a broken bottle lying in the grass, here is the upturned barrel upon which the rabbi stood blessing the recruits. Here is the tavern-keeper, clearing the dishes from the tables. And nothing else remains. A few people stop and ask for a drink of cool water but we go on our silent way."[89]

Such images, Antokol'skii went on to say, evoked in him a new appreciation of the painting by the contemporary French artist Paul Delaroche, *The Return from Golgotha* (1856).[90] This artist, Antokol'skii claimed, expressed the heartbreak of the conscription scene "better than [he] ever could in words." The full scope of horror embodied in the recruitment of Russian Jewish children could apparently be appreciated not in its historical singularity but, Antokol'skii claimed, as part of a Christian pattern of elevating the suffering of one Jewish mother into a paradigm of cosmic significance: "Habit is second nature, someone once said; this is absolutely true.[91] The most awful, most astounding things, if they should happen before our own eyes, inure us to them and make us grow indifferent. Only the few are endowed with the capacity to see the truth in all its nakedness. Go right ahead and compare: take the so-called fact of the 'Slaughter of the Innocents' and the facts that I have related here and we would see that what happens before our very eyes is more awful."[92] The "few" here are artists gifted with the capacity to endow historical events with the eternal significance attached to the collective experience of the past; only the appropriate visual vocabulary, rooted in Christian legend—what Antokol'skii calls the "so-called fact" of the "Slaughter of the Innocents"—could convey the import of "what happens before our very eyes." Thus, the poetic language of Western Christian painting, the same idiom that Antokol'skii visually assaulted in *Ecce homo*, here represented in the work of Delaroche, elevated Antokol'skii's Jewish memories to epic significance and justified his interest in what Stasov dismissed as "old time" Christian myths.

In a letter that he wrote to Kramskoi before the painter had had the chance to see *Ecce homo*, Antokol'skii anticipated the charge that Jesus' skullcap might appear "anachronistic." The arch-realist all of the sudden affirmed, contrary to the conventional reading of *Ecce homo*, that he had no interest in "historical sources," which were "sparse" and, in any case, "irrelevant" to his conception—to make Jesus as he "appears in the nineteenth century."[93] The emphasis on the immediate relevance of the person of Jesus echoed Renan's claim that the "legend" of Christ was more important than the "petty certainty" of the text.[94] Concurrently, Antokol'skii's gesture toward his audience effectively brought "the people" back into his *Jesus before the Judgment of the People*. The skullcap made Jesus visible as a Jew to Antokol'skii's contemporaries. At the same time, the figure's "decidedly stone-like" feet, one of them balanced on the edge of the step, pointed to the alternative possibility that the Jewishness of Jesus was not so easily grounded. The visual relationship between the skullcap and the feet effectively recapitulates the way in which Antokol'skii's epistolary returns enabled radical acts of departure. The claims of homesickness allowed him to assert affective ties to a provincial Jewish world that no longer held him in place. "My heart is in the East," wrote Judah Halevi, "and I am at the edge of the West." In the shadow of Antokol'skii's edgy *Jesus*, we may set the medieval Spanish poet's expression of the historic Jewish desire to "leave all of the good things" of exile for the "dust of a ruined shrine" in its proper light.

V.
In Search of a Usable Aesthetic

One of the central questions asked by this volume is whether the modern Jewish experience has in some sense been a pointedly artistic one. Or, to put it otherwise, what does it mean to define Jewish experience principally in aesthetic terms? The essays by Zachary Braiterman, Mark Kligman, and Hankus Netsky explore different ways in which the aesthetic character of traditional Jewish ritual or custom (such as synagogue worship, liturgy, and wedding celebration) has been adapted and refurbished to fit the sensibilities of distinctly modern circumstances.

In "A Modern Mitzvah-Space-Aesthetic," Zachary Braiterman presents the revered religious philosopher Franz Rosenzweig less as the proponent of an intellectually austere and abstract religious system, as generally assumed, than as the champion of a Judaism reveling in its aesthetic sensuality. Like the subjects of the essays in the section "Siting the Jewish Tomorrow," Rosenzweig offered a prescription for the ideal Jewishness of the future. But in contrast to Soviet and Zionist utopias described there, Rosenzweig's proposal amounted to a restitution of a Jewishness that he believed had already existed in the recent past. Through an examination of Rosenzweig's letters, as well as such familiar works as *The Star of Redemption*, Braiterman demonstrates that Rosenzweig conceived of this Judaism as a complete aesthetic system, one whose emotive power had been virtually neutered by the bourgeois conformism of the modern era. Via its sacred objects, its ritual, and its ceremony, and by sacralizing sight, sound, touch, and taste, Rosenzweig's recovered Judaism would be one that enveloped its participants in layers of sensory stimuli. Judaic aestheticism, as understood by Rosenzweig, had once functioned as both a unifying mechanism that compensated for Jewish "demographic heterogeneity" (i.e., diaspora) and a dividing line separating the feminine domain from "homosocial" experience of male fellowship. With its almost neopagan sensuality, Rosenzweig's "Orthodoxy" was thus designed to suit modern sensibilities in a far more visceral manner than the prosaic ethical monotheism developed by the immediately preceding generations of German Jews.

Like distorted images of "abstruse" theologians such as Rosenzweig, clichéd treatments of American Reform Judaism similarly emphasize the premium it placed on assimilation, ethics, and decorum. But as Mark Kligman demonstrates in his account of one of American Reform Judaism's principal composers, Abraham W. Binder (1895–1967), the Reform movement placed a high value on aesthetics and depended heavily upon the arts—and, above all, music—to produce a distinctively Reform Jewish experience. Yet just what that music should be was subject to considerable debate. Binder formulated his own musical philosophy at a moment when American Reform Judaism was being transformed by the infusion of East European Jewish immigrants, a factor that decisively influenced his understanding of "authentic" Jewish music. That said, Kligman shows that Binder's search for the appropriate American Jewish synagogue sound followed a process of relentless experimentation. The composer drew from disparate and (in light of the conventional image of a Reform movement that dispenses with tradition) counterintuitive resources: Hasidic and Palestinian folk music, Eastern European *hazzanut* and *nusach*, in addition, of course, to romantic and modern art music. Was there something in the American spirit (with its melting pot and cultural pluralist ideologies) that fed this heterogeneous approach? What is certain is that Binder's eclecticism was harnessed to a singular goal: to construct an ever more intensive and "elevating" liturgical experience that, like Rosenzweig's ideal Jewishness, would envelop and spiritually transform the worshiper. Here the art of being Jewish and the art of being modern were intended seamlessly to converge.

These efforts at devising usable Jewish aesthetics, however, were largely theoretical and programmatic. Rosenzweig's sensual Judaism remained embedded in a philosophical text and pedagogical program. And even Binder's synagogue music, despite the composer's talent and commitment, proved ephemeral in its application. In contrast, Hankus Netsky, in "The Evolution of Philadelphia's Russian Sher Medley," describes a creative impulse that operated over the course of several generations of musicians and their fans rather than within the genius of a single individual. In the aesthetic universe of Jewish klezmer musicians, where collaboration and improvisation rule, music is composed in performance, not prior to it. Netsky traces the evolution of one exceptionally well-documented piece of such music, the Philadelphia Russian Sher medley, from its earliest recorded American importation in the 1860s to its near extinction a century later. Through close musicological analyses of rare manuscripts, recordings, and interviews, he demonstrates how Philadelphia musicians adapted the four major components of the medley (expanding some and shortening others, as well as reworking both arrangements and instrumentation) to fit the changing tastes and cultural practices of the local Jewish community. Despite Philadelphia Jewry's rapid acculturation, the *sher* endured there longer than in other East European Jewish immigrant centers and even held on (though barely) long enough to experience a revival via the klezmer rejuvenation of the 1980s and 1990s. The Jewish aesthetic of Netsky's *klezmorim* proved to be not just usable but well used too.

Chapter 13

A Modern Mitzvah-Space-Aesthetic: The Philosophy of Franz Rosenzweig

Zachary Braiterman

What drew Franz Rosenzweig, a champion of so-called German Jewish renaissance, into Judaism and its ritual? Born in 1886 to a middle-class assimilated family from Cassel, Rosenzweig emerges from early letters and diaries as an indulged and precocious son. In particular, the letters detail his relationship with cousins Hans and Rudolf Ehrenberg and with Eugen Rosenstock, all three converts to Christianity. He was tempted to join them, but intended to do so as a Jew, not as a "pagan." According to legend, a visit to an East European *shtibl* in Berlin on Yom Kippur in 1913 overwhelmed young Rosenzweig, who, in a now-famous letter, sent word back to Rudolf Ehrenberg that he was to remain a Jew (*"also ich bleibe Jude"*). The wartime letters and diaries show a young Rosenzweig visiting Jewish communities in Macedonia and Warsaw. They indicate burgeoning commitments to Jewish learning and observance. A student of the famed historian Friedrich Meinecke and the author of a monograph on Hegel and the state, Rosenzweig turned down an academic post in order to run the Free Jewish Lehrhaus in Frankfurt, a position from which he had to resign after being diagnosed with Lou Gehrig's disease. He continued to work and write, at a terrible effort, until his death in 1929.

No doubt there was something saintly about the image of Rosenzweig and his return to Jewish ritual life. Much of the literature about him revolves around ethical thought and the problem of community. What I will argue here is that what drew Rosenzweig to Judaism and Jewish ritual was not truth or ethics or the desire for community per se, but rather sensation and sensual life, theatrical space and drama. Indeed, in his magnum opus, *The Star of Redemption* (1921), as well as in his writings relating to the Jewish Lehrhaus, Rosenzweig sees Judaism as aesthetic in the broadest sense (word-form, color, cloth, and sound, a tactile world of men who cry out in their prayer shawls and death shrouds) and as more basic than art because of the power of ritual to attract and structure sensual life, whether in the synagogue service, understood architecturally and theatrically, or in death. In the words of George Mosse, "death was the final sensuous experience, the necessary climax of a fully lived life."[1] Rosenzweig envisioned Judaism, and the ritual life associated with it, as a sensual spirit in aesthetic terms, first in the lush contours of *Jugendstil*, and later in terms of the more sharply contoured erotic charge and harsh dissonant style of Expressionism.

Rosenzweig's earliest letters show how a fancied image of death stamped a precocious understanding of ritual. The first references to death and its relation to religious ideas and practice in his *Letters and Diaries* took the form of playful jokes. In one 1907 diary entry, Rosenzweig considered the philosophical possibility of denying death. Responding to a hypothetically posed question, "What do you think about death?" Rosenzweig curtly noted, "That it is a bad symptom to think anything about it." He went on to remark how strange it is that he has absolutely no relation to the topic. Now clearly into the joke, the young Rosenzweig proceeded to offer a pseudo-Kantian argument to support the notion of immortality. Qua physiological phenomenon (in this case meaning raw, inert stuff), the human person does not die, because he or she is already dead. Qua noumenon (in this case referring to that eternal part of the soul that constitutes one's own immortal essence), the human person does not die because he or she never lived in time.[2] Ironically, these reflections follow the disavowal of any relation to the subject of death.

The laughing spirit with which the young Rosenzweig considered death is not isolated to this one diary entry. Consider Hermann Badt's 1908 account of Rosenzweig's morning ablutions. Coming to visit late in the morning, Badt found Rosenzweig still in bed. Badt then proceeded to tease Rosenzweig about the length of time he took preparing himself. Badt recorded Rosenzweig's response: a half-serious, half-jesting lecture about the moment of daily awakening from nocturnal death as the greatest and most holy part of the day. In Rosenzweig's eyes, one could never dwell too long on this daily renewal. He described as truly happy the person who not only consciously experiences this daily reawakening but who remains conscious even at the moment of death, stepping from this world to the beyond.[3] Ritual life reflects the light of eternal life into the narrow prism of temporal life. It helps the soul direct its journey toward the goal of death. In Badt's telling, ritual practice heightens the soul's consciousness of life's daily renewal. It prepares the soul for the ultimate step.

In his wartime letters Rosenzweig provides sensuous descriptions of his experiences in terms that reveal the exotic art nouveau allure of the Jewish Orient, whether in the Macedonian city of Uskub, near where he was stationed as a soldier, or in Warsaw, where he visited on furlough. In one 1917 letter to his parents, he described the minarets and domes of Uskub, the Sephardic Friday evening service in "a white plastered synagogue," "ancient melodies," a "beautiful" rendition of "*Lecha Dodi*," the "tenor" of the prayer, and the way "the male congregants wear their *talit.*"[4] In these letters, one discovers the "totally passive" pleasure and the "greatest relaxation" that Rosenzweig took at a bathhouse, where he was massaged by "a wretched, half naked Turk with the appearance of a dwarf."[5] Throughout the wartime letters, Rosenzweig mentions a young local boy named Immanuel Noah, who guided Rosenzweig through the Uskub Jewish community.[6] The Orient (symbolized by the city, synagogue service, baths, and the young boy) bears an exotic, faraway aesthetic. Letters from Warsaw leave the same impression. Rosenzweig described Orthodox Jews at prayer and study. He observed their "attractive costumes and language" and intellectual prowess. "Race pride" shows itself in Rosenzweig's comparison of "the aristocratic" *Ostjuden* to the German Jewish philistine. The letters record the architecture of the Jewish Quarter, the enthusiasm of song and prayer, and the author's visits to the Jewish theater.[7]

Just as a younger Rosenzweig once traveled to Italy to see paintings, a now older Rosenzweig traveled about Uskub and Poland to visit synagogues, religious schools, bathhouses, and garden theaters. Informed by a *Jugendstil* sensibility, the letters home focus on beauty, not the rarefied beauty of art objects but the beauty of everyday life, architectural form, and prayer, which combined theater and costume. One notes as well the faintly homoerotic touch inspired by the sight of male congregants, the half-naked Turk, and the young boy. Rosenzweig sought by means of this lush fin de siècle Orientalism to identify the deepest part of his being, turning later in life away from *Jugendstil* to harsher though no less aesthetic forms of expression. In a frequently cited 1920 letter to his mentor, the historian Friedrich Meinecke, Rosenzweig sought to explain—in aesthetic terms— why he had turned down a university lectureship in order to administer Frankfurt's Free Jewish Lehrhaus program in adult education.[8] Referring to a fellow student from before the war, Rosenzweig wrote, "I remember how sinister my insatiable hunger for 'forms' [*Gestalten*], a hunger without goal or meaning, driven on solely by its own momentum, then appeared to him. The study of history would have only served to feed my hunger for forms [*Gestaltenhunger*], my insatiable receptivity. History to me was a purveyor of forms, no more. No wonder I inspired horror in others as well as in myself."[9] Consistent with Kant's understanding of aesthetic pleasure, Rosenzweig's intellectual appetites presumed no extrinsic purpose apart from their own movement. But the hues are all dark and sinister, like in an Expressionist woodcut. Linking the study of history to aesthetics, Rosenzweig explained that "[s]cientific curiosity and aesthetic appetite [*Stoffhunger*] no longer fill me today, though I was once under the spell of both, particularly the latter." He compared the academic scholar to a "vampire."[10]

Abandoning historical research and "aesthetic appetite," Rosenzweig described himself as having gone to "the vaults of my own being" and its "ancient treasure chest." By this he meant Judaism. Those occasions had been the "supreme moments of my life." But cursory inspection no longer satisfied. Now his hands dug deeper into the bottomless chest. He went away with "treasure," with as "much as his arms could carry." Now he claimed to possess his own talent, mastering it, whereas previously it had possessed him. In fact, the letter shows something else. Now a philosopher, his life had fallen under "the rule of a 'dark drive' which I'm aware that I merely *name* by calling it 'my Judaism.'" His attraction to Judaism was every bit as demonic as the one that had drawn him to historical form and aesthetic appetite.[11]

The architectural reference to "the vaults of my being" is consistent with Rosenzweig's vision of Judaism, as can be seen in the images of Judaism and Christianity in *The Star of Redemption*: Jewish life arises from a single people, whereas Christian life emerges from a conglomeration of individuals, which is why the Christian supposedly needs to draw people together and the Jew does not. By "art," Rosenzweig meant the applied arts of church architecture, church music, and miracle play, not the fine arts, which supposedly sunder creator and consumer from the world, art for art's sake being "an ultimate aside." Using spatial metaphors, Rosenzweig sees fine art as a "prison," a "peculiar realm" spatially set apart from everyday life, whereas the applied arts find their way from "that peculiar realm" "back into life." Anticipating the closing phrase of *The Star of Redemption*, the phrase "into life" is repeated twice in the applied art discussion, to emphasize the point. No "demanding sweetheart," applied art is the "good wife" that prepares a man for "the marketplace" (i.e., everyday life) and public life.[12] Church architecture frees the prisoners, redeeming them. Painters decorate walls, sculptors adorn columns and cornices, draftsmen illuminate holy books. Freed from the confines of ideal space, the applied arts create a "real space" that is centered on revealed spatial directions, fixed points from which radiate a "fixed, immovable, created space, where small and large, middle and end, above and below, east and west are meaningful."[13] For their part, residential, commercial, official buildings, assembly halls, theaters, and inns are all devoted to particular and specialized purposes, their space subdivided according to function. In contrast, church space is uniform, "pure and simple," an oriented space around one basic room. Combining beauty and function, church spaces are "beautiful of form and yet for a purpose."[14] The single room creates the desire for community by anticipating the "feeling of unification in every individual even before this unification itself has been established."[15] By creating real time, music will then elevate that "initial togetherness" into a conscious and active togetherness. The space created by architecture is filled by the chorale, sung in a mighty unison.[16] Words and feelings lose their arbitrary character; they become necessary and durable. The person "speaks, but what he says are not his words but the words set to music which are common to all."[17]

Speaking of the poetry of dance, festive processions, parades, tournaments, and pageants, Rosenzweig recalled Cologne at carnival time, Olympic stadiums, and the Bayreuth stage. It would all sound like fascism were it not for the following: the glance, the simplest gesture, has "the power to dissolve all that is rigid." This includes the rigidity of church space. Dance does not find its way into church. Its enclosed space cannot accommodate the idea of redemption. The idea of redemption opens the circle and turns it into a spiral. It bursts the locked gate as the procession proceeds out of the church confines and into the city. Corpus Christi is the festival of processionals par excellence. The church "must export its cult into the world for the sake of redemption." In doing so, it bursts its own space.[18]

For all its devotion to the spatial arts, the church begins to look as cosmopolitan and uprooted as Judaism, while, ironically, Judaism assumes a much firmer spatial character than Christianity. Indeed, that was probably the precise point: to erase the aesthetics of difference between Judaism and Christianity, but only at the end of the book, and to do so on Jewish terms. Unlike Christian space, Jewish space endures.[19] However, the Jewish life presented in the Judaism chapter of *The Star of Redemption* builds on a liturgical expression whose temporal and lyrical character might lead one to overlook its spatial dimension.

The first hint of Judaism's spatial and visual character comes in the introduction to part III of Rosenzweig's text, which introduces "the possibility of entreating the Kingdom." Rosenzweig's understanding of the cultic prayer presumably common to both Christianity and Judaism relied heavily on metaphors of house, room, and ocular technologies. Observing that the cult "appears merely to build the house in which God may take up residence," he asks, "can it really force the exalted guest to move in?" This prayer of the believer entreating God's presence presumes an undergirding spatial orientation. It occurs *in the midst* of the believing congregation.[20] The Kingdom represents that universal, believing congregation at that messianic point in time when God will have entered into its midst. But where is the Kingdom now? Rosenzweig compared the entreating prayer to a technological device, to "a searchlight" that "illuminates the Kingdom."[21] A startling image, it suggests that the Kingdom does not lie in the future but looms out there now. Unlit and in the dark, it requires lighting. Its invisible existence subsists simultaneously with our own in the present.

Again, at the end of this introduction, Rosenzweig turned to the image of the star. We have not yet seen what he called "the star of redemption." But like the Kingdom, it's out there, simultaneous with our own existence. It too assumes a spatial locus. The "star" is an anagram of absolute truth, a figure that presents the isolated truths of God, world, person, creation, revelation, and redemption all at once. It forms a "material point which moves in space." Only after "telescope and spectroscope have brought it to us do we now know it as we know a tool of our daily use or a painting in our chambers: in familiar perceptions."[22] One adapts the technology of prayer in order to bring these forms, invisible to the naked eye, into visible view.

How does this bear upon Judaism and its relation to Christianity and space? According to Rosenzweig, the Kingdom and "the star of redemption" constitute figures of world redemption and absolute truth that outstrip the limited forms of Judaism and Christianity. This might suggest that the Kingdom's Jewish component remains temporal and the Christian component plastic. But the strategy of referencing Jewish synagogue space in the chapter on Christianity undermines the neat division of Judaism and time on the one hand, against Christianity and space on the other. Significantly, Christianity never comes into view in the Judaism chapter, but Judaism appears repeatedly throughout the Christianity chapter. It is as if Rosenzweig wanted to press the polemical point that Christianity depends on Judaism and not vice versa. The image of "Zion and all the world, Bethlehem-Ephrathah and the 'thousands of Judah'" illustrates the character of church architecture as fixed around a revealed center.[23] A complex image, it situates Judaism and Jewish messianism geographically. Zion stands over and against, set apart from, but in the midst of, the nations of the world. For its part, Bethlehem and Ephraim form a circle within a circle amid the myriads of Judah. Thus conceived, Jewish space forms into a Kingdom patterned upon the image of a circle of its own with a fixed center in the midst of world space.

Plastic objects fill the world of spatial extension and shape Judaism, no less than Christianity. Space overcomes time. That is why Rosenzweig turned to the cultic object after describing the unicellular space of church architecture. In his view, cultic objects "achieve essentiality as objects." In other words, they resist every change in form; their visage remains stable and fixed over time. And oddly enough, this being the Christianity chapter, the first examples provided by Rosenzweig are the Torah scroll and the Scroll of Esther! Ancient documents preserved in ancient form, they do not change. This, in his view, shows how cultic space transforms everything subjective into an abiding, eternal form. This includes anything that might change, anything personal. That too is the effect created by cultic garments. In cultic space, the body does without the expression of personality. One "dresses according to the rule of the space which unites him with others."[24] Again, Rosenzweig referred to "the ancient garb in the Jewish ritual" before considering Catholic and Eastern Orthodox ritual. In short, his wonderful description of cultic space in the Christianity chapter presumes Jewish cultic space, the enduring objects that fill it, and their abiding effect upon the human subject.

Mentions of Jewish ritual space continue to interrupt the chapter on Christianity as Rosenzweig turns to an analysis of gesture. At the very point in the Christianity chapter where dance is discussed, Rosenzweig presents Yom Kippur, "our festival of redemption," when traditionally observant

Jewish congregants fall to the ground, reenacting sacral rites from the time of the Second Temple in Jerusalem. According to Rosenzweig, the Yom Kippur prostration bursts every space, erasing all time. But does it? The aggadah that he cites recounts a miracle that was said to occur in the sanctuary on Yom Kippur. The assembled multitude was said to have crowded so closely that there was no room left to stand. However, at the very moment that those who were standing had to prostrate themselves, "there was endlessly much room left over."[25] The space within the Temple confine had expanded.

Rosenzweig interprets this to mean that Jewish space proves miraculously elastic, open, and durable: "The gates of our Jewish houses of worship may remain closed, for when Israel kneels, there is suddenly room for all mankind in what was hitherto a confined space." In the view expressed here, dance is a cultic act in Judaism. Examples include the holiday of Simhat Torah, when observant Jews dance with the Torah, and "the dance of the Hasid who 'praises God with all his limbs.'"[26] Whereas dance shatters the walls of the church as it proceeds outside the church and into the village, in Judaism, dance occurs inside the synagogue, as the festival procession proceeds into life. Elastic, the synagogue includes all humanity within a narrowly circumscribed space.

The synagogue and cathedral may seem distinctly unmodern or even anti-modern forms. At best, they might call to mind Feininger's *Cathedral of Socialism* or the utopian Expressionism expressed at the Bauhaus before Gropius sacked the more mystically inclined Johannes Itten in favor of the more exacting and rational type of modernism favored by Lazlo Moholy-Nagy. I would argue that the theatricality that informs Rosenzweig's understanding of religious life brings modern Jewish thought into the Bauhaus, where play, theater, and stage theory were taken seriously, as can been seen in Kandinsky's comment on theater space: "That building (architecture), which can be nothing if not colored (painting), and which at any given moment is capable of fusing divisions of space (sculpture), sucks in streams of people through the open doors and lines them up according to a strict schema. All eyes in one direction, all are tuned to a given source. The highest receptive tension waiting to be discharged. This is the outward power of the theater, which only has to be given new form."[27] Theater also constitutes the "outward power" of cultic space in Rosenzweig's work. Like the theater, the cathedral and synagogue fuse all the arts (color, sculpture, architecture, music). They too generate "receptive tension waiting to discharge," directing the eye and tuning the ear in one direction. Ritual life has turned into a kind of theater space, simultaneously optic, sonic, and tactile.

Are theater and theatrical space what attracted Rosenzweig, a thoroughly modern person, to Judaism and Jewish ritual, understood in theatrical terms as a combination of space, cultic objects, costume, and dance? In

"The New Thinking," Rosenzweig compared God, world, and humans in abstract isolation to "the cast, the theater program, which is also not a part of the drama itself and which one nevertheless does well to read before-hand."[28] In *The Star of Redemption*, Rosenzweig referred to drama as an "about-face into life." All that goes in to the work of art stimulates the spectator such that "[t]he door of the personal realm of art opens and discloses the way into life."[29] On a smaller scale, the synagogue provides an applied stage, a drama between love and death through the language of creation, revelation, and redemption. In a word, *The Star of Redemption* becomes a text about creating theater.

The Star of Redemption, the discussion of the holiday cycle presumes what Kalman Bland has called "a fully engaged, well-tempered sensorium."[30] Four of the five senses appear in Rosenzweig's account: taste, touch, sight, sound. "Every mouthful of bread and every sip of wine tastes just as wonderful as the first we ever savored."[31] The sense of taste underlies the "very act of renewing the life of the body" that is ritualized in the common festival meal.[32] The Yom Kippur costume—the death shrouds men traditionally wear under the shawl, "the chiton and tunic of antiquity," the cloth that touches male flesh—is nothing less than the "wholly visible sign" of eternity in time.[33] In their shrouds, the community of men stands "lonely and naked, straight before the throne of God." On Yom Kippur, the person confronts "the eyes of his judge." No longer guilty before man. All sins pardoned. A merciful divine face. "And God lifts up his countenance" to this "united and lonely pleading of men in their shrouds." The sequence concludes in sound. The man "to whom God's countenance" has lifted now "bursts out" into an "exultant profession" that "'[t]he Lord is God': this God of love, he alone is God!'"[34]

The dramatic vision of God vouchsafed on Yom Kippur remains partial, limited to a brief glimpse at God's countenance and the appearance of His "eyes," in anticipation of a more complete vision of Yom Kippur at the end of *The Star of Redemption*. Setting the finale in theatrically architectural space, this last section carries the title "Gate." At the gate, between this world and the next, God's face hovers fully revealed, simultaneously six sense organs (two ears, a nose, two eyes, and a mouth) appearing together like the six-pointed Star of David. Rosenzweig calls it a "mask." Describing the base formed out of the "receptive organs" (ears and nose), Rosenzweig wrote that "they are the building blocks, as it were, which together compose the face, the mask," adding that "[t]he Star of Redemption," now that we know it is a mask, "is become countenance [glancing] at me and out of which I glance." God's truth has put on a human mask, a living form. He turns to look at me. And wearing the same mask, I peer out at Him. The mask work is now complete. Masked, face to face, the subject anticipates God's consummate kiss, like Moses at his death. "Thus does God seal" the truth, with a kiss, "and so too does man."[35]

The image of a mask, along with the accounts of Yom Kippur, assume a highly staged and choreographed expression. All this drama and mask work gets anticipated in the synagogue, week in and week out, year after year. Ritual theater and theatrical ritual create the kind of performance to which one returns again and again. The theatricality of ritual expression is what drew Rosenzweig to its service and made him think it could draw others to it. No wonder that Rosenzweig explicitly compared the synagogue to the theater and concert hall in a 1917 letter to his cousin Richard Ehrenberg. This letter concerned the creation of an Academy for the Science of Judaism that Rosenzweig had proposed in the open letter to Hermann Cohen entitled "It Is Time" (*Zeit Ists*). In the letter to Ehrenberg, Rosenzweig argued that German youth go to school and then to the theater and concert hall. The latter serve as a "magnified object lesson" that projects what they learned at school onto a broader scale. The synagogue should play the same function: a place to project the language and literature learned at school. Clearly, it was not "religion," nor simply moral community, that drew Rosenzweig to religion. Otherwise he would have compared the synagogue to the church, not to the theater and concert hall and the sensory experiences associated with them.

Jewish life as understood by Rosenzweig includes a highly homosocial image of home as a "platform" alongside the space of the synagogue. The description of Jewish life in *The Star of Redemption* includes a very strong emphasis upon men, alternating between the paterfamilias on the one hand, and the relationship between old men and young boys within a community of men outside the home, on the other. Rosenzweig's account of the Sabbath includes the synagogue service but pays more attention to the paterfamilias at home. Six days he has worked, attending to his affairs. Now the manservant and maidservant must also rest. Then "all the house" is free from noise and commanded to rest. Similarly, Passover, Shavuot, and Sukkot, which revolve around a heterosocial common meal eaten at home (during which wine and jest are said to dissolve the "autocracy" of family life into community), are compared to occasions of male fellowship associated with the monastery, lodge, club, and fraternity.[36] Thus, at the festival meal, "The sweet, fully ripened fruit of humanity craves the community of man with man."[37] Similarly, he emphasized the "greeting," which was customary not only after the Jewish festival meal, when guests from the previous night would greet each other in the street, but also at such all-male events as the military parade (saluting the flag, the review before the commander-in-chief).[38] Envisioned in this way, the collective meal and greeting turned a community into an exclusively male compact.

In this intensely gendered body of work, "man" is more than a generic term for humanity. Rosenzweig knew that according to Jewish tradition, only men wear the shroud at their wedding, at the Passover *seder*, and on Yom Kippur, and only men enjoy the privilege of studying Torah. Just prior to the description of the wedding and Yom Kippur shroud, Rosenzweig writes: "Only man needs to be aware that the Torah is the basis of life. When a daughter is born, the father simply prays that he may lead her to the bridal canopy and to good works. For a woman has this basis of Jewish life without having to learn it deliberately over and over, as the man who is less securely rooted in the depth of nature is compelled to do. According to ancient law, it is the woman who propagates Jewish blood."[39] However important her role in determining the Jewish bloodline, she fulfills this role passively and invisibly. Rosenzweig advances the standard apologetic for her exclusion from the study of Torah and observance of its positive time-bound commandments.

The power of sensation and sensual life, an attraction to men, to death, and an intense aesthetic and even erotic appetite formed the dark drive that drove Rosenzweig's approach to Judaism and Jewish life in general and to Jewish ritual law and its observance in particular. Unlike so many at the time, Rosenzweig was able to apply his own aesthetic sensibility to the apparently rigid world of a moribund law. Touching upon the entire gamut of sensual perception, he envisions a tactile world of men in their *talitot*, in their shrouds, a young boy leading Rosenzweig though exotic Uskub, the eros of sexual reproduction, creating a community out of its own viscous substance, a combination of seed and blood. Leora Batnitzky has argued that Rosenzweig did not think that Judaism needed art, which his comparison with Christianity, discussed above, would seem to support. But this claim ignores Rosenzweig's profoundly spatial and even architectural understanding of Judaism, although Batnitzky rightly notes that, according to Rosenzweig, prior to Enlightenment and Emancipation, Judaism was itself a piece of art, not art for art's sake, but wholly art, understood as such—uncanny, self-contained, and luminously beautiful.[40]

The Jewish aesthetic and its architecture provide a new lens through which to understand a critical question about the status and authority of mitzvah in the modern period. In an open letter to Buber, published in *Der Jude* and entitled "The Builders," Rosenzweig had this to say about the law: "From Mendelssohn on, our entire people has subjected itself to the torture of this embarrassing questioning: the Jewishness of every individual has squirmed on the needle point of a 'why.'" Rosenzweig took particular issue with the nineteenth-century neo-Orthodox thinker Samson Raphael Hirsch, who believed that one observed mitzvah because God commanded it at Sinai. He called Hirsch an "architect" who converted this foundation into a protective wall. Piling midrash on top of midrash, aggadah on top of aggadah, Rosenzweig countered, "No doubt the Torah, both written and oral, was given to Moses on Sinai, but was it not created before the creation of the world?" And was it not written in black and white fire? Was not the world created for its sake? Studied by Adam's son Seth? Observed by the patriarchs? Given in seventy languages? It has six hundred and thirteen commandments, "a number that . . . mocks all endeavor to count what is countless."[41] Did it not include everything that later generations came to interpret? Did not its vast scope allow later scholars to interpret the ornamental crownlets and tips of letters, outdoing the comprehension of Moses? Concluding this interrogative barrage, the paragraph ends with an exclamation point: "The Torah, which God himself learns day after day!"[42]

Beauty and sublimity attracted Rosenzweig to mitzvah. Against the Orthodox Hirsch, Rosenzweig took issue with the "pseudo-historical theory of its origin" and the "pseudo-juristic theory of its power to obligate," that is, with God having "commanded" them upon the Jewish people. He also rejected the "pseudo-logical theory of the unity of God" and the "pseudo-ethical theory of the love of one's neighbor" espoused by Abraham Geiger's liberal Judaism, arguing that the essence of Judaism has little to do with the logical rigor of its monotheism or the purity of its ethic. Neither community nor the need for meaning drew Rosenzweig to the observance of mitzvah. Mitzvah was not a means toward a social good but, like love, an end in itself: "miracle does not constitute history, a people is not a juridical fact, martyrdom is not an arithmetical problem, *and love is not social*."[43] Following the architectural logic of "The Builders," one observes the Torah and its commandments because of love, because of their structure, because they are beautiful and sublime, because their number "mocks the endeavor to count what is countless." So Rosenzweig heaped Torah text on top of Torah text to form one great *rhetorical* question. The image of black and white fire shimmers. Like a work of art as understood by Kant, it has no instrumental or extrinsic purpose outside its own remarkable edifice. Indeed, the social world was created for its sake, not the other way around. Builders are architects. In this view, Hirsch had used history and law as "the foundation of a rigid and narrow structure, unbeautiful despite its magnificence."[44] By implication, the Judaism whose magnificence Rosenzweig sought to construct on the foundation of "law" would be the polar opposite: free, open, and beautiful. The concluding statement, "[t]he Torah, which God himself learns day after day!" is carried by an exclamation point in the wake of the questions that precede it. It acts like a judgment, as if to say, "How divine!"

The intersection between ritual and a spatial/visual aesthetic becomes more acute as he drew more and more into the gravitational orbit of Jewish ritual. He wrote to his parents in 1917 about going to the Orthodox Hildesheimer synagogue for the High Holidays of Rosh ha-Shana and Yom Kippur in 1914 because it offered the most beautiful service in Berlin.[45] A 1922 letter to Joseph Prager noted the "great joy" taken in a marvelously beautiful (*wunderschön*) Yom Kippur service arranged for him at his home. He describes the blue room of the family apartment bedecked by a colossal display of cloth and candles, a white and gold cloth spread over a cabinet. He notes further that on the next day, the lighting was natural because the ceiling light had gone out the day before and "fortunately" could not be repaired in time, while that evening, thanks to "another lucky accident," the closing recitations of the *Shema* were preceded by a full five-minute silence because the *neilah* service had concluded some five minutes too soon.[46] The impression left by the event recorded in the letter to Prager depends on a unique combination of halakha and happenstance, the tactile feel of cloth, the shimmering glow of candle and natural light, the intermingling of ritual dictate with silence. At the simplest level, the letter shows great attention to color, light, texture, and sound. More technically, it suggests that the beauty of the mitzvah consists in the way it combines necessity and the accidental. Halakha forbids Jews from turning electricity on and off during the Sabbath and holidays and requires the congregation to conclude the Yom Kippur recitation of the *Shema* at dusk. In Rosenzweig's account, these requirements combine with circumstance to create beautiful effects. The everyday annoyance of an electric light that happened to go out the night before brought natural light into a Yom Kippur space. The inconvenience of the service that happened to end five minutes too soon forced a long and pregnant five-minute silence. The accidental was ordered into a lovely sensory pattern.

Despite the elaborate staging of *The Star of Redemption* and its intensified pathos, there was something unpretentious about the way Rosenzweig drew art out of Jewish life, as seen in his letter to Prager and in his writings from the 1920s. One notes the simple act of judgment that comes near the end of an essay outlining his understanding of adult Jewish education. In "Bildung und kein Ende," Rosenzweig opposed the formulation of plans, proclamations, and programs. He preferred questions, doubt, and desire.[47] "Wait," he counseled, "People will appear who prove by the very fact of their coming that . . . the Jewish human being is alive in them."[48] One should "lose the 'true ring' of dead-sure conviction." Who will come and why? Rosenzweig averred, "I can already hear voices saying: 'How vague, how undefined, how cloudy' . . . I can also hear the voices of those who say, 'How little' . . . But perhaps here and there someone will say longingly, 'How beautiful' and think hesitantly, 'If only such a thing only existed.'"[49] In the same vein, Rosenzweig's "program" remained intentionally vague, pared down, bordering on the abstract. What makes Jewish life—and what makes it beautiful, in Rosenzweig's view—lies between the completely obscure representation of raw, unfiltered sensation and precisely determined cognitive representation.

No doubt this opens modern Jewish thought to the objection that images and eros, "mere beauty," or perhaps more precisely, sheer expression, provide a weak foundation upon which to fashion Jewish life and thought. From the very start, other contributors to the German Jewish Renaissance, such as Hugo Bergmann and Ernst Simon, voiced severe opposition to a form of literary Judaism that could not meet the bar of truth, including

Elias Auerbach's proposal for an educational program that would draw children to the beauty of Jewish customs and literature. In an article entitled "Traditionelles und nationals Judentum," published in *Der Jude* (1916–17), Auerbach stressed the role of aesthetic form and feeling, not religious content and intellect. Simon attacked the program some ten years later, also in *Der Jude*. Under the title "Erziehung zur Tradition," he rejected any educational program based on religious fairy tales (*Storchmärchen*), the eventual exposure of which would bring spiritual catastrophe to those raised upon them.[50] As for Rosenzweig, recall how he rejected a narrowly conceived "aesthetic" of rarefied art objects, mere beauty, and the ideal of art as an independent and autonomous value, in favor of the idea that form, content, beauty, truth, and ethics come together to form a luminous and dissonant whole.

To be sure, critics might still want to skewer Rosenzweig by falling back upon the idea of autonomous art and concluding with Kant that all taste is relative to the individual. Yet Kant also knew that the individual subject seeks to share his or her aesthetic judgment, as did Rosenzweig. The vagueness of the Lehrhaus program, the free beauty of its form, and its lack of fixed contents were meant to surprise and enchant, to elicit a spontaneous response, like the sudden inhalation of air. Rosenzweig hoped that rendering an aesthetic judgment, and sharing it with others, would pull modern Jews into the study of Jewish life. What kind of beauty would this need to be? The pure beauties that had appealed to Kant at the end of the eighteenth century were abstract, nonrepresentational patterns, in whose real existence the subject takes no interest. In contrast, Rosenzweig belonged to a generation who broke with that conception of autonomous beauty divorced from the rigor of truth, ethics, spiritual encounter, and everyday life. Especially in modern times, beauty is not always "beautiful," nor aesthetics always "aesthetic." The attraction to beautiful and erotically charged images allowed Rosenzweig to revel in a sometimes violent expression of harsh judgment and dissonant sound.

While beauty and expression do not represent stable standards upon which to build religious life, they might still prove more durable than theoretical and moral truth claims. Many profoundly beautiful and complex works of art have outlasted the scientific truths and social mores of their time. Art styles can be rejuvenated and transfigured, long after their initial demise. In much the same way, great works of religious thought take on a style of their own. They assume a specific shape and expression that might very well survive the exact truths they present. The same can be said for the Bible and the telegraphically awkward style of the Talmud. As for Rosenzweig, I suspect that readers continue to read him today for the charisma of his personal presence, for the great and complicated beauty of his images of Jewish life, and for the sexual charge that drives his understanding of truth and ethics.

Chapter 14
Reestablishing a "Jewish Spirit" in American Synagogue Music: The Music of A. W. Binder

Mark Kligman

During the first half of the twentieth century, Abraham Wolf Binder (1895–1966) rose to prominence as a prolific composer of synagogue music and champion of Jewish music. According music a central role in religious experience, Binder was concerned that synagogue attendance was waning because congregants had high musical expectations that synagogue music failed to fulfill. Not only could contemporary synagogue music not compete with the concert hall and the radio but, in Binder's view, it was also not Jewish enough.[1] As early as 1927, Binder despaired that music of the synagogue, lacking a "Jewish spirit," was not an expression of the "Jewish soul."[2] Thirty years later, he was still complaining that "extraneous musical influences which had nothing to do with our sacred *nusach ha-tefillah*—our Jewish musical tradition—had invaded this sacred domain. This was alienating our people from the synagogue."[3] Binder attributed the problem to poorly educated composers unfamiliar with the Jewish musical tradition. Binder, who started out as a synagogue musician in New York City, dedicated his career to rectifying the situation by creating a distinctive form of Jewish musical expression. While assimilated Jews during the mid-twentieth century led secular lives in the outside world, Binder wanted them to be drawn to the synagogue by compelling Jewish music. Just what that music should be, as reflected in Binder's compositions and writings, is the subject of this essay.

Creating a Jewish Music for the Reform Synagogue

Binder declared, in forceful terms, "Without a distinctive Jewish art we are not a nation; we cannot speak of a complete culture, nor can we call ourselves a civilization."[4] This idea had never been a raison d'être for Reform synagogue music in America. On the contrary, the ideal way to glorify God in the synagogue was with the repertoire of the concert hall. Accordingly, most nineteenth-century Central European synagogue music basically shed traditional European cantorial music for the more "enlightened" musical repertoire of Protestant hymns and adaptations of classical music. In Binder's view, those composers and their American successors had gone too far. The lack of a "Jewish spirit"[5] enabling congregants to "feel the Jewish soul"[6] deprived them of a "distinctive Jewish art."[7] Binder wanted music to rise to the level of "pure religious art"[8] capable of offering a "religio-musical experience unobtainable in any other manner."[9] The challenge was to create synagogue music that was sophisticated while still rooted in the past, a musical worship experience that drew from tradition while conforming to modern standards of musical taste. Binder's solution was to preserve elements of the Eastern European synagogue tradition, in particular the solo chanting of the *hazzan*, which he considered a hallmark of its authenticity. Cantillation of the Bible had significantly waned in Reform synagogues during the nineteenth century. Likewise, the solo chanting of the liturgy was replaced with composed music for organ and choir.

Binder envisioned a service that would include traditional cantillation as well as newly composed music based on traditional modes and melodies:

> We are here concerned with keeping the music of the synagogue alive and in tune with the development of the musical art. We realize and appreciate the beauty and originality of the cantillation modes of the *Torah* on the Sabbath. We do not advocate any change in that direction whatsoever, outside of the fact that this very important function ought to be performed by one who knows the tropes and can sing them with a beautiful voice. Nor do we wish to interfere with the pure and almost naïve beauty of the *nusach ha-tefillah* as we hear it chanted by the ordinary congregant who is by instinct musically endowed. Our quarrel is with most of the vocal and instrumental music which we hear in many synagogues throughout the country—Orthodox, Conservative, and Reform.[10]

Particularly sensitive to the power of music to set mood, Binder took issue with the "secular atmosphere"[11] created by synagogue music based on foreign sources:

> With regard to music borrowed from foreign sources, let me say that every type of music creates its own specific mood. When we hear Moussorgsky or Rimsky-Korsakov we are immediately transplanted to a Russian atmosphere even if by chance a Hebrew text were set to this music. The same is true of an air or chorus from a French or Italian opera when treated, or rather mistreated, in this manner. Why should such incongruities be permitted when our own musical heritage is so rich?[12]

More specifically, Jewish chant not only gave the music its sacred spirit but also set the mood for each part of the liturgy:

> The tremendous musical structure which our ancestors wrought in our round-the-year liturgy over a period of more than 2,000 years, consists of modes and melodies divided into small motifs, each one designed to create the atmosphere of a particular holiday, prayer, special occasion, or spiritual moment. If this musical tradition

is wrong or absent, a service loses its sacred and traditional spirit. The sacred spirit of our people and its prayers are enshrined in our *nusach ha-tefillah*.[13]

To make traditional liturgy the basis for new compositions was to accord melody a central place in them. More specifically, composers should make use of the proper *nusach* and base harmonization, melody, and rhythm on it.

Binder routinely criticized nineteenth-century composers of synagogue music for not including traditional modes and defined his own role within the history of synagogue music as that of effectively reasserting the essentiality of tradition, which he identified with the "authenticity" and "originality" of the Eastern European liturgical tradition. Why did Binder single out the Eastern European tradition as "authentic" synagogue music? Moreover, what criteria of authenticity did he apply in adopting some features of the Jewish musical past and rejecting others?

A Usable Musical Past

During the period from the 1920s through the 1960s, American Jewry stood at a crossroads between its European past, as exemplified by the East European Jews arriving in large numbers from the 1880s, and its desire for assimilation, an aspiration of the German Jews who had arrived even earlier. This dichotomy was expressed musically as well. The Central European Reform Jewish liturgical music of the nineteenth century used classical music idioms, was metrically driven, and emphasized the singing of hymns as an important communal experience, modeled after the Protestant church. In contrast, Eastern European music was more ornate melodically and made use of vocal improvisation developed in the art of *hazzanut*. By the 1920s, according to the historian of Judaism Michael Meyer, a synthesis was envisioned in which "Reform congregations would give up their Teutonic coldness and the excess of rationalism they had imported from Germany while the Russians and Poles would cast off their inappropriate vestigial orthodoxy."[14] The American style of the first part of the twentieth century, what was called *Minhag* America, combined these approaches. What did such a synthesis sound like?

How Binder envisioned this synthesis can be seen from his assessment, both positive and negative, of the most influential nineteenth-century composers of synagogue music. Chief among these was Salomon Sulzer (1804–90). From 1826 Sulzer officiated at the New Synagogue in Vienna, where his fine musicianship and especially his singing won such admirers as Schubert and Liszt. Sulzer's most important contribution was *Shir Zion*, a collection of his own compositions as well as compositions by others that he had commissioned. *Shir Zion* was published in two volumes in 1840 and 1866, respectively. Sulzer wanted to "purify" traditional Jewish melodies, whose ornate Baroque musical elaborations diminished the dignity of the service. He did this, first, by "refining" the traditional melody, preferring a straightforward lyrical melodic setting of the text to ornate elaboration. This can be seen in the symmetrical phrases in his melodic settings. Second, Sulzer sought to harmonize these melodies within the rules of musical art current in his time. Third, he wrote out the music for the cantor and choir, previously an oral tradition, and eliminated improvisation and congregational singing. Finally, he sought to professionalize the office of the cantor as a musician. Widely respected throughout Central Europe and attracting many important students, Sulzer had an unprecedented and enduring impact on synagogue music.

The Central European synagogue composer and choral director Louis Lewandowski (1821–94), also a self-conscious modernizer, conducted Sulzer's music and carried Sulzer's program of refinement even further. Lewandowski served in Berlin as the music director at the Old Synagogue in the Heidereutergasse, and after 1866 at the New Synagogue. His musical compositions appear in two well-known publications: *Kol Rinah U'T'fillah* (1871), for one and two voices, and *Todah W'simrah* (1876–82), for four voices and soli, with optional organ accompaniment. Lewandowski provided settings of traditional melodies and wrote unique compositions, both with and without *nusach*. His music had a major impact on both Reform and traditional synagogues throughout Europe and America well into the twentieth century.

Few Eastern European synagogues incorporated such musical reforms, preferring to maintain the traditional Eastern European cantorial style, with its traditional melodies and Jewish prayer modes. Still, some cantors did come to Vienna to study with Sulzer and they adapted his musical innovations for the Eastern European synagogue. One such figure, Nissan Blumenthal (1805–1903), who was born in Ukraine, introduced the German style of synagogue music at the Brody Synagogue in Odessa. He founded a choir school in 1841 and developed choral singing in four voices. Eliezer Gerovich (1844–1913), a student of Blumenthal, began as a *hazzan* at the Choral Synagogue in Berdichev. After 1887, he was chief *hazzan* in Rostov-on-Don. In his settings of traditional melodies for cantor and choir, which make use of extremely ornate cantorial phrases, the cantor sings above the choir at climactic moments. In contrast with Sulzer, Gerovich and several other East European synagogue composers of his period did not make use of symmetrical phrases, favoring the melodic freedom of traditional *nusach* instead.

The hallmark of the Eastern European style is the use of recurring melodic fragments that convey a deep emotional feeling to the congregation and ornate musical embellishments that transport the listener into a spiritual realm. Word repetition is not uncommon. Thus, the nicely patterned phrases of Central Europe came to be known as *hazzanut ha-seder* (orderly *hazzanut*), in contrast with the free and ornate Eastern European style, which was known as *hazzanut ha-regesh* or emotional *hazzanut*. It is this latter style that became the foundation for the Golden Age of the Cantorate in America during the first few decades of the twentieth century. This style is epitomized by such cantorial stars as Gerson Sirota and Yossele Rosenblatt. However distinct, *hazzanut ha-seder* and *hazzanut ha-regesh* were also intermingled in the compositions of cantors who were immersed in the Eastern European musical world but had studied with such cantors as Sulzer. Thus, David Nowakowsky (1848–1921), a cantor highly regarded by Binder, was appointed choirmaster and associate cantor in 1870 of the Odessa Synagogue, known as the Broder-Schul. He worked with the cantors Nissan Blumenthal and Pinchos Minkowsky (1859–1924), who worked in Odessa and Ukraine. He is known for his choral compositions, which became Binder's model for a balanced synthesis of Central and Eastern European musical elements that became characteristic of synagogue music in the United States and was later known as *Minhag* America.

American Reform synagogues drew on contemporary European composers, predominantly Sulzer and Lewandowski, as well as on American composers. Nineteenth-century American synagogue innovators included Sigmund Schlesinger (1835–1906) and Edward Stark (1863–1918), whose music was devoid of traditional prayer modes. Schlesinger, an organist at a synagogue in Mobile, Alabama, set texts for the synagogue service to operatic excerpts from Bellini, Donizetti, and Rossini, while Stark, a cantor at Temple Emanuel in San Francisco, used some traditional melodies. His compositions were considered naïve. The Hungarian-born Alois Kaiser (1840–1908) was an apprentice to Sulzer. After stints in Vienna (1859–63) and Prague (1863–66), he immigrated to America, where he served as cantor to Congregation Ohab Shalom in Baltimore. His collections of synagogue music include hymnal compositions, melodies with four-part chorale settings, following the Lutheran model of J. S. Bach.

These cantors and composers, though largely forgotten today, were instrumental in the emergence of *Minhag* America, a term coined by Isaac Mayer Wise, the mid-nineteenth-century progenitor of American Reform Judaism, to refer to a new and specifically American form of Jewish tradition. Originally the title of a prayerbook in 1856, *Minhag* America refers more generally to the Americanization of European Jewish traditions. Convinced that the communal singing of hymns was the quintessential religious experience, the Central Conference of American Rabbis resolved in 1892 to adopt Wise's hymnbook as the official hymnbook of American Jewish Reform congregations. In a discussion of this resolution, rabbis commented that their congregations had to sing so much non-Jewish music because so few Jewish composers valued hymns. At the 1892 conference, one representative, Rabbi Gutman, stated that he fully recognized the power of Christian worship to reside in the communal singing of hymns and encouraged Jews to follow suit. Accordingly, the *Union Prayer Book* of 1892 was followed by the *Union Hymnal* in 1897. By 1912, the first edition of the hymnal was deemed a failure, and rabbis encouraged cantors to devote their efforts to creating a more effective hymnal, which they did in a second edition. Binder became the editor of the third edition of the hymnal, which appeared in 1932. Although a part of many Reform congregations through the 1950s, hymn singing eventually fell out of fashion.

The Composer as a Young Man

Binder was immersed in synagogue music from an early age. His father was a *baal tefilah* (lay prayer leader) who had in turn learned the tradition from his father in Galicia. At the age of four, Abraham sang in his father's High Holiday choir and by six he was singing solos and chanting harmonies. Of his youthful enjoyment of the synagogue and musical fantasies, Binder later recalled that "all fascinated me, and I began to play *shul*, picturing myself as the *hazzan*. Later I dreamed some miracle which would make a choir of singers appear magically, and I would then lead them in the manner that I saw in the large synagogues on the East Side."[15] When Binder was seven, his father had him audition for Cantor Abraham Frachtenberg's choir, one of the large synagogue choirs in Manhattan, where Binder would sing until the age of fourteen. Frachtenberg, who was born in Galatz, Romania, and served as a *meshorer* (singer in a synagogue choir) in Berdichev, had a profound influence on Binder. He not only taught Binder choral conducting but also imbued him with a love for creating music and respect for traditional *nusach*.[16]

The idealization of the Eastern European tradition would permeate all of Binder's writings on synagogue music, no doubt as a result of his upbringing in a traditional Eastern European home, close relationship with his musical father, and singing in Frachtenberg's choir. In his last writing he stated, "The background of *nusach ha-tefillah*, which I inherited from my father and from Abraham Frachtenberg, was to stand me in good stead later on in my career as a synagogue musician."[17] He embarked on that career at the age of eleven, when he started studying piano, organ, and composition at the Settlement Music School. In 1911, at the tender age of sixteen, he became the organist and choir director at Temple Beth El in Greenpoint, Brooklyn, while also teaching harmony at the Neighborhood Music School (now the Manhattan School of Music). In 1916, he formed the Hadassah Choral Union, the first to sing "Palestinian" folk songs in America. A year later, he started a music program at the 92nd Street YMHA, which continued until 1958. In 1919 he received his Bachelor of Music degree from New York College of Music. Subsequent to holding several synagogue music positions, Binder was asked by Rabbi Stephen S. Wise in 1921 to teach at the Jewish Institute of Religion in 1921. Wise, who had seen Binder in a concert at the 92nd Street Y, believed that liturgical music was an important element of the Jewish religious service and provided Binder with a formative environment to further his interest in liturgical music. In 1922 Binder became choirmaster at the newly formed Free Synagogue. Teaching and creating liturgical music gave Binder an opportunity to explore how traditional forms of Jewish music might inspire new musical compositions. He sought to find "authentic" chants for the liturgy and championed Zionist folk songs. Binder studied biblical cantillation and reintroduced it in the Free Synagogue service, in contrast to common Reform practice, which favored reading the biblical text with no intonation. *Biblical Chant*, first published in 1959 (with a second edition in 1963) and still in print and used today, is the standard reference tool for learning the Eastern European melodies for cantillation.

Although his earliest published article was 1927, Binder did most of his writing during the last twenty-five years of his life, from 1941 to 1966. His articles, most of which are about synagogue music, were usually based on lectures that he gave at cantorial and rabbinic conferences, organ and hymn societies, and other forums. Later published in the proceedings of these events, they dealt for the most part with musical style, referring on occasion to the work of a composer, but only once including musical notation (1927). Ever a champion of Jewish music and an educator, Binder wrote for a readership of musicians and cantors, as well as for the interested general reader. These publications are the basis for the discussion of his assessment of the history of synagogue music that follows.

Assessing the History of Synagogue Music

Binder's earliest publication, his 1927 article about the Friday evening Sabbath liturgical prayer "V'shomru," foreshadows an assessment of the history of synagogue music that he would flesh out more fully in the years that followed. His major concerns were the retention of *nusach* in new compositions, the successful harmonization of traditional modal melodies, and the appropriate use of non-Jewish musical sources. Thus, while Binder admired Sulzer and Lewandowski for elevating the artistry of synagogue music, he criticized them for failing to make sufficient use of traditional melodies and not achieving a successful integration of harmony and modal traditions. Even when, on the rare occasion, a traditional Jewish melody did appear, the harmonization made the familiar melody unrecognizable: "In the synagogue music of the nineteenth century much of the true color of synagogue music was lost when the composers of that period attempted to harmonize our traditional music with the existing Western system of harmony. They did not go together."[18] Part of the problem was their overdependence on German church music, as a result of which their compositions lacked Jewish spirit. Thus, while they "were able to weave the traditional motifs through the recitatives for the cantor," rarely "do their choral works indicate that these composers were capable of that abandon, that complete embodiment of the Jewish spirit where we find the Jewish soul expressed. Their choral music was kept in forms with a watchful eye on their musical neighbor—the German church-chorale."[19]

In Binder's view, in emulating church music these composers were also trying to limit or even eliminate the "Oriental" aspects of traditional *nusach*, the mainstay of traditional Eastern European synagogue music. Writing in 1941, Binder observed:

Even the music of the great classicists and pioneers of synagogue choral music— Sulzer, Lewandowski, and [Samuel] Naumbourg—is not thoroughly Jewish in the light in which we understand it today. They created their works during an assimilationist period, and obviously kept off the tracks of synagogal musical tradition to suit the theories of the then active reform rabbis and laymen. Their congregants were taught not to want to hear those "Oriental modes and melodies," but rather tunes in the style of the purely European chorales and folk songs. A large literature of this synagogue music exists.[20]

The dichotomy between the European chorale versus the "Oriental modes" follows the Jewish ethnomusicologist A. Z. Idelsohn's view that the contribution of nineteenth-century Central European composers was to shed the old Oriental layer of the Jewish tradition in favor of an Enlightened and modern European sound.[21] In rare instances of their later works, Sulzer and Lewandowski did follow the innovations of their Eastern European contemporaries, an achievement that Binder acknowledged.[22]

Binder felt that the German style lacked expressiveness and advocated what he called the Eastern European solution, which applied "modern methods of musical composition to the ancient Jewish modes and melodies."[23] He praised East European cantors and musicians who succeeded in making the harmony follow the structure and flow of the traditional modal melodies, an achievement that eluded many a serious musician confronted by "the incongruity between the oriental *melos* of their musical tradition and the German harmonic system which was being employed as harmonic background."[24] From his first statement on the Eastern European style in 1927, Binder consistently idealized the harmonizing of modal melody and praised composers, most of them East Europeans, who were successful in doing so:

The Jewish spirit speaks in their works, without restriction or imitation, without the fear of Wagnerian criticism, such as was aimed at Meyerbeer and Mendelssohn. Everything, everything is felt in [David] Nowakowsky both in solo passages and in his choral treatments. His harmonies are genuinely semitic, containing that wonderful subtlety, coupled with simplicity. In [Samuel] Alman, as well, we feel the Jewish soul; we hear the Talmudic student at study, and all such other beautiful touches that Jewish life reveals . . . We are happy that after them [Sulzer and Lewandowski] came such creative spirits as Naumbourg, [Hirsch] Weintraub, Alman, [Eliezer]

Gerovitch, [Mordechai] Loewenstamm, [Anton] Dunajewski, [Anshel] Schorr, Nowakowsky. They were the builders of a structure which is still being built, and which hopefully will in the future tower to exalted musical heights.[25]

To support his observation, Binder compared seven settings of the "V'-shomru" prayer. He praised the settings by Nowakowsky and Alman for their free rhythm and chant-like phrasing and the enduring value of compositions by Gerovitch, which "remain useful for the modern service even in our own day."[26]

As for late nineteenth-century composers in America? They were not only of modest talent but also bad imitators of Sulzer and Lewandowski:

In our own country, the composers of synagogue music who immigrated here toward the last quarter of the nineteenth century were of rather meager musical stature. Men like Welsh, Kaiser, and Sparger did their best, indeed, but the best they achieved resulted only in a mediocre imitation of Sulzer and Lewandowski. We cannot call men like Kitziger and Schlesinger composers of synagogue music, for they were merely artisan-organists—organists called in to play and direct. With a new liturgy, and no music to suit it, they were forced into an unfortunate situation. In this emergency they had to compose, and nobody attempted to guide them . . . That music is not liturgical and is even anti-liturgical. At its best, it is quasi-operatic, saccharine and sentimental. Many of the tunes in these works were actually lifted from various Italian operas.[27]

To make things worse, Schlesinger had a major impact on the music performed in Reform synagogues: "His music . . . was almost totally devoid of any traditional elements, and more than any other, was responsible for the breakdown of the Jewish musical tradition in the Reform synagogue in this country."[28] Edward Stark was an improvement but lacked the "technical musical equipment needed to deal with the harmonization of a Jewish tune." At best, his compositions resembled those of Sulzer and Lewandowski in planting "synagogue music in an alien harmonic soil in the nineteenth century."[29]

In contrast, Binder viewed Ernest Bloch's symphonic works, particularly his "Jewish Cycle" (1910–13) and the *Avodat Hakodesh* (Sacred Service) (1930–33), as paradigmatic for two reasons: first, his use of a free chant-like melody, one that was not tied to a specific fixed rhythm, and second, his new approach to harmonization (a style of harmonization that was based on the mode of the melody, rather than only on major and minor scales). Bloch's compositions were able to "express the Jewish *melos* with a harmonic background which reflects its true spirit."[30] In this regard, Bloch's approach was consistent with Eastern European composers whom Binder admired for the use of non-Western folk melodies, including Mussorgsky and Rimsky-Korsakov, and Jewish composers who were inspired by them, particularly those associated with the Jewish Folk Music Society of St. Petersburg such as Joseph Achron, Moshe Milner, Solomon Rosowsky, and Jakov Weinberg.[31]

By the mid-1950s, Binder had become more optimistic. Reform congregations had grown in size and hired cantors and music directors, and American Jewish liturgical music had matured: "Instead of operatic tunes, we now have melodies based on our musical tradition—*nusach ha-tefillah.* Instead of the tonic-dominant harmonies characteristic of the nineteenth century, new harmonic efforts are made to retain the character of the Jewish melody. Instead of secular rhythms, we have rhythms related to the Hebrew language."[32] Thanks to research and discussion at the Mailamm Society and Jewish Music Forum with noted musicologists like Eric Werner, composers had a better understanding of "the nature of genuine synagogue music." New liturgical works for the synagogue created from the 1930s through the 1950s were moving in right the direction by emphasizing the use of traditional melodies or cantillation motifs in their compositions. In addition, free chant was being brought back into the synagogue in solos and choral compositions, "thus giving to the synagogue song a quality of authenticity and antiquity" and helping "to create the right atmosphere and spirit of the occasion . . . [S]ome of our modern composers will sometimes use a traditional tune *in toto*; others will compose an original tune in a traditional mode. An important step forward is the use of the correct mode and melody at the right time."[33] At the same time, Binder repeatedly insisted that his approach was but one possible solution, not the ultimate one, though it was an advance over what synagogue composers were creating at the end of the nineteenth century and beginning of the twentieth century.

After forty years of thinking about these issues, Binder offered a succinct summation of his view of the history of Jewish liturgical music:

The background of *nusach ha-tefillah*, which I inherited from my father and from Abraham Frachtenberg, was to stand me in good stead later on in my career as a synagogue musician. At the age of sixteen, I became organist and choir director successively in two small temples for several years. It was then that I began to realize how sterile was the music of Schlesinger and Stark, which was widely sung in those days and I daresay even today. In 1922, when Rabbi Stephen Wise called me to become music director of the Free Synagogue, which at that time held its services in Carnegie Hall, I felt that it was my duty to do something about letting Reform Jews hear some of the works by synagogue masters of the nineteenth century: Sulzer, Lewandowski, Naumbourg, and Nowakowsky. The Reform services had become saturated with music composed for the *Union Prayer Book* by non-Jews.

I soon realized that all was not *kosher* with Sulzer and Lewandowski, either. Somehow, to me, their music did not always create the synagogal atmosphere that I knew. There was what Idelsohn called in their music something *galchish* [non-Jewish]. I know the reason for this was that there was so little genuine *nusach ha-tefillah* in their music. Even when *nusach* was used, it was put behind bars and harmonized with Western tonic-dominant harmonies. To say that I knew all the answers in 1923 would be an error. I am not sure whether I do today, either.[34]

If the great German synagogue composers had put the music "behind bars" by regularizing its rhythms and aligning its tunes with "Western tonic-dominant harmonies," Binder's self-appointed task was to liberate this music from its rhythmic and harmonic prison by employing modal traditional melodies in free rhythm with modal harmonization. How Binder put his ideas and ideals to work in his editions of the *Union Hymnal* and in his own compositions is the subject of what follows.

The *Union Hymnal*

Binder had long wanted to improve hymn singing. Consistent with his approach to synagogue music more generally, he sought to innovate by drawing upon tradition and working within its established structure. The first two editions of the hymnal (1897 and 1912) had helped to make hymn singing a mainstay of America Reform synagogues. By the 1920s, however, the *Union Hymnal* was in need of revision and Binder took responsibility for the third edition. His goal was to create quality "Jewish" music, which for him meant traditional music in a modern fashion, while ensuring congregational participation in the form of group singing, a prime concern of the rabbinic committee overseeing the revision. Binder's solution was to include as many traditional tunes as possible and to invite new synagogue composers to adapt traditional melodies and modes. As he explained in his introduction to the third edition:

One of the main purposes kept constantly in view was to make it as Jewish as possible, and thus meet one of the needs of our modern synagogal life, namely the adaptation of Jewish traditional music to the usage and taste of our own days. This involves a two-fold question: what elements of synagogal melody best express our religious life in music employed by our congregations; and how shall we clothe them in harmony that shall reveal their own peculiar modal character and melodic contours? We would not assert that we have solved these two problems. Not only in this Hymnal, but in our religious-musical life in general, they are still far from a solution. But we have made an earnest effort to proceed in this direction. We have called upon Jewish composers for aid. A considerable number of them have contributed compositions to this collection. Composers were urged to utilize some of the wealth of synagogal melody. This plea found a ready response. Even a superficial glance through the contents of this volume indicates how many of the hymns are based upon traditional melodies.[35]

The third edition consisted of 266 hymns. Like the previous two editions, this one included melodies of Sulzer, Lewandoski, and other prominent composers (Bach, Beethoven, Handel, Haydn, Mozart, Mendelssohn, and Rossini). But, in contrast with the earlier editions, this one also featured melodies by Novakowsky and Alman, consistent with Binder's championing of Eastern European synagogue composers as the bearers of tradition, as well as thirty-four compositions by Binder himself and nine of his arrangements. Binder's approach can be seen in "Into the Tomb of Ages Past,"[36] a hymn text, authored by Penina Moise, which Binder set to a traditional

Rosh Hashanah melody for "Adon Olam" (Figure 14.1). His arrangement of "When the Sabbath,"[37] based on a melody by Jacob Beimel, uses the *HaShem Malakh* mode, which appears in the traditional liturgy for the Friday evening *Kabbalat Shabbat* portion of the prayers (Figure 14.2). Its use here marks the liturgical occasion, consistent with Binder's view that music creates an atmosphere specific to the occasion and that the traditional liturgy constitutes a vast and unique reservoir of musically coded moods.

Binder's Liturgical Compositions

Educated and cosmopolitan Jews were connoisseurs of concert music, and Binder was concerned that synagogue music, while meeting their high expectations, elevate and dignify the synagogue and reestablish it as a center for "Jewish inspiration." In addition to composing synagogue music, Binder created cantatas, chamber works, art songs, choral music, and music for children. His liturgical works for the Reform synagogue, which include eight services and over forty individual liturgical compositions, vary in scope. His larger works include the *Dybbuk Suite* (1956) for chamber ensemble; the Carnegie Sextet in New York and the Philadelphia Orchestra performed this work and several of his other cantatas, including *Esther* and *Hanukkah*.

His eight services for the synagogue stand as his most significant achievement and best evidence of his musical credo in action. The first principle was to "purify and perpetuate" *nusach ha-tefillah*, "not for its own sake, but for what it has meant to our forefathers. What it did for the service in the past, it can do for the synagogue service today."[38] The second principle was "the liberation of the chant from behind the nineteenth century bar lines, and, the search for the proper harmonic background for our synagogue modes."[39]

How Binder realized these principles in his own musical compositions can be seen in "Hashkivenu" (1943), a setting for a Friday evening service (Figure 14.3).[40] Binder's harmonization, which supports the cantorial line, underpins of the traditional modal phrase. His choice of harmonies follows the mode and creates unique colors not commonly found in Western music. The flowing and often recitative cantorial line provides a feeling of freedom. Although not improvised, the melody does exhibit a free rhythm. In this way, Binder blends a modal and free melody, which harkens back to Eastern European *hazzanut*, with written-out phrasing and accompaniment to provide control and order, which are markers of the Central European cantorial style.

In "Bor'chu" (call to prayer) from the *Three-Festival Musical Liturgy* (1962) (Figure 14.4), the melody in the cantorial line is in the traditional *nusach* for the *Shelosh Regalim* (Three Festivals).[41] The modal line is somewhat complex, hovering around two notes D and A. Two separate melodic

New Year

Into the Tomb of Ages Past

Penina Moise

A. W. Binder
Trad. Rosh Hashanah
Adon Olam melody.

1. In - to the tomb of a - ges past. An - oth - er year has now been cast; Shall time un-heed - ed take its flight, Nor leave one ray of high - er light, That on man's pil-grim-age may shine And lead his soul to spheres di-vine?

2. With firm re-solves your spir - it nerve, The God of right a - lone to serve; Speech, tho't and act to reg - u - late, By what His per-fect laws dic-tate; Nor from His ho - ly precepts stray, By world- ly i-dols lured a - way.

3. Peace to the house of Is - ra - el! May joy with - in it ev - er dwell! May sor-row on the op-'ning year, For - get-ting its ac-cus-tomed tear, With smiles a-gain fond kindred meet, With hopes revived, the New Year greet!

168

Figure 14.1. "Into the Tomb of Ages Past" (#157), *Union Hymnal* (Cincinnati: Central Conference of American Rabbis, 1932), p. 168.

The Sabbath

114

When the Sabbath

Marcus Jastrow, alt.

Jacob Beimel
Based on a Traditional Sabbath Mode

Moderato

1. When the Sab-bath, peace-in - vit -ing, Fills our hearts with sa - cred mirth,
2. Here, where wor-ship-pers as-sem-ble, Where God's spir - it 'mongst us dwells,

Then from hea-ven, soul - de - light-ing, Man - na rain - eth down on earth;
Where all lips, re - joic - ing, tremble, And with thanks each bo-som swells,

Then to song all sor-row yield-eth, Loud to God rings up the strain,
Here the dust - born man per-ceiv - eth How to con - quer fear and woe,

Heav - en-born de - vo - tion wield-eth O'er each soul her sway a - gain.
Cho - sen when this earth he leav - eth, End - less Sab - bath bliss to know.

Figure 14.2. "When the Sabbath" (#114), in *Union Hymnal* (Cincinnati: Central Conference of American Rabbis, 1932), p. 119.

HASHKIVENU
Evening Prayer

Figure 14.3. Abraham Wolf Binder, "Hashkivenu," Evening prayer for voice and organ (piano), *Friday Evening Service* (New York: Bloch Publishing Co., 1947). © 1947 Transcontinental Music Publications.

BOR'CHU
Call to Worship

Based on the musical tradition of the synagogue.

Figure 14.4. "Bor'chu," from Abraham Wolf Binder, *Three-Festival Musical Liturgy* (New York: Transcontinental Music Publications, 1962). © 1962 Transcontinental Music Publications.

lines have equal emphasis, thus providing an illusive modal pattern. This dual modal emphasis is followed harmonically. Binder anchors the phrases in both D major and A major, thus providing bitonality, a technique in twentieth-century music of using two tonalities rather than one. This "Bor'-chu" shows the inventive nature of Binder's compositional approach. In a short composition keeping to the traditional structure of a call by the cantor and response by the choir, representing the congregation, he plays with musical possibilities and explores the limits of contemporary musical styles. The ending harmony is a jolting combination of two tonal centers, D and A.

While Binder is credited with inspiring a host of new composers for the

Figure 14.5. Abraham Wolf Binder.

synagogue (Heinrich Schalit, Herber Fromm, Hugo Chaim Adler, Lazare Saminsky, Isadore Freed, and Julius Chajes, among others), little of Binder's music has stood the test of time. Binder's early Shabbat services, *Hibbat Shabbat* (1929) and *Rinnath Sabbath* (1935), while they drew from *nusach* and tradition, have not endured, while his later services, *Morning Service for the New Year* (1951) and *Three-Festival Musical Liturgy* (1962), have continued to be performed to some extent. Parts of these later services are simple, in a more straightforward style (as seen in the "Bor'chu," whereas the earlier services are musically dense, reflecting a more intellectual approach.

Yet despite the failure of his individual compositions to endure, Binder's synthetic approach, philosophy, and musical aesthetic enjoyed enormous influence. The once-a-week Shabbat or occasional holiday experience for Reform Jews was infused with renewed purpose, thanks to him. Since then, musical styles of group singing have changed with the rise of folk music and new forms of congregational participation, particularly the emergence of lay song leaders.[42] By the 1970s, the use of traditional melodies and *nusach* was once again in flux, as were the compositions from the last half of the nineteenth and first half of the twentieth centuries. Though not entirely successful in realizing his ideals, Binder was clear and constant in espousing them. Synagogue music was to transport the listener to a religious realm. Toward the end of his life, he wrote: "What are some of the goals of good synagogue music? The worshiper should be moved to deeper concentration upon prayer, and to more profound devotional feeling. Sacred music should help bring forth all that is good and tender in a human being. When the service is artistically performed, the worshipper undergoes a religio-musical experience unobtainable in any other manner. For this spiritual experience he will surely return!"[43] Beyond the music he himself composed and inspired others to create, it is his vision and approach that have endured.

Chapter 15

The Evolution of Philadelphia's Russian Sher Medley

Hankus Netsky

> *There was a marvelous sher. That was a big deal.*[1]
> —David Raksin, Hollywood film-music composer and former Philadelphia klezmer

This essay traces the history of the Philadelphia Russian Sher medley, the musicians who created it, and the community that reveled to it in their celebrations, from the late nineteenth century to the present. While many other dance tunes, including bulgars, freylekhs, horas, a mezinke medley celebrating the marriage of the youngest daughter, and a dobranotsh, a goodnight waltz, were also unique to the Philadelphia klezmer repertoire, a specific sher medley became identified with this city, even by musicians from elsewhere.[2] This transplanted European klezmer dance medley became known as the Philadelphia Sher, the Philadelphia Sherele, or the Philadelphia Russian Sher.[3]

The sher (from the German *Schar* [crowd] or possibly *Schere* [scissors], or the Russian Sher, as it was known in English, rose to its position of prominence in the nineteenth century and remained an indispensable feature of Philadelphia's Jewish weddings through the 1950s. During the period of mass immigration, the music played at Jewish weddings was a sensitive barometer of the relationship of American Jews to their European past. The decline and eventual disappearance of the music and the dance associated with the sher coincided with a move away from the Yiddish language and toward a self-conscious embrace of American values and styles. By the 1960s, the dance was seldom played at weddings, although it endured at gatherings held by Jewish fraternal organizations. Thus, like so many Eastern European aspects of American Jewish culture, the evolution of the sher has followed a seemingly inevitable path in the direction of entropy, as the dance lost its status as an integral part of a Jewish party. The sher lingered on as a nostalgic commemoration of an older form of expression until the 1970s, when it became a cornerstone in the revival of what has come to be known as klezmer music and the Eastern European Jewish dances associated with that music.

Although processes shaping a musical form are all but hidden from view, whether because they are embodied and rarely verbalized or because of professional secrecy, it is in this case possible through a detailed analysis of the music itself to uncover the forces that shaped them. Thanks to a unique body of evidence, including manuscripts and recordings of Philadelphia's Russian Sher medley, as well as interviews with old-time musicians, one learns that the small klezmer instrumental ensembles of the late nineteenth century gave way to larger ones and, later, to smaller regroupings; that remarkably well constructed codified versions of the medley emerged; that older European-style sections became interspersed with more contemporary material; that, eventually, those codified versions were abandoned in favor of half-remembered fragments; and that a gradual decline in interest led to the dance's disappearance and the medley's obsolescence until younger enthusiasts engineered its recent revival. The history of Philadelphia's sher comprises a vivid sonic portrait of an American Jewish community as reflected in their shifting social relations and ways of making music over the course of a century.[4]

The European Legacy

A set dance for four couples that took fifteen to twenty minutes to complete, the Russian Sher is related to other popular Euro-American social dances, including American square and contra dances and, most notably, the quadrille, a dance of French origin that is found in many forms around the world.[5] The sher is in the tradition of courtship dances that have their roots in Provençal court dance at the time of the Crusades, which embodied a polite "code of social behavior," in contrast with older dances in which men would pick women up and carry them into a circle. The new code of social behavior replaced other more overtly physical expressions of dominance with the bowing or turning that can be seen in the sher.[6]

While little is known about the early history of the sher, a *Scherer oder Schartanz* (Scissors or Crowd Dance) dating from 1562 is found in Böhme's *Collection of German Dances*.[7] This 2/4 dance has a phrase structure similar to the popular Jewish version. The pioneering Soviet Jewish ethnomusicologist Moshe Beregovski hypothesized that Ashkenazic Jews adapted their sher medleys from the (now obscure) German ones, eventually employing characteristic Jewish dance steps and "Easternized" melodies more typical of Eastern Europe, where most Jews lived during the nineteenth century.[8] One of several popular couple dances originally performed by Jewish women, the sher was part of a longstanding athletic tradition of same-sex Jewish dancing, although, in the twentieth century, it functioned primarily as a mixed-couple dance.[9] The most flamboyant and individualistic moves in the sher, as in other Eastern European Jewish dances, were characterized as "shining," a combination of dramatic arm gestures, head tilts, and strutting that gave the dance a strong Eastern European flavor. Particular communities later introduced their own steps and gestures to the sher. In Cuba, for example, dancers would rotate their hips in a way reminiscent of Latin dancing.[10] The sher's demise in America is linked to the advent of American and Latin-style mixed ballroom dancing and Israeli dancing at American Jewish celebrations.

Dancing the *Sher* in Twentieth-Century Philadelphia

How was the sher played in twentieth-century Philadelphia? By the early 1900s, Philadelphia boasted a large and vibrant Jewish community of 240,000, the third largest in America, and most Jews lived in South Philadelphia, a richly diverse ethnic enclave. A large percentage of them came from southern Ukraine and Moldova, long considered heartlands of klezmer music. Jews from this region were inclined toward an ethnic, rather than formally religious, approach to life, which may account in part for the longevity of older "ethnic" celebratory customs, including Eastern European dance and music traditions, in the Philadelphia Jewish community.[11] Many did their best to continue the social affiliations they had brought with them from Europe through their membership in *landsmanshaften* (organizations of Jews from a specific European city or town), synagogues, and burial societies. They also maintained allegiances to musicians who came from their towns or regions. A European town's musical repertoire (and musical business) would often be passed down within a family of American musicians.

Philadelphia's early twentieth-century klezmorim were a mixed group that ranged from self-taught to conservatory trained. They plied their trade in hotel, theater, and radio orchestras and occasionally in recording bands, but the bread and butter of their business was the wedding music scene. Jewish weddings took place in social halls, which by the 1930s had mostly given way to catering halls that doubled as restaurants. Charlotte Kimball Patten, a social worker, described a 1905 Philadelphia Jewish wedding, as follows: "The guests dance till four o'clock, strange old-world dances to tuneless music, peasant dances from Rumania, Austria and Russia; competitive dances between men, circling dances of women whirling, laughing and embracing each other. It is greatly enjoyed by all except the bride, who is often desperately tired and ill after her twenty-four hours' fast."[12]

The sher was a "request number," which meant that the person who requested it was obligated to pay the musicians a substantial tip. The bandleader would then dedicate the number to the patron, who would invite others to join him or her in the dance and serve as the "leader" once it started. In the 1920s and 1930s, shers were usually played for only one set of dancers at a time. This made it a lucrative dance for the musicians, since, over the course of an evening, several different guests or groups of guests would put together sets of their own and commission a sher performance exclusively for their own dancing. In the 1940s, the sher became more of a communal dance, with a large number of wedding guests taking to the floor at a time. In either case, Bernie Uhr (b. 1923), manager of several of Philadelphia's most popular catering institutions and an excellent dancer in his own right, recalls that "the musicians would play a sher till everybody dropped." He also remembers how Philadelphia musicians let the crowd know that the dance was soon to begin: "The musicians played a signal, and then they stopped till everybody got together into (sets), and then the dance started."[13] The "signal" consisted of the first eight measures of the opening phrase of A minor sher #1, culminating in an abrupt ending, as the musicians waited for the dancers to get ready. Joe Borock, a well-respected Philadelphia clarinetist and saxophonist who began his work with Jewish bands in 1945, recalls that all the guests knew the protocol and were ready to contribute funds when the time came: "When you went to a wedding you had to have at least three dollars in your pocket. The first dollar was for the coat-check girl who was usually the daughter of the caterer—if you didn't have a dollar you wouldn't get your clothes back. Number two was for the fiddle-player when he went around to the tables, and the third was for the sher. If the guests didn't have the money for a sher you just sat with your arms folded."[14]

The Structure of the Dance

The dance steps associated with Philadelphia's Russian Sher medley are similar to those of shers found among recent Soviet Jewish immigrants from southern Ukraine. The sher consists of four figures:

Figure 1: "Circle." Couples (with man on left, woman on right) circle right for sixteen counts, then turn around and circle left for sixteen counts, usually ending the figure with a "one, two, three." This figure is often done twice.

Figure 2: "Promenade" in a circle with the woman on the outside for sixteen counts, usually ending with the man turning the woman.

Figure 3: "Crossing." Couples one and three take four steps forward, then four steps back, then eight steps across, usually passing on the right, and turning on the last two counts. Then couples two and four do the same.

> Figure 4: "Leading Out (*aroysfirn*)." The "number one" man "sets up" (gets in position) for eight beats, dances with his partner for eight beats, sets up again for eight beats, dances with his corner (*shokhn*) for eight beats, sets up again, dances with his partner again, and then dances with each of the other women in the circle, continuing the pattern. The tradition of "checking in with one's partner" after dancing with all the other women in the set made the Philadelphia version of the sher unusually long. It was in this portion of the dance that the practice of "shining" (mentioned above) was especially encouraged.

In all versions of the sher, after the four figures were completed, the entire dance would be repeated three more times. Each man would dance with each of the women following the same formula mapped out above. If there were more than one "set" on the dance floor, after everyone completed all the figures, all the participating couples would form a long line and smoothly promenade around the room.[15] Upon completion of the promenade, they would join hands and "thread the needle." This part of the dance required the leader to form a "chain" and lead the front of the line under the arms of dancers in the middle, a pattern that was repeated several times, until everyone was eventually led into a tangled mass. Then, the leader retraced his or her steps, and the chain slowly unraveled.[16] This last part of the dance required participants to become more intimately entwined than some guests cared to be, and, by this point, shers sometimes degenerated into fights. Indeed, the musician Joe Borock observed that fighting was so common that, in his long career, he had never seen a sher get to its conclusion.[17]

Although the choreographed dance figures that compose the sher are invariably eight measures in length, they do not always correlate directly with eight-bar musical phrases. The Eastern European Jewish dance revivalist Michael Alpert makes this point in these instructions to a group of New York–based dancers: "Ideally, [the sher] should have a sense of constant motion, like the gears of a clock, with people always turning. If you're not the one dancing in the middle [you] dance in place. Traditionally, when people do it, the steps are not in sync with the musical phrase; nobody cares about the musical phrase—what's important is the rhythm . . . so that you may do a figure and it takes longer than a phrase, it overlaps, it's a little disconcerting in a certain way. But what's important is the rhythm, and what's important is that you keep dancing."[18]

While the music used for some sher medleys (including those popular among New York musicians) is often composed exclusively of eight-, sixteen-, and thirty-two-measure phrases, a variety of phrase lengths appears in other examples. The typical Philadelphia Sher medley includes at least eight twelve-bar phrases (each repeated so as to create twenty-four bar sections) along with the eight, sixteen, and thirty-two ones. These less symmetrical phrases may represent an attempt on the part of the musicians to provide "signal" phrases to allow the couples enough time to get into position, while also generating clear cues to help the musicians and dancers coordinate the phrasing of the dance steps, even if only approximately, with the phrasing of the music.

As was already noted, the music traditionally played for the sher was usually sequenced in long medleys, which may or may not have been determined before the dancing began. Feldman places the traditional music played for sher medleys within the category of "core" (or uniquely Jewish) klezmer repertoire.[19] The musical material traditionally found in all of these dances is in 2/4 meter and derives entirely from duple subdivisions; there are no triplets, as there would be in the Romanian sirba or bulgar. Other lively traditionally Jewish 2/4 dances include the skotshne and the freylekhs.[20] In Eastern Europe, tunes used for a sher medley in one town might also be used for other dances, such as a freylekhs, in another town. However, once a specific musician established a tune as part of a sher medley, that tune would no longer be played as part of a freylekhs. In this way, particular sher medleys often came to be associated with specific geographical points of origin. This tradition continued in America, with distinctive sher medleys taking root in Milwaukee, New York, and Philadelphia, among other places. Where there was no ancestral klezmer tradition to draw on, or where ancestral traditions were put aside, musicians turned to the New York Russian Sher, which became readily available after being published in 1924 in one of the Kammen Brothers' popular Jewish wedding music folios.

A Brief History of Philadelphia's Russian Sher Medley

While klezmer music research has suffered from a lack of documentation, the music played for the Philadelphia Russian Sher medley prior to its recent revival is exceptionally well documented.[21] I am fortunate to have found eleven different complete manuscript versions and four recorded renditions that, taken together, span over fifty years, from folios hand-copied shortly after 1910 to a recording made at a B'nai Brith (Jewish fraternal organization) function in 1968. I am a klezmer musician myself and come from a family of Philadelphia klezmer musicians, which facilitated my efforts to interview old-time musicians and to observe the klezmer scene in Philadelphia today. The manuscripts, recordings, interviews, and observations that I have gathered come from active and retired musicians from klezmer backgrounds, children and grandchildren of klezmer musicans, and my own relatives. Taken together, they form a series of snapshots from different eras that reveal, in unprecedented detail, not only a history of the Philadelphia Russian Sher medley in the twentieth century but also the history of the musical and cultural sensibilities of the community that played this music and danced to it.

What are the distinctive features of the Philadelphia Russian Sher medley? It was exceptionally long, consistent, and stable. The music played for the Philadelphia sher was usually sequenced in seventeen- to twenty-minute medleys, with fixed key (tonic) relationships, a practice that remained consistent through the 1960s. The effort that Philadelphia's musicians made to adhere to such a consistent structure in these medleys over such a long period of time contrasts with what we know about the practice of musicians in other American cities, where sher medleys generally consisted of two or three set sections, after which the musicians added popular folk, theater, and dance tunes from their common repertoire.[22] As Feldman notes in his study of the bulgar, by the 1940s American musicians had ceased to distinguish between various types of lively wedding dances and were incorporating sirbas and bulgars, as well as the more traditional freylekhs, into their sher medleys.[23] By the late 1960s, a less rigorous approach had also taken hold among some Philadelphia musicians, so much so that knowledge of the entire sher medley from start to finish became a barometer of both one's technical skill as a musician and one's serious commitment to the klezmer scene. If you either "didn't know the sher" or "couldn't make it though the sher," you were, quite plainly, not fit to share the stage with those who did or could.

The stability of the Philadelphia Russian Sher medley reflects the emphasis of Philadelphia's musicians on knowing, memorizing, and retaining the components of the sher, a feat that represented a high level of accomplishment. It was essential that someone, if not the entire band, know the sher by memory because, as can be seen in Harry Swerdlow's popular 1945 hand-notated klezmer folio, the entire piece took up eight full pages of music, with virtually all of the page-turns coming in the middle of musical phrases. In my research, it quickly became obvious who such players were. They needed nothing more than several measures of the opening phrase to launch into an entire eight-page medley by heart. Thus, Berl Freedman, a classically trained violinist from Buki (near Kiev in Ukraine), who served as both contractor and copyist for the orchestra of Philadelphia's Arch St. Yiddish Theater and for Harry Kandel's Victor recording orchestra, only notated the first few measures of the Philadelphia Russian Sher medley in his wedding folio, whereas when it came to other pieces, he wrote them out in their entirety.

Fortunately for the sake of posterity, others were less casual in committing their sher medleys to paper. By the 1920s, as more musicians from outside the traditional klezmer orbit entered the Jewish wedding music scene,

Figure 15.1. Kol Katz Orchestra performing at the Cramer wedding, 6735 N. 16th Street, Philadelphia, October 15, 1950. From left to right: Al Brown (tenor sax), Marvin Katz (trumpet), Kol Katz (drums), Sunny Gale (vocals), Morris Steinberg, piano.

complete manuscript versions of tunes and medleys became more common. Morris Freed, a music store owner, published his nine-page sheet music edition of the Philadelphia Russian Sher medley as he knew it in 1914, while others proudly wrote out their sprawling versions for students and clients. Jerome Adler, a clarinetist, somehow managed to crowd most of his manuscript onto two very densely packed pages, and Joseph Hoffman, a cornetist, fit his onto three pages. Still, despite the existence of printed sources, the form of Philadelphia's Russian Sher medley evolved through a gradual process of accretion, deletion, and innovation.[24] Some of the manuscripts are palimpsests, with traces of earlier markings visible through the most recent revisions. One can attribute much of the music's fluidity to the personal preferences of the musicians, since they played with one another in various constellations and across generations, forming interconnecting circles of musical performance, transmission, and repertoire.

Since there were various versions of the sher that leaders might call up without notice, a sideman had to have lots of sections at his fingertips. The trumpeter Marvin Katz describes the process as he remembers it in the early 1950s:

It all depended on whom you were playing with—the order wasn't always the same and some of the leaders didn't know all of the sections . . . If you were playing with Jerry Adler it was one thing, with Lou Orkin it was another, with Joe Borock it was quite a different thing. If I played with Ray Sheinfeld I would lead it myself. The important thing was to know all of the sections so that nothing would surprise you. The Swerdlow book was the only one that actually had all of the sections, but I didn't have one of those back then, nor did I need one.[25]

There were indeed a lot of sections for a 1950s musician to know, as there had been in the 1920s and 1930s and, undoubtedly, in earlier days as well. Beregovski points out that, in Eastern Europe, "Every *kapelye* (band) had several established tunes it played for the sher,"[26] although there is no evidence that any of the sher medleys he collected were as long or as fixed in sequence as the Philadelphia Russian sher medley.

Not surprisingly, Philadelphia's older klezmer folios contain remnants of earlier shers that musicians brought over from Europe. A Jewish wedding music folio, notated by Berl Freedman around 1930, contains the well-known Berditchever Sher, attributed to the Hasidic *rebbe* Levi Yitzhak of Berditchev, while in the *International Hebrew Wedding Music* folio (first published in New York in 1916 by Wolf Kostakowsky) we find another atractive European-style melody that was seemingly part of the Philadelphia Russian Sher medley at one time. In the c. 1910–15 Harry Kandel manuscript, an otherwise obscure melody (see Figure 15.2) appears as Sher #4, but it is not heard on either of Kandel's sher recordings, nor does it appear in any of the other ten renditions in my possession.

Tunes such as these are indicative of the diverse material that made up the earliest sher medleys played in Philadelphia. By the second decade of the twentieth century, however, they were being abandoned in Philadelphia, while other tunes were entering a mix that would become what we now think of as the Philadelphia Russian Sher medley.

Despite Philadelphia's long retention of the sher medley (in much of its classic complexity), this piece did change over time in relation to changes in Philadelphia's Jewish community. Consequently, in 1915, we see a piece that reflects a community's shared immigrant origins; in the 1930s, we find a medley that mirrors the aesthetics of a second generation, at home in Philadelphia and determined to reconstruct their musical repertoire in a way more consonant with the tastes of their audience. In the 1940s, in contrast, we encounter a community and a sher medley with a more cosmopolitan outlook, and in the 1960s we find a community, music, and dance that are hardly in sync with each other at all. Throughout its history, the piece has remained very much a local phenomenon, a Philadelphia mix that

Figure 15.2. Section of Kandel sher manuscript, 1910–15.

reflects the tastes of that city's close-knit Jewish community and collection of musicians in a soundscape that belongs in Philadelphia's catering halls.

Particular individuals with leadership or entrepreneurial talents played important roles in the history of the Philadelphia Russian Sher medley, starting in the late nineteenth century when the Lemisch family arrived in Philadelphia, bringing with them the shers they played in Jassi (Yiddish: Yass), Romania. By the early 1880s, Selig Itzik Lemisch (1819–91) and his family had become celebrated local party and theater musicians, and at least one of their shers became a cornerstone of all Philadelphia Russian Sher medleys to follow.[27] A 1914 hand-copied manuscript belonging to Meyer Swerdlow, a violinist, cornetist, bandleader, teacher, and family patriarch who wrote tunes out for students who later played in his band, represents an actual bandstand edition of his day, including an early bow to the New York Russian Sher—sixteen bars of it at the very end.[28] Comparing such a manuscript with medleys played elsewhere at the time, we can observe that a *Philadelphia* sher medley—a compilation of material brought over from Europe or crafted locally—had taken shape, with tunes, form and structure unique to musicians of that city.

Critical to an understanding of the transmission and canonization of a Philadelphia sher medley was the shift from Old World European methods (oral transmission, by ear and example) to handwritten manuscripts, followed by printed sheet music and, finally, sound recordings. Thus an account of the history of the Philadelphia Russian Sher medley would need to attend to the impact of the 1914 Freed sheet music edition, which made a version of the medley available for mass dissemination, not only in Philadelphia but also in New York. Freed, the son of a *badkhn* (wedding jester and master of ceremonies) from Brest (today in Belarus), was an amateur composer, a music entrepreneur, and, later, a chess champion of the state of Pennsylvania. He sold copies of his edition at his popular music store, which was located at Fifth and Morris Streets in the center of South Philadelphia's Jewish community, while his Old World father repaired string instruments and bows in the back room. Freed's 1914 sheet music enjoyed great longevity as the model for a 1920 recording by New York's Abe Schwartz Orchestra and as a handy (but outdated) text for musicians who wanted to learn the sher in later years.[29]

While creating the illusion of a definitive and permanent musical form, such sheet music could not, in itself, forestall shifts in popular tastes during the 1920s and 1930s. This resulted in part from the performance of Americanized Jewish music on Jewish radio and in the Yiddish theater or heard on 370 recordings of such icons as the clarinetist Dave Tarras. A close examination of the musical evidence reveals how some, but not all, elements in the 1914 Freed sheet music were supplanted by a more modular construction that strings together much shorter and catchier tunes. Once these changes were consolidated, the younger Swerdlows, for a small price, wrote out a new version of the sher for the 1940s and 1950s generations[30] where, until recently, it sat in club-date wedding music folios, gathering dust and waiting for this collector to find it. In contrast, by the 1960s (as we can hear in a recorded rendition from 1968),[31] the musicians seemed to pay very little attention to manuscripts. Instead, they incorporated other popular Jewish melodies that they learned by ear and by heart. Oral tradition had returned.

Musical Analysis of the Philadelphia Russian Sher Medley

Given its heterogeneous musical elements and structural flexibility, how did the Philadelphia Russian Sher medley manage to retain its musical identity over time? To answer this question, I offer an extended analysis of the historical development of the medley, based upon the following corpus:

the clarinetist Harry Kandel's handwritten Jewish wedding music folio (c. 1910–15)
Morris Freed's 1914 published edition (supplemented by a 1920 Abe Schwartz Orchestra recording)
a 1914 handwritten folio from the cornetist-violinist Meyer Swerdlow
Wolf Kostakowsky's 1916 International Hebrew Wedding Music folio
Harry Kandel's 1918 Victor recordings

a 1927 manuscript version by the cornetist Joseph Hoffman

A 1940s manuscript from the clarinetist Jerome Adler

A 1945 folio from the pianist-drummer Harry Swerdlow

a 1950s manuscript from the clarinetist Lou Orkin

the "official" Jewish dance folio of the popular "Music Associates" Jewish society music agency (1960s), compiled by the trumpeter Norman Yablonsky and notated by copyist Al Boss

A rendition featuring the clarinetist Jerome Adler and the trumpeter Morris Zeft, on a recording made by Alan Shapiro that dates from 1968.

The following analysis of the Philadelphia Russian Sher traces how this music changed and why it took the form that it did in the historical contexts in which it was played.

COMPOSITION

The Philadelphia Russian Sher medley is an imposing piece of music in its own right. Despite all its variety, an internal musical logic ties its parts together, giving the piece not only a sense of unity but also a clear dramatic curve. In addition, within its overall framework, flexibility in combining units allows the musicians to vary the length of the piece in response to the contingencies of each performance situation.

While the nature, number, and sequence of sections vary within each notated version, two organizational systems consistently appear. The first one can be seen in the c. 1910–15 Harry Kandel, 1914 Meyer Swerdlow, 1927 Hoffman, and 1960s Yablonsky manuscripts, where the medleys are divided into shers, which might be thought of as pieces comprising two to five sections (as is also true of European freylekhs). The shers are usually at least thirty-two measures long, including repeats. While musicians didn't always agree as to exactly how many sections constituted each sher, some internal musical logic (motivic or modal coherence, for example) seems to bind the sections together into these larger units.

Roughly two shers correspond to each cycle of the dance. Several additional shers were always needed for the collective promenade and chain ("threading the needle"). The older manuscripts are, in fact, liberally sprinkled with *da capo* ("from the beginning") signs, indicating that bandleaders often repeated each sher in its entirety. Nine of the versions I examined contain at least nine shers, and the longest in my collection (c. 1945 Harry Swerdlow manuscript) consists of thirteen. The exact length of each sher hardly mattered because, as already noted, direct correspondence of phrase length to the dancing was not really an issue, although musicians did keep their eye out for the progress of the dancers, so that they could mark the beginning of the promenade and the "threading the needle" chain.

A second pattern can be seen in the 1914 Freed, 1916 Kostakowsky, 1950s Orkin, and 1940s Adler manuscripts, where the medleys are divided only into short sections separated by double bars. In the 1950s Orkin manuscript, the sections are actually labeled as one through twenty-seven. This contrasting method of dividing up the medley can perhaps be traced to Morris Freed's influential sheet music for the sher, in which the traditional delineation into multisection entities was absent. It was through the 1914 Freed sheet music that the sher became available to everyone (and especially novices) on the Jewish wedding music scene. Nevertheless, for the purpose of this study, I will refer to each complete sher as a unit because shers have traditionally been multisectional entities.

Because so little is known about traditional sequencing of klezmer tunes, this collection of materials is all the more valuable, for it offers some of the only hard evidence of how Jewish dance tunes were joined together in medleys.[32] Given the substantial flexibility of sectional delineation and content—which tunes, how many tunes, how they were sequenced, and how many sections varied—one might ask, how did the piece maintain its overall compositional integrity over the years? One key to the stability of the medley are guideposts within the form that remained relatively consistent throughout the period of my survey. These include the opening section, the Lemisch sher, and the beginning of the New York Russian Sher, all of which became instantly recognizable by the community.

TONALITY

The corpus is also remarkably consistent with respect to the tonal centers found within most complete renditions of the Philadelphia Russian Sher medley over a period of at least fifty years. [33] As early as 1918 (the date of the Kandel recording), four distinct tonal centers, which may be defined as sections with a definite tonic or resolution point and collections of pitches that imply scales or other modal material, divide the piece clearly into four parts:[34]

Part 1: Shers in various forms of A minor[35]
Part 2: Shers that are mostly in A freygish[36]
Part 3: Shers in various types of D minor (usually corresponding to the promenade section of the dance)[37]
Part 4: Shers in D freygish or (after 1940) "Der Nayer Sher" (The New Sher, a 1939 Abe Ellstein composition) in D major[38]

On listening to the medley, one can easily hear the tonal logic of such a structure, and its ordering may show the influence of Western musical formulas.[39] At the same time, this sequence could just as easily reflect the

Freed 1914	A minor		A freygish			D minor
Swerdlow 1914	A minor		A freygish		D minor	
Hoffman 1927	A minor	A freygish	D minor	D freygish	D minor	D frey.
Swerdlow 1945	A minor	A frey.	A mi.	A frey.	D minor	D major
Orkin 1950	A minor	A frey.	A mi.	A frey.	D minor	D major
Yablonsky 1960	A minor	A frey.	A mi.	A frey.	D minor	D major
Zeft Adler-1968	A minor	D minor			D mi. / A mi.	D major

Figure 15.3. Proportional relationship of tonalities in Philadelphia Russian Sher medley, 1914–68.

influence of modal systems such as Turkish *makam*, in which similar modulations and tonal sequences are not uncommon.[40]

In examples spanning the period from 1914 to 1968, the length of each part of the sher varies widely. As early as the 1920s we can see a pattern emerging—the A-minor part becomes shorter, the A-freygish part grows, and the D-minor part becomes much longer. A proportional breakdown of the sher medleys grouped by key center and tonality, using seven of the examples I collected, shows how the key relationships evolved over time (Figure 15.3).

Why does the A-minor part shrink? The A-minor part is essentially old-time European Jewish fiddle music (see below). Short of a 1940s traditionalist revival, which never happened, mid-twentieth-century American musicians were highly unlikely to come up with more material of this sort. At the same time, it was not as difficult for the younger generation to find or compose newer and more modular material in A freygish, D major, and D minor.[41]

As the older generation, the "keepers of the guard" for the Philadelphia klezmer tradition, faded away, the D-minor section (mostly material from the New York Russian Sher medley) grew and eventually came to dominate the medley. As we will see in more detail below, when the musicians and their audiences became more cosmopolitan, the piece lost much of its provincial uniqueness.

MUSICAL STRUCTURE

The sher medley is in four parts. Part 1 consists of the A-minor shers (Figure 15.4), which form a tightly interwoven motivically unified dance medley that sounds as if it might have been written by one composer. Its tonality is complex, with lines that meander through shifting modalities with only occasional nods to consistency. In early years, these tunes were accompanied with fairly static drones (evident in the Freed sheet music), while later renditions incorporated more Westernized harmonies. As the opening part of the Philadelphia Russian Sher medley, the A-minor shers also have a special significance for both the musicians and their audience—they contain the fanfare that serves as the "signal," the signature phrase that immediately tells the audience that a sher is about to begin. It is a phrase that links generations, that registers with the Philadelphia audience in an almost Pavlovian way: It says, "Find your partner and get ready to dance!"

Part 1 actually had tremendous longevity in printed editions. Most of the material in the 1914 Freed sheet music can still be found in manuscripts from the 1940s and 1950s, as well as in the 1960s Yablonsky manuscript. However, interviews and transcriptions of recorded versions reveal that, in practice, musicians did not always play all the sections of the A-minor shers. Why? While these A-minor shers contain many stock phrases that early twentieth-century klezmorim would have known, their quirky hybrid-minor tonalities (A minor and C major, with the sections in minor fluctuating between harmonic minor and a hybrid sort of minor with a lowered ninth scale degree) were not so familiar to American-born club-date musicians, and their phrase structures were, most likely, equally puzzling. In general, these old klezmer tunes were really only intended as fiddle music: A minor is a much better key for instruments from the string family, all of which have open A strings and enhanced resonance in that key, than it is for winds and brass, which are more easily played in flat keys, such as B-flat and E-flat. For a variety of reasons, including the nature of early recording technology, the violin, which had been the key instrument in European klezmer bands, was overtaken by wind and brass instruments in American klezmer ensembles, and some of the older repertoire (including these A-minor shers) did not really suit this new instrumentation.[42]

The A-minor shers ground the Philadelphia Russian Sher medley in Old World march-like freylekhs, with Eastern-sounding melodic swirls that twist, turn, and wind around, evoking bold gestures from a preharmonic past. These dance tunes are technically demanding and relentless in their busy deedle-deedle rhythms, and, no matter what rendition we look at or listen to, they are very much symbolic of a bygone era. Still, they are essential—without them, no medley could be thought of as a Philadelphia sher.

The beginning of the second part of the sher medley provides a stark contrast to the busy A-minor shers discussed above. Here we find an abrupt switch to material in freygish, the expressive hallmark sound of Hasidic Jewish chant (and a cornerstone of popular Jewish music—think "Hava Nagila" or "If I Were a Rich Man"), with the instantly recognizable wailing

Figure 15.4. A minor shers, as printed in Freed 1914 sheet music.

sound preferred by American Jewish ears. In almost every version I collected, the first sher in the A-freygish part is modeled after a section of one
of the Lemisch shers, dating back to the late nineteenth century (Figure
15.5). As mentioned above, this sher may have been among the first to
arrive in Philadelphia. While motivic development in part 2 continues

Figure 15.5. Part 2, A-freygish shers: "Lemisch" sher.

along the lines of part 1, the gradual stepwise unfolding of register, a characteristic typical of older freygish melodies, is the most pronounced compositional feature of the first sher in this section.

The rest of the second section (Figure 15.6) underwent a massive change in the 1930s and 1940s, as a new generation of musicians with less awareness of Middle Eastern–influenced modal traditions crafted new material. In an era when old-fashioned hall weddings gave way to functions held at more modern synagogues and catering houses, many of this section's European sher melodies were displaced by more streamlined, brassy Odessa-style bulgars (Figure 15.7), tunes that also fit better on the clarinet and trumpet, which now dominated the front line. The audience presumably liked the change too; these were the kinds of Jewish dance tunes American Jewish audiences of this generation preferred (and still prefer) to dance to.[43] Even the legendary Dave Tarras, a clarinetist as grounded in the European tradition as any, who, through his recordings, set the standard for all other American klezmorim of his generation, was creating mostly frey-lekhs/bulgar hybrids in this period. It is, therefore, not at all surprising that Philadelphia musicians would do the same.

Part 3, the D-minor section of the Philadelphia Russian Sher medley

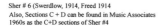

Figure 15.6. More shers in A freygish, as printed in Freed sheet music.

(Figure 15.8), might be seen as a harbinger of encroaching cosmopolitanism—just another manifestation of the ever-growing influence of New York on America's provincial Jews. As noted above, this section tended to grow and grow over the years, even more profoundly in live performance than in manuscript versions. Yet one can hardly blame the musicians and audience for succumbing to the New York Russian Sher medley, which is extremely catchy. Like the Philadelphia medley, its first few strains are interwoven with an intricate compositional logic. Its later inclusion of popular Second-Avenue Yiddish theater tunes became another asset in an American environment where audiences craved the familiar.

Once part 3 does start, there is no consensus on the sequence that should be followed. Four of the manuscripts (1927 Hoffman, c. 1945 Harry

Figure 15.6. (Continued)

Swerdlow, 1950s Orkin, and 1940s Adler) begin with a D-minor freylekhs played only in the Philadelphia sequence. Other versions (including the 1914 Meyer Swerdlow manuscript) move directly into material found in the New York Russian Sher medley. Once the New York sher material has been exhausted, the actual sequencing here has an improvisational quality, and each sher's length varies. Different versions might lead into a popular Odessa bulgar, an early twentieth-century Yiddish theater melody, "Ikh bin a border bay mayn vayb" (I Am a Lodger at my Wife's Place), and the Yiddish folk song "Ikh bin shoyn a meydl in di yorn" (I Am Already a Girl Advanced in Years). All these tunes were also popular among contemporaneous New York musicians.

Over time, Philadelphia musicians gave increasing weight to the New York material and approach. In a 1968 recording by the Jack Shapiro Orchestra (featuring the clarinetist Jerome Adler and the trumpeter Morris Zeft), we find an extended version of the D-minor part. Here, the band, veteran musicians who in previous years would have played many more of the earlier strains, took a left turn immediately after the very first A-minor sher of part 1, skipping the freygish shers of part 2 altogether and heading straight for the D-minor world of New York (with what seems like a rather

Sher #5 (in Adler 1940's Swerdlow 1945, Orkin 1950's, Music Associates 1960's)

Sher #6 (in Adler 1940's, Swerdlow 1945, Orkin 1950's, Music Associates1960's)

Sher #7 (Swerdlow, 1945, Orkin 1950's Music Associates 1960's)

Sher #8 (in Swerdlow 1945, Orkin 1950's)
Sher #7 (in Adler 1940"s)

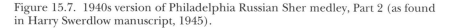

(This Bulgar is also found as Sher #6 (transposed to "D") in Hoffman 1927)

Figure 15.7. 1940s version of Philadelphia Russian Sher medley, Part 2 (as found in Harry Swerdlow manuscript, 1945).

Sher #9 (in Swerdlow 1945, Orkin.1950's), Sher #10 (in Swerdlow 1914), Sher #4 (in Hoffman, 1927), Sher #5 (in Kandel 1918), Sher # 8 (in Adler 1940s and Music Associates 1960s)

Sher #5 (in Hoffman 1927), Ikh Bin A Border Bay Mayn Vayb (I Am a Lodger at My Wife's Place)

Sher #10 (in Swerdlow 1945), Sher #4 (in Adler 1968). Also known as a popular Adeser Bulgar (dance from Odessa).

Figure 15.8. Part 3, D-minor shers.

jarring modulation), and we hear an extemporaneous medley as it unfolds. After opening with the second section of the New York sher and moving on to the usual "Odeser bulgar" and "Ikh bin shoyn a meydl in di yorn," the musicians follow with a medley of popular Jewish melodies, including "A khulem" (A Dream) and "Undzer rebenyu" (Our Rabbi), two well-known folk tunes, "Vu zaynen mayne zibn gute yor?" (Where Are My Seven Good Years?), a popular Yiddish theater song, and a Bessarabian bulgar. This medley, with its occasional moments of conflict, particularly when the

Sher #9 (Swerdlow 1914), Sher #7 (Hoffman 1927), Sher #4 (Kandel 1918), Sher #8 (Orkin 1950's, Music Associates 1960's), Sher #11 (Swerdlow 1945), Sher #10 (Adler 1940's) Sher #1 (Kammen Book #1, NY 1920s)

Sher #12 Swerdlow 1945), Sher #5 (Adler 1968) Ikh Bin Shoyn A Meydl in di Yorn (I Am A Girl Already Advanced in Years)

Figure 15.8. (Continued)

lead players fail at second-guessing each other's next moves, reveals a kind of fluidity and spontaneity that links Philadelphia's mid-twentieth-century klezmorim with the musical culture of preceding generations. By this time (1968), the folios I collected have perhaps become obscure to the musicians themselves, rather than reflections of current performance practices.

Part 4 of Philadelphia's Russian Sher medley (Figure 15.9) moves the music from D minor into a D freygish or major tonality and corresponds to that part of the dance where guests form a chain and "thread the needle," a move similar to one found in early renditions of the New York Russian Sher medley. This final move is the last link in the progression of resolutions that lead up to it and, musically, it feels very much like an arrival. In early manuscripts and recordings, the concluding piece is a lively march-like freylekhs in freygish. In later versions we find "Der Nayer Sher" (The New Sher), a bulgar composed in 1939 by the Julliard-trained composer Abraham Ellstein. Soon after, in a rendition by Ertha Kitt, the same tune became known in English to a wide crossover audience as "The Wedding Samba." Thus, the arrival is not only the resolution of a tonal journey but also the culmination of a chronological one—musically, we finally reach the 1940s, the beginning of a difficult era for immigrant Jewish culture. Soon, the 1940s generation, with their move to suburbia and creation of "mainstream" Judaism (that is, Judaism as a religion mostly devoid of ethnicity) will put dances like the sher on the back burner at best.

In this era, the age of quotas was mostly over; hotels and country clubs lifted their discriminatory barriers; Jews found their way into new kinds of professional and academic careers and eventually into positions of political power. The historian Arthur Hertzberg sums up postwar Jewish aspirations as he saw them: "They were numerous and increasingly wealthy, and ever more 'Jewish.'" . . . [T]hey regarded the Jewish community as their primary home. Yet, they were deeply ambivalent, often without admitting it even to themselves, about their most Jewish emotions . . . What they did as Jews— and more revealing, what they chose not to do, had to fit their dominant purpose: to arrive."[44]

One thing they generally chose not to do was traditional dancing, instead peppering their parties with more recent passions, such as the rumba and the cha-cha. By the 1960s, as it became difficult to find enough knowledgeable guests to do a proper sher, caterers and emcees often found themselves leading the dance. The trumpeter Marvin Katz has pointed out that in this era the dance would often end prematurely because of the participants' advanced ages and their lack of stamina.[45]

By the 1970s, few musicians were familiar enough with klezmer repertoire to make their way through the sher medley in any form. Even the availability of notated versions could not prevent the virtual disappearance of the dance. Nonetheless, a longing for the past could still inspire the inevitable request from an older relative: "There was always one guy who was gonna bug you. He'd come up and say, 'Play the sher, play the sher, play the sher.' You can't get rid of him, so the only thing to do is to play the song. Well, after about the first four phrases of it, you see that nobody's dancing, so you go right back to the beginning and out. I mean, you're not gonna keep going for another twenty minutes when nobody's dancing."[46] Who can really blame such a patron? For those who danced to it in its glory days, the wedding was the sher and the sher was the wedding. To have one without the other was unthinkable.

Over the course of twenty or so minutes, the music of Philadelphia's Russian Sher medley winds through a compressed soundscape that ties together sensibilities spanning the entire immigrant era. Taken as a whole, its parts form an intricately woven tapestry, a significant piece of folk art forged over time through a multigenerational collective vision, with its his-

Sher #5 (in Kandel 1918), Sher #9 (in Hoffman 1927) Sher #3 (in Kostakowsky 1916)

Sher #7 (in Adler 1968)

Der Nayer Sher (in Adler 1940's, Swerdlow 1945, Orkin 1950's, Music Associates1960's, Adler 1968)

[B] (B section from original sheet music)

Figure 15.9. Shers in D freygish and "Der Nayer Sher" ("The New Sher") by Abraham Ellstein. Copyright © 1940 (renewed) by Music Sales corporation (ASCAP). International copyright secured. All rights reserved. Reprinted by permission.

tory sedimented in the music itself. Its richly layered form preserves older aesthetics, even as it innovates to trends in American popular music, on the one hand, and the internal development of this wedding dance, on the other. It is a cultural centerpiece, a paean to continuity, a vehicle through which dancers and musicians exuded pride as they paid tribute to those who came before them, not through a dirge or a prayer, but with a celebratory dance.

List of Musical Sources

All sources are in my possession, courtesy of the individuals designated, unless otherwise indicated. I have transposed all musical examples, with the exception of two facsimiles, already transposed, to concert pitch. Unless otherwise indicated, recordings are 78 rpm and all transcriptions from sound recordings are my own. An asterisk (*) indicates that the musical source contains a complete version of the Philadelphia Russian Sher medley. Sources are listed in chronological order.

c. 1907–8 Solinski Recording

Rumänische Fantasie # 3, recorded in Warsaw, c. 1907–8, with Josef Solinski (violin), tsimblist unknown, Columbia 124161. From the Abner and Mary Schreiber Jewish Music Library, Bertha and Monte H. Tyson Music Department, Gratz College, Melrose Park, Pennsylvania.

* c. 1910–15 Kandel Manuscript

Jewish wedding music folio. Papers of Harry Kandel, Record Group 112, Supplement 39, Sheet Music Collection, YIVO Archives, YIVO Institute for Jewish Research, New York. Harry Kandel immigrated to the United States in 1905 and was well acclimated to America by 1910. Since the manuscript contains only Russian and Yiddish titles, his daughter, Doris, concluded that it was from his early immigrant days or even predates his arrival in America. On the other hand, because of their position in the folio (wedged in on empty staff lines below other tunes), the characteristic "Philadelphia" portions of the sher were in all likelihood added at a later date.

* 1914 Freed Sheet Music

"Sher," *Celebrated Hebrew Wedding Dance*, sheet music for pianoforte solo, edited by Morris Freed (Philadelphia: Morris Freed Music, 1914). Courtesy of the late Jerome Adler.

* 1914 Meyer Swerdlow Manuscript

"Saer" [*sic*], hand-notated cornet folio. Private collection of the late Dr. Samuel Katz, Philadelphia.

* 1916 Kostakowsky Folio

Wolff N. Kostakowsky, *International Hebrew Wedding Music*, violin folio, arranged, revised, bowed, and fingered by Wolff N. Kostakowsky (Brooklyn: Nat Kostakowsky, 1916). Private collection of Henry Sapoznik, New York. In the first edition, not only does Wolff Kostakowsky appear as the compiler of the volume but his name appears as the composer of every piece of music in the collection. Later that year, presumably after protests from other musicians, he removed his name as composer and changed the name of "Celebrated Hebrew Wedding Dance" to "Famous Philadelphia Sherele."

1918 Schwartz Recording

Russian Quadriglia, Pt. 1, 2, performed by Russky Norodny Orkestr (otherwise known as the Abe Schwartz Orchestra). Columbia E 3998: Matrix #: 84103. Recorded February 1918 in New York.

1918 Kandel Recording

Rusiche Shaer (Russian Dance) Part 1 and *Rusiche Shaer (Russian Dance) Part 2,* performed by [Harry] Kandel Orchestra. Victor 72102: Matrix #s: 21666–4 and 21667–5. Recorded June 25, 1918, in New York.

* 1918 Hochman Recording

Rusish Shehr und Kadril, performed by I. J. Hochman and Orchestra. Emerson 1306: Matrix #: 3430–3. Recorded 1918 in New York.

* 1920 Freed/Schwartz Recording

Sher, Part 1 and *Sher, Part 2* (Morris Fried [*sic*], Philadelphia), performed by the Abe Schwartz Orchestra. Columbia E 4905: Matrix #s: 86691–2 and 86692–1. Recorded October 1920 in New York.

1924 Kammen Folio

Kammen International Dance Folio #1, arranged by Jack Kammen and William Scher, compiled by Joseph Kammen (Brooklyn: J. and J. Kammen Music Co., 1924).

* 1927 Hoffman Manuscript

"Sherr," Jewish wedding music folio, notated by Joseph Hoffman. Private collection of Elaine Hoffman Watts, Philadelphia.

c. 1930 Freedman Manuscript

Jewish wedding music folio, notated by Berl Freedman. Private collection of the Nathan Freedman family, Philadelphia.

1939 Ellstein Sheet Music

"Der Nayer Sher," words and music by Abraham Ellstein (New York: Metro Music, New York, 1939).

1940s Adler Manuscript

Foreign Music Collection, bound folio of music hand-copied by Jerome Adler. 80 pages. Courtesy of the late Jerome Adler.

1940s Abe Neff Recording

Russian Sher, performed by Abe Neff Orchestra, recorded in the mid-1940s in Philadelphia, 20th Century Records, Matrix #: 2315A. From the Abner and Mary Schreiber Jewish Music Library, Bertha and Monte H. Tyson Music Department, Gratz College, Melrose Park, Pennsylvania.

* c. 1945 Harry Swerdlow Manuscript

"Shear," Jewish wedding music folio, notated by Harry Swerdlow. Private collection of Joseph Borock, Philadelphia.

* 1950s Orkin Manuscript

Jewish wedding music bound folio, hand-copied by the clarinetist Louis Orkin. 50 pages. Courtesy of Marvin Katz, Philadelphia.

* 1960s Yablonsky Manuscript

Jewish wedding music folio, compiled by the trumpeter Norman Yablonsky and hand-copied by Al Boss, the "official" Jewish dance music folio of the popular "Music Associates" booking agency. Courtesy of Bobby Block, Philadelphia.

1968 Shapiro Recording

Philadelphia Russian Sher medley, performed by Jack Shapiro Orchestra, with Jerome Adler (clarinetist), Morris Zeft (trumpeter), Sam Zager (piano), and Jack Shapiro (percussion). Performed at a B'nai Brith (Jewish fraternal organization) function in Philadelphia. Privately recorded on reel-to-reel tape by Alan Shapiro. Private collection of Alan Shapiro, Philadelphia.

2000 Khevrisa Recording

Khevrisa, *Khevrisa: European Klezmer Music* (Washington, D.C.: Smithsonian Folkways, 2000), SFW CD 40486.

VI.
Hotel Terminus

The inherently unstable interdependency of history and memory has dominated recent discussions of the Holocaust, with aesthetics and the arts figuring importantly in this dynamic. Two essays, Charles Dellheim's "Framing Nazi Art Loot" and Marion Kant's "Lewitan and the Nazification of Dance," examine how Nazi determinations of aesthetic validity helped to decide both the fates of individual Jews and—more surprisingly—the status that their artistic endeavors still retain in our collective consciousness. A third essay, Susan Rubin Suleiman's reading of the Marcel Ophuls's film *Hotel Terminus* (lending its name to this concluding section), describes how the documentarian's self-aware aesthetic pose enabled him to confront a subject that transcends merely factual representation.

Rather than simplify the inherent moral complexities of the Holocaust in terms of elementary dichotomies like truth and denial, memory and forgetting, or property and theft, Charles Dellheim asks why the issue of "Nazi art loot" has lately become so fashionable as a Holocaust morality tale. Its current saliency certainly derives in part from recent exposé of Swiss collaboration during World War II, from recent bitter controversies over reparation payments, and from a glut of lawsuits surrounding Nazi-stolen treasures. Yet Dellheim's essay retreats from this current "surfeit of memory" and its comforting judgments in order to assess the lengthy preceding period of neglect. He reviews the history of depictions of Nazi art theft by recalling the methods and mentalities of a group of United States Army "monuments men" that had been assigned the task of "protecting and salvaging artistic and historical monuments" in Allied-occupied Europe. Dellheim illuminates the role in efforts to recover art masterpieces played by German Jews like Captain James Rorimer (later the director of the Metropolitan Museum) or—even during the war itself—the French partisan Alexandre Rosenberg. Depictions of these men and their activities in subsequent memoirs, monographs, and movies occasion Dellheim's reflections on the reasons behind the conscious and unconscious suppression of the Jewish identities of the principal victims of Nazi art pillaging in postwar culture. This in turn begs the question of why, in the first place, modern European Jews became conspicuous, not so much as practitioners of art but as its dealers, owners, and patrons. What is clear is that the Nazis stole so much art from Jews both because Jews owned so much of it and because anti-Semitism made them all too easy to dispossess. Both factors, as Dellheim indicates, point to the critical function played by art in sustaining many modern Jews' claims to possess the cultural qualifications for legitimate membership in European society—the very status the Nazis set out to destroy.

The dance critic Joseph Lewitan was a Jewish artistic mediator along the lines described by Dellheim. That his important role in the history of twentieth-century German dance has been largely forgotten is also consistent with Dellheim's analysis, in which the significance of modernity's countless Jewish artistic sidemen and middlemen has been occluded. In her rediscovery of Lewitan, Marion Kant makes the added point that Lewitan's field of modern dance was the only avant-garde art form officially embraced by National Socialism, a fact that renders the Jewish critic's role all the more complex. In the hands of choreographers like Mary Wigman and Rudolph von Laban, modern dance aestheticized the Nazis' *Volkisch* and neo-Romantic ideals. Through his pioneering journal *Der Tantz* (founded in 1927), Lewitan combated these tendencies without ever succumbing to a facile rejection of modern dance itself. Yet with the 1933 Nazi seizure of power this precarious balancing act proved impossible to sustain. Accepting the Jewishness imposed upon him by the regime's racial categories, Lewitan eventually fled Germany. But he appeared little at home in overtly Jewish milieus, preferring instead to submerge himself indistinctly into New York's émigré society. It seems that by conferring Jewishness upon him the Nazis had succeeded in rendering Lewitan anonymous, an art-historical non-person, so to speak. Perhaps this is why he did not seek to reconstitute his role in the postwar world of dance criticism. His was the bygone modern dance moment of Weimar Germany: once Nazi appropriation managed to forcibly resolve that moment's internal contradictions (e.g., experimental *and* essentialist, avant-garde *and* nationalist) into a totalistic aesthetics, no room remained for Lewitan's indisputable but highly *individual* place within that history.

The strange paradoxes of Lewitan's biography demonstrate just how slippery the modern art of being Jewish can be—indeed, unimaginably so under the extreme conditions of the Nazi Holocaust. In her essay, with which this volume concludes, Susan Rubin Suleiman dissects the strategy of the documentary filmmaker Marcel Ophuls to "work up" or "process" (in Theodor Adorno's words) a tragedy whose character seems to negate the promise of aesthetic catharsis. Instead of blanket denunciations of the "Holocaust industry," not excluding its busy academic sector, Suleiman offers a constructive approach for winnowing the discussion to its most essential elements. If the production of memory is in itself unstoppable, the question should rather become: "How is memory best enacted or put to public use?" In Suleiman's meticulous unpacking, Ophuls's documentary on the capture and career of the war criminal Klaus Barbie stands as an exemplary—because ambiguous, playful, and reflexive—if inimitable model of the artistic "working through" of this subject matter. Ophuls resorts to "investigative sarcasm" (his term) and employs "expressionist moments" (Suleiman's) to expose his own manipulative role in staging acts of moral denunciation. He thereby succeeds in (helpfully) compromising himself without, at the same time, exonerating his targets. Though Suleiman never suggests that this technique is characteristically Jewish, her appreciation of Ophuls's deployment of it cannot be separated from the status of the director as a former refugee who fled Nazi Europe as a child. And while Ophuls would reject any depiction of his odyssey as a triumphalist morality tale, his painful revisiting of the era has enabled him to transform senseless tragedy into meaningful questioning. In the exploration of modern Jewry's manifold places in the arts, Hotel Terminus (Barbie's notorious headquarters and the title of Ophuls's film) thus becomes not a final destination but a point of departure.

Chapter 16
Framing Nazi Art Loot

Charles Dellheim

You can live with that?
With what?
That it's all been left in the dark?

—Bernhard Schlink, *"Girl with Lizard"*[1]

"Does the painting of that Jewish girl have to hang there? Does the boy have to sleep under the painting of that Jewish girl?" asked the boy's mother.[2] The disputed object depicted a girl and a lizard "looking at each other and not looking at each other, the girl gazing dreamily toward the lizard, the lizard directing its vacant, glistening eyes toward the girl." The boy "had no idea what a Jewish girl was," but that didn't stop him from missing the painting of the girl when his parents abruptly ended his naps at age nine.[3] When he wrote a description of the picture for a homework assignment in eighth grade, his father made clear that it was "not for other people . . . If only because other people are envious," he explained to his son, "it's best not to show them your treasures . . . Either it makes them sad because they don't have them, or they turn greedy and want to take them away from you."[4]

In the course of Bernhard Schlink's story "Girl with Lizard," we learn that the painting in question was the work of Rene Dalmann, a surrealist French artist living in Germany, and that the model was his wife, Lydia, a cabaret dancer whose father was a Jewish doctor who had converted to Orthodoxy. Last seen at the Nazis' *Degenerate Art* exhibition in Munich in 1937, *Girl with Lizard* was considered "missing" if not destroyed. Though the Dalmanns fled Germany to Strasbourg before World War II, all traces of the couple disappeared with the Nazi occupation of the artist's native city.

The mysterious provenance of *Girl with Lizard* was tied to the hidden Nazi past of the boy's father and to his family's declining fortunes. When the story begins, the father, a judge of the municipal court, enjoyed his local importance and visibility. But the boy senses a distance separating his parents from other people. "They were on their guard."[5] For good reason, as it turned out: the father is forced to resign from the bench and takes a job at an insurance company that he ends up losing because of drunkenness. Unbeknown to his son, what precipitated his father's fall was the discovery that when he was a judge during the war he had condemned to death an officer (a friend, no less) for having helped Jews escape from the police.

Girl with Lizard, the boy's father tells him, is his legacy, but it soon proves tainted. The Nazi provenance of the painting symbolizes the ruined inheritance of the children who must live with their fathers' sins; it is an emblem of German guilt and dishonor. When the boy inherits the picture during his third year at university, he investigates its history, while hiding it under the bed except when he is alone. He finally asks his mother the inevitable question that the judge had done everything to evade. "I want to know how my father came by a painting by René Dalmann . . . I want to know why he made such a secret of the painting."[6] His mother replies that the painting was a gift from Jews with forged papers, whom his father had helped during the war when he was on the military court in Strasbourg.

Unconvinced by this explanation, the boy ponders whether he should look for the Dalmanns' heirs and give them the painting; sell it and make his life easier with the money; or do good with it.[7] The story ends with a less than satisfactory solution: the boy burns the painting on the beach and returns home. The burning is a ritual sacrifice and an act of atonement. Though the protagonist punishes himself by destroying his beloved portrait, he fails to make restitution of any sort.

Bernhard Schlink's powerful tale epitomizes the mounting concern with Nazi art loot. Rarely does a month go by now without articles in the press about stolen pictures and bitter disputes over their ownership. It is common knowledge that countless pictures were plundered from Jews in Nazi-occupied Europe. Acquired by hook or crook, by ignorant or unscrupulous individuals and institutions—art dealers, collectors, and museums—thousands of these works of art were never returned to their rightful owners. The fate of plundered art has become a cause célèbre. It has even penetrated popular culture: Nazi art looting figured in an episode of the television show *The West Wing*. For all the recent publicity about the fate of Nazi stolen art, the pillaging of Jewish-owned art collections has been well known, at least in certain circles, since the end of World War II. But why the tremendous resurgence of interest in plundered art more than five decades after the crimes took place? That question points to a larger historical problem: how and why the issue of stolen art emerged, faded, and resurfaced in the United States.

Presented originally as spoils of war documenting German perfidy, Nazi stolen art has become an emblem recalling Jews' shattered European legacy. What began mainly as a story about Nazis stealing art treasures recovered by courageous "monuments men" has gradually been cast as a Jewish tragedy. Whereas Nazi art theft was first regarded as an assault on national cultural legacies, it has now become a chapter in the story of the Shoah. The fate of the "last prisoners of war," in the words of Elan Steinberg of the World Jewish Congress, has become a touchstone for memory— memories of belonging and betrayal, courage and collaboration. The changing frames of Nazi art loot reflect to some extent the broad pattern postulated by Peter Novick in *The Holocaust in American Life* (1999): the movement of the Shoah from the relative margins of American Jewish culture toward its symbolic core.[8]

Looting and Recovery

Art treasures have long been numbered among the choicest booty of war and booty of empire; the name of Lord Elgin alone hammers home the fact.[9] In certain respects, Nazi art pillaging resembled other conquerors' aesthetic crimes. The Russians, after all, also looted an enormous amount of art during World War II. Like other plunderers, Nazi leaders were driven on the one hand by the hunger for personal gain and on the other hand by dreams of national grandeur.[10]

What is distinctive about the Nazi case, though, is a combination of massive scale, careful planning, systematic organization, ideological hatred, and above all, racial anti-Semitism. Captain Lane Faison of the Office of Strategic Services Art Looting Investigation Unit (OSS ALIU) insisted that Nazi looting was different from that in any previous war because it was "officially planned and expertly carried out . . . to enhance the cultural prestige of the Master Race."[11] Whereas Faison neglects to mention that Nazi art looting was part of the solution to the "Jewish problem," the journalist Janet Flanner leaves no doubt that the Germans looked on "looted art on an ideological basis—almost all the victims were French, Dutch, Austrian and Belgian Jews, and Poles and Russians of any faith."[12] It is worth remembering, therefore, that if the Nazis singled out Jewish-owned collections, they also confiscated the art of other suspect *untermenschen*, notably the Poles.

Nevertheless, Jews had a special, if hardly privileged, place in Nazi ideology. Fired by intellectual hatred and material greed, art looting was an essential element in the Nazi war against the Jews. It was also part of a sustained effort to proclaim the dominance of a certain notion of German culture by eliminating alleged Jewish threats to it. The ideological basis of Nazi art looting stemmed partly from German anti-modernism. The unbearable cultural prominence of Jews was a leitmotif of anti-Semitic ideology from Richard Wagner's complaints about Jews in music to Adolf Hitler's howls about Jews in art. The incursion of Jews into an aesthetic realm once dominated by non-Jews, especially by aristocrats and their minions, became a pretext for an inconceivably furious backlash. As parvenus in search of aesthetic hegemony and cultural "*lebensraum,*" certain Nazis were particularly eager to sweep away Jewish competitors from the temple of art. They condemned Jews for peddling "degenerate" modern art and besmirching hallowed Christian old masters. The irony was that if assimilating Jews had turned to art partly as an emblem of citizenship, the Nazis stripped them of their citizenship as a prelude to confiscating their art and taking their lives.

The plunder of Jewish-owned art collections began in Vienna in 1938 and spread with the Nazi occupation of Europe. For all the voracious greed and intense wrangling of Nazis bent on getting their hands on whatever art they could get away with, looting was not simply a matter of individual acts of violence and theft. Indeed, what is most characteristic about Nazi art plundering was the high degree of bureaucratic organization embodied in meticulous lists.[13]

Ironically, the looting of old masters inadvertently affirmed the aesthetic choices of the very Jews derided in, and denounced by, official Nazi cultural policy. If imitation is the sincerest form of flattery, looting may be the most vicious. While heaping contempt on "Jewish taste," Nazis happily seized paintings owned by the French Rothschilds; among them were Vermeer's *The Astronomer,* Frans Hals's *Lady with a Rose,* and Chardin's *Portrait of a Young Girl.*

The fate of stolen art treasures received a flurry of attention toward the end of World War II and in its immediate aftermath. As D-day approached, the risk of damage to art and architecture became a matter of mounting concern. "Shortly we will be fighting our way across the Continent of Europe in battles designed to preserve our civilization," announced General Eisenhower. "Inevitably, in the path of our advance will be found historical monuments and cultural centers which symbolize to the world all that we are fighting to preserve."[14] Of course, military imperatives took precedence over aesthetic considerations. When Captain James Rorimer, a medievalist art historian charged with protecting historic monuments, complained about the dangers facing Mont-St.-Michel, one colonel responded irritably: "You idiot . . . This is twentieth-century war. Who gives a damn about medieval walls and boiling pitch?"[15] Even so, "the lure of discovering hidden treasures, together with the desire for sure-fire attendant publicity, appealed to many commands," especially after V-E day, Rorimer pointed out.[16]

Generally, American officials and journalists reported art looting as a war story that offered additional and abundant proof of Nazi vice and Allied virtue. The richest published accounts were Janet Flanner's wonderful *New Yorker* reports, later published in *Men and Monuments.* Flanner focused on the perpetrators, Hitler and Goering, as well as their dealers Karl Haberstock and Hans Posse. But she did not ignore the Jewish victims whose collections were stripped by the Nazis. An occasional newspaper article also focused on the Nazis' cultural war against the Jews. One such piece, preserved in James Rorimer's papers, reported the recovery in the American-occupied zone of "a priceless collection of Jewish book and ceremonial objects, seized in half a dozen countries by Jew-baiting Nazis." The contrast between the splendor of the sacred objects and the squalor of their location could hardly have been greater: "From damp, rat-infested cellars and many other hiding places have been brought 130,000 volumes of Hebrew literature, Torah scrolls, ancient, illuminated manuscripts dating back to the fourteenth century."[17]

At first, Nazi art loot was framed in terms of the wonders of recovered art and the heroism of the "monuments men" who salvaged them. The tasks of preservation and recovery fell to the American Commission for the Protection and Salvage of Artistic and Historic Monuments in War Areas. Authorized by Franklin Delano Roosevelt in June 1944, the Roberts Commission, as it was known, was staffed mainly by art historians in the military. This band of army officers included Lane Faison, Theodore Rousseau, John Skelton, Craig Hugh Smyth, and James Rorimer, who already were, or soon became, eminent figures in the art world, some as academic art historians, others as museum directors and curators. After the war, many of them wrote essays or memoirs about their activities.

Among these works is James Rorimer's *Survival; The Salvage and Protection of Art in War* (1950). Written with Gilbert Rabin, it furnishes a vivid look at one "monuments man's" perception of Nazi art loot. Even in the 1960s, when Rorimer was director of the Metropolitan Museum, he always wore army boots with the custom made suits from Madrid or London that he favored.[18] Was this military touch merely a flash of sartorial idiosyncrasy? Was it an emblem of the war service for which Rorimer was awarded the Bronze Star and then the Legion d'Honneur? Or was it an indication that Rorimer saw his mission at the museum in military terms?

In all events Rorimer, like many of his fellow "monuments men," was a protégé of Paul J. Sachs. Sachs had left the family investment bank, Goldman Sachs, to return to Harvard as a dollar-a-year man and trained a generation of museum directors and curators at the Fogg. Like Sachs, Rorimer hailed from "our crowd," the German Jewish elite. He came to Harvard armed with an introduction from Walter Sachs, Paul's brother, that presented him as a "very attractive" young man with a leaning to the fine arts.[19] The young Rorimer came by the inclination honestly. His father, Louis Rorimer, was Cleveland's leading interior designer; his firm made everything from replicas of sixteenth-century tapestries to more sedate decorations for the Statler Hotels. James Rorimer's aesthetic education began, then, as a family affair; it involved frequent trips to Europe, including tours of Germany, where his father had studied in the 1890s.

After graduating from Harvard in 1927, Rorimer went to work at the Metropolitan Museum and remained there for the rest of his career, except for his stint in the military. At the age of twenty-nine, Rorimer became head of the newly created Medieval Department. The young connoisseur quickly succeeded, with John D. Rockefeller's mighty backing, in building a masterpiece, the Cloisters. Jim Rorimer's brilliant career at the Metropolitan culminated in the directorship that he held proudly from 1957 until his death in 1966.[20]

But anti-Semitism and social insecurity dogged him. The "flashing brown-black eyes which darted about constantly," in Thomas Hoving's words, did more than allow Rorimer to sustain his obsessive, loving watch over the display of art objects and the physical face of the museum. They also enabled him to watch his back in an institution that was happier to find room for the donations of Jewish collectors than to seat them on its blue-blooded board. Thus, Rorimer tried—evidently with little success—to hide his own Jewish provenance. And he advised the young Henry Geldzahler, the son of Belgian refugees from Hitler, to do the same.[21] After a particularly brutal exchange at a meeting of the board of trustees on May 11, 1966, Rorimer cursed his principal tormentor, the Hudson Valley grandee Roland B. Redmond. When Tom Hoving asked his boss what was behind Redmond's latest fulminations, Rorimer, purple-faced with fury, mentioned anti-Semitism: "The man's just petty, mean, and insulting. It's as if he's trying to kill me. I hate the bastard—I hate all of them!"[22] Later that night, Rorimer died of a cerebral hemorrhage.

The issue of Rorimer's health had surfaced in 1941, when the Army turned him down because of high blood pressure. Not easily deterred, he pulled some well-placed strings (including John D. Rockefeller, Robert Lehman, and Paul Sachs) to overturn the decision. After military intelligence had a look at this thirty-seven-year-old "Jewish gentlemen," Rorimer was finally allowed to enlist as a private; he became a commissioned officer soon after.[23] Writing to his mentor, Paul Sachs, who was also involved with the effort to salvage art and architecture in the European theater, Rorimer happily noted in December 1944: "Here I have the job of jobs as far as my background and desire are concerned . . . the most fortunate possible solution of many situations. To have had the opportunity of following the armies with Advance Section and arriving here on the first day of the liberation helped very much with establishing contacts which are proving valuable in carrying out directives and desires."[24] Rorimer eventually became chief of section in the Western Military District. Early on, he was charged with protecting buildings, especially in Paris, but he soon became involved in recovering stolen art.

Katherine Rorimer recalled that *Survival* was a "difficult book" for her husband to write. It involved "boiling down thousands of pages of wartime horrors generated from his daily reports to the War Department in Washington." Much of the documentation was still classified as "top secret" and the "subject matter was all grim."[25]

Aside from the occasional cloak-and dagger detective story flourish, the narrative of *Survival* is simple and straightforward. It "begins with Jim's landing on the Normandy coasts with the U.S. invasion and progresses through the embattled countryside to Paris."[26] Rorimer's narrative gives no quarter to Nazis or their French collaborators. Nor does it make excuses for the misdeeds of American soldiers lacking in "simple good manners and Christian principles."[27] But Rorimer also singles out heroic museum officials, above all Rose Valland, the assistant curator at the Jeu de Paume, whose "blind devotion to French art made no allowance for any thoughts of personal danger." Led to the door by the Germans with a frequency that bordered on the comic, she managed each time to return to the museum that they used to store prized art loot.[28]

Survival focuses on the quest to discover Nazi stolen art in the face of immense practical difficulties. The extent of Nazi art looting and the hateful greed that drove it dawned only gradually on the Allies. "It was some time before we gained an impression of what had transpired," Rorimer observed. "Works of art could no longer be thought of in ordinary terms"; the quantities of art they had to reckon with were "a roomful, a carload, a castle full."[29]

Survival is framed from the perspective of an art historian with a military assignment and an aesthetic mission. Furthermore, it is the work of a curator known for his intense love of, and personal connection to, art objects. It is the work of a student of Paul Sachs, with little interest in the iconographical concerns that drove German refugee scholars such as Erwin Panofsky or Edgar Wind. Rorimer regarded plundered art as part of the national heritage as opposed to individual property. Recovery necessarily looms larger than restitution in his story largely because that was the "monuments men's" brief.

How did Rorimer deal with the Jewish dimension of Nazi art looting? Though the story focuses on the fate of plundered art as opposed to the travails of its owners, Rorimer makes clear, for instance, that Nazis stripped the homes of Henry and Edouard de Rothschild. Nevertheless, *Survival* is not a Jewish story, much less a Holocaust narrative. In this respect, it is typical of early postwar attitudes. The "survivors" that Rorimer's title alludes to are stolen works of art rather than victims of the Shoah. He rightly points out that the Germans didn't take only Jewish properties in France. "Though the property of Jews was taken more methodically, and suffered less on this account since it was usually handled by either experts of self-styled experts, many treasures were looted by individuals from more than twenty-five chateaux I could mention."[30]

Usually, Rorimer passes over the religious or ethnic background of the Nazis' victims. Take, for example, how he tells the story of one of his unit's most remarkable finds. Outside a sprawling monastery at Buxheim, Captain Rorimer came upon an extraordinary repository of stolen art including Watteaus and Bouchers, Davids and Goyas, Delacroixs and Renoirs. Among the seemingly endless spoils of war were "cases stamped with the symbol D-W, representing the collection of M. David-Weill, President of the Museum of France."[31] But Rorimer declines to point out a critical fact: the Nazis looted David-Weill's collection because they regarded the Parisian banker as a Jew rather than a Frenchman.

It would be unfair to suggest that Rorimer simply overlooked the Nazi war against the Jews. But references to it were more abundant in an earlier draft of *Survival* found in the Rorimer papers in the Archives of American Art in Washington, D.C. Whether Jewish issues were toned down because of the author's anxieties or the publisher's strictures is a matter of speculation, however. In the published narrative, the Jewish owners of stolen art figured at various points, though usually without comment. When Rorimer returned to Munich (a city he knew well) on May 7, 1945, only a few days after its capture by the Seventh Army, he scrutinized Pinakothek records devoted to acquisitions since the Nazi rise to power. "I noted at random a Tyrolese painting of the year 1470. It was entered as coming from a Jew. No name was given. The agent was Helbing, and the sale and purchase price was only 250 marks."[32] It is only in an appendix that we find a list of the major Jewish collections that had been plundered by the Nazis.[33]

Sites of Forgetfulness

Although individuals and families continued to press for the restitution of Nazi stolen art, the issue faded from public view soon after the end of World War II. American policy was partly responsible for what did, and did not, happen. Returning plundered art to the nation where it had been stolen rather than to individual owners may have been a reasonable strategy, but it opened the way for considerable abuse. Was the Dutch government, for instance, entitled to art works owned by Jews who died in the concentration camps? On another front, the advent of the Cold War made the American government especially eager to employ former Nazis in the crusade against Russian Communism. Battling the "Red Menace" was more pressing than raising inconvenient questions about who stole what from Jews.

The return of the majority of the "monuments men" to the States by 1946–47 was also unfortunate if not ill-advised. Their departure left the task of restitution more often than not to those who really didn't want it to happen. Governments, museums, auction houses, dealers, and collectors had little motive—save honesty and honor—to admit that they had made dubious acquisitions, much less to offer compensation to Jews. The efforts of bodies such as the French Commission de Récuperation Artistique were usually half-hearted and inadequate. But they did return numerous works to their rightful owners—perhaps just enough to buy off powerful collectors and stave off scandal.

Even if the will of such commissions had been exemplary—and that was hardly true—the task of restitution would have remained formidable. Locating stolen art was no easy matter especially if it passed through multiple jurisdictions. Determining whether "sales" of art were forced or "voluntary," the product of necessity or proof of collaboration, was especially ticklish. The principal obstacle, however, especially for refugees and camp survivors, was producing proof of ownership. The quest for restitution demanded substantial time, energy, patience—and luck. And so large dealers and influential collectors retrieved much of their looted art, but minor players rarely fared so well. Few had the time or connections to batter away at government bureaucracies with little interest in their cases.

Finally, the shadow of the Holocaust inevitably colored what was done, and not done, with Nazi stolen art. There is good reason to believe that the desire to get past the catastrophe of the war dampened interest in the fate of Nazi art loot, along with far weightier concerns. Disregarding the provenance of plundered art and the moral claims of the living was, apparently, part of what the French call the "right to forget." Next to the murder of millions, after all, keeping stolen masterpieces was small beer indeed. And there were, needless to say, a great many more pressing issues in the postwar world. Who would have had the audacity to focus on the whereabouts of stolen art in the face of displaced persons who had lost everything? How, in good conscience, could Jewish communal organizations focus their attention on, say, a lost Klimt, rather than make provisions for Viennese survivors or search for their relatives?

Nevertheless, the issue of Nazi stolen art did not totally fade from public view in the 1950s and 1960s, as evidenced by a clipping in James Rorimer's papers from an unexpected venue—*Variety*. The article reported that Burt Lancaster would star in a French picture "about how the French resistance saved art treasures from being sent to Germany during the last war . . . Pic will be eligible for French Film Aid and will have mostly Yank coin behind it . . . it has Britain thesp Paul Scofield in the cast as well as locals."[34]

John Frankenheimer's film *The Train* (1964) was adapted loosely from Rose Valland's memoir, *Le front de l'Art: Défense des collections françaises 1939–1945* (1961). Hailed by Rorimer for her brave campaign to save French art, Valland devoted part of her memoir to the confiscation of "Israélite," that is, Jewish-owned, collections such as that of Adolph Schloss, and to the administrative battles to save such holdings.[35]

The Train did nothing of the sort, however. Though it is far superior to the run-of-the-battle Hollywood war movie, *The Train* is longer on panache than accuracy. Rather than focus on the story of Nazi art looting, *The Train* fixes on a dramatic tale of recovery. It derives its plot from an actual incident. On August 1, 1944, as the Allies pushed toward Paris, the Germans packed up the stolen art that remained in the Jeu de Paume; the 148 cases of Nazi loot took up nearly fifty-two railway cars. For nearly four weeks, the French Resistance managed to limit the progress of the art train.

The Train illustrates how Jews were written out of the story of Nazi stolen art; it omits the pillaging of Jewish-owned collections that figures so prominently in Valland's memoir. The opening scenes take place in and around the Jeu de Paume, one of the principal Nazi repositories for stolen art. Although the film begins with haunting shots of an array of modern paintings, it offers little explanation of how and why the booty got there in the first place, much less to whom it had belonged. As Captain von Waldheim (Paul Scofield) looks on, the curator, Mlle. Villard (Suzanne Flom), stares at a modern picture. Offering nothing more than a veiled reference to the Jewish provenance of its owners, she notes mournfully notes: "It was part of the Klugmann collection." Unmoved by, but not unaware of, what has happened, von Waldheim simply responds, "Was." The captain adds that as "a loyal officer" he should have no sympathy for "degenerate art," but his reverential stance suggests a very different attitude to the painting.

Far from depicting von Waldheim as a stock Nazi brute, The Train portrays him as a civilized and humane aesthete. In fact, the actual person upon whom the character was based, Baron von Behr, was an aristocratic social climber dedicated to high living rather than high art. Determined to advance his own interests by catering to Goering's appetite for art and power, von Behr and his wife pushed their way into the highest circles of Occupied Paris. Supposedly awash in champagne, the von Behrs committed suicide before the Allies entered Paris.

The Train focuses on the struggle of the French Resistance to prevent the Germans from taking art treasures to Berlin. Though French railway workers are initially reticent to risk lives to safeguard art pictures, Mlle. Vallard's pleadings and the murder of one of their Resistance colleagues soon changes their minds. Labiche (Burt Lancaster) and his compatriots come to see the stolen works of Renoir and Cézanne, Picasso and Braque, Degas and Matisse as "the glory of France," "our special vision," and "our trust." Recapturing the train, then, becomes a matter of national honor, saving France's cultural heritage, and outwitting the Nazis. Rather than focus on Vichy collaboration, The Train represents the French as victims striking back against Nazi oppression and not as quislings collaborating with the occupying power. It shows how Labiche and his compatriots ultimately succeed against great odds in derailing the Germans in more ways than one; they capture the art train and keep its treasures in France and for France.

Censoring the Jewish dimension of Nazi art looting was not simply a matter of opting for suspense in The Train. For the denouement of this unusually exciting film omits what is perhaps the most poignant, dramatic episode in the real-life saga of the art train. On August 27, 1944, a detachment of General Leclcerq's army, led by Captain Alexandre Rosenberg, captured the train in the Paris suburb of Aulnay. No liberator could have been more suitable than Alexandre Rosenberg, whose father, Paul Rosenberg, was a leading Parisian dealer of Jewish origin. Opening the cars of the train, Captain Rosenberg came upon a host of Picassos, Braques, and Matisses, many of which he had last seen in his family home and gallery at rue la Boétie. *The Train* glosses over this beautiful irony. Instead, it ends with a statutory face-off between the victorious Labiche and the vanquished von Waldheim. Refusing to follow standard Hollywood formulae, however, *The Train* pictures the German officer as an art lover and the French railway man as courageous but philistine. From start to finish, then, *The Train* represents Nazi art looting in terms of a battle between the French and the Germans. The Jewish victims remain obscure or forgotten.

In Search of Lost Time

Not until the mid-1990s did the restitution of Nazi art loot surface as an important public issue—a problem demanding a solution. It is the memory of the Holocaust that provides the current frame of Nazi art loot. Contemporary narratives emphasize the victimization of Jews and the necessity of restitution. The principal cause of renewed interest in stolen art was clearly the growing centrality of the Shoah in contemporary consciousness (as exemplified by a variety of memorials and films ranging from the United States Holocaust Memorial Museum in Washington, D.C., to *Schindler's List*).[36] This concern is itself a symptom of the cultural obsession with survivors and memory, roots and identity. And it has a strong material basis: the struggle to recover Nazi art loot is part of a larger battle for financial restitution from governments and corporations.

But other factors also spurred the new concern with Nazi stolen art. First, the opening of confidential archival files closed for fifty years facilitated the work of journalists and scholars. Lynn Nicholas's pioneering study of art looting and recovery, *The Rape of Europa*, mined American government records along with other sources. Hector Feliciano's *The Lost Museum*, which was based more on interviews than archives, drew attention to the fact that the French had never returned countless works of art to their rightful owners. Second, the revelation that the legendarily clean Swiss provided Hitler with not only an alpine money laundry but also a clearinghouse for pillaged art has provoked justified outrage. Third, mounting indignation at the colonial appropriation of native people's art and artifacts fed into interest in Nazi pillaging and, to a point, sympathy for its Jewish victims. Fourth, the enormous inflation of art prices in recent years, especially for French Impressionist canvases, has made the prospect of restitution all the more attractive to potential claimants and all the more worrying to the current owners of tainted works. Fifth, the legal complexities and potential fees involved in recovering, say, a Picasso or a Rembrandt have attracted a small but growing band of lawyers and investigators. What is a labor of love for some is a source of billable hours for others.

Finally, family piety, Jewish pride, aesthetic devotion, and financial interests—all these drive the quest to recover Nazi art loot. The aging of survivors, and indeed their children and grandchildren, has made them particularly eager to recover palpable remains of an otherwise crushed inheritance. The slaughtered dead are gone, but the art they collected lives after them. In short, stolen art works have become what Pierre Nora has called "sites of memory." These sites exist because of an absence of settings in which memory is a real part of everyday experience.[37] Pillaged art, remembered or recovered, constitutes traces of a vanished life and indeed vanished lives. The art that once adorned the walls of family homes, now occupied by others if not destroyed, offers a path to a bygone time. Pictures and sculptures furnish an aesthetic equivalent of Proust's famous madeleine, now rendered bittersweet. Unlike specifically religious vestiges of the world before the Shoah, stolen art works are emblems of citizenship, proof of national belonging, cosmopolitan sympathies, and aesthetic taste. In short, art collections symbolize certain Jews' participation in secular culture.

"Thou shalt remember," the Jewish imperative, colors the drive to recapture Nazi art loot. Hence, restitution becomes both a moral duty and a psychological necessity. A documentary by the British producer Anne Webber, who is now chair of the European Commission on Looted Art, embodies the new frame of Nazi art loot.[38] The aptly titled *Making a Killing* (1998) refers both to the murder of Jews and to the profits of art. It tells the story of the Gutmanns, a prominent German Jewish banking family who fled to the Netherlands. These Protestant converts no longer considered themselves Jews. The Nazis disagreed. When, in 1943, Friedrich and Lilli Gutmann refused to sign over their art collection, the Nazis confiscated their art and sent them to concentration camps where they died.

Making a Killing dramatically reveals how Nazi art loot has become a touchstone for memory, and restitution, a surrogate for recapturing the past. It focuses on the struggle of the Gutmanns' children, Bernard and Lili, and Bernard's sons, Nick and Simon Goodman, to recover a stolen Degas. In 1987, the Chicago pharmaceutical magnate Daniel Searle legally purchased Degas's *Landscape with Smokestack* for US$850,000. At the film's outset, the narrator proclaims that unfinished business remains: it is too late to try the perpetrators who murdered the Gutmanns, but it may be possible to recover the art. The place on the wall where the Degas once hung in their house remains empty. "So little of our old life remains," Lili Gutmann remarks. How much easier it is to reconstruct the past through art one remembers in heart and mind than through pieces of paper. But the battle for restitution makes her ill and anxious. No such unease seemed to affect her nephew, Simon Goodman, who told a reporter: "My family was murdered, their possessions destroyed or stolen. These works are all that is left of our heritage, so we want the painting back."[39]

Making a Killing indicts the art world's "conspiracy of silence," the complicity of art dealers, auction houses, and museum officials who turned a blind eye to Nazi art loot. It also indicts Dutch government officials who blocked the Gutmann family's claims and queries. The film shows the formidable legal and financial obstacles that prevent most claimants from pressing their cases. The Goodmans' attorneys faulted Daniel Searle for not adequately researching the provenance of the Degas. For their part, Searle's attorneys claimed that the heirs had not been diligent enough in their search for the stolen painting. In August 1998, the parties reached a Solomonic out of court settlement: they divided the estimated US$1.1 million value of the Degas between the two "owners." Searle, a trustee of the Art Institute of Chicago, donated his half of the painting's value to the museum, which purchased rights to the other portion from the Goodmans and Lili Gutmann.

The restitution of Nazi stolen art is also the theme of Daniel Silva's recent best-selling thriller, *The English Assassin* (2002). Its hero, Gabriel Allon, whose parents were murdered in Auschwitz, is an art restorer and sometime Israeli agent. He works with Julian Isherwood, a Jewish art dealer in London. Isherwood, who is also an Israeli "helper," was a refugee from Paris, where his father, Samuel Isakowitz, had a gallery on rue la la Boétie in the eighth arrondissement, the hub of the art trade. After the fall of France, the Nazis pillaged the Isakowitz gallery and also the Bordeaux warehouse where Isakowitz *père* had stored much of his collection. They worked on a tip from a collaborationist dealer who received a 5 percent commission. (The story closely resembles what actually happened to Paul Rosenberg's goods.) Julian's parents managed to smuggle him out of the country but they themselves were arrested and sent to Sobibor in 1943, where they were killed immediately. Changing his name but not his loyalties, Isherwood became an expert on Nazi stolen art.

The English Assassin explores Switzerland's role as a trading house for art that Nazis had stolen from Jews. The plot turns on the mystery behind the murder of a wealthy, influential Swiss broker and art collector, Augustus Rolfe, and the theft of certain paintings. As Gabriel unravels the mystery, he works with Rolfe's daughter, Anna, an eminent violinist who loathed her father. Searching Rolfe's Zurich villa, Gabriel comes upon a photograph of Rolfe with Goering and Hitler on an alpine terrace—an emblem of Swiss collaboration with the Nazis. As payment for services rendered to the Reich, Rolfe was allowed to buy (for next to nothing) art that had been stolen from Jews. In a Swiss bank vault, Gabriel and Anna discover Rolfe's hidden booty, sixteen pictures including works by Monet, Picasso, Degas, van Gogh, Renoir, and Bonnard. "Even Gabriel, a man used to working · with priceless art, was overwhelmed by the sheer volume of it."[40] When

Julian Isherwood later examines the treasure trove, he is amazed to find his father's initials, S.I., on the back of one of the paintings, a Renoir portrait of a young girl with flowers. Anna apologizes on behalf of the Rolfe family and immediately returns the stolen picture to him.

The vault also contains a letter from Augustus Rolfe addressed to Gabriel. The remorseful banker admitted that the paintings were "acquired with a veneer of legality but quite illegally. When I 'purchased' them, I was aware that they had been confiscated from the collections of Jewish dealers and collectors in France."[41] As wracked by guilt as he was once driven by greed, Rolfe found in Yom Kippur inspiration for making amends to the injured parties. And so he asked Gabriel to return the works to their rightful owners or, if they could not be located, to hang the pictures in Israeli museums. But Rolfe also warned Gabriel that a small circle of elite Swiss bankers (to which he had belonged) "want the past to remain exactly where it is—entombed in the bank vaults of the Bahnhofstrasse—and they will stop at nothing to achieve their end."[42] In fact, the bankers succeeded in murdering a Swiss professor, Emil Jacobi, the disavowed conscience of the nation who had devoted himself to uncovering and publicizing Switzerland's wartime collaboration with the Nazis.

In *The English Assassin*, Gabriel Allon figures as the antithesis of the Swiss bankers who wish to keep the past buried. Virtually cut off from his past (his parents killed by the Nazis, his son murdered, and his wife disfigured by a Palestinian terrorist), the archangel Gabriel is an art restorer, symbolically and literally, who returns art loot.

The campaign to recover Nazi stolen art, however, has not been confined to literary thrillers and documentary films. What began largely as an individual effort to recover Nazi art loot is fast becoming institutionalized. The residues of personal or familial memory are now the stuff of collective action. Long neglected by Jewish communal organizations, the issue of stolen art is now very much on their dockets, largely thanks to the increasingly militant attitude of leaders such as Edgar Bronfman, Jr., toward Holocaust reparations. In 1997, the World Jewish Congress and the World Jewish Restitution Organization established the Commission on Art Recovery. Its mission, according to Chairman Ronald Lauder, is to "help bring a small measure of justice into the lives of families whose art was seized . . . the problem of stolen art must be recognized as a moral issue."[43]

But negotiating between conflicting goods is not simple—as Lauder himself had cause to discover. In January 1998, Manhattan District Attorney Robert Morgenthau issued a grand jury subpoena to prevent the Museum of Modern Art from returning two pictures by Egon Schiele (*Portrait of Wally* and *Dead City*) to their "owner," the Leopold Foundation in Vienna, at the end of an exhibition. The injunction placed Lauder in a particularly uncomfortable position. For this devoted collector of Viennese modernism was already planning the Neue Gallerie, his temple of modern German and

Austrian art, which opened in late 2001 in the former Vanderbilt mansion on Fifth Avenue in New York. In addition to being the chairman of the Commission on Art Recovery, Lauder was also the head of MoMA's board of trustees. Faced with an apparent conflict of interest, Lauder declined to recuse himself. Rather, he backed MoMA's plan to return the Schieles to the Leopold Foundation despite their dark provenance.

Robert Morgenthau, the scion of one of America's most distinguished German Jewish families, had his own agenda. His father, Henry Morgenthau, FDR's Secretary of Treasury during World War II, had advocated the deindustrialization of Germany. Robert Morgenthau himself had led the drive to found the recently established Museum of Jewish Heritage in New York. His extraordinary intervention was a response to pleas from the heirs of Lea Bondi Jaray, who fled Austria after the Anschluss, and the heirs of Fritz Grünbaum, who died in Dachau. In 1938, an Austrian Nazi, who had benefited from the "aryanization" of Jaray's gallery, seized *Wally* along with much else. Mistakenly identified as part of another looted art collection, *Wally* was given to the Belvedere, the Austrian National Gallery, after the war. Then, in 1954, Dr. Ruldolf Leopold acquired the picture, despite the fact, according to Lea Bondi Jaray, that he knew that the picture was rightfully hers.

All the involved parties in New York claimed that they wanted to determine the ownership of the pictures, but MoMA officials and their advocates argued that if Morgenthau's suit succeeded, it would limit the ability of New York's art institutions to mount major exhibitions and display great art borrowed from abroad. Though Morgenthau blocked the return of the looted Schieles, the New York State Court of Appeals overturned the subpoena. But the U.S. Attorney's New York office weighed in on the dispute, claiming the painting had been illegally imported under the National Stolen Property Act. Just when the return of the looted Schieles to Vienna seemed unstoppable, in April 2002, the chief judge of the Federal District Court in Manhattan, Michael B. Mukasey, ruled that *Portrait of Wally* was stolen property. He ordered a trial to determine the rightful owner.[44]

Caught red-handed with stolen art, governments, museums, dealers, collectors, and auction houses are under intense pressure to address the problem of the "last prisoners." The Seattle Museum of Art is but one of several institutions that have returned Nazi art loot, in this case a stolen Matisse. The Museum of Modern Art, the Tate Gallery, and the Getty Museum, among others, established websites for their collections to help locate stolen art. In 1998, the Art Loss Register in London, a commercial company, established a Holocaust-claims detective service. Though the Art Loss Register purports to take no commission on such claims, its interests are with the art trade, the auction houses, and gallery owners who supposedly fund its researches.[45] Nevertheless, the Art Loss Register was instrumental in helping to locate a number of stolen works, notably Monet's *Water Lilies, 1904,* which the Nazis looted from the collections of Paul Rosenberg.

The debate on the restitution of art may be one of the last acts of the Shoah. There is good reason to welcome the quest to recover plundered art, but the preoccupation with restitution poses certain dangers. Critics such as Abraham Foxman of the Anti-Defamation League and Gabriel Schoenfeld of *Commentary* have argued that the focus on recovering property desecrates the memory of the Shoah. Mixing meaning, memory, and money is a risky business.

What is missing in the current frame of Nazi stolen art is at least as telling as what is present. The danger of dwelling on the darkly enthralling story of how Nazis and collaborators got their hands on Jewish-owned art collections is that it may obscure the experiences, dreams, and fate of their collectors. Much as the concern with the mass murder of Jews during the Shoah may inadvertently efface the lives that Jews built in pre–World War II Europe, the concern with Nazi stolen art may draw attention away from the cultural activities of individual Jews. For the story of Jewish art dealers and collectors is not simply or primarily a story of affluent Jews buying art that Nazis confiscated along with all their other worldly possessions. Rather, the crux of the story is how and why certain individuals and families of Jewish origin became arbiters of taste, interpreters and traffickers of old masters and modern art alike. In other words, how did certain Jews acquire so many old and modern masterpieces in the first place? That is the untold story of Nazi art looting.

Restitution is not simply a matter of regaining stolen masterpieces; it is also a matter of remembering stolen lives. Following the trail of plundered art necessarily takes us back to the Nazi war against the Jews, but stopping there is historically and ethically dubious. The past cannot be recaptured, but plundered art may yet help us remember that Jews were actors in European culture and not simply its victims. As Julian Isherwood tells Gabriel Allon in *The English Assassin*: "The paintings can't talk, but their provenance *can* . . . Provenance, after all is everything."[46]

Chapter 17

Joseph Lewitan and the Nazification of Dance in Germany

Marion Kant

This is the story of a forgotten man. Joseph Lewitan, one of the most important modern dance critics in Germany during the interwar years, has been virtually lost to history, a casualty of the fate of dance and those who wrote about it during the Nazi period.[1] German modern dance was the only modern art form celebrated by the Nazis, in contrast with modern literature, visual art, and music, which were considered "degenerate." However, once the Nazis declared Lewitan "Jewish," his writing on modern German dance became "Jewish" too. How German modern dance came to enjoy pride of place in the Nazi regime's "New Order" and how Germany's leading dance critic became an involuntary Jew is the subject of this essay.

Early Years

Joseph Lewitan was born in Russia in 1894. He studied jurisprudence at the Imperial University in St. Petersburg and was awarded a degree from its law faculty in November 1915. A year later, Lewitan started working for the Regional Military Equipment Committee of the North Western Region, securing food, clothes, military goods, weapons, and ammunition for the Imperial Russian Army, which was fighting the Germans during World War I.[2] After the Bolshevik Revolution, Lewitan joined a governmental cultural teaching cooperative, where he worked as an instructor of education for the People's Commissariat of Education for cooperatives in the Northern Region, as his calling card stated.[3]

Lewitan left Soviet Russia for Helsingfors on January 8, 1920, and immigrated to Berlin in April 1920.[4] He joined the Russian émigré community in Berlin, a center of Russian life outside Soviet Russia at the time. Fleeing the upheaval of the Bolshevik revolution and ensuing civil war, and seeking a safe haven far from politics, this talented Russian lawyer chose an unlikely discipline—dance, and specifically ballet—within which to develop his many skills as manager, linguist, and aesthete. His lover, Evgenia Eduardova, a former *coryphée* (ballet dancer) at the Maryinski Theater in St. Petersburg, also fled to Berlin. She brought her entire household with her, including not only her husband but also her admirers, maids, cooks, and circle of friends. With Lewitan's support, indeed with his expertise and under his guidance, she opened a ballet school, which would in time become one of the most influential institutions for professional ballet training in Northern Germany. Even more important than his role as *éminence grise* in a leading ballet school was Lewitan's contribution to the world of publishing.

Der Tanz

While we do not know precisely when Lewitan decided to create a dance journal, it must have been soon after he moved to Berlin in 1920. Lewitan envisioned a serious professional journal on dance that would cover all aspects and all genres of dance: ballet/theatrical dance; free dance; modern German dance, including chamber dance as well as group and solo dance; the new genre of community dance; social dance or ballroom dance (at the time swing or jazz dance, the waltz, fox-trot, Charleston); acrobatics; any dance in entertainment; dance in other countries and regions, national dances and national dance styles (so-called folk dance); and competitions. He encouraged a boldly multidisciplinary approach that would include history and aesthetics, anthropology and ethnography, psychology and sociology. And he took responsibility for everything about the journal, from concept to execution, including production and distribution, the business aspects (funding, contributors, honorariums, subscribers, and prices), commissioning articles and writing articles, as well as editing them. He took ideas from early drafts through to their final versions. He found photographs and illustrations and designed the pages of the magazine.

In October 1927, nine months after he had established the legal basis for the journal, the first issue of *Der Tanz: Monatsschrift für Tanzkultur* (Dance: A Monthly Journal for Dance Culture) appeared.[5] *Der Tanz* was unprecedented in Germany, not only in its aspirations but also because of its willingness to address a deeply divided dance scene. There were two other journals with which it might be compared: the English *Dancing Times*, the oldest dance journal, which was established in 1910 and boasted a worldwide readership;[6] and *Severnyii Vestnik*, a Russian experiment whose editor, Akim Volynskii, helped shape Lewitan's views on the arts and approach to dance writing.[7] Between the English model of impartial judgment and cool, but exact observation and the Russian model of passionate involvement and intervention arose the ideal fusion, a German model of democratic argument and philosophical debate. This ideal was difficult to realize in the stormy political context of the Weimar Republic, where dance, which figured in extreme experiments to transform everyday life, was itself torn by contentious artistic debates.[8]

Ballet as a theatrical art, and modern dance, mostly practiced outside the theater, were enemies from the turn of the century over issues of *Weltanschauung* and *Lebensweise*, an ideological war carried out on the human body and ways to move. Modernists attacked ballet as outmoded and decadent. They considered its formal properties an impediment to the "natural" flow of movement and lacking in significant meaning. Balletomanes considered modern dance barbaric with respect to its form and crazy in its conception of the body. They faulted modern dancers for being arrogant and escapist in their engagement with contemporary issues and faith in the power of modern dance to redeem humanity. The bitterness was so great that the two sides barely talked to one another—not even on a personal level. Lewitan entered the dance debate at a point when advocates of German modern dance were trying to renew the dance scene through dance education, preferably without ballet.[9]

Dance Wars

Lewitan's aim—to provide a public forum for these concerns and build bridges across factions—was daring. The journal demanded tolerance of different views and interest in a wide range of achievements. Lewitan gathered together an impressive group of writers, invited anyone with the requisite expertise to contribute, and even persuaded bitter rivals to publish work in his magazine or at the very least to offer statements. Lewitan himself served as editor, columnist (*Tänzerische Tagesfragen*), main critic (*Tanzabende*), compiler of notes on dance (*Arabesken*), and frequent commentator on social dance. He did not sign his name to these contributions and frequently wrote under the pseudonym "Bescapi", the master in E. T. A. Hoffmann's *Prinzessin Brambilla*.[10] Bescapi stood for a program that united conflicting ideas: a romantic and at the same time modern approach to art.

The two central pillars in Lewitan's magazine were dance pedagogy (teaching dance and training dancers) and dance criticism (description, interpretation, and evaluation of actual dance works). It was in the area of criticism that he made a name for himself. The city of Berlin did not lack critical voices. But Lewitan's stood out because he did not let his personal preferences prevent the journal from exploring a wide range of dance forms in their own terms, whether in scholarly articles or critical reviews.

Lewitan was not only erudite—he was knowledgeable in dance history, aesthetics, and technique—but also open to everything that had to do with dance in Berlin. He paid close attention to movement, while also considering music, costume, lighting, space, and narrative. He wrote about what he saw clearly and soberly, while not hesitating to take a stand, a delicate balance to maintain. Lewitan was not particularly enthusiastic about German modern dance and disliked what many of the modern German dancers stood for, but that did not prevent him from closely following their careers. Lewitan's true passion was modern ballet Russian-style (he admired such artists as Nikolai Legat and Assaf Messerer), but precisely for that reason he went out of his way to note the limits of modern ballet.

During the approximately seven years that Lewitan covered dance and ballet in Germany, he monitored, reviewed—and increasingly—reported. Written immediately after the performance, the reviews were a direct response, a spontaneous impression, and in their entirety they form an important chronicle of contemporary dance of the time. In contrast, his reports included extensive commentary and analysis, and over time they got longer and more elaborate to the point of becoming short political essays. For a while, the brief reviews and long reports appeared together. But as the political situation in Germany deteriorated and Lewitan grew increasingly desperate, he turned more often to the essay form. It is in these essays, his reports on the dance congresses (*Tänzerkongresse*), to be discussed, and his commentaries on the state of dance in the present and for the future that some of his most important ideas were developed— above all, the notion of a "third way" in dance. Lewitan envisioned a kind of new dance that would draw on the technical foundations and formal aesthetic properties of modern ballet and the adventurousness of modern dance performance.

Lewitan, like many of his fellow artists and critics in Germany at the time, wanted to insulate art from contemporary politics, which was, in his opinion, contaminating every aspect of life. To be above politics was itself a political act, as Lewitan realized when he requested balanced articles on Soviet Russia or the Jews in Palestine and insisted on representing a diversity of views and maintaining a respectful tone. In time he learned to accept politics in art. Amid the turbulence of the 1920s, the "objective" criticism in *Der Tanz* aimed less to celebrate an artist, though of course this could and did happen, but more to enlighten the reader. The critic's role was not only to speak to the dance world about itself but also to expose audiences to serious thought about dance—and especially contemporary dance—as an art form.[11]

Lewitan and Jewish Dance

While Lewitan commissioned articles from faraway countries, those on Jewish dance were particularly noteworthy. The German readers of *Der Tanz* would have had the opportunity to see Habima, which had been to Berlin on several occasions in the 1920s, greatly impressing the German artistic world.[12] What they would have made of M. Berchin-Benedictoff's article on Jewish dance is difficult to say. According to Berchin-Benedictoff, although Jews had always danced, they were anomalous in the history of dance because of their diaspora experience. While life in the diaspora had inter-nationalized them, life in the "ghettos" had also made them dependent on their hosts, which distorted their relationship to Jewish heritage. As a result, Jewish youth were drawn to the culture of the larger society, a ten-dency that Berchin-Benedictoff associated with the "de-nationalization" of the Jews. What Jews needed most urgently, in his view, was dance that expressed their national consciousness. Where better to create a true national dance than in Palestine?

However, the form that such dance should take was a point of conten-tion. Baruch Agadati, the most important proponent of the new national Jewish dance, while drawing on the entirety of Jewish history, from biblical times to the present, made use of the grotesque. This was a mistake, accord-ing to Berchin-Benedictoff, because the grotesque epitomized ghetto oppression and Jewish "restlessness." Fortunately, though, Agadati was gradually overcoming this limitation, as could be seen in the new national dance of the Jews of Palestine, a utopian attempt to synthesize ancient Jew-ish dance, however it was imagined, and modern dance based on ballet technique. Whether Berchin-Benedictoff was a real person or just Lewitan in disguise, we do not know. What we do know is that as editor, he was making a place for Jewish dance within the pages of *Der Tanz* and envi-sioning a future for Jewish dance in Palestine rather than Europe; he was projecting an idealistic Zionist vision of a brighter future in dance. If noth-ing else, then, Lewitan's bold inclusion of Jewish dance is an indication for an ongoing inner debate about Judaism and its place in a modern world. He had, after all, also to find his place and he had to find it as a Jew.[13]

Dance Congresses

The 1927, 1928, and 1930 dance congresses in Magdeburg, Essen, and Munich, respectively, marked the rising hopes as well as the complete disil-lusionment of dancers in Germany. These events were organized mainly by Rudolf von Laban and his pupils. Laban is considered the father of Ger-man modern dance and the driving force behind the reorganization of the dance landscape. Throughout the 1920s Laban and his disciple, Mary Wig-man, had campaigned for the institutionalization of dance. He envisioned a college of dance dedicated to the teaching of modern and avant-garde styles based on his theories.[14] The college was finally founded under the Nazis, with Laban as director.

The sina qua non of a German enterprise such as this was the construc-tion of a "*theoretische Grundlage*" (a theoretical basis); Lewitan watched its evolution and never doubted its necessity, though, as a Russian Jew, he did not necessarily agree with its premises. During the 1920s, Laban's dance "science," which he had established as a discipline in his schools and in the Choreographisches Institut in Essen and Berlin, consisted of *choreosophy*, a philosophy dedicated to ethical and aesthetical aspects of dance as community service and educational means; *choreography*, the description and study of dance and movement in order to notate it; and *choreology*, a method for studying the governing laws and inner logic of space and time elements in movement.[15] Lewitan objected that choreosophy, which was supposed to enable "us to understand dance in its cultural context with the means offered by contemporary life," was not at all a *Wissenschaft*, a science, because it had neither an epistemology nor a methodology.[16] In his view, choreosophy actually posed a danger because it would encourage dilettantism and obscurantism rather than scientific approaches to dance.

Laban's ideas were given a wide hearing at the three dance congresses. Lewitan's views on them can be seen from his report on the 1928 dance congress in Essen, which featured major addresses on the future of dance by Laban and Wigman, both of whom denounced ballet. Wigman argued that ballet was degenerate, belonged to a past age, and should be banned from any contemporary theatrical establishment. Existing theaters were suitable neither as architectural spaces in which to perform nor as institutions for which young dancers should be trained. The alternative that she proposed was "absolute dance." She spoke apodictically about "absolute dance" as the dance form of the future and real expression of modernity.[17] Absolute dance was to arise exclusively from the inner logic of movement. It was neither theatrical dance nor was it intended for the theater. A former Laban pupil, Wigman was now his greatest rival.

Laban, in his lecture "Das chorische Kunstwerk" (Choric Artwork), offered a competing alternative: the movement choir.[18] Laban envisioned choral works executed by amateur or professional dance choirs, who would celebrate the true spirit of community and lead dancers into another world, whether real or otherworldly. Ideally, the movement choirs would perform not in theaters but in dance temples. Through physical activity, participants would achieve spiritually heightened states and soulful embodiments of the principles of communion. Above all, Laban envisioned a dancing community as the antidote to the ills of civilization and utopian model for a society made whole by art.

In contrast, Kurt Jooss, a choreographer who was also a Laban pupil, called for an "objective basis . . . for practical artistic questions" and pragmatic approach.[19] The structure and function of the institution of theater was to be the starting point of all future artistic activities because one had to work with, and not against, a historically developed institution. Moreover, Jooss rejected the distinction between "theater dance" and "dance theater," relegated Wigman's "absolute dance" to a subcategory of theatrical dance, and absorbed it into his own *Tanztheater*. In this way, Jooss tried to overcome the rift between modern dance and ballet, which he saw as two sides of one coin, not two distinct genres.

From *Der Tanz*, it becomes clear that Lewitan considered the proposal to abolish theater fruitless and had become impatient with Wigman's extremism and Laban's narrow-mindedness. Lewitan called for tolerance in the search for solutions to overcome the acute political and social divisions in dance. Interestingly enough, Kurt Jooss' concept, a true theoretical and practical compromise, as much a "third way" in choreography as Lewitan's efforts in journalism and dance criticism—and an affront to Wigman—did not impress Lewitan. It was Laban whom he considered the most influential and hence the most likely figure to succeed, not Jooss, whom he saw as offering but a slight modification of Laban's thoughts. This was one of Lewitan's few misjudgments but, as events were to show, it was a spectacular one—politically, aesthetically, as well as personally.

For Lewitan, the Essen congress was an unmistakable demonstration of the decline of modern dance in Germany. Looking back on the first quarter of the twentieth century, he bemoaned the absence of an acceptable theoretical framework for the new dance. It was time to announce the end of the revolutionary past. Instead of inflation, dance needed a period of deflation, in which dancers should strive toward clarity and stability, which could be achieved only if professional dance began in school and ended on stage. There were too many *Tanzbühnen* (dance groups aspiring to performance without solid foundations) and too few good schools to teach them the basics. The future of dance required an investment in quality pedagogy.

A month after his report on the congress, in September 1928, Lewitan, in an afterthought, warned his readers that the *Tanzdeflation*, or deflation of dance, was not happening. He wanted his readers to learn from the past. At the beginning of the twentieth century, Isadora Duncan, while revolutionizing dance, also opened the floodgates to dance inflation, that is, to amateurism and to a pointless rebellion against existing artistic values. Not everybody could or should dance, in Lewitan's view, because truly outstanding and original works could only be created on a solid technical foundation. Moreover, the divide between ballet and modern dance was misguided, because ballet could also be modern and modern dancers needed disciplined training.

Then, in October 1928, Lewitan questioned whether Laban could live up to his claim to have created the dance system for the future and philosophical framework for it. Entitled "Der Kampf um den Tanz," which evoked Laban's slogan of combat and reverberated with the *Kulturkampf* that was shaking up Germany, the essay analyzed several lectures in which Laban presented his entire dance system. Lewitan was open to reform, but he wanted it to be a collaborative process, not the proclamation of a "genius." Public debate was central to that process. But Laban and his disciples were not open to debating Laban's complex belief system, an obscure mixture of occult thought, scientific claims, and quasi-scientific methods. It had been devised as a secret cultic religion for a community that fought the evils of civilization. Inspired by the cultural pessimism of Nietzsche and Spengler, Laban and Wigman developed their movement concepts into systems of substantial cultural criticism. Dance for Laban was a means to build healthy communities and heal the wounds inflicted by a corrupt and evil society. For Wigman, dance was the representation of her national culture, which would prevent democracies such as the Weimar Republic from destroying the inner values of a Germanic society. Lewitan failed to comprehend that it was already far too late for any corrections. The systems were in place; they had been fully developed. Lewitan thought that art could be a form of reasoned thought; Laban knew that his dance was a religion.

The German Dance Scene

Whereas Lewitan had been resolute, yet always polite and eager to communicate through his writing, the dance critic André Levinson had been more frank about the German dance scene and the Essen congress. Lewitan liked Levinson's intelligent remarks, even if he did not consider them entirely new. The two men had much in common. Both came from St. Petersburg, had studied law, and fled the Bolsheviks. Both were admirers of ballet and wrote and discussed dance from an educated and enlightened philosophical background. Both were Jewish with clearly Jewish names that marked their descent. Levinson lived in Paris, the other place for Russian refuges.

In a 1929 issue of *Theater Arts Monthly*, an American journal, Levinson expressed concerns about the German modern dance scene: "The modern dance has become a national institution in Germany. Many indeed would make its practice and propagation an affair of state . . . At the bottom, the modern German dance is fiercely aware of its racial originality. It isolates itself in bitter pride from the rest of the world and proclaims its novelty by renouncing all tradition."[20] He then proceeded to speak of "cults," "idols," and "obliviousness to the past." He made fun of the "furia Germanica" and "genius of the race," which he saw as distortions of the mind more than of the body. He warned: "The youth of Germany brings a kind a fanaticism to these theatrical diversions. What you would take for a technical exercise or an extravagant joke turns out to be a mystic article of faith."[21] Levinson also elaborated on the rival groups, on the split of the modern guild, and on the enmity and jealousy between Laban and Wigman and their zealous followers. Their fight concerning the philosophical foundations of dance would have far-reaching consequences. Levinson confirmed Lewitan's recognition that modern dance in Germany was about much more than mere movement principles. At stake was nothing less than the German *Weltanschauung*. While Levinson had a firm theoretical grip on the basic principles of German modern dance, he (and Lewitan) had a poor practical understanding of how dance could become part of a murderous machinery.

Levinson's judgment of Laban was not favorable, but his verdict on Mary Wigman was worse. She represented everything that should be banned from serious art: she behaved like a "high-priestess" and "manipulator," managed her performances with "despotic detail," and moved within a "lay mystery."[22] Even more than Laban, Wigman represented Germanic ideals. Levinson questioned the false religiosity, the "conceptions which substitute overstatement in expression for 'the pure act of metamorphosis,'" and the actual inability to express or interpret "things of the soul."[23] That was why he found the performances of all those German dancers "insufferably tedious, rotten with intellectual vainglory, vitiated in its humanity by the inflation of its feeling."[24] There must be something very wrong with the German elite if it enjoyed such "questionable artifices."[25]

There came an immediate and furious response from Mary Wigman, entitled "Das Land ohne Tanz" (The Land without Dance). In her magazine, *Die Tanzgemeinschaft* (The Dance Community), she explained to the "young dancers in Germany" that Levinson's was a most revealing essay "since it shows very clearly with what destructive nastiness a person impregnated with Latin culture and aesthetics regards the struggle of German dancers to form the meaning of their lives . . . What I find remarkable in Mr. Levinson's essay is the reflection of the entire German dance movement as seen by a man who lacks authentic German orientation."[26] How could such people ever understand "Germanic intensity of sensibility and expression"? Wigman racialized the aesthetic differences that had provoked the conflict between herself and Levinson. Indeed, for Wigman, race was the key to understanding the German rejection of classical ballet, with its emphasis upon formal beauty, in contrast with the aesthetics of German modern dance. Wigman and Laban had turned criticism into a Jewish vice.[27] Lewitan did not respond directly to Levinson's attack and Wigman's hostile outburst. But in his reviews of German modern dance, he agreed with Levinson's criticisms, though in milder terms.

While Lewitan and Levinson could not have anticipated the terror of Nazism in 1929, each in his own way sensed the danger of the ideas of Laban and Wigman and, in particular, their practical application of dance aesthetics. Wigman condemned her critics as "un-German," a code word for Jewish, and denied them the capacity, on racial grounds, to understand German modern dance. Initially simply an annoying Russian ballet advocate, Lewitan and people like him had now become "Jewish critics." That these "Jews" used irony and sarcasm in their dance writing showed that they could not take a sacred art seriously. Both Levinson and Lewitan tried to rescue what they saw in Laban (partly because Wigman seemed so much worse), by comparing his achievements to those of ballet and treating his work as a continuation rather than a break in the evolution of dance, notwithstanding Laban's protests against the idea of a continuous history of dance. Laban had consistently tried to "invent" a new dance and a new dance history that would sever modern dance from its historical roots.[28]

Levinson failed to recognize that Laban's and Wigman's disagreements and competition arose from their closeness, not their differences. Both defined themselves as breaking with tradition and history; both were cultists; and both were extreme in their visions. Where, then, did they part ways? Laban invented a theory and set out to demonstrate it through art, while Wigman derived her theory from her art. Laban built a new religion with dance; his dance groups and movement choirs were fashioned after the model of Masonic secret sects and were experiments carried out according to a strict plan or theory. Wigman derived her theory in the course of ecstatic, Dionysian experiences of movement in the agony of creation.

Ironically, while German dancers were soaking up nationalist ideologies in summer dance camps, closely knit dance groups, and dance communities—in short, while they were turning the art of movement into a nationalist weapon—Lewitan and Levinson were observing, analyzing, criticizing, and writing about the dance scene; many of those writing for *Der Tanz* reflected a growing awareness of the right-wing tendencies of modern German dance advocates and their potential to join forces with conservative and nationalist movements.[29]

The third dance congress gathered in Munich, in June 1930. That August, Lewitan summarized the spirit of the gathering in an article called "Aschermittwoch" (Ash Wednesday), which refers to the first day of the period in which Catholics prepare for the resurrection of Jesus Christ.[30] Ash Wednesday marks the end of carnival and start of fasting. As symbol of repentance and cleansing, ash is strewn on one's head. Lewitan had chosen a powerful metaphor for the congress. His meticulous account of the six-day assembly culminated in an explosive expression of disappointment, disillusionment, and rage. He had found the theoretical contributions and performance pieces inadequate on every level. Only minor subjects had been presented, as though there were no vital matters to consider; the discussion neither addressed nor reflected any of the pressing problems in the dance world and was far from suggesting any solutions. Not only was this a poor sequel to the Essen congress but also all expectations for general betterment had been crushed. Lewitan lamented the inability of dancers and choreographers to leave their narrow convictions behind. The glimpse of solidarity at Essen had yielded to complete bleakness. The hope that dancers would unite to overcome their social difficulties had evaporated. No rethinking of pedagogical questions, no redefinition of strategies in theater had taken place. In addition, the congress had been an informational and organizational disaster. Responsible for this fiasco was the modern dance camp, with its leaders, Laban and Wigman.[31] Their chore-

ographies lacked any artistic distinction and direction. Some were acceptable, some were mediocre, some were simply bad. Very few started from
promising ideas, one or two raised hopes, but only because they left the
well-trodden paths of their masters. Finally, there was the so-called high
point of the congress, Wigman's *Totenmal*, a choreographic work that celebrated the heroic deaths of German soldiers in World War I ("Zum Gedäch-
tnis der Gefallenen im Weltkrieg") in cultic form. But this too was a
disaster: "The biggest scandal was that Mary Wigman, the leader of a generation of dancers in Germany, was part and parcel of this bluff. It was more
than a scandal: it was unworthy and an abuse of the art of dance, an offence
against the obligations, which her position dictates."[32]

At the end of the congress, Laban and Wigman issued a declaration on
the necessity of a *Tanzhochschule,* or College of Dance, that would eliminate
unwanted art, in this case ballet, the old enemy. This announcement
sounded the death knell for Lewitan's dream of a rapprochement between
ballet and modern dance.

Dance of the Future

In November 1930, despite all his pessimism, Lewitan wrote "Der Tanz von
Morgen" (The Dance of Tomorrow).[33] If nobody else was willing, then he
would envision what dance might look like. Dance had to reflect the social
and political changes that were transforming Germany and dancers had to
become engaged. What some regarded as modern dance was no longer
modern, Expressionism had become an anachronism, and primitive feelings and gestures were passé. Dance belonged to a much larger realm, and
the dance of the future should be understood as unity, as totality, as new
simplicity, not because it was poor or empty, but because it was complex.
An immense knowledge of detail and technique would be necessary; arti-
sanship would be required. The majority of dancers would have to learn a
lot more before they would be able to convey this message. The dance of
the future would have to be part of today's civilization: "Dance can accomplish this undertaking by submitting itself to the laws of time and space—
the new synthesis."[34] Lewitan's visions and desperate cries for unity were
not heard.

Two years later, Lewitan referred again to the dance of the future. This
time, in June 1932, his optimism about finding a future dance, about promoting something worthwhile, had faded. Lewitan proclaimed modern
dance bankrupt: "We, with our occidental glory, are standing at the abyss.
We speak of the crisis of capitalism, of the parliamentary system, of the
state, of the economy. We are beggars, we have shot all our ammunition;
we live from loans and extensions; we are a typical example of complete
decadence . . . We are uninventive and unimaginative."[35] The new artistic

forms were pale imitations of old content. There were no dancers who portrayed the world being torn apart.

There was, however, *one* dancer through whom one could glimpse the catastrophe of the time: Valeska Gert, whose grotesque dances and satirical sketches and portraits pointed to the terrors of being human and alive in the late 1920s. She danced social criticism and demanded that "absolute dance" turn to reality and incorporate the tensions of a fragile world. If, in Wigman's estimation, Gert's dances were non-art, "*Un-Kunst*," then surely Gert was "Jewish." During the Weimar period, Valeska Gert had been one of the most outspoken opponents of Wigman, whose dances, Gert claimed, reeked of blood and sweat. Her caricatures, performed in night clubs and cabarets, poked fun at Wigman's attempt to turn dance into a sacred device. Valeska Gert was indeed Jewish and, like Lewinson, who had praised her grasp of modernity, she too had to flee after the Nazis came to power. Though Lewitan had revised many of his views by the early 1930s, he had not changed his position on Kurt Jooss's artistic merits. Jooss did not feature in the "Dance of the Future." Only in the mid-1930s had Lewitan become sufficiently acquainted with Jooss and his aesthetics to act as the Ballet Jooss's tour manager.[36]

Humiliation

In January 1933, the Nazis seized power. Hitler became Reich Chancellor. The Reichstag burned and the concentration camps were filled with Hitler's political enemies. The first racial laws were passed. The Gesetz zur Wiederherstellung des Berufsbeamtentums (Law for the Reestablishment of the Professional Civil Service) "cleansed" the civil administration in Germany of its Jewish employees. *Der Tanz* reflected these growing political tensions, without fully grasping their impact. Issues for the first several months of 1933 had been prepared before the Nazis came to power. Then, in April 1933, the *Schriftleitung*, the editor—that is, Lewitan—proclaimed that the "revolutionary political events of the last weeks . . . have to be evaluated as the will of the people. They represent an upsurge of the national spirit in all cultural areas. A mighty impulse sweeps through the country and brings about a self-deliberation of the national characteristics."[37] Lewitan concluded with the hope that Germany could be the leading "Volk" among the dancing "Völker."

It is difficult to understand why Lewitan wrote such a column. In his private papers he never stated or supported similar views. Even more confusing is that he was contemplating emigration even as he was writing the editorial. Whether he was being diplomatic and did not want to make even more enemies or whether he was being pragmatic in order to postpone the point at which his journal would be taken from him is hard to judge.

One month later, in May 1933, Lewitan lost all his positions in the

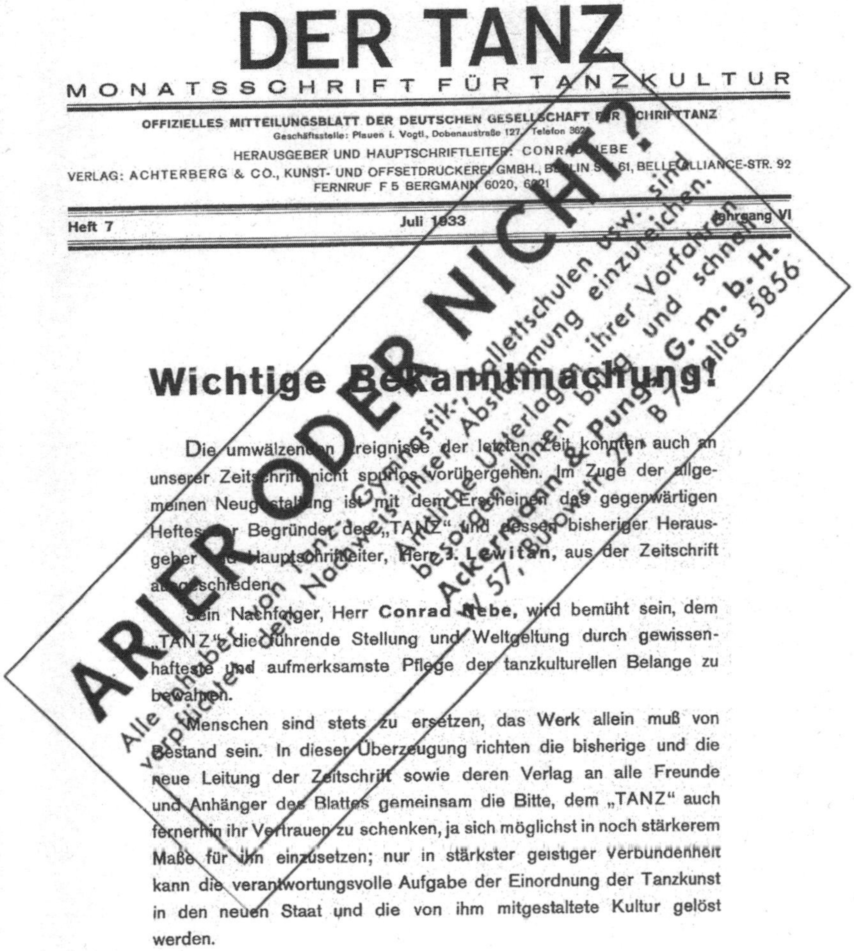

DER TANZ

MONATSSCHRIFT FÜR TANZKULTUR

OFFIZIELLES MITTEILUNGSBLATT DER DEUTSCHEN GESELLSCHAFT FÜR SCHRIFTTANZ

Geschäftsstelle: Plauen i. Vogtl., Dobenaustraße 127, Telefon 3626

HERAUSGEBER UND HAUPTSCHRIFTLEITER: CONRAD NEBE

VERLAG: ACHTERBERG & CO., KUNST- UND OFFSETDRUCKEREI GMBH., BERLIN SW 61, BELLE-ALLIANCE-STR. 92

FERNRUF F 5 BERGMANN 6020, 6021

Heft 7 Juli 1933 Jahrgang VI

Wichtige Bekanntmachung!

Die umwälzenden Ereignisse der letzten Zeit konnten auch an unserer Zeitschrift nicht spurlos vorübergehen. Im Zuge der allgemeinen Neugestaltung ist mit dem Erscheinen des gegenwärtigen Heftes der Begründer des „TANZ" und dessen bisheriger Herausgeber und Hauptschriftleiter, Herr **J. Lewitan**, aus der Zeitschrift ausgeschieden.

Sein Nachfolger, Herr **Conrad Nebe**, wird bemüht sein, dem „TANZ" die führende Stellung und Weltgeltung durch gewissenhafteste und aufmerksamste Pflege der tanzkulturellen Belange zu bewahren.

Menschen sind stets zu ersetzen, das Werk allein muß von Bestand sein. In dieser Überzeugung richten die bisherige und die neue Leitung der Zeitschrift sowie deren Verlag an alle Freunde und Anhänger des Blattes gemeinsam die Bitte, dem „TANZ" auch fernerhin ihr Vertrauen zu schenken, ja sich möglichst in noch stärkerem Maße für ihn einzusetzen; nur in stärkster geistiger Verbundenheit kann die verantwortungsvolle Aufgabe der Einordnung der Tanzkunst in den neuen Staat und die von ihm mitgestaltete Kultur gelöst werden.

ARIER ODER NICHT?

Alle Inhaber von Tanz-, Gymnastik-, Ballettschulen usw. sind verpflichtet, den Nachweis ihrer Abstammung einzureichen. Amtliche Unterlagen ihrer Vorfahren besorgen Ihnen billig und schnell

Ackermann & Pung G. m. b. H.

W 57, Bülowstr. 27 B 7 Pallas 5856

Figure 17.1. The July 1933 issue of *Der Tanz* announces that Josef Lewitan, founder and editor of the journal, has "resigned." Marion Kant has superimposed an advertisement for a service to trace Aryan ancestry that actually appears inside the magazine.

Reichsbund zur Pflege des Gesellschaftstanzes (Association of Social Dancing). In July 1933, *Der Tanz* announced on its front page that it was undergoing a general reorganization and that Herr J. Lewitan had left the journal. "People can always be replaced, the oeuvres, the work only is of importance."[38] The new editor officially dismissed Lewitan although he still owned the journal.

Though Lewitan had never underestimated the Nazis, he did become increasingly melancholy and depressed. He fought for his civil rights to retain a measure of dignity. On December 1, 1934, he described how he felt. He could hardly stand the nerve-wracking tension of complete uncertainty: "Times of fantastic energy changed with times of complete apathy, when I do not want to do anything. Negotiations here, talks there; soon I see myself in faraway lands, on some kind of Galapagos Island, and then again here, in this place."[39] He had enough political insight to anticipate that he would have to leave Germany, but he hesitated. There were bureaucracies everywhere, German, French, or British; there were visa permits and work permits. From 1934 onward, he considered emigration, not as a serious option but as an existential one. Where would he go? Where could he go? He hid behind his Russian passport, yet knew that his Jewish identity would determine his options.

Between 1935 and early 1938, Lewitan left Berlin about thirteen times, returning each time to a worse situation. Nazi legislation made his moves in and out of the country increasingly difficult. He had to apply frequently for new passports. They would become invalid with every new law and would only be issued with new permission to stay in the country. His German passport is stamped with seven passport extensions and renewals of permits. He fled and came back and fled again. His letters capture his state of mind:

I want to get rid of the journal, which still belongs to me, but don't know how to.[40]

My plans for the future are in the air.[41]

I want to leave but don't know where to go to.[42]

Meanwhile the attacks came from all sides. Fritz Böhme, critic of the *Deutsche Allgemeine Zeitung* and one of the foremost supporters of Laban (and later his theoretician), declared ballet "un-German" in form and content and urged his fellow Germans to get rid of ballet and its "anti-German spirit" as fast as possible. Who were these representatives of the ballet, anyway? Russians, Frenchmen, Jews.[43]

This was bad enough, but worse followed. Böhme, who had developed grand plans for German dance, wrote to Minister Joseph Goebbels in the Ministry of Popular Enlightenment and Propaganda and sent a detailed plan for the inclusion of dance in the National Socialist movement. He established similar roots for Nazism and German dance and outlined how dance could help to shape a National Socialist future. "Dance is a racial question," Böhme concluded, and he proposed various practical measures. Cleansing the dance scene of its "racial antipodes," Jews and Negroes, was one obvious and urgent task. Jews had undermined German dance for far too long by insisting on "international dance" and "[d]ance criticism had relied in the past largely on Jewish connections." The Jews were a "destructive force in life," who had conquered the press and had to be removed from all positions of influence. German dance deserved good German observation instead of critical thought. Together with Laban and Wigman,

German dancers were ready to further the course of racial values and serve as the perfect expression of the Nazi movement.

Despite public humiliations in Germany, Lewitan was named one of the officers of the International Society of Dance at the International Dance Competition in Vienna in June 1934. On March 13, 1935, he quietly stepped down and invited Laban to take his place as vice-president of the society.[44]

Officially Jewish

In January 1933, Lewitan was officially made a Jew according to Nazi racial politics and racial legislation. Jossif Davidovitsch Lewitan was born in Aleksandrovskoye, a shtetl, probably in Lithuania. His father, David Lewitan, and his mother, Rose Shapiro, suddenly appeared on his documents and identified him as a Jew, an Israelite. All certificates stating who he was and what he had been became invalid, useless. Lewitan had to reapply to the Polizeipräsident (president of the police force) of Berlin for a passport and identification papers. He received a new passport in 1935. His nationality, Russian, was changed to "staatenlos," or stateless.

The next and final blow came when Mary Wigman launched a campaign against *Der Tanz* in October 1935. In a letter to Goebbels's Ministry of Propaganda, she, together with her school manager, complained about the "Jewish" journal *Der Tanz*.[45] Lewitan, who continued to guide the journal and manage its affairs in the background, had published a report by a former pupil of Wigman. This dancer, who had followed her Zionist calling and had settled for a time in Palestine, was giving classes in Alexandria. Her article appraised the dance situation under the new Nazi regime. It had not been nasty about Wigman at all; on the contrary, the pupil seemed to want to protect her beloved teacher from the Nazi danger. Incensed by the idea that she needed protection, Wigman and her school manager demanded a safeguard against any further attempts to "undermine" the relationship between her and the Nazi state.[46] Wigman went as far as to demand that the "German dancers sever their links to that journal" and asked the ministry to take practical steps against *Der Tanz*.[47]

In June 1936, Lewitan sold the journal. The sale took place under the procedures of *Arisierung,* or Aryanization. Lewitan, without his journal, without any work at all, was now "free"—free to emigrate, that is. He traveled to Austria, Switzerland, France, Great Britain, in search of work, in search of a life. He acted as tour manager for the Jooss Ballet when it performed in Vienna in the spring of 1937. While he was traveling with the Jooss Ballet, he also organized trips for Habima, the Hebrew art theater.[48] Lewitan was familiar with the troupe, from times long past when he had lived in Russia and from their visits to Berlin in the 1920s. In 1924, they had staged the play *Belshazzar* in Hebrew. After the group split in New York, one part returned to Berlin once more.[49] The ties between Lewitan and the members of this group had never been cut, and in the spring of 1938 he arranged performances in Vienna and Prague, stations during their third important tour to Europe. But he did not find these tasks satisfying. First, he had too many problems with affidavits himself; as a Jew he always encountered difficulties in obtaining permissions. Second, he found the troupe's artistic program disappointing and finally broke off the relationship.[50] His future was not with Habima.

With recommendations from Pierre Tugal, from the Archive internationale de la danse, and Pierre Michaut, Secretaire Général de l'Association des ecrivains et critiques de la danse, Lewitan tried to secure his existence in Paris.[51] He used his German passport to travel abroad until it expired; then he applied for French identification papers and rented a flat in Paris. From October 1937, the entries in his German passport show stamps from French, Austrian, Belgian, and Swiss consulates all over Europe, an indication that they were no longer being issued in Berlin. Sometime between the end of 1937 and the beginning of 1938, Lewitan left Germany for good. On July 22, 1938, his German passport and his resident's permit for Germany became invalid. At the end of July, Evgenia Eduardova followed her lover to Paris. She left her ballet school, the most prestigious in Berlin, in the hands of her daughter-in-law and former pupil, Sabine Ress. The life of a refugee did not suit her and her efforts to set up a ballet studio in Paris were unsuccessful, but she endured both because she could not live without Lewitan.[52]

Lewitan accepted the fact of being Jewish. He had never denied it. He had, for instance, not changed his unmistakably "Jewish" name, unlike his idol Volynskii.[53] He did not hesitate to associate with Habima, even if he did not pursue a permanent career with the company. If assimilation would not work, if he was denied a chance to integrate into the society that he had chosen, then Lewitan would make the best of being different. One thing was vital: not to give up, but to fight for whatever rights he could. In 1934 he joined two Zionist organizations: the Berliner Zionistische Vereinigung and the Zionistischer Landesschekel-Verband. He also joined the Jewish cultural association, the Reichsverband der Jüdischen Kulturbünde in Deutschland.

After Lewitan left Germany and became a refugee, his existence was determined by bare survival. Thanks to his Russian connections, he met Wladimir Wengeroff, also a Russian refugee and a well-known avant-garde film director and manager who had made a name working for the UFA, the famous German film studio.[54] Wengeroff employed Lewitan in his Westi-Film company in Paris. Lewitan also became a member of the Organisation Sioniste de France.[55]

Just days before the German Wehrmacht paraded on the Champs-Elysée on June 14, 1940, Lewitan left the firm and Paris. He lost his correspondence, his archive, and his art collections "when the Germans overran France."[56] The only thing he took with him wherever he went was a small oil painting depicting an idyllic Russian landscape, made by his uncle, the impressionist artist Isaac Lewitan.[57] Lewitan fled to Carcassone in the south of France.

Lewitan's biography, insofar as it can be reconstructed from passports, permits, and a few remaining scraps of paper, shows his struggle to survive while on the move. He reached St. Gaudens in July 1940, was interned in the camp in Récébédou, and was released only after agreeing to join the French Foreign Legion. For a short period he worked as an agricultural laborer for Monsieur Kosma Dubine. First quarterly, then monthly, then weekly, then daily, he had to register with the local police and apply for the *récépisse*, on which a refugee's life depended.[58] Over and over again, he walked most of the way to Marseille and back again to queue at the embassies that were prepared to issue affidavits. After obtaining permission to enter Cuba on February 26, 1942, but not the transit visa through Portugal, he missed the last boat to the Caribbean island. Visa after visa, affidavit after affidavit became useless because some important paper was always missing. Eventually, Lewitan acquired a transit visa to Morocco. Along with Evgenia Eduardova, he left Marseille on May 14, 1942, and landed in Casablanca on May 20.

Evgenia converted to Judaism and the couple was married in a Jewish ceremony in Casablanca in September 1943. In Morocco, Lewitan was engaged in many activities of Jewish and Zionist life and represented the electoral area of Morocco at the twenty-second Zionist Congress in Basle in 1946. As soon as American and British forces landed in North Africa on November 8, 1942, Lewitan offered his organizational talents to the U.S. Naval Construction Battalion and, by late November 1942, he was acting as their base purchasing agent. His outstanding work earned him several commendations. It also, finally, paved the way for Lewitan and Eduardova to enter the United States on May 14, 1947, and become American citizens. They anglicized their names and resided on Manhattan's Upper West Side.[59]

Lewitan worked as a Russian translator for the United Nations from 1949 to 1968. Constantly traveling, constantly moving, Lewitan crossed the continents: the Americas, Europe, Africa. As a translator, he belonged to the delegation that discussed disarmament in London in 1956. He helped supervise elections in Togo in March and April of 1958; thereafter he was sent to the Ivory Coast for a similar task. He visited Israel both as a translator for the UN and several times in the 1960s as a tourist, dividing his attention between Jewish and Christian sites. Also in the 1960s, he returned to Germany and Austria to take the waters and restore his health.

Wherever he went, he remained an emigrant, a wanderer, unsettled. After the war he became less and less committed to a Jewish identity and Zionism, for which he had fought so vigorously during the late 1930s and 1940s. Lewitan, now well into his fifties, seemed to feel most at home in the Russian refugee community in New York.[60] He returned to Russian culture: he spoke Russian, he wrote in Russian, he made a living translating into the Russian language, he celebrated Russian holidays. He wrote a dozen reviews for one of the Russian newspapers on visiting theater companies, on the various *Sleeping Beauty* productions coming into town, or on other romantic jewels of ballet. But he never again integrated wholly into any community; he never again published a dance magazine; he never again advocated criticism as part of a social program. He did write, though infrequently, for some American dance journals, but his interest seemed to trickle away. If he had bigger plans, he did not complete them; if he had hopes to return to Europe to live there, he did not succeed. In New York, Lewitan, like so many refugees, was confronted with the shattered remains of his life. Did he search for something that would restore his importance? Was he alienated by a society that glorified youth, knew little of history, and saw the past as a burden? Did he look back or forward? We simply do not know. Lewitan, who in French exile had called himself an *homme des lettres*, was invisible in America, where there were all too many refugees like himself; and he was forgotten in Germany, where there were too few refugees willing to return.

After 1945, Laban, Wigman, and their followers and admirers systematically eradicated from the record the fact that the great figures of German modern dance had been enthusiastic Nazis. They either lied directly or allowed others to lie for them, cloaking the entire era with silence, a silence into which Lewitan disappeared. They had less reason than ever to remember the "Jewish" critic and even more reason to forget him. Since the politics of the entire period were simply repressed, Lewitan, the critic of modern dance, could once more become the outsider, the man who lacked Germanic feelings and failed to understand the essence of German modernity.[61]

Issues of the journal *Der Tanz* are scattered all over Germany. No library possesses a complete collection. More recently, several scholars, who knowingly or not take up Laban's and Wigman's view of history, describe Lewitan as "conservative," "orientated towards the traditional," "belonging to the old school," and misunderstanding the new movement. He appears in these accounts as a "condemning" and "acidly complaining" critic of German modern dance and the inadequacy of modern German dancers.[62] His critical attitude toward modern dance in Germany is blamed for allegedly paving the way for the Nazis and their aggressive and violent journalistic style. It is assumed that modern dance per se is a positive development; hence anyone questioning the modernity of German dance must be a forerunner of the Nazis. In a final and mad distortion, he thus is blamed for paving the way for Nazism in dance criticism.

Joseph Lewitan died on one of his journeys, in Paris on April 9, 1976, at the age of eight-two.

History, Memory, and Moral Judgment in Documentary Film: On Marcel Ophuls's *Hotel Terminus: The Life and Times of Klaus Barbie*

Susan Rubin Suleiman

> *The hell with "teaching" the Holocaust! Denounce and be angry!*
> —*Marcel Ophuls* [1]

> *Memory loves a movie.*
> —*Patricia Hampl* [2]

In an essay published more than forty years ago, Theodor Adorno asked the question: What does it mean to "work up," to "process," or—as the English translation puts it—to "come to terms with" the past? (Was bedeutet: Aufarbeitung der Vergangenheit). The word "Aufarbeitung," Adorno wrote in 1959, had already become a highly suspect *Schlagwort*, a "slogan," for it did not imply a "serious working through of the past, the breaking of its spell through an act of clear consciousness."[3] "Working through," which is here contrasted with the suspect "working up," is Freud's word for overcoming resistance to difficult material: to work through such material (*durcharbeiten*) requires effort. Although Adorno himself did not use the Freudian term (instead, he said *verarbeiten*, yet another word for "working up" or "processing"), the translators got his meaning right. For Adorno insists, in this essay, on the difference between a genuine working through of the past in the psychoanalytic sense (further on, he defines psychoanalysis as "critical self-reflection") and a mere "turning the page" on the past, which is actually a desire to wipe it from memory. That kind of "working up" is false and ineffective, as well as self-deceptive: "The attitude that it would be proper for everything to be forgotten and forgiven by those who were wronged is expressed by the party that committed the injustice," Adorno notes with dry irony.[4]

In the West Germany of 1959, those words had a special significance. Although the Adenauer government had recognized, early on, Germany's responsibility for the Nazi persecution of the Jews and had signed an agreement in 1952 to pay reparations to Holocaust survivors, the general mood in the country was not in favor of remembering. As many historians have noted, the main goal in West Germany after the war was " 'normalcy' at all costs."[5] The assumption of responsibility for the "Jewish question" did not, it has been argued, carry with it a full recognition of the "Nazi question": the role of National Socialism and of anti-Semitism in German life and politics before the war, and their prolongation within the postwar period.[6] (In East Germany, the situation of memory was even worse, as Jeffrey Herf has shown.)[7] Adorno's essay reminded his fellow Germans that their desire to "get free of the past," while understandable (for "one cannot live in its shadow"), could not be satisfied as long as "the past one wishes to evade is still so intensely alive."[8]

The solution, according to Adorno, was enlightened pedagogy on a mass scale, a pedagogy at once "turned toward the subject"—focusing on individual psychology and aiming for increased self-consciousness and "subjective enlightenment" on the part of individuals—and turned toward objective arguments about history: "Let us remind people of the simplest things: that open or disguised revivals of fascism will bring about war, suffering, and poverty."[9] That particular reminder may be useful even today—though one may wonder whether Adorno wasn't being overly optimistic in trusting in the power of rational argument, based on self-interest, to counteract the emotional appeals of racism and xenophobic nationalism.

But another aspect of Adorno's essay, his emphasis on the need for remembrance, may strike one as no longer pertinent: for haven't we—we Western Europeans and Americans—experienced, in the past decade and more, not an excess of forgetting but rather a "surfeit of memory"? Charles Maier, whose essay by that title has often been quoted, argued in 1992 that the current obsession with memory, especially with the memory of World War II and the Holocaust, in Germany and elsewhere, "is a sign not of historical confidence but of a retreat from transformative politics."[10] For Maier, the fascination with memory, which today often takes the form of group memories vying with each other for recognition of their suffering, "reflects a new focus on narrow ethnicity" and acts as an obstacle to democracy.[11] (For Adorno, by contrast, democracy required a self-critical working through of the past.) No wonder that Maier concludes his essay with the flippant but serious wish: "I hope that the future of memory is not too bright."[12]

As a historian, Maier is of course not in favor of forgetting. But he pits history against memory: the historian, even the postmodern historian who has rejected "naive positivism," seeks causal explanations for events. The "retriever of memory" has no such imperative. The historian seeks understanding, whereas the rememberer seeks emotion—specifically, according to Maier, the emotion of melancholy. Practical democrat that he is, Maier distrusts such emotion as a "collective self-indulgence," seeing in it an "addiction to memory" that is potentially "neurasthenic and disabling."[13]

Although Maier's critique is open to debate in its details and its choice of metaphors (is melancholy the only emotion associated with memory? is drug addiction the right analogy?), its general argument seems to be a shared one; the last few years have brought extended critiques of memory, and especially of memories of World War II and the Holocaust, by other historians as well. In the United States, Peter Novick's book *The Holocaust in American Life* develops the charge that the emphasis on memory of that event has acted as a block against perceiving—and attempting to act on— more current problems, whether concerning human rights or other urgent issues.[14] In France, Henry Rousso—who gained international acclaim for his 1987 book *The Vichy Syndrome*, which traces the history of the memory of the Occupation years in postwar France—has deplored, in his more recent works, the "obsession with memory" and the "judaeo-centrism" of current memories of Vichy.[15] This judaeo-centrism, according to him, not only splinters national memory into rival group memories; it is also an anachronistic distortion of history, for the "Jewish question" was not central to Vichy as Vichy saw itself.[16] Most recently, Rousso has insisted on the rights and responsibilities of the historian as opposed to the witness, in terms that recall Maier's insistence on the necessary primacy of history over memory, of understanding over emotion.[17]

Personally, I find these recent critiques of memory, together with the foregrounding of the need for continued historical research, on the whole salutary. They are a corrective to the "sacralization" of memory, the "duty to remember," which can all too quickly degenerate into kitsch, the very opposite of critical self-reflection. Claude Lanzmann, explicating his masterpiece *Shoah* (1985), has insisted on the "obscenity" of any attempt to "understand" the Holocaust, that is, to find causal, historical explanations for it. Lanzmann seeks, instead, to relive the most unfathomable aspects of the Holocaust (the organization and industrialization of mass murder on an unprecedented scale) by an active process of witnessing, a joint enterprise of survivors and those who receive—in reverence and awe—the survivors' testimony.[18] Lanzmann's idea about the "obscenity of understanding" appeared attractive to many people (at least, among literary scholars) when it was first formulated; and Lanzmann's film is a brilliant enactment of it. But the idea, and even the film insofar as it is its enactment, have come under strong criticism in recent years: the refusal to "understand," as Dominick LaCapra has argued in an extended critique, has its limits, both ethical and aesthetic.[19]

Finally, the emphasis on memory has been justly criticized because it can lead not only to dogmatism and kitsch but to political instrumentalization of every kind, including some very bad kinds. As has often been pointed out about the bloody ethnic wars in the former Yugoslavia, collective memories of ethnic humiliation or of religious conflict can be put to cynical political uses. In a different register, the bitter debates of recent years over the Holocaust memorial in Berlin can be considered as examples of the political instrumentalization of memory, in addition to being (in some instances) critiques of it.[20]

As salutary as the recent critiques of memory may be, however, there is also a sense in which they miss the point. For the "obsession with memory," by the very fact that it is an obsession, is not something that can be made to go away. Whether in the purely private realm, as manifested by the increasing practice of diary and memoir writing, most of which will never reach publication, or in the public realm, as manifested by the unabated interest in (and production of) memorials, anniversaries, documentaries, public commemorations, and literary memoirs—including especially the historical memoir that recounts an individual experience in a time of collective crisis or trauma—memory and memorialization continue to be central preoccupations in Europe and the United States.

The question we might salutarily ask, therefore, is not (or not only) "why the obsession with memory?" or "when will it fade?" but rather "*how* is memory enacted or put to public use?" A poetics of memory, rather than a history or a politics. And, I would add, an ethics too—not only "how" but to what good end? The question then becomes: How is memory *best* enacted or put to public use? But since all poetics and ethics are situated (in the Sartrean sense: located and given meaning in a specific time and place), history and politics come back another way: How is memory best served at a given moment, in a specific place? And who does the judging, to what end?

At this point, we encounter once again Adorno's idea about critical self-reflection. It is a good point from which to launch a discussion of Marcel Ophuls's Academy Award-winning documentary, *Hotel Terminus: The Life and Times of Klaus Barbie.*

Other People's Memories

Hotel Terminus was first screened at Cannes in 1988 and was immediately recognized as a major work, winning the Academy Award for best documentary the following spring. It is readily available on video (unlike most of Ophuls's other films), but in movie theaters it had very short runs, both in Europe and in the United States; and surprisingly few people have seen it.[21] Aside from being a difficult and brilliant work, it is, I think, a film that makes many viewers on both sides of the Atlantic uncomfortable. It is that lack of comfort that will be my focus in discussing the film.

But first, a bit of historical background. Klaus Barbie, born in 1913 in

Bad Godesberg in the Rhineland, into a family that came from the Saar region near the French border, was head of the German Security Police (SIPO-SD) in Lyon during the German Occupation of France, from November 1942 to late August 1944. Known as "the butcher of Lyon" because of his cruelty, Barbie was responsible for the torture and deportation of many hundreds of Jews and members of the Resistance during that period. In particular, he was known as the man who had arrested and tortured to death the best-known hero of the Resistance, Jean Moulin. After the war, Barbie disappeared from view; it came to light much later that for several years he had worked for the American Army's Counter-Intelligence Corps (CIC) in Germany, which was deep into the Cold War almost as soon as World War II had ended. In 1951, the CIC helped him escape from Europe via the "rat line," the notorious escape route for former Nazis organized by members of the Catholic Church. In 1952 and again in 1954, he was tried for his war crimes in France and condemned to death in absentia.

In the early 1970s, Barbie was tracked down in South America: under the false name of Klaus Altmann, he was living at ease with his family in Bolivia and Peru, involved in shady business deals and very close to the military rulers in La Paz. In the late 1970s, pressure built up for his extradition to France, thanks in large part to the efforts of Beate and Serge Klarsfeld. But Altmann, interviewed by French newspaper and television reporters, denied categorically that he was Barbie; and he was confident in the protection of the Bolivian government. The French government, under conservative president Giscard d'Estaing, was not overly eager to press the matter. It was only in February 1983, after changes in regime both in France (where socialist president François Mitterrand was elected in 1981) and in Bolivia (where President Siles Zuazo replaced the military junta in late 1982), that Barbie was flown back to France and incarcerated at Montluc Prison in Lyon, the scene of his own earlier exploits (this was for symbolic reasons—he was transferred out of Montluc into a more secure prison a week later).[22]

The arrest and return of Klaus Barbie to Lyon, more than forty years after he first arrived there and set up his headquarters in the luxurious Hotel Terminus (which gave its name to Ophuls's film), caused an immense uproar in France. His trial took over four years to prepare, and at times it was not certain that it would take place. The trial—which unfolded over an eight-week period between mid-May and early July 1987—was a watershed in the history of French memories of World War II; and in the history of French jurisprudence as well, for the case brought about a new definition of "crimes against humanity" in French law. By an interesting coincidence, the trial took place the same year as the publication of Rousso's *Le syndrome de Vichy,* which ended with the claim that the memory of Vichy had become, since the early 1970s, a national obsession.[23]

What were the reasons for the French "obsession"? Probably the most important was the disappearance of Charles de Gaulle from the political scene and the demythologizing of the Gaullist version of wartime France as a "nation of resisters." The Gaullist myth of a France united against the occupant—all save for a few traitors who received their just punishment—had served a useful unifying function in the decades following the war; but it was definitively laid to rest in the early 1970s. Robert Paxton's 1972 book *Vichy France* (translated immediately into French) documented the Vichy regime's more than eager collaboration with the Germans, as well as the deep ideological and political divisions that had existed in French society during the decades preceding the war; Marcel Ophuls's groundbreaking 1971 film, *The Sorrow and the Pity,* based on dozens of interviews with people who remembered those years, showed the very wide range of choices, most of them indubitably less than heroic, made by the citizens of France during the Occupation.[24]

The other important reason for the obsession with Vichy was the emergence of a new extreme right in French politics (Jean-Marie Le Pen's Front National), along with a French brand of Holocaust negationism (represented by Robert Faurisson and others). This provoked a strong reaction, from liberal intellectuals as well as from a wider segment of the population.[25] At the same time, a certain part of the extreme left embraced the negationist theses as a way of supporting the Palestinians against Israel. Whatever the exact position one adopted, the Holocaust loomed large— this at a time when the accelerating memory of the Holocaust was becoming an international as well as a French phenomenon.

During the four years that preceded the Barbie trial, the national obsession was given ample opportunity to grow and develop. The list of charges against Barbie required plaintiffs and witnesses, producing an immense amount of testimony and public attention.[26] The trial also brought to the fore a painful aspect of the collective memory of the Resistance around the person of Jean Moulin, whose arrest along with six other Resistance leaders in June 1943 was known to be the result of a betrayal.[27] Internal dissensions within the Resistance—among Gaullists, communists, and several other factions—were gleefully emphasized by Barbie's defense team, headed by the well-known lawyer Jacques Vergès.

Vergès, who had represented a number of Algerian terrorists in the 1960s and later, was pursuing his own agenda in defending Barbie: he wanted to use the trial as a way of putting France itself on trial, not for what it had done under Vichy but for the tortures it had practiced during the Algerian war. Furthermore, Maître Vergès sought to exacerbate possible conflicts between Jewish plaintiffs and plaintiffs who had been tortured or deported as members of the Resistance. At stake here was an important point of jurisprudence, for at first the prosecution excluded all charges *except* those brought by Jewish victims. Barbie's crimes against *résistants* came under the heading of war crimes rather than crimes against humanity and had therefore expired under the statute of limitations. Besides, in his trials of the 1950s, Barbie had already been condemned for a number of war crimes, and he couldn't be tried for the same crimes twice.

Maître Vergès was overjoyed when, acting on the request of various Resistance groups, the French Supreme Court of Appeals (Cour de Cassation) ruled in December 1985 that certain charges could be maintained even though they featured crimes of torture or deportation against *résistants*, not only against Jews. In effect, this ruling changed the definition of "crime against humanity" in France, and was criticized for that reason by a number of intellectuals. Alain Finkielkraut, for example, argued that the ruling played into the hand of Vergès, for it seemed to say to the Jews: "You ask us to suffer with you, but your memories are not ours, and your narcissistic lamentations do not bring tears to our eyes."[28] According to Finkielkraut, by extending the definition of crimes against humanity, the ruling actually fomented rivalry among group memories and group suffering. In his view, the murder of the Jews in the Holocaust was a universal concern, not simply a "narcissistic lamentation"; therefore, the definition of crimes against humanity did not need to be expanded.

Of course, Alain Finkielkraut is Jewish.

That's a horrible thing to say, isn't it? But it is what Jacques Vergès, and not only he, would say (and did say, in different words) in response to Finkielkraut's argument. Or so Finkielkraut would say. Or so I say that Finkielkraut would say.

With those multiple twists in mind, we are ready to talk about Marcel Ophuls's *Hotel Terminus.*[29]

The film opens with a dark screen, then the names of the American producers appear with piano music on the sound track: someone is playing, haltingly, the opening bars of the slow movement of Beethoven's *Pathétique* sonata. After another credit line, and another stop and start in the music, a black and white photo appears: three men in medium close-up, evidently at a party, laughing; the one on the left, a young man, has his arm around the shoulder of the one in the middle, who holds up a wine glass in a toast; he is wearing what looks like a party hat; his other hand holds an upraised cane. The camera zooms in on him, the music fades, and we hear a man's voice speaking English with a German accent: "We had a New Year's Party almost fifteen years ago, and Barbie was sitting at the end of the table." The camera cuts to a medium close-up of a youthful, jovial-looking man sitting on a sofa, and his name and occupation flash on the screen: Johannes Schneider-Merck, import-export. "And then I said that this bastard Hitler had, you know, betrayed the idealism of German youth. He jumped up, furious, and shouted, 'In my presence, nobody insults the Führer!'" In the middle of this sentence, the camera cuts back quickly to the close-up of the man with the party hat, who is now identified as Klaus Barbie, then back to

Figure 18.1. Opening image of *Hotel Terminus:* Barbie (center) and two friends celebrating at a New Year's party in Peru in the 1970s. Copyright © 1988 The Memory Pictures Company.

a close-up of Schneider-Merck; the attentive viewer may have noticed that this jovial interviewee is the young man in the opening photo, with his arm around Barbie.

The fact that Ophuls chooses to open his motion picture (in living color) with a black-and-white still photograph is significant. The photograph, an informal snapshot taken decades after Barbie's crimes in Lyon and more than a decade before his trial and the making of this film, emphasizes the passage of time and the huge distance between the historical subject of the film (the Nazi criminal Barbie) and those who speak about him or try to follow his tracks forty years later. The snapshot, freezing one intermediate moment (and a New Year at that) in that huge temporal lapse, may be a figure for memory—or more exactly, for the multiple, necessarily incomplete memories, of many people ranging over time and place, that will constitute the substance of the film.[30]

Schneider-Merck continues his story: "His face turned red, it was like something exploded in him—it was something he really believed in, there was no arguing: 'The Führer is Number One,' you know, and I'm sure that in his prison cell in Lyon, he has got . . ." Schneider-Merck, laughing, draws a frame with his fingers to suggest a photo, and the camera cuts to a close-up of the Christmas decoration on the side table next to him; another voice, that of the interviewer Marcel Ophuls, has said something, but one cannot catch the words. Schneider-Merck: "Has he got a photo?" Ophuls: "I don't know!" and both men laugh. "Maybe we should send him one for Christmas!" Schneider-Merck jokes. The camera now cuts to a view of a prison, evidently the prison in Lyon, and the film's title appears over the image.

In the meantime, some music has been playing. Exactly at the moment when Schneider-Merck, mimicking Barbie, says, "The Führer is Number One," the pure voices of the Vienna Boys Choir are heard singing a plaintive song in German. To French or American viewers, the song is probably not familiar—but to most Germans it is well known, a folk song, a love song: "Wenn ich ein Vöglein wär / und auch zwei Flüglein hätt / Flög ich zu dir / Weils aber nicht kann sein / Weils aber nicht kann sein / Bleib ich allhier" (If I were a bird and had two wings, I would fly to thee. But since that cannot be, but since that cannot be, I will stay here).[31]

Speak of multiple twists: a former close friend, now one no longer, recalls Barbie's love of the Führer and shares a laugh with the filmmaker. Schneider-Merck, involved in an unspecified kind of import-export enterprise, will explain later that Barbie and his pals cheated him out of half a million Deutschmarks, which he had entrusted to them as part of a currency speculation. No one in this tale has very clean hands, certainly not its narrator.[32] Yet the viewer, like the filmmaker, has shared a laugh with him at Barbie's expense. But upon reflection, the viewer may wonder: What exactly did Schneider-Merck mean, at that party long ago, when he said that Hitler had betrayed the idealism of German youth? "He had, you know, betrayed . . ." But what do we know? Did Hitler betray German youths' idealism by leading them into the war? Or by losing the war? Did their idealism embrace Nazi ideas, for example about the danger of the "Jewish race"?

Schneider-Merck addresses his "you know" not to us but to Marcel Ophuls, son of the German Jewish emigré filmmaker Max Ophuls—Max was born in Saarbrücken, Barbie's land, in 1902 and left Germany with his wife and young son (Marcel, five years old at the time) in 1933. Marcel Ophuls knows German folk songs, as well as French ones and American ones. "I don't have any roots," he has said about himself, "but I have ties . . . very deep ties to the Anglo-Saxon world and to America. I have traditional ties through my mother and father to Germany."[33] Does Marcel Ophuls know what German youths' idealism was, and how Hitler had betrayed it? Later in the film, while interviewing one of the former American intelligence agents who had employed Barbie after the war, Ophuls asks him, somewhat aggressively: "What is a Nazi idealist?" The agent had called Barbie, in a memo he wrote for the State Department in 1947, "a Nazi idealist"—now, almost forty years later, he tells Ophuls that he doesn't remember what he meant by that phrase but wishes he could rewrite it. "Yes, perhaps especially right now," Ophuls replies cruelly.

But he is not cruel to Schneider-Merck; in fact, he shares a joke with him. We too laugh—until we start to wonder why we're laughing.

Then there is the music. Does the beautiful old love song allude, ironically, to Barbie, who longs to fly to his beloved Führer? Or does it allude, with different degrees of irony, to anyone whose wings have been clipped: Barbie in his prison cell, idealists who have been betrayed, import-exporters of doubtful integrity who have been cheated, Jews who were expelled from home? The next song we will hear in the film, a few sequences after this, is another folk song sung by the Vienna Boys' Choir: "Ade nun mein lieb Heimatland" (Farewell now, my beloved homeland). It was sung by political exiles after the 1848 Revolution, as well as by those who left or were made to leave after 1933.[34] Ophuls puts it on the sound track over images of the village of Izieu, near Lyon, from where forty-four children were deported to Auschwitz in April 1944 on Klaus Barbie's orders—the most damaging of the charges brought against him at his 1987 trial.[35]

"Farewell now, my beloved homeland." After shots of the village and the building where the children lived, we see black-and-white photos of some of the children: a little brown-haired girl, a young boy. There follows a montage of voices without music, talking about Barbie. Then the song starts again—but this time we're in the border city of Trier, where Klaus Barbie went to high school. As the camera pans over the city with the song on the sound track, the filmmaker's voice is heard, reading a letter written by Klaus Barbie in 1934: "Like my mother, I am a child of the Eifel [region]." The camera cuts to the old German farmer Johannes Otten, who knew Barbie as a child and calls him affectionately *der Bub,* "the boy." In the Izieu sequence we have just seen, a French farmer said he remembered "the little Jews" of the children's home, with the same song playing on the sound track.

Is Ophuls suggesting, with that parallelism, that the boy Barbie and the children of Izieu were alike? That the "butcher of Lyon" was once a lovable boy who had to leave his homeland? Are we supposed to feel sorry for him (Otten recalls that Barbie's father, a teacher, became very violent when drunk—he beat the boy), the way we feel sorry for the children of Izieu? Or is the parallelism ironic, suggesting not similarity but difference: Barbie was a boy who left home, but he grew to a ripe old age in exile; the children of Izieu were gassed upon arrival at Auschwitz, and it was Barbie who had sent them there.

Similarly, we might ask what role the *Pathétique* sonata plays in the opening sequence. Later, several people who knew Barbie in Bolivia will remark that he was a fine musician, a masterful pianist. Is Ophuls giving us, ironically, the familiar trope about "Nazis who listened to Beethoven after a day's work of killing"? Is he mocking the torturer who plays the most cliched melody of Beethoven, and stumblingly at that? Or is he seriously wondering what relation can exist between sublime music and crimes against humanity?[36]

The film does not answer these questions, certainly not explicitly. This does not mean that it adopts a position of moral relativism—Ophuls has stated that he's "very Manichean."[37] But the moral judgments the film proposes must be arrived at through work, and struggle, by both filmmaker and viewer. On the filmmaker's part, the work and struggle are not only in the filming but in the montage. "I intervene enormously in the editing, for it's there that the narrative is formed," Ophuls said in an interview about this film. "*Hotel Terminus* is by far the most difficult thing I've done in my life. I'm quite pleased and optimistic to have been able to come out of it alive, I really thought I'd drop dead in that godforsaken editing studio in Billancourt."[38] He wrote five different scripts at the editing stage and barely considers the film finished.

The brilliance of Ophuls's editing lies in its capacity to pose uncomfortable questions for the viewer—or, to put it another way, its capacity to force the viewer into uncomfortable subject positions in relation to the material. Never—or at least, not for long—do we have a chance, in this film, to bask in righteous indignation or moral superiority, not even toward a villain like Barbie. The extremely rapid and complex montage of soundtrack and images not only demands close attention but creates a destabilizing effect on the viewer's understanding, on his or her moral certainties, and even, I would say, on his or her sense of self. "Whom do I believe and who do I think is lying? Whose ideas do I share? Whom do I identify with? Where are my loyalties?" These are among the questions that Ophuls obliges the viewer to confront with his editing.

Like all his documentary films, *Hotel Terminus* is what theorists call an interactive documentary, whose standard form is the interview, or generally multiple interviews.[39] Already in *The Sorrow and the Pity*, Ophuls had perfected his technique of "dialectical montage" in editing the interview material: this consists of cutting up the individual interviews and juxtaposing various pieces, so that the statements of one witness are qualified, or even totally contradicted, by those of another witness (or several others) in quick succession. In some cases, it is the insertion of documentary footage, or of an unrelated film clip or a musical sound track that produces the dialectical effect, qualifying visually or aurally what is being said by the interviewee. Since Ophuls refuses voice-over or "voice of God" commentary in his films, whatever meaning the viewer derives must be deduced from his juxtapositions; and if the juxtapositions are rapid as well as dialectical, the viewer is kept off balance.

Contributing to the viewer's sense of instability, narrative and visual fragmentation are much more present in *Hotel Terminus* than in *The Sorrow and the Pity*. Geographically and temporally, *The Sorrow and the Pity* focuses on the city of Clermont-Ferrand between 1940 and 1944, whereas *Hotel Termi-*

nus moves among five countries (France, Germany, the United States, Bolivia, Peru) on three continents, covering a period of more than forty years. In *Sorrow*, the languages are almost exclusively French and English (with a few short sequences in German); in *Hotel Terminus*, we hear substantial amounts of German (with some dialects) and Spanish, as well as French and English, including English spoken with a wide range of accents. As for dramatis personae, the final credits for *Hotel Terminus* list ninety-five people seen and heard in the film—and since some items on the list are plural ("citizens of Marburg"), the number we actually see and hear is even greater, a hundred or more. (*The Sorrow and the Pity*, only seven minutes shorter, lists thirty-five interviewees). For anyone not familiar with at least some aspects of the Barbie case, and even for someone who is, a first reaction to *Hotel Terminus* may be nothing short of bewilderment at the succession of voices and faces, not to mention musical motifs, landscapes, and inserted elements. If the filmmaker had to struggle with his editing, so does the viewer.

Paradoxically, however, this is not a flaw in the film. On the contrary, by means of his montage, Ophuls creates what I would call (harkening back to my earlier question about "public use") a *good* public use of memory. *Hotel Terminus* presents an unusually wide range of individual memories (or lack of memories, whether genuine or feigned) referring to a man who, by the force of circumstance, looms large historically. Around the figure of Barbie, individual memory, collective memory, and historical memory converge, and often clash: the film's subtitle turns out to be serious as well as parodic—this really is a film about the "life and times" of Klaus Barbie, on a world stage. Ophuls's editing emphasizes both his and the viewer's difficulty in confronting and evaluating the testimonies he gathers (or fails to gather, in some cases). But the issues as he presents them are not undecidable; they are merely not to be resolved without a struggle.

Is the struggle only intellectual, a matter of critical judgment? Ophuls has stated, somewhat haughtily, that his films are not intended for people with less than a high school education. But he added, in the same interview, that the "man in the street" is often more canny [*malin*] and attentive to difficult works than he is given credit for being.[40] In fact, the viewer is summoned not only to evaluate critically but to situate him- or herself affectively, as a subject—an ethical subject as well as the subject of aesthetic perception—in relation to the film's rendering of "other people's memories." I want to suggest, in what follows, that Ophuls achieves this by putting himself into the action—in front of the camera as well as behind it.

The Filmmaker's Self

As film theorists have pointed out, the interactive documentary allows for a wide range of interventions on the part of the filmmaker, who can participate more or less noticeably in the interviews. At one end of the interactive spectrum is what Patricia Hampl has called the "memoir film," where the filmmaker and his or her friends and family are the real subject of the story.[41] At the other end is what Bill Nichols calls the "masked interview," where the filmmaker is neither seen nor heard in the final cut but has in fact instigated the conversation and simply edited signs of him/herself out of it.[42] In a film whose proclaimed subject is a historical event or personage, one would expect a relatively unobtrusive presence on the part of the filmmaker, closer to the "masked interview" than to the memoir film.

Ophuls, however, has—with increasing insistence and provocativeness from *Hotel Terminus* on—played against this expectation. Already in the *The Sorrow and the Pity*, his presence was clearly felt. Although that film showed only a handful of *images* of the filmmaker, he was present in almost every interview as a voice: respectful toward some, witheringly ironic toward others, and adopting a wide range of tones in between. The range of attitudes communicated by Ophuls's voice is one indication of the moral spectrum of the film: at the positive (respectful) end, we find Pierre Mendès-France, who joined de Gaulle in London after escaping from a French prison, and the peasant Grave brothers, members of the Resistance who were denounced and deported; at the negative (ironic) end is Marius Klein, the merchant who put an ad in the papers around 1941 to inform people that despite his name, he was not Jewish. Between these extremes, Ophuls's expressive voice modulates from that of neutral information-seeker (as when he inquires from the owner of a movie theater what kinds of films were played during the Occupation) to that of calm adversary, as when he corrects some "facts" advanced in defense of the collaborationist prime minister Pierre Laval by his son-in-law. These interview techniques were one element that made *The Sorrow and the Pity* a groundbreaking documentary—its influence on Claude Lanzmann's *Shoah* is obvious in this regard, as in some others.

Hotel Terminus uses the same interview techniques but adds to them a new set of procedures that emphasize the filmmaker's visual presence and subjective responses. Recalling the many scenes in *Shoah* where Lanzmann appears in the frame, we might see in Ophuls's self-representations a piece of reverse influence: he started filming *Hotel Terminus* just around the time that *Shoah* came out (1985) and has himself drawn a parallel between his subjective interventions and Lanzmann's.[43] (He also interviews Lanzmann briefly in the film, in what appears to be a homage and a gesture of solidarity more than anything else.) But Ophuls has suggested, as well, that it was the subject he was dealing with that dictated his (as well as Lanzmann's) choices: "I feel frustration, bitterness, and revolt, and because I believe that documentaries should reflect the mood of the moment, it's all up there on the screen."[44] Can one make a film about other people's memories of

Klaus Barbie without putting one's own self and emotions into the film? Ophuls's answer is no.

I propose to call those moments of self-representation and subjective expression where the filmmaker's self comes strongly into play the *expressionist moments* of the film. While this is a somewhat loose definition, it allows us to discount those scenes where Ophuls is visible without any strong affect involved. As suggested by Ophuls himself in the remark I quoted above, frustration and anger are the strongest affects displayed; but there are a few others. In my view, these expressionist moments are the most original—as well as the most problematic—moments in the film, aesthetically and thematically. Furthermore, it is in these moments of visually highlighted subjectivity that Ophuls points the viewer to the central moral issues raised by his work.

Old Nazis

The first "expressionist moment" consists of three sequences in succession, linked by a single theme. The series occurs quite early in the film, just after the lengthy segment Ophuls devotes to Jean Moulin and the problem of his arrest and betrayal. Returning to an earlier interview with Daniel Cordier, a distinguished-looking man who was Moulin's young assistant in 1943 and who is now his respected biographer, Ophuls asks him, off-screen: "Do you think that the Moulin case has overshadowed other tortures: the Holocaust, deportation, the death camps?" Cordier answers that indeed, Barbie owes his "glory, in quotation marks," to Moulin—otherwise, he was just an ordinary torturer. "Atrocious but ordinary," Ophuls ventures. "Yes, atrocious, monstrous, but altogether ordinary—he did what thousands of other Nazis did or would have liked to do." As Cordier speaks this sentence, the camera cuts to a view of Ophuls from the back, reaching the top of a staircase. On the landing, an elderly man stands in the doorway, expecting him. Ophuls (after a quick cut that elides any preliminaries) addresses him in German: "I'd like to ask you—what crimes against the Reich could a two-year old girl commit?" The man gestures with his hand as if to say "not that again" and starts to shut the door, then opens it partially and says: "That little girl . . . I didn't even look." At this point, an identifying tag appears on the screen: "Karl-Heinz Muller, former Gestapo chief in Toulouse." Muller continues: "Whoever was there, signed. If I had separated the two-year-old girl . . ." Then, abruptly: "Oh what's the use!" and shuts the door as Ophuls cries: "*Bitte!*" "Please!" Ophuls turns toward the camera, with an odd smile on his face; in the meantime, a chorus has started on the sound track, in English: "Joy to the world, the Lord has come!" *"Fröhliche Weihnacht"* (Merry Christmas), Ophuls says to the door, as the camera cuts to a sign that reads *"Frohes Fest"* (Happy Holiday), in a store window.

In a perceptive essay on this film (with whose main argument I don't

Figure 18.2. Ophuls, rebuffed by Karl-Heinz Müller, former Gestapo chief. From *Hotel Terminus*. Copyright © 1988 The Memory Pictures Company.

agree), Richard Golsan refers to this scene as one of several filmed in Germany, in which "Ophuls abandons any real pretense of objectivity" and uses "heavy-handed techniques to make his case."[45] Indeed, the irony of the Christmas carol, and more generally of the Christmas motif here and throughout the film, may be called heavy-handed. But what, exactly, is the "case" Ophuls is making in this scene? That old Nazis continue to live among their neighbors, undisturbed? That old Nazis don't like to be reminded of their crimes? Neither of those cases had to be made, I think, to European or American audiences circa 1985. If that were solely—or even principally—the point of the scene, Ophuls's efforts would seem to be wasted, or at the very least, not cost effective: too much effort for the point. But what if the point of this scene were something different: for example, the encounter between an old Nazi and an aggressive Jewish filmmaker who doesn't even introduce himself or ask to be admitted before launching into a "question" designed to get the door slammed in his face? What if the point were precisely to lead to the odd smile with which the filmmaker glances at the camera as he is left standing there? And what if, furthermore, the point of the scene were to prod the viewer to exclaim: "Hey, you staged all that! That was a mise-en-scène!"

In a long interview with a French film journal in 1988, Ophuls stated a general rule of documentary film: "One shouldn't do any staging [*mise-en-scène*]."[46] Critics who find his irony too heavy-handed are responding to what they perceive as Ophuls's own transgression of this rule.[47] The reason for the rule is important, for it distinguishes the documentary genre from fiction: the seriousness and authenticity of documentary as a representation of reality demands that the filmmaker eschew techniques of "make believe." As if he were replying to this criticism, Ophuls adds in the same interview: "In *Hotel Terminus*, the only moments where there is staging it's comedy, and it's so obvious that I hope people will be amused by it."[48] In other words, there is no deception involved since the staging is obvious.[49]

Ophuls does not consider the scene with Muller as staging, because he couldn't really plan or control it: there was a possibility that Muller would not slam the door in his face.[50] The example he mentions in the above interview is a scene later in the film, clearly a mise-en-scène, in which he and his German assistant Dieter Reifarth mimic one of the many refusals they are receiving from people in Bavaria who claim they never knew Barbie and have nothing to say. This scene is broadly farcical, with Ophuls playing a Munich lady who is at first very interested when she hears of a documentary being made, but as soon as she finds out it what it is about, she retreats behind feigned absence of memory and lack of knowledge about politics. Ophuls has explained, in various interviews, that in *Hotel Terminus* his main difficulty was how to deal with people who either claimed forgetfulness and ignorance or else constantly lied and "manipulated." The farcical scene of mimicry in Bavaria (one of the major "expressionist moments" in the film) was one way he found to express his frustration. "There's no contradiction in handling often tragic subjects in depth and the idea of game playing. On the contrary, I see no other way out," Ophuls told an interviewer in 1995.[51]

In psychoanalytic terms, we might speak of such "playing" as a defense against overwhelming feelings of sadness and anger. In a 1988 essay titled "The Sorrow and the Laughter," Ophuls tells the story of a woman he once met in London, whom he employed to dub one of his films into English. She was a survivor of several Nazi and Soviet concentration camps, and "between takes she would tell me of her own experiences . . . Most of her stories turned out to be uproariously funny, I'm sorry to say."[52] But of course, he is not sorry at all. Mrs. Pravda's (for that, he claims, was her name: Mrs. Truth) way of coping with tragedy is exactly his own. Immediately following the above remark, he states what can be considered one of his aesthetic credos: "The reason Ernst Lubitsch's *To Be or Not to Be* is the greatest film ever made on National Socialism is that he debunks it, makes it ridiculous." As for his own films: "through the method of investigative sarcasm, you can make a point against the horror but also demystify the horror at the same time."[53]

Aside from being an outlet for personal feeling, "playing" in a documentary is a sign of self-consciousness about the form. As Ophuls put it to his 1995 interviewers, it is a way of "stressing the form, putting it up front"—a tendency he sees as "part of the maturing process."[54] In this self-reflexive mode, which Bill Nichols mentions as one of the canonical modes of the contemporary documentary genre, the filmmaker "speaks to us less about the historical world . . . than about the process of representation itself."[55] By mimicking the woman who refuses to be interviewed, Ophuls emphasizes his own role—as well as his own difficulties—as a documentary filmmaker. I would say, however, that in this process he *also* "speaks to us about the historical world." For he prefaces his little farce scene with a somewhat less farcical direct address to the camera: "This is February something or other 1986, and we are still in Bavaria . . . I represent Memory Pictures." Here, metacommentary about the process of representation merges with commentary about the historical world: Ophuls suggests that the willed forgetfulness of some Germans in 1986 refers not only to the "Nazi past," the years before and during the war, but also (maybe especially) to the continuing survival of Nazism. It is significant that this sequence, explicitly dated (February 1986), was shot during the early days of the historians' debate (*Historikerstreit*) that was being waged heatedly in the German press at that very time, a debate that concerned precisely the origins and the historical meaning of Nazism.[56]

Of course, we could say that the farcical scene is heavy-handed, like the scene with the old Nazi—but the question about the "case" Ophuls is making can be asked here as well, and even more so the question of his own position with regard to it. If his "case" is that we should condemn all those who claim to have forgotten the past (and who include, as the film makes clear, not only former Nazis but many others, of various ages and nationalities), then we might see Ophuls's heavy-handedness as a method of forcible recall, with all the aggressiveness and sadism that such methods imply. Clowning an old Munich housewife with a dubious past, the filmmaker affirms his own superiority, just as he does in more overt fashion in other scenes where he confronts reluctant or "forgetful" individuals (like the former American agent Robert Taylor, who called Barbie a Nazi idealist) with past actions they would rather not think about. One critic has compared Ophuls's role to that of a psychoanalyst bringing repressed memories to light.[57] But the sadism of such scenes suggests a different comparison, one that Ophuls himself has made. He has compared his role to that of an "interrogator," noting the "cruel enjoyment" (*jouissance méchante*) that both he and the viewer could take from his playing that role[58]—precisely the role that, as we hear over and over from witnesses, Klaus Barbie was so good at. But if we allow that association to surface, then the notion of the filmmaker's "heavy-handedness" takes on a new, more troubling, meaning; it becomes both a sign and a cause of the viewer's discomfort—and I would guess that Ophuls intended it as such, whether consciously or not.

In a quite amazing passage in his 1988 interview, Ophuls remarked on a certain similarity between himself and Klaus Barbie: "It's true that there is, between Barbie and me, at least one point of identification (or maybe several, I too yell a lot, but I don't torture . . .), it's the cosmopolitan aspect. Both born in Germany, followed by a diaspora. His is the diaspora of the torturers, mine is the other one. But our knowledge of languages, of the way people think in other countries [. . .] He's a man of considerable intelligence, a man who knows the mentality of those he deals with, and who used his knowledge professionally . . . Well, me too."[59] If the viewer has enjoyed Ophuls's sadism, whether overt or farcical—and inevitably, one has, as Ophuls knows—then the viewer must also say "me too."

Odd and uncomfortable couplings, whose implications go far. I don't mean toward a facile conclusion about "complicity between victim and perpetrator," but rather toward the question of what it takes to genuinely "work through" a subjective relation to the Holocaust. Ophuls's film suggests—and brilliantly enacts—the proposition that any attempt to deal with that question involves making one's own fears, angers, and prejudices visible, both to oneself and others. That means, for a filmmaker, not standing back behind the protection of the camera, with the illusion of objectivity and the inevitable superiority that that affords, but putting oneself at least occasionally in front of it, even if it makes one look bad—like a sadistic interrogator, or like an "aggressive Jew" who gets the door slammed in his face; or, simply, weak, sad, or ridiculous.

That brings us back to the old Nazi Karl-Heinz Muller and the silly grin on Ophuls's face as he stands by the door. He looks at once sheepish and triumphant, for if he could not fully predict what would happen in this scene, he was ready for the rebuff and knew it would yield "something to show"—otherwise, why would he have asked Muller that question, with no preliminary *politesse?* But Ophuls also looks, by the same token, manipulative, somewhat obnoxious (does he have to play "Joy to the World" just then?), angry—and anger impedes control, whether of one's own behavior or that of others.

The theme is "failed encounters with old Nazis living in retirement." Ophuls repeats it with the two sequences immediately following this one, in a crescendo of anger and loss of control, matched by increasing emphasis on his own role. After Muller, he tries to interview a man named Steingritt, who worked for Barbie in Lyon (he participated in the arrest of Jean Moulin) and who was tried after the war and served time in jail. We see Ophuls gesturing to the cameraman to follow him as he climbs the steps in the hallway of Steingritt's apartment building. Steingritt, who has come downstairs, puts a piece of paper up to block the camera; Ophuls chases him into the stairwell and is finally stopped by the closing of the elevator door as Steingritt rides away. "Why won't you talk to me? You don't even know what I want to ask." Ophuls keeps saying. "Leave me in peace, I've served my time. And stop filming!" Steingritt responds. The sequence ends with a striking image: Ophuls staring at the closed elevator door, whose

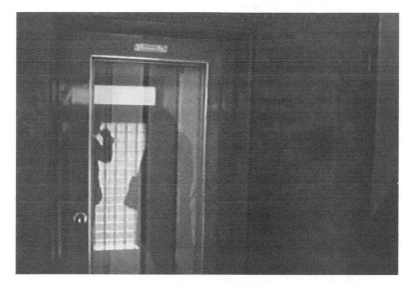

Figure 18.3. Steingritt evades Ophuls. From *Hotel Terminus.* © 1988 Memory
Pictures Company.

glass reflects his own silhouette and the outside door, then walking out of
the building as "Joy to the World" starts up again.

In this scene, the emphasis is less on the filmmaker's superiority or
aggressiveness than on his weakness. The old Nazi gets the better of
him—he blocks the camera's view and attacks Ophuls verbally. Rather than
being in the position of sadist, Ophuls appears here in the position of victim: the other man won't allow him to ask a single question. Of course, in
one sense Ophuls is still in control, since he controls the camera and the
editing—but what he chooses to show us is the scene of his own humiliation and lack of control. The look on his face this time is not smirking, but
grim.

The third sequence in what I am calling the initial expressionist moment
("failed encounters with old Nazis") is the longest, and it stages the filmmaker's self in the most complex way of the three. It begins with Serge
Klarsfeld, who has acted as the "expert informant" about all three of these
former Nazis in intercut shots, and who explains that Bartelmus, Barbie's
assistant for Jewish affairs in Lyon, was tried after the war but condemned
to only ten years in prison—which proves, says Klarsfeld, that crimes
against Jews were not even considered as serious as war crimes at the time.
The camera cuts to a road with a sign indicating entrance to a town, then
to rooftops, a row of houses, a street sign (*Friedhofstrasse*: Cemetery Street).
Off-screen, we hear Ophuls's voice, very low and polite: "Frau Bartelmus?"

Figure 18.4. Searching for Herr Bartelmus. From *Hotel Terminus.* Copyright © 1988 The Memory Pictures Company.

A woman's voice answers. He would like to speak with Herr Bartelmus, Ophuls tells her. Yes, she knows, she answers, but her husband has no comment. Cut to Ophuls, wearing a raincoat and matching cap, walking in a vegetable garden. As he bends over rows of vegetables, he calls out repeatedly, in a loud voice: "Herr Bartelmus? Herr Bartelmus?" A double mug shot, front and profile, of a brutal-looking man, evidently Bartelmus at the time of his postwar trial, appears on the screen. A woman's voice, coming from in front of the vegetable garden offscreen, asks Ophuls what he's doing there. Looking for Bartelmus, he answers. "You won't find him there," she says coolly, then asks him to leave the premises: private property. The camera cuts to her balcony, and we see her from afar as Ophuls leaves the garden and stands below: a youngish woman, born after the war.

The camera is now behind Ophuls, as he looks up at her—a balcony scene, but this Juliet is indifferent. "His past [*Vergangenheit*] doesn't interest you?" Ophuls asks. "No, it doesn't interest me," she answers. Cut to a man's voice, then a close-up of an elderly man in profile, shaking his head—he is speaking in Bavarian dialect: "I'm not at all interested, not at all interested." The camera cuts to another youngish woman, a gas station attendant who has just filled up Ophuls's car. "You're doing it for the sensationalism, that's what I think," she says as she walks back to the pump, then takes the money handed to her by Ophuls's assistant; Ophuls and another assistant stand looking at her. "Old people should be left in peace, not hounded from place to place," the woman continues. Cut to the old man who is "not interested." We hear Ophuls's voice, evidently asking about something he has just said and that we haven't heard: "What do you mean?" "You're selling pictures," the man answers. "And what about the children who never grew old?" Ophuls asks, as the camera cuts to a young girl opening the door of a ground-floor apartment. "Do you think it will help the children if you make an old man's last years difficult?"—it's the gas station attendant speaking again, and the camera pans over to her in medium close-up, with Ophuls and his assistant listening.

Cut now to an extreme close-up, the eyes and nose only, of the frontal mug shot of Bartelmus we saw previously, with Ophuls's voice on the sound track: "So your husband had nothing to do with arresting Jews?" Mrs. Bartelmus, unseen, replies as the camera pulls back to show the whole face in the photograph: "I can't say Yes or No. It was something that happened not only in Lyon, and it wasn't just Barbie who was responsible. Frenchmen too were involved." The camera cuts to another black-and-white photo: two French policemen on the left, one on the right, and between them a young man wearing a suit and matching cap, with a scared look on his face. This is evidently a wartime roundup, a *rafle*, and the French police are in charge.

What has happened here? The sequence starts like the other two, with Ophuls rebuffed and angry; sarcastically, he clowns the bumbling but clever detective looking for his prey in a vegetable patch (his attitude and his raincoat may remind one of Inspector Columbo, one of Ophuls's heroes, as he has stated in interviews).[60] In the balcony scene, he gets a young German woman to state that the old Nazi's past doesn't interest her, presumably producing a negative effect on the viewer. Then, in the gas station, the situation turns: Ophuls himself becomes the accused, "You're selling pictures." Do the accusations make the accusers look bad—ordinary Germans denying responsibility, still not interested in the past? That may well be. But in a telling way, the accusations hit home: Ophuls *is* making a picture, and he will sell it. Are the murdered children of Izieu only an alibi, a justification for "selling pictures"?

At the opening of *Hotel Terminus* at Cannes, Ophuls recounts in "The Sorrow and the Laughter," he was confronted during intermission by a tearful elderly woman, "small and rather stout" and full of gratitude—she wanted to tell him about the nightmares and sleepless nights his film had revived in her. His own reaction, however, was one of embarrassment, and a desire for distance from this victim. "Ever since, much against my will, I've become 'specialized' in films about old Nazis, collaborators, and their victims, I've tried learning to cope with such encounters," he writes stiffly. Victims of the Nazis who see his films tend to "project their own desperate feelings" into them, reacting to his own "mostly professional involvement in intensely emotional ways," he adds. "How could I explain to that lady in the lobby . . . after she had rolled up the sleeve of her summer blouse to show me the concentration camp number tattooed on her wrist . . . that my main satisfaction was that the audience had *laughed* in the right places and my main concern was that it would continue reacting favorably to my film?"[61] This anecdote, told by Ophuls, puts him in a curiously unattractive light. Instead of siding with the grateful survivor, he insists on his difference from her: his own involvement in the material is "mostly professional"—he wants his film to meet with critical success, and that is his main concern.

This may, of course, be an elaborate defense on Ophuls's part—a defense against his own "desperate feelings" (he has spoken of "fits of paranoia" he experienced while making the film) as well as against the pain of identifying with a concentration camp survivor.[62] But in addition to being defensive, Ophuls's statement confirms the accusations thrown at him by the "ordinary Germans" at the gas station: he is acting out of self-interest, "selling pictures."

It is precisely in order to counter this accusation, we may surmise, that Ophuls brings us back, at the end of the sequence, to Bartelmus, the brutal man in the mug shot. The filmmaker may be selling pictures, but this man's past should not be forgotten. In a final twist, however, Mrs. Bartelmus's rejoinder brings both Ophuls and the viewer up short: "the French too were involved." Yes, they were: Ophuls gives us the photo of the roundoup with French policemen, bringing the sequence to a close.

The filmmaker is not innocent, and neither are the French, yet Barbie and his henchmen are guilty. Barbie and his henchmen are guilty, even though the filmmaker is not innocent and neither are the French. However one turns the phrase, the truth that emerges is uncomfortable. But it is the truth we are asked to grapple with here.

If I have dwelt at such length on this first "expressionist moment" and on the associations it calls up, it is not only because I admire Ophuls's complex artistry. It has been to show that the moments of the filmmaker's highlighted self-representation in this film are also the moments when questions of moral judgment are posed in the most acute and compelling way. These questions concern not only the enormously difficult subject of guilt and responsibility in the Holocaust, and of the proper way to approach it today, but also the role of documentary filmmaking in representing those very questions. This is not to say that they don't arise at other moments in the film, for they do. But they attain particular force, and are explored with particular acuity, in those scenes where the filmmaker's subjectivity is expressed not through indirect means (by the editing, music, placing of witnesses in the frame, and all the other cinematic means at his disposal) but directly, visible on screen as a corporeal presence. It is when the filmmaker himself becomes a "social actor" (the name given to people filmed in a documentary) that the moral *and* aesthetic issues raised by the film are most clearly highlighted.

"*Un film de juif*"?

As a final example, which will also lead us toward a conclusion—and, as it were, to the heart of the matter—I want to focus on a brief but intense expressionist moment from the second half of the film. It occurs as Ophuls is tracking Barbie's escape to Bolivia after the war, by way of the so-called rat line operated out of Rome, which furnished many Nazis with falsified travel documents. Ophuls interviews Ivo Omrcamin, a Croatian living in the United States who was closely involved with the operation of the "rat line." In a typical dialectical montage, Omrcamin's statements are intercut with those of a very different interviewee, the Brooklyn district attorney and former congresswoman Elizabeth Holtzman—a handsome woman dressed in blue, sitting at an oval table in her office. Ophuls is only heard with Omrcamin, but he is also seen with Holtzman. At one point, Omrcamin says, in his heavily accented English: "There is that segment of the Jews who will never stop before turning the last stone, and such Jews are helped by immense riches in this country [who] want to prosecute Barbie." Ophuls's voice, smooth, encouraging, asks one of those questions he is famous for, letting witnesses reveal the ugliest things about themselves: "You think they're a vengeful people . . . ?" "Oh, yes," says Omrcamin. Ophuls repeats: "The revengeful ones." Omrcamin, looking pleased, adds emphatically, pumping his arm up and down: "To fabricate the crime and then accuse somebody of having committed those crimes—and hang them!" Ophuls's voice, strangely quiet, responds: "I see."

Next we are back in Elizabeth Holtzman's office, and the camera slowly zooms from a full view of Ophuls, sitting facing Holtzman and seen in half profile, to a close-up of Holtzman as Ophuls asks, very slowly, in a low voice: "Do you ever get the feeling, Ms. Holtzman, that, um, only . . . Jews and old Nazis are still interested in . . . Jews and old Nazis?" Her reply is quick: "Actually, not. Actually, the whole problem of Nazis in America was brought to my attention by a non-Jew who was horrified, as a human being, that for example our government could protect Nazi war criminals living here and allow them to stay here." After another dialectical cut to Omrcamin, who accuses Holtzman of opportunism—she wants to get reelected in Brooklyn, where the "vengeful Jews" live—Holtzman continues, speaking straight into the camera: "There is a view that somehow the Holocaust is simply a Jewish problem—when indeed the dangers of the Holocaust affected millions of non-Jews as well. And the threat that it represents today is to *all* humanity, not only to Jews."

Holtzman functions, in what looks like a deliberately staged scene, as the spokesperson for what we might call the moral and philosophical credo of the film, its ethical center: the Holocaust concerns all humanity, not only Jews. She says this in reply to Ophuls, who, in the quietest, most depressed moment of the film, wonders whether "only Jews and old Nazis" are still

Figure 18.5. Ophuls with Elizabeth Holtzman. From *Hotel Terminus*. Copyright © 1988 The Memory Pictures Company.

interested in that event. He has just been told, by the negationist Croatian exile, that the Holocaust is a Jewish invention. Unable to reply anything except "I see," Ophuls turns to Elizabeth Holtzman, a fellow Jew. She reassures him that not only Jews are interested in the Holocaust and makes an eloquent case for the universally human relevance of that historical event. But just to destabilize matters, Omrcamin indicts her for acting out of crassly political motives.

So here we have the moral heart of the matter: whose concern is the Holocaust? Ophuls, in his interview with Jean-Pierre Jeancolas, stated that he was constantly aware, during the shooting of the film, "including during my fits of paranoia in the streets of Germany, France, and Bolivia," of something that bothered him greatly: "I felt the aspect of 'Ah! a Jewish film!' [*un film de juif*] weighing on me."[63] "*Un film de juif*" is more exactly translated as "a film by a Jew, for Jews"—in other words, not a film of *human* concern or interest, but merely another piece to add to the storehouse of group memories and to the skirmishes of identity politics. What really bothered him, Ophuls explained, was the thought that this "Ah! a Jewish film" feeling existed "on both sides of the camera"—not only on the part of those he interviewed, which would be understandable, but on the part of those who assisted him, in Germany and elsewhere. "It drove me crazy, at times."

Whose concern is the Holocaust? Who should remember, or want to remember, the Holocaust? The gas station attendant in Germany says, "leave the old men in peace, don't exploit them for your profit." Marcel Cruat, a French billiard player in Lyon, tells Ophuls right at the beginning of the film: "Personally, I'm not one for vengeance, and forty years is a long time." Besides, his own family was not touched by the deportations, "if you see what I mean." Much later, Paul Schmitt, the warden of the Montluc prison who first received Barbie when he was returned to France, tells Ophuls: "If you want my opinion as an average Frenchman, *un français moyen*, forty years is a long time—if they had wanted to kill him earlier, they would have." Are the memory of the Holocaust and the demand for justice purely matters of self-interest, then? That's what the negationist Omrcamin claimed: the Jews care about the Holocaust because they are "the revengeful ones"—and besides, there was no Holocaust. Elizabeth Holtzman contradicted him, reassuring the filmmaker that his film was not just a "*film de juif.*" But earlier, we heard the "average" French billiard player affirm that he had nothing against Barbie because his family was not "affected by the deportations." And soon we will hear Barbie's Bolivian bodyguard and friend, Alvaro de Castro, telling Ophuls (in the next-to-last of the great expressionist moments in the film) that Barbie had some Jewish friends in Bolivia—those who weren't angry, who didn't keep a grudge, "*sin rancore.*" Ophuls, who has just lost his temper with de Castro ("Look at at me! Do you know that I'm a Jew? Do I look Jewish? Did Barbie teach you how to recognize a Jew?") will repeat, incredulous: "The Jews are not full of anger? This is what Barbie thought?" De Castro replies: "So he said." But we next hear an anecdote from a German acquaintance of Barbie: he once saw Barbie attacked and almost hurled to his death from a balcony by a German Jew, who recognized him and screamed that his whole family had been wiped out by the Nazis.

Klaus Barbie, as he was boarding the plane that took him back to France, gave a last television interview in Bolivia, which Ophuls reproduces. The white-haired old man, unbowed and unrepentant, says in excellent Spanish: "I have forgotten. If they haven't forgotten, it's their concern. I in any case have forgotten." That brings us right back to where we started: "The attitude that it would be proper for everything to be forgotten and forgiven by those who were wronged is expressed by the party that committed the injustice." That was Adorno, in 1959; and that was Klaus Barbie, in 1983.

And what do people say today? The Omrcamins and the David Irvings are still with us, as are the "average citizens"—of France, of Germany, of Bolivia, of the United States—who think that all moral judgments are a question of self-interest. These average citizens are not "assassins of memory," as Pierre Vidal-Naquet has called the negationists. But they are impatient: they want to "turn the page on the past" before working through it.

Fortunately, there are also others—like the non-Jews who first alerted Elizabeth Holtzman to the problem of Nazi war criminals in the United

Figure 18.6. Ophuls with Simone Lagrange. From *Hotel Terminus*. Copyright © 1988 The Memory Pictures Company.

States, or like Jews who write denunciatory books about the genocide in Rwanda in the 1990s or about King Leopold's genocide in the Congo a century ago.[64]

Ophuls knows this too. At the end of *Hotel Terminus*, after the trial and condemnation of Klaus Barbie—for he was tried, however belatedly, and condemned to life imprisonment for crimes against humanity—the filmmaker stands at the top of the stairs with Simone Lagrange, one of the witnesses he truly respects, a survivor of Auschwitz who was arrested with her parents by Barbie's men when she was a schoolgirl. She and Ophuls have been talking about two of the neighbors she remembers from that time: Madame Serre, who still lives in the building and whom we have just heard conversing with them from her upstairs window (yet another "balcony scene"), and Madame Bontout, now deceased. When Barbie's men were leading the family down the stairs, Simone Lagrange says, Madame Serre stayed carefully behind her locked door; Madame Bontout (how lucky Ophuls is with names: Mrs. Goodall) opened her door and tried to pull the young girl inside, only to receive a slap in the face that sent her reeling. As the filmmaker and the woman stand perched on top of the staircase, another woman's voice (the voice of Jeanne Moreau) informs us that "this motion picture is dedicated to the late Madame Bontout, a good neighbor."

From which one might conclude two things. It is better to be a good neighbor than a bad neighbor, even if it gets you a slap in the face. And in order to have the right to say that, one must earn it—which means that, like the filmmaker, one must be willing to engage in critical self-reflection, just as Adorno said. Only then will we viewers, individually and collectively, be able to "put the past behind us and turn the page."

That would be the cautiously upbeat ending. But following Ophuls's own dialectical lead, I want to end on a somewhat less stable and less comforting note, by returning once again to Ophuls's anecdote about his encounter with the Auschwitz survivor at the screening of *Hotel Terminus* in Cannes. As we recall, Ophuls distanced himself from the emotional victim, affirming his own cool professionalism. And he went even further. After the woman, in an angry outburst, screamed, "I want all Germans killed, they're all alike," Ophuls bid her goodbye: "At that point, I was unable to repress the urge to tell that unhappy woman that the intermission was over, that my wife was waiting for me in the theater, and that *my wife is German*. I know I shouldn't have done it."[65] Why not? Because it was sadistic? The woman, silenced, walked back into the theater, where she started a commotion with her shouts: "They should all be killed!" Then other members of the audience got into the act, berating the woman, supporting her, or bringing up their own memories of the Resistance. Finally, it was Ophuls himself who, in an effort to calm things down and get the film back on the screen, announced that from his perspective, "any concentration-camp survivor was entitled to any opinion she might have about Germans," or about anything else.

Earlier, he wanted nothing more than to affirm his difference from this woman; now, he took her side. This intricate dance of closeness and distance, identification and disavowal, may be a more just image on which to conclude than that of a page finally turned. For the viewer as for the filmmaker, questions persist: Where do I stand? Whom do I resemble? Maybe, where memory of the Holocaust is concerned, no "turning of the page" is yet possible.

Or is that just a Jewish obsession?

Notes

Introduction

"Introduction" © 2008 Barbara Kirshenblatt-Gimblett and Jonathan Karp

1. Notable recent examples in the field of art history include Margaret Olin, *The Nation without Art: Examining Modern Discourses on "Jewish Art"* (Lincoln: University of Nebraska Press, 2001); Catherine M. Soussloff, ed., *Jewish Identity in Modern Art History* (Berkeley: University of California Press, 1999); Matthew Baigell and Milly Heyd, eds., *Complex Identities: Jewish Consciousness and Modern Art* (New Brunswick, N.J.: Rutgers University Press, 2001); Samantha Baskind, *Raphael Soyer and the Search for Modern Jewish Art* (Chapel Hill: University of North Carolina Press, 2004); and the many substantial catalogues produced by The Jewish Museum in New York to accompany their art exhibitions.

2. This seminar was the most recent in a series of efforts by Richard I. Cohen and Ezra Mendelsohn over the last fifteen years to encourage work on this topic. These efforts include two important collections of essays on this topic: Ezra Mendelsohn and Richard I. Cohen, eds., *Art and Its Uses: The Visual Image and Modern Jewish Society*, Studies in Contemporary Jewry, 6 (Oxford: Oxford University Press, 1990), and Ezra Mendelsohn, ed., *Modern Jews and Their Musical Agendas*, Studies in Contemporary Jewry, 9 (Oxford: Oxford University Press, 1993). In spring 1996 they convened a research group dedicated to visual culture and modern Jewish Society at the Institute for Advanced Jewish Studies, Hebrew University, Jerusalem. Since then, each has published a major work on the subject: Richard I. Cohen, *Jewish Icons: Art and Society in Modern Europe* (Berkeley: University of California Press, 1998), and Ezra Mendelsohn, *Painting a People: Maurycy Gottlieb and Jewish Art* (Hanover, N.H.: Brandeis University Press, published by University Press of New England, 2002).

3. Theodore K. Rabb and Jonathan Brown, "The Evidence of Art: Images and Meaning in History," *Journal of Interdisciplinary History* 17, 1 (1986):5. Like the work in this volume, these publications emerge from symposia designed to foster interchange across fields.

4. Svetlana Alpers, "Foreword," *Representations*, no. 12 (1985):1.

5. Editor's introduction [W. J. T. Mitchell], "Essays toward a New Art History," *Critical Inquiry* 15 (Winter 1989):226.

6. W. J. T. Mitchell, "What Do Pictures 'Really' Want?," *October* 77 (Summer 1996):82. On the "new art history," see Thomas DaCosta Kaufman, "What Is New about the 'New Art History,'" in *The Philosophy of the Visual Arts*, ed. Philip Alperson (New York: Oxford University Press, 1992), pp. 515–20. On visual culture studies, see W. J. T. Mitchell, "Showing Seeing: A Critique of Visual Culture," *Journal of Visual Culture* 1, 2 (2002):165–82, and Nicholas Mirzoeff, *An Introduction to Visual Culture* (London: Routledge, 1999). For recent efforts to address these concerns in relation to Jewish studies, see Shelley Hornstein, Laura Levitt, and Laurence J. Silberstein, eds., *Impossible Images: Contemporary Art after the Holocaust* (New York: New

York University Press, 2003), which "seeks to contribute to the emerging field of Jewish cultural studies" and, to that end, brings together "artists, architects, art historians, art and architectural historians, curators, cultural critics, literary scholars, and religious studies specialists," out of "concern that Jewish studies scholars critically engage with works of visual culture and the representational problems that this entails" (pp. 1–2). Leora Faye Batnitzky and Barbara Mann, eds., *Icon, Image, and Text in Modern Jewish Culture*, special issue of *Jewish Studies Quarterly* 11, 3 (2004) explores the nature of visuality in modern Jewish culture from interdisciplinary perspectives.

7. Susan McClary, "Constructions of Subjectivity in Schubert's Music," in *Queering the Pitch: The New Gay and Lesbian Musicology*, ed. Philip Brett, Elizabeth Wood, and Gary Thomas (New York: Routledge, 1994), p. 212. On the "new musicology," which has much in common with ethnomusicology, see the special issue of *Journal of Musicology* 15, 3 (1997):291–352, which is dedicated to "Contemporary Music Theory and the New Musicology," and Philip V. Bohlman, "Ethnomusicology's Challenge to the Canon; the Canon's Challenge to Ethnomusicology," in *Disciplining Music*, ed. Katherine Bergeron and Philip V. Bohlman (Chicago: University of Chicago Press, 1992), pp.116–36. Noteworthy recent studies of Jewish music include Gila Flam, *Singing for Survival: Songs of the Lodz Ghetto, 1940–45* (Urbana: University of Illinois Press, 1992); Jehoash Hirshberg, *Music in the Jewish Community of Palestine, 1880–1948: A Social History* (New York: Oxford University Press, 1996); Kay Kaufman Shelemay, *Let Jasmine Rain Down: Song and Remembrance among Syrian Jews* (Chicago: University of Chicago Press, 1998); David Michael Schiller, *Bloch, Schoenberg, and Bernstein: Assimilating Jewish Music* (Oxford: Oxford University Press, 2003); Philip V. Bohlman, *Jewish Music and Modernity: Music and Cultural Contestation in Central Europe* (Oxford: Oxford University Press, 2003). For a comprehensive survey and bibliography, see Edwin Seroussi et al, "Jewish Music," in *Grove Music Online*, ed. L. Macy, http://www.grovemusic.com (accessed July 29, 2004).

8. On performance studies, see Barbara Kirshenblatt-Gimblett, "Performance Studies," in *The Performance Studies Reader*, ed. Henry Bial (London: Routledge, 2004), pp. 43–55; Richard Schechner, *Performance Studies: An Introduction* (London: Routledge, 2002); Diana Taylor, *The Archive and the Repertoire: Performing Cultural Memory in the Americas* (Durham, N.C.: Duke University Press, 2003); and Mark Franko and Annette Richards, eds., *Acting on the Past: Historical Performance across the Disciplines* (Hanover, N.H.: Wesleyan University Press, published by University Press of New England, 2000). For recent efforts to bring this perspective into Jewish studies, see the special issue of *American Jewish History* 91, 1 (2003) on "Jews and Performance," ed. Edna Nahshon, which includes articles on subjects ranging from *Death of a Salesman* and Paul Robeson's "Hassidic Chant" to the American-Israel Pavilion at the New York World's Fair, 1964–65 and the film *Avalon*. The historian Arthur A. Goren has done pioneering work on the role of performance in Jewish public culture; see, for example, *The Politics and Public Culture of American Jews* (Bloomington: Indiana University Press, 1999). Recent studies of Jews and theater include Glenda Abramson, *Drama and Ideology in Modern Israel* (New York: Cambridge University Press, 1998); Edna Nahshon, *Yiddish Proletarian Theatre: The Art and Politics of the Artef, 1925–1940* (Westport, Conn.: Greenwood Press, 1998); Jeffrey Veidlinger, *The Moscow State Yiddish Theater: Jewish Culture on the Soviet Stage* (Bloomington: Indiana University Press, 2000); Freddie Rokem, *Performing History: Theatrical Representations of the Past in Contemporary Theatre* (Iowa City: University of Iowa Press, 2000); Joel Berkowitz, *Shakespeare on the American Yiddish Stage* (Iowa City: University of Iowa Press, 2002); and Joel Berkowitz, ed., *The Yiddish Theatre: New Approaches* (Oxford: Littman Library of Jewish Civilization, 2003). For a thor-

ough survey of the field, see Ahuva Belkin, and Gad Kaynar, "Jewish Theatre," in *The Oxford Handbook of Jewish Studies*, ed. Martin Goodman, Jeremy Cohen, and David Jan Sorkin (New York: Oxford University Press, 2002), pp. 870–910.

9. See Jonathan Boyarin and Daniel Boyarin, eds., *Jews and Other Differences: The New Jewish Cultural Studies* (Minneapolis: University of Minnesota Press, 1997). See also the wide range of expressive practices represented in Michael Steinlauf and Anthony Polonsky, eds., *Focusing on Jewish Popular Culture in Poland and Its Afterlife*, Polin: Studies in Polish Jewry, 16 (Oxford: Littman Library of Jewish Civilization, 2003), which includes studies of postcards, cartoons, and photography, traditional wedding music and Yiddish world beat, Yiddish theater, and the Yiddish press. Jenna Weissman Joselit has amply demonstrated the value of close attention to vernacular aesthetic culture, both tangible and intangible, in *The Wonders of America: Reinventing Jewish Culture, 1880–1950* (New York: Hill and Wang, 1994), as well as in Jenna Weissman Joselit and Susan L. Braunstein, eds., *Getting Comfortable in New York: The American Jewish Home, 1880–1950* (New York: The Jewish Museum, 1990). For earlier periods, see Lawrence Fine, ed., *Judaism in Practice: From the Middle Ages through the Early Modern Period* (Princeton, N.J.: Princeton University Press, 2001), which, in contrast with a tendency in Jewish studies to stress intellectual religious achievements, focuses on "religious practices and religious experience" as evidence of the "embodied nature of Jewish religion." Approaches include "literary, anthropological, phenomenological, and gender studies, as well as the methods of comparative religion" (p. 1).

10. See Susan Tumarkin Goodman, ed., *The Emergence of Jewish Artists in Nineteenth-Century Europe* (New York: Merrell in association with The Jewish Museum, 2001).

11. Mendelsohn, *Painting a People*, p. 208. Mendelsohn goes on to explore "a universalist tradition among Jewish artists, both in Europe and America," which he links to a concern among Jewish artists since the mid-nineteenth century with rendering "scenes of conciliation among various ethnic and religious groups," which "[f]or some of them, at least . . . was very much a Jewish vision, an ideal whose roots were to be found in the prophetic tradition of Judaism."

12. Compare with Mendelsohn's analysis of the contrasting reception of Gottlieb by Jewish and Polish Christian critics, *Painting a People*, pp. 151–66.

13. On the role of exhibition, museums, and participation in world's fairs in furthering Jewish interests, see Jeffrey Feldman, "Within the Glass Case and Beyond: The Social Construction of Jewish Museum Objects," *Wiener Jahrbuch für jüdische Geschichte, Kultur & Museumswesen* 1, 1 (1994):39–54; Grace Cohen Grossman, *Judaica at the Smithsonian: Cultural Politics as Cultural Model*, Smithsonian Studies in History and Technology, no. 52 (Washington, D.C.: Smithsonian Institution Press, 1997); and Barbara Kirshenblatt-Gimblett, "Exhibiting Jews," *Destination Culture: Tourism, Museums, and Heritage* (Berkeley: University of California Press, 1998), pp. 79–128.

14. See Olin, *The Nation without Art*. See also Seroussi's introduction to the "Jewish Music" entry in *Grove Music Online*, http://www.grovemusic.com (Accessed July 29, 2004): "'Jewish music' as a concept emerged among Jewish scholars and musicians only in the mid-19th century with the rise of modern national consciousness among European Jews, and since then all attempts to define it have faced many difficulties. The term 'Jewish music' in its nation-oriented sense was first coined by German or German-trained Jewish scholars, among whom the most influential in this respect was A. Z. Idelsohn (1882–1938)."

15. Harold Rosenberg, "Is There a Jewish Art?" *Commentary* 42, 1 (1966):60.

16. Arthur C. Danto, "Body and Soul," *The Nation* 279, 3 (2004):40.

17. See, for example, Martin Jay, *Downcast Eyes: The Denigration of Vision in Twentieth-Century French Thought* (Berkeley: University of California Press, 1993), pp. 33–36.

18. On court Jews, see Vivian B. Mann and Richard I. Cohen, eds., *From Court Jews to the Rothschilds: Art, Patronage, and Power, 1600–1800* (Munich: Prestel-Verlag, for The Jewish Museum, 1996). On unrepresentability, see Saul Friedländer, *Probing the Limits of Representation: Nazism and the "Final Solution"* (Cambridge, Mass: Harvard University Press, 1992), and Berel Lang, *Holocaust Representation: Art within the Limits of History and Ethics* (Baltimore: Johns Hopkins University Press, 2000).

19. This subject has been extensively discussed with reference to Martin Heidegger and to post-Holocaust French thought, especially the work of Emmanuel Levinas. See Jay, *Downcast Eyes*, pp. 270, 550–86.

20. See, for example, Bland, *The Artless Jew*; Leora Faye Batnitzky, *Idolatry and Representation: The Philosophy of Franz Rosenzweig Reconsidered* (Princeton, N.J.: Princeton University Press, 2000), and for earlier periods, Marc Bregman, "Aqedah: Midrash as Visualization," *Journal of Textual Reasoning* 2, 1 (2003), http://etext.lib.virginia.edu/journals/tr/volume2/bregman.html (accessed August 5, 2004), which is followed by responses from other scholars; Jacob Isaac Leshem, "The Recognition of Aesthetic Beauty in Judaism" (Hebrew), in *Ha-Yahadut ve-ha-omanut*, ed. David Cassuto (Ramat Gan: Makhon le-Yahadut u-le-mahashavah bat zemanenu, 1988), pp. 71–80; Elliot R. Wolfson, *Through a Speculum that Shines: Vision and Imagination in Medieval Jewish Mysticism* (Princeton, N.J: Princeton University Press, 1994); Vivian B. Mann, *Jewish Texts on the Visual Arts* (New York: Cambridge University Press, 2000); and Kathleen Biddick, *The Typological Imaginary: Circumcision, Technology, History* (Philadelphia: University of Pennsylvania Press, 2003).

21. Sander Gilman, "R. B. Kitaj's 'Good Bad' Diasporism and the Body in American Jewish Postmodern Art," in *Complex Identities: Jewish Consciousness and Modern Art*, ed. Matthew Baigell and Milly Heyd (New Brunswick, N.J.: Rutgers University Press, 2001), p. 221.

22. Sidra DeKoven Ezrahi, "The Grapes of Roth: Diasporism from Portnoy to Shylock," in *Booking Passage: Exile and Homecoming in the Modern Jewish Imagination* (Berkeley: University of California Press, 2000), pp. 221–33.

23. See Nicholas Mirzoeff, ed., *Diaspora and Visual Culture: Representing Africans and Jews* (New York: Routledge, 2000), and Howard Wettstein, ed., *Diasporas and Exiles: Varieties of Jewish Identity* (Berkeley: University of California Press, 2002).

24. See Jonathan Boyarin and Daniel Boyarin, *Powers of Diaspora: Two Essays on the Relevance of Jewish Culture* (Minneapolis: University of Minnesota Press, 2002).

25. See also Robert S. Wistrich, "The Demonization of the Other in the Visual Arts," *Demonizing the Other: Antisemitism, Racism, and Xenophobia*, ed. Robert S. Wistrich (Berkeley: University of California Press, 1999), pp. 44–72, and, for an earlier period, Frank Felsenstein, *Anti-Semitic Stereotypes : A Paradigm of Otherness in English Popular Culture, 1660–1830* (Baltimore: Johns Hopkins University Press, 1995).

26. See Brian Cheyette and Laura Marcus, eds., *Modernity, Culture and 'the Jew'"* (Cambridge: Polity Press, 1998), for a discussion of the ambivalent figure of "the Jew" in modernity from postcolonial and postmodern perspectives within a largely British cultural studies framework.

27. See Goodman, *The Emergence of Jewish Artists in Nineteenth-Century Europe*; David Sorkin, *The Transformation of German Jewry, 1780–1840* (New York: Oxford University Press, 1987), and, for the earlier period, Jonathan Karp, "The Aesthetic Difference: Moses Mendelssohn's *Kohelet Musar* and the Inception of the Berlin Haskalah," in *Dialogues between Past and Present: Cultural Reconfigurations in Medieval*

and Modern Jewish History, ed. Ross Brann and Adam Sutliffe (Philadelphia: University of Pennsylvania Press, 2004), pp. 93–102. For the turn of the nineteenth century, see Steven Beller, "The World of Yesterday Revisited: Nostalgia, Memory, and the Jews of Fin-de-Siècle Vienna," *Jewish Social Studies* 2, 2 (1996):37–53.

28. Abraham Wolf Binder, "The Sabbath in Music," in *Studies in Jewish Music: Collected Writings of A. W. Binder*, ed. Irene Heskes (New York: Bloch Publishing Company), p. 90.

29. For a parallel effort to create a national Jewish style of modern synagogue architecture, see Steven Fine, "Arnold Brunner's Henry S. Frank Memorial Synagogue and the Emergence of 'Jewish Art' in Early Twentieth-Century America," *American Jewish Archives Journal* 54, 2 (2004):47–70. For recent studies of American synagogue music, see Judah Michael Cohen, "Becoming a Reform Jewish Cantor: A Study in Cultural Investment" (Ph.D. dissertation, Harvard University, 2002); Jeffrey A. Summit, *The Lord's Song in a Strange Land: Music and Identity in Contemporary Jewish Worship* (New York: Oxford University Press, 2000); and Mark Slobin, *Chosen Voices: The Story of the American Cantorate* (Urbana: University of Illinois Press, 1989).

30. See Michael Berkowitz, *Zionist Culture and West European Jewry before the First World War* (New York: Cambridge University Press, 1993), and Gilya Gerda Schmidt, *The Art and Artists of the Fifth Zionist Congress, 1901: Heralds of a New Age* (Syracuse, N.Y.: Syracuse University Press, 2003).

31. An excellent example of this convergence is Tamar Katriel, *Performing the Past: A Study of Israeli Settlement Museums* (Mahwah, N.J: Lawrence Erlbaum Associates, 1997).

32. Recent studies of lived space and cultural production in Palestine and Israel include [Arieh] Bruce Saposnik, "From Babel and Uganda to the Promised Land: The Creation of a National Hebrew Culture in the Jewish Yishuv in Palestine, 1903–1914" (Ph.D. dissertation, New York University, 2002); Susan Slyomovics, *The Object of Memory: Arab and Jew Narrate the Palestinian Village* (Philadelphia: University of Pennsylvania Press, 1998); and Rafi Segal and Eyal Weizman, eds., *A Civilian Occupation: The Politics of Israeli Architecture*, rev. ed. (Tel Aviv: Babel and Verso, 2003).

33. Howard S. Becker, *Art Worlds* (Berkeley: University of California Press, 1982), p. x.

34. Ibid., p. xi.

35. It should be noted that Jewish engagements with dance, of all the arts, have received the least attention. For example, *The Oxford Handbook of Jewish Studies* (2002) includes substantial articles on art, architecture, and archaeology, theater, music, and cinema, but nothing on dance. For a laudatory effort to address this gap, see the excellent dance issue of *Jewish Folklore and Ethnology Review* 20, 1–2 (2000), edited by Judith Brin Inger, which includes articles on "Jewish dance" in Renaissance Italy, Hasidic dance, Israeli dance, and Jewish involvement with modern dance, among others, as well as an extensive annotated bibliography. Notable recent contributions to the study of Jews and dance in the modern period include Julia L. Foulkes, "Angels 'Rewolt!'": Jewish Women in Modern Dance in the 1930s," *American Jewish History* 88, 2 (2000):233–52; Naomi M. Jackson, *Converging Movements: Modern Dance and Jewish Culture at the 92nd Street Y* (Hanover, N.H.: University Press of New England, 2000); Nina S. Spiegel, "Jewish Cultural Celebrations and Competitions in Mandatory Palestine, 1920–1947: Body, Beauty, and the Search for Authenticity" (Ph.D. dissertation, Stanford University, 2001); Elke Kaschl, *Dance and Authenticity in Israel and Palestine: Performing the Nation* (Leiden: Brill, 2003); and Dina Roginsky, "Performing Israeliness: Nationalism, Ethnicity, and Israeli 'Folk and Ethnic' Dance" (Ph.D. dissertation, Tel Aviv University, 2004).

36. "The Work Itself" was the subject of two recent conferences. The first was

organized by the Département de Sociologie de l'Université Pierre Mendes France de Grenoble in November 1999. Becker's contribution appears as "L'Oeuvre elle-même," in *Vers une sociologie des œuvre: Cinquièmes rencontres internationales de sociologie de l'art de Grenoble,* ed. Jean-Olivier Majastre, Alain Pessin, Pascale Ancel, Yvonne Neyrat, and Gisèle Peuchlestrade (Paris: L'Harmattan, 2001), pp. 449–63. Becker organized a second conference, "The Work Itself," for the Arts Program, Social Science Research Council, New York, in September 2003. The papers presented there appear in *Art from Start to Finish,* ed. Howard S. Becker, Robert R. Faulkner, and Barbara Kirshenblatt-Gimblett (Chicago: University of Chicago Press, 2005). For a parallel development in the field of musicology, see Scott Burnham, "Theorists and 'The Music Itself,'" *Journal of Musicology* 15, 3 (1997):316–29.

37. M. Meskimmon, "Visuality: The New, New Art History?" *Art History* 20, 2 (1997):331–35.

38. Roger Kimball, "The Rape of the Masters," *New Criterion* 22, 4 (December 2003), http://www.newcriterion.com/archive/22/dec03/masters.htm (accessed August 5, 2004).

39. Rose Rosengard Subotnik, "On Grounding Chopin," in *Music and Society: The Politics of Composition, Performance, and Reception,* ed. Richard D. Leppert and Susan McClary (New York: Cambridge University Press, 1987), p. 106. For a history of the notion of music's autonomy, see Susan McClary, "The Blasphemy of Talking Politics during Bach Year," in *Music and Society,* pp. 13–62. The locus classicus for the notion of the radical autonomy of art is, of course, Theodor W. Adorno, *Aesthetic Theory,* ed. Gretel Adorno and Rolf Tiedemann (Minneapolis: University of Minnesota Press, 1997), first published in German in 1970.

40. See David Carrier, *Principles of Art History Writing* (University Park: Pennsylvania State University Press, 1991).

41. Becker, "The Work Itself," in *Art from Start to Finish,* pp. 21–30.

42. For recent work on the klezmer revival, see Mark Slobin, *Fiddler on the Move: Exploring the Klezmer World* (New York: Oxford University Press, 2000), and Mark Slobin, ed., *American Klezmer: Its Roots and Offshoots* (Berkeley: University of California Press, 2002).

43. Stuart Hall, "Notes on Deconstructing 'the Popular,'" in *People's History and Socialist Theory,* ed. Raphael Samuel (London: Routledge, 1981), pp. 227–40.

44. For recent contributions to the study of Jews and cinema in the United States, see J. Hoberman, *Bridge of Light: Yiddish Film between Two Worlds* (New York: Museum of Modern Art and Schocken Books, 1991); Michael Paul Rogin, *Blackface, White Noise: Jewish Immigrants in the Hollywood Melting Pot* (Berkeley: University of California Press, 1996); and J. Hoberman and Jeffrey Shandler, eds., *Entertaining America: Jews, Movies, and Broadcasting* (Princeton, N.J.: Princeton University Press for The Jewish Museum, 2003). For a survey of the field and bibliography, see Moshe Zimerman, "Jewish and Israeli Film Studies," in *The Oxford Handbook of Jewish Studies,* pp. 912–942. On the Holocaust and media, a topic about which much has been written, see, among others, Jeffrey Shandler, *While America Watches: Televising the Holocaust* (New York: Oxford University Press, 1999).

45. Recent contributions to the study of Jews in American popular performance and media include Harley Erdman, *Staging the Jew: The Performance of an American Ethnicity, 1860–1920* (New Brunswick, N.J.: Rutgers University Press, 1997); Jeffrey Paul Melnick, *A Right to Sing the Blues: African Americans, Jews, and American Popular Song* (Cambridge, Mass.: Harvard University Press, 1999); Michael Alexander, *Jazz Age Jews* (Princeton, N.J.: Princeton University Press, 2001); Michael Billig, *Rock 'n' Roll Jews* (Syracuse, N.Y.: Syracuse University Press, 2001); and Andrea Most, *Making Americans: Jews and the Broadway Musical* (Cambridge, Mass.: Harvard University Press, 2004).

Chapter 1. Theater as Educational Institution

1. A more extensive discussion of the intellectuals' efforts to reform the Yiddish theater can be found in Bettina Warnke, "Reforming the New York Yiddish Theater: The Cultural Politics of Immigrant Intellectuals and the Yiddish Press, 1887–1910" (Ph.D. dissertation, Columbia University, 2001).

2. For a detailed analysis of the Jewish radicals' indebtedness to Russian populism and their literary and political writings in New York, see Steven Cassedy, *To the Other Shore: The Russian Jewish Intellectuals Who Came to America* (Princeton, N.J.: Princeton University Press, 1997).

3. "Di yidishe bine, ire 'behelfer' un behelfers helfer," *Folksadvokat*, November 23, 1888. All translations from Yiddish are my own unless otherwise noted.

4. B. Weinstein, "Di ershte yidishe teater-forshtelung in amerike," in *Teater zikhroynes*, reprinted in *Hintern forhang*, ed. Zalmen Zylbercweig (Vilna: Kletzkin, 1928), pp. 69–72.

5. The information on and quote from Barsky's article is taken from Elias Tcherikower, *Geshikhte fun der yidisher arbeter bavegung in di fareynikte shtatn*, vol. 2 (New York: YIVO, 1945), pp. 378–79.

6. Melech Epstein, *Jewish Labor in U.S.A.* (New York: Trade Union Sponsoring Committee, 1950), p. 129.

7. Abraham Cahan, *Arbayter tsaytung*, April 11, 1890, as quoted in Nora Levin, *While Messiah Tarried: Jewish Socialist Movements, 1871–1917* (New York: Schocken, 1977), p. 143.

8. Moyshe Katz, "Y. Gordins fardinst af der nyu yorker yidisher bine," *Suvenir tsu Yankev Gordins tsen-yorikn yubileyum* (New York: n.p., 1901), pp. 12–13.

9. For Ostrovskii's comparing theater to a *"narodnaia shkola"* (as in Yiddish, it literally means "people's school"), see Eugene Anthony Swift, "Theater for the People: The Politics of Popular Culture in Urban Russia, 1861–1917" (Ph.D. dissertation, University of California, Berkeley, 1992), p. 49. See also Gary Thurston, *The Popular Theatre Movement in Russia, 1862–1919* (Evanston, Ill.: Northwestern University Press, 1998).

10. Jacob Gordin, "Nokh vos darf men teater?" in Gordin, *Ale shriftn fun Yankev Cordin*, vol. 4 (New York: Hebrew Publishing Co., 1910), pp. 112–13.

11. On the role and function of literature as advocated by the radical Russian intelligentsia, see Jeffrey Brooks, *When Russia Learned to Read: Literacy and Popular Literature, 1861–1917* (Princeton, N.J.: Princeton University Press, 1985), pp. 317–22.

12. Abraham Cahan, "Di yidishe bine: Sibiriya in yunyon teater," *Arbayter tsaytung*, November 20, 1891.

13. Ibid., November 27, 1891.

14. Jacob Gordin, "Vegn di [*sic*] drama 'Pogrom,'" *Arbayter tsaytung*, April 15, 1892.

15. Cahan, "Di yidishe bine: Sibiriya in yunyon teater."

16. Gordin, "Vegn di drama 'Pogrom.'"

17. Bernard Gorin, *Geshikhte fun yidishn teater*, 2 vols. (New York: Literarisher ferlag, 1918). The Progressive Dramatic Club was founded in 1902 and saw itself as the spiritual heir to the Fraye yidishe folksbine. See "Progresiv dramatik klub," in *Leksikon fun yidishn teater*, vol. 3, ed. Zalmen Zylbercweig (New York: Elisheva, 1959), pp. 1857–66.

18. Jacob Gordin, "Di fraye yidishe folksbine: undzer platform," *Fraye yidishe folksbine*, vol. 1 (n.d.), pp. 2–3. The organization was inspired by the Berlin-based, socialist Freie Volksbühne, which was devoted to raising workers' understanding of drama and appreciation of art.

19. It broke up in the fall of 1897 when Gordin and several of his friends resigned over the decision to have Kobrin's first play staged. See Leon Kobrin, *Erinerungen fun a yidishn dramaturg*, vol. 1 (New York: Komitet far Kobrins shriftn, 1925), pp. 13–20, and Joel Entin, "Leon Kobrin der dramaturg," in Leon Kobrin, *Dramatishe shriftn* (New York: Leon Kobrin bukh-komitet, 1952), pp. xiv–xviii.

20. Benjamin Feigenbaum, "Di 'kenigin' fun ale yidishe dramas," *Abend blatt*, August 22, 1898.

21. Moyshe Katz, "Di yidishe kenigin Lir oder Mirele Efrosi [*sic*]," *Forverts*, August 28, 1898.

22. "Moyshe Kats," in Zylbercweig, *Leksikon fun yidishn teater*, vol. 4, p. 2932.

23. Abraham Cahan, *Bleter fun mayn lebn*, vol. 4 (New York: Forverts Association, 1928), p. 382. His recollection is based on a *Forverts* article published on April 25, 1904.

24. Attitudes toward the dance halls are discussed by Kathy Peiss, *Cheap Amusements: Working Women and Leisure in Turn-of-the-Century New York* (Philadelphia: Temple University Press, 1986); and for the intellectuals' critique of music halls, see my article, "Immigrant Popular Culture as Contested Sphere: Yiddish Music Halls, the Yiddish Press, and the Processes of Americanization, 1900–1910," *Theatre Journal* 48 (1996):321–35.

25. Khayim Malits, "Yidishe myuzik hols in nyu york," *Amerikaner*, November 30, 1906.

26. Jacob Gordin, "Di tsukunft fun yidishn teater," *Tsukunft* 11 (February 1906):81–85.

27. Ibid., p. 84.

28. Ibid.

29. The centrality of the "child" paradigm in the intellectuals' descriptions of early Yiddish theater and its audience is discussed in detail in my essay "The Child Who Wouldn't Grow Up: Yiddish Theatre and Its Critics," in *Yiddish Theatre: New Approaches*, ed. Joel Berkowitz (Oxford: Littman Library of Jewish Civilization, 2003), pp. 201–16.

30. Bernard Gorin, "Varum di yidishe bine hot zikh a tsi geton tsurik?" *Amerikaner*, February 15, 1907.

31. Abraham Cahan, "Yidishe shund-pyesn," *Forverts*, October 24, 1908.

32. Reflecting the intellectuals' focus on *shund* successes, Gorin barely mentions Kaminska's performances or those of Pinski's play in the chapter "Harts, neshome, pintele" in his *Geshikhte*, vol. 2, pp. 203–31.

33. "Vos zol men ton vegn dem yidishn teater?" *Forverts*, November 8, 1908. See also Bernard Gorin, "Di tsushtende fun der yidisher bine," *Tsukunft* 15 (May 1910):313–319.

34. S. Raskin, ["Yankev Gordin iz toyt"], *Der groyser kundes*, June 18, 1909. That sentiment also found expression on the Yiddish music hall stage, where the song "Gordin has died. Hurrah! Hurrah!" was performed. Y. Kirshenboym, "Luis Kremer velkher hot gekenigt in vodevil iz itst a 'fargesener,'" *Morgen zhurnal*, November 17, 1939.

Chapter 2. Film and Vaudeville on New York's Lower East Side

1. Advertisement for Grand Street Music Hall, *Forward*, December 13, 1909. The paper was known as *Forverts* in Yiddish and as the *Jewish Daily Forward* in English.

2. Quoted in Richard Abel, "The Perils of Pathé or the Americanization of American Cinema," in *Cinema and the Invention of Modern Life*, ed. Leo Charney and Vanessa R. Schwartz (Berkeley: University of California Press), p. 202.

3. See Hadassa Kosak, *Cultures of Opposition: Jewish Immigrant Workers, New York City, 1881–1905* (Albany: State University of New York Press, 2000).

4. Irving Howe, *The World of Our Fathers: The Journey of the East European Jews to America and the Life They Found and Made* (1976; New York: Schocken, 1990), pp. 287–324; Gerald Sorin, *A Time for Building: The Third Migration, 1880–1920* (Baltimore: Johns Hopkins University Press, 1992), pp. 109–35.

5. Daniel Soyer, "Class Conscious Workers as Immigrant Entrepreneurs: The Ambiguity of Class among Eastern European Jewish Immigrants to the United States at the Turn of the Twentieth Century," *Labor History* 42, 1 (2001):45–59.

6. Ibid., p. 46.

7. John Collier, "Cheap Amusements," *Charities and Commons*, April 11, 1908, 74.

8. Judith Thissen, "Oy Myopia!: A Reaction from Judith Thissen on the Singer-Allen Controversy," *Cinema Journal* 36, 4 (1997):104–6. For locations of nickelodeons in Manhattan and details about ownership, see Ben Singer, "Manhattan Nickelodeons: New Data on Audiences and Exhibitors," *Cinema Journal* 34, 3 (Spring 1995):5–35.

9. William Uricchio and Roberta E. Pearson, *Reframing Culture: The Case of the Vitagraph Quality Films* (Princeton, N.J.: Princeton University Press, 1993), p. 24.

10. Abel, "The Perils of Pathé," p. 202.

11. Richard Abel, " 'Pathé Goes to Town': French Films Create a Market for the Nickelodeon," *Cinema Journal* 35, 1 (1995):3–26.

12. Abel, "The Perils of Pathé," pp. 194–200.

13. Ibid., p. 200.

14. "The People's Institute Motion Picture Show Report" (n.d., around March 1910), Jacob A. Riis Neighborhood Settlement Records, box 10, folder 7 (motion pictures and vaudeville shows 1909–10), Rare Books and Manuscript Division, New York Public Library, New York; "Report to the Health Committee" (February 1910), National Board of Review of Motion Pictures Records, Subject Papers, box 170, folder 1 (papers relating to the formation and the subsequent history of the NBRMP, 1908–15)," Rare Books and Manuscripts Division, New York Public Library, New York.

15. "East Side Neighborhood Association," Jacob A. Riis Neighborhood Settlement Records, box 15, folder 5, Rare Books and Manuscripts Division, New York Public Library, New York.

16. "Censorship for Moving Pictures," *Survey* 22, April 3, 1909, 9.

17. Thomas Bedding, "Vaudeville Vitiates the Picture," *Moving Picture World*, June 11, 1910, quoted in Ben Singer, "New York, Just Like I Pictured It . . . ," *Cinema Journal* 35, 3 (1996):118. For a detailed discussion of the relation between vaudeville and film, see Singer's article and also Robert C. Allen, "Manhattan Myopia," *Cinema Journal* 35, 3 (Spring 1996):84–95.

18. Miriam Hansen, *Babel and Babylon: Spectatorship in American Silent Film* (Cambridge, Mass.: Harvard University Press, 1991), p. 94.

19. Ibid., p. 84.

20. For a recent overview of the underlying debate in film history, see Melvyn Stokes, "Introduction: Reconstructing American Cinema's Audiences," in *American Movie Audiences: From the Turn of the Century to the Early Sound Era*, ed. Melvyn Stokes and Richard Maltby (London: BFI Publishing, 1999), pp. 1–10. See also Singer, "Manhattan Nickelodeons," pp. 5–6.

21. On the "Americanization of American Cinema," see Richard Abel, *The Red Rooster Scare: Making Cinema American, 1900–1910* (Berkeley: University of California Press, 1999), esp. pp.118–40, 151–74.

22. Nina Warnke, "Immigrant Popular Culture as Contested Sphere: Yiddish

Music Halls, the Yiddish Press, and the Processes of Americanization, 1900–1910," *Theatre Journal* 48 (1996):321–35.

23. Quoted in ibid., p. 329.

24. Ibid., p. 324.

25. Advertisements Grand Street Music Hall, *Forward*, August 11 and 22, and September 9, 1905; Khayim Malits, "Yidishe myuzik hols in nyu york," *Der Amerikaner*, November 30, 1906; "Fun vanen nehmen zikh unzere verayti ektors," *Forward*, February 24, 1906.

26. Singer, "Manhattan Nickelodeons," p. 22.

27. "Vu zaynen ahingekumen di yidishe myuzik hols?" *Forward*, May 24, 1908.

28. "Ibid., and "Vu zaynen ahingekumen di yidishe myuzik hol 'stars'?" *Forward*, November 26, 1908.

29. In 1910, American Federation of Labor delegates urged local unions to "use all legitimate means . . . to discourage the exhibition of such moving pictures that falsely pretend to represent instances in connection with our movement." Quoted in Steven J. Ross, "The Revolt of the Audience: Reconsidering Audiences and Reception during the Silent Era," in Stokes and Maltby, eds., *American Movie Audiences*, p. 96. For a detailed analysis of labor and radical film production, see Steven J. Ross, *Working Class Hollywood: Silent Film and the Shaping of Class in America* (Princeton, N.J.: Princeton University Press, 1998).

30. "Der muving piktshur trost," *Tageblatt*, January 6, 1909; "Muving piktshurs in lebens-farben," *Tageblatt*, December 17, 1909; and "Shiken bilder durkh elektrik," *Tageblatt*, January 23, 1910.

31. Andrew Heinze, *Adapting to Abundance: Jewish Immigrants, Mass Consumption and the Search for American Identity* (New York: Columbia University Press, 1990), p. 150.

32. "Golden rul theater iz zikher," *Tageblatt*, December 16, 1908. It should be emphasized in this context that neither the *Tageblatt* nor the *Morgen zhurnal* was subject to pressure from local film exhibitors, who might have used advertising as leverage to produce favorable publicity. Movie theaters rarely advertised in the Yiddish press before 1913–14.

33. "Der unglik oyf rivington strit," editorial, *Forward*, December 15, 1908.

34. "Grend theater thut zikh on in di bgodim fun muving piktshurs," *Warheit*, September 5, 1909.

35. "Adler, miler un kompani," *Forward*, September 8, 1909.

36. "Vos thut zikh in theater?," *Tageblatt*, November 19, 1910.

37. "Di muving piktshur frage," *Tageblatt*, March 20, 1911.

38. For a detailed analysis, see Judith Thissen, "Charlie Steiner's Houston Hippodrome: Moviegoing on New York's Lower East Side, 1909–1913," in *American Silent Film: Discovering Marginalized Voices*, ed. Greg Bachman and Thomas Slater (Carbondale: Southern Illinois University Press, 2002), pp. 44–47.

39. "Lazt nit ayere kinder gehn aleyn in di muving piktshur pletser," *Forward*, May 13, 1910. See also "2 yidishe boys fershikt in sing-sing als kadeten," *Forward*, January 31, 1910; "2 maydlekh ferfihrt in a muving piktshur plats," *Forward*, December 23, 1910; and "Vider di gefahr fun di muving piktshurs," *Forward*, editorial, Febuary 2, 1911. For the general context in which these concerns about movies and white slavery were articulated, see Janet Staiger, *Bad Women: Regulating Sexuality in Early Cinema* (Minneapolis: University of Minnesota Press, 1995), pp. 44–52, 99–103, 120–28.

40. "Durkh muving piktshurs beganvenen zey a hoyz," *Forward*, January 11, 1910; "Lernt zikh ganvenen durkh muving piktshurs," *Forward*, June 6, 1910; and "Kinder veren banditen fun muving piktshurs," *Forward*, June 11, 1910.

41. "Muving piktshurs un di kinder," *Tageblatt,* January 30, 1911; "Di muving piktshur frage," *Tageblatt,* March 20, 1911.

42. Moving Picture World, December 6, 1913, p. 1132.

43. "Der yidisher kristmes: Der vehtog fun unzer gas," *Tageblatt,* December 23, 1913. For a description of the film and its production context, see Patricia Ehrens, *The Jews in American Cinema* (Bloomington: Indiana University Press, 1984), pp. 46–47.

44. "Eybi's muving piktshurs," *Warheit,* October 30, November 6 and 9, 1912.

45. Roger Chartier, *On the Edge of the Cliff: History, Language, and Practices* (Baltimore: Johns Hopkins University Press, 1997), p. 77.

Chapter 3. Of Maestros and Minstrels

1. See generally Barbara Tischler, *An American Music: The Search for an American Musical Identity* (New York: Oxford University Press, 1986). Pioneering treatments of Jews and American musical modernism and of Tin Pan Alley respectively appear in MacDonald Smith Moore, *Yankee Blues: Musical Culture and American Identity* (Bloomington: Indiana University Press, 1985), and Jeffrey Melnick, *A Right to Sing the Blues* (Cambridge, Mass: Harvard University Press, 1999). My account—though indebted to both—differs in its transatlantic emphasis on the image of the Jewish middleman.

2. For general background, see Walter P. Zenner, *Minorities in the Middle: A Cross-Cultural Analysis* (Albany: State University of New York Press, 1991); Jonathan Karp, *The Politics of Jewish Commerce: Economic Thought and Emancipation in Europe, 1638–1848* (New York: Cambridge University Press, 2007). For recent discussions of Jewish occupational overrepresentation, see Yuri Slezkine, *The Jewish Century* (Princeton, N.J.: Princeton University Press, 2004), and David A. Hollinger, "Rich, Powerful, and Smart: Jewish, Overrepresentation Should Be Explained Rather Than Mystified or Avoided," *Jewish Quarterly Review* 94, 4 (2004):592–602.

3. See Derek Penslar, *Shylock's Children: Jewish Economics and Identity in Modern Europe* (Berkeley: University of California Press, 2001), pp. 94–121.

4. Albert S. Lindemann, *Esau's Tears: Modern Antisemitism and the Rise of the Jews* (New York: Cambridge University Press, 1997), pp. 115–18, 187–90.

5. Thomas Kessner, *The Golden Door: Italian and Jewish Immigrant Mobility in New York City, 1880–1915* (New York: Oxford University Press, 1977); Daniel Soyer, "Class Conscious Workers as Immigrant Entrepreneurs: The Ambiguity of Class among Eastern European Jewish Immigrants to the United States at the Turn of the Century," *Labor History* 42, 1 (2001):45–59; Andrew Heinze, *Adapting to Abundance: Jewish Immigrants, Mass Consumption, and the Search for American Identity* (New York: Columbia University Press, 1990).

6. Evyatar Friesel, *Atlas of Modern Jewish History* (New York: Oxford University Press, 1990), p. 139.

7. Edward Pessen, "The Great Songwriters of Tin Pan Alley's Golden Age: A Social, Occupational, and Aesthetic Inquiry," in *A Celebration of American Music: Words and Music in Honor of H. Wiley Hitchcock,* ed. Richard Crawford, R. Allen Lott, and Carol Oja (Ann Arbor: University of Michigan Press, 1990), pp. 184–85.

8. M. Witmark and Sons; Shapiro-Bernstein; Marks and Stern; Leo Feist; Snyder and Waterhouse (later Snyder, Waterhouse, and Berlin); T. B. Harms (by 1900 controlled by Max Dreyfus); Chas. K. Harris; Harry Von Tilzer; and Jerome Remick are the most important.

9. Isaac Goldberg, *Tin Pan Alley: A Chronicle of Popular Music* (New York: F. Unger, 1961), p. 111.

10. Quoted in David Suisman, "The Sound of Money: Music, Machines, and Markets, 1890–1925" (Ph.D. dissertation, Columbia University, 2002), p. 44.

11. Pessen, "The Great Songwriters," p. 185.

12. Gerald Bordman, *Jerome Kern: His Life and Music* (New York: Oxford University Press, 1980), p. 10; Arnold Shaw, *The Jazz Age: Popular Music in the 1920s* (New York: Oxford University Press, 1987), p. 164; John Tasker Howard, *Our American Music* (New York: Thomas Y. Crowell, 1946), p. 673.

13. David Ewen, *All the Years of American Popular Music* (Englewood Cliffs, N.J.: Prentice Hall, 1977), p. 271; Howard, *Our American Music*, p. 665; Shaw, *Jazz Age*, p. 173; Yip Harburg, "From the Lower East Side to 'Over the Rainbow,'" in *Creators and Disturbers: Reminiscences by Jewish Intellectuals of New York*, ed. Bernard Rosenberg and Ernest Goldstein (New York: Columbia University Press, 1982), p. 142; Howard, *Our American Music*, p. 671; Edward Jablonski, *Harold Arlen: Rhythm, Rainbows and Blues* (Boston: Northeastern University Press, 1996), p. 9; Howard, *Our American Music*, p. 675.

14. Charles Schwartz, *Gershwin: His Life and Music* (New York: Bobbs-Merrill, 1973), p. 5. The lyricist Edgar "Yip" Harburg recalled that "[c]ompared to most of us, the Gershwins were affluent; Ira had an allowance, and money to buy magazines, books, and records." See Harburg, "From the Lower East Side to 'Over the Rainbow,'" p. 141.

15. Shaw, *Jazz Age*, p. 158.

16. "Otto Harbach," in *Webster's New World Dictionary of Music*, ed. Nicholas Slonimsky and Richard Kassel (New York: Macmillan, 1998), 207; Shaw, *Jazz Age*, p. 173; Ewen, *All the Years*, pp. 435, 339.

17. Quoted in Laurence Bergreen, *As Thousands Cheered: The Life of Irving Berlin* (New York: Da Capo Press, 1996), p. 46.

18. Lawrence W. Levine, *Highbrow/Lowbrow: The Emergence of Cultural Hierarchy in America* (Cambridge, Mass.: Harvard University Press, 1988), pp. 90–91; William J. Mahar, *Behind the Burnt Cork Mask: Early Blackface Minstrelsy and Antebellum American Popular Culture* (Urbana: University of Illinois Press, 1999), pp. 2–5, 101–56.

19. From the recording by Arthur Collins and Byron C. Harlan (Columbia A801), found in Irving Berlin, *The Songs of Irving Berlin for Voice and Piano*, vol. 1 (Boca Raton, Fla.: Masters Music, 1980), pp. 22–25; Charles Hamm, *Irving Berlin: Songs from the Melting Pot: The Formative Years, 1907–1914* (New York: Oxford University Press, 1997), pp. 74–75.

20. Hamm, *Irving Berlin*, pp. 76, 200–201.

21. Irving Berlin, *Ragtime Opera Medley* (New York: Wakison, Berlin & Snyder, 1914), *http://www.thepeaches.com/music/composers/berlin/songography.html*.

22. Janell R. Duxbury, *Rockin' the Classics and Classicizin' the Rock: A Selectively Annotated Discography* (Westport, Conn.: Greenwood Press, 1985).

23. Chuck Berry, "Roll Over Beethoven," Chess Records single 1626 (1956).

24. Thomas L. Riis, *More Than Just Minstrel Shows* (Brooklyn: Institute for Studies in American Music, 1992), pp. 8–9.

25. Ann Douglas, *Terrible Honesty: Mongrel Manhattan in the 1920s* (New York: Farrar, Straus and Giroux, 1995), p. 349.

26. Quoted in Hamm, *Irving Berlin*, p. 212.

27. Quoted in ibid., pp. 107–9.

28. Bordman, *Jerome Kern*, pp. 112 ff.

29. Mark Slobin, *Tenement Songs: The Popular Music of the Jewish Immigrants* (Urbana: University of Illinois Press, 1982), p. 41.

30. Burton W. Peretti, *The Creation of Jazz: Music, Race, and Culture in Urban America* (Urbana: University of Illinois Press, 1992), pp. 71–75.

31. Quoted in Bergreen, *As Thousands Cheered*, p. 121.

32. Simone Luzzatto, *Discourse on the Jews of Venice* (Hebrew), trans. Dan Lattes (Jerusalem, 1954), p. 90.

33. Fyodor Dostoevsky, *The Diary of a Writer* (New York: George Brazillier, 1954), p. 642.

34. Quoted in Adrienne Fried Block, "Dvořák, Beach, and American Music," in *Celebration of American Music*, p. 257.

35. Ibid., pp. 258–62; Moore, *Yankee Blues*, pp. 81–82.

36. See Werner Sollors, *Beyond Ethnicity: Consent and Descent in American Culture* (New York: Oxford University Press, 1986), pp. 66–75.

37. Van Wyck Brooks, *America's Coming of Age* (New York: B. W. Huebsch, 1915), pp. 14, 15, 34.

38. Cited in Goldberg, *Tin Pan Alley*, pp. 252–53.

39. Carl Van Vechten, "The Great American Composer," in *Interpreters and Interpretations* (New York: Alfred A. Knopf, 1917), pp. 269–70.

40. On Rosenfeld, see Hugh M. Potter, *False Dawn: Paul Rosenfeld and Art in America, 1916–1946* (Ann Arbor: University of Michigan Press, 1980), pp. 187–88.

41. Gilbert Seldes, "Cakes and Ale Return to Favor," *Vanity Fair*, May 1924, 50.

42. Gilbert Seldes, *The Seven Lively Arts* (New York: Sagamore Press, 1957), p. 99. On the ultimate cultural superiority of Jews to Negroes, see Gilbert Seldes, "The House of Esau," *Nation*, October 5, 1921, 374.

43. A 1933 recording was made by The Funnyboners and appears on the CD *From Avenue A to the Great White Way* (New York: Columbia/Legacy, 2002). Ira Gershwin's less discreet first draft appears in Edward Jablonsky and Lawrence D. Stewart, eds., *The Gershwin Years* (New York: Doubleday, 1958), p. 56.

44. Ira Gershwin, *Lyrics on Several Occasions* (New York: Limelight Editions, 1997), pp. 177–81.

45. Marc Blitzstein, "Popular Music—An Invasion: 1923–1933," *Modern Music* 2 (January–February 1933):101.

46. Ibid., p. 99.

47. Ibid., p. 100.

48. Ibid., p. 102.

49. James Lincoln Collier, *The Making of Jazz: A Comprehensive History* (London: Papermac, 1981), pp. 177–81, esp. 180. See also James Lincoln Collier, *The Reception of Jazz in America: A New View* (Brooklyn: Institute for Studies in American Music, 1988), p. 17.

50. See the brief tribute to Paul Whiteman and references therein by Terry Teachout, "King of the Jazz Age," *Commentary*, December 2003, 58–61.

51. As Louis Armstrong wrote in 1936, "The reason swing musicians insist upon calling the music 'swing music' is because they know how different it is from the stale brand of jazz they're so sick of hearing. But in the early days, when jazz was born, jazz wasn't that way at all." Quoted in Alain Locke, *The Negro and His Music* (1936; Port Washington: Kennikot Press, 1968), pp. 93–94.

52. Quoted in Moore, *Yankee Blues*, p. 160.

53. Waldo Frank, "Jazz and Folk Art," *The American Jungle 1925–1936* (New York: Farrar and Rhinehart, 1937), pp. 122–23.

54. Seldes, *Lively Arts*, p. 249.

55. Constant Lambert, *Music Ho! A Study of Music in Decline* (London: Faber and Faber, 1937), p. 142; Goldberg, *Tin Pan Alley*, pp. 267–68.

56. Eric A. Gordon, *Mark the Music: The Life and Work of Mark Blitzstein* (New York: St. Martin's Press, 1989), p. 41.

57. Ibid., pp. 29, 42–43.

58. Ibid., p. 20.

59. These errors appeared as late as 1967. See *Encyclopedia Judaica*, s.v. "Antheil" and "Whiteman."

60. Virgil Thomson, "The Cult of Jazz," *Vanity Fair*, June 1925, 54; Virgil Thomson, "Enter: American-Made Music," *Vanity Fair*, October 1925, 124.

61. Darius Milhaud, *My Happy Life: An Autobiography*, trans. Donald Evans, George Hall, and Christopher Palmer (London: M. Boyars, 1995), pp. 109, 146–47.

62. Ernst Krenek, *Music Here and Now*, trans. Barthold Fles (New York: W. W. Norton, 1939), pp. 253–61.

63. Aaron Copland, *Our New Music: Leading Composers in Europe and America* (New York: McGraw-Hill, 1941), p. 227.

64. A. Walter Kramer, "Louis Gruenberg," *Modern Music* 8 (November–December 1930):4–5.

65. Howard Pollack, *Aaron Copland: The Life and Work of an Uncommon Man* (New York: Henry Holt, 1999), p. 120.

66. Robert F. Nisbett, "Louis Gruenberg's American Idiom," *American Music* 3, 1 (Spring 1985):38–39.

67. Goldberg, *Tin Pan Alley*, pp. 293–94.

68. Quoted in Pollock, *Aaron Copland*, p. 519.

69. Pollock, *Aaron Copland*, p. 519. Mason's views are explored at length in Moore's *Yankee Blues*, pp. 128–68, esp. 133–47. Cowell's remarks appear in his "Bericht aus Amerika," *Melos: Zeitschrift für Musik* 12 (December 1930): 526.

70. Rosenfeld, "Musical Chronicle," *Dial*, February 1926, 175.

71. Thomson, "The Cult of Jazz," p. 54.

72. R. W. S. Mendl, *The Appeal of Jazz* (London: P. Allan, 1927), pp. 164–65. Mendl believed jazz "consists more of interpretation than does any other form of music." See also Kathy Ogren, *The Jazz Revolution: Twenties America and the Making of Jazz* (New York: Oxford University Press, 1989), pp. 155–56.

73. Milhaud, *My Happy Life*, p. 110.

74. Mendl, *Appeal of Jazz*, p. 47.

75. Thomson, "How Modern Music Gets that Way," *Vanity Fair*, April 1925, 102.

76. Quoted in Pollock, *Aaron Copland*, p. 114. One might ask why the same would not apply to most classical works as well.

77. Quoted in Charles Hamm, "A Blues for the Ages," in *Celebration of American Music*, p. 347.

78. Otto Kahn, *Of Many Things: Being Reflections and Impressions on International Affairs, Domestic Topics and the Arts* (New York: Boni and Liveright, 1926), pp. 65–71; Mary Jane Phillips-Matz, *The Many Lives of Otto Kahn* (New York: Macmillan, 1963), pp. 226–29.

79. Bergreen, *As Thousands Cheered*, pp. 190–91.

80. Quoted in Pollock, *Aaron Copland*, p. 107.

81. See Michael Denning, *The Cultural Front: The Laboring of American Culture in the Twentieth Century* (London: Verso Press, 1996).

82. But see Jeffrey Magee, "Before Louis: When Fletcher Henderson Was the 'Paul Whiteman of the Race,'" *American Music* 18, 4 (Winter 2000):391–425. It should be noted that jazz musicians like Duke Ellington and James P. Johnson were also attempting to build sophisticated compositional frameworks as settings for but not as replacements of individual improvisations.

Chapter 4. May Day, Tractors, and Piglets

Note on transliteration: When quoting Yiddish from published material, I use the YIVO system for the romanization of Yiddish. When quoting from a recorded interview in Yiddish, I try to reflect the basic features of the speaker's pronunciation.

1. Grigorii B., interview, New York, April 1999.
2. L. Rosenblum, "Der kleyner pioner," *Pioner* 1 (1926):18.
3. Grigorii B., interview, New York, April 1999.
4. Anne Gorsuch, *Youth in Revolutionary Russia: Enthusiasts, Bohemians, Delinquents* (Bloomington: Indiana University Press, 2000), p. 1.
5. Mordechai Altshuler, *Soviet Jewry on the Eve of the Holocaust: A Social and Demographic Profile* (Jerusalem: Yad Vashem, 1998), p. 56.
6. Ibid., p. 48.
7. Ibid., pp. 89–97.
8. Elias Schulman, *A History of Jewish Education in the Soviet Union* (New York: Ktav, 1971), pp. 97–122; Zvi Y. Gitelman, *Jewish Nationality and Soviet Politics* (Princeton, N.J.: Princeton University Press, 1972), p. 337.
9. About 45 percent of Ukrainian Jewish children attended Yiddish schools in 1926, and about 50 percent of Jewish children in Byelorussia. See Schulman, *A History of Jewish Education*, pp. 148–51.
10. Anna Shternshis, "From the Eradication of Illiteracy to Workers' Correspondents: Yiddish Language Mass Movements in the Soviet Union," *East European Jewish Affairs* 32 (2002):120–37, esp. pp. 125–27.
11. Schulman, *A History of Jewish Education*, p. 72.
12. The most notable were Itsik Fefer, Moyshe Kotlyar, and Fayvl Sito, *Ferzn un tshastushkes* (Kiev: Ukrmelukhisher farlag, 1937); Rive Boyarskaya, *Klingen hemerlekh* (Moscow: Melukhe-Farlag, Muzikalishe serie, 1925).
13. Calculations are based on information retrieved from the catalogue of the Russian State Library in Moscow.
14. The interviews are currently being transcribed. Some texts are located at the Frankel Center for Judaic Studies at the University of Michigan, Ann Arbor. If not indicated in the text, all other interviews are in the author's possession and are available upon request.
15. Most of my respondents wanted their names to be published, yet some requested that they remain anonymous. I provide only their first names and initials to protect their privacy. I conducted mostly individual interviews, as well as a few group interviews. Group interviews, generally less revealing, did have some advantages, such as when people reminded each other of various events and artistic pieces that they otherwise might not have mentioned.
16. No author, *Zamlbukh fun kinder lider* (Homel: Melukhe farlag, 1921), p. 3.
17. "Forvort," in M. Limone, *30 lider far kinder* (Minsk: Vaysruslendisher melukhe-farlag, 1928), p. 3.
18. Vladimir Papernyi, *Kul'tura dva* (Moscow: Novoye literaturnoye obozrenie, 1996), pp. 72–100.
19. *Zamlbukh fun kinder lider*, p. 6.
20. I. Katsenelson, "Marsh," in *Zamlbukh fun kinder lider*, p. 6.
21. Ian Derbaremdiker, interview, New York, February 1999.
22. Itsik Fefer, "Ruft di kinder afn shlyakh," in Y. Bakst and M. Gnesin, *Naye lider* (Moscow: Tsenterfarlag, 1927), p. 12.
23. Tsirl B., interview, Moscow, June 2001.
24. Fifteen respondents spoke about this phenomenon.
25. Rive Boyarskaya, *Kleyne boyers* (Moscow: Der Emes, 1938), p. 20.
26. Sheila Fitzpatrick, *Everyday Stalinism: Ordinary Life in Extraordinary Times, Soviet Russia in the 1930s* (New York: Oxford University Press, 1999), p. 9.
27. Semyon S., interview, New York, August 1999.
28. Mariya K., interview, Moscow, June 2001.

29. The text of the song is published in Limone, *30 lider far kinder*, pp. 16–17.

30. Matvey G., interview, Berlin, June 2002.

31. Papernyi, *Kul'tura dva*, pp. 260–61.

32. Boyarskaya, *Kleyne boyers*, p. 28.

33. Z. Smolyansky, "Fabrik Lid," in S. Polonsky, *Far yugnt* (Moscow: Tsentraler felker farlag fun fssr, 1931), p. 15.

34. Faina M., interview, Moscow, June 2001.

35. Boyarskaya, *Klingen hemerlekh*, p. 29.

36. Ibid., p. 3.

37. Boyarskaya, "Traktor," in *Kleyne boyers*, p. 13.

38. E. Spivak, "Arbeter un poyer," in Polonskii, *30 lider far kinder* (Moscow: Der Emes, 1930), p. 13.

39. N. Gladilin, "Krim," *Pioner* 6 (1928):13.

40. "Khazerlekh [Piglets]," in R. Boyarskaya, *Lomir zingen, lider mit notn* (Moscow: Der Emes 1940), p. 15. Music by R. Boyarskaya, text by L. Kvitko.

41. Mikhail B., interview, New York, June 1999.

42. David Hofshteyn, "Birobidzhan," in Boyarskaya, *Lomir zingen, lider mit notn,* p. 47.

43. Efim G., interview, New York, February 1999.

44. For methods of Soviet indoctrination, see Peter Kenez, *The Birth of the Propaganda State: Soviet Methods of Mass Mobilization, 1917–1929* (Cambridge: Cambridge University Press, 1985). For propaganda in Russian popular culture, see Richard Stites, *Russian Popular Culture: Entertainment and Society since 1900* (Cambridge: Cambridge University Press, 1992). For political folklore, see Frank Miller, *Folklore for Stalin: Russian Folklore and Pseudo-folklore of the Stalin Era*, Studies of the Harriman Institute (Armonk: M. E. Sharpe, 1990).

45. Anna Shternshis, *Soviet and Kosher: Jewish Popular Culture in the Soviet Union, 1923–1939* (Bloomington: Indiana University Press, 2006), chap. 2.

46. Six respondents from religious families mentioned that at least one family member forbade children to sing Communist songs in their presence.

47. Y. Dobrushin and A. Yuditsky, *Yidishe folks-lider* (Moscow: Der Emes, 1940), p. 426.

Chapter 5. Performing the State

"Performing the State: The Jewish Palestine Pavilion at the New York World's Fair, 1939/40" © 2008 Barbara Kirshenblatt-Gimblett

1. On the history of Jewish participation in world's fairs, see Barbara Kirshenblatt-Gimblett, "Exhibiting Jews," in *Destination Culture: Tourism, Museums, and Heritage* (Los Angeles: University of California Press, 1998), pp. 79–128. On Holy Land displays at world's fairs, see Barbara Kirshenblatt-Gimblett, "A Place in the World: Jews and the Holy Land at World's Fairs," in *Encounters with the "Holy Land": Place, Past and Future in American Jewish Culture*, ed. Jeffrey Shandler and Beth S. Wenger (Philadelphia: National Museum of American Jewish History; Center for Judaic Studies, University of Pennsylvania; and the University of Pennsylvania Library, 1997), pp. 60–82.

2. I am indebted here to J. L. Austin's notion of performative utterance in *How to Do Things with Words*, 2nd ed., ed. Marina Sbisa and J. O. Urmsson (Cambridge, Mass.: Harvard University Press, 1975).

3. *Grover Aloysius Whalen, Mr. New York: The Autobiography of Grover A. Whalen* (New York: Putnam, 1955), p. 211.

4. Ibid., p. 176.

5. Ibid.

6. Frank Monaghan, *Official Guide Book of the New York World's Fair*, 3rd ed. (New York: Exposition Publications, 1939), p. 24.

7. Ibid., p. 37.

8. Ibid., p. 215.

9. From their inception in 1851 until 1940, world's fairs took place before, during, or after the Crimean War, American Civil War, the series of wars relating to German unification, Philippine-American War, Russo-Japanese war, Boer War, Russian Revolution, World War I, World War II, and the armed conflicts in the various colonial empires throughout this period.

10. From the speech delivered by Grover Whalen at a ceremony at the Fair grounds on March 25, 1930. "Fair to Be Opened on a Note of Peace," *New York Times*, March 26, 1939, p. 1.

11. Quotations are from, respectively, Roland Robertson, "Social Theory, Cultural Relativity and the Problem of Globality," in *Culture, Globalization, and the World-System: Contemporary Conditions for the Representation of Identity*, ed. Anthony D. King (Minneapolis: University of Minnesota Press, 1997), p. 78; and Michael Billig, *Banal Nationalism* (London: Sage Publications, 1995), p. 83. On the notion of mutual recognition, see Anthony Giddens, *The Consequences of Modernity* (Stanford, Calif.: Stanford University Press, 1990). The case of the Soviet Union is instructive: the Soviet Union, which had only just been recognized by the United States in 1933, was the first government to sign up for the 1939 New York World's Fair in March 1937. See Anthony Swift, "The Soviet World of Tomorrow," *Russian Review* 57, 3 (1998): 365.

12. Billig, *Banal Nationalism*, p. 83.

13. The Fair was organized into thematic zones, including, among others, amusement, communications, community interests, and government. It was not a perfect arrangement. For various reasons, Sweden and Turkey ended up in the Food zone, Florida in the Amusement zone, and Masterpieces of Art in the Communication and Business Systems zone.

14. Billig, *Banal Nationalism*, p. 83.

15. Cited by Daniel Shimshoni, *Israeli Democracy: The Middle of the Journey* (New York: Free Press and Collier Macmillan, 1982), p. x.

16. It was not until May 1937 that the Bureau International des Expositions "recognized the New York World's Fair as the *one* international exposition for 1939," In fact, the Golden Gate Exposition in San Francisco, while not as big as the New York World's Fair, took place at the same time. Monaghan, *Official Guide Book*, p. 123.

17. Ibid. This figure is at variance with the *Guide*'s maps, descriptions, and index, as well as with other accounts.

18. Francis Edmonds Tyng, *Making a World's Fair: Organization, Promotion, Financing, and Problems, with Particular Reference to the New York World's Fair of 1939–1940* (New York: Vantage Press, 1958), p. 37.

19. Jewish participation at the Wembley fair is discussed more fully in Kirshenblatt-Gimblett, "Exhibiting Jews," pp. 118–19.

20. *The Jewish Chronicle*, April 25, 1924.

21. Memorandum from W. H. Stanley to J. M. Killeen, October 7, 1937, Palestine, box 535, New York World's Fair Collection, New York Public Library.

22. *Seattle Sunday Times* (August 6, 1939), quoted by Nicholas J. Cull, "Overture to an Alliance: British Propaganda at the New York World's Fair, 1939–1940," *Journal of British Studies* 36, 3 (1997):345.

23. Ibid., p. 335.

24. Ibid., pp. 333–34. On his world's fair activities, see Sol Bloom, *The Autobiography of Sol Bloom* (New York: G. P. Putnam's Sons, 1948), pp. 119, 133–40.

25. Ibid., p. 344. Without a state and an army, the only authority that the Jewish Palestine Pavilion could put forward was moral authority.

26. Letter from Frederick B. Lyon to Julius C. Holmes, September 16, 1938, Pal-

estine, Government Participation, box 535, New York World's Fair Collection, New York Public Library. The letter to the high commissioner is dated August 13, 1938.

27. Harvey D. Gibson, chairman of the 1940 New York World's Fair, represented the Soviet withdrawal as follows: the Soviets made unreasonable demands, would not play by the Fair rules, insisted that their flag fly highest, used their own accounting methods, and threatened to demolish their pavilion if their demands were not met. Much had been conceded to get their participation for the 1939 fair, in the hope that other countries would follow the Soviet lead. (Harvey D. Gibson, *Harvey D. Gibson: An Autobiography* [North Conway, N.H.: Reporter Press, 1951], p. 326.) Swift, "The Soviet World of Tomorrow," pp. 378–79, argues that the Soviet Union decided not to return for the 1940 season because American public opinion had turned against it after it invaded Finland, a neutral country; unlike its occupation of Poland, the Soviet Union's invasion of Finland was not seen as an attempt to hold Hitler at bay, but rather as a break with the Western democracies.

28. Kathryn Maddrey, *Official Guide Book: The World's Fair of 1940 in New York* (New York: Rogers-Kellog-Stillson, 1940), p. 14.

29. The American Common is an example of what Philip Gleason characterizes as the ideological phase in the history of what came to be known as American "identity." Philip Gleason, "Americans All: World War II and the Shaping of American Identity," *Review of Politics* 43, 4 (1981):483–518.

30. Cull, "Overture to an Alliance," p. 353, characterizes British participation in the New York World's Fair as "the first salvo in what became a desperate British diplomatic struggle to draw the United States into World War II," adding that "In retrospect, the British contribution to the New York World's Fair stands as the high point in Britain's interwar policy of national projection. It was the single greatest effort made in the single most important struggle to overcome the forces of U.S. isolation."

31. "Denmark to Keep Its Exhibit at Fair," *New York Times*, April 10, 1940, p. 26.

32. Cull, "Overture to an Alliance," p. 352, citing the *New York Times*, May 22, 1940.

33. Even before the 1939 fair opened, Austria was invaded by Germany in March 1938 and did not participate in the Fair. Czechoslovakia, which had lost Sudetenland as a result of the Munich Pact of September 1938, was persuaded (and assisted financially) to take part in the Fair. Czechoslovakia's situation only got worse. On March 15, 1939, two weeks before the 1939 fair officially opened, the Germans marched into Prague. During the 1939 fair season (April 30 to October 31), the Nazis, and then the Soviets, invaded Poland. Between the two fairs (November 1, 1939 to May 10, 1940), the Soviets invaded Finland, were expelled from the League of Nations, and bombed Sweden. The Nazis invaded Denmark, France, Belgium, Luxembourg, and the Netherlands. During the 1940 fair (May 11 to October 27), Italy declared war on Britain and France and invaded Egypt and Greece. The Soviets took Lithuania, Latvia, and Estonia. The Nazis bombed Britain, attacked Norway, and entered Romania.

34. *Jewish Palestine Pavilion, New York World's Fair, 1939*. No other publication information is indicated. The pages are not numbered.

35. This pageant traveled to New York, Philadelphia, Detroit, and Cleveland. It had been preceded by his Hanukkah pageant in 1932 in Chicago and was followed by *The Eternal Road* in 1937, a grandiose biblical epic that lost money. Weisgal's repeated proposals for a pageant at the New York World's Fair, preserved in the records of the Fair at New York Public Library, were never accepted. On the pageants that Weisgal did produce, see Atay Citron, "Pageantry and Theater in the Service of Jewish Nationalism in the United States 1933–1946" (Ph.D. dissertation, New York University, 1989); Stephen J. Whitfield, "The Politics of Pageantry, 1936–

1946," *American Jewish History* 84, 3 (1996):221–51; Arthur Goren, "Celebrating Zion in America," in *Encounters with the "Holy Land,"* ed. Shandler and Wenger, pp. 41–59; and Kirshenblatt-Gimblett, "Exhibiting Jews."

36. Meyer Weisgal, . . . *So Far: An Autobiography* (New York: Random House, 1971), pp. 106–7.

37. Ibid., p. 107.

38. Ibid., p. 142.

39. Ibid., p. 149.

40. Jewish Charter members of the New York World's Fair 1939, Inc., included the following luminaries. Unless otherwise indicated, they were American born. Harry F. Guggenheim was an aviation pioneer and founder of *Newsday.* Arthur Lehman, an investment banker and art collector, played a leading role in the Federation of Jewish Philanthropies of New York and the American Jewish Joint Distribution Committee. His brother Herbert was governor of New York State during the 1930s. Henry Morgenthau, Sr., was a real estate lawyer and agent, philanthropist, and diplomat. Morgenthau came to the United States from Germany in 1866. He served as ambassador to Turkey between 1913 and 1916, during which time he raised money to help Jewish settlers in Palestine. President Wilson sent him to Poland in 1919 to investigate atrocities committed against Jews. A Reform Jew, he helped found and then served as president of the Free Synagogue. His son Henry Morgenthau, Jr., was secretary of the Treasury under Roosevelt. David Sarnoff, who arrived in the United States from Russia in 1900, played an instrumental role in the development of radio and then television as mass media. He became president of RCA in 1930. RCA was represented at the New York World's Fair by its own spectacular building, from which, in April 1939, Sarnoff "conducted the first public television broadcast." Percy S. Straus was president of Macy's at the time of the Fair, and Felix M. Warburg, who was born in Germany, was an investment banker, philanthropist, lover of art, and leader in the Jewish community. He helped establish the American Jewish Joint Distribution Committee, the Federation for the Support of Jewish Philanthropic Societies in New York, the Jewish Agency, and the Palestine Emergency Fund. He was an active force in providing relief to Jewish communities in Europe and Palestine during and after the two world wars. He supported Jewish settlement in Palestine, but not a Jewish state. Robert D. Kohn, the architect for Temple Emanu-El (built in 1929), chaired the Theme Committee and served on the Board of Design. Albert Einstein, who was born in Germany, chaired the Local Advisory Committee on Science.

41. The most ambitious study of the Temple of Religion is Jesse T. Todd, "Imagining the Future of American Religion at the New York World's Fair, 1939–40" (Ph.D. dissertation, Columbia University, 1996).

42. Synagogue Council of America, "The Jewish Exhibits at the World's Fair, Jews of All Nations, Their Contributions to the Making of America," folder p3.7, Synagogue Council of America, Jewish Organizations Participation, box 211, New York World's Fair Collection, New York Public Library.

43. Monaghan, *Official Guide Book,* p. 35.

44. Ibid., p. 36.

45. Ibid.

46. Program for B'nai B'rith Day, New York World's Fair, September 8, 1940, Temple of Religion, "in response to the proclamation of President Franklin D. Roosevelt for a 'day of Prayer,'" Program Correspondence, 1940, Temple of Religion, box 7, New York World's Fair Collection, New York Public Library.

47. Weisgal, . . . *So Far,* p. 150.

48. Ibid., pp. 158, 161.

49. Carmela Rubin, *Aryeh el-Hanani: Rav omanuyot* (Tel Aviv: Bet Reuven, 1993).

50. [Meyer Weisgal], . . . *Facts about the Jewish Palestine Pavilion at the N. Y. World's Fair—1939* (New York: Palestine Exhibits, Inc., 1939), p. 6. On the significance of this architectural icon, see Tamar Katriel and Eliza Shenhar, "Tower and Stockade: Dialogic Narration in Israeli Settlement Ethos," *Quarterly Journal of Speech* 76 (1990):359–80.

51. . . . *Facts about the Jewish Palestine Pavilion*, p. 6.

52. The New York World's Fair produced an extraordinary body of reflection on the nature of exhibition, particularly at international expositions but also in relation to museums See, for example, Carlos E. Cummings, *East Is East and West Is West: Some Observations on the World's Fairs of 1939 by One Whose Main Interest Is Museums*, Bulletin of the Buffalo Society of Natural Sciences, vol. 20 (East Aurora, N.Y.: Printed by the Roycrofters, 1940).

53. On the history of public relations in this period, see Edward L. Bernays, *Crystallizing Public Opinion* (New York: Boni and Liveright, 1923), and Edward L. Bernays, *Propaganda* (New York: Liveright, 1928).

54. David H. Shapiro, *From Philanthropy to Activism: The Political Transformation of American Zionism in the Holocaust Years, 1933–1945* (Oxford: Pergamon Press, 1994), p. xi.

55. Ibid., p. 19.

56. On the difference between strategy and tactic, see Michel de Certeau, *The Practice of Everyday Life* (Berkeley: University of California Press, 1984).

57. Only recently has attention turned to such tactical phenomena. Arthur A. Goren has led the way with his work on Jewish public culture in the United States. See his essay, "Celebrating Zion in America," in *Encounters with the "Holy Land,"* ed. Shandler and Wenger, pp. 41–59; and Arthur A. Goren, *The Politics and Public Culture of American Jews* (Bloomington: Indiana University Press, 1999). See James L. Gelvin, "Zionism and the Representation of 'Jewish Palestine' at the New York World's Fair, 1939–1940," *International History Review* 22, 1 (2000):37–64, for an analysis of the Jewish Palestine Pavilion at the New York World's Fair as a window on a critical moment in the history of American Zionism.

58. Any effort to answer this question cannot be separated from the process of their disenfranchisement. See Benny Morris, *Righteous Victims: A History of the Zionist-Arab Conflict, 1881–1998* (New York: Alfred A. Knopf, 1999), and Rashid Khalidi, *Palestinian Identity: The Construction of Modern National Consciousness* (New York: Columbia University Press, 1997).

59. Edward Said, "Projecting Jerusalem," *Journal of Palestine Studies* 25, 1 (1995): 8.

60. Ibid., p. 7. This passage has been quoted by critics of the ineffectuality of Arab and Arab-American reactions to Israel's claims to Jerusalem in its recent Epcot pavilion. See, for example, "Framing Jerusalem," *Jerusalem Quarterly File* 6 (1999), at http://www.jerusalemquarterly.org/details.php?cat=7&id=68 (date of last access: January 1, 2007). As with the 1939 New York World's Fair, Israel projects and the Arabs react. Thus, Khaled Turaani, executive director of American Muslims for Jerusalem, stated that "if the Arab League can not stand up to Mickey Mouse, how can they stand up to Israel's attempts to annex Jerusalem?" He called on "Saudi Arabia and Morocco to use their exhibits to right the wrongs committed by the Israeli exhibit." Quoted by Rasha Saad, "Dealing with Disney," *Al-Ahram Weekly Online* (Cairo), 449 (September 30–October 6, 1999), at http://weekly.ahram.org .eg/1999/449/re3.htm (date of last access: January 1, 2007). Expo 2000 in Hanover, which included Palestinian and Israeli exhibits, would be worthy of study in this context. The Palestinian exhibit was enclosed within the walls of Jerusalem. The Israeli exhibit, hastily assembled, was entitled "Isr@el from Holy Land to

Whole-E-Land" and featured computer terminals. The website was still "under construction" in 2004 at http://www.israelexpo.net/, when last accessed on February 11, 2004. It has since been retired.

61. Doug Suisman, Steven N. Simon, Glenn E. Robinson, C. Ross Anthony, and Michael Schoenbaum, *The Arc: A Formal Structure for a Palestinian State* (Santa Monica, Calif.: Rand Corporation, 2005), p. 5.

Chapter 6. Was There Anything Particularly Jewish about "The First Hebrew City"?

I would like to thank Hagit Lavsky for her inspiring and helpful remarks.

1. A. Z. Ben-Yishai, *Tel-Aviv: Ir va-em be-yisrael* (Jerusalem: Keren Hayesod, 1936), p. 3. And see Barbara E. Mann, *A Place in History: Modernism, Tel Aviv, and the Creation of Jewish Urban Space* (Stanford, Calif.: Stanford University Press, 2006), pp. 1–25.

2. Hayyim Nahman Bialik, *Divrei Bialik al ha-universitah ha-ivrit* (Jerusalem: Agudat Shoharei Ha-universitah, 1935), p. 45. And see Aharon Kellerman, "Cultural and Economic Characteristics of Jerusalem and Tel-Aviv," in *Society and Settlement: Jewish Land of Israel in the Twentieth Century* (Albany: State University of New York Press, 1993), p. 154; Amiram Gonen, " Keyzad kam 'merkaz ha-aretz' be-eretz-yisrael," in *Kalkalah ve-hevrah bimei ha-mandat, 1918–1948*, ed. Avi Bareli and Nahum Karlinsky (Beer Sheva: Merkaz Moreshet Ben-Gurion, 2003), p. 468; Maoz Azaryahu, *Tel-Aviv ha-ir ha-amitit: Mytografyah vehistoryah* (Beer Sheva: Ben Gurion Research Institute, 2005), pp. 249–64.

3. Shalom Asch, "Tel-Aviv," *Yediot iriyat Tel-Aviv Tarzav* (1936):116.

4. Edmond Fleg, *The Land of Promise* (New York: T. Werner Laurie, 1933), pp. 128–30. Also see Anat Helman, "European Jews in the Levant Heat: Climate and Culture in 1920s and 1930s Tel-Aviv," *Journal of Israeli History* 22, 1 (2003):84.

5. Eliezer Schweid, *Emunat am yisrael ve-tarbuto* (Jerusalem: Sh. Zack, 1976), pp. 164–68.

6. For instance, see Amos Rapoport, *Human Aspects of Urban Form* (Oxford: Pergamon, 1977), p. 31; Jack L. Nasar, *The Evaluating Image of the City* (Thousand Oaks, Calif.: Sage, 1998), p. 1.

7. Avner Holzman, "Tarbut noledet: Ha-safrut ha-ivrit u-pulmus ha-tarbut batenu'ah ha-ziyonit be-reshitah," in *Idan ha-ziyonut*, ed. Anita Shapira, Jehuda Reinharz, and Jay Harris (Jerusalem: Merkaz Zalman Shazar, 2000), pp. 145–47.

8. Shalom Razabi, "Pulmus shelilat ha-galut bi-shenot ha-sheloshim u-mekorotav," *Ha-ziyonut* 18 (1994):307.

9. Gideon Shimoni, "Behinah mehadash shel 'shelilat ha-galut' kera'ayon u-ma'aseh," in *Idan ha-ziyonut*, pp. 45–52.

10. For instance, see Yael Zerubavel, *Recovered Roots: Collective Memory and the Making of Israeli National Tradition* (Chicago: University of Chicago Press, 1995), pp. 20–28; Israel Bartal, "The Ingathering of Traditions: Zionism's Anthology Projects," *Prooftexts* 17 (1997):84–85.

11. Although the formal difference between the words is only slight. See Avraham Even-Shoshan, *Hamilon ha-ivri ha-merukaz* (Jerusalem: Am Oved/Zmora-Bitan/Kineret, 2001), pp. 92, 100–101.

12. David Horowitz and Moshe Lissak, *Mi-yishuv le-medinah* (Tel Aviv: Am Oved, 1977), p. 341. Also see Gideon Biger, "Ha-geografyah ha-politit shel ha-behirot le-iriyat tel-aviv bi-tekufat ha-mandat," *Merhavim* 4 (1991):87–101.

13. Itamar Even-Zohar, "The Emergence of Native Hebrew Culture in Palestine, 1882–1948," in *Essential Papers on Zionism*, ed. Jehuda Reinharz and Anita Shapira (New York: New York University Press, 1996), p. 733.

14. Diana Crane, *The Production of Culture: Media and the Urban Arts* (Newbury Park: Sage, 1992), p. 112.

15. Zohar Shavit, "Introduction," in *Bniyatah shel tarbut ivrit be-eretz-yisrael*, ed. Zohar Shavit (Jerusalem: Israeli National Science Academy, 1999), p. 3.

16. Gershon Shaked, *Hasiporet ha-ivrit*, vol. 2 (Tel Aviv: Hakibbutz Hameuchad, 1983), pp. 287, 351–53; Pinchas Ginosar, "Ha-safrut ha-ivrit ve-tenu'at ha-po'alim ha-eretz-yisraelit bimei ha-aliyah ha-shelishit" (Ph.D. dissertation, Tel Aviv University, 1987), pp. 424–25; Gideon Ofrat, *Adamah, adam, dam* (Tel Aviv: Tcherikover, 1980), pp. 15–17; Ben-Ami Feingold, "Teatron umaavak," *Cathedra* 74 (1995): 140–56.

17. Ofrat, *Adamah*, p. 21; Zali Gurevich and Gideon Aran, "Al ha-makom," *Alpayim* 4 (1991):22.

18. Gurevich and Aran, "Al ha-makom," p. 28.

19. Menahem Shemi, "Al eretzyisraeliyut ba-tziyur," *Ketuvim* 34, 14 (May 1928):1.

20. Eliyahu Newman, "Ha-omanut be-eretz yisrael bi-shnat tarzad [1934]," in *Sefer ha-shanah shel eretz yisrael bi-shnat tarzah* [1935], ed. Asher Barash (Tel Aviv: Shem Publications, 1935), p. 310.

21. Binyamin Tamuz, Dorit Levitte, and Gideon Ofrat, *Sipurah shel omanut yisrael* (Givatayim: Massada, 1980), pp. 53–127.

22. Film footage from *"Moledet"* newsreels, V/70–71, Jerusalem Cinemateque; *Baruch Agadati: oman ha-rikud ha-ivri* (Tel Aviv: Hedim, 1925); *Davar*, April 21, 1927; *Tesha ba-erev*, November 17, 1938.

23. *Iton meyuhad* (33) Elul 1937, 6. Also *Haaretz*, January 14, 1934.

24. Yizhak Loffbine, "Tel-Aviv," *Hapo'el haza'ir*, May 11, 1934, p. 6. Moshe Glikson, from "Le-ma'an Tel Aviv," in *Ir ha-pelaot*, ed. A. Vardy (Tel Aviv: Hashahar, 1928), p. 80.

25. Ben-Yishai, *Tel-Aviv*, pp. 8–9. On the Sabbath controversy, see Anat Helman, "Torah, avodah u-vatei-kafeh," *Cathedra* 105 (2002):85–110; Azaryahu, *Tel-Aviv*, pp. 88–89.

26. On Purim, see Batya Carmiel, *Tel-Aviv be-tahposet va-keter* (Tel Aviv: Eretz Israel Museum, 1999). Also see Yaacov Shavit and Shoshana Sitton, *Staging and Stagers in Modern Jewish Palestine: The Creation of Festival Lore in a New Culture, 1882–1948* (Detroit: Wayne State University Press, 2004), pp. 88–104.

27. Y. Ben-Naftali, "Tel Aviv ratzah leselihoth," *Hed ha-am* (Fall 1924):6.

28. *Hayishuv*, February 26, 1925, pp. 7–8. Decisions no. 2610 (October 24, 1937) and no. 3870 (July 20, 1938), File no. 9/4–5, Tel Aviv–Jaffa Municipal Archive, Tel Aviv. And see Adinah Meyer-Maril, "Beit ha-knesset ha-gadol be-tel-aviv u-terumato shel Alex Bearwald le-hakamato," *Cathedra* 57 (1990):116–19.

29. I draw on Raymond Williams, *The Sociology of Culture* (New York: Schocken Books, 1982), p. 13, and Ernst Gellner, *Nations and Nationalism* (Oxford: Blackwell, 1983), p. 92, for the idea of "culture" in its wider anthropological sense, designating the unique styles of behavior, concepts, social practices, and communication in a certain community.

30. See Steven M. Lowenstein, *Frankfurt on the Hudson* (Detroit: Wayne State University Press, 1989), pp. 163–64, for a similar definition of "Jewish culture" in America.

31. *Yediot iriyat tel-aviv, sefer hashanah tarzaz* (1937):105; *Hapo'el haza'ir*, January 12, 1923, p. 6. And see Bazalel Amikam, *Nirim rishonim* (Jerusalem: Yad Izhak Ben-Zvi, 1980), p. 17.

32. Anat Helman, " 'Even the Dogs in the Streets Bark in Hebrew': National Ideology and Everyday Culture in Tel-Aviv," *Jewish Quarterly Review* 42, 3–4 (2002):359–82.

33. *Iton meyuhad*, Sivan 20, 1937, p. 2; *Hashomer haza'ir*, January 11, 1936, pp. 6–7. And see Anat Helman, "East or West? Tel-Aviv in the 1920s and 1930s," in *People of the City: Jews and the Urban Challenge*, ed. Ezra Mendelsohn (Oxford: Oxford University Press, 1999), p. 69. Odessa—where Bialik, Dizengoff, and other Tel Aviv leaders arrived from—was also regarded as a positive model, but Odessa itself was known as Russia's most "European" (i.e., Western) city. See Patricia Herlihy, *Odessa: A History* (Cambridge, Mass.: Harvard University Press, 1986), pp. 143–44; and Steven Zipperstein, *The Jews of Odessa: A Cultural History, 1794–1881* (Stanford, Calif.: Stanford University Press, 1985), p. 29; Joachim Schlor, "Odessa and Warsaw: Studies in the Pre-History of Tel-Aviv," in *Jewish Studies in a New Europe*, ed. Ulf Haxen, Hanne Trautner-Kramann, and Karen Lisa Goldschmidt Salamon (Copenhagen: Reitzel, 1998), pp. 706–7.

34. Letter from Berkovich to Rokakh, July 23, 1932, file no. 4/2641, Tel Aviv–Jaffa Municipal Archive, Tel Aviv. Also see his letter to the mayor, September 1924, file no. 3/64a, Tel Aviv–Jaffa Municipal Archive, Tel Aviv.

35. *Haaretz*, February 4, 1926.

36. A. Krolnik, translation from *Der Tag*, in *Ir ha-pelaot*, ed. Vardy, pp. 69–70.

37. *Haaretz*, April 15, 1921; letter from the municipal secretary, August 1926, file no. 4/3562, Tel Aviv–Jaffa Municipal Archive, Tel Aviv. Quotation is from *Ideal Travel Talks: Palestine 1934* (compilation of documentary footage), prod. Edelheit Productions, item no. VT DA 139 B, Steven Spielberg Jewish Film Archive, The Hebrew University, Jerusalem.

38. Shalom Asch, translation from *Der Haynt*, in *Ir ha-pelaot*, ed. Vardy, p. 65.

39. Asch, "Tel-Aviv," p. 116.

40. Itamar Even-Zohar, "Tahalikhei maga ve-hit'arvut be-hivatzrut ha-tarbut ha-ivrit ha-hadashah," in *Nekudot tazpit: Tarbut ve-hevrah be-eretz-yisrael*, ed. Nurit Gertz (Tel Aviv: Open University, 1988), p. 130.

41. Picture no. 33323, Lavon Institute for Labour Research Archive, Tel Aviv.

42. A. Vardy, "Ha-ger," in *Ir ha-pelaot*, ed. Vardy, p. 49.

43. Loffbine, "Tel-Aviv," p. 4. "Hagigot hazi ha-yovel," *Yediot iriyat Tel-Aviv*, anniversary issue (1933–34):310. Also see Azaryahu, *Tel-Aviv*, pp. 79–84.

44. Asch, translation from *Der Haynt*, in *Ir ha-pelaot*, ed. Vardy, p. 65.

45. Asch, "Tel-Aviv," p. 116.

46. Ludwig Lewisohn, translation from "Israel," in *Ir ha-pelaot*, ed. Vardy, p. 76.

47. Abraham Cahan, translated comment, in *Ir ha-pelaot*, ed. Vardy, pp. 91–92. And see Yaacov N. Goldstein, *Pulmus Cahan (1925–1926)* (Jerusalem: Merkaz Dinur, 1999), pp. 29–48.

48. A. Z. Ben-Yishai, "Leil ha-neital," in *Ir ha-pelaot*, ed. Vardy, p. 52.

49. Y. Greenbaum, "Tel-Aviv," *Yediot iriyat Tel-Aviv tarzag* (1933):245–46.

50. Meir Berlin, "Al shem he-atid," *Yediot iriyat Tel-Aviv tarzad* (1934):263.

51. Marcia Gitlin, "A South African's Impression of Palestine," *South African Jewish Chronicle*, June 30, 1933, file no. 4/3563a, Tel Aviv–Jaffa Municipal Archive, Tel Aviv. Similar claims in *Ha'olam*, February 14, 1930.

52. See Michael Roman, "Ma'avaro shel ha-merkaz ha-demografi ve-hakalkali mi-yerushalayim le-tel-aviv," in *Yerushalayim ba-toda'ah u-va'asiyah ha-ziyonit*, ed. Hagit Lavsky (Jerusalem: Merkaz Zalman Shazar, 1989), p. 222; Gonen, "Keyzad kam," pp. 444, 462, 464–88.

53. Loffbine, "Tel-Aviv," p. 6; *Palestine Post*, May 7, 1934.

54. Meir Dizengoff, *Al Tel-Aviv ve-orhot hayehah* (Tel Aviv: Iriyat Tel-Aviv, 1934), p. 2.

55. Eliezer Steinman, "Eimah," in *Ir ha-pelaot*, p. 53. The relationship between Tel Aviv Jews and Jaffa Arabs deteriorated dramatically after the outbreak of the Arab Revolt in 1936.

56. Gonen, "Keyzad kam," p. 462; Mann, *A Place in History*, p. 144.

57. Baruch Kimmerling, "Between Premordial and the Civil Definition of Collective Identity: Eretz Israel and the State of Israel," in *Comparative Social Dynamics*, ed. E. Cohen, M. Lissak, and U. Almog (Boulder, Colo.: Westview Press, 1985), p. 273. This nonlocal Jewish aspect of Zionism would be severely criticized in the 1940s and 1950s by the nativist ideological-artistic movement "The Canaanites."

Chapter 7. Re-Routing Roots

1. Judith Katzir, *Closing the Sea*, trans. Barbara Harshav (New York: Harcourt Brace Jovanovich, 1992), p. 118.

2. Establishing accurate estimates of audiocassette sales is virtually impossible. Sources for the estimates in this essay include interviews with Meir Reuveni and Moshe Ben Mosh, owners of audiocassette companies; newspaper articles; interviews with Danny Yadin, managing director of NMC, one of Israel's largest commercial recording companies; and interviews with owners of the audiocassette booths in the marketplace. The difficulty of obtaining accurate estimates is further complicated by the large numbers of pirated copies of audiocassettes, often on sale side by side with the official product. As one leading Mediterranean Israeli music composer/performer recently said in a newspaper interview: "We gave the defense ministry the exact location of the factory [that was pirating CDs] and we hoped the IDF [Israeli Defence Force] would go in, blow it up and destroy the factory." *Yedioth Ahronot* quoted in *Ha'aretz, Friday Magazine,* January 9, 2004, p. 4.

3. The singer's name is romanized variously as Um Kulthum, Om Kalsoum, Umm Kulthoum, Om Kalthoum, Umm Kalsum, and Oum Kalthum. I spell it as Umm Kulthum in this text or, in the case of quotations, as the name appears in the original source.

4. On the audiocassette music phenomenon, see Peter Lamarche Manuel, *Cassette Culture: Popular Music and Technology in North India* (Chicago: University of Chicago Press, 1993). From Meir Reuveni I learned that it was actually the invention of the four-way duplicator that was crucial to the audiocassette revolution in Israel, as it allowed quicker duplication and distribution of product. Meir Reuveni, interview, Tel Aviv, January 11, 1991.

5. "Ketourna Masala," performed by Etnix and Zehava Ben, *Ketourna Masala* (Tel Aviv: Helicon Records, 1991), no. Hl8085.

6. *Muwwal* is the Arabic term for the opening introductory segment of a song in which the performer often introduces the modes (*makamat*) that will be heard. While drawing on the features of the traditional *muwwal*, Argov's adaptation is both shorter and more contained.

7. Amnon Shiloah and Erik Cohen, "The Dynamics of Change in Jewish Oriental Ethnic Music in Israel," *Ethnomusicology* 27, 2 (May 1983):227–52, is just one example of the "popularization trend" noted in Oriental music. Also see Amnon Shiloah and Erik Cohen, "Major Trends of Change in Jewish Oriental Ethnic Music in Israel," *Popular Music* 5 (1985):199–223.

8. Jeffrey Halper, Edwin Seroussi, and Pamela Kidron, "*Musika Mizrakhit*: Ethnicity and Class Culture in Israel," paper presented at Forum for Socio-Musicological Sciences, Tel Aviv, 1988. They draw on Gans's notion of "taste public," which he defines as "a subcultural aggregate defined primarily by its shared aesthetic values and its choice of cultural products and expressions." Herbert Gans, *Popular Culture and High Culture: An Analysis of Evaluation and Taste* (New York: Basic Books, 1974), p. 12.

9. Pierre Bourdieu, "The Field of Cultural Production, or: The Economic World

Reversed," in *The Field of Cultural Production* (New York: Columbia University Press, 1993), pp. 29–73.

10. In the Israeli context, one of the avenues for elite acceptance is previous participation in the various military entertainment ensembles (*lahaqot tsvayot*). "[O]rganizationally, the salient phenomena in Israeli music were the Army Entertainment Ensembles, which served as a channel for the distribution of ideologically saturated music, and as a credential mechanism for performers: most Israeli performers, entertainers and actors who succeeded during the 1970's were graduates of these ensembles." Motti Regev, "Israeli Rock, or a Study in the Politics of 'Local Identity,'" *Popular Music* 11, 1 (1992):2.

11. Motti Regev and Edwin Seroussi, *Popular Music and National Culture in Israel* (Berkeley: University of California Press, 2004), p. 194.

12. Ibid., p. 195. In one stunning example, they claim that Asher Reuveni "hid" the fact that Musika Mizrahit had been in existence for years before his 1973 wedding in order to claim his wedding as the genesis point for the genre. My ethnographic research indicates, to the contrary, that Reuveni was referring to the reproduction of taped copies of the music at his wedding as having moved the music distribution process forward.

13. Yehudit Ravitz, interview, Tel Aviv, December 20, 1986.

14. Aron Marko Rothmuller, *The Music of the Jews* (London: Valentine, Mitchell, 1953), p. 150. Rothmuller states: "These songs of Yemenite Jews have a special attraction for the Israeli musicians because it is generally accepted that they have come down from comparatively ancient times, and in many respects are much closer to ancient Jewish song than those of other Jewish communities." Also see Itamar Even-Zohar, "The Emergence of a Native Hebrew Culture in Palestine: 1882–1948," *Poetics Today* 11, 1 (1990):175–91, an excellent critique of practitioners and observers such as Rothmuller.

15. Whether in the realm of foodways, textiles, architecture, or music, Arab and Mizrahi Jewish cultural forms were sometimes appropriated by Ashkenazi Jews and used within the context of their everyday lives. The issue here is not whether Eastern forms were the object of romanticization (or as Edward Said calls it, the Orientalization of the East) but who controlled the aesthetic means of representation, production, and distribution. See Edward Said, *Orientalism* (New York: Random House, 1978); Natan Shahar, "The Eretz Israeli Song and the Jewish National Fund," in *Modern Jews and Their Musical Agendas*, vol. 9, *Studies in Contemporary Jewry*, ed. Ezra Mendelsohn (Jerusalem: Institute of Contemporary Jewry, Hebrew University, 1993), pp. 78–91; and Natan Shahar, "The Israeli Song, 1920–1950: Musicological and Socio-Musical Aspects" (Ph.D. dissertation, Hebrew University, 1989).

16. Chaim Moshe and Asher Reuveni, interview, Tel-Aviv, August 5, 1984.

17. Zohar Argov, *Elinor* (Tel Aviv: Reuveni Brothers, 1980), audiocassette, no. 43/1.

18. Zohar Argov, quoted in Michael Ohad, "Libi Ba'Mizra (My heart Is in the East)," *Ha'aretz*, September 25, 1981, p.17.

19. Ibid.

20. Moshe Ben Mosh, quoted in Liat Amran, "Ha'aliato Ve'Niflato Shel Ha'Zemer Ha'Mizrahi Zohar Argov" (The Rise and Fall of the Mizrahi Song Idol Zohar Argov), unpublished final school paper, Kibbutz Ein Tzurim, Hevrat Ha'Noa'ar, 1991, p. 53. Private collection of Amy Horowitz, Columbus, Ohio, courtesy of Edwin Seroussi, Jerusalem. See the ethnomusicologist Avraham Amzaleg's description of Zohar Argov's vocal techniques as justification for his place as the leading Mizrahi singer. Upon his death in prison in November 1987, dozens of newspapers articles proclaimed him the posthumous "king" of Mizrahi singers, and an annual memorial concert marks his place in Mizrahi cultural history.

21. Katerina Clark and Michael Holquist, *Mikhail Bakhtin* (Cambridge, Mass.: Belknap Press of Harvard University Press, 1984), pp. 276, 319.

22. Ohad, "Libi Ba'Mizrah?," p. 17.

23. "Jerusalem Shel Zahav controversy" in the English edition of *Ha'aretz,* May 6, 2005, discussed recent revelations that Nomi Shemer's most famous song, "Jerusalem of Gold," was drawn from the work of a Catalan singer whom she had heard perform live in Tel Aviv in the early 1960s.

24. See Edwin Seroussi's discussion of Mediterranean categories in "*Yam Tikhoniyut:* Transformations of the Mediterranean in Israeli Music," in *Mediterranean Mosaic: Popular Music and Global Sounds,* ed. Goffredo Plastino (New York: Routledge, 2003), pp. 179–97.

25. Rino Tsror, "The Neighborhood Abandoned Hebrew Rino Tsror," *Maariv sof ha-shavuah,* weekend supplement, June 1991 (unpaginated).

26. Yoel Rekem, interview, Jerusalem, October 13, 1992.

27. Computer music compositional tools such as sequencing and quantizing became available in the early 1980s. These were employed, sometimes poorly, by composers who were not fluent in the musical styles they were exploring. See the NPR series "Techno Pop," especially parts 5 and 6 at http://www.npr.org/programs/morning/features/2002/technopop

28. Zehava Ben, *Tipat Mazal* (A Drop of Luck) (Tel Aviv: Eli Banai Productions, 1992), audiocassette, ref. no. 67.

29. *Tipat Mazal* (A Drop of Luck), dir. Ze'ev Revah, perf. Zehava Ben, prods. Yoram Globus and Bo'az Davidzon, screenplay by Hanan Peled and Ze'ev Revah, music by Dov Seltzer, videocassette, Globus grup, dist. Noah Films, 1992, 90 minutes.

30. Zehava Ben, *Zehava Ben Shara Aravit* (Zehava Ben Sings Arabic) (Tel Aviv: Eli Banai Productions, 1995), CD.

31. In a television interview with Rino Tsror (May 24, 2005) Zehava Ben confessed that after fifteen years of hard work with Banai she had been left with a pile of unpaid bills, income tax agents after her, and the bank about to repossess her home.

32. *Zehava Ben: The Solitary Star,* in Hebrew and Arabic, with English subtitles, prod. dir. Erez Laufer, prod. Dalia Migdal, documentary video, Idan Productions, dist. Ergo Media, 1997, 59 minutes.

33. Zehava Ben, *Zehava Ben Shara Aravit: Enta Omri* (Zehava Ben Sings Arabic: You Are My Life) (Helicon: Tel Aviv, 1995), CD.

34. Kirin Narayan, "Songs Lodged in Some Hearts: Displacements of Women's Knowledge in Kangra," in *Displacement, Diaspora, and Geographies of Identity,* ed. Smadar Lavie and Ted Swedenburg (Durham, N.C.: Duke University Press, 1996), p. 187: "As ethnomusicologists have observed, gender and other planes of social differentiation are mapped onto musical spheres." Narayan cites Ellen Koskoff, "An Introduction to Women, Music, and Culture," in *Women and Music in Cross-Cultural Perspective,* ed. Ellen Koskoff (Urbana: University of Illinois Press, 1989), pp. 1–24.

35. Zehava Ben, telephone interview by Amy Horowitz and Esther Namdar, Tel Aviv, September 1, 2002.

36. Ibid.

37. See "Zehava Ben to Appear on al Jazeera," *Jerusalem Post,* November 12, 2003, accessible at *Freepublic.com,* http://209.157.64.200/focus/f-news/1020516/posts/ (date of last access: January 16, 2004). I want to observe here that goods (in this case, the virtual Zehava Ben in the form of a television broadcast to the Arab world) circulate when people cannot.

Chapter 8. The "Wandering Jew" from Medieval Legend to Modern Metaphor

A different version of this essay with additional illustrations appeared in French in the catalogue *Le Juif errant: Un témoin du temps,* ed. Laurence Sigal-Klagsbald and Richard I. Cohen (Paris: Adam Biro and Musée d'art et d'histoire du Judaïsme, 2001).

1. George K. Anderson, *The Legend of the Wandering Jew* (Hanover: Brown University Press, 1965), pp. 1–10. Anderson's comprehensive study provides a basis for any future scholarship on this phenomenon. See also Edgar Knecht, *Le mythe du Juif errant: Essai de mythologie littéraire et de sociologie religieuse* (Grenoble: Presses Universitaires de Grenoble, 1977).

2. Frank Felsenstein, *Anti-Semitic Stereotypes: A Paradigm of Otherness in English Popular Culture, 1660–1830* (Baltimore: Johns Hopkins University Press, 1995), p. 62.

3. Galit Hasan-Rokem, "L'image du Juif errant et la construction de l'identité Européenne," in the exhibition catalogue *Le Juif errant: Un témoin du temps,* ed. Laurence Sigal-Klagsbald and Richard I. Cohen (Paris: Adam Biro and Musée d'art et d'histoire du Judaïsme, 2001), pp. 72–73.

4. A classic case is Eugène Sue's anti-clerical and anti-Jesuit novel, *Le Juif errant,* which appeared in serial form in the journal *Constitutionnel* from June 25, 1844 to July 12, 1845. The first edition of the novel was published in Paris by Paulin, in 1844. It was reprinted many times in various languages in the nineteenth and twentieth centuries. Sue's novel placed the Wandering Jew alongside the forces that attempted to curtail the Jesuit influence.

5. It is interesting to point out that Champfleury and Anderson shared a common perspective—an appreciation for what they considered the "true" folktale and their dislike of the many diverse forms and configurations the legend took, literally and visually.

6. Champfleury, *Histoire de l'imagerie populaire* (1869; Paris: E. Dentu, 1886); Luce Abélès, *Champfleury: L'art pour le peuple* (Paris: Ministère de la Culture, de la Communication, des Grands Travaux et du Bicentenaire, 1990). The latter is an exhibition catalogue.

7. Sigal-Klagsbald and Cohen, eds., *Le Juif errant.* As this essay was going to press, another article treating aspects of the visual material on the Wandering Jew appeared; see Ziva Amishai-Maisels, "Menasseh Ben Israel and the 'Wandering Jew,'" *Ars Judaica* 2 (2006):59–82.

8. Gaël Milin, *Le cordonnier de Jérusalem: La véritable histoire du Juif errant* (Rennes: Presses Universitaires de Rennes), pp. 65–108.

9. Fredric Jameson, *Postmodernism, or, The Cultural Logic of Late Capitalism* (Durham, N.C.: Duke University Press, 1991); Robert Darnton, *The Great Cat Massacre and Other Episodes in French Cultural History* (New York: Basic Books, 1984).

10. Jonathan I. Israel, *European Jewry in the Age of Mercantilism, 1550–1750,* rev. ed. (Oxford: Clarendon Press, 1991); also see Shmuel Ettinger, "The Beginnings of the Change in the Attitude of European Society towards the Jews," in *Scripta Hierosolymitana* 7 (Jerusalem: Magnes Press, 1961), pp. 193–219.

11. *The Wandering Jew, or, The shoe-Maker of Jerusalem who Lived when our Saviour Jesus Christ was Crucified, and Appointed by Him to Live till He Comes again; Together with His Travels, Manner of Living, Adventures, &c; to which is Added, His True Description of Christ* (London: Aldermary Church Yard, Bow-Lane, c. 1720), p. 4; see also Felsenstein, *Anti-Semitic Stereotypes,* pp. 43–47, 58–89; Anderson, *The Legend,* pp. 60–66.

12. *The Wandering Jew,* p. 8.

13. *The Wandring [sic] Jew's Chronicle: A Brief History of the Remarkable Passages from*

WILLIAM the Conqueror, to this present Reign (London: T. Norris, n.d. [c. 1720]). A copy appears in the Wandering Jew Collection, gift of W. Easton Louttit, Jr., B1753, Special Collections, John Hay Library, Brown University, Providence, Rhode Island (henceforth cited as the Louttit Wandering Jew Collection). Another version is found in the Library of the Jewish Theological Seminary, New York, which lists the date of printing c. 1714.

14. Isaiah Shachar, "The Emergence of the Modern Pictorial Stereotype of 'The Jews' in England," in *Studies in the Cultural Life of the Jews in England*, vol. 5 (Folklore Research Center Studies), ed. Dov Noy and Issachar Ben-Ami (Jerusalem: Magnes Press, 1975), pp. 331–65. This pioneering study on caricatures and rhetoric of the Jews has often been overlooked by scholars.

15. Quoted in Felsenstein, *Anti-Semitic Stereotypes*, p. 62.

16. Marsha Schuchard has recently argued that he became associated with a group of Kabbalist Freemasons, a claim that seems somewhat exaggerated. See David B. Ruderman, *Jewish Enlightenment in an English Key: Anglo-Jewry's Construction of Modern Jewish Thought* (Princeton, N.J.: Princeton University Press, 2000), pp. 152–66.

17. This image of Gordon, along with others of him, appeared in the exhibition *The Jew as Other: A Century of English Caricature, 1730–1830* (New York: Library of The Jewish Theological Seminary, 1995), p. 50. See also pp. 47–52.

18. Anderson, *The Legend of the Wandering Jew*, pp. 162–66.

19. Barbara Ann Day-Hickman, *Napoleonic Art: Nationalism and the Spirit of Rebellion in France (1815–1848)* (Newark: University of Delaware Press, 1998).

20. Frédéric Maguet, "Le développement du thème du Juif errant dans l'imagerie populaire en France et en Europe," in *Le Juif errant*, ed. Sigal-Klagsbald and Cohen, pp. 90–107.

21. Ibid., pp. 202–3.

22. Champfleury, *Histoire de l'imagerie populaire*, p. 61.

23. I follow Linda Nochlin, "Gustave Courbet's *Meeting*: A Portrait of the Artist as a Wandering Jew," *Art Bulletin* 49 (1967):209–22; for the image, see *Le Juif errant*, ed. Sigal-Klagsbald and Cohen, p. 24.

24. Nochlin, "Gustave Courbet's *Meeting*," pp. 219–20.

25. In a review of paintings at the New Gallery in London in 1888, this one was cited, clearly for its connection to Jewish life. See the *Jewish Standard*, June 15, 1888, p. 2. Two versions of the painting exist—one in oil, and another in pastel on paper, mounted on canvas. The painting was also exhibited in 1888 at the Royal Manchester Institution. Its whereabouts today is unknown. In response to my request, the De Morgan Foundation in London was unable to track down the painting.

26. Judy Oberhausen, "Evelyn Pickering De Morgan and Spiritualism: An Interpretive Link," *Journal of Pre-Raphaelite Studies* 3 (1994):1–11; see further literature there.

27. On Evelyn Pickering De Morgan, see Jan Marsh and Pamela Gerrish Nunn, *Pre-Raphaelite Women Artists* (London: Thames and Hudson, 1999), pp. 139–44; Catherine Gordon, *Evelyn De Morgan: Oil Paintings* (London: De Morgan Foundation, 1996); and Oberhausen, "Evelyn Pickering De Morgan and Spiritualism," pp. 1–11.

28. G. E. Bentley, Jr., *The Stranger from Paradise: A Biography of William Blake* (London: Yale University Press, 2001).

29. Quotes from Moreau, in Sigal-Klagsbald and Cohen, eds., *Le Juif errant*, pp. 204–7.

30. Hans Mühlestein and Georg Schmidt, *Ferdinand Hodler: Sein Leben und sein Werk* (Zurich: Unionsverlag, 1983); Sharon L. Hirsh, *Hodler's Symbolist Themes* (Ann Arbor: UMI Research Press, 1983), pp. 13–14; Peter Wegmann, *Caspar David Fried-*

rich to Ferdinand Hodler: A Romantic Tradition, Nineteenth-Century Paintings and Drawings from the Oskar Reinhart Foundation, ed. and trans. Margaritha Russell (Frankfurt am Main: Insel Verlag, 1993).

31. Champfleury commented briefly on this work, wondering whether Kaulbach introduced the figure as a result of a childhood recollection of "naive images." See Champfleury, *Histoire de l'imagerie,* p. 56. This may indeed be the case as popular images of the Wandering Jew (*der ewige Jude*) could be seen in Germany, though they were much less common than in France. See the image of Ahasuerus among Jewish professions in the broadsheet *Unser Verkehr,* Germany, mid-nineteenth century, reproduced in Sigal-Klagsbald and Cohen, eds., *Le Juif errant,* p. 143. *Der ewige Jude* is seen among fifteen individuals, ostensibly representing professions of Jews in Germany.

32. Avraham Ronen, "Kaulbach's Wandering Jew: An Anti-Jewish Allegory and Two Jewish Responses," *Assaph* 3 (1998):243–62, esp. p. 250.

33. Christian Lenz, *The Neue Pinakothek, Munich* (London: Scala, 1995), p. 71.

34. Photocopies of some of these works are extant in the Louttit Wandering Jew Collection. See the lithograph by J. G. Schreiner, *Der ewige Jude aus der Zerstörung Jerusalems* (Munich: Joseph Aumüller); and another lithograph by an unknown artist, *Der ewige Jude* (Stuttgart: Krais und Hoffmann), in which the three demons are seen pursuing the Wandering Jew energetically. See also Sigal-Klagsbald and Cohen, eds., *Le Juif errant,* pp. 187, 189, 192.

35. Eduard Fuchs, *Die Juden in der Karikatur* (München: Albert Langen Verlag, 1921). Fuchs, who showed only a few images of the Wandering Jew, gave Doré's prominence, adding a color illustration, facing p. 144. Compare with Ronen, "Kaulbach's Wandering Jew," p. 257, n. 14.

36. On negative associations with the color red, see Ruth Mellinkoff, "Judas's Red Hair and the Jews," *Journal of Jewish Art* 9 (1982):31–46.

37. For a discussion of Lewis, see Anderson, *The Legend,* pp. 177–81. On the mark of Cain, Anderson claimed that "very often Ahasuerus appears in nineteenth-century popular picturizations with this red cross gleaming or flaming on his forehead" (p. 179) but offers no references, and I have rarely come across such depictions. See also Ruth Mellinkoff, *The Mark of Cain* (Berkeley: University of California Press, 1981), pp. 38–40.

38. For a similar image, though relating to the arrival of the Wandering Jew in the United States and its implications for more established Americans, see *Judge,* 1892, published in Elie Kedourie, *The Jewish World: Revelation, Prophesy, and History* (London: Thames and Hudson, 1979), p. 245, plate number 40, and a figure in *Pèlerin,* published in Norman L. Kleeblatt, ed., *The Dreyfus Affair: Art, Truth, and Justice* (Berkeley: University of California Press, 1987), p. 56. For further discussion on this issue, see Pierre Birnbaum, "Le retour du Juif Errant: Juif errant, Juif de cour et Juif d'Etat," in *Le Juif errant,* ed. Sigal-Klagsbald and Cohen, pp. 127–37. See also Gale B. Murray, "Toulouse-Lautrec's Illustrations for Victor Joze and Georges Clemenceau and Their Relationship to French Anti-Semitism of the 1890's," in *The Jew in the Text: Modernity and the Construction of Identity,* ed. Linda Nochlin and Tamar Garb (London: Thames and Hudson, 1995), pp. 56–82; literal references to Dreyfus as a "wandering Jew" appear in Mary Louise Roberts, *Disruptive Acts: The New Woman in Fin-de-Siècle France* (Chicago: University of Chicago Press, 2002), pp. 134–35; also see pp. 112–14. In both of these works, contemporaries (1880s) denote Sarah Bernhardt as a Wandering Jewess, though I have yet to find visual representations to this effect.

39. Quotations are taken from Charcot's *Leçons du midi* 2, pp. 347–48, 352–53, as they appeared in Jan Goldstein, "The Wandering Jew and the Problem of Psychi-

atric Anti-Semitism in Fin-de-Siècle France," *Journal of Contemporary History* 20 (1985):521–52, esp. p. 540. "Cartophilus" is commonly spelled "Cartaphilus."

40. Henry Meige, *Étude sur certains névropathes voyageurs: Le Juif errant à la Salpê-trière* (Paris, 1893), p. 4; the thesis was reprinted (Paris: Editions du Nouvel Objet, 1993) with an introduction by Lucien Israël and illustrations by Michel Clardi.

41. Ibid., pp. 16, 19–20. Anderson, in *The Legend*, pp. 406–7, simply dispensed with Meige, calling his work a "wild theory" and thus devoting only a few lines to it.

42. Most of the images in Meige appeared in Champfleury, *Histoire de l'imagerie*. His own drawings appear on pp. 25, 29. See Birnbaum, "Le retour du Juif Errant," in *Le Juif errant*, ed. Sigal-Klagsbald and Cohen, pp. 127–37; also see Sander Gilman, *The Jew's Body* (New York: Routledge, 1991), pp. 71–80; and Jay Geller, "The Unmanning of the Wandering Jew," *American Imago* 49 (1992):227–62.

43. *Le Charivari*, June 20, 1936.

44. Pierre Birnbaum, *Les Fous de la République* (Paris: Fayard, 1992), following p. 216, no. 2. See also Birnbaum, "Le retour du Juif Errant," in *Le Juif errant*, ed. Sigal-Klagsbald and Cohen, pp. 136–37; and Ilan Greilsammer, *Blum* (Paris: Flammarion, 1996), pp. 183–92.

45. Streicher's infamous *Der Sturmer* published in February 1936 a caricature of *Der ewige Kain* in which Cain (whose appearance resembles typical anti-Semitic caricatures) is seen escaping from the scene of a murder he has apparently committed. The caption reads: "During thousands of years the Jew added murder upon murder. The Jew will not cease to murder until his path is blocked by international justice."

46. Reproduced in Sigal-Klagsbald and Cohen, eds., *Le Juif errant*, p. 135. The Yad Vashem Archive has in its possession a copy of the material shown in the 1937 exhibition. See the exhibition poster, no. FA-196, Yad Vashem Archives, Jerusalem. Also see the image by Vicky (Victor Weisz) in Rosamunde Neugebauer, "Der ewige Wanderer—eine Leitfigur der Bildkunst im Exil?," *Kunst und Politik. Jarhbuch der Guernica-Gesellschaft. Schwerpunkt: Kunst im Exil, 1933–1945*, Bd. 3 (2001):13.

47. *Der ewige Jude*, exhibition brochure (München: Zentralverlag der NSDAP, 1937); Frank Stern, "Der ewige Jude—Stereotype auf der europäischen Wander-ung," in the exhibition catalogue *Die Macht der Bilder: Antisemitische Vorurteile und Mythen* (Wien: Jüdisches Museum der Stadt Wien, 1995), pp. 117–21.

48. See the argument made by Paul Rose on the meaning of Ahasuerus in German thought. Paul Lawrence Rose, *Revolutionary Antisemitism in Germany: From Kant to Wagner* (Princeton, N.J.: Princeton University Press, 1990), pp. 23–43.

49. Given the scope of this essay, my comments will only briefly illustrate some of the ways several artists transformed the meaning of the legend.

50. This interpretation would seem to conform to Nossig's writings on the natural sciences and Judaism and the contribution of Moses to Jewish health. See Mitchell Hart, "Moses the Microbiologist: Judaism and Social Hygiene in the Work of Alfred Nossig," *Jewish Social Studies* 2 (1995):72–97.

51. Reuven Brainin, "Jewish Art: Alfred Nossig," *Hador* 1, 7 (1901):9–11, and *Hador* 1, 8 (1901):8–10 (Hebrew); Avner Holtzman, *Melekhet Mahashevet, Tehiyat ha-Umah: Ha-Sifrut ha-'Ivrit le-Nokhah ha-Omanut ha-Plastit* (Tel Aviv: Zmora-Bitan and Haifa University Press, 1999). Also see Shmuel Almog, "Alfred Nossig: A Reappraisal," *Studies in Zionism* 7 (1983):1–29; Ezra Mendelsohn, "From Assimilation to Zionism: The Case of Alfred Nossig," *Slavonic and Eastern Review* 117 (1971):512–34.

52. *The Jewish Chronicle Supplement*, November 9, 1906; Julia Weiner, "Jewish Women Artists in Britain, 1700–1940," in the exhibition catalogue *Rubies and Rebels: Jewish Female Identity in Contemporary British Art*, ed. Monica Bohm-Duchen and Vera

Grodzinski (London: Lund Humphries, 1996), pp. 30–39, 62–63; Julia Weiner, "A Brush-Up for Anglo-Jewry," *Manna* 58 (Winter 1998):28–30.

53. Benjamin Harshav, "The Role of Language in Modern Art: On Texts and Subtexts in Chagall's Paintings," *Modernism/Modernity* 1, 2 (1994):51–87, esp. p. 62.

54. Ziva Amishai-Maisels, "The Artist as Refugee," in *Art and Its Uses: The Visual Image and Modern Jewish Society* 6 (Studies in Contemporary Jewry), ed. Ezra Mendelsohn and Richard I. Cohen (New York: Oxford University Press, 1990), p. 62.

55. Ziva Amishai-Maisels, "Chagall and the Jewish Revival: Center or Periphery?" in the exhibition catalogue *Tradition and Revolution: The Jewish Renaissance in Russian Avant-Garde Art 1912–1928*, 2nd ed., ed. Ruth Apter-Gabriel (Jerusalem: Israel Museum, 1988), pp. 80–83.

56. Vivianne Barsky, " 'Home is where the Heart is': Jewish Themes in the Art of R. B. Kitaj," in *Art and Its Uses*, ed. Mendelsohn and Cohen, p. 150.

57. According to Ziva Amishai-Maisels, *The Jew, Etc.* was originally called the *Wandering Jew.* See her *Depiction and Interpretation: The Influence of the Holocaust on the Visual Arts* (Oxford: Pergamon Press, 1993).

58. See his conversation with Julian Riós in Riós, *Kitaj: Pictures and Conversations* (London: Hamish Hamilton, 1994), p. 189.

59. Following Barsky, "Jewish Themes in the Art of R. B. Kitaj," p. 171; however, Marco Livingstone claims that the philosopher is Michael Podro. See Livingstone, *Kitaj* (London: Phaidon Press, 1992), p. 39.

60. Barsky, "Jewish Themes," p. 171.

61. Riós, *Kitaj*, p. 189.

Chapter 9. Diasporic Values in Contemporary Art

1. R. B. Kitaj, *First Diasporist Manifesto* (London: Thames and Hudson, 1989), p. 89.

2. Sidra DeKoven Ezrahi, *Booking Passage: Exile and Homecoming in the Modern Jewish Imagination* (Berkeley: University of California Press, 2000), p. 228.

3. Ibid.

4. Ben Katchor, *The Jew of New York* (New York: Pantheon Books, 1998).

5. The term was coined by W. E. B. Du Bois in *The Souls of Black Folk* (1903; New York: Penguin Books, 1995) to convey the multiple and conflicted social psyche of African Americans. Henry Louis Gates notes that "double consciousness, once a disorder, is now the cure." See "Both Sides Now," *New York Times Book Review*, May 4, 2003, p. 31.

6. Yitzhak Baer, *Galut*, trans. Robert Warshow (New York: Schocken Books, 1947); A. B. Yehoshua, "The Golah: The Neurotic Solution," in *Between Right and Right*, trans. Arnold Schwartz (Garden City, N.Y.: Doubleday, 1981), pp. 21–74; Arnold M. Eisen, *Galut: Modern Jewish Reflections on Homelessness and Homecoming* (Bloomington: Indiana University Press, 1986). The postmodern literature on diaspora is extensive. For seminal essays, see James Clifford, "Diaspora," *Cultural Anthropology* 9 (1994):302–38; William Safran, "Diasporas in Modern Societies: Myths of Homeland and Return," *Diaspora* (Spring 1991):83–99; Jon Stratton, "(Dis)placing the Jews: Historicizing the Idea of Diaspora," *Diaspora* 6, 3 (1997):301–29; and Kachig Tölölyan, "Rethinking Diaspora(s): Stateless Power in the Transnational Moment," *Diaspora* 5, 1 (1996):3–36.

7. For an anti-diasporic position and insistence on Israel's "authenticity" as the site of Jewish culture, see Gershon Shaked, "Alexandria: On Jews and Judaism in America," *Jerusalem Quarterly* 49 (Winter 1989):47–84.

8. Simon Dubnow, "The Affirmation of the Diaspora," in *Nationalism and History, Essays on Old and New Judaism*, ed. and trans. Koppel S. Pinson (Cleveland:

Meridian Books, 1961), p. 188. See also "Autonomism, the Basis of the National Program" (1901), pp. 131–42, in the same volume.

9. Dubnow, "Affirmation of the Diaspora," pp. 186–87.

10. Ezrahi, "The Grapes of Roth: Diasporism from Portnoy to Shylock," in *Booking Passage*, pp. 221–33.

11. Janet Wolff identifies the figure in "The Impolite Boarder: 'Diasporist' Art and its Critical Response," in *Critical Kitaj: Essays on the Work of R. B. Kitaj*, ed. James Aulich and John Lynch (New Brunswick, N.J.: Rutgers University Press, 2001), p. 29.

12. Kitaj, *First Diasporist Manifesto*, p. 19.

13. Ibid., p. 25.

14. Ibid., p. 101.

15. Ibid., pp. 29–31.

16. A major retrospective of Kitaj's work at the Tate Gallery in 1987 was panned by British critics for being, to the artist's mind, "too Jewish and parochial." On the anti-Semitic character of the critical response, see Wolff, "Impolite Boarder," pp. 29–43.

17. Kitaj, *First Diasporist Manifesto*, p. 29.

18. Andrew Benjamin, "Kitaj and the Question of Jewish Identity," in *Art, Mimesis and the Avant-Garde: Aspects of a Philosophy of Difference* (London: Routledge, 1992), pp. 89–90.

19. Wolff, "Impolite Boarder," pp. 41–42.

20. Benedict Anderson, *Imagined Communities: Reflections on the Origins and Spread of Nationalism*, rev. ed. (London: Verso Editions, 1991). For a discussion of the distribution issues of class and media in diasporic production, see Paul Gilroy, "Cruciality and the Frog's Perspective: An Agenda of Difficulties for the Black Arts Movement in Britain," in *Small Acts: Thoughts on the Politics of Black Culture* (London: Serpent's Tail, 1993), pp. 100–101.

21. Jonathan Sarna, "The Mythical Jewish Columbus and the History of America's Jews," in *Religion in the Age of Exploration*, ed. Bryan le Beau and Menachem Mor (Omaha, Neb.: Creighton University Press, 1992), pp. 81–95.

22. Cyrus Adler and Isidore Singer, eds., *The Jewish Encyclopedia: A Descriptive Record of the History, Religion, Literature, and Customs of the Jewish People from the Earliest Times to the Present Day* (first published by Funk and Wagnalls, 1901–06; New York: Ktav Publishing House, 1964).

23. For an account of beadwork production and the Native economy, see Jolene Rickard, *Across Borders: Beadwork in Iroquois Life* (Washington, D.C.: National Museum of the American Indian, 2002).

24. Jean Gagnon, "The Space to Say," in . . . *from the Transit Bar* / . . . *du transitbar*, ed. Vera Frenkel and Jean Gagnon (Toronto: Power Plant; Ottawa: National Gallery of Canada, 1994), pp. 11–17.

25. Ibid., p. 12.

26. Irit Rogoff, "Moving On: Migration and the Intertextuality of Trauma," in . . . *from the Transit Bar*, pp. 243–67.

Chapter 10. Modern? American? Jew?

Excerpt from "Modern? American? Jew? Museum and Exhibitions of Ben Shahn's Late Paintings" by Diana L. Linden in *Prospects*, vol. 30 (2005), pp. 665–84. Copyright © 2005 Cambridge University Press. Reprinted with permission.

I thank Jack Salzman, editor of *Prospects*, for allowing me to reprint this excerpt here. My thanks to Dora Apel, David Brody, John Davis, Judy Endelman, Todd

Endelman, Jonathan Karp, Norman Kleeblatt, Anthony Lee, and Peter Ross for their suggestions and criticisms. The curatorial, education, and public relations staffs at The Jewish Museum, the Museum of Modern Art, the Whitney Museum of American Art, and the DIA all graciously answered numerous questions. I would especially like to thank Susan Chevlowe, independent curator; and Nancy Jones, director of education, Jennifer Czajkowski, associate educator, and Rebecca Hart, assistant curator of modern and contemporary art, all at the DIA. Earlier versions of this chapter were presented at the American Studies Association Annual Meeting, Montreal, October 1999, and at the Center for Advanced Judaic Studies Conference, University of Pennsylvania, May 2001. I would like to thank David Ruderman and the staff of the CAJS for the opportunity to spend 2000–2001 there.

1. See Kenneth W. Prescott's exhibition catalogue, *Ben Shahn: A Retrospective, 1898–1969* (New York: The Jewish Museum, 1976). The itinerary for the retrospective, which circulated from October 1977 through January 1978, was as follows: in 1977 at The Jewish Museum, New York, October 20–January 2; Georgia Art Museum, University of Georgia, Athens, January 27–March 17; Maurice Spertus Museum of Judaica, Chicago, April 11–May 29; University Art Museum, University of Texas at Austin, June 23–August 11; Cincinnati Art Museum, September 5–October 24; and the Amon-Carter Museum, Fort Worth, November 17, 1977–January 15, 1978.

2. Deborah Martin Kao, Laura Katzman, and Jenna Webster, *Ben Shahn's New York: The Photography of Modern Times* (New Haven, Conn.: Yale University Press, 2000), and Alejandro Anreus, ed., *Ben Shahn and the Passion of Sacco and Vanzetti* (New Brunswick, N.J.: Rutgers University Press, 2001), an exhibition catalogue with contributions by Laura Katzman, Diana L. Linden, Frances K. Pohl, and Nunzio Pernicone.

3. Susan Chevlowe, ed., *Common Man, Mythic Vision: The Paintings of Ben Shahn* (New York: The Jewish Museum, and Princeton, N.J.: Princeton University Press, 1998), an exhibition catalogue with contributions by Chevlowe, Diana L. Linden, Stephen Polcari, and Frances K. Pohl. See also Stephen Polcari, *Abstract Expressionism and the Modern Experience* (Cambridge: Cambridge University Press, 1991).

4. Matthew Baigell, who does acknowledge Shahn's abstract expressionist context, claims that, along with Barnett Newman, Shahn created the most significant body of Jewish religious art of any American artist during the 1950s and 1960s. See Matthew Baigell, "Ben Shahn's Postwar Jewish Paintings," in *Artist and Identity in Twentieth-Century America* (Cambridge: Cambridge University Press, 2001), pp. 212–31, 282–84, and, in the same volume, "Barnett Newman's Stripe Paintings and Kabbalah: A Jewish Take," pp. 232–42, 284–85.

5. Irving Sandler, *The Triumph of American Painting: A History of Abstract Expressionism* (New York: Harper and Row, 1970).

6. Joan Rosenbaum, "Foreword," in *Common Man, Mythic Vision*, pp. vi–x.

7. See my essay, "Ben Shahn's New Deal Murals: Jewish Identity in the American Scene," in *Common Man, Mythic Vision*, pp. 37–66.

8. For studies that treat Shahn's FSA/RA photographs, and specifically his southern photographs, see Susan H. Edwards, "Ben Shahn and the American Racial Divide," in *Intersections: Lithography, Photography, and the Traditions of Printmaking*, ed. Kathleen Stewart Howe (Albuquerque: University of New Mexico Press, 1998), pp. 77–85, and "Ben Shahn: The Road South," *History of Photography* 19,1 (Spring 1995):13–19. For a discussion of the formal relationship between Rivera's and Shahn's work, see Francis V. O'Connor, "The Influence of Diego Rivera on the Art of the United States during the 1930s and After," in the exhibition catalogue *Diego Rivera: A Retrospective* (Detroit: Detroit Institute of Arts, 1986), pp. 166–70.

9. On the Jersey Homesteads mural, see my essay, "Ben Shahn's New Deal Murals: Jewish Identity in the American Scene," pp. 41–50.

10. See my essay, "What Becomes an Icon Most? The Critical Reception to Ben Shahn's *The Passion of Sacco and Vanzetti*," in *Ben Shahn and the Passion of Sacco and Vanzetti*, pp. 89–108, 136–38, on the critical and popular reception to Shahn's series from the 1930s to the present day.

11. Adam D. Weinberg," Introduction," in *Frames of Reference: Looking at American Art, 1900–1950, Works from the Whitney Museum of American Art*, ed. Beth Venn and Weinberg (New York: Whitney Museum of American Art, and Berkeley: University of California Press, 1999), p. 11.

12. On the politics of exhibition, see Ivan Karp and Steven D. Lavine, eds., *Exhibiting Cultures: The Poetics and Politics of Museum Display* (Washington, D.C.: Smithsonian Institution Press, 1991).

13. Barbara Haskell, *The American Century: Art and Culture, 1900–1950* (New York: Whitney Museum of American Art, in association with W. W. Norton, 1999). This volume accompanied an exhibition, which included several of Shahn's works: two FSA/RA photographs, *Musgrove Brothers, Westmoreland Country, Penn.* (1935) and *Cotton Pickers* (1935); a poster entitled *Years of Dust* (1937) for the FSA/RA; *Bartholomeo Vanzetti and Nicola Sacco* (1931–32), tempera on paper on board, and *The Passion of Sacco and Vanzetti* (1931–32), tempera on canvas; *This Is Nazi Brutality* (1942), a poster for the OWI; and *Reconstruction* (1945).

14. Serge Guilbaut, *How New York Stole the Idea of Modern Art*, trans. Arthur Goldhammer (Chicago: University of Chicago Press, 1983).

15. Clement Greenberg, "Art," *Nation* (November 1, 1947), pp. 481–82.

16. Frances K. Pohl, *Ben Shahn: New Deal Artist in a Cold War Climate, 1947–1954* (Austin: University of Texas Press, 1989), in particular pp. 147–72.

17. For information on Shahn's affiliation with the CIO-PAC, see Frances K. Pohl, *Ben Shahn with Ben Shahn's Writings* (San Francisco: Pomegranate Art Books, 1993), pp. 21–22, and her *Ben Shahn*, pp. 9–33. See also Kenneth W. Prescott, *Prints and Posters of Ben Shahn* (New York: Dover Publications, 1982), pp. viii, pl. viii. In 1962, MoMA's International Council organized and traveled the exhibition *Ben Shahn: Graphics* to Baden-Baden, Zagreb, Ljubljana, Stockholm, Lund, and Jerusalem.

18. Ann Eden Gibson, *Abstract Expressionism: Other Politics* (New Haven, Conn.: Yale University Press, 1997).

19. Carol Duncan, *Civilizing Rituals: Inside Public Art Museums* (London: Routledge, 1995), pp. 104–5.

20. Ibid., p.108.

21. Kirk Varnedoe with Pepe Karmel, *Jackson Pollock* (New York: Museum of Modern Art, 1998). This is an exhibition catalogue. MoMA lent the following works to the exhibition: *Common Man, Mythic Vision: Portrait of Myself When Young* (1943); *Liberation* (1945); *Pacific Landscape* (1945); and *Father and Child* (1946). Regrettably, MoMA withdrew its paintings from the Detroit exhibition, as did a few other lenders.

22. Pohl, *Ben Shahn*, p. 28.

23. Ben Shahn, *The Shape of Content* (Cambridge, Mass.: Harvard University Press, 1957), p. 48.

24. Joan Rosenbaum, "Foreword," in *Common Man, Mythic Vision*, ed. Chevlowe, p. viii.

25. On the importance of seeing Shahn within postwar American art and appreciating his formal accomplishments, see Anthony W. Lee, "Exhibition Review: Ben Shahn," *Apollo* (October 2000):63–64 (based on the Detroit venue), and Jonathan Weinberg, "Ben Shahn: Picture Maker," *Art Journal* 60, 1 (Spring 2000):104–7.

26. Laura Katzman, "Art in the Atomic Age: Ben Shahn's Stop H Bomb Tests," *Yale Journal of Criticism* 2, 1 (1998):139–58.

27. Polcari, "Ben Shahn and Postwar American Art," in *Common Man, Mythic Vision*, p. 73.

28. Clipping, Ben Shahn Papers, 1879–1990, Archives of American Art, Smithsonian Institution, Washington, D.C.

29. Laura Katzman, "The Politics of Media: Painting and Photography in the Art of Ben Shahn," *American Art* 7, 1 (1993):60–87.

30. Pohl, *New Deal Artist in the Cold War Era*, pp. 49–50.

31. Conversation with Rebecca Hart, assistant curator, modern and contemporary art, Detroit Institute of Arts, September 21, 1999.

32. See Ziva Amishai-Maisels, "Ben Shahn and the Problem of Jewish Identity," *Jewish Art* 12–13 (1986–87):304–19. I presented this argument as "Zion in the Garden State: Ben Shahn's Mural for the Jersey Homesteads" at the Fogg Art Museum, Harvard University, February 2000. The DIA unfortunately missed a great opportunity by neglecting to link Rivera's *Detroit Industry* murals with the Shahn exhibition; for example, they did not place directional signs to Shahn's *Soapbox* in the Rivera court, and vice versa.

33. Clipping, "Attractions in the Galleries," *New York Sun*, April 16, 1932, Edith Gregor Halpert Collection, Archives of American Art, Smithsonian Institution, Washington, D.C.

34. Diego Rivera, "The Revolutionary Spirit in Modern Art," *Modern Quarterly* 6 (Autumn 1932):56–57.

35. Clipping, "Current Exhibitions: Extensive One-Man Show by Ben Shahn at the Modern Museum," *New York Sun*, October 3, 1947, James Thrall Soby Papers, Museum of Modern Art, New York City.

36. Hilton Kramer, "Publicizing Social Causes of Canvas," *New York Times*, November 7, 1976, p. D23.

37. Arthur Liebman, *Jews and the Left* (New York: John Wiley, 1978).

38. Frances K. Pohl, "Allegory in the Work of Ben Shahn," in *Common Man, Mythic Vision*, pp. 44–45. The ad "Wine, diamonds, ships, prayer shawls and you—The State of Israel" appeared in *Time* (February 5, 1951):44–45. As Pohl mentions, Ziva Amishai-Maisels believes that Shahn's *Sound in the Mulberry Tree, 1948*, which includes in Hebrew a quotation from 2 Samuel, is the artist's indirect reference to the founding of the state of Israel. See Amishai-Maisels, "Ben Shahn and the Problem of Jewish Identity," pp. 304–19. Matthew Baigell argues that Shahn's three *Allegory* paintings, as well as his genre painting *Sound in the Mulberry Tree, 1948*, are among the artist's "[v]ery strong, but very coded statements made in support of the still young, new country, Israel." See Baigell's "Ben Shahn's Postwar Jewish Paintings," in *Artist and Identity in Twentieth-Century America*, pp. 213–31.

39. Amishai-Maisels, "Ben Shahn and the Problem of Jewish Identity," pp. 304–19.

40. Shahn, *The Shape of Content*, pp. 41–42.

41. Peter Novick, *The Holocaust in American Life* (New York: Houghton Mifflin Company, 1999), p. 7.

Chapter 11. Max Liebermann and the Amsterdam Jewish Quarter

Research for this essay was begun in the course of the seminar "Visual Culture and Modern Jewish Society" held at the Institute for Advanced Studies at The Hebrew University, Jerusalem, in 1996, in which I participated as Norman and Rosita Winston Foundation Fellow. I am most grateful to the organizers, Richard I.

Cohen and Ezra Mendelsohn, and to the members of the seminar for making this a memorable and fruitful experience.

1. The literature on Liebermann has grown very large in recent years, after a hiatus during the period of the National Socialist dictatorship. The principal titles among these writings are Erich Hancke's biography, *Max Liebermann: Sein Leben und seine Werke*, 2nd ed. (Berlin: Bruno Cassirer, 1914; 2nd ed., Berlin, 1923); the massive exhibition catalogue *Max Liebermann in seiner Zeit* (Berlin; Nationalgalerie and Munich Haus der Kunst, 1979–80); and Matthias Eberle's *Max Liebermann: Werkverzeichnis der Gemälde und Ölstudien* (Munich: Hirmer, 1996), 2 vols. The artist's writings were published under the title *Gesammelte Schriften von Max Liebermann* (Berlin: Bruno Cassirer, 1922) and those after that date have been edited by Günter Busch in *Die Phantasie in der Malerei* (Frankfurt am Main: S. Fischer, 1978). Among the more valuable general publications devoted to the painter and his work in the recent past, the following deserve mention: Günter Busch, *Max Liebermann: Maler, Zeichner, Graphiker* (Frankfurt am Main: S. Fischer, 1986), and catalogues of the exhibitions mounted on the occasion of the 150th anniversary of Liebermann's birth: *Was vom Leben übrig bleibt, sind Bilder und Geschichte. Max Liebermann zum 150. Geburtstag. Rekonstruktion der Gedächtnisaustellung der Berliner Jüdischen Museum von 1936* (Berlin: Stiftung "Neue Synagoge Berlin-Centrum Judaicum," 1997); *Max Liebermann: Der Realist und die Phantasie* (Hamburger Kunsthalle, Städtische Galerie im Städelschen Kunstinstitut Frankfurt am Main, Museum der Bildenden Künste Leipzig, 1997/1998) (Hamburg: Dölling und Galitz, 1997); and *Max Liebermann und die französischen Impressionisten* (Jüdisches Museum der Stadt Wien, 1998) (Düsseldorf: DuMont, 1998).

2. Madeleine van Strien-Chardonneau, *Le Voyage de Hollande: Récits de voyageurs français dans les Provinces-Unies, 1748–1795* (Studies on Voltaire and the Eighteenth Century, no. 318) (Oxford: Voltaire Foundation at the Taylor Institution, 1994), pp. 44, 65–66, 374–75, 438–39.

3. *The Diary of John Evelyn*, ed. E. S. de Beer (London: Oxford University Press, 1959), pp. 25–26. See also on this subject Yosef Kaplan, "'*Gente Politica*': The Portuguese Jews of Amsterdam vis-à-vis Dutch Society," in *Dutch Jews as Perceived by Themselves and by Others* (Proceedings of the Eighth International Symposium on the History of the Jews in the Netherlands), ed. Chaya Brasz and Yosef Kaplan (Cologne: Brill, 2001), pp. 21–40.

4. These data are drawn from Selma Leydesdorff, *We Lived with Dignity: The Jewish Proletariat of Amsterdam, 1900–1940* (Detroit: Wayne State University Press, 1987), p. 82. The area is also described by Mozes Heiman Gans, *Memorbook: History of Dutch Jewry from the Renaissance to 1940* (Baarn: Bosch and Keuning, 1977), pp. 637ff., and more impressionistically in the recent book by Geert Mak, *Amsterdam* (Cambridge, Mass.: Harvard University Press, 2000), pp. 158–59.

5. Edmondo de Amicis, *Holland* (Philadelphia: Henry T. Coates and Co., 1894), pp. 76–78, a translation of the thirteenth Italian edition of this immensely popular work, initially published in 1874. On the author, see the article of L. Strappini in *Dizionario biografico degli Italiani*, 33 (Rome: Istituto della Enciclopedia Italiana, 1987), pp. 232–40. A guidebook of 1838 recommends a visit to the Jewish Quarter with an even greater wealth of picturesque detail; see W. J. Olivier, *Manuel des étrangers à Amsterdam* (Amsterdam: Diederichs, 1838), pp. 51–52, cited in a German translation in the exhibition catalogue by Jüdisches Museum der Stadt Wien, *Max Liebermann und die französischen Impressionisten*, p. 134.

6. The painting (Collection Vera Eisenberger KG, Vienna) was shown in the exhibition *The Emergence of Jewish Artists in Nineteenth-Century Europe*. The catalogue of the same title (London: Merrell; New York: in association with The Jewish

Museum, 2001) was edited by Susan Tumarkin Goodman. See p. 106, catalogue entry no. 57, for the painting, and p. 169 for information about the artist.

7. Staller and Witsen's views here mentioned are in the Joods Historisch Museum, Amsterdam. On the former, see the brief entry in H. Vollmer, *Allgemeines Lexikon der bildenden Künstler des XX. Jahrhunderts* (Leipzig: E. A. Seemann, 1953–61), vol. 4, p. 340; on the latter, the entry in U. Thieme and Felix Becker, *Allgemeine Lexikon der bildenden Künstler,* vol. 36, pp. 118–19. The sculptor Mendez da Costa (1865–1939) also took the Jewish Quarter as the subject for a number of his works. See Christiaan J. Roosen, "Joseph Mendez da Costa: The Revitalization of Dutch Sculpture," in *Dutch Jewish History* 3, ed. Jozeph Michman (Netherlands Institute for Research on Dutch Jewry; Assen: Van Gorcum, 1993), vol. 3, pp. 261–71. According to Roosen, some of these sculptures were displayed in a 1916 exhibition at the Stedelijk Museum that documented the disappearance of the Jewish Ghetto. See p. 270, n. 21.

8. Some of these photographs are reproduced in Mozes Heiman Gans, *De oude Amsterdamse Jodenhoek in Foto's, 1900–1940* (Baarn: Te Have, 1974), and in the same author's *Memorbook,* pp. 637ff.

9. See Leydesdorff, *We Lived with Dignity,* pp. 90ff.

10. "In meinem 43 jährigen Hollandfahren habe ich einen ähnlich schlechten Sommer noch nicht erlebt. Ich fürchte daher, dass die diesjährige Ernte demgemäss ausfallen und die Preise sehr in die Höhe gehn werden (bei der starken Nachfrage). Also decken Sie Ihren Bedarf so bald als möglich. Judenstrassen überhaupt nicht mehr aufzutreiben und neue Malen unmöglich, da das Judenviertel eigentlich aufgehört hat, zu existieren." Quoted from the Berlin Nationalgalerie and Munich Haus der Kunst exhibition catalogue *Max Liebermann in seiner Zeit,* p. 107.

11. Review of Frits Lugt, "Mit Rembrandt in Amsterdam," *Kunst und Künstler* 19, 7 (1921), reprinted in *Max Liebermann, Vision der Wirklichkeit: Ausgewählte Schriften und Reden,* ed. Günter Busch (Frankfurt am Main: Fischer Taschenbuch, 1993), p. 162. On the larger historical background, see now Michael Zell, *Reframing Rembrandt: Jews and the Christian Image in Seventeenth-Century Amsterdam* (Berkeley: University of California Press, 2002).

12. The source of information on the painter's visit to the Jewish Quarter is Erich Hancke's biography, *Max Liebermann,* p. 120. On Allebé, who was director of the Amsterdam Academy from 1880 to 1916, see Thieme and Becker, *Allgemeine Lexikon,* vol. 1, p. 204.

13. The drawing, inscribed *Judenviertel in Amsterdam* (present whereabouts unknown), is published in Erich Hancke, "Mit Liebermann in Amsterdam," *Kunst und Künstler* 12 (1914):11. It was then in the possession of the artist.

14. Zurich, private collection. See Eberle, *Werkverzeichnis,* vol. 1, pp. 129–30, no. 1876/32. The painting bears the date 1877 but was likely executed in the previous year.

15. Hancke, *Mit Liebermann in Amsterdam,* pp. 14–16. The passage deserves to be cited in the original German: "Er wollte mir nun auch die Synagoge zeigen, wo er die Studien zu Christus im Tempel gemacht hat. Unterwegs erzählte er von der Zeit, wo er noch mit Allebé Freitag abends hinzugehen pflegte, in jene alte berühmte Synagoge, wo Spinoza in dem Bann getan wurde [. . .] und sahen nach den Fenstern, durch die man die brennenden Lichter erblickte und Liebermann sprach von seiner Familie und deren Frömmigkeit. Auch er selbst sei früher am Sonnabend nie mit einer Zigarre über die Strasse gegangen, wozu ich aus meiner Errinerung ergänzen kam, als er sogar diesem Freitag zur Ehren stets den Zylinder trug. Als wir ausgeraucht hatten, traten wir hinein, blieben aber am Eingang stehen."

16. A most detailed and illuminating treatment of the painting and its history is

found in Katrin Boskamp, *Studien zum Frühwerk von Max Liebermann* (Studien zur Kunstgeschichte, Bd. 88) (Hildesheim: G. Olms, 1994), pp. 75ff. See also the entry in Eberle, *Werkverzeichnis*, 1, pp. 159–62, no. 1979/3; and Ziva Amishai-Maisels, "Origins of the Jewish Jesus," in *Complex Identities: Jewish Consciousness and Modern Art*, ed. Matthew Baigell and Milly Heyd (New Brunswick, N.J.: Rutgers University Press, 2001), pp. 66–69.

17. Birmingham Museum and Art Gallery. On this picture, see the exhibition catalogue *The Pre-Raphaelites* (London: Tate Gallery, 1984), pp.158–60, no. 85.

18. H. Knackfuss, *Adolf von Menzel* (Künstler Monographien, 7) (Bielefeld: Velhagen und Klasing, 1912), pp. 45–46. Menzel and Liebermann's compositions are compared by Richard Muther in *Geschichte der Malerei im XIX. Jahrhundert* (Munich: G. Hirth, 1894), vol. 3, pp. 632–33.

19. Knackfuss, *Adolf von Menzel*, p. 46.

20. Letter to Alfred Lichtwark, dated June 5, 1911, in Max Liebermann, *Siebzig Briefe*, ed. Franz Landsberger (Berlin: Schocken Verlag, 1937), p. 50, letter no. 32: "Die Juden schienen mir zu charakteristisch; sie verleiten zur Karikatur—in welchen Fehler mir Menzel verfallen zu sein scheint." The painter's comments on Rembrandt's portrayal of Jews contained in a letter to Landsberger (October 1, 1925) are also germane to this issue (*Siebzig Briefe*, pp. 68–71).

21. In a letter to Fritz Stahl, dated April 17, 1915, Liebermann writes: "Die ekelhaften Anwürfe von Anti- und Semiten, als ich den Christus im Tempel gemalt hatte, haben mich für immer von biblischen Stoffen . . . abgehalten." Quoted from Berlin Nationalgalerie and Munich Haus der Kunst, *Max Liebermann in seiner Zeit*, p. 107.

22. Eberle, *Werkverzeichnis*, vol. 1, pp. 270–72, no. 1884/25. The term *Judengasse* literally means a Jewish street, but refers more generally to a Jewish quarter.

23. Georg Hermann, "Max Liebermann," in *Jüdische Künstler*, ed. Martin Buber (Berlin: Jüdischer Verlag, 1903), pp. 111–36.

24. On this episode, see Peter Paret, *The Berlin Secession* (Cambridge, Mass.: Belknap Press of Harvard University, 1980), pp. 170–82.

25. Eberle, *Werkverzeichnis*, vol. 2, pp. 640–41, no. 1905/8. Hancke notes that Hugo von Tschudi, the director of the museum in Berlin, who was favorably inclined toward modern developments in German art, wanted to acquire the painting but was persuaded by "Bedenken, die mit der Kunst nichts zu schaffen haben" not to do so, a continuing sign of the hostility that the painter still encountered in official circles. See Hancke, *Max Liebermann*, pp. 437ff.

26. Some of these drawings are discussed by Hancke, *Max Liebermann*, pp. 491ff., and Hans-Jürgen Imiela, *Max Liebermann als Zeichner* (Mainz: Kunstgeschichtliches Institut der Johannes-Gutenberg-Universität Mainz, 1970), pp. 28ff.

27. Gustav Schiefler, *Das graphische Werk von Max Liebermann*, 2nd ed. (Berlin: Bruno Cassirer, 1914), pp. 89ff, nos. 57, 66–67, 70–75, 77, 80, 113, 147–49.

28. Illustrated in the exhibition catalogue *Max Liebermann in seiner Zeit*, p. 36, figs. 30–31.

29. Hancke, *Mit Liebermann in Amsterdam*, repeated in Hancke, *Max Liebermann*, and Hans Ostwald, *Das Liebermann-Buch* (Berlin: Franke, 1930), pp. 322–24.

30. The Magdeburg painting, apparently lost in World War II, is inventoried by Eberle, *Werkverzeichnis* 2, pp. 686–87, no. 1907/5. A previously unrecorded version of this composition from a private collection in Israel, which recently appeared on the art market (*Israeli and International Art* [Sotheby's, Tel Aviv, Israel, April 9, 1999, p. 29, lot 28A]), appears to be an inauthentic copy of the lost painting once in the possession of Henry B. Simms in Hamburg (Eberle, *Werkverzeichnis*, vol. 2, p. 687, no. 1907/6). On Pissarro's city views, see Richard A. Bretell, "Camille Pissarro and

Urban View Painting: An Introduction," in the exhibition catalogue *The Impressionist and the City: Pissarro's Series Painting*, ed. Richard A. Bretell and Joachim Pissarro (New Haven, Conn.: Yale University Press, 1993), pp. xv–xxxvi, and nos. 35–37. See also on this topic Robert L. Herbert, *Impressionism: Art, Leisure, and Parisian Society* (New Haven, Conn.: Yale University Press, 1988), pp. 1–32; Joel Isaacson, "Monet's Views of Paris," *Bulletin of the Allen Memorial Art Museum* (November 1993):81ff., and Meyer Schapiro, *Impressionism: Reflections and Perceptions* (New York: G. Braziller, 1997), pp. 144–52.

31. The Frankfurt painting is catalogued by Eberle, *Werkverzeichnis*, vol. 2, pp. 724–25, no. 1908/9. The large version (Cologne Kaufhof Holding AG), pp. 754–56, bears no. 1909/1. Hancke, *Max Liebermann*, p. 445, found the sharper focus to have a deadening effect, and other critics have tended to share his critical view.

32. Hans Rosenhagen, *Max Liebermann* (Künstler-Monographien 45) (Bielefeld: Velhagen und Klasing, 1900). The *Judengassen* are discussed on p. 78 of the second, expanded edition of the work, which appeared in 1927. On the relations of the author with Liebermann, see M. Fuhr, "'. . . der Liebe Gott und Rosenhagen': Die Briefe Max Liebermann an seinen Biographen Hans Rosenhagen," *Niederdeutsche Beiträge zur Kunstgeschichte* 37 (1998):157–97.

33. Karl Scheffler, *Max Liebermann* (Munich: R. Piper and Co., 1906), pp. 15–19. Liebermann's sensitivity and resentment over his failure to be fully accepted by the upper strata of German society led him, according to this author, who compares the painter to Ahasuerus in the legend of the Wandering Jew, to compensate by making his Jewishness even more exaggerated and ostentatious. Scheffler's book was revised and reissued several times, the latest edition (Wiesbaden: Insel-Verlag, 1953) appearing almost twenty years after the author's death.

34. Gustav Pauli, *Max Liebermann: Des Meisters Gemälde* (*Klassiker der Kunst*, 19) (Stuttgart: Deutsche Verlagsanstalt, 1911), p. xl: "Dass er ein Jude ist und sich mit Stolz als Sohn einer alten reinen Rasse fühlt, kommt fur uns, die wir vor seinen Bilder stehen, nur wenig in Betracht, denn diese Bilder reden unsre Muttersprache und haben ihre besten Anregungen dem urgermanischen Boden der Niederlände entnommen."

35. Hancke, *Max Liebermann*, p. 8: "Es hat an Vermutungen über ihre Herkunft nicht gefehlt, wobei man besonders seine Rassenabstammung in Betracht zog."

36. Ibid., p. 500: "es spricht wohl viel historisches mit, das Gedenken an die Geschichte diese Ortes und der Rasse, die ihn bewohnt, an die Tragik des 'alten Volkes'."

37. Ostwald, *Liebermann-Buch*, pp. 326–28.

38. Hancke, *Mit Liebermann in Amsterdam*, pp. 14–16; Hancke, *Max Liebermann*, p. 496; and Ostwald, *Liebermann-Buch*, pp. 322–24.

39. Gustave Le Bon, *Psychologie des foules* (Bibliothèque de philosophie contemporaine), 5th ed. (Paris: F. Alcan, 1905), pp. 16ff., 43–44. On the importance of traditions in the behavior of crowds, Le Bon asserts that they represent "la synthèse de l'âme de la race" (pp. 70ff.). On the psychology of crowds in nineteenth-century thought, see also Suzanna Barrows, *Distorting Mirrors: Visions of the Crowd in Late Nineteenth-Century France* (New Haven, Conn.: Yale University Press, 1981), and J. S. McClelland, *The Crowd and the Mob: From Plato to Canetti* (London: Unwin Hyman, 1989). For a recent application to the history of art, see Stefan Jonsson, "Society Degree Zero: Christ, Communism, and the Madness of Crowds in the Art of James Ensor," *Representations* 75 (2001):1–32.

40. Liebermann, *Siebzig Briefe*, p. 35, no. 17.

41. Ostwald, *Liebermann-Buch*, p. 326; Ellen Spickernagel, *Max Liebermann: Judengasse in Amsterdam, 1908* (Kleine Werkmonographie), p. 22; Städelsches Kunstinstitut und Städtische Galerie, Frankfurt am Main, s.d.

42. George Eliot, *Daniel Deronda* (London: W. Blackwood, 1876). My quotation is from the Penguin Classics edition, ed. Barbara Hardy (London: Penguin Books, 1967), p. 414. On this topic, see William Baker, *George Eliot and Judaism* (Salzburg: Institut für Englische Sprache und Literatur, Universität Salzburg, 1975), chapter 6, pp. 117ff., and Anne Aresty Naman, *The Jew in the Victorian Novel* (New York: AMS Press, 1980), chapter 5, pp. 161ff.

43. Heinrich Heine, "Der Rabbi von Bacherach," in *Heines Sämtliche Werke* 5 (Leipzig: Tempel, 1914), vol. 5, pp. 439–40; J. W. H. Stoffers, "Juden und Ghetto in der deutschen Literatur bis zum Ausgang des Weltkrieges" (Ph.D. dissertation, Catholic University of Nijmegen, 1939), pp. 68–69.

44. Johan Wolfgang Goethe, *Aus meinem Leben: Dichtung und Wahrheit* (Gedenkausgabe der Werke: Briefe und Gespräche 10), ed. Ernst Beutler (Zurich: Artemis Verlag, 1948), p. 166; Stoffers, *Juden und Ghetto*, pp. 69–70. For more recent literary reflections of the ghetto, see Dan Miron, *The Image of the Shtetl and Other Studies of Modern Jewish Literary Imagination* (Syracuse, N.Y.: Syracuse University Press, 2000).

45. Joachim Schlör, "Berlin II. Traum-und Notstand der Juden," in *Deutsch-jüdische Passagen: Europäische Stadtlandschaften von Berlin bis Prag*, ed. Willi Jasper and Julius H. Schoeps (Hamburg: Hoffmann und Campe, 1996), pp. 63–81.

46. Martin Buber, *Die jüdische Bewegung: Gesammelte Aufsätze und Ansprachen, 1900–1915* (Berlin: Jüdischer Verlag, 1916), pp. 12, 59: "Das Blühen und Wachsen jenseits des Ghettos war unseren Ahnen unbekannt und verhasst wie der wunderbare Menschenleibs." On these ideas, see also the commentary of Ritchie Robertson, *The "Jewish Question" in German Literature, 1749–1939* (Oxford: Clarendon Press, and New York: Oxford University Press, 1999), p. 388.

47. In the letter to Fritz Stahl, Liebermann wrote: "Ob ich Jude und reich bin, was schiert das meine Kunst? Nichts ist mir verhasster als die Vermengung von religiösen oder sozialen Begriffen mit der Kunst." On this matter, see H. Simon, "Liebermann und sein Judentum," in *Max Liebermann: Der Realist und die Phantasie*, pp. 41–48; and Chana C. Schütz, "Max Liebermann as 'Jewish' Painter: The Artist's Reception in His Time," in the exhibition catalogue *Berlin Metropolis: Jews and the New Culture, 1890–1918*, ed. Emily D. Bilski (Berkeley: University of California Press, 1999), pp. 99, 146–63.

Chapter 12. Rome and Jerusalem

Thanks to the members of the seminar of the Center for Advanced Judaic Studies, University of Pennsylvania, and to my colleagues at the Davis Center, at the History Department of Princeton University, as well as to the members of the Slavic Department at Wesleyan University, where I presented earlier versions of this chapter. Thanks to Laura Engelstein, Carol Armstrong, and Bob Crews for their astute and trenchant criticism and most importantly, to Noam M. Elcott for helping me see. All translations from Russian and French are my own, unless otherwise indicated. Quotations from the New Testament are from the New Jerusalem Bible; quotations from the Hebrew Bible are taken from *Tanakh: The Holy Scriptures, the New JPS Translation According to the Traditional Hebrew Text* (Philadelphia: Jewish Publication Society, 1988).

1. See Wayne A. Meeks, "The Man from Heaven in Johannine Sectarianism," *Journal of Biblical Literature* 91 (1972):44–72.

2. See Paula Fredriksen, *From Jesus to Christ: The Origins of the New Testament Images of Jesus* (New Haven, Conn.: Yale University Press, 1988), p. 23.

3. Ibid., p. 22.

4. There is a prodigious literature on *Andachtsbilder*; the seminal study remains

Erwin Panofsky, "'Imago Pietatis': Ein Beitrag zur Typengeschichte der 'Schmerzensmanns' und der 'Maria Mediatrix,'" in *Festschrift für Max J. Friedländer zum 60. Geburtstage* (Leipzig: E. A. Seemann, 1927), pp. 261–308. See also Sixten Ringbom, *From Icon to Narrative: The Rise of the Dramatic Close-Up in Fifteenth-Century Devotional Painting* (Åbo: Åbo akademi, 1965), and Hans Belting, *Das Bild und sein Publikum im Mittelalter: Form und Funktion früher Bildtafeln der Passion* (Berlin: Mann, 1981).

5. On the image of Christ as Man of Sorrows, see, for example, Louis M. La Favia, *The Man of Sorrows: Its Origin and Development in Trecento Florentine Painting* (Rome: Sanguis, 1980).

6. Jeffrey Hamburger, "The Visual and the Visionary: The Image in Late Medieval Monastic Devotions," *Viator* 20 (1989):161–82, here 176. On the relationship between the gospel text and Passion iconography, see James H. Marrow, *Passion Iconography in Northern European Art of the Late Middle Ages and Early Renaissance* (Kortrijk: Van Ghemmert, 1979).

7. Hamburger, "The Visual and the Visionary," 176.

8. On the development of the theology of the *vera icon*, see Ewa Kuryluk, *Veronica and Her Cloth: History, Symbolism and Structure of a "True" Image* (Oxford: Basil Blackwell, 1991), and Herbert L. Kessler, "Pictures Fertile with Truth: How Christians Managed to Make Images of God without Violating the Second Commandment," *Journal of the Walters Art Gallery* 49/50 (1991–92):53–65.

9. See, for example, Christopher M. S. Johns, *Antonio Canova and the Politics of Patronage in Revolutionary and Napoleonic Europe* (Berkeley: University of California Press, 1998), on the career of Antonio Canova (1757–1822), whose work set the precedent for the development of sculpture in the public life of Victorian Europe. See also Anne M. Wagner, *Jean-Baptiste Carpeaux: Sculptor of the Second Empire* (New Haven, Conn.: Yale University Press, 1986). On the neoclassical revival in nineteenth-century European sculpture, see Francis Haskell and Nicholas Penny, *Taste and the Antique: The Lure of Classical Sculpture, 1500–1900* (New Haven, Conn.: Yale University Press, 1981). On neoclassicism more generally, see Suzanne K. Marchand, *Down from Olympus: Archeology and Philhellenism in Germany, 1750–1970* (Princeton, N.J.: Princeton University Press, 1996).

10. On the nineteenth-century development of graveside devotional sculpture, see Philippe Ariès, *The Hour of Our Death*, trans. Helen Weaver (New York: Knopf, 1980), pp. 524–38.

11. This important distinction comes from the work of Joseph Koerner; see his "The Mortification of the Image: Death as a Hermeneutic in Hans Baldung Grien," *Representations* 10 (1985):52–101, especially p. 93.

12. On Antokol'skii's Jesus as "Jewish," see Ziva Amishai-Maisels, "The Jewish Jesus," *Journal of Jewish Art* 9 (1982):84–104, as well as her "Origins of the Jewish Jesus," in *Complex Identities: Jewish Consciousness and Modern Art*, ed. Matthew Baigell and Milly Heyd (New Brunswick, N.J.: Rutgers University Press, 2001), pp. 51–86, and her *Depiction and Representation: The Influence of the Holocaust on the Visual Arts* (Oxford: Pergamon, 1993), pp. 178–79. On the "historical" elements of *Ecce homo*, see Mirjam Rajner, "The Awakening of Jewish National Art in Russia," *Jewish Art* 16–17 (1990–91):98–121, especially pp. 112–14. On the "human Jesus" of *Ecce homo*, see the work of Antokol'skii's Soviet biographer, E. V. Kuznetsova, *M. M. Antokol'skii, zhizn' i tvorchestvo* (Moscow: Iskusstvo, 1989), pp. 87–94.

13. See Amishai-Maisels, "Origins of the Jewish Jesus," p. 55, and Rajner, "The Awakening of Jewish National Art in Russia," p. 112.

14. On the earliest precedent of the skullcapped Jesus in Christian iconography, see Michael Bachmann, "Jesus mit dem Judenhut: Ikonographische Notizen," *Zeitschrift für Theologie und Kirche* 100 (2003):378–98.

15. Elizabeth Kridl Valkenier, *Ilya Repin and the World of Russian Art* (New York: Columbia University Press, 1990), p. 36. Both Amishai-Maisels and Rajner point out Antokol'skii's so-called debt to Repin's historical realism; see Amishai-Maisels, "Origins of the Jewish Jesus," p. 55, and Rajner, "The Awakening of Jewish National Art in Russia," pp. 111–12. In fact, the ironic use of the skullcap in Antokol'skii's *Ecce homo* violates the normative aesthetic of Russian historical painting.

16. Rajner, "The Awakening of Jewish National Art in Russia," p. 113. The problem with Rajner's assertion is that Antokol'skii's discussion of his "sources" in his correspondence, upon which Rajner relies without qualification, does not exhaust the evidence of the art itself. As I will argue below, Antokol'skii's programmatic avowal of interest in history, both in his letters to Russian friends and colleagues and in his public pronouncements, reflects the self-conscious construction of a discourse about the politics of Russian art that often explicitly contradicts what one might call the poetics of Antokol'skii's style.

17. Amishai-Maisels, "Origins of the Jewish Jesus," p. 55.

18. See Kuznetsova, *M. M. Antokol'skii*, p. 92.

19. In earlier sketches, Antokol'skii wound the ropes several times around Jesus' chest; see ibid., p. 87, and Amishai-Maisels, "Origins of the Jewish Jesus," p. 55. Neither scholar accounts for the shift away from the "oppressed look" of the initial version; clearly, Antokol'skii saw the disposition of the ropes as critical to his conception of the sculpture as a whole.

20. See Uri Ehrlich, *The Non-Verbal Language of Jewish Prayer* (Hebrew) (Jerusalem: Hebrew University Magnes Press, 1999), chapter 7.

21. Mishnah, Yoma 7:5. See also Michael D. Swartz, "The Semiotics of the Priestly Vestments in Ancient Judaism," in *Sacrifice in Religious Experience*, ed. Albert I. Baumgarten (Leiden: Brill, 2002), pp. 57–80.

22. On the taboo of the heart "seeing" the genitals, see TB, Berakhot 25b; see also the discussion in Ehrlich, *The Non-Verbal Language of Jewish Prayer*, pp. 132–35.

23. See TB, Shabbat 9b–10a, as well as later midrashic sources cited in Ehrlich, *The Non-Verbal Language of Jewish Prayer*, p. 133, n. 21, for the phrase "[to] gird oneself for prayer" (Heb. *hoger 'atzmo ba-tefilah*). The biblical source for the idea that prayer requires a form of military readiness is the verse: "Prepare to meet your God, O Israel," (Amos 4:12), i.e., on the field of battle.

24. The practice had fallen into disuse in the medieval period; see Ehrlich, *The Non-Verbal Language of Jewish Prayer*, p. 135. Nevertheless, the *Set Table* (1565–66), the authoritative legal code for modern Eastern and Central European Jewry, ruled that one was obliged to wear an additional belt during prayer; see *Shulhan 'arukh*, "Orah hayim," 9:2. On the basis of this ruling, the third generation of Hasidic masters revived the talmudic custom as a mark of their special "faithfulness" and an aid to proper concentration. See Louis Jacobs, *Hasidic Prayer* (New York: Schocken, 1973), pp. 47–48, 104–20, on the Hasidic preoccupation with warding off "alien thoughts" during prayer.

25. For a discussion of what one might call the "partition (Heb. *mehitsah*) principle," which extends to virtually every aspect of Jewish devotion, see Ehrlich, *The Non-Verbal Language of Jewish Prayer*, p. 141. Compare this effect in Antokol'skii's *Ecce homo* with the devotional meaning of curtains in Christian iconography, characteristically associated with *revelatio*, the unveiling of Jesus' divinity; see Johann Konrad Eberlein, "The Curtain in Raphael's Sistine *Madonna*," *Art Bulletin* 65 (1983): 61–77.

26. Swartz, "The Semiotics of the Priestly Vestments in Ancient Judaism," p. 73.

27. See TB, Zevahim 88b.

28. See Kuznetsova, *M. M. Antokol'skii*, p. 66; on *Peter the Great*, p. 82.

29. See Leo Steinberg, *The Sexuality of Christ in Renaissance Art and Modern Oblivion* (Chicago: University of Chicago Press, 1996), pp. 149–51.

30. Renan, *Vie de Jésus*, in *Oeuvres complètes de Ernest Renan*, ed. Henriette Psichari (Paris: Calmann-Lévy, 1947), vol. 4, p. 116.

31. See Albert Schweitzer, *The Quest of the Historical Jesus: A Critical Study of Its Progress from Reimarus to Wrede*, trans. W. Montgomery (1906; New York: Macmillan, 1968), pp. 79–80.

32. Renan, *Vie*, p. 81.

33. Renan went to Palestine in 1860–61, as the director of the Commission for the Exploration of Ancient Phoenicia; see Edward W. Said, *Orientalism* (New York: Pantheon, 1978), pp. 130–48.

34. Renan, *Vie*, p. 356.

35. T. Colani, "Examen de la vie de Jésus de M. Renan," published in 1864, in *Revue de théologie*, cited in Schweitzer, *Quest*, p. 189.

36. The formative text here is Renan's "Prayer on the Acropolis" (1876): see Pierre Vidal-Naquet, "Renan et le miracle grec," in *La démocratie grecque vue d'ailleurs: Essais d'historiographie ancienne et moderne* (Paris: Flammarion, 1990), pp. 245–64. I am indebted to Tony Grafton for this reference. See also Peter Heinegg, "Hebrew or Hellene? Religious Ambivalence in Renan," *Texas Quarterly* 18 (1975):120–36, especially p. 126. On the "frail harmony" between Hebraism and Hellenism in Renan's view of Jesus, see David C. J. Lee, *Ernest Renan: In the Shadow of Faith* (London: Duckworth, 1996), chapter 7.

37. Renan, *Vie*, p. 110.

38. Ibid., p. 142.

39. Ibid., pp. 201–2.

40. Ibid., p. 187.

41. Ibid., pp. 202, 336.

42. Ibid., pp. 363–64.

43. On the narrative "magic" of the text, see Terence R. Wright, "The Letter and the Spirit: Deconstructing Renan's *Life of Jesus* and the Assumptions of Modernity," *Religion and Literature* 26 (1994):55–71, especially pp. 67–68

44. Compare Renan, *Vie*, p. 364.

45. See Koerner, "Mortification of the Image," p. 94.

46. See Elizabeth Kridl Valkenier, *Russian Realist Art, the State and Society: The Peredvizhniki and Their Tradition* (Ann Arbor, Mich.: Ardis, 1977).

47. On the highly fraught relationship between the state and late imperial Russian educated society, reform-minded intellectuals, scientists and liberal professionals, see the ground-breaking work of Laura Engelstein, *The Keys to Happiness: Sex and the Search for Modernity in Fin-de-Siècle Russia* (Ithaca: Cornell University Press, 1992) and, most recently, Michael D. Gordin, *A Well-Ordered Thing: Dmitrii Mendeleev and the Shadow of the Periodic Table* (New York: Basic, 2004), chapter 6.

48. See I. S. Zil'bershtein, "Rabota I. E. Repina nad kartinoi *Otkaz ot ispovedi pered kazniiu*," in *I. E. Repin: Nauchnaia konferentsiia posviashchennaia velikomu russkomu khudozhniku Il'e Efimovichu Repinu v sviazi s 20-letiem so dnia ego smerti, sbornik dokladov i materialov* (Moscow: Akademiia khudozhestv SSSR, 1952), pp. 47–90, and G. G. Pospelov, "Narodovol'cheskaia seriia I. E. Repina (ot personazhei-tipov k puti lichnosti)," in *Russkoe iskusstvo XIX veka, voprosy pominamii vremeni* (Moscow: Iskusstvo, 1997), pp. 144–83. For the historical background of revolutionary activity in late imperial Russia, see Franco Venturi, *Roots of Revolution: The History of the Populist and Socialist Movements in Nineteenth-Century Russia*, trans. Francis Haskell (New York: Grosset and Dunlap, 1966).

49. Pospelov, "O ponimanii vremeni v zhivopisi 1870–1890kh godov: Kartiny

posviashchennye sud'bam lichnosti," in *Tipologiia russkogo realizma vtoroi poloviny XIX veka*, ed. G. Iu. Sternin (Moscow: Nauka, 1979), pp. 169–217.

50. N. A. Dmitrieva, "Peredvizhniki i impressionisty," in *Iz istorii russkogo iskusstva vtoroi poloviny XIX-nachala XX veka*, ed. E. A. Borisova, G. G. Pospelov, and G. Iu. Sternin (Moscow: Iskusstvo, 1978), p. 30.

51. Pospelov, "O ponimanii vremeni," p. 201.

52. On Kramskoi's relationship to the Wanderers, see S. N. Gol'dshtein, *Ivan Nikolaevich Kramskoi: Zhizn i tvorchestvo* (Moscow: Iskusstvo, 1965). On the tension between reality and realism in his work, particularly on the spiritual value that he attached to the latter, see Pospelov, "O ponimanii vremeni," pp. 183–89.

53. The most reliable account of Antokol'skii's career is Kuznetsova's biography, *M. M. Antokol'skii, zhizn' i tvorchestvo*. My conclusions and interests differ substantially from hers. I focus here on details that Kuznetsova bases on sources other than Antokol'skii himself. Given his preoccupation with his personal mythology, Antokol'skii's statements cannot be taken at face value, particularly when it comes to Vilna, as I will discuss.

54. This second version is at the Tretiakov Gallery, Moscow. There is another version, dated 1902, housed at the former Museum of Religion and Atheism at the Kazan Cathedral, St. Petersburg

55. The standard Russian-language biography of Stasov is A. K. Lebedev and A. V. Solodovnikov, *Vladimir Vasilievich Stasov: Zhizn' i tvorchestvo* (Moscow: Iskusstvo, 1976); see also Michael W. Curran, "Vladimir Stasov and the Development of Russian National Art: 1850–1906" (Ph.D. dissertation, University of Wisconsin, Madison, 1965).

56. On the relationship between Stasov and Antokol'skii, see A. K. Lebedev and G. K. Burova, *Tvorcheskoe sodruzhestvo: M. M. Antokol'skii i V. V. Stasov* (Leningrad: Khudozhnik RSFSR, 1968).

57. On Antokol'skii's time in Rome, see Kuznetsova, *M. M. Antokol'skii*, chapter 2, as well as the short sketch by O. Krivdina, "Antokol'skii v Italii," *Khudozhnik* 19 (1977):43–46.

58. On the Mamontov circle, see D. Z. Kogan, *Mamontovskii kruzhok* (Moscow: Izobrazitel'noe iskusstvo, 1970), and Stuart Grover, "Savva Mamontov and the Mamontov Circle, 1870–1905: Art Patronage and the Rise of Nationalism in Russian Art" (Ph.D. dissertation University of Wisconsin, Madison, 1971).

59. The best account of the place of Abramtsevo as the "school" of modern Russian art remains Camilla Gray, *The Russian Experiment in Art, 1863–1922*, rev. ed. (London: Thames and Hudson. 2002), pp. 11–28.

60. V. V. Stasov, *Mark Matveevich Antokol'skii: Ego zhizn', tvoreniia, pis'ma i stat'i* (Moscow: M. O. Vol'f, 1905). This book forms only a small part of Antokol'skii's substantial and still unexplored epistolary, publicistic, and literary legacy, which Stasov intended to bring to light before he died in 1906. This volume, the earliest and sole example of a sustained correspondence between a Jewish provincial turned European cultural hero and his Russian friends, patrons, and colleagues, represents an unparalleled experiment in the construction and reception of Jewishness in Russian-educated society of the late imperial period.

61. Antokol'skii's correspondence would not seem to support Amishai-Maisels's argument that anti-Semitism motivated Kramskoi's critique of the sculpture, a premise that leads to her misreading, in my view, of Antokol'skii's rejoinder. See Amishai-Maisels, "Origins of the Jewish Jesus," pp. 57–60, and Rajner, "The Awakening of Jewish National Art in Russia," p. 102.

62. On the conventions governing the representation of God in Russian icon painting, see N. P. Kondakov, *Russkaia ikona* (Prague: Seminarium kondakovium,

1931), vol. 3, pp. 50–86, as well as B. A. Uspenskii, "Semiotika ikony," in *Semiotika iskusstva* (Moscow: Shkola "Yazyki russkoi kul'tury," 1995), pp. 221–94; B. B. Bychkov, *Russkaia srednevekovaia estetika XI–XVII veka* (Moscow: Mysl', 1995), pp. 588–615; and O. Iu. Tarasov, *Ikona i blagochestie: Ocherki ikonnogo dela v imperatorskoi Rossii* (Moscow: Progress-Traditsiia, 1995), chapter 1. On the rare appearance of the suffering Christ in Russian Orthodox iconography, see N. V. Pokrovskii, *Evangelie v pamiatnikakh ikonografii preimushchestvenno vizantiiskikh i russkikh* (Moscow: Progress-Traditsiia, 2001), pp. 394–96. On the rarity of representations of Jesus in Russian religious sculpture, see the discussion of church architecture in A. G. Romm, *Russkie monumental'nye reliefy* (Moscow: Iskusstvo, 1953), pp. 12–20, 22–23, 30–32, 40, 53–54. On Orthodox attitudes toward religious sculpture in general, see Uspenskii, "Semiotika ikony," and his *Filologicheskie razyskanii a v oblasti slavianskikh drevnostei* (Moscow: Moscow University, 1982), pp. 112–13.

63. "Beseda chervertaia (ob ikonnom pisanii)," in *Zhitie protopopa Avvakuma im samim napisannoe i drugie ego sochineniia*, ed. N. K. Gudzii (Moscow: Gosud. izd. khudozhestvennoi literatury, 1960), pp. 135–36.

64. On Peter's decree, see "Iz istorii russkoi skul'ptury," *Istoricheskaia letopis'* 1 (1914):874–76. On the beginnings of secular neoclassical sculpture in Russia during the Petrine period, see James Cracraft, *The Petrine Revolution in Russian Imagery* (Chicago: University of Chicago Press, 1997), pp. 220–31.

65. Cracraft, *The Petrine Revolution*, pp. 230–31.

66. See N. N. Bulich, *Ocherki po istorii russkoi literatury i prosveshcheniia s nachala XIX veka* (St. Petersburg: M. M. Stasiulevich, 1902), vol. 1, pp. 340–46, and A. N. Veselovskii, *Zapadnoe vliianie v novoi russkoi literature* (Moscow: I. N. Kushnerev, 1916), p. 93.

67. Janet Kennedy, "The Neoclassical Ideal in Russian Sculpture," in *Art and Culture in Nineteenth-Century Russia*, ed. Theofanis Georges Stavrou (Bloomington: Indiana University Press, 1983), pp. 194–210.

68. On Russian art students in Rome, see N. N. Kovalenskaia, *Russkii klassitsizm: Zhivopis', skul'ptura, grafika* (Moscow: Iskusstvo, 1964), pp. 334–80.

69. Pospelov, "O ponimanii vremeni," p. 200.

70. See the letter to the landscape painter F. A. Vasiliev (1850–73), dated November 8, 1871, in A. A. Suvorin, *Ivan Nikolaevich Kramskoi, ego zhizn', perepiska i khudozhestvenno-kriticheskie stat'i* (St. Petersburg: A. A. Suvorin, 1888), p. 77.

71. Letter to Vasiliev, July 5, 1872, in Suvorin, *Ivan Nikolaevich Kramskoi*, p. 97.

72. Letter to Vasiliev, August 9, 1872, in Suvorin, *Ivan Nikolaevich Kramskoi*, p. 102, and again to Vasiliev, October 10, 1872, in ibid., p. 105.

73. Suvorin, *Ivan Nikolaevich Kramskoi*, p. 382.

74. For the image of the "sandal straps," see Kramskoi's letter to his patron, the merchant art collector P. M. Tretiakov (1832–98), cited in Pospelov, "O ponimanii vremeni," p. 200.

75. Letter to Repin, January 6, 1874, in Suvorin, *Ivan Nikolaevich Kramskoi*, p. 193.

76. Letter to Vasiliev, December 1, 1872, in Suvorin, *Ivan Nikolaevich Kramskoi*, p. 112. See also the letter to A. D. Chirkin, December 27, 1873, in ibid., pp. 185–88.

77. Stasov, *Antokol'skii*, p. 15.

78. The quotation is from a letter to Vasiliev, January 7, 1873; Kramskoi was already planning the trip, which finally took place three years later. See Suvorin, *Ivan Nikolaevich Kramskoi*, p. 124.

79. Letter to Tretiakov, April 23, 1876, in Suvorin, *Ivan Nikolaevich Kramskoi*, p. 277.

80. Letter to Repin, August 26, 1874, in Suvorin, *Ivan Nikolaevich Kramskoi*, p. 228.

81. See Stasov, *Antokol'skii*, pp. 175–76, and Suvorin, *Ivan Nikolaevich Kramskoi*, pp. 230–31.

82. For a picture of Germanicus, see Haskell and Penny, *Taste and the Antique*, pl. 114.

83. Unpublished letter, cited in Lebedev and Burova, *Tvorcheskoe sodruzhestvo*, pp. 59–61.

84. Stasov, *Antokol'skii*, p. 99.

85. See, for instance, Stasov, "Vstupitel'naia lektsiia g. Prakhova v universitete (1874 g)," in *Izbrannye sochineniia v trekh tomakh* (Moscow: Iskusstvo, 1952), vol. 1, pp. 260–61.

86. See Stasov, *Antokol'skii*, pp. 101–7.

87. Ibid., p. 104.

88. Ibid., p. 112.

89. Ibid., pp. 105–6.

90. Ibid., p. 106. Antokol'skii's remark about the visual power of Delaroche's painting is all the more ironic since he probably never saw it. The last work Delaroche ever painted, *Return from Golgotha*, was exhibited only once in the Salon of 1857 and then disappeared into a private collection until the 1980s, when it was bought by the Museé Départemental de l'Oise. See Stephen Benn, *Paul Delaroche: History Painted* (Princeton, N.J.: Princeton University Press, 1997), 268–73. In fact, Antokol'skii's description of the mothers trudging woefully home after their children are taken away to be recruited reproduces almost verbatim a written description of *Return from Golgotha*, featured in an essay devoted to Delaroche. Authored by the French publicist Eugène de Mirecourt, the piece was published in 1871 as the nineteenth installment of his *Histoire contemporaine, portraits et silhouettes du XIXe siècle*, a series that featured short popular biographies of eminent nineteenth-century French personalities. See Eugène de Mirecourt, *Delaroche, Decamps* (Paris: Librairie des contemporains, 1871), pp. 48–51.

91. Antokol'skii is quoting Pascal's *Pensées*. The full citation reads: "Habit is a second nature that destroys the first. But what is nature? Why is habit not natural? I am very much afraid that nature itself is only a first habit just as habit is a second nature." See *Pensées*, trans. A. J. Krailsheimer (New York: Penguin, 1995), no. 26.

92. Stasov, *Antokol'skii*, p. 106.

93. The letter is dated January 28, 1874; see ibid., p. 112.

94. On the "legend" of Jesus in Renan's view of Christianity, see Bernard Reardon, "Ernest Renan and the Religion of Science," in *Religion in the Age of Romanticism: Studies in Early Nineteenth-Century Thought* (Cambridge: Cambridge University Press, 1985), p. 263.

Chapter 13. A Modern Mitzvah-Space-Aesthetic

A slightly different version of this article appears in Zachary Braiterman, *The Shape of Revelation: Aesthetics and Modern Jewish Thought* (Stanford University Press, 2007).

1. George Mosse, *Nationalism and Sexuality: Respectability and Abnormal Sexuality in Modern Europe* (New York: H. Fertig, 1985), p. 44.

2. Franz Rosenzweig, *Der Mensch und sein Werk: Gesammelte Schriften*, vol. 1, *Briefe und Tagebücher* (The Hague: Martinus Nijhoff, 1979), p. 74 (henceforth cited as *Briefe und Tagebücher*).

3. Ibid., p. 85.

4. Ibid., pp. 381–82.

5. Ibid., p. 386.

6. Ibid., pp. 390, 392, 448, 530–31, 570.

7. Ibid., especially pp. 564–67.

8. See also Eric Santner, *On the Psychotheology of Everyday Life: Reflections on Freud and Rosenzweig* (Chicago: University of Chicago Press, 2001), pp. 15–19.

9. Nahum Glatzer, ed., *Franz Rosenzweig: Life and Thought* (New York: Schocken, 1953), p. 95.

10. Ibid., p. 97.

11. Ibid.

12. Franz Rosenzweig, *The Star of Redemption*, trans. William W. Hallo (Notre Dame, Ind.: Notre Dame University Press, 1970), p. 354.

13. Ibid., pp. 355–56.

14. Ibid., p. 356.

15. Ibid., p. 357.

16. Ibid., p. 361.

17. Ibid., pp. 362, 262–63.

18. Ibid., pp. 370–73.

19. To understand this about Judaism, however, one must go to the Christianity chapter, not the Judaism chapter. This structural oddity has nothing to do with Judaism or Christianity per se but with the highly schematic construction of a text whose author assigned eternity to Judaism and space to Christianity. A great failure of *The Star of Redemption* is its inability to account for the spatial character of Judaism in a systematic way. Instead, readers must detect hints scattered not in the Judaism chapter, where they belong, but exiled in the Christianity chapter.

20. Rosenzweig, *The Star of Redemption*, p. 292.

21. Ibid., p. 293.

22. Ibid., p. 295.

23. Ibid., p. 355.

24. Ibid., p. 356.

25. Ibid., p. 372.

26. Ibid., p. 373.

27. Wassily Kandinsky, "Abstract Synthesis on the Stage," in *Complete Writings on Art*, ed. Kenneth C. Lindsay and Peter Vergo (New York: DaCapo Press, 1994), p. 505.

28. Franz Rosenzweig, "The New Thinking," in *The New Thinking*, ed. and trans. Alan Udoff and Barbara E. Galli (Syracuse, N.Y.: Syracuse University Press, 1999), p. 81.

29. Rosenzweig, *The Star of Redemption*, p. 248.

30. Kalman P. Bland, *The Artless Jew: Medieval and Modern Affirmations and Denials of the Visual* (Princeton, N.J.: Princeton University Press, 2000), p. 91

31. Rosenzweig, *The Star of Redemption*, p. 312.

32. Ibid., p. 316.

33. Ibid., pp. 325–26.

34. Ibid., p. 327.

35. Ibid., p. 42

36. Ibid., p. 315.

37. Ibid., p. 316.

38. Ibid., pp. 322–23.

39. Ibid., p. 326.

40. Leora Faye Batnitzky, *Idolatry and Representation: The Philosophy of Franz Rosenzweig Reconsidered* (Princeton, N.J.: Princeton University Press, 2000), pp. 90–101.

41. Ibid.

42. Franz Rosenzweig, "The Builders," in On *Jewish Learning*, ed. Nahum N. Glatzer (New York: Schocken Books, 1955), pp. 78–79.

43. Ibid., p. 80 (emphasis added).

44. Ibid.

45. Rosenzweig, *Briefe und Tagebücher*, pp. 446–47.

46. Glatzer, *Franz Rosenzweig*, pp. 120–21.

47. Glatzer, *On Jewish Learning*, p. 70.

48. Ibid., pp. 68–69.

49. Ibid., p. 71.

50. Cited by Eleonore Lappin, *Der Jude, 1916–1928* (Tübingen: Mohr Siebeck, 2000), pp. 400–401.

Chapter 14. Reestablishing a "Jewish Spirit" in American Synagogue Music

1. Abraham Wolf Binder, "A Perspective on Synagogue Music in America," *Journal of Church Music* (January 1964), reprinted in *Studies in Jewish Music: Collected Writings of A. W. Binder*, ed. Irene Heskes (1971; New York: Bloch Publishing Company, 2001), pp. 274–75.

2. Abraham Wolf Binder, "V'Shomru: A Century of Musical Interpretations," in *Israel Abrahams Memorial Volume* (1927), reprinted in *Studies in Jewish Music*, p. 64.

3. Abraham Wolf Binder, "The Jewish Music Movement in America," in *American Jewish Tercentenary Celebration* (1952/54), reprinted in *Studies in Jewish Music*, p. 227.

4. Abraham Wolf Binder, "The Sabbath in Music," in *Sabbath: The Day of Delight*, ed. Abraham E. Millgram (1944), reprinted in *Studies in Jewish Music*, p. 90.

5. Binder, "V'Shomru," p. 64.

6. Abraham Wolf Binder, "Changing Values in Synagogue Music," *Bulletin of the Jewish Music Forum* (1941), reprinted in *Studies in Jewish Music*, p. 81.

7. Binder, "The Sabbath in Music," p. 90.

8. Binder, "Changing Values in Synagogue Music," p. 84.

9. Abraham Wolf Binder, "New Trends in Synagogue Music," *Journal of the Central Conference of American Rabbis* (January 1955), reprinted in *Studies in Jewish Music*, p. 235.

10. Binder, "Changing Values in Synagogue Music," pp. 79–80.

11. Abraham Wolf Binder, "My Ideas and Theories in My Synagogue Compositions," lecture delivered to the Jewish Liturgical Music Society of America, March 12, 1964, reprinted in *Studies in Jewish Music*, p. 306.

12. Binder, "Changing Values in Synagogue Music," p. 81.

13. Binder, "New Trends in Synagogue Music," pp. 230–31.

14. Michael A. Meyer, *Response to Modernity: A History of the Reform Movement in Judaism* (New York: Oxford University Press, 1988), p. 298.

15. Binder, "My Ideas and Theories in My Synagogue Compositions," pp. 304–5.

16. Ibid., p. 305.

17. Ibid.

18. Binder, "New Trends in Synagogue Music," p. 232.

19. Binder, "V'Shomru," p. 64.

20. Binder, "Changing Values in Synagogue Music," p. 80.

21. A. Z. Idelsohn, "The Influence of Moderate-Reform upon Synagogue Song during the Nineteenth Century in Central and Western Europe," in *Jewish Music in Its Historical Development* (New York: Henry Holt, 1929), pp. 246–95.

22. Binder, "Changing Values in Synagogue Music," p. 80.

23. Binder, "The Sabbath in Music," p. 107.

24. Abraham Wolf Binder, "The Music of the Synagogue: An Historical Survey," in *Diapason: American Guild of Organists* (Fall 1945), reprinted in *Studies in Jewish Music*, p. 95.

25. Binder, "V'Shomru," p. 64.

26. Binder, "New Trends in Synagogue Music," p. 233.

27. Binder, "Changing Values in Synagogue Music," p. 81.

28. Abraham Wolf Binder, "Jewish Music: An Encyclopedic Survey," in *The Jewish People: Past and Present*, vol. 3 (New York: Jewish Encyclopedic Handbooks, Central Yiddish Culture Organization, 1952), reprinted in *Studies in Jewish Music*, p. 163.

29. Binder, "New Trends in Synagogue Music," p. 231.

30. Binder, "The Sabbath in Music," p. 95.

31. Binder, "The Music of the Synagogue," p. 95; Binder, "New Trends in Synagogue Music," p. 232.

32. Binder, "New Trends in Synagogue Music," p. 230.

33. Ibid., p. 232.

34. Binder, "My Ideas and Theories in My Synagogue Compositions," pp. 305–6.

35. Abraham Wolf Binder, "Preface," *Union Hymnal: Songs and Prayers for Jewish Worship*, 3rd ed., revised and enlarged, ed. Abraham Wolf Binder (New York: Central Conference of American Rabbis, 1932), p. vi.

36. A.W. Binder, "Into the Tomb of Ages Past " (#157), *Union Hymnal*, p. 168.

37. Jacob Beimel, "When the Sabbath" (#114), *Union Hymnal*, p. 119.

38. Binder, "My Ideas and Theories in My Synagogue Compositions," p. 307.

39. Ibid., p. 310.

40. Abraham Wolf Binder, "Hashkivenu," Evening prayer for voice and organ (piano), in *Friday Evening Service* (New York: Bloch Publishing Co., 1947).

41. Abraham Wolf Binder, *Three-Festival Musical Liturgy* (New York: Transcontinental Music Publications, 1962), p. 9.

42. See Judah Michael Cohen, "Becoming a Reform Jewish Cantor: A Study in Cultural Investment" (Ph.D. dissertation, Harvard University, 2002), and Jeffrey A. Summit, *The Lord's Song in a Strange Land: Music and Identity in Contemporary Jewish Worship* (New York: Oxford University Press, 2000).

43. Binder, "New Trends in Synagogue Music," p. 235.

Chapter 15. The Evolution of Philadelphia's Russian Sher Medley

Unless otherwise indicated, all interviews were conducted by Hankus Netsky in Philadelphia.

1. David Raksin, telephone interview, March 1998.

2. The bulgar is a lively Rumanian couples dance in duple meter, the freylekhs is a duple freestyle Jewish circle dance, and the hora is a slower Romanian circle dance in 3/8 meter.

3. We can find evidence of this in the 1916 Kostakowsky folio. A sher medley entitled "Celebrated Hebrew Wedding Dance" is found in Wolff N. Kostakowsky, *International Hebrew Wedding Music*, violin folio, arranged, revised, bowed, and fingered by Wolff N. Kostakowsky (Brooklyn: Nat Kostakowsky, 1916), private collection of Henry Sapoznik, New York. The name of the sher medley was changed to "Famous Philadelphia Sherele" in a subsequent edition that year and can be found on pp. 154–55. The opening two sections of the piece are variants on the sher that always opens the Philadelphia medley.

4. Although there is an emerging scholarly literature on klezmer music traditions in particular communities, no one has focused exclusively on the American incarnation of the Russian Sher. One of the most important contributions to the study of a single genre of this music literature is Walter Zev Feldman, "Bulgareasca/Bulgarish/Bulgar: The Transformation of a Klezmer Dance Genre," in *American Klezmer: Its Roots and Offshoots*, ed. Mark Slobin (Berkeley: University of California Press, 2002), pp. 84–126.

5. In several recorded versions, such as the 1918 Schwartz recording and the 1918 Hochman recording, the dance is actually called a Russian quadrille.

6. Joan Lawson, *European Folk Dance* (London: Sir Isaac Pitman and Sons Ltd., 1953), p. 14.

7. Franz Magnus Böhme, *Geschichte des Tanzes in Deutschland: Beitrag zur deutschen Sitten-, Literatur- und Musikgeschichte*, 2 vols., reprint of the Leipzig 1886 edition (Hildesheim: Gg Olms, Breitkopf and Härtel, 1967).

8. Moshe Beregovski, *Jewish Instrumental Folk Music*, trans. and ed. Mark Slobin, Michael Alpert, and Robert Rothstein (Syracuse, N.Y.: Syracuse University Press, 2001). Beregovski was head of the ethnomusicological section of the Institute of Jewish Proletarian Culture of the Ukrainian Academy of Sciences from 1930 until it was closed in 1948 (the exact dates are in some dispute). Mark Slobin writes that Beregovski recontextualized "the Jews as a part of a rich inter-ethnic musical network within a given region," in his introduction to *Old Jewish Folk Music: The Collections and Writings of Moshe Beregovski*, ed. and trans. Mark Slobin (Philadelphia: University of Pennsylvania Press, 1982), p. 3. Unlike many Jewish ethnographers who preceded him, Beregovski created his own detailed musical transcriptions, was deeply interested in the musician's entire cross-cultural repertoire, and ensured that his collecting expeditions in the Southern Ukraine led to the publication of several pivotal volumes, first published in Russian in the 1930s and more recently translated into English and published in the United States, as cited here.

9. Same-sex dancing figures prominently in biblical accounts of Jewish dance. See "Dancing," *JewishEncyclopedia.com*, http://jewishencyclopedia.com/view.jsp?artid=29&letter=D&search=dancing. See also Zvi Friedhaber, "The Dance with the Separating Kerchief," *Dance Research Journal* 17, 2 and 18, 1 (1985–86):65–69. For more citations, see *Helen's Yiddish Dance Page*, http://www.angelfire.com/ns/helenwinkler/ (date of last access: January 16, 2004).

10. Edward Kagansky, interview, Boston, July 2000. Similar hip movements have been noted in the version of the quadrille danced in Martinique. See Julian Gerstin, "Musical Revivals and Social Movements in Contemporary Martinique: Ideology, Identity, Ambivalence," in *The African Diaspora*, ed. Ingrid Monson (New York: Garland Publishing, 2000), pp. 295–328.

11. Robert P. Tabak, "The Transformation of Jewish Identity: The Philadelphia Experience, 1919–1945" (Ph.D. dissertation, Temple University, 1990), p. 23.

12. Charlotte Kimball Patten, "Amusements and Social Life: Philadelphia," in *The Russian Jew in the United States*, ed. Charles S. Bernheimer (Philadelphia: John Winston Co., 1905).

13. Bernie Uhr, telephone interview, Boston–Atlantic City, July 1998. According to the clarinetist Marty Levitt, a similar kind of signal (in this case, four bars taken from one of the cadential passages) was traditionally used in New York. Marty Levitt, interview, Brooklyn, November 2003.

14. Joseph Borock, interview, St. Agathe, Canada, August 1997.

15. Such a promenade is a component of many Russian folk dances. See Lawson, *European Folk Dance*, p. 88.

16. Chain dances may have their roots in the idea of breaking a circle so that evil might leave or good might come in. See ibid., p. 20.

17. Borock, interview. Michael Alpert has suggested that members of the "patron's" set would routinely fight with dancers who joined in uninvited (without paying). Michael Alpert, personal communication, New York, November 2003.

18. Michael Alpert, dance session, New York, 1988. More recently, a great deal of discussion has emerged over coordination of dance and music in the sher (see the archives section of *Klezmershack.com*, at http://www.klezmershack.com, November 17–19, 2003 [date of last access: January 16, 2004]). More recently, when teaching people to dance to klezmer music, Michael Alpert has encouraged dancers to fill out their phrases with "shining" when they're ready to move on and the musical phrase has not yet concluded. Michael Alpert, personal communication, Boston and New York, November 2003.

19. Feldman, "Bulgareasca/Bulgarish/Bulgar," p. 113.

20. The sirba is a lively Romanian circle dance. The skotshne is another duple-metered Jewish dance.

21. On the lack of documentation of klezmer music, see Mark Slobin, *Fiddler on the Move* (New York: Oxford University Press, 2000), p. 93. Because Jewish music archives contain almost no documentation, I have relied almost entirely on private collections.

22. Max Epstein, interview, Florida, December 1997; Sid Beckerman, personal communication, Parksville, New York, December 1998; Ray Musiker, personal communication, St. Agathe, Canada, August 1999. Only Marty Levitt, one of the more traditional Jewish wedding musicians on the New York scene, continued to play full-length through-composed New York shers through the 1950s. Marty Levitt, interview, Brooklyn, November 2003.

23. Feldman, "Bulgareasca/Bulgarish/Bulgar," pp. 115–16.

24. Ciaran Carson, *Last Night's Fun* (New York: North Point Press, 1996), p. 90.

25. Marvin Katz, personal communication, Philadelphia, December 2002. His reference to "all of the sections" refers only to those sections that were current in the 1950s. He was impressed that one manuscript actually seemed to include all the sections that were commonly played in the period when he was active.

26. Beregovski, *Jewish Instrumental Folk Music*, p. 11.

27. This sher, mailed from Philadelphia to a non-Jewish former student of Lemisch who was living in Belz, Bessarabia, at the time, is preserved in a collection of Moldavian dance music compiled by the Romanian composer and musicologist Boris Iakovlevich Kotliarov: *O skripichnoi kul'ture v Moldavii* (Kishinev: Gos.izd-vo Moldavii, 1955), p. 74. Walter Zev Feldman, personal communication, New York City, 2003.

28. *Saer,* from facsimile of 1914 Mayer Swerdlow music manuscript book, collection of Hankus Netsky.

29. "Sher," *Celebrated Hebrew Wedding Dance,* sheet music for pianoforte solo, edited by Morris Freed (Philadelphia: Morris Freed Music, 1914). Courtesy of the late Jerome Adler. "Sher, Part 1" and "Sher, Part 2" (Morris Fried [*sic*], Philadelphia), performed by the Abe Schwartz Orchestra, Columbia E 4905: Matrix #s: 86691-2 and 86692-1, recorded October 1920 in New York.

30. "Shear," Jewish wedding music folio, notated by Harry Swerdlow, 1945. Private collection of Joseph Borock, Philadelphia.

31. Philadelphia Russian Sher medley, performed by Jack Shapiro Orchestra, with Jerome Adler (clarinetist), Morris Zeft (trumpeter), Sam Zager (piano), and Jack Shapiro (percussion). Performed at a B'nai Brith (Jewish fraternal organization) function in Philadelphia, 1968. Privately recorded on reel-to-reel tape by Alan Shapiro. Private collection of Alan Shapiro, Philadelphia.

32. Mark Slobin, *Fiddler on the Move,* p. 98.

33. On the compositional logic of form in klezmer dance tunes, see Slobin [Beregovski], *Jewish Instrumental Folk Music,* pp. 20–21; Slobin, *Fiddler on the Move,* pp. 102–6; Feldman, "Bulgareasca/Bulgarish/Bulgar," pp. 101–11; and Joel Edward Rubin, "The Art of the Klezmer: Improvisation and Ornamentation in the Commercial Recordings of New York Clarinetists Naftule Brandwein and Dave Tarras 1922–1929" (Ph.D. dissertation, City University of London, 2001), pp. 173–249.

34. Readers should take special note of these four parts, for in what follows I will organize my historical and musicological analysis around them.

35. I use the term "minor" to refer to tunes in harmonic minor; melodic minor; a kind of hybrid extended melodic minor; a minor scale with a raised fourth degree similar to the pitch collection in the cantorial *shteyger* (mode) *mi shebeyrekh* (The One who blessed); Turkish *makam nikriz*; and the pitch collection Beregovski calls "altered dorian." Some of my informants have referred to the altered dorian as the "Jewish scale" or "Jewish minor."

36. The pitch collection called freygish by European klezmorim is closely related to makam hijaz, a sound also heard frequently in Greek dance music and folksong. Some American klezmorim think of this tonal grouping as a harmonic minor scale starting on the fifth degree, while others think of it as an altered form of major, because of the major third in its lower tetrachord, which implies its harmonization with a major chord.

37. The tonal groupings in the D-minor section are mostly in natural or harmonic minor, although many of the cadences in this section have lowered second degrees.

38. The term "major" refers to Western major scales (labeled from here on as Maj1) and to typical Romanian pitch groupings that include the major scale's lower pentachord with a different upper tetrachord, which corresponds to the *Adonoy Molokh* (God is King) cantorial *shteyger*. As was already noted, a similar tonal progression can also be found in New York Russian Shers, from D melodic minor to D harmonic minor to D freygish. The consistent use of D as the tonic in New York sher medleys may explain why Kostakowsky prints his version of the Philadelphia sher in the key of D, even though the original version was most likely in A. See the 1916 Kostakowsky folio.

39. Although I did previously call it provincial, Philadelphia was, after all, a major American city, and while the melodic content of the medley derives from Eastern European modal rather than harmonic traditions, the musicians who put these medleys together in Philadelphia were using harmonic accompaniments. Aware of Western harmonic practice, they may have built their sequences of sections around musical concepts that, to the Western ear, imply a dominant to tonic relationship (in the case of A freygish moving to D) and the equivalent of a parallel minor to major shift in the case of A minor moving to A freygish. Thus, an initial A-minor tonality gives way to A freygish (which implies A dominant 7), that eventually "resolves" to D minor. Subsequently, D minor gives way to D freygish or D major. Thus, the tonal groupings found in the Philadelphia Russian Sher medley are not in any way random and in fact exhibit similar tonal principles to those found in Bach's *Well-Tempered Clavier* (minor followed by parallel major) and Beethoven's sonatas (dominant/tonic)!

40. For more on Turkish makam, see Karl Signell, *Makam: Modal Practice in Turkish Art Music* (Seattle: Asian Music Publications/University of Washington Press, 1977), p. 79.

41. While much of the string-oriented European klezmer repertoire was in A, the clarinet- and trumpet-centered American klezmer repertoire was almost always

in D, giving rise to the nickname "D minor" that was used among American club-date musicians for the entire genre.

42. Henry Sapoznik postulates that the clarinet took over as the top klezmer instrument in America because it sounded better on recordings. See Sapoznik, *Klezmer! Jewish Music from Old World to Our World* (New York: Schirmer Books, 1999). One can also point to the decline of the violin as a Jewish folk instrument (and the rise of the Jewish concert violinist), and the popularity of the clarinet/trumpet/trombone combination as the frontline in many kinds of American popular and ethnic music ensembles.

43. See Feldman, "Bulgareasca/Bulgarish/Bulgar," for more on this phenomenon.

44. Arthur Hertzberg, *The Jews in America* (New York: Simon and Schuster, 1989), p. 316.

45. Marvin Katz, personal communication, Philadelphia, May 2003.

46. Marty Portnoy, interview, Cherry Hill, N.J., December 2000.

Chapter 16. Framing Nazi Art Loot

I would like to thank Ezra Mendelsohn and Jonathan Karp for their valuable comments on an earlier version of this chapter.

1. Bernhard Schlink, "Girl with Lizard," in *Flights of Love* (New York: Random House, 2001).

2. Ibid., p. 3.

3. Ibid.

4. Ibid., p. 12.

5. Ibid., p. 7.

6. Ibid., p. 39.

7. Ibid., pp. 48–49.

8. Peter Novick, *The Holocaust in American Life* (Boston: Houghton Mifflin, 1999).

9. A well-known work on looting is E. R. Chamberlin, *Loot! The Heritage of Plunder* (London: Thames and Hudson, 1983).

10. On Nazi art looting, see especially Lynn Nicholas, *The Rape of Europa: The Fate of Europe's Treasures in the Third Reich* (New York: Alfred A. Knopf, 1994); Hector Feliciano, *The Lost Museum: The Nazi Conspiracy to Steal the World's Greatest Works of Art* (New York: Basic Books, 1995); Jonathan Petropoulos, *Art as Politics in the Third Reich* (Chapel Hill: University of North Carolina Press, 1996); Elizabeth Simpson, ed., *The Spoils of War: World War II and Its Aftermath, the Loss, Reappearance and Recovery of Cultural Property* (New York: Harry Abrams, 1997). Konstantin Akinsha and Grigorii Kozlov, *Beautiful Loot: The Soviet Plunder of Europe's Art Treasures* (New York: Random House, 1995) examines the Soviet "response."

11. Quoted in Nicholas, *Rape of Europa*, p. 381.

12. Janet Flanner, *Men and Monuments* (New York: Harper and Row, 1957), pp. 220–21.

13. On Nazi cultural policy, see especially Petropoulos, *Art as Politics*, pp. 19–74, and Stephanie Barron, ed., *"Degenerate Art": The Fate of the Avant-Garde in Nazi Germany* (Los Angeles: Los Angeles County Museum of Art; New York: H. N. Abrams, 1991).

14. See James Rorimer and Gilbert Rabin, *Survival: The Salvage and Protection of Art in War* (New York: Abelard Press, 1950), p. x. Rabin's role seems to have been purely editorial.

15. Rorimer and Rabin, *Survival*, p. 37.

16. Ibid., p. 161.

17. "Recovery of Priceless Jewish Collection Stolen by Nazis," August 16, 1945, James J. Rorimer Papers, 1923–62, microfilm reel 2800, Archives of American Art, Smithsonian Institution, Washington, D.C. (henceforth cited as Rorimer Papers).

18. Thomas Hoving, *Making the Mummies Dance: Inside the Metropolitan Museum of Art* (New York: Simon and Schuster, 1993), p. 19.

19. See letter from Walter Sachs to Paul Sachs, November 8, 1923, Paul Sachs Papers, Fogg Art Museum Archives, Harvard University, Cambridge.

20. On Rorimer, see Calvin Tompkins, *Merchants and Masterpieces: The Story of the Metropolitan Museum of Art* (New York: Henry Holt, 1989), pp. 256–61, 326–33, 345–46.

21. Hoving, *Making the Mummies Dance*, p. 327.

22. Ibid., p. 21.

23. Letter from Merrill Coseo (War Department) to Mrs. Marshall, May 1, 1943, Rorimer Papers, microfilm reel 2800.

24. Letter from James Rorimer to Paul Sachs, December 10, 1944, Rorimer Papers, microfilm reel 2800.

25. Letter from Katherine Rorimer to Paul J. Karlstan, October 29, 1982, Rorimer Papers, microfilm reel 2800.

26. Ibid.

27. Rorimer and Rabin, *Survival*, p. 248.

28. Ibid., pp. 108–16.

29. Ibid., p. 182.

30. Ibid., p. 102.

31. Ibid., p. 164.

32. Ibid., p. 221. The reference is probably to the Alte Pinakothek.

33. Ibid., *Survival*, pp. 259–69.

34. See *Variety*, July 16, 1963.

35. See Rose Valland, *Le Front de l'art: Défense des collections françaises 1939–45* (Paris: Réunion des Musées Nationaux, 1997), pp. 148–53.

36. See especially Novick, *Holocaust in American Life*, and James Young, *The Texture of Memory: Holocaust Memorials and Meanings* (New Haven, Conn.: Yale University Press, 1993).

37. Pierre Nora, ed., *Realms of Memory: Rethinking the French Past*, vol. 1, trans. Arthur Goldhammer (New York: Columbia University Press, 1996), chapter 1.

38. I am grateful to Anne Webber for granting me an interview and providing useful background information. See also "A Curator of Lost Artwork and Found Memories," a profile of Webber by Warren Hoge, in the *New York Times*, May 25, 2002.

39. *Making a Killing*, 1998, produced by Anne Webber, made for Channel 4 in the United Kingdom.

40. Daniel Silva, *The English Assassin* (New York: G. P. Putnam, 2002), p. 227.

41. Ibid., p. 229.

42. Ibid.

43. For Lauder's comments and for general background information, see the Commission on Art Recovery's website, http://www.comartrecovery.org/.

44. The most recent developments in the case are summarized by Celestine Bohlen, "Judge Revives Case of Nazi-Looted Art," *New York Times*, April 27, 2002, p. B9. For Mukasey's decision, see *United States v. Portrait of Wally*, *New York Law Journal* 227 (April 19, 2002):25ff.

45. Interview with Sarah Jackson, Art Loss Register, by Charles Dellheim. She kindly provided background information and publicity materials on "Historic Claims."

46. Silva, *English Assassin*, p. 16.

Chapter 17. Joseph Lewitan and the Nazification of Dance in Germany

1. The German critic Horst Koegler acknowledged in 1972 that Lewitan was one of three influential writers in 1920s Germany; see Koegler, *Tanz in den Abgrund, Berliner Ballett um 1930*, The other two were Artur Michel and Fritz Böhme. Radio transcript for SFB (Sender Freies Berlin), May 22, 1972, in the Joseph D. Lewitan and Eugenia Eduardova Collection (1918–74), (S) *MGZMD 14, item 32, Jerome Robbins Dance Division, New York Public Library for the Performing Arts, New York. In subsequent citations, this collection is abbreviated as the Lewitan and Eduardova Collection. Short biographies on Lewitan have been included in the *Rossiskaya Evreiskaya Encyklopaedia*, the *International Biographical Dictionary of Central European Émigrés 1933–1945*, and the *Handbuch zur deutschsprachigen Emigration 1933–1945, Volume 2, The Arts, Sciences and Literature*, ed. Herbert A. Strauss (New York), Werner Röder and K. G. Saur (Munich: Institut für Zeitgeschichte; New York: Research Foundation for Immigration, 1999), pp. 722, 1107; s.v. *Tanz* by Laure Guilbert-Deguine. In these volumes, Lewitan is classified as one of the most eminent writers on dance in Germany and as a victim of the Nazis.

2. Scrapbook, undated, Lewitan and Eduardova Collection, item 39.

3. Ibid.

4. The Russische Delegation für Angelegenheiten der russischen Kriegsgefangenen und Rückwanderer in Deutschland testified on Lewitan's twenty-sixth birthday that he was a Russian citizen, according to documents he delivered to the department for civil matters, in Berlin's *Uhlandstraße*. On these grounds he could claim a German *Fremdenpass* and a certificate that allowed permanent stay in Berlin. Later he received a *Nansen-Passport*. See Scrapbook, undated, Lewitan and Eduardova Collection, item 39. Fridtjof Nansen was a scientist and humanitarian. Working for the Red Cross, Nansen came to be known in connection with his invention of a particular legal document that bore his name and became an internationally recognized identity card. Lenin deprived the thousands of Russians who had fled to the West after the civil war of their nationality. The Red Cross proposed using Nansen's name on a special passport for refugees. The League of Nations approved the idea in 1922, at the same time appointing Nansen as its first High Commissioner for Refugees. Carriers of the Nansen passport were, for instance, artists such as Igor Stravinsky, Sergey Rachmaninov, Marc Chagall, and Anna Pavlova.

5. In February 1926, the revised regulations for the deed of partnership had been accepted by the Berlin authorities. See Scrapbook, undated, item 39, Lewitan and Eduardova Collection. Lewitan began his career with the backing of one of the Russian émigré publishing houses, the renowned Ladyshnikov company.

6. Quoted from the website *Dancing Times*, at http://www.dancing-times.co.uk/dancingtimes.html (date of last access: January 8, 2004).

7. Lewitan translated Volynskii's *Kniga Likovanii: Azbuka klassichesogo tantsa* from 1925 into German as *Buch des Jubels*. He published several excerpts of his translation in the magazine *Der Tanz* in 1933. His translation was reprinted as Akim Wolynski, *Buch des Jubels* (Wilhelmshafen: Florian Noetzel Verlag, 1990).

8. This debate can be followed in books such as the following: Marianne Aubel and Hermann, *Der künstlerische Tanz unserer Zeit* (Königstein and Leipzig: K. R. Langewiesche, 1928); Rudolf Bach, *Das Mary-Wigman-Werk* (Dresden: C. Reissner, 1933); Oskar Bie, *Der Tanz* (Berlin: Bard, Marquardt and Co., 1906); Ernst Blass, *Das Wesen der neuen Tanzkunst* (Weimar: E. Lichtenstein, 1922); Fritz Böhme, *Der Tanz der Zukunft* (Munich: Delphin Verlag, 1926); Hans Brandenburg, *Der Moderne Tanz* (Munich: G. Müller,1913); Rudolf von Delius, *Mary Wigman* (Dresden: C. Reissner, 1925); Isadora Duncan, *Der Tanz der Zukunft* (Jena: E. Diederichs,

1903); Valeska Gert, *Mein Weg* (Leipzig: A. F. Devrient, 1931); Emile Jaques-Dalcroze, *Der Rhythmus als Erziehungsmittel für das Leben und die Kunst* (Basel: Helbring and Lichtenhahn, 1907); Rudolf Laban, *Die Welt des Tänzers: Fünf Gedankenreigen* (Stuttgart: Walter Seifert, 1920); John Schikowski, *Geschichte des Tanzes* (Berlin: Büchergilde Gutenberg, 1926); Karl Storck, *Der Tanz* (Bielefeld and Leizpzig: Velhagen and Klasing,1903); Werner Suhr, *Der Künstlerische Tanz* (Leipzig: C. F. W. Siegel, 1922); Frank Thiess, *Der Tanz als Kunstwerk* (Munich: Delphin Verlag, 1920); Mary Wigman, *Deutsche Tanzkunst* (Dresden: C. Reissner, 1935); Fritz Winther, *Körperbildung als Kunst und Pflicht* (Munich: Delphin Verlag, 1914).

The relatively small and often short-lived dance magazines devoted to particular teaching methods offer insights into the specific goals and programs of certain schools and groups: *Gymnastik und Tanz: Amtliches Organ des Reichsverbandes Deutscher Turn-, Sport- und Gymnastiklehrer* (later a publication of the Dance and Gymnastics *Fachschaft*, 1926–43); *Körperrhythmus und Tanz: Mitteilungsblatt der Jutta Klamt Gemeinschaft* (1929–36); *Die Tanzgemeinschaft* (1929–30); and *Schrifttanz: Eine Vierteljahrsschrift* (1928–31, reprint Hildesheim 1991).

9. How dance can become a means to establish and instill behavioral patterns can most clearly be followed in dance manuals of past centuries in which dances are advertised and their teaching methods in relation to expected behavior are explained. The study and analysis of manuals can be undertaken within sociological or historical frames. These models offer insights into the social practice of dance. An interesting historical study by William Hardy McNeill, *Keeping Together in Time: Dance and Drill in Human History* (Cambridge, Mass.: Harvard University Press, 1995), looks at the close interaction of dance, drill, and the acceptance of order through movement practice.

10. E. T. A. Hoffman, *Prinzessin Brambilla: Ein Capriccio nach Jakob Callot* (Breslau: J. Max, 1821).

11. The playwright Bertolt Brecht and the theater director Erwin Piscator, both contemporaries of Lewitan, employed a very similar attitude to critical thinking, which they embraced within the theater ensemble in the personage of the dramaturge.

12. Habima, an early Hebrew-language theater, was established in Moscow in 1917, moved to Palestine in 1931, and became the national theater of Israel in 1958.

13. M. Berchin-Benedictoff, "Der jüdische Tanz," *Der Tanz* (March 1929), pp. 3–4.

14. The German term for a college of dance is *Tanzhochschule*.

15. Many of Laban's terms developed alongside each other and occasionally replaced one another, their definitions evolving over many years. Choreology originally had three subdisciplines: choreutics, the actions of bodies in space; eukinetics, the study of dynamics and rhythm; and kinetography, dance notation. The distinction between choreology and choreosophy was also difficult and vague. See Isa Partsch-Bergsohn, *Modern Dance in Germany and the United States: Crosscurrents and Influences* (Chur, Switzerland: Harwood Academic Publishers, 1994), for a description of choreology, "the study of the grammar and syntax of the language of movement" (p. 29). See also Valerie Preston-Dunlop, *Rudolf Laban: An Extraordinary Life* (London: Dance Books, 1998), where she describes "rule-governed base to movement as one of man's fundamental modes of communication" (p. 37).

16. Josef Lewitan, "Der Kampf um den Tanz," *Der Tanz* (October 1928), pp. 2–3.

17. Mary Wigman, "Der neue künstlerische Tanz und das Theater," in *". . . jeder Mensch ist ein Tänzer": Ausdruckstanz in Deutschland zwischen 1900 und 1945*, cd. Hedwig Müller and Patricia Stöckemann (Giessen: Anabas Verlag, 1993), p. 77. See also

Artur Michel, "The Development of the New German Dance," in *Modern Dance,* ed. Mary Wigman, Martha Graham, et al. (New York: E. Weyhe, 1935), pp. 5–8.

18. Rudolf Laban, "Das chorische Kunstwerk," in *". . . jeder Mensch ist ein Tänzer,"* p. 88.

19. Kurt Joos, "Tanztheater und Theatertanz," in *". . . jeder Mensch ist ein Tänzer,"* p. 76.

20. André Levinson, "The Modern Dance in Germany," *Theatre Arts Monthly* 13, 2 (February 1929):143–53.

21. Levinson, "The Modern Dance in Germany," p. 147.

22. Ibid., p. 151.

23. Ibid., p. 152.

24. Ibid.

25. Ibid.

26. Mary Wigman, "Das Land ohne Tanz," *Die Tanzgemeinschaft: Vierteljahreszeitschrift für tänzerische Kultur* 1, 3 (1929):12–13.

27. Throughout her career Wigman used the word "Jewish" as invective, as verbal abuse: her diary is full of diatribes against "Jews." At the same time, she decided who was to be "Jewish." Some of her favorite pupils were, ethnically speaking, "Jewish," but she made them "un-Jewish" because she liked them. Others became "Jewish" if she disliked them. On Wigman's relationship to Jews and her anti-Semitism, see Hedwig Müller's paper presented at the conference "Tanz und Politik" (Dance and Politics), Cologne, Germany, January 30, 2003, organized by the Mary Wigman Society and the Tanzarchiv Cologne.

28. Laban, *Die Welt des Tänzers,* p. 24.

29. Alexander Lewitan, "Zerbrecht die Retorte!," and A. Verin, "Die Kurve," in *Der Tanz* (January 1933), pp. 5, 6.

30. Joseph Lewitan, "Aschermittwoch" (Ash Wednesday), *Der Tanz* (August 1930), pp. 2–3

31. Deutscher Tänzerbund e.V. [eingetragener Verein], Deutsche Tanzgemeinschaft e.V., and Chorische Bühne e.V. were the forces behind the 1930 congress. Rudolf von Laban and Mary Wigman presided in the honorary committee.

32. Lewitan, "Aschermittwoch," p. 3

33. Joseph Lewitan, "Der Tanz von Morgen" (The Dance of Tomorrow), *Der Tanz* (November 1930), pp. 2–3

34. Ibid.

35. Joseph Lewitan, "Der Bankrott. Einige Worte über Formlosigkeit und Geistlosigkeit" (Bankrupt. Remarks on Formlessness and Lack of Intellectuality), *Der Tanz* (June 1932), pp. 4–5

36. Lewitan had considerable experience and an excellent reputation as tour organizer. He had looked after many companies visiting Berlin in the 1920s, among others Anna Pavlova and her ensemble.

37. Joseph Lewitan, Grundsätzliches (Editorial), *Der Tanz* (April 1933), p. 13

38. "July 1933—Important announcement!" *Der Tanz* (July 1933), p. 1

39. Joseph Lewitan, letter to Friderica Derra de Moroda, December 1, 1934, Korrespondenz betr. *Der Tanz,* Special Collection, letter no. 81, Friderica Derra de Moroda Dance Archives, University of Salzburg, Salzburg. All subsequent citations of this collection are abbreviated as the Derra de Moroda Archives.

40. Joseph Lewitan, letter to Friderica Derra de Moroda, January 17, 1935, letter no. 87, Derra de Moroda Archives.

41. Joseph Lewitan, letter to Friderica Derra de Moroda, March 13, 1935, letter no. 97, Derra de Moroda Archives.

42. Joseph Lewitan, letter to Friderica Derra de Moroda, June 6, 1936, letter no. 139, Derra de Moroda Archives.

43. Fritz Böhme, "Ist das Ballett deutsch?" *Deutsche Allgemeine Zeitung*, April 25, 1933.

44. Joseph Lewitan, letter to Friderica Derra de Moroda, March 13, 1935, letter no. 97, Derra de Moroda Archives.

45. Lilian Karina and Marion Kant, *Hitler's Dancers: German Modern Dance and the Third Reich*, with a documentary appendix, selected and edited by Marion Kant (Oxford: Berghahn Books, 2003), p. 227, document no. 22.

46. Ibid.

47. Ibid.

48. A reference letter reads: "Mr. Josef Lewitan is a member of the administrative staff of the Habimah Theatre. We shall very greatly appreciate any assistance that can be given him." It is dated December 10, 1937, and signed by A. Baratz and M. Gnessin. See Scrapbook, undated, Lewitan and Eduardova Collection, item 39.

49. Mendel Kohansky, *The Hebrew Theatre: Its First Fifty Years* (New York: Ktav Publishing House, 1969); and Emanuel Levy, *The Habima, Israel's National Theater, 1917–1977: A Study of Cultural Nationalism* (New York: Columbia University Press, 1979).

50. Lewitan had joined several Jewish and Zionist organizations in Berlin. He indicated that Habima's aesthetic and political program was too narrow for his liking and that he sought a more direct way to make an impact. A former member of Habima voiced a similar criticism: "At the time, European Jewry was in a state of bewilderment. Old social forms were giving way to the new. This affected European Jewry to such a degree that the people felt helpless and insecure. Habima, though it pretended to be a social theater, did little to discharge its obligation to the confused Jewish masses. Our plays did not deal even remotely with the social and economic Jewish problem." Raikin Ben-Ari, *Habima*, trans. A. H. Gross and I. Soref (New York: Thomas Yoseloff, 1957), p. 171.

51. Pierre Tugal, letter to Joseph Lewitan; and Pierre Michaud, letter to Joseph Lewitan, both dated October 23, 1937; see Scrapbook, undated, Lewitan and Eduardova Collection, item 39.

52. Lilian Karina, "Recollections," in *Hitler's Dancers*, p. 40.

53. Volynskii was born Chaim Leib Flekser and incorporated his birth province, Volynia, into his name. See Stanley Rabinowitz, "A Room of His Own: The Life and Work of Akim Volynskii," *Russian Review* 50, 3 (July 1991):291.

54. The UFA, Universum-Film AG, was founded on November 18, 1917.

55. As member of the Organisation sioniste de France, Fédération du Maroc, Lewitan represented the electoral area of Morocco at the Zionist Congress in Basle in 1946. See Scrapbook, undated, Lewitan and Eduardova Collection, item 47.

56. Joseph Lewitan, letter to Seymor Barofsky, May 9, 1970, in Scrapbook, undated, Lewitan and Eduardova Collection, item 1.

57. Circumstantial evidence points to a family connection.

58. The Récépisse de demande de carte d'identité was issued by the police prefect and was an application for an identity card. As identity cards were not or hardly ever handed out to refugees at that time the récépisse equaled a permit to stay and was effectively an identity document itself. Lewitan never received a French identity card.

59. Scrapbook, undated, Lewitan and Eduardova Collection, item 5.

60. I gathered this impression after looking at the Lewitan collection in the YIVO Institute for Jewish Research, New York (see RG 735 Lewitan).

61. Katja Erdman-Rajski, *Gret Palucca, Tanz und Zeiterfahrung in Deutschland im 20 Jahrhundert: Weimarer Republik, Nationalsozialismus, Deutsche Demokratische Republik* (Hildesheim: Deutsches Tanzarchiv Cologne and Georg Olms Verlag AG, 2000), pp. 69, 179, 219, 222, 243, 246, 247.

62. See Karl Toepfer, *Empire of Ecstasy: Nudity and Movement in German Body Culture, 1910–1935* (Berkeley: University of California Press, 1997), pp. 310, 313.

Chapter 18. History, Memory, and Moral Judgment in Documentary Film

Chapter 18, "History, Memory, and Moral Judgment in Documentary Film: On Marcel Ophul's *Hotel Terminus: The Life and Times of Klaus Barbie*," © 2002 Susan Rubin Suleiman. This essay was first published in *Critical Inquiry* 28, 2 (Winter 2002): 509–41. An earlier version was delivered as an Ernst Fraenkel Lecture at the Freie Universität in Berlin on February 14, 2001, and was published by the university as part of the Fraenkel series in 2002. It is also part of my book *Crises of Memory and the Second World War* (Cambridge, Mass.: Harvard University Press, 2006). I wish to thank colleagues as well as the staff and the librarians of the Center for Advanced Judaic Studies at the University of Pennsylvania, where I spent the spring 2001 semester as a fellow and where this essay was largely written.

1. Michel Ciment, "Joy to the World! An Interview with Marcel Ophuls," *American Film* 13, 10 (September 1988):38–43. The quote appears on p. 42.

2. Patricia Hampl, "Memory's Movies," in *Beyond Document: Essays on Non-Fiction Film*, ed. Charles Warren (Middletown, Conn.: Wesleyan University Press, 1996), p. 54.

3. Theodor Adorno, "What Does Coming to Terms with the Past Mean?" in *Bitburg in Moral and Political Perspective*, ed. Geoffrey Hartman, trans. Timothy Bahti and Geoffrey Hartman (Bloomington: Indiana University Press, 1986), p. 115. The German version of the essay is in Theodor Adorno, *Erziehung zur Mündigkeit*, ed. Gerd Kadelbach (Frankfurt: Suhrkamp, 1972), pp. 10–28.

4. Adorno, "What Does Coming to Terms with the Past Mean?" p. 115.

5. Moishe Postone, "After the Holocaust: History and Identity in West Germany," in *Coping with the Past: Germany and Austria after 1945*, ed. Kathy Harms, Lutz R. Reuter, and Volker Durr (Madison: University of Wisonsin Press, 1990), p. 238.

6. Anson Rabinbach, "Beyond Bitburg: The Place of the 'Jewish Question' in German History after 1945," in *Coping with the Past*, pp. 192–94. For a detailed and nuanced account of Adenauer's and other West German politicians' positions in the 1950s, which presents similar conclusions, see Jeffrey Herf, *Divided Memory: The Nazi Past in the Two Germanys* (Cambridge, Mass.: Harvard University Press, 1997), chapter 8. The situation changed dramatically in the 1960s, especially after the student movement of 1968.

7. Herf, *Divided Memory*, chapter 5.

8. Adorno, "What Does Coming to Terms with the Past Mean?" p. 115.

9. Ibid., p. 128.

10. Charles S. Maier, "A Surfeit of Memory? Reflections on History, Melancholy and Denial," *History and Memory* 5, 2 (Winter 1995):150.

11. Ibid.

12. Ibid., p. 151.

13. Ibid., pp. 137, 141.

14. Peter Novick, *The Holocaust in American Life* (Chicago: University of Chicago Press, 1999).

15. Henry Rousso, *Le syndrome de Vichy, de 1944 à nos jours*, 2nd ed. (Paris: Seuil, 1990), English reprint, *The Vichy Syndrome: History and Memory in France since 1944*, trans. Arthur Goldhammer (Cambridge, Mass.: Harvard University Press, 1994); Eric Conan and Henry Rousso, *Vichy, un passé qui ne passe pas* (Paris: Fayard, 1994), English reprint, *Vichy: An Ever-Present Past*, trans. Nathan Bracher (Hanover, N.H.: University Press of New England, 1998); Henry Rousso, *La hantise du passé: Entretiens*

avec Philippe Petit (Paris: Eds. Textuel, 1998), English reprint, *The Haunting Past: History, Memory and Justice in Contemporary France,* trans. Ralph Schoolcraft (Philadelphia: University of Pennsylvania Press, 2002).

16. The argument about Judaeo-centrism is made most explicitly in Conan and Rousso, *Vichy, un passé qui ne passe pas,* pp. 269–74.

17. Rousso, *La hantise du passé,* pp. 122ff.

18. Claude Lanzmann, "The Obscenity of Understanding: An Evening with Claude Lanzmann," in *Trauma: Explorations in Memory,* ed. Cathy Caruth (Baltimore: Johns Hopkins University Press, 1995), pp. 200–220; and Claude Lanzmann, "Hier ist kein Warum," in *Au sujet de Shoah: Le film de Claude Lanzmann,* ed. Bernard Cuau (Paris: Belin, 1990).

19. Dominick LaCapra, *History and Memory after Auschwitz* (Ithaca, N.Y.: Cornell University Press, 1998), chapter 4.

20. For informative accounts of the debates over the Berlin memorial, see James Young, *At Memory's Edge: After-Images of the Holocaust in Contemporary Art and Architecture* (New Haven, Conn.: Yale University Press, 2000), and Caroline Wiedmer, *The Claims of Memory: Representations of the Holocaust in Contemporary Germany and France* (Ithaca, N.Y.: Cornell University Press, 1999).

21. This was only an impression of mine, based on conversations and informal polling of audiences as I lectured on the film. The impression is confirmed by an article by the film's producer, John S. Friedman, who notes that despite its critical success, the film had very limited distribution and did not earn back its production costs. See Friedman, "*Hotel Terminus,* le point de vue d'un producteur," *Images documentaires* 18/19 (1994):39.

22. My account here is based in part on Erna Paris's *Unhealed Wounds: France and the Klaus Barbie Affair* (New York: Grove Press, 1985), chapters 2–6. Paris's book appeared two years before the actual trial but is informative and reliable about Barbie's earlier career and the efforts to extradite him. Another account of Barbie's activities, especially detailed and suspenseful about his years in Bolivia and Peru, is provided in *The Nazi Legacy: Klaus Barbie and the International Fascist Connection,* ed. Magnus Linklater, Isabel Hilton, and Neal Ascherson (New York: Holt, Rinehart and Winston, 1984).

23. Rousso devotes a whole chapter to the Barbie case, including an excellent explanation of the legal issues involved, and alludes to Barbie often throughout the book; the 1990 edition has even more on the trial. For a virtual day-by-day account of the trial, based on dispatches by the French news daily *Libération,* see Sorj Chalandon and Pascale Nivelle, *Crimes contre l'humanité: Barbie Touvier Bousquet Papon* (Paris: Plon, 1998), pp. 13–164.

24. Robert Paxton, *Vichy France: Old Guard and New Order* (New York: Columbia University Press, 1972); Marcel Ophuls, *Le chagrin et la pitié* (screenplay) (Paris: Alain Moreau, 1980). The film was released in 1971.

25. An early and passionate intellectual response to negationism in France was Pierre Vidal-Naquet's *Les assassins de la mémoire* (Paris: La Découverte, 1987), written at the time of the Barbie case; English reprint, *Assassins of Memory,* trans. Jeffrey Mehlman (Columbia University Press, 1992). For a detailed historical account, see Valérie Igounet, *Histoire du négationnisme en France* (Paris: Seuil, 2000).

26. The best-known memoir provoked by the Barbie trial is Lucie Aubrac's *Ils partiront dans l'ivresse* (Paris: Seuil, 1984), English reprint, *Outwitting the Gestapo,* trans. Konrad Bieber and Betsy Wing (Lincoln: University of Nebraska Press, 1992); see also Lise Lesèvre, *Face à Barbie: Souvenirs-cauchemers de Montluc à Ravensbrück* (Paris: Pavillon, 1987). The trial was the first one to be filmed, in France; in the fall of 2000, the French cable channel Histoire obtained legal permission to broadcast

seventy hours, or slightly less than half of the trial, accompanied by commentaries by historians. The public impact of these broadcasts (repeated in June–July 2001) has yet to be evaluated.

27. Actually, seven others were arrested with Moulin, but René Hardy escaped on the way to prison; since Hardy is generally thought to be the one who betrayed Moulin, his escape appears to have been prearranged.

28. Alain Finkielkraut, *Remembering in Vain: The Klaus Barbie Trial and Crimes against Humanity*, trans. Roxanne Lapidus with Sima Godfrey (New York: Columbia University Press, 1992), p. 32.

29. There is no published screenplay for this film; my quotations in what follows are based on multiple viewings of the two-part video. Considering Ophuls's importance as a filmmaker, it is surprising how little serious critical attention his work has received. Aside from a few articles I will cite below, and aside from brief appearances in general works on the history of French film or on films of the Holocaust, I have found no critical commentaries on *Hotel Terminus*—and none at all that devote detailed analysis to its formal procedures. Even *The Sorrow and the Pity* has received little close scrutiny from film analysts, despite its acknowledged importance. The best sources, so far, for detailed commentary on Ophuls's work are the interviews and articles he has given to French and American film journals. One scholarly journal did devote a special issue to Ophuls's work: *Images documentaires* 18/19 (1994).

30. The role of photographs as figures for memory, especially in relation to the Holocaust, has been amply studied and theorized of late. See especially Marianne Hirsch, *Family Frames: Photography, Narrative, and Postmemory* (Cambridge, Mass.: Harvard University Press, 1997), and Barbie Zelizer, *Remembering to Forget: Holocaust Memory through the Camera's Eye* (Chicago: University of Chicago Press, 1998). Ophuls uses still photos—of Barbie at various times and settings, and of his victims during the war—throughout *Hotel Terminus*.

31. I am grateful to Dr. Marion Kant, a musicologist and a fellow, with me, at the Center for Advanced Judaic Studies at the University of Pennsylvania in the spring of 2001, for her help in identifying the German folk songs Ophuls uses in the film.

32. For a detailed account of Schneider-Merck's relations with Barbie, see Linklater et al., *The Nazi Legacy*, chapters 11–12. As his revenge for being defrauded, Schneider-Merck played a significant role in the identification of Altmann as Barbie. Ophuls appears to have made important use of *The Nazi Legacy* in choosing interviewees and constructing his film.

33. Reported by Melinda Camber Porter, *Through Parisian Eyes: Reflections on Contemporary French Arts and Culture* (New York: Oxford University Press, 1986), pp. 10–11.

34. Dr. Marion Kant informs me that German Jewish exiles (including her father) sang this song in an emigrants' choir in London in the 1930s and early 1940s.

35. See Serge Klarsfeld, *Les enfants d'Izieu: Une tragédie juive* (Paris: Beate Klarsfeld Foundation, 1984).

36. Ophuls's use of music in his films (one recalls Maurice Chevalier's songs in *The Sorrow and the Pity*), and in *Hotel Terminus* in particular, deserves a separate study. The sentimental folk songs, all sung by the Vienna Boys Choir (in addition to the two songs already mentioned, there are two more traditional "wanderers' songs": "Muss i' denn, muss i' denn," which was taken up by Elvis Presley in the 1960s, and "Das Wandern ist des Müllers Lust"), function as veritable leitmotifs. For a study of the role of music in memory-films about the Holocaust, see Jean-Louis Pautrot, "Music and Memory in Film and Fiction: Listening to *Nuit et Brouillard, Lacombe Lucien*, and *La ronde de nuit*," *Dalhousie French Studies* 55 (November 2001):168–82.

For a study of Ophuls's use of film clips from Hollywood musicals in a later film, *November Days* (1990), see Nora M. Alter, "Marcel Ophuls' *November Days*: German Reunification as 'Musical Comedy,'" *Film Quarterly* 51, 2 (1997–98):32–43. Ophuls uses a few musical clips, notably the sound track from a Fred Astaire film, in *Hotel Terminus* as well.

37. Richard Porton and Lee Ellickson, "The Troubles He's Seen: An Interview with Marcel Ophuls," *Cinéaste* 21, 3 (1995):11.

38. Jean-Pierre Jeancolas, "Entretien avec Marcel Ophuls sur Hotel Terminus," *Positif* 331 (September 1988):29. Unless otherwise indicated, all translations from the French are my own. Interestingly, Ophuls says that it's the editing that "almost killed" him, although—as he recounts earlier in this interview—he was physically attacked on a beach in Rio on his way back from Bolivia. He blacked out during the attack and had to undergo an operation in Paris. Even now, he still has some "troubles de mémoire" (p. 26).

39. For a thorough discussion of the various modes of documentary film, see Bill Nichols, *Representing Reality: Issues and Concepts in Documentary* (Bloomington: Indiana University Press, 1991), pp. 32–75; on the interactive mode, pp. 44–56.

40. Marcel Ophuls, "Faut-il fusiller Speer au lieu de le filmer?" (Should we shoot Speer instead of filming him?), *Positif* 200 (December 1977–January 1978):115.

41. Hampl, "Memory's Movies," pp. 51–77.

42. Nichols, *Representing Reality*, p. 51.

43. Ophuls in Ciment, "Joy to the World"; the allusions to Lanzmann are on pp. 41, 42.

44. Ibid., p. 42.

45. Richard Joseph Golsan, "Revising *The Sorrow and the Pity*: Marcel Ophuls' *Hotel Terminus*," in *Vichy's Afterlife: History and Counterhistory in Postwar France* (Lincoln: University of Nebraska Press, 2000), p. 87. Golsan's general argument is that by widening his scope to include Germany, the United States, and South America, Ophuls gets "sidetracked" in this film, away from the question of "Klaus Barbie, his wartime crimes in Lyon, and France's efforts to come to terms with these crimes" (p. 77). In my reading, the wide scope is precisely the point of the film, not a "sidetracking." Rather than letting France off the hook, the wider perspective shows that other countries too were implicated, if not directly then indirectly by protecting Nazis after the war. In my view, Ophuls does not "revise" *The Sorrow and the Pity* with this film; rather, he extends and enlarges his inquiry.

46. Jeancolas, "Entretien avec Marcel Ophuls," p. 27.

47. A particularly trenchant critique (which nonetheless recognized the importance of the film) appeared in the Massachusetts Institute of Technology (MIT) student paper, *The Tech*; see Manavendra Thakur, "Hotel Terminus Is Sidetracked by Director Ophuls' Pent-Up Feelings," February 7, 1989, pp. 16 and 21, on the web at http://www-tech.mit.edu/V109/N1/hotel.01a.html.

48. Jeancolas, "Entretien avec Marcel Ophuls," pp. 27–28.

49. One can contrast this with the famous scene in Lanzmann's *Shoah*, where Lanzmann stages a haircut by Abraham Bomba, who cut women's hair in the gas chamber in Treblinka. For a critique of this mise-en-scéne, see LaCapra, *History and Memory after Auschwitz*, p. 96.

50. Personal telephone conversation, June 7, 2001. Ophuls confirmed on this occasion that his first words to Muller were indeed the aggressive question about the little girl (in other words, the preceding cut did not clide a greeting); when I asked whether he expected that the question would get the door slammed in his face, he said he thought there was a fifty-fifty chance, but at least he would have

something to show. Thus, although technically not a mise-en-scène, the scene appears retroactively as one.

51. Porton and Ellickson, "The Troubles He's Seen," p. 9.

52. Ophuls, "The Sorrow and the Laughter," *Premiere* (November 1988), 115.

53. Ibid.

54. Porton and Ellickson, "The Troubles He's Seen," p. 9. Ophuls says here that the "big change" in this direction came with his 1990 film *November Days* (about the fall of the Berlin Wall); as I am trying to show, however, it actually dates from *Hotel Terminus*.

55. Nichols, *Representing Reality*, p. 56.

56. For a good account of the historians' debate, see Rabinbach, "Beyond Bitburg," pp. 206–14. For an overview of recent German debates about Nazism in Germany, see Régine Robin, "La honte nationale comme malédiction: Autour de l'affaire 'Walser-Bubis,'" *Revue Internationale et Stratégique* 3 (Spring 1999):45–69.

57. Jay Cantor, "Death and the Image," in *Beyond Document*, ed. Warren, p. 39.

58. Jeancolas, "Entretien avec Marcel Ophuls," p. 25.

59. Ibid., p. 26.

60. See, for example, "*Un cinéaste sur la piste de Klaus Barbie*," interview with Michel Ciment, *Le Point* 836 (September 26, 1988):159–62.

61. Ophuls, "The Sorrow and the Laughter," p. 112.

62. "Un cinéaste sur la piste de Klaus Barbie."

63. Jeancolas, "Entretien avec Marcel Ophuls," p. 26.

64. Philip Gourevitch, *We Wish to Inform You That Tomorrow We Will Be Killed with Our Families: Stories from Rwanda* (New York: Farrar, Straus and Giroux, 1998); Adam Hochschild, *King Leopold's Ghost: A Story of Greed, Terror, and Heroism in Colonial Africa* (Boston: Houghton Mifflin, 1998).

65. Ophuls, "The Sorrow and the Laughter," p. 115.

Notes on Contributors

ZACHARY BRAITERMAN is Associate Professor of Religion at Syracuse University, where he teaches modern Jewish philosophy and thought. He is the author of *(God) After Auschwitz: Tradition and Change in Post-Holocaust Jewish Thought* (1998) and *The Shape of Revelation: Aesthetics and Modern Jewish Thought* (2007).

WALTER CAHN is Carnegie Professor of the History of Art (Emeritus) at Yale University. A Fulbright scholar and Guggenheim fellow, he is the author of a number of books including *The Romanesque Wooden Doors of Auvergne* (1974); *Masterpieces: Chapters on the History of an Idea* (1979); *Romanesque Bible Illumination* (1982); *Romanesque Manuscripts: The Twelfth Century* (1996); and *Studies in Medieval Art and Interpretation* (2000).

RICHARD I. COHEN holds the Paulette and Claude Kelman Chair in French Jewry Studies at The Hebrew University in Jerusalem. He is the author of *The Burden of Conscience: French-Jewish Leadership during the Holocaust* (1987) and *Jewish Icons: Art and Society in Modern Europe* (1998). His edited books include the diary of Raymond-Raoul Lambert, *Carnet d'un témoin, 1940–1943* (1985); *The French Revolution and Its Historical Impact* (1991, in Hebrew); *Art and Its Uses: The Visual Image and Modern Jewish Society*, with Ezra Mendelsohn (1990); *From Court Jews to the Rothschilds: Art, Patronage, and Power, 1600–1800*, with Vivian B. Mann (1996); *Le Juif errant: Un témoin du temps*, with Laurence Sigal-Klagsbald (2001); *Art and History* (2007, Hebrew); *The Jewish Contribution to Civilization: Reassessing an Idea*, with Jeremy Cohen (2007).

CHARLES DELLHEIM is Professor of History and Chair of the Department of History at Boston University. He received his Ph.D. in history from Yale University. His major publications include *The Disenchanted Isle: Mrs. Thatcher's Capitalist Revolution* (1995); *The Face of the Past: The Preservation of the Medieval Inheritance in Victorian England* (1982); and "The Creation of a Company Culture: Cadburys, 1861–1931," *American Historical Review* (1987). He has held fellowships from the National Endowment for the Humanities, Harvard University Graduate School of Business Administration, and the Center for Advanced Judaic Studies at the University of Pennsylvania. Currently, he is finishing a book that examines the rise and fall of Jewish art dealers in modern Europe. His essay "A Yankees Fan in Red Sox Nation" appeared in *Commentary,* April 2005.

ANAT HELMAN is a Lecturer in the Department of Jewish History, Institute of Contemporary Jewry, and Cultural Studies program at The Hebrew University. She was the recipient of the Moses Aaron Dropsie postdoctoral fellowship at the Center for Advanced Judaic Studies, University of Pennsylvania. Her book on the cultural history of Mandate-era Tel Aviv is forthcoming, and her essays have appeared in journals such as *Historical Journal of Film, Radio and Television, Jewish Quarterly Review, Urban History, Zion, Journal of Israeli History, Middle Eastern Studies, Journal of Modern Jewish Studies,* and *Journal of Urban History.*

AMY HOROWITZ is currently a scholar in residence at the Ohio State University Mershon Center for International Security Studies and the Melton Center for Jewish Studies. She teaches courses on music, globalization, and disputed territories, and on the cultures of Jerusalem through the International Studies Program at Ohio State University. Her research projects have focused on Mediterranean Israeli music, and U.S. protest music as responsible citizenship. She was awarded her Ph.D. in folklore from the University of Pennsylvania and holds an M.A. in Jewish studies from New York University. Her book, *Mediterranean Israeli Music: The Politics of the Aesthetic,* is forthcoming. Research support includes the Center for Advanced Judaic Studies at the University of Pennsylvania, the National Endowment for the Arts, and the Smithsonian Institution. She is the founder of Roadwork: Center for Cultures in Disputed Territory, a non-profit community-based cultural arts organization, and received a Grammy in 1997 for the reissue of *The Anthology of American Folk Music.*

MARION KANT earned her Ph.D. in musicology at Humboldt University in Berlin and teaches at the University of Pennsylvania. Her publications include *Giselle,* commissioned by the State Opera, Berlin (2001), and *Hitler's Dancers: German Modern Dance and the Third Reich* (2003). She is the editor of *The Cambridge Companion to Ballet* (2007). Together with musicians Marshall Taylor and Samuel Hsu, she has organized and presented a series of concerts commemorating *Entartete Musik,* music forbidden by the Nazis.

JONATHAN KARP is Associate Professor in the departments of Judaic Studies and History at Binghamton University of the State University of New York (SUNY). He is the author of *The Politics of Jewish Commerce: Economic Thought and Emancipation in Europe* (2007) and *Philosemitism in History,* co-edited with Adam Sutcliffe (forthcoming). He is currently completing

The Rise and Demise of the Black-Jewish Alliance: A Class-Cultural Analysis. In the fall of 2006, he was Brownstone Visiting Professor at Dartmouth College.

BARBARA KIRSHENBLATT-GIMBLETT is University Professor and Professor of Performance Studies at the Tisch School of the Arts, New York University, where she chaired her department for over a decade. Her publications include *Destination Culture: Tourism, Museums, and Heritage* (1998); *Image Before My Eyes: A Photographic History of Jewish Life in Poland, 1864–1939* (1977), with Lucjan Dobroszycki; *Art from Start to Finish* (2005), co-edited with Howard S. Becker and Robert R. Faulkner; *Museum Frictions: Public Cultures/Global Transformations* (2006), co-edited with Ivan Karp and Corinne Kratz et al.; and *They Called Me Mayer July: Painted Memories of a Jewish Childhood in Poland Before the Holocaust* (2007), with Mayer Kirshenblatt. A recipient of the Guggenheim Fellowship, she was a research fellow at the Center for Advanced Judaic Studies at the University of Pennsylvania (2001), a Winston Fellow at the Institute for Advanced Studies at The Hebrew University in Jerusalem (1996), and a Getty Scholar at the Getty Center for the History of Art and the Humanities (1991–92). She currently co-convenes, with Jeffrey Shandler, the Working Group on Jews, Media, and Religion at New York University's Center for Religion and Media.

MARK KLIGMAN is Professor of Jewish Musicology at Hebrew Union College–Jewish Institute of Religion in New York City, where he teaches in the School of Sacred Music. He holds a Ph.D. in ethnomusicology from New York University. His forthcoming book is *Maqam and Liturgy: Ritual, Music, and Aesthetics of Syrian Jews in Brooklyn.* Kligman's publications include articles and entries in *American Jewish Yearbook* (2001), *Worship Music: A Concise Dictionary* (2000), and *The Encyclopedia of Judaism* (2000). He has published on Sephardic liturgical music and on contemporary Jewish music. He was Research Fellow and Visiting Professor at the Center for Advanced Judaic Studies, University of Pennsylvania.

DIANA L. LINDEN received her Ph.D. in art history from the City University of New York, Graduate Center, and her M.A. in the same field at Williams College. A former member of the Brooklyn Museum's education department, she has taught American art history and museum studies at the University of Michigan–Ann Arbor, Pomona College, Pitzer College, and the University of Southern California. Her forthcoming book on Ben Shahn's New Deal murals has been supported by the Getty Research Institute, the Lucius N. Littauer Foundation, and the Memorial Fund for Jewish Education. She has published articles and catalog essays on African American art, the New Deal mural projects, public art, and museum practices, as well as on Ben Shahn's art and career.

OLGA LITVAK is Associate Professor of Judaic Studies and directs The Center for Jewish Studies at SUNY Albany. She is the author of *Conscription and the Search for Modern Russian Jewry* (2006). She currently serves as the painting and sculpture editor of the *YIVO Encyclopedia of Jews in Eastern Europe* and is writing a biography of Sholem Aleichem and a book on visual culture and Russian-Jewish modernism.

HANKUS NETSKY teaches jazz, contemporary improvisation, and Jewish music at the New England Conservatory in Boston, where he also earned his master's and bachelor's degrees. He has received the Louis Krasner and Lawrence Lesser awards for excellence in teaching. Founder and director of the Klezmer Conservatory Band, he also serves as research director of the Klezmer Conservatory Foundation, a non-profit organization dedicated to research in and perpetuation of Yiddish music. As a multi-instrumentalist and composer, he has composed music for film, theatre, and radio and produced numerous recordings. He received his Ph.D. in ethnomusicology at Wesleyan University in 2004. His book on Philadelphia's klezmer tradition is forthcoming from Temple University Press.

ANNA SHTERNSHIS is Assistant Professor of Yiddish and Yiddish Literature in the Department of Germanic Languages and Literatures at the University of Toronto. She received her Ph.D. from Oxford University in 2001. The recipient of a postdoctoral fellowship at the Center for Advanced Judaic Studies, University of Pennsylvania, she is the author of *Soviet and Kosher: Jewish Popular Culture in the Soviet Union, 1923–1939* (2006). Her articles have appeared in journals such as *East European Jewish Affairs, Jews in Russia and Eastern Europe, Russian Review,* as well as in the anthology *The Shtetl: Image and Reality* (2000).

SUSAN RUBIN SULEIMAN is the C. Douglas Dillon Professor of the Civilization of France and Professor of Comparative Literature at Harvard University. Her most recent book is *Crises of Memory and the Second World War* (2006). Other books include *Budapest Diary: In Search of the Motherbook* (1996); *Risking Who One Is: Encounters with Contemporary Art and Literature* (1994); *Subversive Intent: Gender, Politics, and the Avant-Garde* (1990); *Authoritarian Fictions: The Ideological Novel as a Literary Genre* (1983); the edited volume *Exile and Creativity: Signposts, Travelers, Outsiders, Backward Glances* (1998); and the co-edited anthology *Contemporary Jewish Writing in Hungary* (2003).

JUDITH THISSEN is Assistant Professor of Media History at Utrecht University in the Netherlands. She is currently completing a book entitled *Moyshe Goes to the Movies: Jewish Immigrants, Popular Entertainment, and Ethnic Identity in New York City, 1880–1917.* She was a visiting Fulbright scholar at

New York University in the Department of Cinema Studies, a research fellow at the Center for Advanced Judaic Studies at the University of Pennsylvania, and a visiting professor in the Department of History, University of California, Los Angeles. Her work has been published in *Cinema Journal*, *KINtop*, and *Theatre Survey* as well as in several anthologies, including *American Movie Audiences: From the Turn of the Century to the Early Sound Era* (1999) and *American Silent Film: Discovering Marginalized Voices* (2002).

NINA WARNKE is Assistant Professor of European Studies at Vanderbilt University. She received her Ph.D. from Columbia University in 2001. She has taught Yiddish and German studies at Columbia University, Indiana University, and the University of Texas at Austin. Her publications on Yiddish theater have appeared in *American Jewish History*, *YIVO Annual*, and *Theatre Journal*, as well as in the anthologies *Yiddish Theatre: New Approaches*, edited by Joel Berkowitz, and *Sholem Asch Reconsidered*, edited by Nanette Stahl. She is currently completing a book on the immigrant Yiddish theater and Yiddish press in New York.

CAROL ZEMEL is Professor of Art History and was for five years Chair of the Department of Visual Arts at York University. She is the author of several books on Vincent van Gogh, most recently *Van Gogh's Progress: Utopia and Modernity in Late Nineteenth Century Art* (1997). She is the recipient of a National Endowment for the Humanities research fellowship and a research fellowship at the Center for Advanced Judaic Studies, University of Pennsylvania. Her current scholarship focuses on issues of diaspora in modern Jewish visual culture and on the production of visual images under conditions of trauma. These essays are the basis for two books: *Graven Images: Visual Culture and Modern Jewish History* and *In Extremis: The Necessity of Art*.

Acknowledgments

This volume grew out of the 2000–2001 research year dedicated to modern Jewry and the arts at the Center for Advanced Judaic Studies at the University of Pennsylvania. We wish to express our appreciation to Richard I. Cohen and Ezra Mendelsohn, who provided the intellectual leadership for this research year. They have consistently fostered the study of Jews and the arts through their own stellar scholarship and indefatigable efforts to support the work of others. To David Ruderman, visionary director of the Center for Advanced Judaic Studies, we owe a profound debt of gratitude for encouraging adventurous new directions in Jewish studies and providing such an intellectually stimulating and collegial setting for our work. The Center staff provided outstanding support. We would especially like to thank Sheila Allen, Administrative Coordinator; Etty (Esther) Lassman, Administrative Assistant to the Fellows; and the Center's dedicated librarians, Arthur Kiron, Seth Jerchower, and Judith Leifer. We would also like to express our warm appreciation to Anurima Banerji and Brigitte Sion for their able assistance with the preparation of the manuscript.